Commentaries
on
Equity Jurisprudence

Commentaries
on
Equity Jurisprudence
As Administered
In
England and America

By

JOSEPH STORY

One of the Justices of the Supreme Court of the United States,
and Dane Professor of Law in Harvard University

" Chancery is ordained to supply the Law, not subvert the Law "
- Lord Bacon
" His ergo ex partibus juris, quidquid aut ex ipsa re, aut ex simili,
aut ex majore, minoreve, nasci videbitur, attendere, atque elicere,
pertentando unamquamque partem juris, oportebit. "
-Cic. De Invent. Lib. 2, cap 22.

THIRTEENTH EDITION
BY
MELVILLE M. BIGELOW, PH. D.

IN FOUR VOLUMES

Volume II

BeardBooks
Washington, D.C.

CHAPTER VII.

CONSTRUCTIVE FRAUD.

258. HAVING thus considered some of the most important cases of actual or meditated and intentional fraud in which Courts of Equity are accustomed to administer a plenary jurisdiction for relief, we may now pass to another class of frauds, which, as contradistinguished from the former, are treated as legal or constructive frauds. By constructive frauds are meant such acts or contracts as, although not originating in any actual evil design or contrivance to perpetuate a positive fraud or injury upon other persons, are yet, by their tendency to deceive or mislead other persons, or to violate private or public confidence, or to impair or injure the public interests, deemed equally reprehensible with positive fraud, and therefore are prohibited by law as within the same reason and mischief as acts and contracts done malo animo. Although at first view the doctrines on this subject may seem to be of an artificial if not of an arbitrary character, yet upon closer observation they will be perceived to be founded in an anxious desire of the law to apply the principle of preventive justice so as to shut out the inducements to perpetrate a wrong, rather than to rely on mere remedial justice after a wrong has been committed. By disarming the parties of all legal sanction and protection for their acts, they suppress the temptations and encouragements which might otherwise be found too strong for their virtue.

259. Some of the cases under this head are principally so treated because they are contrary to some general public policy or to some fixed artificial policy of the law. Others again rather grow out of some special confidential or fiduciary relation between all the parties or between some of them, which is watched with especial jealousy and solicitude because it affords the power

and the means of taking undue advantage or of exercising undue influence over others. And others again are of a mixed character, combining in some degree the ingredients of the preceding with others of a peculiar nature; but they are chiefly prohibited because they operate substantially as a fraud upon the private rights, interests, duties, or intentions of third persons, or unconscientiously compromit, or injuriously affect the private interests, rights, or duties of the parties themselves.

260. And in the first place let us consider the cases of constructive fraud which are so denominated on account of their being contrary to some general public policy or fixed artificial policy of the law.[1] Among these may properly be placed contracts and agreements respecting marriage (commonly called marriage brokage contracts), by which a party engages to give another a compensation if he will negotiate an advantageous marriage for him. The civil law does not seem to have held contracts of this sort in such severe rebuke; for it allowed proxenetæ, or match-makers, to receive a reward for their services, to a limited extent.[2] And the period is comparatively modern in which a different doctrine was engrafted into the common law and received the high sanction of the House of Lords.[3]

261. The ground upon which Courts of Equity interfere in cases of this sort is not upon any notion of damage to the individuals concerned, but from considerations of public policy.[4]

---

[1] See Mr. Cox's note to Osmond v. Fitzroy, 3 P. Will. 131; Newland on Contracts, ch. 33, p. 469, &c. By being contrary to public policy we are to understand that in the sense of the law they are injurious to, or subversive of, the public interests. See Chesterfield v. Janssen, 1 Atk. 352; s. c. 2 Ves. 125.

[2] Cod. Lib. 5, tit. 1, l. 6.

[3] Hall and Kean v. Potter, 3 P. Will. 76; 1 Eq. Cas. Abridg. 89, F; s. c. 3 Lev. 411; Show. Parl. Cas. 76; 1 Fonbl. Eq. B. 1, ch. 4, § 10; Grisley v. Lother, Hob. R. 10; Law v. Law, Cas. temp. Talb. 140, 142; Vauxhall Bridge Company v. Spencer, Jac. R. 67. In Boynton v. Hubbard, 7 Mass. R. 112, Mr. Chief Justice Parsons said: 'We do not recollect a contract which is relieved against in chancery as originally against public policy which has been sanctioned in Courts of Law as legally obligatory on the parties. For although it has been said in chancery that marriage brokage bonds are good at law but void in equity, yet no case has been found at law in which those bonds have been holden good.' But see Grisley v. Lother, Hob. R. 10, and a case cited in Hall v. Potter, 3 Levinz, R. 411, 412; 1 Fonbl. Eq. B. 1, ch. 4, § 10, note (r).

[4] 1 Fonbl. Eq. B. 1, ch. 4, § 10, note (r); Newland on Contracts, ch. 33,

Marriages of a suitable nature and upon the fairest choice are of the deepest importance to the well-being of society; since upon the equality and mutual affection and good faith of the parties much of their happiness, sound morality, and mutual confidence must depend. And upon these only can dependence be placed for the due nurture, education, and solid principles of their children. Hence every temptation to the exercise of an undue influence or a seductive interest in procuring a marriage should be suppressed; since there is infinite danger that it may, under the disguise of friendship, confidence, flattery, or falsehood, accomplish the ruin of the hopes and fortunes of most deserving persons, and especially of females. The natural consequence of allowing any validity to contracts of marriage brokage would be to introduce improvident, ill-advised, and often fraudulent matches, in which advantage would be taken of youth and inexperience and warm and generous affections. And the parties would be led on until they would become the victims of a sordid cunning, and be betrayed into a surrender of all their temporal happiness; and thus perhaps be generally prepared to sink down into gross vice and an abandonment of conjugal duties. Indeed contracts of this sort have been not inaptly called a sort of kidnapping into a state of conjugal servitude;[1] and no acts of the parties can make them valid in a Court of Equity.[2]

262. The public policy of thus protecting ignorant and credulous persons from being the victims of secret contracts of this sort would seem to be as perfectly clear as any question of this nature well can be. And the surprise is not that the doctrine should have been established in a refined, enlightened, and Christian country, but that its propriety should ever have been made matter of debate. It is one of the innumerable instances in which the persuasive morality of Courts of Equity has subdued the narrow, cold, and semi-barbarous dogmas of the common law.

---

pp. 469 to 472. ' Marriage brokage bonds which are not fraudulent on either party are yet void because they are a fraud on third persons, and a public mischief, as they have a tendency to cause matrimony to be contracted on mistaken principles, and without the advice of friends, and they are relieved against as a general mischief for the sake of the public.' Per Parsons, Ch. Just. in Boynton v. Hubbard, 7 Mass. 112.

[1] Drury v. Hooke, 1 Vern. 412.

[2] Shirley v. Martin, cited by Mr. Cox, in 3 P. Will. 75; s. c. 1 Ball & Beatty, 357, 358.

The Roman law, while it admitted the validity of such contracts in a qualified form, had motives for such an indulgence founded upon its own system of conjugal rights, duties, and obligations, very different from what in our age would be deemed either safe or just or even worthy of toleration.

263. Be the foundation of the doctrine however what it may, it is now firmly established that all such marriage brokage contracts are utterly void, as against public policy;[1] so much so that they are deemed incapable of confirmation,[2] and even money paid under them may be recovered back again in a Court of Equity.[3] Nor will it make any difference that the marriage is between persons of equal rank and fortune and age; for the contract is equally open to objection upon general principles, as being of dangerous consequence.[4] Indeed some writers treat contracts of this sort as involving considerations of turpitude, and entitled to be classed with others of a highly vicious nature.[5]

264. The doctrine has gone even further; and, with a view to suppress all undue influence and improper management, it has been held that a bond given to the obligee as a remuneration for having assisted the obligor in an elopement and marriage without the consent of friends is void, even though it is given voluntarily after the marriage, and without any previous agreement for the purposes; for it may operate an injury to the wife, as well as give encouragement to a grossly iniquitous transaction, calculated to disturb the peace of families and to involve them in irremediable distress.[6] It approaches indeed very nearly to the case of a premium in favor of seduction.

---

[1] Arundel v. Trevillian, 1 Rep. Ch. 47 [87]; Drury v. Hooke, 1 Vern. R. 412; Hall v. Potter, 3 Lev. 411; s. c. Shower, Parl. Cas. 76; Cole v. Gibson, 1 Ves. 507; Debenham v. Ox, 1 Ves. 276; Smith v. Aykerill, 3 Atk. 566; Hylton v. Hylton, 2 Ves. 548; Stribblehill v. Brett, 2 Vern. 446; s. c. Prec. Ch. 165; 1 Bro. Parl. Cas. 57; Roberts v. Roberts, 3 P. Will. 74, note (1); Id. 75, 76; Law v. Law, 3 P. Will. 391, 394; Williamson v. Gihon, 2 Sch. & Lefr. 357; 1 Eq. Cas. Abridg. 98, F.

[2] Cole v. Gibson, 1 Ves. 503, 506, 507; 1 Fonbl. Eq. B. 1, ch. 4, § 10, note (s); Roberts v. Roberts, 3 P. Will. 74, and Cox's note (1).

[3] Smith v. Bruning, 2 Vern. 392; 1 Fonbl. Eq. B. 1, ch. 4, § 10; Goldsmith v. Bruning, 1 Eq. Abridg. 89, F.

[4] 1 Fonbl. Eq. B. 1, ch. 4, § 10; Newland on Contracts, ch. 33, pp. 470, 471.

[5] Newland on Contracts, ch. 33, p. 469.

[6] Williamson v. Gihon, 2 Sch. & Lefr. 356, 362.

265. Of a kindred nature, and governed by the same rules, are cases where bonds are given or other agreements made as a reward for using influence and power over another person to induce him to make a will in favor of the obligee, and for his benefit; for all such contracts tend to the deceit and injury of third persons, and encourage artifices and improper attempts to control the exercise of their free judgment.[1] But such cases are carefully to be distinguished from those in which there is an agreement among heirs or other near relatives to share the estate equally between them whatever may be the will made by the testator; for such an agreement is generally made to suppress fraud and undue influence, and cannot truly be said to disappoint the testator's intention if he does not impose any restriction upon his devisee.[2]

266. Upon a similar ground secret contracts made with parents or guardians or other persons standing in a peculiar relation to the party, whereby, upon a treaty of marriage, they are to receive a compensation or security or benefit for promoting the marriage, or giving their consent to it, are held void. They are in effect equivalent to contracts of bargain and sale of children and other relatives, and of the same public mischievous tendency as marriage brokage contracts.[3] They are underhand agreements, subversive of the due rights of the parties, and operating as a fraud upon those to whom they are unknown, and yet whose interests are controlled or sacrificed by them. And as marriages are of public concern and ought to be encouraged, so nothing can more promote this end than open and public agreements on marriage treaties, and the discountenance of all others which secretly impair them.[4]

267. Thus where a bond was taken by a father from his son upon his marriage, it was held void as being obtained by undue

---

[1] Debenham v. Ox, 1 Ves. 276.

[2] Beckley v. Newland, 2 P. Will. 181; Harwood v. Tooker, 2 Sim. R. 192; Wethered v. Wethered, Id. 183; post, § 785.

[3] 1 Fonbl. Eq. B. 1, ch. 4, § 10; Keat v. Allen, 2 Vern. R. 588; s. c. Prec. Ch. 267; 1 Madd. Ch. Pr. 231, 232.

[4] Roberts v. Roberts, 3 P. Will. 74, and Mr. Cox's note (1); Payton v. Bladwell, 1 Vern. R. 240; Redman v. Redman, 1 Vern. R. 348; Gale v. Lindo, 1 Vern. R. 475; Cole v. Gibson, 1 Ves. 503; Morrison v. Arbuthnot, 1 Bro. Ch. R. 547, note; s. c. 8 Bro. Parl. Cas. 247 (by Tomlins); 1 Fonbl. Eq. B. 1, ch. 4, §§ 10, 11.

influence or undue parental awe.[1] So where a party upon his marriage with the daughter of A, gave the latter a bond for a sum of money (in effect a part of his wife's portion on the marriage) in order to obtain his consent to the marriage, it was held utterly void.[2] So where upon a marriage a settlement was agreed to be made of certain property by relations on each side and after the marriage one of the parties procured an underhand agreement from the husband to defeat the settlement in part, it was set aside, and the original settlement carried into full effect.[3] In all these and the like cases Courts of Equity proceed upon the broad and general ground that that which is the open and public treaty and agreement upon marriage shall not be lessened or in any way infringed by any private treaty or agreement.[4] The latter is a meditated fraud upon innocent parties, and upon this account properly held invalid. But it has a higher foundation in the security which it is designed to throw round the contract of marriage, by placing all parties upon the basis of good faith, mutual confidence, and equality of condition.[5]

268. The same principle pervades the class of cases where persons, upon a treaty of marriage, by any concealment or misrepresentation mislead other parties, or do acts which are by other secret agreements reduced to mere forms or become inoperative. In all cases of such agreements relief will, upon the same enlightened public policy, be granted to the injured parties. For equity insists upon principles of the purest good faith; and nothing could be more subversive of it than to allow parties, by holding out false colors, to escape from their own solemn engagements.[6]

[1] 1 Fonbl. Eq. B. 1, ch. 4, §§ 10, 11; Williamson v. Gihon, 2 Sch. & Lefr. 362; Anon. 2 Eq. Abr. 187.

[2] Keat v. Allen, 2 Vern. R. 588; 1 Fonbl. Eq. B. 1, ch. 4, § 11; 1 Eq. Cas. Abr. 90, F. 5.

[3] Payton v. Bladwell, 1 Vern. R. 240; Stribblehill v. Brett, 2 Vern. R. 445; Prec. in Ch. 165.

[4] 1 Fonbl. Eq. B. 1, ch. 4, § 11; 1 Eq. Cas. Abr. 90, F. 5, 6.

[5] Lamlee v. Hanman, 2 Vern. 499, 500; Pitcairne v. Ogbourne, 2 Ves. 375; Neville v. Wilkinson, 1 Bro. Ch. R. 543, 547; 1 Fonbl. Eq. B. 1, ch. 4, § 11, and note (x).

[6] 1 Fonbl. Eq. B. 1, ch. 4, § 11, and note; Lamlee v. Hanman, 2 Vern. 499; McNeil v. Cahill, 2 Bligh, R. 228; England v. Downs, 2 Beav. R. 522.

269. Thus where a parent declined to consent to a marriage with the intended husband on account of his being in debt, and the brother of the latter gave a bond for the debt to procure such consent, and the intended husband then gave a secret counter bond to his brother to indemnify him against the first, and the marriage proceeded upon the faith of the extinguishment of the debt, the counter bond so given was treated as a fraud upon the marriage (contra fidem tabularum nuptialium), and all parties were held entitled as if it had not been given.[1]

270. So where a parent upon a marriage of his son made a settlement of an annuity or rent charge upon the wife in full of her jointure, and the son secretly gave a bond of indemnity, of the same date, to his parent, against the annuity or rent charge, it was held void as a fraud upon the faith of the marriage contract; for it affected to put the female party contracting for marriage in one situation by the articles, and in fact put her in another and worse situation by a private agreement.[2] So where a brother on the marriage of his sister let her have a sum of money privately, that her fortune might appear to be as much as was insisted on by the other side, and the sister gave a bond to the brother to repay it, the bond was set aside.[3]

271. And where upon a treaty of marriage a party to whom the intended husband was indebted concealed his own debt and misrepresented to the wife's father the amount of the husband's debts, the transaction was treated as a fraud upon the marriage, and the creditor was prevented by injunction from enforcing his debt, although it did not appear that there was any actual stipulation on the part of the wife's father in respect to the amount of the husband's debts.[4] Upon this occasion the Lord Chancellor said: ' The principle on which all these cases have been decided is that faith in such contracts is so essential to the happiness both of the parents and children, that whoever treats

---

[1] Redman v. Redman, 1 Vern. 348; Scott v. Scott, 1 Cox, R. 366; Turton v. Benson, 1 P. Will. 496; Morrison v. Arbuthnot, 8 Brown, Parl. Cases, p. 247, by Tomlins; 1 Bro. Ch. R. 447, note.

[2] Palmer v. Neave, 11 Ves. 165; Scott v. Scott, 1 Cox, R. 366, 378; Lamlee v. Haman, 2 Vern. 466.

[3] Gale v. Lindo, 2 Vern. 475; Lamlee v. Hanman, 2 Vern. 499; 1 Fonbl. Eq. B 1, ch. 2, § 11.

[4] Neville v. Wilkinson, 1 Bro. Ch. R. 543; s. c. 3 P. Will. 74, Mr. Cox's note; 1 Fonbl. Eq. B. 1, ch. 4, § 11, note (x); 3 Ves. 461; 16 Ves. 125.

fraudulently on such an occasion shall not only not gain but
even lose by it.[1]   Nay he shall be obliged to make his representation good; and the parties shall be placed in the same situation as if he had been scrupulously exact in the performance of
his duty.'[2]

272. In all these cases and those of a like nature the distinct
ground of relief is the meditated fraud or imposition practised
by one of the parties upon third persons by intentional concealment or misrepresentation.   And therefore if the parties act
under a mutual innocent mistake, and with entire good faith,
the concealment or misrepresentation of a material fact will not
induce the court to compel the party concealing it or affirming
it to make it good, or to place the other party in the same situation as if the fact were as the latter supposed.[3]   There must be
some ingredient of fraud, or some wilful misstatement or concealment which has misled the other side.

273. Upon a similar ground a settlement secretly made by a
woman in contemplation of marriage of her own property to her
own separate use without her intended husband's privity will be
held void, as it is in derogation of the marital rights of the husband,[4]

[1] Ibid.   See also Montefiori v. Montefiori, 1 W. Black. R. 363; s. c. cited
1 Bro. Ch. R. 548.

[2] Ibid.   See also Thompson v. Harrison, 1 Cox, R. 344; Eastabrook v.
Scott, 3 Ves. 461; Scott v. Scott, 1 Cox, R. 366; Hunsden v. Cheyney, 2 Vern.
R. 150; Beverley v. Beverley, 2 Vern. 133; Montefiori v. Montefiori, 1 W.
Black. R. 363; 1 Fonbl. Eq. B. 1, ch. 4, § 11, note (x); Vauxhall Bridge v.
Spencer, Jac. R. 67.

[3] Merewether v. Shaw, 2 Cox, R. 124; Scott v. Scott, 1 Cox, R. 366; 1
Fonbl. Eq. B. 1, ch. 4, § 11; Pitcairne v. Ogbourne, 2 Ves. 375.

[4] 1 Fonbl. Eq. B. 1, ch. 4, § 11, and note (z); Id. ch. 2, § 6, note (o); Jones
v. Martin, 3 Anst. R. 882; s. c. 5 Ves. 266, note; Fortescue v. Hennah, 19
Ves. 66; Bowes v. Strathmore, 2 Bro. Ch. R. 345; s. c. 2 Cox, R. 28; 1
Ves. jr. 22; 6 Bro. Par. Cas. (by Tomlins) 427; Ball v. Montgomery, 2
Ves. jr. 194; Carlton v. Earl of Dorset, 2 Vern. 17; Gregor v. Kemp, 3 Swanst.
R. 404, note; Goddard v. Snow, 1 Russell, R. 485; England v. Downs, 2
Beavan, R. 522.   On this occasion Lord Langdale said: 'Joan Mason was a
widow with three children, and, under the will of her first husband, she was
entitled to some freehold and leasehold property, to some furniture, and to
the stock in trade with which she carried on business as a victualler.   Contemplating a second marriage, she considered that she ought to make a provision for her children by the first, and being informed that a will which she
had made would upon her marriage become ineffectual, she made a settlement, and thereby provided that a portion of her freehold property should
be subjected to her own power of appointment, but that subject to such
power of appointment that part of her estate over which the power extended,

and a fraud upon his just expectations.[1] (a)   And a secret
conveyance made by a woman under like circumstances in favor

together with all the rest of her property, should be limited to her own
separate use for her life, with remainder for her three daughters in the manner
therein mentioned.   In the execution of this settlement, so far as it made provision for her children, she was performing a moral duty; in the circumstances
in which she was placed it was clearly her duty, before she placed herself
and her property in the power of her second husband, to secure a provision
for her children by her first husband, from whom her property was derived;
but in performing a duty towards her children she had no right to act fraudulently towards her second husband.   If a woman, entitled to property, enters
into a treaty for marriage, and during the treaty represents to her intended
husband that she is so entitled that upon the marriage he will become
entitled jure mariti, and if, during the same treaty, she clandestinely conveys
away the property in such manner as to defeat his marital right and secure
to herself the separate use of it, and the concealment continues till the marriage
takes place, there can be no doubt but that a fraud is thus practised on the
husband, and he is entitled to relief.   The equity which arises in cases of this
nature depends upon the peculiar circumstances of each case as bearing
upon the question whether the facts proved do or do not amount to sufficient evidence of fraud practised on the husband.   It is not doubted that
proof of direct misrepresentations, or of wilful concealment with intent to
deceive the husband, would entitle him to relief; but it is said that mere
concealment is not, in such a case, any evidence of fraud, and that if a man
without making any inquiry as to a woman's affairs and property thinks fit
to marry her, he must take her and her property as he finds them, and has
no right to complain if in the absence of any care on his part she has
taken care of herself and her children without his knowledge.   This proposition however cannot be admitted as stated; and clearly a woman in such
circumstances can only reconcile all her moral duties by making a proper
settlement on herself and her children, with the knowledge of her intended
husband.   If both the property and the mode of its conveyance, pending the
marriage treaty, were concealed from the intended husband, as was the case

---

[1] Ibid.; Lance v. Norman, 2 Ch. Rep. 41 [79]; Blanchet v. Foster, 2 Ves.
264; England v. Downs, 2 Beav. R. 522.

(a) See Lewellin v. Cobbold, 1 Smale & G. 376; Wrigley v. Swainson, 3 DeG. & S. 458; Chambers v. Crabbe, 34 Beav. 457 ; Goddard v. Snow, 1 Russ. 485; Baker v. Jordan, 73 N. Car. 145; Williams v. Carle, 2 Stockt. 543 ; Duncan's Appeal, 43 Penn. St. 67; Jordan v. Black, Meigs, 142; McAfee v. Ferguson, 9 B. Mon. 475; Goodson v. Whitfield, 5 Ired. Eq. 163; Tisdale v. Bailey, 6 Ired. Eq. 358; Logan v. Simmons, 3 Ired. Eq. 487.   So of the converse case of an ante-nuptial conveyance by a man with intent to defeat his intended wife of her rights in his property after marriage.   Kelly v. McGrath, 70 Ala. 75; Littleton v. Littleton, 1 Dev. & B. 327; Leach v. Duvall, 8 Bush, 201; Petty v. Petty, 4 B. Mon. 215.   Also of the case of conveyances by a husband in fraud of his wife pending proceedings for divorce.   Blenkinsopp v. Blenkinsopp, 1 DeG. M. & G. 495.

of a person for whom she is under no moral obligation to provide would be treated in the like manner. But if she should only reasonably provide for her children by a former marriage, under circumstances of good faith, it would be otherwise.[1] In like manner if previous to her marriage a woman should represent herself to her intended husband to be possessed of property, which she should secretly convey away before the marriage, the husband would be entitled to relief against such conveyance.[2] However circumstances may occur which may deprive the husband of any remedy, as if before the marriage he acquires a knowledge of the prior settlement, or if he has so conducted himself after the settlement that the wife cannot without dishonor to herself live with him. (a)

---

in Goddard v. Snow, there is still a fraud practised on the husband. The non-acquisition of property of which he had no notice is no disappointment, but still his legal right to property actually existing is defeated, and the vesting and continuance of a separate power in his wife over property which ought to have been his, and which is, without his consent, made independent of his control, is a surprise upon him, and might, if previously known, have induced him to abstain from the marriage. Nevertheless cases have occurred in which concealment, or rather the non-existence of communication to the husband, has not been held fraudulent, and whether fraud is made out must depend on the circumstances of each case; as an unmarried woman has a right to dispose of her property as she pleases, and as a conveyance made immediately before her marriage is prima facie good, it is to be impeached only by the proof of fraud.' Taylor v. Pugh, 1 Hare, R. 608, 613, 616; De Manneville v. Crompton, 1 Ves. & Beam. 354.

[1] Ibid.; King v. Cotton, 2 P. Will. 357, 674; St. George v. Wake, 1 Mylne & Keen, 610; England v. Downs, 2 Beav. R. 522; De Manneville v. Compton, 1 Ves. & Beam. 354.

[2] England v. Downs, 2 Beav. R. 542.

(a) Antenuptial conveyances by the intended wife are however presumptively valid. Strathmore v. Bowes, 1 Ves. jr. 22, 38. Such conveyances or settlements are invalid if it appear (1) that intermarriage was in the contemplation of the parties at the time, (2) that the woman executed the same in contemplation of the future marriage, and (3) that she concealed the same from her husband. If the husband establish these facts, the conveyance or settlement will not stand against his marital rights. Goddard v. Snow, 1 Russ. 485; Strathmore v. Bowes, 2 Cox, 28; s. c. 2 Brown, C. C. 345. If then the husband had sufficiently early notice before the marriage of the purpose of the intended wife to execute a settlement, he cannot afterwards object, assuming that nothing afterwards passed to justify the husband in supposing that the purpose would not be carried out. Wrigley v. Swainson, 3 DeG. & S. 458.

In Strathmore v. Bowes, supra, it was laid down by Buller, J., as the result of the authorities as to convey-

274. It is upon the same ground of public policy that contracts in restraint of marriage are held void.[1] A reciprocal engagement between a man and a woman to marry each other is unquestionably good.[2] But a contract which restrains a person from marrying at all, or from marrying anybody except a particular person, without enforcing a corresponding reciprocal obligation on that person, is treated as mischievous to the general interests of society, which are promoted by the encouragement and support of suitable marriages.[3] Courts of Equity have in

---

[1] Hartley v. Rice, 10 East, R. 22; Lowe v. Peers, 4 Burr. 2225; Woodhouse v. Shipley, 2 Atk. 539, 540; Newland on Contracts, ch. 33, pp. 472 to 476.

[2] Cock v. Richards, 10 Ves. 438; Key v. Bradshaw, 2 Vern. 102.

[3] 1 Fonbl. Eq. B. 1, ch. 4, § 10; Baker v. White, 2 Vern. 215; Woodhouse

---

ances by women not previously married, or by widows without children, that if the wife were guilty of any fraud, as e. g. by professing to the husband that there was nothing to interfere with his rights, any conveyance executed by her in prejudice of such representation would be invalid. That however was deemed the extent of the cases; the mere non-disclosure of an antenuptial conveyance would not of itself make the transaction impeachable. Nor when provision was made by a widow for the children of a former marriage would the deed be invalid. Contra where the conveyance was made with intent to deceive the husband, though the grantees are innocent. Tisdale v. Bailey, 6 Ired. Eq. 358; Goodson v. Whitfield, 5 Ired. Eq. 163; Logan v. Simmons, 3 Ired. Eq. 487.

Though a settlement then by an intended wife be voluntary, and not disclosed to the husband, it is not for that reason necessarily fraudulent. The courts will consider the nature of the provision, the situation of the husband in point of pecuniary means, and any other facts which tend to show that no fraud could reasonably be considered to have been intended. The equity which arises in cases of this kind depends upon the peculiar circumstances of each case. Gregory v. Winston, 23 Gratt. 102 ; Bigelow, Fraud, 49–51.

Actual intent to deceive the husband appears to be unnecessary; it is enough, so far, if after the commencement of a treaty of marriage the intended wife should have disposed of her property without the knowledge of her intended husband. Taylor v. Pugh, 1 Hare, 608; supra, pp. 273, 274, note. Indeed it appears to be no good objection to the husband's claim that he did not know that his wife had the particular property until after the marriage. Ib. But it is said that if the husband had made retirement from the treaty of marriage impracticable, as by inducing the wife to cohabit with him before marriage, he could not object to her antenuptial conveyances. Ib.

An obligation founded on a valuable consideration entered into by the wife pending a treaty of marriage cannot be set aside by the husband merely because it was concealed from him ; though if it was fraudulently entered into by the wife, with knowledge in the other party, it would be void against the husband. Gregory v. Winston, 23 Gratt. 102, 123; Blanchet v. Foster, 2 Ves. sen. 264.

this respect followed, although not to an unlimited extent, the doctrine of the civil law that marriage ought to be free.[1] (a)

v. Shipley, 2 Atk. 595; Lowe v. Peers, 4 Burr. 2225; Cock v. Richards, 10 Ves. 429; Key v. Bradshaw, 2 Vern. 102; Atkins v. Farr, 1 Atk. R. 287; s. c. 2 Eq. Abridg. 247, 248.

[1] Dig. Lib. 35, tit. 1, l. 62, 63, 64; Key v. Bradshaw, 2 Vern. 102; 1 Fonbl. Eq. B. 1, ch. 4, § 10.

(a) *Conditions in Restraint of Marriage.* — Notwithstanding the many expressions of the books, it is doubtful whether much now remains of the once generally accepted rule that conditions in restraint of marriage in gifts and contracts are void. In the first place all the exceptions of the Roman law, from which the doctrine was derived, were admitted by the Ecclesiastical Courts, and the Courts of Common Law and of Equity have always looked upon the doctrine with disfavor, and have been continuously narrowing its application. See e. g. Stackpole v. Beaumont, 3 Ves. jr. 89; Jones v. Jones, 1 Q. B. D. 279; Commonwealth v. Stauffer, 10 Barr, 350; Cornell v. Lovett, 35 Penn. St. 100; Hogan v. Curtin, 88 N. Y. 162. Swinburne enumerates ten exceptions to the doctrine. Wills, part 4, sec. 12.

The English Ecclesiastical Courts, having jurisdiction of the distribution of the personal estate of decedents, early adopted, apparently with little regard to difference of circumstances (Stackpole v. Beaumont, 3 Ves. jr. 89, 96; infra, § 278), the rule of the Roman law that, subject to the familiar exceptions, conditions imposing restraint upon marriage were of no effect and would be disregarded. And it appears to have been a matter of no consequence whether the condition was precedent or subsequent ; the distinction of the English law upon this subject was not taken by the Roman law, and the ecclesiastical judges did not, at first at least, adopt it.

The Courts of Common Law and of Equity however were restless under the views of the ecclesiastical judges; and the Law Courts having jurisdiction of the real estate of decedents, and the Court of Chancery having in various ways to treat both of the personalty and the realty of decedents, while both of these courts had jurisdiction, to the exclusion of the Ecclesiastical Courts, over contracts, it resulted that every opportunity was improved of laying down exceptions or qualifications to a doctrine which the courts were not quite bold enough to repudiate altogether. To this end the intention of the testator or donor came to be looked into more and more, and if possible to be allowed effect. This alone would seem to have been a virtual abandonment of the Roman rule; that rule apparently looked to the effect of the gift, and then governed regardless of the giver's intention.

The Courts of Common Law and of Equity began to say that the question whether the donor had made a gift over to a third person on breach of the condition concerning marriage might be taken into account; that is, the existence or non-existence of a gift over would have a bearing upon the question whether the donor really *intended* to have the condition enforced, or, as it was rather blindly said, to have it act merely in terrorem (what fear could there be if the condition was not to be enforced?). Though sometimes it was said that the reason why a condition with a gift over was good was because of the interest of the donee over; but this was only another way of saying that the donor's intention

275. Where indeed the obligation to marry is reciprocal, although the marriage is to be deferred to some future period,

would be respected. The first donee could not take a larger interest, to the detriment of the donee over, in the absence of evidence of any purpose in the giver to enlarge the gift in any case. 2 Jarman, Wills, 44, note (Bigelow's ed.). 'Different reasons,' said Sir William Grant, in Lloyd v. Branton, 3 Mer. 108, 'have been assigned for allowing this operation to a bequest over. Some have said that it afforded a clear manifestation of the intention of the testator not to make the declaration of forfeiture merely in terrorem, which might otherwise have been presumed. Others have said it was the interest of the legatee over, which made the difference, and that the clause ceased to be merely a condition of forfeiture, and became a conditional limitation, to which the court was bound to give effect.' See Dickson's Trust, 1 Sim. N. s. 37, 45. Whether the one or the other or neither of these views be correct, the passage shows that the judges were feeling for the donor's intention.

At the same time the distinction which had grown up in other cases between conditions precedent and conditions subsequent began to be drawn into the question; and it was said by Courts of Law and by Courts of Equity alike that if the condition was precedent, especially if followed by a gift over, it was binding, though the rule of the ecclesiastical judges was allowed to have greater play if the condition was subsequent. But even in this case if there was a gift over, the judges sometimes considered that the condition was intended to be binding and must be respected, as the case before Sir William Grant just cited shows. The adoption therefore of the distinction between conditions precedent and conditions subsequent was further indication of the desire of the courts to

put the case as far as possible upon the ground of intention.

Indeed this is manifested as much by the cases in which the condition is declared to be in terrorem only as by those in which it is held binding. This will be seen by the following propositions of Mr. Jarman: He submits that conditions *precedent* to marry with consent, unaccompanied by a bequest over in default, are in terrorem, except in three cases: (1) Where the legatee takes a provision or a legacy in the alternative of marrying without consent. Creagh v. Wilson, 2 Vern. 573; 1 Eq. Cas. Abr. 111, pl. 5; Gillet v. Wray, 1 P. Wms. 284. The principle in Creagh v. Wilson, Jarman says, is that the testator did not intend the gift to be in terrorem only. (2) Where marriage with consent is but one of two events on either of which the legatee will be entitled to the legacy. Hemmings v. Munckley, 1 Bro. C. C. 303; s. c. 1 Cox, 39; Scott v. Tyler, 2 Bro. C. C. 431. See Gardiner v. Slater, 25 Beav. 509, case of a gift over. (3) Where marriage with consent is confined to minority. Stackpole v. Beaumont, 3 Ves. 89; 2 Jarman, Wills, 46, 47 (5th Am. ed.). See also Hogan v. Curtin, 88 N. Y. 162. It may be added that in Younge v. Furse, 8 DeG. M. & G. 756, a condition precedent not to marry under twenty-eight was held valid, though there was no gift over and nothing else to bring the matter within any of the three cases of Jarman.

When at last English judges reached the point of declaring that the real question in a particular case was whether a testator intended to discourage marrying or not (Jones v. Jones, 1 Q. B. D. 279, 281, Blackburn, J.), and to decide the case, as in Jones v. Jones, upon the answer to that question, a step only remained to declaring

there may not be as between the parties any objection to the contract in itself, if in all other respects it is entered into in good

that the donor's intention should govern. That step however cannot be said to have been taken until the courts — going further than to say that if no intention to discourage marrying appears, the donor's purpose must prevail — declare that a direct attempt to persuade a donee not to marry at all, and providing a forfeiture if the donor's will is not complied with, must be respected. Mr. Justice Blackburn seems all but prepared to take the step. He says, ' There is, I *admit*, strong authority that when the object of the will is to restrain marriage and promote celibacy,' the condition is not good. Jones *v.* Jones, supra.

Perhaps among the chief English authorities the case is nowhere put more strongly than long ago by Powell in the 7th ed. of Swinburne on Wills, p. 483 (part 4, sec. 12), where he says of a condition requiring assent to marriage that the law of England, in disregarding the condition, ' does not proceed upon the ground that the condition is unlawful, and therefore to be rejected, for,' he declares, ' there are three sorts of conditions only to be rejected: first, such as are repugnant; secondly, such as are impossible in their creation; thirdly, such as are mala in se; and this condition of marrying with consent does not come under any one of these three heads. It therefore seems merely a rule of construction or legal presumption that such clauses annexed to absolute legacies of personal property are merely cautionary.' And he adds that if the gift is not absolute, but is followed by a gift over, the presumption that it was meant to be cautionary is overturned. This he considers as the result of all the old authorities.

Turning to the American cases, quite as strong a disposition will be found to prevail against adopting broadly the doctrine that conditions in restraint of marriage are void. Many of the courts have, in cases of *personalty*, followed the in terrorem doctrine; but it will generally be found that the decisions to that effect proceed upon the ground that there was no intention to make the condition effective. Bannerman *v.* Weaver, 8 Md. 517; Gough *v.* Manning, 26 Md. 347, 362; Waters *v.* Tazewell, 9 Md. 292. If however there is a gift over, the condition is effective (see Hogan *v.* Curtin, 88 N. Y. 162), at least in the case of a gift to the husband or wife of the donor. Hawkins *v.* Skeggs, 10 Humph. 81; Gough *v.* Manning, supra; Duddy *v.* Gresham, 2 L. R. Ir. 442, 464, 465. And this too probably even in the case of a condition subsequent. The condition is not treated in any of these cases as a thing to be repudiated in itself; it is either treated as no condition at all, for want of the manifestation of a sufficient purpose in omitting a gift over, or it is held valid. If the question should arise for the first time, a gift of personalty to the donor's wife or widow on condition of remaining single might well be upheld, though followed by no gift over.

With regard to gifts of *realty*, over which the Ecclesiastical Courts never had jurisdiction, a condition in a gift in restraint of marriage is valid (Hogan *v.* Curtin, 88 N. Y. 162, where there was no gift over), at least in the case of a gift to the donor's widow. Duddy *v.* Gresham, 2 L. R. Ir. 442, 465; Commonwealth *v.* Stauffer, 10 Barr, 350; Cornell *v.* Lovett, 35 Penn. St. 100; Luigart *v.* Ripley, 19 Ohio St. 24; Clark *v.* Tennison, 33 Md. 85; Duncan *v.* Philips, 3 Head, 415; Hughes *v.* Boyd, 2 Sneed, 512; Vaughan *v.* Lovejoy, 34 Ala. 437; Snider *v.* Newsom, 24 Ga. 139; Chapin

faith and there is no reason to suspect fraud, imposition, or undue influence.[1]　But even in these cases, if the contract is de-

[1] Lowe v. Peers, 4 Burr. 2229, 2230; Key v. Bradshaw, 2 Vern. 102.

v. Marvin, 12 Wend. 538; Pringle v.
Dunkley, 14 Smedes & M. 16; Dumey
v. Schoeffler, 24 Mo. 170; Allen v.
Jackson, 1 Ch. D. 399. The same
rule applies to a condition in a gift
to a husband in restraint of another
marriage by him. Allen v. Jackson,
supra; Bostick v. Blades, 59 Md. 231.
And the condition is good though there
be no gift over. Ib.; Cornell v. Lovett,
35 Penn. St. 100, 104; Commonwealth
v. Stauffer, supra.

Another way by which our courts,
following the suggestions of English
judges, have sought to escape the
doctrine of the ecclesiastical judges,
and to carry out the donor's purpose,
has been by construing the gift, when
possible, as a limitation of the estate
of the donee rather than as a condition
against marriage. Thus it is held
that where land is given to A 'until
marriage,' or to A 'and in the event
of marriage' then over, the gift is
good, because a man may give as
small an estate as he will. Otis v.
Prince, 10 Gray, 581; Selden v. Keen,
27 Gratt. 576; Maddox v. Maddox,
11 Gratt. 804; Lloyd v. Branton, 3
Mer. 108; Morley v. Rennoldson, 2
Hare, 570; Harmon v. Brown, 53 Ind.
207; Randall v. Marble, 69 Maine,
310; Dawson v. Oliver-Massey, 2 Ch.
D. 753. But in Jones v. Jones, 1
Q. B. D. 279, 282, it is declared by
Blackburn, J., that the validity of a
gift of land cannot turn upon the question whether the disposition amounts
to a limitation or not, though it might
be otherwise of a gift of personalty.
See 4 Kent, 127. It has been held of a
condition subsequent, in the case of a
gift not to the donor's wife or husband,
that the limitation over must be good
as such for the purpose of cutting down
the prior estate on marriage. Otis v.

Prince, and Randall v. Marble, supra,
where the limitation over was to
'heirs,' who would have taken any-
how. There was not sufficient indication that the condition was intended
to be effective; though if the gift over
had been held good, the courts would
perhaps have veiled their real meaning
by saying that it was the interest of the
donee over that governed, rather than
the purpose to restrain marriage.

The result is that where the courts
can discover in the written instrument
— that must govern, it seems — any
other intention than that of a clearly
designed discouragement of marriage,
they will respect that intention. It
appears to make no difference that
the nature of the gift may have an
obvious tendency that way, as indeed
has been the case in nearly every instance in which the provision of the
donor has been held absolute; if there
is no clear design to prevent marriage,
the intention will be upheld. And in
almost every case the courts either
find the want of any such design,
and hence uphold the condition, as
where it is precedent, or they find
that the supposed condition is no condition at all but only a wish, which,
like a precatory trust, need not be
complied with. See Duddy v. Gresham, 2 L. R. Ir. 442, 464, 465.

When it has come to this, that
nothing is left of the Roman rule
except where a clear design to discourage marrying is expressed, as held
in Jones v. Jones, — where, though the
obvious and natural effect of a particular gift is to prevent marriage,
that fact is disregarded unless there
is a plain and real intent, — it seems
quite time, with Powell, ut supra, to
drop a rule altogether which never
had a sufficient reason for its existence

signed by the parties to impose upon third persons, as upon
parents, or friends standing in loco parentis or in some other
particular relation to the parties, so as to disappoint their bounty
or to defeat their intentions in the settlement or disposal of their
estates, there, if the contract is clandestine and kept secret for
this purpose, it will be treated by Courts of Equity as a fraud
upon such parents or other friends, and as such be set aside;
or the equities will be held the same as if it had not been entered into.[1] The general ground upon which this doctrine is

[1] Woodhouse *v.* Shipley, 2 Atk. 535, 539; Cock *v.* Richards, 10 Ves. 436,
438.

in the English law, and to permit the
case to stand on the donor's intention, whatever it may be. Indeed the
reasoning of the better authorities
comes quite to this result. Stackpole
v. Beaumont, 3 Ves. jr. 89; Commonwealth *v.* Stauffer, 10 Barr, 350. In
working out the question of intention,
when not clearly expressed, the consideration whether there is a gift over,
and whether the condition is precedent
or subsequent, might have a bearing.
If there is no gift over, and the condition is subsequent, with nothing
more, it might be inferred that it was
not intended to make the condition
absolute; if on the other hand there
is a gift over, or if the condition is
precedent, the contrary might well be
inferred. But the mere circumstance
that there is or is not a gift over
should not be *decisive.* See 4 Kent,
127; Dickson's Trust, 1 Sim. N. S.
37; Parsons *v.* Winslow, 6 Mass. 169,
181; Cornell *v.* Lovett, 35 Penn. St.
100, 104. See Hogan *v.* Curtin, 88
N. Y. 162. When however the intention is found, it is submitted as a
legitimate conclusion of the reasoning
of the judges against the Roman rule,
if not as the natural effect of the cases
themselves, that that intention should
be allowed to prevail, though it be
considered of a particular gift that
the donor clearly designed to discourage the donee, not merely from
marrying without consent (as to which

see Hogan *v.* Curtin, supra), but from
marrying altogether. Such a case as
the last indeed can hardly arise except
where there is a provision either
(1) for the wife or the husband of
a grantor or a testator, or (2) for a
person who is desired to enter monas-
tic life (in what other case would a
premium be avowedly offered to per-
petual singleness?); and in the first
of these cases the better authorities
agree, as we have seen, that the intention of the grantor or testator to
have the condition effective will be
upheld if clear, though, at least in
a case of realty, there be no gift over.
Nor is there any real ground in this
country why the same rule should not
apply to personalty. The second case
does not appear to have arisen except
in regard to the widow of a donor
(Duddy *v.* Gresham, 2 L. R. Ir. 442),
and is not very likely to arise. If
however it should arise, and it should
appear that the donor has made a
clear gift over, in case his will be not
respected, to another not as 'heir,'
his intention will probably be allowed
to prevail. The whole question seems
therefore within the control of the
grantor or testator.

Query whether hostility to monasti-
cism may not have influenced the
Protestant ecclesiastics in adopting
the Roman rule? Or was that rule
adopted before the Reformation?

the restraint of it were a mere political regulation applicable to the circumstances of the Roman Empire at that time, and inapplicable to other countries. After the civil war the depopulation occasioned by it led to habits of celibacy. In the time of Augustus the Julian law, which went too far, and was corrected by the Lex Papia Poppæa, not only offered encouragement to marriage but laid heavy impositions upon celibacy. That being established as a rule in restraint of celibacy (it is an odd expression), and for the encouragement of all persons who would contract marriage, it necessarily followed that no person could act contrary to it by imposing restraints directly contrary to the law. Therefore it became a rule of construction that these conditions were null. It is difficult to apply that to a country where there is no law to restrain individuals from exercising their own discretion as to the time and circumstances of the marriage which their children or objects of bounty may contract. It is perfectly impossible now, whatever it might have been formerly, to apply that doctrine, not to lay conditions to restrain marriage under the age of twenty-one, to the law of England; for it is directly contrary to the political law of the country. There can be no marriage, under the age of twenty-one, without the consent of the parent.'

279. It is highly probable that this view of the origin of the English doctrine as to conditions in restraint of marriage, annexed to gifts, legacies, and other conveyances of interests, is historically correct.[1] But whether it be so or not, it may be

---

[1] See Scott v. Tyler, 2 Bro. Ch. R. 487; s. c. 2 Dick. R. 712; Clarke v. Parker, 19 Ves. 13; Reynish v. Martin, 3 Atk. 330, 331, 332; 1 Roper on Legacies, by White, ch. 13, § 1, p. 654. Lord Thurlow, in Scott v. Tyler (2 Dick. R. 716 to 721), has traced out with much learning and ability the gradual introduction and progress of the civil-law doctrine, through the instrumentality of the canon law, into the law of England. I gladly extract a portion of his statements, as they may tend to instruct the student more exactly in a branch of the law confessedly not without some anomalies. 'The earlier cases,' said he, 'refer in general terms to the canon law as the rule by which all legacies are to be governed. By that law undoubtedly all conditions which fell within the scope of this objection, the restraint of marriage, are reputed void; and, as they speak, " pro non adjectis." But those cases go no way towards ascertaining the nature and extent of the objection. Towards the latter end of the last and beginning of the present century the matter is more loosely handled. The canon law is not referred to (professedly at least) as affording a distinct and positive rule for annulling the obnoxious conditions. On the contrary they are treated as partaking of the force allowed them by

affirmed without fear of contradiction that the doctrine on this
subject at present maintained and administered by Courts of

the law of England. But in respect of their imposing a restraint of marriage
they are treated at the same time as unfavorable and contrary to the common
weal and good order of society. It is reasoned that parental duty and affection are violated when a child is stripped of its just expectations; that such
an intention is improbably imputed to a parent, particularly in those instances
where there was no misalliance, as in marriage with the houses of Bellases,
Bertie, Cecil, and Semphile, which the parent, if he had been alive, would
probably have approved. These ideas apply indifferently to bequests of lands
and of money, and were in fact so applied in one very remarkable case. Nay,
to avoid the supposed force of these obnoxious conditions, strained construc-
tions were made upon doubtful signs of consent, and every mode of artificial
reasoning was adopted to relax their rigor. This was thought more practicable by calling them conditions subsequent; although if that had made such
difference, they were and indeed must have been generally conditions precedent, as being the terms on which the legacy was made to vest. At length it
became a common phrase that such conditions were only in terrorem. I do
not find it was ever seriously supposed to have been the testator's intention to
hold out the terror of that which he never meant should happen, but the court
disposed of such conditions so as to make them amount to no more. On the
other hand some provisions against improvident matches, especially during
infancy, or to a certain age, could not be thought an unreasonable precaution
for parents to entertain. The custom of London has been found reasonable,
which forfeits the portion on the marriage of an infant orphan without consent. The Court of Chancery is in the constant habit of restraining and pun-
ishing such marriages. And the Legislature has at length adopted the same
idea, as far as it was thought general regulation could in sound policy go. In
this situation the matter was found about the middle of the present century, when
doubts occurred which divided the sentiments of the first men of the age.
The difficulty seems to have consisted principally in reconciling the cases, or
rather the arguments on which they proceeded. The better opinion, or at
least that which prevailed, was, that devises of land, with which the canon
law never had any concern, should follow the rule of the common law, and
that legacies of money, being of that sort, should follow the rule of the canon
law. Lands devised, charges upon it, powers to be exercised over it, money
legacies referring to such charges, money to be laid out in lands (though I do
not find this yet resolved), follow the rule of the common law; and such
trusts are to be executed with analogy to it. Mere money legacies follow the
rule of the canon law, and all trusts of that nature are to be executed with
analogy to that. But still, if I am not mistaken, the question remains un-
resolved, What is the nature and extent of that rule as applied to conditions
in restraint of marriage? The canon law prevails in this country only so far as
it hath been actually received with such ampliations and limitations as time and
occasion have introduced, and subject at all times to the municipal law. It is
founded in the civil law; consequently the tenets of that law also may serve
to illustrate the received rules of the canon law. By the civil law the provision of a child was considered as a debt of nature, of which the laws of civil
society also exacted the payment; insomuch that a will was regarded as
inofficious, which did not in some sort satisfy it. By the positive institu-

Equity (for it has undergone some important changes) is far better adapted to the exigencies of modern society throughout Christendom than that which was asserted in the Roman law. While it upholds the general freedom of choice in marriages, it at the same time has a strong tendency to preserve a just control and influence in parents in regard to the marriages of their children, and a reasonable power in all persons to qualify and restrict their bounty in such a manner and on such conditions as the general right of dominion over property in a free country justifies and protects upon grounds of general convenience and safety.

280. The general result of the modern English doctrine on this subject (for it will not be found easy to reconcile all the cases)[1] may be stated in the following summary manner.　Conditions annexed to gifts, legacies, and devises in restraint of marriage are not void if they are reasonable in themselves, and do not directly or virtually operate as an undue restraint upon the freedom of marriage.　If the condition is in restraint of marriage generally, then indeed as a condition against public policy and the due economy and morality of domestic life it will be held utterly void.[2]　And so if the condition is not in restraint of marriage generally, but still the prohibition is of so rigid a nature or so tied up to peculiar circumstances that the party upon whom it is to operate is unreasonably restrained in the

---

tions of that law, it was also provided, " Si quis cælibatus vel viduitatis conditionem hæredi legatariove injunxerit; hæres legatariusve e conditione liberi sunto; neque eo minus delatam hæreditatem, legatumve, ex hac lege, consequantur."　In ampliation of this law it seems to have been well settled in all times, that if instead of creating a condition absolutely enjoining celibacy or widowhood, the same be referred to the advice or discretion of another, particularly an interested person, it is deemed a fraud on the law, and treated accordingly; that is, the condition so imposed is holden for void.　Upon the same principle, in further ampliation of the law, all distinction is abolished between precedent and subsequent conditions; for it would be an easy evasion of such a law if a slight turn of the phrase were allowed to put it aside.　It has rather therefore been construed that the condition is performed by the marriage, which is the only lawful part of the condition, or by asking the consent, for that also is a lawful condition; and for the rest the condition, not being lawful, is holden " pro non adjecta."

[1] Scott v. Tyler, 2 Bro. Ch. R. 487; 2 Dick. R. 718; Stackpole v. Beaumont, 3 Ves. 95; 1 Foubl. Eq. B. 1, ch. 4, § 10, note (q).

[2] Keily v. Monck, 3 Ridgw. Parl. R. 205, 244, 247, 261; 1 Fonbl. Eq. B. 1, ch. 4, § 10, note (q); Pratt v. Tyler, 2 Bro. Ch. R. 487; Harvey v. Aston, Com. Rep. 726; s. c. 1 Atk. 361.

choice of marriage, it will fall under the like consideration.[1] Thus where a legacy was given to a daughter on condition that she should not marry without consent, or should not marry a man who was not seised of an estate in fee simple of the clear yearly value of £500, it was held to be a void condition, as leading to a probable prohibition of marriage.[2]

281. But the same principles of public policy which annul such conditions when they tend to a general restraint of marriage, will confirm and support them when they merely prescribe such reasonable and provident regulations and sanctions as tend to protect the individual from those melancholy consequences to which an over-hasty, rash, or precipitate match would probably lead.[3]   If parents, who must naturally feel the deepest solicitude for the welfare of their children, and other near relatives and friends, who may well be presumed to take a lively interest in the happiness of those with whom they are associated by ties of kindred or friendship, could not, by imposing some restraints upon their bounty, guard the inexperience and ardor of youth against the wiles and delusions of the crafty and the corrupt who should seek to betray them from motives of the grossest selfishness, the law would be lamentably defective, and would, under the pretence of upholding the institution of marriage, subvert its highest purposes.   It would indeed encourage the young and the thoughtless to exercise a perfect freedom of choice in marriage ; but it would be at the expense of all the best objects of the institution, the preservation of domestic happiness, the security of private virtue, and the rearing of families in habits of sound morality and filial obedience and reverence. Such a reproach does not belong to the common law in our day ; and least of all can it be justly attributed to Courts of Equity.

282. Mr. Fonblanque has with great propriety remarked : ' The only restrictions which the law of England imposes are such as are dictated by the soundest policy and approved by the purest morality.   That a parent, professing to be affectionate, shall not be unjust ; that, professing to assert his own claim, he

---

[1] Keily v. Monck, 3 Ridgw. Parl. R. 205, 244, 247, 261; 1 Eq. Abridg. p. 110, Condition, C. in Marg.;   Morley v. Rennaldson, 2 Hare, R. 570.

[2] Keily v. Monck, 3 Ridgw. Parl. R. 205, 244, 247, 261; 1 Chitty, Eq. Dig. Marriage, W.

[3] 1 Fonbl. Eq. B. 1, ch. 4, § 10, note (q).

shall not disappoint or control the claims of nature nor obstruct the interests of the community ; that what purports to be an act of generosity shall not be allowed to operate as a temptation to do that which militates against nature, morality, or sound policy, or to restrain from doing that which would serve and promote the essential interests of society : [these] are rules which cannot reasonably be reprobated as harsh infringements of private liberty, or even reproached as unnecessary restraints on its free exercise.   On these considerations are founded those distinctions which have from time to time been recognized in our Courts of Equity respecting testamentary conditions with reference to marriage.' [1]

283. Godolphin also has very correctly laid down the general principle : 'All conditions against the liberty of marriage are unlawful.   But if the conditions are only such as whereby marriage is not absolutely prohibited but only in part restrained, as in respect to time, place, or person, then such conditions are not utterly to be rejected.' [2]   Still this language is to be understood with proper limitations ; that is to say, that the restraints upon marriage, in respect to time, place, or person, are reasonably asserted.   For it is obvious that restraints as to time, place, and person may be so framed as to operate a virtual prohibition upon marriage, or at least upon its most important and valuable objects.   As for instance a condition that a child should not marry until fifty years of age ; [3] or should not marry any person inhabiting in the same town, county, or state ; or should not marry any person who was a clergyman, a physician, or a lawyer, or any person except of a particular trade or employment ; for these would be deemed a mere evasion or fraud upon the law. [4]

284. On the other hand some provisions against improvident matches, especially during infancy, or until a certain age of discretion, cannot be deemed an unreasonable precaution for parents and other persons to affix to their bounty. [5]   Thus a legacy given to a daughter to be paid her at twenty-one years of age if she does

[1] 1 Fonbl. Eq. B. 1, ch. 4, § 10, note (q).
[2] Godolphin's Orphan's Legacy, Pt. 1, ch. 15, § 1.
[3] But see 1 Roper on Legacies, ch. 13, § 2, p. 716, edit. by White.
[4] See Scott v. Tyler, 2 Dick. R. 721, 722; 2 Brown, Ch. R. 488.
[5] Scott v. Tyler, 2 Dick. R. 719.

not marry until that period, would be held good; for it post-
pones marriage only to a reasonable age of discretion.[1] (a)   So a
condition, annexed to a gift or legacy, that the party should not
marry without the consent of parents or trustees or other persons specified, is held good, for it does not impose an unreasonable restraint upon marriage; and it must be presumed that
the person selected will act with good faith and sound discretion
in giving or withholding consent.[2]   The civil law indeed seems
on this point to have adopted a very different doctrine; holding that the requirement of the consent of a third person, and
especially of an interested person, is a mere fraud upon the
law.[3]

285. Other cases have been stated which are governed by the
same principles. Thus it has been said that a condition not to
marry a widow is no unlawful injunction; for it is not in general
restraint of marriage. So a condition that a widow shall not
marry is not unlawful, neither is an annuity during widowhood
only.[4] A condition to marry, or not to marry, Titius or Mævia
is good. So a condition prescribing due ceremonies and a due
place of marriage is good. And so any other conditions of a

[1] See Stackpole v. Beaumont, 3 Ves. 96, 97; Scott v. Tyler, 2 Dick. R. 721,
722, 724.

[2] Desbody v. Boyville, 2 P. Will. 547; Scott v. Tyler, 2 Bro. Ch. R. 431,
485; 2 Dick. R. 712; Clarke v. Parker, 19 Ves. 1; Lloyd v. Branton, 3 Meriv.
R. 108; Dashwood v. Bulkley, 10 Ves. 229.

[3] Lord Thurlow in Scott v. Tyler, 2 Dick. R. 720; Ayliffe, Pand. B. 3, tit.
21, p. 374.

[4] Conditions requiring widowhood were generally void by the civil law when
the legacy was to the party herself, but not where it was to a third person.
Ayliffe, Pand. B. 3, tit. 21, p. 374.   ' Legatum alii sub conditione sic relictum;
Si uxor nuptui se post mortem mariti non collocaverit, contractis nuptiis, conditione deficit, ideoque peti nequaquam potest.' Cod. Lib. 6, tit. 40, l. 1;
Pothier, Pand. Lib. 35, tit. 1, n. 35. In Parsons v. Winslow (6 Mass. R. 169),
where the legacy was during widowhood and life, without any bequest over,
the court held the condition to be in terrorem only; and that the legatee took,
notwithstanding a second marriage. But see Scott v. Tyler, 2 Dick. R. 721,
722; s. c. 2 Brown, Ch. R. 488; Harvey v. Aston, 1 Atk. 379; Marples v.
Bainbridge, 1 Madd. R. 590; Richards v. Baker, 2 Atk. 321; 1 Roper on
Legacies, by White, ch. 13, § 2, p. 721, 722.

(a) Beaumont v. Squire, 21 L. J. Q. B. 123; Younge v. Furse, 8 DeG. M. & G. 756. In the last case marriage was to be postponed until the age of twenty-eight.

similar nature, if not used evasively as a covert purpose to restrain marriage generally.[1]

286. But Courts of Equity are not generally inclined to lend an indulgent consideration to conditions in restraint of marriage ;[2] and on that account (being in no small degree influenced by the doctrines of the civil and canon law) they have not only constantly manifested an anxious desire to guard against any abuse to which the giving of one person any degree of control over another might eventually lead, but they have on many occasions resorted to subtleties and artificial distinctions in order to escape from the positive directions of the party imposing such conditions.

287. One distinction is between cases where in default of a compliance with the condition there is a bequest over, and cases where there is not a bequest over, upon a like default of the party to comply with the condition. In the former case the bequest over becomes operative upon such default, and defeats the prior legacy.[3] (a) In the latter case (that is, where there is no bequest over) the condition is treated as ineffectual, upon the ground that the testator is to be deemed to use the condition in terrorem only, and not to impose a forfeiture, since he has failed to make any other disposition of the bequest upon default in the condition.[4] (b)

288. Another distinction is taken between conditions in re-

---

[1] Scott v. Tyler, 2 Bro. Ch. R. 488; 2 Dick. R. 721, 722; Godolp. Orp. Leg. Pt. 3, ch. 17, §§ 1 to 10; Ayliffe, Pand. B. 3, tit. 21, p. 374.

[2] See Long v. Dennis, 4 Burr. R. 2052. Lord Mansfield, in Long v. Dennis, 4 Burr. R. 2055, said, ' Conditions in restraint of marriage are odious, and are therefore held to the utmost rigor and strictness.' Lord Eldon seems to have disapproved of this generality of expression, in Clarke v. Parker, 19 Ves. 19.

[3] Clarke v. Parker, 19 Ves. 13; Lloyd v. Branton, 3 Meriv. R. 108, 119; 1 Fonbl. Eq. B. 1, ch. 4, § 10, note (q); Wheeler v. Bingham, 3 Atk. 368; Malcolm v. O'Callaghan, 2 Madd. R. 350; Chauncey v. Graydon, 2 Atk. 616.

[4] Harvey v. Aston, 1 Atk. 361, 375, 377; Reynish v. Martin, 3 Atk. 330; 1 Wilson, R. 130; 1 Fonbl. Eq. B. 1, ch. 4, § 10, note (q); Pendarvis v. Hicks, 2 Freeman, R. 41; Pullen v. Ready, 2 Atk. R. 587; Long v. Dennis, 4 Burr. 2055; 1 Eq. Abridg. 110, C.; Parsons v. Winslow, 6 Mass. R. 169; 1 Roper on Legacies by White, ch. 13, § 1, pp. 654 to 660; Id. § 2, pp. 687, 715 to 727; Eastland v. Reynolds, 1 Dick. R. 317.

(a) But where the condition of a devise was the giving a bond not to marry or cohabit with certain persons, with a devise over, the court refused to enforce the condition because it tended to inquiries that might disturb the peace of another family. Poole v. Bott, 11 Hare, 33.

(b) But see Dickson's Trust, 1 Sim. N. S. 37.

straint of marriage annexed to a bequest of personal estate, and the like conditions annexed to a devise of real estate, or to a charge on real estate, or to things savoring of the realty. In the latter cases (touching real estate) the doctrine of the common law as to conditions is strictly applied. If the condition be precedent, it must be strictly complied with in order to entitle the party to the benefit of the devise or gift. If the condition be subsequent, its validity will depend upon its being such as the law will allow to devest an estate. For if the law deems the condition void as against its own policy, then the estate will be absolute, and free from the condition. If on the other hand the condition is good, then a non-compliance with it will defeat the estate in the same manner as any other condition subsequent will defeat it.[1] (a)

289. But if the bequest be of personal estate, a different rule seems to have prevailed, founded in all probability upon the doctrines maintained in the Ecclesiastical Courts, and derived from the canon and civil law.[2] If the condition in restraint of marriage be subsequent and general in its character, it is treated as the like condition is at law in regard to real estate, as a mere nullity, and the legacy becomes pure and absolute. (b) If it be only a limited restraint (such as to a marriage with the consent of parents, or not until the age of twenty-one) and there is no bequest over upon default, the condition subsequent is treated as merely in terrorem, and the legacy becomes pure and absolute.[3] But if the restraint be a condition precedent, then it admits of a very different application from the rule of the common law in similar cases as to real estate. For if the condition regard real

---

[1] Co. Litt. 206, a & b; Id. 217, a; Id. 237, Harg. and Butler's note (152); Bertie v. Faulkland, 3 Ch. Cas. 130; s. c. 2 Freeman, R. 220; 2 Vern. R. 333; 1 Eq. Cas. Abridg. 108, margin; Harvey v. Aston, Com. R. 726; s. c. 1 Atk. 261; Reynish v. Martin, 3 Atk. 330, 332, 333; Fry v. Porter, 1 Mod. R. 300; Long v. Rickets, 2 Sim. & Stu. R. 179; Popham v. Bamfield, 1 Vern. R. 83; 1 Foubl. Eq. B. 1, ch. 4, § 10, note (q); Graydon v. Hicks, 2 Atk. 16; Peyton v. Bury, 2 P. Will. 626; 1 Roper on Legacies, by White, ch. 13, § 1, pp. 650, 666; Id. § 2, pp. 687 to 727; post, § 290, note 2.

[2] 1 Roper on Legacies, by White, ch. 13, § 1, pp. 650 to 660; Scott v. Tyler, 2 Bro. Ch. R. 487; 2 Dick. R. 712; Stackpole v. Beaumont, 3 Ves. 96.

[3] Lloyd v. Branton, 3 Meriv. R. 117; Marples v. Bainbridge, 1 Madd. R. 590; 1 Roper on Legacies, by White, ch. 13, § 1, p. 654, &c.; Id. § 2, pp. 715, 747; Garret v. Pretty, 2 Vern. R. 293; Wheeler v. Brigham, 3 Atk. 364.

(a) See 2 Jarman, Wills, 44 et seq. (5th Am. ed.).

(b) 2 Jarman, Wills, 48 (5th Am. ed.).

estate and be in general restraint of marriage, there, although it is void, yet, as we have seen, if there is not a compliance with it, the estate will never arise in the devisee. But if it be a legacy of personal estate under like circumstances, the legacy will be held good and absolute as if no condition whatsoever had been annexed to it.

290. Whether the same rule is to be applied to legacies of personal estate upon a condition precedent not in restraint of marriage generally, but of a limited and qualified and legal character, where there is no bequest over, and there has been a default in complying with the condition, has been a question much vexed and discussed in Courts of Equity, and upon which some diversity of judgment has been expressed. There are certainly authorities which go directly to establish the doctrine that there is no distinction in cases of this sort between conditions precedent and conditions subsequent. In each of them if there is no bequest over, the legacy is treated as pure and absolute, and the condition as made in terrorem only. The civil law and ecclesiastical law recognize no distinction between conditions precedent and conditions subsequent as to this particular subject.[1] On the other hand there are authorities which seem to inculcate a different doctrine, and to treat conditions precedent as to legacies of this sort upon the same footing as any other bequests or devises at the common law; that is to say, that they are to take effect only upon the condition precedent being complied with, whether there be a bequest over or not.[2]

---

[1] See Harvey v. Aston, 1 Atk. 375; s. c. Com. Rep. 738; Reynish v. Martin, 3 Atk. R. 332.

[2] The former doctrine (that is, that there is no difference between conditions precedent and conditions subsequent as to this point) was maintained by Lord Hardwicke in Reynish v. Martin, 3 Atk. 330, and was recognized by Lord Clare in Keily v. Monck, 3 Ridgw. R. 263, and by Sir Thomas Plumer in Malcolm v. O'Callaghan, 2 Madd. R. 349, 353. See also Garbut v. Hilton, 1 Atk. 381. But the contrary doctrine is indicated in Hemmings v. Munckley, 1 Bro. Ch. 303; Scott v. Tyler, 2 Bro. Ch. R. 488; 2 Dick. R. 723, 724; Stackpole v. Beaumont, 3 Ves. 89. See also Knight v. Cameron, 14 Ves. 388; Clarke v. Parker, 19 Ves. 13; Elton v. Elton, 1 Ves. 4. Mr. Roper, in his work on Legacies (1 Roper on Leg. by White, ch. 13, § 1, pp. 654 to 660; Id. § 2, pp. 715 to 727), is of opinion that the weight of authority is with the latter doctrine; and so is Mr. Hovenden in his Supplement to Vesey, jr., Vol. 1, p. 353, note to 3 Ves. 89. See also Mr. Saunders's note to Harvey v. Aston, 1 Atk. 381. A distinction has also been taken between cases of personal legacies and cases of portions charged on land. In the former, the condition may

291. But whichever of these opinions shall be deemed to maintain the correct doctrine, there is a modification of the strictness of the common law as to conditions precedent in regard to personal legacies which is at once rational and convenient, and promotive of the real intention of the testator. It is, that where a literal compliance with the condition becomes impossible, from unavoidable circumstances and without any default of the party, it is sufficient that it is complied with as nearly as it practically can be, or (as it is technically called) cy pres. This modification is derived from the civil law and stands upon the presumption that the donor could not intend to require impossibilities, but only a substantial compliance with his directions as far as they should admit of being fairly carried into execution. It is upon this ground that Courts of Equity constantly hold, in cases of personal legacies, that a substantial compliance with the condition satisfies it, although not literally fulfilled. Thus if a legacy upon a condition precedent should require the consent of three persons to a marriage, and one or more of them should die, the consent of the survivor or survivors would be deemed a sufficient compliance with the condition.[1] And a fortiori this doctrine would be applied to conditions subsequent.[2] (a)

perhaps be dispensed with, at least under some circumstances; in the latter, the condition must be complied with, to entitle the party to take, although there may be no devise over. See Harvey v. Aston, 1 Atk. R. 361; s. c. Com. Rep. 726; Cas. T. Talb. 212.

[1] Swinburne on Wills, Pt. 4, § 7, n. 4, p. 262; 1 Roper on Legacies, by White, ch. 13, § 2, pp. 691, 692. See Clarke v. Parker, 19 Ves. 1, 16, 19.

[2] See 1 Roper on Legacies, ch. 13, § 2, p. 691; Peyton v. Bury, 2 P. Will. 626; Graydon v. Hicks, 2 Atk. 16, 18; Aislabie v. Rice, 3 Madd. R. 256; Worthington v. Evans, 1 Sim. & Stu. R. 165.

(a) A condition in a devise that if the devisee 'shall marry contrary to the order and established rules of the people called Quakers, such devise' shall cease and be void is held valid. Haughton v. Haughton, 1 Molloy, 611. So a condition is lawful requiring the donee not to marry a Scotchman. Perrin v. Lyon, 9 East, 170. Or a papist. Duggan v. Kelly, 10 Irish Eq. 295; 1 Eq. Cas. Abr. 110, pl. 2. So of a gift by a father to his daughter 'during her separation from her husband,' the parties at the time living separate. Cooper v. Remsen, 5 Johns. Ch. 459. On the reconciliation of the parties and the return of the wife before the father's death it was held that the gift did not take effect, though there was a separation again after the death of the father. But a condition intended to induce husband and wife to separate or to get divorced is void on grounds of public policy. Wren v. Bradley, 2 DeG. & S. 49; Brown v. Peck, 1 Eden, 140; Tennant v. Braie, Tothill, 141 (p. 78 of 2d ed.).

292. Another class of constructive frauds, and so deemed because inconsistent with the general policy of the law, is that of bargains and contracts made in restraint of trade. (*a*)   And here the known and established distinction is between such bargains and contracts as are in general restraint of trade and such as are in restraint of it only as to particular places or persons.   The latter, if founded upon a good and valuable consideration, are valid.   The former are universally prohibited.   The reason of this difference is, that all general restraints upon trade have a tendency to promote monopolies and to discourage industry, enterprise, and just competition, and thus to do mischief to the party by the loss of his livelihood and the subsistence of his family, and mischief to the public by depriving it of the services and labors of a useful member.[1]   But the same reasoning does not apply to a special restraint not to carry on trade in a particular place, (*b*) or with particular persons, or for a limited

[1] Mitchell *v.* Reynolds, 1 P. Will. 181, where the subject is most elaborately considered.   See also Pierce *v.* Fuller, 8 Mass. R. 223; Morris *v.* Colman, 18 Ves. 436.

(*a*) An association of carriers or forwarders to regulate the price of freight and passage, with provisions prohibiting the members from engaging in similar business out of the association, is considered within the mischief of general restraints upon trade.   Stanton *v.* Allen, 5 Denio, 434.   See Oregon Nav. Co. *v.* Winsor, 20 Wall. 64.   So of combinations among workmen and employers to demand or to pay only certain prices for labor with a penalty on breach.   Hilton *v.* Eckersley, 6 El. & B. 47, 66.   See Bowen *v.* Matheson, 14 Allen, 499; Carew *v.* Rutherford, 106 Mass. 1; Morris Coal Co. *v.* Barclay Coal Co., 68 Penn. St. 173.   A contract by a municipality not to license more than one market is void.   Gale *v.* Kalamazoo, 23 Mich. 344.   So of an agreement by a lessee of a coal mine not to give or accept any order on any store except that of a lessor.   Crawford *v.* Wick, 18 Ohio St. 190.   So of an agreement for a 'corner' in stocks.   Sampson *v.* Shaw, 101 Mass. 145.

(*b*) Ropes *v.* Upton, 125 Mass. 258 (that equity will restrain a violation of the agreement); Morgan *v.* Perhamus, 36 Ohio St. 517 (same effect); Guerand *v.* Dandelet, 32 Md. 561; Warfield *v.* Booth, 33 Md. 63; Boutelle *v.* Smith, 116 Mass. 111; Dean *v.* Emerson, 102 Mass. 480 ; McClurg's Appeal, 58 Penn. St. 51; Doty *v.* Martin, 32 Mich. 468; Hubbard *v.* Miller, 27 Mich. 15.   Secus by some cases if it apply to a whole State.   More *v.* Bonnet, 40 Cal. 251; Wright *v.* Rider, 36 Cal. 342.   Contra, if reasonable, Beal *v.* Chase, 31 Mich. 490, in which the subject is ably and exhaustively considered.

A person selling a copyright, a patent right, or a goodwill, or the like, may clearly impose upon himself such restriction as may be necessary to protect the purchaser, so long as it is reasonable, though the restriction be not local.   Morse Twist Co. *v.* Morse, 103 Mass. 73; Taylor *v.* Blanchard, 13 Allen, 370; Leather Cloth Co. *v.* Lorsont, L. R. 9 Eq. 345; Beal *v.* Chase,

reasonable time, (*a*) for this restraint leaves all other places and persons and times free to the party to pursue his trade and employment.[1] (*b*) And it may even be beneficial to the country that a particular place should not be overstocked with artisans or other persons engaged in a particular trade or business,[2] or a

[1] Rannie *v.* Irvine, The Jurist, (1844), vol. 8, p. 1051.

[2] Ibid.; Davis *v.* Mason, 5 T. R. 118; Chesman *v.* Nainby, 3 Bro. Parl. Cas. 349; Shackle *v.* Baker, 14 Ves. 468; Crutterell *v.* Lye, 17 Ves. 336; Harrison *v.* Gardner, 2 Madd. R. 198; Pierce *v.* Fuller, 8 Mass. R. 223; Perkins *v.* Lyman, 9 Mass. R. 522; Stearns *v.* Barrett, 1 Pick. R. 443; Palmer *v.* Stebbins, 3 Pick. R. 188; Pierce *v.* Woodward, 6 Pick. R. 206.

supra. But see Allsopp *v.* Whistcroft, L. R. 15 Eq. 59.

Indeed it has been declared in England that there is no absolute rule that a contract in restraint of trade without limit of space is invalid. The question is whether the restraint extends further than is reasonably necessary to protect the party in whose favor the restriction is made. Rousillon *v.* Rousillon, 14 Ch. D. 351; Leather Cloth Co. *v.* Lorsont, L. R. 9 Eq. 345. See Hitchcock *v.* Coker, 6 Ad. & E. 438, 454; Ward *v.* Byrne, 5 Mees. & W. 548, 561; Tallis *v.* Tallis, 1 El. & B. 391; Mallan *v.* May, 11 Mees. & W. 653, 667. To the same effect, Beal *v.* Chase, 31 Mich. 490. In the first case cited, Fry, J., denied Allsopp *v.* Whistcroft, L. R. 15 Eq. 59, upon this point. He also denied that where from its terms a contract in restraint of trade might be either good or bad, it was to be presumed, prima facie, bad, as had been declared to be the rule by the court in Mitchel *v.* Reynolds, 1 P. Wms. 181, 191.

However if the terms of a contract in restraint of trade are hard or complex, equity may refuse to aid in the enforcement of it though it would be good at law. Keeler *v.* Taylor, 53 Penn. St. 467.

The fact that a plaintiff has not attempted to prevent certain unimportant breaches of a contract not to carry on a certain trade, will not prevent his obtaining an injunction in a case otherwise proper. Richards *v.* Revett, 7 Ch. D. 224.

In regard to the right of the seller of the business to solicit the old customers after the sale, see Walker *v.* Mottram, 19 Ch. D. 355; Leggott *v.* Barrett, 15 Ch. D. 306 (overruling Ginesi *v.* Cooper, 14 Ch. D. 596, which extended the prohibition in Labouchere *v.* Dawson, L. R. 13 Eq. 322, against such solicitation); Dawson *v.* Beeson, 22 Ch. D. 504.

(*a*) The restraint may be without limit as to time if it relates only to a particular place, and is not unreasonable. Catt *v.* Tourle, L. R. 4 Ch. 651; Perkins *v.* Clay, 54 N. H. 518; Hubbard *v.* Miller, 27 Mich. 15.

(*b*) See Sainter *v.* Ferguson, 7 C. B. 716; Hartley *v.* Cummings, 5 C. B. 247; Mallan *v.* May, 11 Mees. & W. 653; Hastings *v.* Whitby, 2 Ex. 611; Nichols *v.* Stratton, 10 Q. B. 346; Green *v.* Price, 13 Mees. & W. 695, 698; Rannie *v.* Irvine, 7 Man. & G. 969; Lange *v.* Work, 2 Ohio St. 519; Gilman *v.* Dwight, 13 Gray, 356; Dean *v.* Emerson, 102 Mass. 480; Harms *v.* Parsons, 32 Beav. 328; Benwell *v.* Inns, 24 Beav. 307; Edmonds *v.* Plews, 6 Jur. N. S. 1091. So of an agreement not to make a particular article. Gillis *v.* Hall, 2 Brewst. 342. But see Taylor *v.* Blanchard, 13 Allen, 370. So of a covenant by a vendor of land not to sell marl off his adjacent land. Brewer *v.* Marshall, 4 C. E. Green, 537, court not unanimous.

particular trade may be promoted by being for a short period limited to a few persons, especially if it be a foreign trade recently discovered and it can be beneficial but to a small number of adventurers.[1] And for a like reason a person may lawfully sell a secret in his trade or business and restrain himself from using that secret.[2] (a)

293. Upon analogous principles agreements whereby parties engage not to bid against each other at a public auction, especially in cases where such auctions are directed or required by law, as in cases of sales of chattels or other property on execution, are held void; for they are unconscientious and against public policy, and have a tendency injuriously to affect the character and value of sales at public auction and to mislead private confidence. They operate virtually as a fraud upon the sale.[3] (b) So if under-bidders or puffers are employed at an auction to enhance the price (c) and deceive other bidders, and they are in fact misled, the sale will be held void as against public policy.[4] (d)

[1] Perkins v Lyman, 9 Mass. R. 522, 530.

[2] Bryson v. Whitehead, 1 Sim. & Stu. 94.

[3] Jones v. Caswell, 3 John. Cas. 29; Doolin v. Ward, 6 John. R. 194; Wilbur v. Howe, 8 John. 444; 1 Fonbl. Eq. B. 1, ch. 4, § 4, note (x).

[4] See Howard v. Castle, 6 T. R. 642; Bramlet v. Alt, 3 Ves. 619, 623, 624; Conolly v. Parsons, Id. 624, note; Smith v. Clarke, 12 Ves. 577. But see Bexwell v. Christie, Cowp. R. 395; Twining v. Morrice, 2 Bro. Ch. R. 326; 1 Madd. Ch. Pr. 257; Jeremy on Eq. Jurisd. B. 3, Pt. 2, ch. 3, § 1, p. 390; 2 Kent, Comm. Lect. 39, pp. 537, 538 (5th ed.); Steele v. Ellmaker, 11 Serg. & Rawle, 86.

(a) Peabody v. Norfolk, 98 Mass. 452.

(b) But persons who wish to make a joint purchase may authorize one to bid for them, if there is no agreement not to compete. National Bank v. Sprague, 5 C. E. Green, 159. Contra of an agreement between two bidders for a public contract, to divide the profits whichever was successful. Atcheson v. Mallon, 43 N. Y. 147. An agreement to pay a mail contractor for repudiating his bargain is void. Weld v. Lancaster, 56 Maine, 453; Stevens v. Perrier, 12 Kans. 297.

(c) Secus if the object is not to enhance the price, but to prevent a sacrifice of the property, or if there is any other honest or reasonable purpose. Phippen v. Stickney, 3 Met. 387. See Veazie v. Williams, 8 How. 134; Latham v. Morrow, 6 B. Mon. 630. As to one by-bidder qu. See Mortimer v. Bell, L. R. 1 Ch. 10.

(d) Where property is advertised to be sold 'without reserve,' the announcement is understood to exclude any interference by the vendor, direct or indirect, which under any circumstances can affect the right of the highest bidder, whatever the amount of his bid, to be declared the purchaser. Robinson v. Wall, 2 Phill. Ch. 372. See further Green v. Baverstock, 14 C. B. N. s. 204; National Bank v. Sprague, 5 C. E. Green, 159; Mortimer v. Bell, L. R. 1 Ch. 10; Dimmock v. Hallett, L. R. 2 Ch. 21.

293 *a*. So where contracts are entered into between parties pending a bill in Parliament for the charter of a corporation for private purposes (as for example a railway), and the agreement is to be concealed from Parliament in order to procure the bill to be passed without the knowledge thereof, and thereby to produce a false impression or to mislead or suppress inquiry, or to withdraw public opposition thereto on grounds of public or private general interest, such contracts will be held void as a constructive fraud upon Parliament as well as upon the public at large.[1] (*a*)

294. In like manner agreements which are founded upon violations of public trust or confidence or of the rules adopted by courts in furtherance of the administration of public justice are held void. Thus an agreement made for a remuneration to

---

[1] Lord Howden *v.* Simpson, 10 Adolph. & Ell. 743 ; Simpson *v.* Lord Howden, 1 Keen, R. 583; s. c. 3 Mylne & Craig, R. 97; The Vauxhall Bridge Co. *v.* Earl Spencer, 2 Madd. R. 356; s. c. Jac. R. 64.

(*a*) See Petre *v.* Eastern Counties Ry., 1 Railw. Cas. 462; Shrewsbury *v.* North Staff. Ry. Co., L. R. 1 Eq. 593 ; Caledonian Ry. Co. *v.* Helmsburgh Trustees, 2 Macq. 391. In like manner a contract to procure the passage of an act of the Legislature by any sinister means, or by exerting personal influence with the members, is invalid. Clippinger *v.* Hepbaugh, 5 Watts & S. 315; Wood *v.* McCann, 6 Dana, 366 ; Pingry *v.* Washburn, 1 Aik. 264; Edwards *v.* Grand Junc. Ry. Co., 1 Mylne & C. 650; Marshall *v.* Baltimore & O. R. Co., 16 How. 314; Smith *v.* Applegate, 3 Zabr. 352. See Mills *v.* Mills, 40 N. Y. 543; Frost *v.* Belmont, 6 Allen, 152; Trist *v.* Child, 21 Wall. 441. So of an agreement to perform services in obtaining a contract from an executive department. Tool Co. *v.* Norris, 2 Wall. 45. Or of an agreement by an officer of a foreign government to use his influence in obtaining contracts with his government. Oscanyan *v.* Arms Co., 103 U. S. 261. See Cappell *v.* Hall, 7 Wall. 542 ; Meguire *v.* Corwine, 101 U. S. 108; Hope *v.* Hope, 8 DeG. M. & G. 731. Of the same objectionable nature is a contract to procure signatures and obtain a pardon for a criminal. Hatfield *v.* Gulden, 7 Watts, 152. But perhaps the case would be different if the agreement is only for the use of proper means to obtain signatures. Formby *v.* Pryor, 15 Ga. 258. A contract to abandon the prosecution of a petition presented to the House of Commons against the return of a member accused of bribery is illegal. Coppock *v.* Bower, 4 Mees. & W. 361. So where a city charter prohibited any member of the council from being interested in any contract payment for which was to be made by vote of such council, and a member by secret arrangement with a contractor became interested in such a contract, it was held that a note given by the contractor to the member for his share of the profits was void even in the hands of an innocent assignee. Bell *v.* Quinn, 2 Sandf. 146. See Bowes *v.* Toronto, 11 Moore, P. C. 463; Miles *v.* McIlwraith, 8 App. Cas. 120.

commissioners appointed to take testimony and bound to secrecy by the nature of their appointment upon their disclosure of the testimony so taken is void.[1] So an assignment of the half-pay of a retired officer of the army is void; for it operates as a fraud upon the public bounty.[2] (a) So an assignment of the fees and profits of the office of keeping a house of correction and of the profits of the tap-house connected with it is void; for the former plainly tends to oppression and extortion, and the latter to increase riot and debauchery among the prisoners.[3] (b) Agreements founded upon the suppression of criminal prosecutions fall under the same consideration. They have a manifest tendency to subvert public justice.[4] So wager contracts which are contrary to sound morals, or injurious to the feelings or interests of third persons, or against the principles of public policy or duty,

[1] Cooth v. Jackson, 6 Ves. 12, 31, 32, 35.

[2] Stone v. Liddledale, 2 Anst. 533; M'Carthy v. Goold, 1 Ball & Beatty, R. 389. See Davis v. Duke of Marlborough, 1 Swanst. R. 74, 79; Osborne v. Williams, 18 Ves. 379.

[3] Methwold v. Walbank, 2 Ves. 238.

[4] Johnson v. Ogilby, 3 P. Will. 276, and Cox's note (1); Newland on Contr. ch. 8, p. 158.

(a) See Price v. Lovett, 20 L. J. Ch. 270; s. c. 4 Eng. L. & E. 110; Ex parte Huggins, 21 Ch. D. 85. A pension given an officer upon retiring from office is property, and is subject to the claims of creditors, at least where they offer a reasonable allowance to the pensioner out of the fund. Ex parte Huggins, supra.

'There are no doubt some salaries and pensions which are not assignable. But when this is so, it is always referable to one of two grounds. It is said to be contrary to public policy that payments made to induce persons to keep themselves ready for the service of the Crown, as the half-pay of officers in the army or navy, or payments for actual service rendered to the Crown, should be assigned. The other class is that of pensions, like the retiring allowance of a beneficed clergyman, which are by statute expressly made not assignable.' Ib. Jessel, M. R. p. 91. See Gibson v. East India Co., 5 Bing. N. C. 262; Innes v. East India Co., 17 C. B. 351; Ex parte Hawker, L. R. 7 Ch. 214; Wells v. Foster, 8 Mees. & W. 149; Ex parte Wicks, 17 Ch. D. 70; Cooper v. Regina, 14 Ch. D. 311.

(b) So of an agreement by a party to a suit to pay a witness a certain sum for his attendance, and more if the party promising succeeds in the suit. Dawkins v. Gill, 10 Ala. 206; Patterson v. Donner, 48 Cal. 369, 379. Or of an agreement to pay a board of public officers, for their personal benefit, a certain sum for doing an act in their official duty. Odineal v. Barry, 24 Miss. 9. So also of a contract by a deputy sheriff to pay the sheriff a certain sum as the price of his appointment. Ferries v. Adams, 23 Vt. 136.

are void.[1]　So are contracts which have a tendency to encourage champerty.[2]

295. Another extensive class of cases falling under this head of constructive fraud respects contracts for the buying, selling, or procuring of public offices.   It is obvious that all such contracts must have a material influence to diminish the respectability, responsibility, and purity of public officers, and to introduce a system of official patronage, corruption, and deceit, wholly at war with the public interests.[3] (a)   The confidence of officers may thereby not only be abused and perverted to the worst purposes, but mischievous arrangements may be made to the injury of the public, and persons may be introduced or kept in office who are utterly unqualified to discharge the proper functions of their stations.[4]   Such contracts are justly deemed contracts of moral turpitude,[5] and are calculated to betray the public interests into the administration of the weak, the profligate, the selfish, and the cunning. They are therefore held utterly void as contrary to the soundest public policy, and indeed as a constructive fraud upon the government.[6]   It is acting against the spirit of the constitution of a free government, by which it ought to be served by fit and able persons, recommended by the proper officers of the government for their abilities and from motives of disinterested purity.[7]   It has been strongly remarked that there

[1] De Costa v. Jones, Cowp. 729; Atherford v. Beard, 2 T. Rep. 610; Gilbert v. Sykes, 16 East, R. 150; Hartley v. Rice, 10 East, 22; Allen v. Hearn, 1 T. Rep. 56; Shirley v. Shankey, 2 Bos. & Pull. 130.

[2] Power v. Knowler, 2 Atk. 224.

[3] 1 Fonbl. Eq. B. 1, ch. 4, § 4, note (u); Chesterfield v. Janssen, 1 Atk. 352; s. c. 2 Ves. 124, 156; Boynton v. Hubbard, 7 Mass. R. 119; Hartwell v. Hartwell, 4 Ves. 811, 815.

[4] Chesterfield v. Janssen, 1 Ves. 155, 156; s. c. 1 Atk. 352; Newland on Contracts, ch. 33, pp. 477 to 482.

[5] Morris v. McCulloch, 2 Eden, R. 190; s. c. Ambler, R. 435; Law v. Law, 3 P. Will. 391; s. c. Cas. T. Talb. 140; Harrington v. Du Chastel, 2 Swanst. 167, note; s. c. 1 Bro. Ch. R. 124.

[6] Bellamy v. Burrow, Cas. T. Talb. 97; Harrington v. Du Chastel, 1 Bro. Ch. R. 124; s. c. 2 Swanst. R. 167, note; Garforth v. Fearon, 1 H. Black. 327, 329; Palmer v. Bate, 6 Moore, R. 28; s. c. 2 Bro. & Bing. 673; Waldo v. Martin, 4 B. & Cressw. R. 319; Parsons v. Thompson, 1 H. Black. 322, 326.

[7] Morris v. McCulloch, 2 Eden, R. 190; s. c. Ambler, R. 432, 435; Ive v. Ash, Prec. Ch. 199; Co. Litt. 234 a; East India Company v. Neave, 4 Ves. 173, 181, 184; Hartwell v. Hartwell, 4 Ves. 811.

(a) Hunter v. Nolf, 71 Penn. St. 282.

is no rule better established (it should be added, in law and reason, for unfortunately it is often otherwise in practice) respecting the disposition of every office in which the public are concerned than this, 'deter digniori.' On principles of public policy no money consideration ought to influence the appointment to such offices.[1] (a) It was observed of old that the sale of offices accomplished the ruin of the Roman Republic. 'Nulla alia re magis Romana Respublica interiit, quam quod magistratus officia venalia erant.'[2]

296. Another class of agreements which are held to be void on account of their being against public policy are such as are founded upon corrupt considerations or moral turpitude, whether they stand prohibited by statute or not; for these are treated as frauds upon the public or moral law.[3] The rule of the civil law on this subject speaks but the language of universal justice. 'Pacta quæ contra leges constitutionesque, vel contra bonos mores fiunt, nullam vim habere, indubitati juris est.'[4] It is but applying a preventive check by withholding every encouragement from wrong and aiming thereby to enforce the obligations of virtue. For although the law as a science must necessarily leave many moral precepts without due enforcement as rules of imperfect obligation only, it is most studious not thereby to lend the slightest countenance to the violations of such precepts. Wherever the divine law, or the positive law, or the common law prohibits the doing of certain acts or enjoins the discharge of certain duties, any agreement to do such acts or not to discharge such duties is against the dearest interests of society, and therefore is held void; for otherwise the law would be open to the just reproach of winking at crimes and omissions or tolerating in one form what it affected to reprobate in another.[5] Hence all agreements, bonds, and securities, given as a price for future (b) illicit intercourse (præmium pudoris), or for the commission of a

---

[1] Lord Kenyon in Blackford v. Preston, 8 T. Rep. 92; Newland on Contracts, 478.   [2] Cited Co. Litt. 234 a.
[3] Newland on Contracts, ch. 32, p. 469, &c.; 1 Fonbl. Eq. B. 1, ch. 4, § 5.
[4] Cod. Lib. 2, tit. 3, l. 6.
[5] 1 Fonbl. Eq. B. 4, ch. 4, § 4, and notes (s), (y).

(a) An agreement to share the emoluments of an office is illegal. Martin v. Wade, 37 Cal. 168.

(b) Or for past illicit intercourse if not under seal. Beaumont v. Reeve, 8 Q. B. 483. See Vallance v. Blagdon, 26 Ch. D. 353.

public crime, or for the violation of a public law, or for the omission of a public duty, (a) are deemed incapable of confirmation or enforcement upon the maxim 'Ex turpi contractu non oritur actio.'[1]

296 a. But where a party to an illegal or immoral contract comes himself to be relieved from that contract or its obligations, he must distinctly and exclusively state such grounds of relief as the court can legally attend to ; and he must not accompany his claim to relief, which may be legitimate, with other claims and complaints which are contaminated with the original immoral purpose ; for if he sets up as a ground of relief the non-fulfilment of the illegal contract on the other side, and thereby that he is released from his obligation to perform it, that shows that he still relies upon the immoral contract and its terms for relief, and therefore the court will refuse it.[2]

297. Other cases might be put to illustrate the doctrine of Courts of Equity in setting aside the agreements and acts in fraud of the policy of the law.   Thus if a devise is made upon a secret trust for charity in evasion of the statutes of mortmain, it will be set aside.[3] So if a parent grant an annuity to his son to qualify him to kill game, he will not be permitted by tearing off the seal to avoid the conveyance.[4] So if a person convey an estate to another to qualify him to sit in Parliament or to become a voter, he will not be permitted to avoid it upon the ground of its having been done by him in fraud of the law, and upon a secret agreement that it shall be given up.[5] So conveyances made of estates in trust, in order to secure the party from forfeitures for treason or felony, will be set aside against the Crown,

---

[1] 1 Fonbl. Eq. B. 1, ch. 4, § 4, and notes (s), (y); Walker v. Perkins, 3 Burr. 1568; Franco v. Bolton, 3 Ves. 370; Clarke v. Perrain, 2 Atk. 333, 337 ; Whaley v. Norton, 1 Vern. R. 483; Robinson v. Gee, 1 Ves. R. 251, 254; Gray v. Mathias, 5 Ves. 286; Ottley v. Browne, 1 Ball & Beatt. 360; Battersley v. Smith, 3 Madd. R. 110; Thompson v. Thompson, 7 Ves. 470; St. John v. St. John, 11 Ves. 535, 536.   But see Spear v. Hayward, Prec. Ch. 114.

[2] Bates v. Chester, 5 Beav. R. 103.

[3] Strickland v. Aldrich, 9 Ves. 516; Muckleston v. Bruen, 6 Ves. 52.

[4] 1 Madd. Ch. Pract. 242; Curtis v. Perry, 6 Ves. 747; Birch v. Blagrave, Ambler, R. 264, 265.

[5] See The Duke of Bedford v. Coke, 2 Ves. 116, 117; 3 P. Will. 233; 1 Madd. Ch. Pr. 243.

(a) A contract to indemnify an office for *past* neglect of duty is held lawful. Hall v. Huntoon, 17 Vt. 244.

but they will be good against the party. So contracts affecting public elections are held void; so are assignments of rights or property, pendente lite, when they amount to or partake of the character of maintenance or champerty, and are reprehended by the law.[1]

298. And here it may be well to take notice of a distinction, often but not universally acted on in Courts of Equity, as to the nature and extent of the relief which will be granted to persons who are parties to agreements or other transactions against public policy, and therefore are to be deemed participes criminis. In general (for it is not universally true),[2] where parties are concerned in illegal agreements or other transactions, whether they are mala prohibita or mala in se, Courts of Equity, following the rule of law as to participators in a common crime,[3] will not at present interpose to grant any relief; acting upon the known maxim, 'In pari delicto potior est conditio defendentis, et possidentis.'[4] (a)　But in cases where the agreements or other trans-

---

[1] Waller v. Duke of Portland, 3 Ves. 494; Stevens v. Bagwell, 15 Ves. 139; Strachan v. Brander, 1 Eden, R. 303; 18 Ves. 127, 128.

[2] The relief granted in Courts of Equity in cases of usury constitutes an exception. Smith v. Bromley, Doug. R. 695, note; Id. 697, 698. In this case Lord Mansfield said: 'If the act is in itself immoral, or a violation of the general laws of public policy, there the party paying shall not have this action [to recover back the money]; for where both parties are equally criminal against such general laws the rule is "Potior est conditio defendentis." But there are other laws which are calculated for the protection of the subject against oppression, extortion, deceit, &c. If such laws are violated, and the defendant takes advantage of the plaintiff's condition or situation, there the plaintiff shall recover. And it is astonishing that the Reports do not distinguish between the violation of the one sort and the other.' Id. p. 697; Astley v. Reynolds, 2 Str. R. 915. See 1 Fonbl. Eq. B. 1, ch. 2, § 13, and note (r); 1 Madd. Ch. Pr. 241, 242; Browning v. Morris, Cowp. R. 790.

[3] Buller, N. P. 131, 132.

[4] See Bromley v. Smith, Doug. R. 697, note; Id. 698; Vandyck v. Herritt, 1 East, R. 96; Hanson v. Hancock, 8 T. Rep. 575; Browning v. Morris, Cowp. R. 790; Osborne v. Williams, 18 Ves. 379; Buller, N. P. 131, 132; 1 Fonbl.

(a) As in the case of a contract executed on Sunday. Berry v. Planters' Bank, 3 Tenn. Ch. 69. So of participation in a devastavit. Halsley v. Fultz, 76 Va. 671. And of profits from illegal trading. Dunham v. Presley, 120 Mass. 285; Snell v. Dwight, Ib. 9. For further illustration see Blasdel v. Fowle, 120 Mass. 447; Pettiton v. Hipple, 90 Ill. 420 (wagers); Smith v. White, L. R. 1 Eq. 626 (lease of premises for prostitution); De Wolf v. Pratt, 42 Ill. 198; Olin v. Bate, 98 Ill. 53 (college degrees); Marlatt v. Warwick, 4 C. E. Green, 439; Cutter v. Tuttle, Ib. 549, 562; Compton v. Bunker Hill Bank, 96 Ill. 301. But equity will

actions are repudiated on account of their being against public
policy, the circumstance that the relief is asked by a party who
is particeps criminis is not in equity material. The reason is
that the public interest requires that relief should be given, and
it is given to the public through the party.[1] (a)   And in these

Eq. B. 1, ch. 4, § 4, note (y); Bosanquet v. Dashwood, Cas. T. Talb. 37, 40,
41. I say, at present; for there has been considerable fluctuation of opinion,
both in Courts of Law and Equity, on this subject. The old cases often gave
relief both at Law and in Equity, where the party would otherwise derive an
advantage from his iniquity. But the modern doctrine has adopted a more
severely just and probably politic and moral rule, which is, to leave the parties
where it finds them, giving no relief and no countenance to claims of this
sort. See the cases at law, Tompkins v. Bernet, 1 Salk. 22; Bromley v.
Smith, Doug. R. 695, note; Collins v. Blantern, 2 Wils. R. 347; Lowry v.
Bourdieu, Doug. R. 468; Marak v. Abel, 3 Bos. & Pull. 35; Vandyck v. Herritt, 1 East, R. 96; Lubbock v. Potts, 7 East, R. 449, 456; Browning v.
Morris, Cowp. R. 750; Hanson v. Hancock, 8 T. Rep. 575; McCullum v.
Gourley, 8 John. R. 147; Buller, N. P. 181; 1 Fonbl. Eq. B. 1, ch. 4, § 4, and
note (y); Buller, N. P. 131, 132; Inhab. of Worcester v. Eaton, 11 Mass. R.
368, 376, 377; Phelps v. Decker, 10 Mass. R. 267, 274. And in equity see
the cases of Neville v. Wilkinson, 1 Bro. Ch. R. 543, 547, 548; Jacob, R. 67;
Watts v. Brooks, 3 Ves. jr. R. 612; East India Company v. Neave, 5 Ves.
173, 181, 184; Thompson v. Thompson, 7 Ves. 469; Knowles v. Haughton,
11 Ves. 168; St. John v. St. John, 11 Ves. 535, 536; Osborne v. Williams,
18 Ves. 379; Bosanquet v. Dashwood, Cas. T. Talb. 37; Rider v. Kidder, 10
Ves. 366; Rawdon v. Shadwell, Ambler, R. 269, and Mr. Blunt's notes. In
the case of Phelps v. Decker (10 Mass. R. 274), it was broadly laid down that
'by the common law deeds of conveyance or other deeds made contrary to the
provisions of a general statute, or for an unlawful consideration, or to carry
into effect a contract unlawful in itself, or in consequence of any prohibitory
statute, are void, ab initio, and may be avoided by plea; or on the general
issue, non est factum, the illegality may be given in evidence.' But in a later
case the doctrine was qualified; and the court took the distinction between
bonds and contracts sought to be enforced, and actual conveyances of lands or
other property. The former might be avoided; the latter were treated as
actual transfers, and governed by the same rule as the payment of money or
the delivery of a personal chattel. Inhabitants of Worcester v. Eaton, 11
Mass. 375 to 379.

[1] St. John v. St. John, 11 Ves. 535, 536; Bromley v. Smith, Doug. R. 695,

enforce a naked declaration of *trust*
between parties to a deed executed
in fraud of creditors, though it will
not enforce a contract of the kind.
Ownes v. Ownes, 8 C. E. Green, 60;
Harvey v. Varney, 98 Mass. 118. See
Eyre v. Eyre, 4 C. E. Green, 42;
infra, § 371. Still the distinction
between an attempt to enforce a contract, as in the cases cited, and an

attempt to get relief from one, either
before or after the contract has been
performed, as in the cases now to
be mentioned in the text, is to be
noticed.

(a) Reynell v. Sprye, 1 DeG. M. &
G. 660; Cox v. Donnelly, 34 Ark. 762;
Hale v. Sharpe, 4 Cold. 275; Breath-
wit v. Rogers, 32 Ark. 758.

cases relief will be granted, not only by setting aside the agreement or other transaction, but also in many cases by ordering a repayment of any money paid under it.[1] (a)   Lord Thurlow indeed seems to have thought that in all cases where money had been paid for an illegal purpose it might be recovered back, observing that if courts of justice mean to prevent the perpetration of crimes, it must be not by allowing a man who has got possession to remain in possession, but by putting the parties back to the state in which they were before.[2]   But this is pushing the doctrine to an extravagant extent, and effectually subverting the maxim, 'In pari delicto potior est conditio defendentis.' The ground of reasoning upon which his Lordship proceeded is exceedingly questionable in itself ; and the suppression of illegal contracts is far more likely in general to be accomplished, by leaving the parties without remedy against each other, and by thus introducing a preventive check naturally connected with a want of confidence, and a sole reliance upon personal honor. And so accordingly the modern doctrine is established.   Relief is not granted where both parties are truly in pari delicto, unless in cases where public policy would thereby be promoted.[3] (b)

697, 698; Hatch v. Hatch, 9 Ves. 292, 298; Roberts v. Roberts, 3 P. Will. 66, 74, and note (1); Browning v. Morris, Cowp. R. 790; Morris v. McCulloch, 2 Eden, R. 190, and note Id. 193.

[1] See Goldsmith v. Bruning, 1 Eq. Abridg. Bonds, &c. F. 4, p. 89; 1 Fonbl. Eq. B. 1, ch. 2, § 13, and note; Smith v. Bruning, 2 Vern. R. 392; Morris v. McCulloch, Ambler, R. 432; s. c. 2 Eden, R. 180.   Money paid will not in all cases be ordered to be paid back.   For instance a bond given for future illicit intercourse will be decreed to be set aside; but money paid under the bond will not, under all circumstances, be directed to be repaid. See Newland on Contracts, ch. 33, pp. 483 to 492; Hill v. Spencer, Ambler, R. 641, and Id. App. 836 (Blunt's edition); Nye v. Mosely, 6 B. & Cressw. 133; Dig. Lib. 12, tit. 5, l. 4, § 3.   See also cases of gaming before the statute in Chesterfield v. Janssen, 2 Ves. 137, 138.   See also Inhabitants of Worcester v. Eaton, 11 Mass. R. 376, 377.

[2] Neville v. Wilkinson, 1 Bro. Ch. R. 547, 548; 18 Ves. 382.

[3] See the remarks of Lord Eldon in Rider v. Kidder, 10 Ves. 366; Smith v. Bromley, Doug. R. 696, note.

(a) Or a cancellation of instruments. Breathwit v. Rogers, 32 Ark. 758; Darst v. Brockway, 11 Ohio, 462, 471.

(b) The fact that an assignment is *intended* for an illegal purpose not carried into execution will not prevent the assignor from recovering back the property. Symes v. Hughes, L. R. 9 Eq. 475.   Nor can the Statute of Frauds be set up as a defence to such a case. Lincoln v. Wright, 4 DeG. & J. 16; Haigh v. Kaye, L. R. 7 Ch. 469.

Where the directors of a corporation

299. Even in cases of a præmium pudicitiæ, the distinction has been constantly maintained between bills for restraining the woman from enforcing the security given, and bills for compelling her to give up property already in her possession under the contract. At least there is no case to be found where the contrary doctrine has been acted on, except where creditors were concerned. And in this respect the English law seems to have had a steady regard to the policy of the Roman Jurisprudence.[1]

300. And indeed in cases where both parties are in delicto,

---

[1] Rider v. Kidder, 10 Ves. 366. The Roman law has stated some doctrines and distinctions upon this subject which are worthy of consideration. I shall quote them without commenting upon them. They are partially cited in 1 Fonbl. Eq. B. 1, ch. 4, § 4, note (y). Three cases are put. (1) Where the turpitude is on the part of the receiver only; and there the rule is, ' Quod si turpis causa accipientis fuerit, etiamsi res secuta sit, repeti potest.' Dig. Lib. 12, tit. 5, l. 1, § 2. (2) Where the turpitude is on the part of the giver alone; and there the rule is the contrary. 'Cessat quidem condictio, quum turpiter datur.' Pothier, Pand. Lib. 12, tit. 5, art. 8. (3) Where the turpitude affects both parties; and there the rule is, ' Ubi autem et dantis et accipientis turpitudo versatur, non posse repeti dicimus; veluti si pecunia detur, ut male judicetur.' Dig. Lib. 12, tit. 5, l. 3; Pothier, Pand. Lib. 12, tit. 5, n. 7. The reason given is, 'In pari causa possessor potior haberi debet.' Dig. Lib. 50, tit. 17, l. 128; Pothier, Pand. Lib. 12, tit. 5, n. 7. Several other examples are given under this head. ' Idem, si ob stuprum datum sit; vel si quis, in adulterio deprehensus, redemerit se, cessat enim repetitio. Item, si dederit fur, ne proderetur; quoniam utriusque turpitudo versatur, cessat repetitio.' Dig. Lib. 12, tit. 5, l. 4; Pothier, Pand. Lib. 12, tit. 5, n. 7. ' Cum te propter turpem causam contra disciplinam temporum meorum, domum adversariæ dedisse profitearis; frustra eam tibi restitui desideras; cum in pari causa possessoris conditio melior habeatur.' Cod. Lib. 4, tit. 7, l. 2; Pothier, Pand. Lib. 12, tit. 5, l. 7. ' Sed quod meretrici datur, repeti non potest. Sed nova ratione, non ea, quod utriusque turpitudo versatur, sed solius dantis;' a new reason, which Pothier as well as Ulpian seems to doubt. See Dig. Lib. 12, tit. 5, l. 4, § 3; Pothier, Pand. Lib. 12, tit. 5, n. 7, and nota (6). On the other hand, when the money had not been paid or the contract fulfilled, the Roman law deemed the contract void. 'Quamvis enim utriusque turpitudo versatur, ac solutæ quantitatis cessat repetitio, tamen ex hujusmodi stipulatione, contra bonos mores interposita, denegandas esse actiones juris auctoritate demonstratur.' Cod. Lib. 4, tit. 7, l. 5; Pothier, Pand. Lib. 12, tit. 5, n. 9.

invest its funds in an illegal manner, though with the assent of the corporation, the corporation may follow the funds in equity, the consent being ultra vires. Great Eastern Ry. Co. v. Turner, L. R. 8 Ch. 149. But where money illegally borrowed by a corporation has been applied to its benefit, with the consent of the shareholders, the corporation cannot set up the illegality. In re Magdalena Nav. Co., Johns. 690; In re Cork Ry. Co., L. R. 4 Ch. 748.

concurring in an illegal act, it does not always follow that they stand in pari delicto; for there may be, and often are, very different degrees in their guilt.[1] One party may act under circumstances of oppression, imposition, (a) hardship, undue influence, or great inequality of condition or age; so that his guilt may be far less in degree than that of his associate in the offence.[2] (b) And besides, there may be on the part of the court itself a necessity of supporting the public interests or public policy in many cases, however reprehensible the acts of the parties may be.[3] (c)

301. In cases of usury this distinction has been adopted by Courts of Equity. All such contracts being declared void by the statute against usury, Courts of Equity will follow the law

[1] Smith v. Bromley, Doug. R. 696; Browning v. Morris, Cowp. R. 790; Osborne v. Williams, 18 Ves. 379.

[2] Bosanquet v. Dashwood, Cas. T. Talb. 37, 40, 41; Chesterfield v. Janssen, 2 Ves. 156, 157; Osborne v. Williams, 18 Ves. 379.

[3] See Woodhouse v. Meredith, 1 Jac. & Walk. 224, 225; 1 Fonbl. Eq. B. 1, ch. 4, § 4, note (y); Bosanquet v. Dashwood, Cas. T. Talb. 37, 40, 41; Smith v. Bromley, Doug. R. 696, note; Browning v. Morris, Cowp. R. 790; Morris v. McCulloch, 2 Eden, 190, and note 193.

(a) An agreement executed under a threat of prosecuting the plaintiff's son for forgery was ordered to be delivered up for cancellation in Bayley v. Williams, 4 Giff. 638.

(b) See Pinckston v. Brown, 3 Jones, Eq. 494; Poston v. Balch, 69 Mo. 115; Harrington v. Grant, 54 Vt. 236; Davidson v. Carter, 55 Iowa, 117.

(c) In W—— v. B——, 32 Beav. 574, a daughter concurred with her father in a covenant to surrender copyholds by way of mortgage to one who had loaned money to the father; part of the consideration being the permission of the father to the mortgagee to continue visits to the daughter, whom he was seducing or had seduced. Upon bill and cross-bill to enforce and to set aside the contract the court at first considered that it could not interfere for either party, but ultimately ordered the deed to be cancelled, the grantee to pay costs in both cases. In another case a man being deserted by his wife, and not having heard of her for two years, supposed her to be dead, and married another. Subsequently learning that his first wife was alive, and supposing that he was liable to be prosecuted for bigamy, he conveyed his lands to another, with the understanding that the grantee should hold it for his use. The grantee finally refused to reconvey, though the grantor had remained in possession four years and had paid off a mortgage on the premises. The court now held the transaction not illegal, and that the grantor was entitled to a reconveyance both on the ground of a resulting trust in his favor and the fraud of the grantee. Davies v. Otty, 35 Beav. 208. So equity will enforce between the parties a naked declaration of trust by the grantee of a deed executed in fraud of creditors. Ownes v. Ownes, 8 C. E. Green, 60. See Harvey v. Varney, 98 Mass. 118; post, § 371.

in the construction of the statute. If therefore the usurer or lender come into a Court of Equity seeking to enforce the contract, the court will refuse any assistance and repudiate the contract.[1] But on the other hand if the borrower comes into a Court of Equity seeking relief against the usurious contract, the only terms upon which the court will interfere are that the plaintiff will pay the defendant what is really and bona fide due to him, deducting the usurious interest; and if the plaintiff do not make such offer in his bill, the defendant may demur to it, and the bill will be dismissed.[2] (a) The ground of this distinction is, that a Court of Equity is not positively bound to interfere in such cases by an active exertion of its powers; but it has a discretion on the subject, and may prescribe the terms of its interference, and he who seeks equity at its hands may well be required to do equity. And it is against conscience that the party should have full relief, and at the same time pocket the money loaned, which may have been granted at his own mere solicitation.[3] (b) For then a statute made to prevent fraud and oppression would be made the instrument of fraud. But in the other case, if equity should relieve the lender who is plaintiff, it would be aiding a wrong-doer who is seeking to make the court the means of carrying into effect a transaction manifestly wrong and illegal in itself.[4]

302. And upon the like principles, if the borrower has paid the money upon an usurious contract, Courts of Equity (and

[1] 1 Fonbl. Eq. B. 1, ch. 1, § 3, note (h); Fanning v. Dunham, 5 John. Ch. R. 142, 143, 144.

[2] 1 Fonbl. Eq. B. 1, ch. 1, § 3, note (h); Id. B. 1, ch. 4, § 7, note (k); Mason v. Gardner, 4 Bro. Ch. R. 436; Rogers v. Rathbun, 1 John. Ch. R. 367; Fanning v. Dunham, 5 John. Ch. R. 142, 143, 144.

[3] Scott v. Nesbit, 2 Bro. Ch. R. 641; s. c. 2 Cox, R. 183; Benfield v. Solomons, 9 Ves. 84.

[4] 1 Fonbl. Eq. B. 1, ch. 1, § 3, note (h); Id. B. 1, ch. 4, § 7, and note (k).

(a) Sporrer v. Eifler, 1 Heisk. 633; Williams v. Fitzhugh, 37 N. Y. 444; Ruddell v. Ambler, 18 Ark. 369; Noble v. Walker, 32 Ala. 456; Uhlfelder v. Carter, 64 Ala. 527; Ware v. Thompson, 2 Beasl. 66. Contra in Wisconsin. Cooper v. Tappan, 4 Wis. 362. And see Bissell v Kellogg, 60 Barb. 617. But where the party setting up the usury is acting on the defensive, it seems he need not offer to pay what is justly due. Union Bank v. Bell, 14 Ohio St. 200; Kuhner v. Butler, 11 Iowa, 419. See Spain v. Hamilton, 1 Wall. 604; Hart v. Goldsmith, 1 Allen, 145; Smith v. Robinson, 10 Allen, 130.

(b) Thomas v. Cooper, 31 Eng. L. & E. 526.

indeed Courts of Law also)[1] will assist him to recover back the excess paid beyond principal and lawful interest; but not further. (a) For it is no just objection to say that he is particeps criminis, and that ' volenti non fit injuria.' It would be absurd to apply the latter maxim to the case of a man who from mere necessity pays more than the other can in justice demand, and who has been significantly called the slave of the lender. He can in no just sense be said to pay voluntarily. And as to being particeps criminis, he stands in vinculis, and is compelled to submit to the terms which oppression and his necessities impose on him.[2] Nor can it be said, in any case of oppression, that the party oppressed is particeps criminis; since it is that very hardship which he labors under, and which is imposed upon him by another, that makes the crime.[3]

303. In regard to gaming contracts it would follow, a fortiori, that Courts of Equity ought not to interfere in their favor, but ought to afford aid to suppress them, since they are not only prohibited by statute, but may justly be pronounced to be immoral, as the practice tends to idleness, dissipation, and the ruin of families.[4] No one has doubted that under such circumstances a bill in equity might be maintained to have any gaming security delivered up and cancelled.[5] But it was at one time held that if the money were actually paid in a case of gaming, Courts of

[1] 1 Fonbl. Eq. B. 1, ch. 4, § 7, and note (k); Smith v. Bromley, Doug. R. 696, note; Browning v. Morris, Cowp. R. 792; Bond v. Hays, Ex'r, 12 Mass. R. 34.

[2] Smith v. Bromley, Doug. 696, note; Bosanquet v. Dashwood, Cas. Temp. Talb. 39; Browning v. Morris, Cowp. R. 790; Rawden v. Shadwell, Ambler, R. 269, and Mr. Blunt's notes; 1 Fonbl. Eq. B. 1, ch. 4, § 8, note (k).

[3] Lord Chancellor Talbot in Bosanquet v. Dashwood, Cas. Temp. Talb. 41. The same principle applies to cases of annuities set aside for want of a memorial duly registered; and an account of the consideration paid, and payments made, will be taken, and the balance only will be required to be paid upon a decree to give up the security. Holbrook v. Sharpey, 19 Ves. 131.

[4] 1 Fonbl. Eq. B. 1, ch. 4, § 6, and note (c). See Robinson v. Bland, 2 Burr. 1077.

[5] Rawden v. Shadwell, Ambler, R. 269, and Mr. Blunt's notes; Woodroffe v. Farnham, 2 Vern. 291; Wynne v. Callendar, 1 Russ. R. 23; Baker v. Williams, cited in Blunt's note to Ambler, R. 269; Portarlington v. Soulby, 3 Mylne & Keen, 104.

(a) The borrower may maintain a bill to compel the return of securities left as collateral to a usurious debt, though he might defend the debt at law. Peters v. Mortimer, 4 Edw. Ch. 279.

Equity ought not to assist the loser to recover it back upon the ground that he is particeps criminis. Lord Talbot on one occasion said: ' The case of gamesters, to which this (of usury) has been compared, is no way parallel; for there both parties are criminal. And if two persons will sit down and endeavor to ruin one another, and one pays the money, if after payment he cannot recover it at law I do not see that a Court of Equity has anything to do but to stand neuter; there being in that case no oppression upon the party as in this.'[1] (a)

304. But it is difficult to perceive why upon principle the money should not be recoverable back, in furtherance of a great public policy, independently of any statutable provision. It has been decided that if money is paid upon a gaming security it may be recovered back, for the security is utterly void.[2] Why is not the original gaming contract equally void? And if it be, why is it not equally within the rule, and the policy on which the rule is founded?

305. The civil law contains a most wholesome enforcement of moral justice upon this subject. It not only protects the loser against any liability to pay the money won in gaming, but if he has paid the money, he and his heirs have a right to recover it back at any distance of time; and no presumption or limitation of time runs against the claim. ' Victum in aleæ lusu, non posse conveniri. Et, si solverit, habere repetitionem, tam ipsum, quam hæredes ejus, adversus victorem et ejus hæredes; idque perpetuo, et etiam post triginta annos.'[3] Thirty years was the general limitation of rights in other cases.

306. Questions are also often made as to how far contracts which are illegal by some positive law, or which are declared so upon principles of public policy, are capable, as between the par-

---

[1] Bosanquet v. Dashwood, Cas. Temp. Talb. 41; 1 Fonbl. Eq. B. 1, ch. 4, § 6; Rawden v. Shadwell, Amb. R. 269; Wilkinson v. L'Eaugier, 2 Y. & Coll. 366. It has been recently held in England that money knowingly lent to game is not recoverable. McKimell v. Robinson, 3 Mees. & Welsb. 434.

[2] 1 Fonbl. Eq. B. 1, ch. 4, § 6, and note (c).

[3] Cod. Lib. 3, tit. 43, l. 1; 1 Fonbl. Eq. B. 1, ch. 4, § 6, note (c).

(a) Thomas v. Cronie, 16 Ohio, 54. See also Raguert v. Cowles, 14 Ohio, 38; White v. Buss, 3 Cush. 448; Machir v. Morse, 2 Gratt. 257; Brua's Appeal, 55 Penn. St. 294; Spalding v. Preston, 21 Vt. 9; Adams v. Gay, 19 Vt. 358. But in some of the States statutes give the loser a right to recover back money paid. See also Diggle v. Higgs, 2 Ex. D. 422; Tremble v. Hill, 5 App. Cas. 342.

ties, of a substantial confirmation. This subject has been already alluded to, and will be again touched in other places. The general rule is that wherever any contract or conveyance is void either by a positive law or upon principles of public policy, it is deemed incapable of confirmation upon the maxim, 'Quod ab initio non valet, in tractu temporis non convalescit.'[1] But where it is merely voidable, or turns upon circumstances of undue advantage, surprise, or imposition, there, if it is deliberately and upon full examination confirmed by the parties, such confirmation will avail to give it an ex post facto validity.[2] (a)

307. Let us in the next place pass to the consideration of the second head of constructive frauds, namely, of those which arise from some peculiar confidential or fiduciary relation between the parties. (b)   In this class of cases there is often to be found some intermixture of deceit, imposition, overreaching, unconscionable advantage, or other mark of direct and positive fraud. But the principle on which Courts of Equity act in regard thereto stands independent of any such ingredients, upon a motive of general public policy; and it is designed in some degree as a protection to the parties against the effects of overweening confidence and self-delusion, and the infirmities of hasty and precipitate judgment. These courts will therefore often interfere in such cases, where but for such a peculiar relation they would either abstain wholly from granting relief or would grant it in a very modified and abstemious manner.[3] (c)

[1] Vernon's case, 4 Co. R. 2, b.

[2] Newland on Contracts, ch. 25, p. 496 to 503; Chesterfield v. Janssen, 2 Ves. 125; s. c. 1 Atk. 301; Roberts v. Roberts, 3 P. Will. 74, Mr. Cox's note; Cole v. Gibson, 1 Ves. 507; Crone v. Ballard, 3 Bro. Ch. R. 120; Cowen v. Milner, 3 P. Will. 292, note (C); Cole v. Gibbons, 3 P. Will. 289; 1 Fonbl. Eq. B. 1, ch. 2, § 13, note (r); Id. ch. 2, § 14, note (v), and the note to § 263.

[3] See Goddard v. Carlisle, 9 Price, R. 169; Gallatiani v. Cunningham, 8 Cowen, R. 361.

(a) Whiting v. Hill, 23 Mich. 399; Davis v. Henry, 4 W. Va. 571; Morris v. Morris, 41 Ga. 271.

(b) A relation of confidence between the parties appears to be sufficient, in most cases at least, to found jurisdiction in equity in favor of the party in the dependent position. See Pratt v. Tuttle, 136 Mass. 233; Badger v. McNamara, 123 Mass. 117;

Makepiece v. Rogers, 11 Jur. N. s. 314; s. c. 34 L. J. Ch. 396, as to principal and agent. But as to that see Barry v. Stevens, 31 Beav. 258, and Phillips v. Phillips, 9 Hare, 471, which is regretted by Lord Justice Turner, so far as it is opposed to Makepiece v. Rogers, supra. See post, § 462, note.

(c) But equity will not do injus-

308. It is undoubtedly true, as has been said, that it is not upon the feelings which a delicate and honorable man must experience, nor upon any notion of discretion to prevent a voluntary gift or other act of a man whereby he strips himself of his property, that Courts of Equity have deemed themselves at liberty to interpose in cases of this sort.[1] (a) They do not sit, or affect to sit, in judgment upon cases as custodes morum, enforcing the strict rules of morality. But they do sit to enforce what has not inaptly been called a technical morality. If confidence is reposed, it must be faithfully acted upon, and preserved from any intermixture of imposition. If influence is acquired, it must be kept free from the taint of selfish interests, and cunning and overreaching bargains. If the means of personal control are given, they must be always restrained to purposes of good faith and personal good. Courts of Equity will not therefore arrest or set aside an act or contract merely because a man of more honor would not have entered into it. There must be some relation between the parties which compels the one to make a full discovery to the other or to abstain from all selfish projects. But when such a relation does exist, Courts of Equity, acting upon this superinduced ground in aid of general morals, will not suffer one party, standing in a situation of which he can avail himself against the other, to derive advantage from that circumstance; for it is founded in a breach of confidence.[2] The general principle which governs in all cases of this sort is, that if a confidence is reposed and that confidence is abused, Courts of Equity will grant relief.[3] (b)

[1] Huguenin v. Baseley, 14 Ves. 290.

[2] Fox v. Mackreth, 2 Bro. Ch. R. 407, 420

[3] Gartside v. Isherwood, 1 Bro. Ch. R. App. 560, 562; Osmond v. Fitzroy, 3 P. Will. 129, 131, Cox's note. See The English Quarterly Magazine for May, 1843, Vol. 29, Pt. 2, p. 362 to 378.

tice; and if the case is not one of actual fraud, equity may impose the strongest terms as a condition of relief. Thus in setting aside a sale where there was no actual fraud, equity will require the return of the purchase-money, or that the conveyance shall stand as security therefor. Coiron v. Millaudon, 19 How. 113; Tompkins v. Sprout, 55 Cal. 31; Bean v. Smith, 2 Mason, 296.

(a) In the absence of fraud, mis-take, or undue influence, equity will not set aside a gift where no relation of confidence exists between the parties. Willamin v. Dunn, 93 Ill. 511.

(b) See Taylor v. Taylor, 8 How. 200; Thornber v. Sheard, 12 Beav. 589; Hoghton v. Hoghton, 15 Beav. 278; Blandy v. Kimber, 24 Beav. 148; Leavitt v. La Force, 71 Mo. 353. And the presumptions are all in favor of the party in the dependent position. Smith v. Kay, 7 H. L. Cas. 750.

309. In the first place, as to the relation of parent and child. (*a*) The natural and just influence which a parent has over a child renders it peculiarly important for courts of justice to watch over and protect the interests of the latter; and therefore all contracts and conveyances whereby benefits are secured by children to their parents are objects of jealousy, and if they are not entered into with scrupulous good faith, and are not reasonable under the circumstances, they will be set aside, unless third persons have acquired an interest under them; especially where the original purposes for which they have been obtained are perverted, or used as a mere cover.[1] (*b*) But we are not to indulge

---

[1] Young *v.* Peachey, 2 Atk. 254; Glissen *v.* Ogden, Ibid. 258; Corking *v.* Pratt, 1 Ves. 400; Hawes *v.* Wyatt, 3 Bro. Ch. R. 156; 1 Madd. Ch. Pract. 244, 245; Carpenter *v.* Heriot, 1 Eden, R. 338; Blackborn *v.* Edgely, 1 P. Will. 607; Blunden *v.* Barker, 1 P. Will. 639; Morris *v.* Burroughs, 1 Atk. 402; Tendril *v.* Smith, 2 Atk. 85; Heron *v.* Heron, 2 Atk. R. 160. See Jenkins *v.* Pye, 12 Peters, R. 241.

(*a*) As to cases of other blood relationships, see Beauland *v.* Bradley, 2 Smale & G. 339; Hewitt *v.* Crane, 2 Halst. Ch. 159; Van Meter *v.* Jones, 2 Green's Ch. 520; Fish *v.* Cleland, 33 Ill. 238; Cleland *v.* Fish, 43 Ill. 282; Sears *v.* Shafer, 2 Seld. 268; Todd *v.* Grove, 33 Md. 188; Ranken *v.* Patton, 65 Mo. 378; Boyd *v.* De la Montagnie, 73 N. Y. 498 (husband and wife); White *v.* Smith, 51 Ala. 405; Taylor *v.* Johnston, 19 Ch. D. 603. It was held in Taylor *v.* Johnston that in the absence of evidence of the exercise of control or influence on the part of the donee, or of the existence of the relation of guardian and ward between the donor and the donee, a gift of her property within a month before her death by an infant of twenty years, of business habits, firm will, and ability to manage her own affairs, to a relative with whom she had been living from the time of her father's death till her own death, five months, was not invalid.

On the other hand where three brothers induced their sister, who had a reversionary interest in land devised by their father to the brothers for life, to release her interest to them without consideration, but upon a belief, induced by the brothers, that the father intended to devise the land to the brothers in fee, the release was set aside; it appearing that the sister was in feeble health, and had always relied on her brothers for advice. Sears *v.* Shafer, 2 Seld. 268. See also Boney *v.* Hollingsworth, 23 Ala. 690; Hewitt *v.* Crane, 2 Halst. Ch. 159, 631.

It is apprehended that all such cases are to be distinguished from gifts by children to parents, in that there can be no presumption or suspicion of unfairness on the mere relationship, such as may arise on the relation of parent and child.

(*b*) See Baker *v.* Tucker, 17 Jur. 771; Wood *v.* Rabe, 96 N. Y. 414; Miller *v.* Simonds, 72 Mo. 669; Ranken *v.* Patton, 65 Mo. 378; Bainbrigge *v.* Browne, 18 Ch. D. 188; Maitland *v.* Irving, 15 Sim. 437; Archer *v.* Hudson, 7 Beav. 551; Berdoe *v.* Dawson, 34 Beav. 603; Bury *v.* Oppenheim, 26 Beav. 594; Turner *v.* Collins, L. R. 7 Ch. 329; Wright *v.* Vanderplank,

undue suspicions of jealousy, or to make unfavorable presumptions as a matter of course in cases of this sort. ‘It is undoubtedly the duty of courts carefully to watch and examine the circumstances attending transactions of this kind when brought under review before them, to discover if any undue influence has been exercised in obtaining the conveyance. But to consider a parent disqualified to take a voluntary deed from his child without consideration, on account of their relationship, is assuming a principle at war with all filial as well as parental duty and affection; and acting on the presumption that a parent, instead of wishing to promote the interest and welfare, would be seeking to overreach and defraud his child. Whereas the presumption ought to be, in the absence of all proof tending to a contrary conclusion, that the advancement of the interest of the child was the object in view; and to presume the existence of circumstances conducing to that result. Such a presumption harmonizes with the moral obligations of a parent to provide for his child, and is founded upon the same benign principle that governs cases of purchases made by parents in the name of a child. The prima facie presumption is that it was intended as an advancement to the child, and so not falling within the principle of a resulting trust. The natural and reasonable presumption in all transactions of this kind is, that a benefit was intended the child, because in the discharge of a moral and parental duty. And the interest of the child is abundantly guarded and protected by keeping a watchful eye over the transaction to see that no undue influence was brought to bear upon it.’ [1] (a)

---

[1] Jenkins v. Pye, 12 Peters, R. 253, 254. The opinion of the court in this case was delivered by Mr. Justice Thompson, and immediately preceding the

8 DeG. M. & G. 133; Hoghton v. Hoghton, 15 Beav. 278; Kempson v. Ashbee, L. R. 10 Ch. 15, 21. The rule applies equally to a person who has put himself in loco parentis. Archer v. Hudson, supra.

(a) It is laid down that when a deed conferring a benefit on a father is executed by a child not emancipated, if the deed is afterwards impeached by the child the onus is on the father to show that the child had independent advice, and that he executed the deed with full knowledge of its contents, and with free intention to give the father the benefit conferred. Bainbrigge v. Browne, 18 Ch. D. 188. And this rule operates equally against volunteers and purchasers with notice. Ib. But not against others. Ib.; Kempson v. Ashbee, L. R. 10 Ch. 15, 21. See further in regard to the general doctrine that a child’s gift to a parent will be narrowly scrutinized,

310. In the next place, as to the relation of client and attorney or solicitor. It is obvious that this relation must give rise to great confidence between the parties, and to very strong influences over the actions and rights and interests of the client.[1] The situation of an attorney or solicitor puts it in his power to

passage cited in the text, he said: ' But the grounds mainly relied upon to invalidate the deed were, that being from a daughter to her father rendered it, at least prima facie, void; and if not void on this ground, it was so because it was obtained by the undue influence of paternal authority. The first ground of objection seeks to establish the broad principle that a deed from a child to a parent conveying the real estate of the child ought, upon considerations of public policy growing out of the relation of the parties, to be deemed void : and numerous cases in the English chancery have been referred to which are supposed to establish this principle. We do not deem it necessary to travel over all these authorities; we have looked into the leading cases, and cannot discover anything to warrant the broad and unqualified doctrine contended for on the part of the appellees. All the cases are accompanied with some ingredient showing undue influence exercised by the parent, operating upon the fears or hopes of the child, and sufficient to show reasonable grounds to presume that the act was not perfectly free and voluntary on the part of the child; and in some cases, although there may be circumstances tending in some small degree to show undue influence, yet if the agreement appears reasonable, it has been considered enough to outweigh light circumstances, so as not to affect the validity of the deed. It becomes the less necessary for us to go into a critical examination of the English chancery doctrine on this subject, for should the cases be found to countenance it, we should not be disposed to adopt or sanction the broad principle contended for, that the deed of a child to a parent is to be deemed, prima facie, void.'

[1] Walmesley v. Booth, 2 Atk. R. 25; 1 Fonbl. Eq. B. 1, ch. 4, § 12, note (k). See also Barnesly v. Powel, 1 Ves. 284; Bulkley v. Wilford, 1 Clark & Finn. R. 102, 177 to 181; Id. 183; ante, § 218; Edwards v. Meyrick, 2 Hare, R. 260, 268.

Wallace v. Wallace, 2 Dru. & W. 470; Rhodes v. Cook, 2 Sim. & S. 489; Baker v. Bradley, 2 Smale & G. 531; Wright v. Vanderplank, 2 Kay & J. 1; s. c. 8 DeG. M. & G. 133. Family arrangements have been looked upon with more indulgence in favor of the grantee than other cases. Wallace v. Wallace, supra; Baker v. Bradley, supra; Hartopp v. Hartopp, 21 Beav. 259. See Head v. Godlee, Johns. 536; Jenner v. Jenner, 2 DeG. F. & J. 359; Field v. Evans, 15 Sim. 375. The converse case of a gift or conveyance from parent to child may, on a reversal of the duties of the parties, equally require scrutiny. Comstock v. Comstock, 57 Barb. 453; Deem v. Phillips, 5 W. Va. 168; Day v. Day, 84 N. Car. 408; Thorn v. Thorn, 51 Mich. 167; McKinney v. Hensley, 74 Mo. 326; Harrington v. Grant, 54 Vt. 236; Highberger v. Stiffler, 21 Md. 352; Simpler v. Lord, 28 Ga. 52; Glover v. Hayden, 4 Cush. 580; Belcher v. Belcher, 10 Yerg. 121; Martin v. Martin, 1 Heisk. 644. But presumptively such a gift is perfectly good. Millican v. Millican, 24 Texas, 424, 446; Sanfley v. Jackson, 16 Texas, 579; Leddel v. Starr, 5 C. E. Green, 274.

avail himself not only of the necessities of his client, but of his good nature, liberality, and credulity to obtain undue advantages, bargains, and gratuities. Hence the law, with a wise providence, not only watches over all the transactions of parties in this predicament, but it often interposes to declare transactions void which between other persons would be held unobjectionable.[1] It does not so much consider the bearing or hardship of its doctrine upon particular cases, as it does the importance of preventing a general public mischief which may be brought about by means, secret and inaccessible to judicial scrutiny, from the dangerous influences arising from the confidential relation of the parties.[2] By establishing the principle that while the relation of client and attorney subsists in its full vigor the latter shall derive no benefit to himself from the contracts, or bounty, or other negotiations of the former,[3] (a) it supersedes the necessity of any inquiry into the particular means, extent, and exertion of influence in a given case; a task often difficult, and ill-supported by evidence which can be drawn from any satisfactory sources.[4] This doctrine is not necessarily limited to cases where

---

[1] 1 Madd. Ch. Pr. 94; Welles v. Middleton, 1 Cox, R. 112, 125; 3 P. Will. 131, Cox's note (1); Wright v. Proud, 13 Ves. 136; Wood v. Downes, 18 Ves. 126; ante, § 219.

[2] Wood v. Downes, 18 Ves. 126; ante, § 219; De Montmorency v. Devereux, 7 Clark and Finn. 188.

[3] Wood v. Downes, 18 Ves. 126; Jones v. Tripp, Jac. Rep. 322; Goddard v. Carlisle, 9 Price, R. 169; Edwards v. Meyrick, 2 Hare, R. 68.

[4] See Welles v. Middleton, 1 Cox, R. 125; Wright v. Proud, 13 Ves. 137. See Cheslyn v. Dalby, 2 Younge & Coll. 194, 195. In the case of Hunter v. Atkins (3 M. & Keen, 113), Lord Brougham made the following remarks on this subject: ' There is no dispute upon the rules which, generally speaking, regulate cases of this description. Mr. Alderman Atkins is either to be regarded in the light of an agent confidentially entrusted with the management of Admiral Hunter's concerns, a person at least in whom he reposed a very special confidence, or he is not. If he is not to be so regarded, then

---

(a) Tomson v. Judge, 3 Drew. 306; In re Holmes, 3 Giff. 337; O'Brien v. Lewis, 4 Giff. 221; Walker v. Smith, 29 Beav. 394; Morgan v. Minett, 6 Ch. D. 638; Savery v. King, 5 H. L. Cas. 627; McMahan v. Smith, 6 Heisk. 167; Mason v. Ring, 3 Abb. App. Dec. 210; Polson v. Young, 37 Iowa, 136; Zeigler v. Hughes, 55 Ill. 288. See further Salmon v. Cutts, 4 DeG. & S. 128; Robinson v. Briggs, 1 Smale & G. 188; Brock v. Barnes, 40 Barb. 521; Pearson v. Benson, 28 Beav. 598; Williamson v. Moriarty, 19 Week. R. 818; Corley v. Stafford, 1 DeG. & J. 238; Hobday v. Peters, 6 Jur. N. s. 794; Cowdry v. Day, 5 Jur. N. s. 1199; Reickhoff v. Brecht, 51 Iowa, 633; Pearce v. Gamble, 72 Ala. 341.

the contract or other transaction respects the rights or property in controversy, in the particular suit in respect to which the

a deed of gift or other disposition of property in his favor must stand good, unless some direct fraud were practised upon the maker of it; unless some fraud either by misrepresentation or by suppression of facts misled him, or he was of unsound mind when the deed was made. If the alderman did stand in a confidential relation towards him, then the party seeking to set aside the deed may not be called upon to show direct fraud; but he must satisfy the court, by the circumstances, that some advantage was taken of the confidential relation in which the alderman stood. If the alderman stood towards the admiral in any of the known relations of guardian and ward, attorney and client, trustee and cestui que trust, &c., then in order to support the deed he ought to show that no such advantage was taken; that all was fair; that he received the bounty freely and knowingly on the giver's part, and as a stranger might have done. For I take the rule to be this: There are certain relations known to the law as attorney, guardian, trustee; if a person standing in these relations to client, ward, or cestui que trust takes a gift or makes a bargain, the proof lies upon him that he has dealt with the other party, the client, ward, &c., exactly as a stranger would have done, taking no advantage of his influence or knowledge, putting the other party on his guard, bringing everything to his knowledge which he himself knew. In short the rule rightly considered is, that the person standing in such relation must, before he can take a gift, or even enter into a transaction, place himself in exactly the same position as a stranger would have been in; so that he may gain no advantage whatever from his relation to the other party beyond what may be the natural and unavoidable consequence of kindness arising out of that relation. A client, for example, may naturally entertain a kindly feeling towards an attorney or solicitor by whose assistance he has long benefited; and he may fairly and wisely desire to benefit him by a gift, or without such an intention being the predominating motive, he may wish to give him the advantage of a sale or a lease. No law that is tolerable among civilized men — men who have the benefits of civility without the evils of excessive refinement and overdone subtlety — can ever forbid such a transaction, provided the client be of mature age and of sound mind, and there be nothing to show that deception was practised, or that the attorney or solicitor availed himself of his situation to withhold any knowledge or to exercise any influence hurtful to others and advantageous to himself. In a word, standing in the relation in which he stands to the other party, the proof lies upon him (whereas in the case of a stranger it would lie on those who opposed him) to show that he has placed himself in the position of a stranger; that he has cut off, as it were, the connection which bound him to the party giving or contracting; and that nothing has happened which might not have happened had no such connection subsisted. The authorities mean nothing else than this when they say, as in Gibson v. Jeyes (6 Ves. 277), that attorney and client, trustee and cestui que trust, may deal, but it must be at arm's length; the parties putting themselves in the situation of purchasers and vendors, and performing (as the court said, and I take leave to observe, not very felicitously or even very correctly) all the duties of those characters. The authorities mean no more, taken fairly and candidly towards the court, when they say, as in Wright v. Proud (15 Ves. 138), that an attorney shall not take a gift from his client

attorney or solicitor is advising or acting for his client; but it may extend to other contracts and transactions disconnected therefrom, or at least where from the attendant circumstance there is reason to presume that the attorney and solicitor possessed some marked influence, ascendency, or other advantage over his client in respect to them.[1]

while the relation subsists, though the transaction may be not only free from fraud but the most moral in its nature; a dictum reduced in Hatch v. Hatch (9 Ves. 296) to this, that it is almost impossible for a gift from client to attorney to stand, because the difficulty is extreme, of showing that everything was voluntary and fair, and with full warning and perfect knowledge; for in Harris v. Tremenheere (15 Ves. 40) the court only held that in such a case a suspicion attaches on the transaction and calls for minute examination.'

[1] See Edwards v. Meyrick, 2 Hare, R. 60, 68. Mr. Vice-Chancellor Wigram here said: 'It was not insisted in argument that a solicitor is under an actual incapacity to purchase from his client. There is not in that case the positive incapacity which exists between a trustee and his cestui que trust; but the rule the court imposes is, that inasmuch as the parties stand in a relation which gives or may give the solicitor an advantage over the client, the onus lies on the solicitor to prove that the transaction was fair. Montesquieu v. Sandys, 18 Ves. 302; Cane v. Lord Allen, 2 Dow, 289. The rule is expressed by Lord Eldon (6 Ves. 278. See also Sugden, Vend. & Pur. Vol. 3, p. 238, ed. 10) to be, that if the attorney "will mix with the character of attorney that of vendor, he shall, if the propriety of the transaction comes in question, manifest that he has given his client all that reasonable advice against himself that he would have given him against a third person." It was argued that the rule I have referred to has no application unless the defendant was the plaintiff's solicitor in hac re, and this argument is no doubt well founded. Jones v. Thomas, 2 Y. & Coll. 498; Gibson v. Jeyes, 6 Ves. 266, 278. It appears to me however that the question whether Meyrick was the solicitor in hac re is one rather of words than of substance. The rule of equity which subjects transactions between solicitor and client to other and stricter tests than those which apply to ordinary transactions is not an isolated rule, but is a branch of a rule applicable to all transactions between man and man in which the relation between the contracting parties is such as to destroy the equal footing on which such parties should stand. In some cases, as between trustee and cestui que trust, the rule goes to the extent of creating a positive incapacity; the duties of the office of trustee requiring on general principles that that particular case should be so guarded. The case of solicitor and client is however different. In the case of Gibson v. Jeyes there was evidence that the client was of advanced age and of much infirmity, both in mind and body, that the consideration was inadequate, and of various other circumstances. Lord Eldon there shows how each of those circumstances gave rise to its appropriate duty on the part of the attorney. In other cases where an attorney has been employed to manage an estate, he has been considered as bound to prove that he gave his employer the benefit of all the knowledge which he had acquired in his character of manager or professional agent, in order to sustain a bargain made for his own advantage. Cane v. Lord Allen, 2 Dow, 294. But as the communication of such knowledge by

311. On the one hand it is not necessary to establish that there has been fraud or imposition upon the client; (a) and on

the attorney will place the parties upon an equality, when it is proved that the communication was made, the difficulty of supporting the transaction is quoad hoc removed. If on the other hand the attorney has not had any concern with the estate respecting which the question arises, the particular duties to which any given situation of confidence might give rise cannot of course attach upon him, whatever may be the other duties which the mere office of attorney may impose. If the attorney, being employed to sell, becomes himself the purchaser, his duties and his interests are directly opposed to each other, and it would be difficult — and without the clearest evidence that no advantage was taken by the attorney of his position, and that the vendor had all the knowledge which could be given him in order to form a judgment, it would be impossible — to support the transaction. In other cases the relation between the parties may simply produce a degree of influence and ascendency, placing the client in circumstances of disadvantage, as where he is indebted to the attorney and is unable to discharge the debt. The relative position of the parties in such a case must at least impose upon the attorney the duty of giving the full value for the estate, and the onus of proving that he did so. If he proves the full value to have been given, the ground for any unfavorable inference is removed. The cases may be traced through every possible variation until we reach the simple case where, though the relation of solicitor and client exists in one transaction, and therefore personal influence or ascendency may operate in another, yet, the relation not existing in hac re, the rule of equity to which I am now adverting may no longer apply. The nature of the proof therefore which the court requires must depend upon the circumstances of each case according as they may have placed the attorney in a position in which his duties and his pecuniary interests were conflicting, or may have given him a knowledge which his client did not possess or some influence or ascendency or other advantage over his client, or, notwithstanding the existence of the relation of attorney and client, may have left the parties substantially at arm's length and on an equal footing: this seems deducible from the cases. Gibson v. Jeyes; Hatch v. Hatch, 9 Ves. 292; Welles v. Middleton, 1 Cox, 112; s. c. cited 18 Ves. 127; Wood v. Downes, 18 Ves. 120; Bellew v. Russell, 1 Ba. & Be. 96; Montesquieu v. Sandys; Cane v. Lord Allen; Hunter v. Atkins, 3 Myl. & K. 113. I have therefore to consider the position in which these parties actually stood to each other. And I certainly am not treating the case of the plaintiff too strictly when I exclude all considerations which the bill does not state as having existed; and according to the statements in the bill, it does not appear that the defendant had any peculiar or exclusive knowledge of these particular farms or the value of them or that he had undertaken any particular duties respecting them which were opposed to his becoming a purchaser. No equity appears to me to arise except that which might arise from the mere possibility of the relation of attorney and

(a) In Morgan v. Minett, 6 Ch. D. 638, Bacon, V. C., decided, that while the relation exists the attorney *cannot* take a gift from his client, though there be no fraud, misrepresentation, or even suspicion; following Tomson v. Judge, 3 Drew. 306, and commenting on Hunter v. Atkins, 3 Mylne & K. 113. But that is too strong.

the other hand it is not necessarily void throughout, ipso facto. (*a*) But the burthen of establishing its perfect fairness, adequacy, and equity is thrown upon the attorney, upon the general rule that he who bargains in a matter of advantage with a person placing a confidence in him is bound to show that a reasonable use has been made of that confidence ; a rule applying equally to all persons standing in confidential relations with each other.[1] (*b*) If no such proof is established, Courts of Equity treat the case as one of constructive fraud.[2] In this respect there is said to be a distinction between the case of an attorney and client, and that of a trustee and cestui que trust. (*c*) In

client giving the attorney some influence or ascendency over the client, and the circumstance that the plaintiff was pressed by him to pay his bill of costs. On the evidence in the cause I am satisfied that the only ground upon which I can proceed is this bare relation between the parties. Taking the obligations of the defendant to stand as high as the relative position of the parties enables me to place them, — admitting the defendant to be the attorney in hac re, — I cannot consider that he is bound to do more than prove that he gave the full value for the estate.' Post, § 313.

[1] Gibson *v.* Jeyes, 6 Ves. 278; Montesquieu *v.* Sandys, 18 Ves. 313; Bellew *v.* Russell, 1 B. & Beatty, R. 104, 107; Harris *v.* Tremenheere, 15 Ves. 34, 39; Cane *v.* Lord Allen, 2 Dow, R. 289, 299; Edwards *v.* Meyrick, 2 Hare, R. 60. The like rule applies to counsel employed as a confidential adviser; for he is disabled from purchasing for his own benefit charges on his client's estate without his permission, and the disability will continue as long as the reason exist, although the confidential employment may have ended. Carter *v.* Palman, 8 Clark & Finn. 657, 706.

[2] See Jones *v.* Thomas, 2 Y. & Coll. 498. In this case it was held that where an account is decreed to be taken between an attorney and his client, in the course of which the attorney has taken securities from the client, the attorney must not only prove the securities, but the consideration for which they were given. Champion *v.* Rigby, 1 Russ. & Mylne, 539.

(*a*) For cases in which the transaction between attorney and client was upheld see Moss *v.* Bainbrigge, 6 DeG. M. & G. 292; Blagrave *v.* Routh, 2 Kay & J. 509; Clanricarde *v.* Henning, 30 Beav. 175; Johnson *v.* Fesemeyer, 3 DeG. & J. 13; Porter *v.* Peckham, 44 Cal. 204; Howell *v.* Ransom, 11 Paige, 538; Evans *v.* Ellis, 5 Denio, 640; Nesbit *v.* Lockman, 34 N. Y. 167.

(*b*) See Smith *v.* Kay, 7 H. L. Cas. 750; Holmes's Estate, 3 Giff. 337; Walker *v.* Smith, 29 Beav. 394; Spencer *v.* Topham, 22 Beav. 573; Lewis *v.*

Hillman, 3 H. L. Cas. 706; Nesbit *v.* Lockman, 34 N. Y. 167; Jennings *v.* McConnell, 17 Ill. 148; Bayliss *v.* Williams, 6 Coldw. 440. The attorney should show that his client had competent and independent (or at least sufficient) advice. Rhodes *v.* Bate, L. R. 1 Ch. 257. And so doubtless of all other cases of special relations of confidence. Tyrrell *v.* Bank of London, 8 Jur. N. s. 849; s. c. 31 L. J. Ch. 369.

(*c*) See however Morgan *v.* Minett, 6 Ch. D. 638.

the former, if the attorney, retaining his connection, contracts with his client, he is subject to the onus of proving that no advantage has been taken of the situation of the latter.   But in the case of a trustee it is not sufficient to show that no advantage has been taken ; but the cestui que trust may set aside the transaction at his own option.[1]   The reason of this distinction, which savors somewhat of nicety if not of subtilty, seems to be that in the case of clients the rule is general, and applicable to all contracts, conveyances, and negotiations between the attorney and client, and is not limited to the property about which the attorney is retained, or the suit in which he is acting.   In the case of a trustee the rule giving the cestui que trust an option is limited to the purchase of the trust property, and as to other property it would seem that the rule is the same as in other fiduciary relations ; that is, at most it only shifts the burthen of proof from the seller to the buyer, to show the entire fairness of the transaction, or leaves the seller to establish presumptively that there has been some irregularity in the bargain, or some influence connected with the relation under which it has been made.[2]

312. Thus if a bond is obtained by an attorney from a client who is poor and distressed, and it does not appear to be for a full and fair consideration, it will be set aside as obtained by undue influence from his station.[3] (a) Upon a like ground a bond taken by an attorney from his client for a specific sum will not

---

[1] Cane v. Lord Allen, 2 Dow, 289, 299; post, § 322. See the remarks of Lord Brougham, in Hunter v. Atkins, 3 Mylne & Keen, R: 113; ante, § 310, note, where he seems to put the cases of client and attorney, guardian and ward, trustee and cestui que trust, upon the same general footing, and governed by the same rule. The same distinction is stated in Edwards v. Meyrick, 2 Hare, R. 60, 68, 69; ante, § 310, note.

[2] See post, § 313; Montesquieu v. Sandys, 18 Ves. R. 302, 318.

[3] Proof v. Hines, Cas. T. Talb. 111; Walmesley v. Booth, 2 Atk. 29.

(a) So of all securities. Brown v. Bulkley, 1 McCart. 451. As to lapse of time and acquiescence see Blagrave v. Routh, 8 DeG. M. & G. 620; Shaw v. Neale, 20 Beav. 157. The same weight ought not to be given perhaps to lapse of time as in ordinary cases, while the relation continues. Gresley v. Mousley, 5 Jur. N. S. 583; s. c. 4 DeG. & J. 78; 3 DeG. F. & J. 433. If a solicitor propose to take any contract from his client for compensation beyond what the law provides, he should inform his client on the point. Lyddon v. Moss, 5 Jur. N. S. 637; s. c. 4 DeG. & J. 104; Morgan v Higgins, 5 Jur. N. S. 236; s. c. 1 Giff. 270.

be allowed to stand as a security, except for the amount of fees
and charges due to the attorney; for it is the general policy of
courts of justice in cases between client and attorney to protect
the suitors, and not to suffer any advantage to be taken of them
by securities of this sort.[1]   And for the same reason a judgment
obtained by a solicitor against his client for security for costs
will be overhauled even after a considerable lapse of time.[2] So
a gift made to an attorney, pendente lite (for it would be otherwise if the relation had completely ceased), will be set aside as
arising from the exercise of improper influence;[3] for it has been
said with great force that there would be no bounds to the
crushing influence of the power of an attorney who has the
affairs of a man in his hand, if it were not so.[4]   And sales made
and annuities granted to attorneys under similar circumstances
will upon the same principles of public policy be set aside, at
least unless they are established to have been transacted uberrima fide.[5] (a)

313. Indeed the general principle is so well established, that
Lord Eldon on one occasion said: ' It is almost impossible in the
course of the connection of guardian and ward, attorney and
client, trustee and cestui que trust, that a transaction shall stand,
purporting to be bounty for the execution of an antecedent
duty.'[6] (b)   But where the relation is completely dissolved, and

[1] Newman v. Payne, 4 Bro. Ch. R. 350; s. c. 2 Ves. jr. 200; Langstaffe v.
Taylor, 14 Ves. 262; Wood v. Downes, 18 Ves. 120, 127; Pitcher v. Rigby,
9 Price, R. 79.

[2] Draper's Company v. Davis, 2 Atk. 295.

[3] Oldham v. Hand, 2 Ves. 259; Welles v. Middleton, 1 Cox, 112, 125;
Harris v. Tremenheere, 15 Ves. 34; Wood v. Downes, 18 Ves. 120, 127;
Morse v. Royal, 12 Ves. 371.

[4] Welles v. Middleton, 1 Cox, R. 125; Hatch v. Hatch, 9 Ves. 292, 296.

[5] Harris v. Tremenheere, 15 Ves. 34; Gibson v. Jeyes, 6 Ves. 266; Wood
v. Downes, 18 Ves. 120; Bellew v. Russell, 1 Ball & Beatt. 104.

[6] Hatch v. Hatch, 9 Ves. 296, 297. Mr. Maddock, in 1 Madd. Ch. Pr. 95,
note (f), has suggested that what is said as to an attorney, in Morse v. Royal,
12 Ves. 371, and in Wright v. Proud, 13 Ves. 138, does not seem warranted

(a) But testamentary dispositions
stand on a better footing towards the
donee. Hindson v. Weatherill, 5 DeG.
M. & G. 301; Walker v. Smith, 29
Beav. 394. Compare however § 320,
note, as to guardian and ward.

(b) The rule does not touch small
gifts. Rhodes v. Bate, L. R. Ch. 257.
But it applies to a solicitor's clerk as
well as to the solicitor himself. Hobday v. Peters, 28 Beav. 349; s. c. 6
Jur. N. s. 794.   See Nesbit v. Lockman, 34 N. Y. 167, where a gift to a
clerk was held good.

the parties are no longer under the antecedent influence, but deal with each other at arm's length, there is no ground to apply the principle, and they stand upon the rights and duties common to all other persons.[1] (a) And the same rule will or may apply where the transaction is totally disconnected with the relation, and concerns objects and things not embraced in, or affected by, or dependent upon, that relation,[2] and there is an absence of all other circumstances which may create a just suspicion as to the integrity and fairness of the transaction.

314. Similar considerations apply to the case of a medical adviser and his patient. For it would be a meagre sort of justice to say that the sort of policy which has induced the court to interfere between client and attorney should be restricted to such cases; since as much mischief might be produced, and as much fraud and dishonesty be practised, if transactions were permitted to stand which arose between parties in equally confidential relations.[3] (b)

by the authorities. I confess myself at a loss precisely to understand what Mr. Maddock intended by this remark. Surely he could not mean to say that a gift to an attorney, while that relation continued, could not be avoided unless fraud or imposition were proved, for that would be contradicted by the doctrine maintained in several cases. Welles v. Middleton, 1 Cox, R. 125; Hatch v. Hatch, 9 Ves. 296, 297; Gibson v. Jeyes, 6 Ves. 276; Wood v. Downes, 18 Ves. 123; Oldham v. Hand, 2 Ves. 259; Montesquieu v. Sandys, 18 Ves. 313. See also Bellew v. Russell, 1 Ball & Beatt. R. 104, 107; Harris v. Tremenheere, 14 Ves. 34, 42; Walmesley v. Booth, 2 Atk. 29, 30. See also Wendell v. Van Rensselaer, 1 John. Ch. R. 350; Hylton v. Hylton, 2 Ves. 547, as cited by Lord Eldon, 18 Ves. 126; Newland on Contracts, ch. 31, p. 453, &c.; Welles v. Middleton, 1 Cox, R. 125; 18 Ves. 126.

[1] Gibson v. Jeyes, 6 Ves. 277; Oldham v. Hand, 2 Ves. 259; Montesquieu v. Sandys, 18 Ves. 313; Walmesley v. Booth, 2 Atk. 29, 30; Wood v. Downes, 18 Ves. 126, 127.

[2] Montesquieu v. Sandys, 18 Ves. 313; Newland on Contracts, ch. 31, pp. 456, 457, 458; Howell v. Baker, 4 John. Ch. R. 118; Edwards v. Meyrick, 2 Hare, R. 60, 68; Jones v. Thomas, 2 Younge & Coll. 498; Gibson v. Jeyes, 6 Ves. R. 266, 278; ante, § 310.

[3] Dent v. Bennett, 2 Keen, R. 539; s. c. 4 Mylne & Craig, 269, 276, 277; Gibson v. Russell, 2 Younge & Coll. N. R. 104; s. c. The Jurist (English), Oct. 7, 1843, p. 875. But see Pratt v. Barker, 1 Sim. R. 1.

(a) If a solicitor has obtained leave to bid at his client's sale, that does away with the fiduciary relation, and he is no longer bound to disclose all material facts. Boswell v. Coaks, 23 Ch. D. 302.

(b) Bellage v. Souther, 9 Hare, 534. See however Dogget v. Lane, 12 Mo. 215.

315. In the next place, the relation of principal and agent. This is affected by the same considerations as the preceding, founded upon the same enlightened public policy.[1] In all cases of this sort the principal contracts for the aid and benefit of the skill and judgment of the agent, and the habitual confidence reposed in the latter makes all his acts and statements possess a commanding influence over the former. Indeed in such cases the agent too often so entirely misleads the judgment of his principal, that while he is seeking his own peculiar advantage he seems but consulting the advantage and interests of his principal ; placing himself in the odious predicament so strongly stigmatized by Cicero : ' Totius autem injustitiæ nulla capitalior est, quam eorum qui, cum maxime fallunt, id agunt, ut viri boni esse videantur.' [2] It is therefore for the common security of all mankind that gifts procured by agents and purchases made by them from their principals should be scrutinized with a close and vigilant suspicion. And indeed considering the abuses which may attend any dealings of this sort between principals and agents, a doubt has been expressed whether it would not have been wiser for the law in all cases to have prohibited them, since there must almost always be a conflict between duty and interest on such occasions.[3] Be this as it may, it is very certain that agents are not permitted to become secret vendors or purchasers of property which they are authorized to buy or sell for their principals ; (a) or by abusing their confidence to acquire unreasonable gifts or advantages ; [4] (b) or indeed to deal validly

[1] 1 Fonbl. Eq. B. 1, ch. 3, § 12, note (k); Benson v. Heathom, 1 Younge & Coll. N. R. 326.

[2] Cic. de Offic. Lib. 1, ch. 13; Huguenin v. Baseley, 14 Ves. 284.

[3] Dunbar v. Tredennick, 2 Ball & Beatt. R. 319 ; Norris v. Le Neve, 3 Atk. R. 38.

[4] See Church v. Mar. Ins. Co. 1 Mason, R. 341; Barker v. Mar. Ins. Co., 2 Mason, R. 369; Woodhouse v. Meredith, 1 Jac. & Walk. 204, 222; Massey v. Davies, 2 Ves. jr. 318; Crowe v. Ballard, 3 Bro. Ch. R. 120; Lees v. Nuttall, 1 Russ. & Mylne, 53; s. c. 1 Tamlyn, R. 282.

(a) See Parker v. Nickerson, 112 Mass. 195; s. c. 137 Mass. 487, 497; Kimber v. Barber, L. R. 8 Ch. 56 ; Tyrrell v. Bank of London, 10 H. L. Cas. 26; Lewis v. Hillman, 3 H. L. Cas. 607; Jeffries v. Wiester, 2 Sawy. 135; Ingle v. Hartman, 37 Iowa, 274; Ruckman v. Bergholz, 37 N. J. 437; Bain v. Brown, 56 N. Y. 285; Tynes v. Grimstead, 1 Tenn. Ch. 508; Uhlrich v. Muhlke, 61 Ill. 499. So of purchasers from the agent with notice. Young v. Hughes, 32 N. J. Eq. 372.

(b) See Gower v. Andrew, 59 Cal. 119.

with their principals in any cases, except where there is the most entire good faith and a full disclosure of all facts and circumstances, and an absence of all undue influence, advantage, or imposition.[1] (a)

316. Upon these principles if an agent sells to his principal his own property as the property of another, without disclosing the fact, the bargain, at the election of the principal, will be held void.[2] So if an agent employed to purchase for another purchases for himself, he will be considered as the trustee of his employer.[3] (b) Therefore if a person is employed as an agent to purchase up a debt of his employer, he cannot purchase the debt upon his own account, for he is bound to purchase it at as low a rate as he can, and he would otherwise be tempted to violate his duty.[4] The same rule applies to a surety who purchases up the debt of his principal. And therefore in each case if a purchase is made of the debt, the agent or surety can entitle himself, as against his principal, to no more than he has actually paid for the debt.[5] So if an agent discover a defect in the title

[1] See Crowe v. Ballard, 3 Bro. Ch. R. 117; Purcell v. Macnamara, 14 Ves. 91; Huguenin v. Baseley, 14 Ves. 273; Watt v. Grove, 2 Sch. & Lefr. 492; Fox v. Mackreth, 2 Bro. Ch. R. 400; s. c. 2 Cox, R. 320; Coles v. Trecothick, 9 Ves. 246; Lowther v. Lowther, 13 Ves. 102, 103; Seley v. Rhodes, 2 Sim. & Stu. R. 49; Morret v. Paske, 2 Atk. 53; Green v. Winter, 1 John. Ch. R. 27; Parkist v. Alexander, 1 John. Ch. R. 394. The case of Cray v. Mansfield, 1 Ves. R. 379, has been very justly doubted by Mr. Belt, as not consistent with established principles. See Belt's Supplement, 167.

[2] Gillett v. Peppercorne, 3 Beav. R. 78, 83, 84.

[3] Lees v. Nuttall, 1 Russ. & M. 53; s. c. 1 Tamlyn, R. 282; post, § 327; Taylor v. Salmon, 2 Mees. & Cromp. 139; s. c. 4 Mylne & Craig, 139; Torrey v. Bank of New Orleans, 9 Paige, R. 619; Van Epps v. Van Epps, 9 Paige, R. 327; post, §§ 1201 a, 1211 a.

[4] Reed v. Norris, 2 Mylne & Craig, 361, 374.

[5] Ibid.

(a) See Cleveland Ins. Co. v. Reed, 1 Biss. 180; Krutz v. Fisher, 8 Kans. 90; s. c. 9 Kans. 501; White v. Ward, 26 Ark. 445; Glenwaters v. Miller, 49 Miss. 150; Condit v. Blackwell, 7 C. E. Green, 481; McMahon v. McGraw, 26 Wis. 614; Beck v. Kantorowicz, 3 Kay & J. 230. Where a partnership or joint-stock company is in contemplation, and a promoter purchases property to sell to the associates, he acts as quasi agent, and cannot sell at an advance without full disclosure. Short v. Stevenson, 63 Penn. St. 95; Densmore Oil Co. v. Densmore, 9 Am. Law Reg. N. s. 96; Beck v. Kantorowicz, supra. But persons about to enter into partnership do not ordinarily stand in a situation of confidence. Uhler v. Semple, 5 C. E. Green, 288.

(b) Wentworth v. Lloyd, 32 Beav. 467; s. c. 10 H. L. Cas. 589.

of his principal to land, he cannot misuse it to acquire a title for himself; if he do, he will be held a trustee for his principal.[1]

316 a. In all cases of purchases and bargains respecting property directly and openly made between principals and agents the utmost good faith is required. The agent must conceal no facts within his knowledge which might influence the judgment of his principal as to the price or value; and if he does, the contract will be set aside.[2] (a) The question in all such cases does not turn upon the point whether there is any intention to cheat or not; but upon the obligation, from the fiduciary relation of the parties, to make a frank and full disclosure.[3] Of course, upon the principles already stated, if the relation of principal and agent has wholly ceased, the parties are restored to their common competency to deal with each other. It is also to be understood, as a just qualification of the whole doctrine, that the principal may, at his election, deem the bargain made or act done by his agent valid or not, and that the agent cannot himself avoid it on that ground.[4]

317. In the next place, as to the relation of guardian and ward. In this most important and delicate of trusts the same principles prevail, and with a larger and more comprehensive efficiency. It is obvious that during the existence of the guardianship the transactions of the guardian cannot be binding upon the ward if they are of any disadvantage to him; and indeed the relative situation of the parties imposes a general inability to deal with each other.[5] (b) But Courts of Equity

[1] Rengo v. Binns, 10 Peters, R. 269.

[2] Farnam v. Brooks, 6 Pick. R. 212.

[3] Ibid.

[4] Story on Agency, § 210, and cases there cited.

[5] See 3 P. Will. 131, Cox's note 1; 1 Fonbl. Eq. B. 1, ch. 2, § 12, note (k); 1 Madd. Ch. Pr. 102, 103; Dawson v. Massey, 1 Ball & Beatt. R. 226.

(a) Tyrrell v. Bank of London, 10 H. L. Cas. 26; Kimber v. Barber, L. R. 8 Ch. 56; Parker v. Nickerson, 112 Mass. 195; s. c. 137 Mass. 487, 497.

(b) Everitt v. Everitt, L. R. 10 Eq. 405; Sullivan v. Blackwell, 28 Miss. 737. To entitle a ward to set aside a conveyance made by him after majority to his guardian he must repay the sum given him for the property. Wickiser v. Cook, 85 Ill. 68. But a purchaser of ward's land under a void decree of sale obtained by the guardian cannot insist upon the ward's returning to him the purchase-money as a condition to setting aside the sale, when the money never went into the ward's hands, but was fraudulently appropriated by the guardian. Reynolds v. McCurry, 100 Ill. 356.

proceed yet farther in cases of this sort. They will not permit transactions between guardians and wards to stand, even when they have occurred after the minority has ceased and the relation become thereby actually ended, if the intermediate period be short, unless the circumstances demonstrate, in the highest sense of the terms, the fullest deliberation on the part of the ward, and the most abundant good faith (uberrima fides) on the part of the guardian. (a) For in all such cases the relation is still considered as having an undue influence upon the mind of the ward, and as virtually subsisting, especially if all the duties attached to the situation have not ceased; as if the accounts between the parties have not been fully settled, or if the estate still remains in some sort under the control of the guardian.[1] (b)

318. Lord Hardwicke has expounded the general ground of this doctrine in a clear manner. 'Where,' says he, 'a man acts as guardian, or trustee in nature of a guardian, for an infant, the court is extremely watchful to prevent that person's taking any advantage immediately upon his ward's coming of age, and at the time of settling accounts, or delivering up the trust because an undue advantage may be taken. It would give an opportunity, either by flattery or force, by good usage unfairly meant or by bad usage imposed, to take such an advantage. And therefore the principle of the court is of the same nature with relief in this court on the head of public utility; as in bonds obtained from young heirs, and rewards given to an attorney pending a cause, and marriage brokage bonds. All depends upon public utility; and therefore the court will not

---

[1] Dawson v. Massey, 1 Ball & Beatt. R. 229; Wright v. Proud, 13 Ves. 136; Wedderburn v. Wedderburn, 4 Mylne & Craig, 41.

(a) See Ranken v. Patton, 65 Mo. 378. But there is no absolute disability on the part of the guardian to take a gift or conveyance from the ward. Doe v. Hassell, 68 N. Car. 213; Lee v. Howell, 69 N. Car. 200; Meek v. Perry, 36 Miss. 190. If the guardian can show that he dealt with the ward in perfect fairness, taking no advantage of the relation or of his superior knowledge, exercising no influence, and giving the ward all needful information, the transaction will stand, if the ward was able to act intelligently for himself. Meek v. Perry, supra. Disinterested advice appears necessary in all these relations of trust. McClure v. Lewis, 72 Mo. 314.

(b) Hylton v. Hylton, 2 Ves. 548; Maitland v. Backhouse, 16 Sim. 58; Revett v. Harvey, 1 Sim. & S. 502; Waller v. Armistead, 2 Leigh, 11; Eberts v. Eberts, 55 Penn. St. 110. See Kittredge v. Betton, 14 N. H. 401; Tucke v. Buchholz, 43 Iowa, 415.

suffer it, though perhaps in a particular instance there may not
be any actual unfairness.' [1] (a)   His Lordship afterwards added:
' The rule of the court as to guardians is extremely strict, and
in some cases does infer some hardship; as where there has
been a great deal of trouble, and he has acted fairly and honestly, that yet he shall have no allowance.   But the court has
established that, on great utility, and on necessity, and on this
principle of humanity, that it is a debt of humanity that one
man owes to another, as every man is liable to be in the same
circumstances.' [2]

319. Lord Eldon has expressed himself even in a more em-
phatic manner on this subject.   ' There may not be,' says he,
' a more moral act, one that would do more credit to a young
man beginning the world, or afford a better omen for the future
than if a trustee having done his duty, the cestui que trust,
taking it into his fair, serious, and well-informed consideration,
were to do an act of bounty like this.   But the court cannot
permit it, except quite satisfied that the act is of that nature for
the reason often given; and recollecting that in discussing
whether it is an act of rational consideration, an act of pure
volition uninfluenced, — that inquiry is so easily baffled in a court
of justice, — that, instead of the spontaneous act of a friend uninfluenced, it may be the impulse of a mind misled by undue
kindness or forced by oppression, and the difficulty of getting
property out of the hands of the guardian or trustee thus increased.   And therefore if the court does not watch these transactions with a jealousy almost invincible in a great majority of
cases, it will lend its assistance to fraud, where the connection is
not dissolved, the account not settled, everything remaining
pressing upon the mind of the party under the care of the guardian or trustee.' [3]   The same principles are applied to persons standing in the situation of quasi guardians or confidential
advisers.[4] (b)

---

[1] Hylton v. Hylton, 2 Ves. 548, 549; Pierce v. Waring, cited ibid. and in
1 Ves. 380; 1 P. Will. 120, Cox's note; 1 Cox, R. 125; Wright v. Proud, 13
Ves. 136, 138; Wood v. Downes, 18 Ves. 126.

[2] Hylton v. Hylton, 2 Ves. 548, 549.   [3] Hatch v. Hatch, 9 Ves. 297.

[4] Revett v. Harvey, 1 Sim. & Stu. R. 502.

(a) See Sullivan v. Blackwell, 28
Miss. 737; Hawkins's Appeal, 32
Penn. St. 263.

(b) Tucke v. Buchholz, 43 Iowa,
415; Quinton v. Frith, L. R. 2 Ir. Eq.
396; Espey v. Lake, 10 Hare, 260.

320. In the cases to which these principles have been applied in order to set aside grants and other transactions (*a*) between guardian and ward, two circumstances of great importance have generally concurred : first, that the grants and transactions have taken place immediately upon the ward's attaining age ; and secondly, that the former influence of the guardian has been demonstrated to exist to an undue degree ; or, in other words, that the parties have not met upon equal terms.[1] If therefore the relation has entirely ceased, not merely in name but in fact, (*b*) and if sufficient time has elapsed to put the parties in complete independence as to each other, and if a full and fair settlement of all transactions growing out of the relation has been made, there is no objection to any bounty or grant conferred by the ward upon his guardian.[2] Indeed in such cases it is only the performance of a high moral duty recommended as well by law as by natural justice.

321. In the next place, with regard to the relation of trustee and cestui que trust, or rather beneficiary, or fide-commissary, as we could wish the person beneficially interested might be called, to escape from the awkwardness of a barbarous foreign idiom.[3] In this class of cases the same principles govern as in

---

[1] See Dawson *v.* Massey, 1 Ball & Beatt. 229, 232, 236; Aylward *v.* Kearney, 2 Ball & Beatt. R. 463.

[2] Hylton *v.* Hylton, 2 Ves. 547, 549.

[3] The phrase 'cestui que trust' is a barbarous Norman law French phrase; and is so ungainly and ill adapted to the English idiom, that it is surprising that the good sense of the English legal profession has not long since banished it and substituted some phrase in the English idiom furnishing an analogous meaning. In the Roman law the trustee was commonly called 'hæres fiduciarius'; and the cestui que trust, 'hæres fidei commissarius,' which Dr. Halifax has not scrupled to translate ' fide-committee.' (Halifax, Anal. of Civil Law, ch. 6, § 16, p. 34; Id. ch. 8, §§ 2, 3, pp. 45, 46.) I prefer fide-commissary as at least equally within the analogy of the English language. But 'beneficiary,' though a little remote from the original meaning of the word, would be a very appropriate word, as it has not as yet acquired any general use in a different sense. Hæres fidei commissarius was sometimes used in the civil law to denote the trustee. See Vicat, Vocab. voce, Fidei commissarius. The French law calls the cestui que trust, fidei commissaire. See Ferriere

---

(*a*) Testamentary dispositions in favor of a guardian by his ward have been held to fall within the same category. Meek *v.* Perry, 36 Miss. 190; Garvin *v.* Williams, 50 Mo. 206. But compare § 312, note, as to cases of attorney and client.

(*b*) Kittredge *v.* Betton, 14 N. H. 401.

cases of guardian and ward, with at least as much enlarged liberality of application, and upon grounds quite as comprehensive. Indeed the cases are usually treated as if they were identical.[1] A trustee is never permitted to partake of the bounty of the party for whom he acts, except under circumstances which would make the same valid, if it were a case of guardianship. A trustee cannot purchase of his cestui que trust, unless under like circumstances ; or, to use the expressive language of an eminent judge, a trustee may purchase of his cestui que trust, provided there is a distinct and clear contract, ascertained to be such after a jealous and scrupulous examination of all the circumstances, and it is clear that the cestui que trust intended that the trustee should buy, and there is no fraud, no concealment, and no advantage taken by the trustee of information acquired by him as trustee. (a) But it is difficult to make out such a case where the exception is taken, especially when there is any inadequacy of price or any inequality in the bargain.[2] And therefore if a trustee, though strictly honest, should buy for himself an estate of his cestui que trust, and then should sell it for more, according to the rules of a Court of Equity, from general policy, and not from any peculiar imputation of fraud, he would be held still to remain a trustee to all intents and purposes, and not to be permitted to sell to or for himself.[3] (b)

Dict. voce, Fidei commissaire. Merlin, Repertoire, voce, Substitution, et Substitution fidei commissaire. Dr. Brown uses the word, 'fidei commissary,' 1 Brown, Civil Law, 190, note.

[1] Hatch v. Hatch, 9 Ves. 292, 296, 297 ; Newland on Contracts, ch. 32, p. 459, &c.; Jeremy on Eq Jurisd. B. 1, ch. 1, § 3, p. 142, &c.; 1 Fonbl. Eq. B. 1, ch. 2, § 12, note (k); Farnam v. Brooks, 9 Pick. R. 212. See also Bulkley v. Wilford, 2 Clark & Finn. R. 102, 177 to 183; ante, §§ 317, 320.

[2] Ante, § 310; Coles v. Trecothick, 9 Ves. 246; Fox v. Mackreth, 2 Bro. Ch. R. 400; Gibson v. Jeyes, 277 ; Whichcote v. Lawrence, 3 Ves. 740; Campbell v. Walker, 5 Ves. 678; Ayliffe v. Murray, 2 Atk. R. 59 ; Hawley v. Cramer, 4 Cowen, R. 717; Van Epps v. Van Epps, 9 Paige, R. 207; Scott v. Davis, 4 Mylne & Craig, 87.

[3] See Fox v. Mackreth, 2 Brown, Ch. R. 400; s. c. 2 Cox, R. 320, 327;

(a) See Morse v. Hill, 136 Mass. 60; Julian v. Reynolds, 8 Ala. 680; Stallings v. Freeman, 2 Hill, Ch. 401; Pratt v. Thornton, 28 Maine, 355; McCartney v. Calhoun, 17 Ala. 301; Marshall v. Stephens, 8 Humph. 159; Beeson v. Beeson, 9 Barr. 279; McKinley v. Irvine, 13 Ala. 681; Franks v. Bollans, L. R. 3 Ch. 717; Hamilton v. Young, 7 L. R. Ir. 289, 299. Part only of the cestuis que trust may avoid the sale. Morse v. Hill, supra.

(b) But after a fair and honest sale to a third person the trustee may in

322. But we are not to understand, from this last language, that to entitle the cestui que trust to relief it is indispensable to show, that the trustee has made some advantage where there has been a purchase by himself; and that, unless some advantage has been made, the sale to the trustee is good. That would not be putting the doctrine upon its true ground, which is, that the prohibition arises from the subsisting relation of trusteeship.[1] The ingredient of advantage made by him would only go to establish that the transaction might be open to the strong imputation of being tainted by imposition or selfish cunning.[2] But the principle applies, however innocent the purchase may be in a given case.[3] It is poisonous in its consequences. The cestui que trust is not bound to prove, nor is the court bound to decide, that the trustee has made a bargain advantageous to himself. The fact may be so, and yet the party not have it in his power distinctly and clearly to show it. There may be fraud, and yet the party not be able to show it. It is to guard against this uncertainty and hazard of abuse, and to remove the trustee from temptation, that the rule does and will permit the cestui que trust to come, at his own option and without showing essential injury, to insist upon having the experiment of another sale.[4] (a) So that in fact, in all cases where a purchase has been made by a trustee on his own account of the estate of his cestui que trust, although sold at public auction, it is in the option of the cestui que trust to set aside the

Prevost v. Gratz, 1 Peters, Cir. R. 367, 368; s. c. 6 Wheat. R. 481; Hamilton v. Wright, 6 Clark & Finn. 111, 133; Edwards v. Meyrick, 2 Hare, R. 60, 68; Hawley v. Cramer, 4 Cowen, R. 717. Quære, does the doctrine extend to all purchases made by a trustee from the cestui que trust, or is it limited to purchases of the trust estate?

[1] See Newland on Contracts, ch. 32, p. 461; Ex parte Lacey, 6 Ves. 625, 626; 1 Madd. Ch. Pr. 92, 93; Chesterfield v. Janssen, 2 Ves. 138.

[2] See Campbell v. Walker, 5 Ves. 678; 13 Ves. 601.

[3] Ex parte James, 8 Ves. 337, 345; Ex parte Bennett, 10 Ves. 381, 385; Cane v. Lord Allen, 2 Dow, R. 289, 299; ante, § 311.

[4] Davoue v. Fanning, 2 John. Ch. R. 252, where Mr. Chancellor Kent has examined the cases with a most exemplary diligence. Ex parte Bennett, 10 Ves. 381, 385, 386; ante, § 311.

good faith, after the lapse of considerable time at least, buy from him. Baker v. Peck, 9 Week R. 472; Stephen v. Beall, 22 Wall. 329.

(a) See Hamilton v. Young, 7 L. R. Ir. 289, 299; Brookman v. Rothschild, 3 Sim. 153; Gillett v. Peppercorne, 3 Beav. 78; Newcomb v. Brooks, 16 W. Va. 32.

sale, whether bona fide made or not.[1] So a trustee will not be
permitted to obtain any profit or advantage to himself in managing the concerns of the cestui que trust, but whatever benefits or profits are obtained will belong exclusively to the cestui
que trust.[2] In short it may be laid down as a general rule
that a trustee is bound not to do anything which can place
him in a position inconsistent with the interests of the trust, or
which have a tendency to interfere with his duty in discharging it.[3] (a) And this doctrine applies not only to trustees
strictly so called, but to other persons standing in like situation ;
such as assignees and solicitors of a bankrupt or insolvent estate,
who are never permitted to become purchasers at the sale of the
bankrupt or insolvent estate.[4] (b) It applies in like manner to
executors and administrators, (c) who are not permitted to purchase up the debts of the deceased on their own account ; but
whatever advantage is thus derived by them, by purchases at an
undue value, is for the common benefit of the estate.[5] Indeed

---

[1] Campbell v. Walker, 5 Ves. 678, 680; 13 Ves. 601; Ex parte Lacey, 6
Ves. 625; Ex parte Bennett, 10 Ves. 381, 385, 386; Morse v. Royal, 12 Ves.
355; Whitcomb v. Minchin, 5 Madd. R. 91; Belt's Supplement, pp. 11, 12.

[2] Saagar v. Wilson, 4 Serg. & Watts, 102.

[3] Hamilton v. Wright, 9 Clark & Finn. R. 111, 123.

[4] Ex parte Lacey, 6 Ves. 625; Ex parte James, 8 Ves. 337; Ex parte
Bennett, 10 Ves. 381; Davoue v. Fanning, 2 John. Ch. R. 252; Lady Ormond
v. Hutchinson, 13 Ves. 47; Farnam v. Brooks, 9 Pick. 202.

[5] Ex parte Lacey, 6 Ves. 628; Ex parte James, 8 Ves. 346; Green v. Winter,

---

(a) A trustee of a leasehold interest who obtains a renewal of the lease
must hold the same in trust for the
cestui que trust. Gabbett v. Lawder,
11 L. R. Ir. 295, 299; O'Brien v.
Egan, 5 L. R. Ir. 633. And this is true
of a purchase by the trustee of the reversion. Ib., distinguishing Randall
v. Russell, 3 Mer. 190, Hardman v.
Johnson, 3 Mer. 347, and Norris v.
Le Neve, 3 Atk. 26, as not being purchases by parties in a fiduciary situation. See also Giddings v. Giddings,
3 Russ. 241; Buckley v. Lavauze,
Lloyd & G. t. Plunk. 327; Trumper v.
Trumper, L. R. 14 Eq. 295; s. c. L. R.
8 Ch. 870. In O'Brien v. Egan, supra,
this doctrine of graft was extended
and applied to the case of a new lease
obtained some time after the expiration of the first, and after the right of
the party entitled as cestui que trust
had ceased. And the only fiduciary
relation in the case consisted in the
fact that if the lessee died before the
first lease ran out, the plaintiff would
be entitled in remainder. The event
did not happen. See also Gower v.
Andrew, 59 Cal. 119, employer and em-
ployé, and renewal of lease by the latter.

(b) Nor can an assignee buy in
a debt of the bankrupt. Pooley v.
Quilter, 2 DeG. & J. 327.

(c) Gabbett v. Lawder, 11 L. R. Ir.
295, renewal of lease. An attorney of
an executor in going on the executor's
behalf and advising is in the same situation. Reed v. Peterson, 91 Ill. 288, 295.

the doctrine may be more broadly stated, that executors or administrators will not be permitted, under any circumstances, to derive a personal benefit from the manner in which they transact the business or manage the assets of the estate.[1] (a) And if a trustee misapply the funds of his cestui que trust or beneficiary, and purchase a judgment or other security therewith, the latter has an election to take such judgment or security, or to call upon the trustee to make good the original fund.[2] (b)

323. There are many other cases of persons standing in regard to each other in the like confidential relations in which similar principles apply. Among these may be enumerated the cases which arise from the relation of landlord and tenant, (c) of partner and partner, (d) of principal and surety, and various others,

1 John. Ch. R. 27; Forbes v. Ross, 2 Bro. Ch. R. 430; Hawley v. Mancius, 7 John. Ch. R. 174.

[1] Schieffelin v. Stewart, 1 John. Ch. R. 620; Brown v. Brewerton, 4 John. Ch. R. 303; 4 Dow, Parl. R. 131; Evartson v. Tappan, 1 John. Ch. R. 497; Hawley v. Mancius, 7 John. Ch. R. 174; Cook v. Coolingridge, Jac. R. 607, 621; Jeremy on Equity Jurisd. B. 1, ch. 1, § 3, p. 142, &c.; 1 Fonbl. Eq. B. 2, ch. 7, § 6, note (p); Id. § 7, and note (r). Trustees are not voluntarily allowed a compensation in England for their services, unless specially provided for in the creation of the trust; but their duties and services are treated as gratuitous and honorary. A different rule prevails in many if not all of the States of this Union. See post, § 1268.

[2] Steele v. Babcock, 1 Hill (N. Y.), R. 527.

(a) Moses v. Moses, 50 Ga. 9; Goodwin v. Goodwin, 48 Ind. 584; Sheldon v. Rice, 30 Mich. 296; Green v. Sargent, 23 Vt. 466; Ebelmesser v. Ebelmesser, 99 Ill. 541; Kruse v. Steffens, 47 Ill. 112; Ives v. Ashley, 97 Mass. 198; Seackel v. Litchfield, 13 Allen, 417; Harper v. Mansfield, 58 Mo. 17; Lytle v. Beveridge, 58 N. Y. 593; Staples v. Staples, 24 Gratt. 225; Crubb v. Bray, 36 Wis. 336; Humphreys v. Burleson, 72 Ala. 1. See however for some qualification of the rule, Wilson v. Miller, 30 Md. 82; Frazer v. Lee, 42 Ala. 25; and especially Stallings v. Foreman, 2 Hill, Ch. 401, establishing the right of an administrator to buy at his own sale at a fair price. Huger v. Huger, 9 Rich. Eq. 217, 224, 225.

(b) And releases and confirmations of the acts of trustees even after the termination of the trust will be narrowly scrutinized; unless the cestui que trust was fully informed of the facts, such acts will not be binding. Burrows v. Walls, 5 DeG. M. & G. 233. See also Lloyd v. Atwood, 3 DeG. & J. 614. But if with full knowledge the cestui que trust has acquiesced for a long time, e. g. in improper investments of the trust fund, the trustee will not be chargeable with losses arising thereby. Griffiths v. Porter, 25 Beav. 236; Liddell v. Norton, 21 Beav. 183; West v. Sloan, 3 Jones Eq. 102. But this supposes of course that the beneficiary was of capacity to understand, and did understand, what was going on.

(c) See Matthew's Appeal, 104 Penn. St. 444.

(d) See Tyrrell v. Bank of London, 10 H. L. Cas. 26; s. c. 8 Jur. N. S.

where mutual agencies, rights, and duties are created between the parties by their own voluntary acts or by operation of law. (a)

849; 31 L. J. Ch. 369; Brown v. Kennedy, 9 Jur. N. s. 1163; s. c. 33 L. J. Ch. 71, and 33 Beav. 133; Jones v. Dexter, 130 Mass. 380; Freeman v. Freeman, 136 Mass. 260; Dean v. McDowell, 8 Ch. D. 345 (C. A.). But the mere fact that a partner secretly engages in some business in violation of the partnership articles, and derives a profit therefrom, will not entitle his associates to treat the same as belonging to the partnership. Whether they can do so will depend upon the question whether the obnoxious trade is within the scope of the partnership business. Dean v. McDowell, supra. And this rule covers the case not merely of using the partnership funds in the secret trade, it covers the case of making use of information which the partnership is entitled to, and it covers the case of profits got by means of the position in the partnership. Ib.

An administrator of a deceased partner may call upon the surviving partner for an account in equity of the profits received by him since the death of his associate from the sale of patents belonging to the partnership. Freeman v. Freeman, 136 Mass. 260; Yates v. Finn, 13 Ch. D. 839. See Willett v. Blanford, 1 Hare, 253; Watney v. Wells, L. R. 2 Ch. 250.

(a) The relation of mortgagor and mortgagee falls within the category. See Prees v. Coke, L. R. 6 Ch. 645; Villa v. Rodriguez, 12 Wall. 323, 339; Morris v. Nixon, 1 How. 118; 4 Kent, 143. A mortgagee cannot, in exercising a power of sale, purchase the property on his own account (except perhaps under circumstances which would be proper in the case of a purchase by a trustee). Nor can the agent of the mortgagee buy for him or for himself. Martinson v. Clowes, 21 Ch. D. 857. So of the case of pledgor

and pledgee. See Hayward v. National Bank, 96 U. S. 611; Chouteau v. Allen, 70 Mo. 290. A director of a company stands also in a fiduciary situation. He cannot retain a consideration received by him from the promoters as an inducement to become a director. And if the consideration has been a gift of fully paid-up shares, he may be compelled not only to restore the shares but to account to the company for the highest value they have reached since he received them. McKay's Case, 2 Ch. D. 1; Pearson's Case, 5 Ch. D. 336; Bagnall v. Carlton, 6 Ch. D. 371; Nant-y-glo Iron Works Co. v. Grave, 12 Ch. D. 738 (Bacon, V. C. doubting Hall v. Hallett, 1 Cox, 134).

But contracts made by a director in his own interest and contrary to his duty are voidable only, and will stand until repudiated by the company. Thomas v. Brownville R. Co., 109 U. S. 522, 524; Twin Lick Co. v. Marbury, 91 U. S. 587; Union Pacific R. Co. v. Credit Mobilier, 135 Mass. 367. And if the stockholders seek directly to impeach the transaction, as by cross bill, they must still do equity by those with whom the contract was made, making compensation for all honest outlay of which the company will have the benefit. Ib.; Wardell v. Union Pacific R. Co., 4 Dillon, 339; s. c. 103 U. S. 651. As to the jurisdiction of equity over directors misapplying the funds of the company, see Lyman v. Bonney, 118 Mass. 222; s. c. 101 Mass. 562; Brewer v. Boston Theatre, 104 Mass. 378.

And where a contract is entered into between a corporation and a third person, and the control of the contract secured by a director of the company, to the knowledge of all for a purpose not improper, to be carried out by an assignment to others, which purpose

But it would occupy too much space to go over them at large, and most of them are resolvable into the principles already commented on.[1] (a)   On the whole the doctrine may be generally stated that wherever confidence is reposed, and one party has it in his power in a secret manner for his own advantage to sacrifice those interests which he is bound to protect, he will not be permitted to hold any such advantage.[2] (b)

[1] See 1 Hovenden on Frauds, ch. 6, pp. 199, 209; Id. vol. 2, ch. 20, p. 153, ch. 21, p. 171; Maddeford v. Anstwick, 1 Sim. R. 89; 1 Chitty, Dig. Fraud, vii; Oliver v. Court, 8 Price, R. 127; Farnam v. Brooks, 9 Pick. R. 212.

[2] Jeremy on Eq. Jurisd. B. 3, Pt. 2, ch. 3, § 2, p. 395; Griffiths v. Robins, 3 Madd. R. 191.

has been carried out as intended and the contract performed in good faith by the assignees, the circumstance that the contract was at first entered into or controlled by a director will not be ground for avoiding it in the hands of the assignees.   Union Pacific R. Co. v. Credit Mobilier, 135 Mass. 367, 376. Further as to the invalidity of transactions of directors having an interest in contracts of the company with third persons, see Kitchen v. St. Louis Ry. Co., 69; Pearson v. Concord R. Co., 16 Reporter, 463; Gilman R. Co. v. Kelly, 77 Ill. 426, 432–434; Flagg v. Manhattan Ry. Co., 21 Am. Law Reg. N. S. 785, and note; In re Ambrose Tin Co., 14 Ch. D. 390, 394; Cumberland Coal Co. v. Sherman, 8 Law Reg. 333.

An individual who has bargained for the purchase of patents, upon an undertaking to make payment for the same out of the net profits to arise from selling the patented articles, becomes thereby a quasi trustee towards the vendor, and can be called to account in equity for the profits so received.   Pratt v. Tuttle, 136 Mass. 233; Badger v. McNamara, 123 Mass. 117, 119; Foley v. Hill, 2 H. L. Cas. 28, 35; Padwick v. Stanley, 9 Hare, 627, 628; Hemings v. Pugh, 4 Giff. 456, 459; Moxon v. Bright, L. R. 4 Ch. 292, 295; Mackenzie v. Johnston, 4 Madd. 373. But this is not true of

a corporation (or it should seem of any company or person) acting merely as agent for the purchaser, though the purchaser may own most of the stock therein.   Pratt v. Tuttle, supra.

Again though there be nothing in the relation of the parties tending to show influence on the one side and dependence on the other, it may still be shown that confidence existed and was betrayed; and the court will look upon the transaction in the same light as if it had grown out of one of the special relations.   Smith v. Kay, 7 H. L. Cas. 750. On the relation of pastor and parishioner see Ford v. Hennessey, 70 Mo. 580; In re Welsh, 1 Redf. 238; Lyon v. Home, L. R. 6 Eq. 655.

In all cases of relations of confidence the burden of proof is upon the party standing in the superior situation; he must make out the perfect fairness of the transaction.   Smith v. Kay, supra; Rhodes v. Bate, L. R. 1 Ch. 252; Tomson v. Judge, 3 Drew. 306; supra, § 311.

(a) See Bentley v. Craven, 18 Beav. 75; Perens v. Johnson, 3 Smale & G. 419; Richie v. Cowper, 28 Beav. 344; Clegg v. Edmonson, 8 DeG. M. & G. 787; Clements v. Hall, 2 DeG. & J. 173.

(b) See Storrs v. Scougale, 48 Mich. 388; Schultz's Appeal, 80 Penn. St. 396; Leavitt v. La Force, 71 Mo. 353; Gower v Andrew, 59 Cal. 119.

324. The case of principal and surety however, as a striking illustration of this doctrine, may be briefly referred to. The contract of suretyship imports entire good faith and confidence between the parties in regard to the whole transaction. Any concealment of material facts, or any express or implied misrepresentation of such facts, (a) or any undue advantage taken of the surety by the creditor either by surprise or by withholding proper information, will undoubtedly furnish a sufficient ground to invalidate the contract. (b) Upon the same ground the creditor is in all subsequent transactions with the debtor bound to equal good faith to the surety.[1] (c) If any stipulations therefore are made between the creditor and the debtor which are not communicated to the surety and are inconsistent with the terms of his contract, or are prejudicial to his interests therein, they will operate as a virtual discharge of the surety from the obligation of his contract.[2] And on the other hand if any stipulations for additional security or other advantages are obtained between the creditor and the debtor, the surety is entitled to the fullest benefit of them.[3]

325. Indeed the proposition may be stated in a more general

[1] See Cecil v. Plaistow, 1 Anstr. R. 202; Leicester v. Rose, 4 East, R. 372; Pidcock v. Bishop, 3 B. & Cressw. 605; Smith v. Bank of Scotland, 1 Dow, R. 272; Bank of United States v. Etting, 11 Wheat. R. 59.

[2] See King v. Baldwin, 2 John. Ch. R. 554, and the cases there cited; s. c. 17 John R. 384; Nisbet v. Smith, 2 Bro. Ch. R. 583.

[3] Hayes v. Ward, 4 John. Ch. R. 123; Mayhew v. Crickett, 2 Swanst. R. 186, and the authorities cited, p. 191, note (a); Boultbee v. Stubbs, 18 Ves. 23; Ex parte Rushforth, 10 Ves. 409, 421; post, § 499.

(a) It is not clear whether, to discharge the surety, the misrepresentation or the concealment should have been fraudulent or not. Perhaps the better view is that if the creditor was aware of the truth concerning the matter misrepresented to or concealed from the surety, the latter will be discharged whether there was fraud or not; but contra if he was not aware of it, unless there was fraud. 2 Story, Contracts, § 1125 (5th ed.), where the cases are examined. See Davies v. London Ins. Co., 8 Ch. D. 469 (ante, § 215, and note); Pidcock v. Bishop, 3 Barn. & C. 605; Stone v. Compton, 5 Bing. N. C. 142; Railton v. Mathews, 10 Clark & F. 935; Hamilton v. Watson, 12 Clark & F. 119; Phillips v. Foxall, L. R. 7 Q. B. 666; Campbell v. Moulton, 30 Vt. 667; Denison v. Gibson, 24 Mich. 186; Dawson v. Lawes, Kay, 280.

(b) A collusive and fraudulent confession of judgment by the principal debtor will be void as to the surety. Wright v. Hake, 38 Mich. 525.

(c) Boschert v. Brown, 72 Penn. St. 372.

form, that if a creditor does any act injurious to the surety or in-consistent with his rights, or if he omits to do any act (*a*) when required by the surety which his duty enjoins him to do, and the omission proves injurious to the surety, — in all such cases the lat-ter will be discharged, and he may set up such conduct as a de-fence to any suit brought against him, if not at law, at all events in equity.[1] (*b*)

326. It is upon this ground that if a creditor without any communication with the surety and assent on his part should afterwards enter into any new contract with the principal incon-sistent with the former contract, or should stipulate in a binding manner upon a sufficient consideration for further delay and postponement of the day of payment of the debt, that will ope-rate in equity as a discharge of the surety.[2] (*c*)   But there is no

[1] The proposition is thus qualified, because in a variety of cases it is cer-tainly very questionable whether the defence can be asserted at law, though there is no doubt that it can be asserted in all cases in equity.   It has indeed been said by a learned court, that there is nothing in the nature of a defence by a surety to make it peculiarly a subject of equity jurisdiction; and that whatever would exonerate a surety in one court, ought to exonerate him in the other.   The People *v.* Janssen, 7 John. Rep. 332; S. P. 2 John. Ch. R. 554, 557. But this doctrine does not seem to be universally adopted; and certainly it has not been acted upon in England to the extent which its terms seem to import.   See Theobald on Principal and Surety, pp. 117 to 138.

[2] Skip *v.* Huey, 3 Atk. 91; Boultbee *v.* Stubbs, 18 Ves. 20; Ludlow *v.* Simond, 2 Cain. Cas. Err. 1; King *v.* Baldwin, 2 John. Ch. R. 554; 17 John. R. 384; Ex parte Gifford, 6 Ves. 805; Rees *v.* Berrington, 2 Ves. jr. 540; Blake *v.* White, 1 Younge & Coll. 420.   Quære, whether a surety on a bond for the fidelity of a party for an indefinite period can by notice to the obligee terminate his liability.   See Gordon *v.* Gordon, 2 Sim. R. 253; s. c. 4 Russ. R. 581; Bonser *v.* Cox, 6 Beav. R. 379.

(*a*) It is held in Camp *v.* Bost-wick, 20 Ohio St. 337, that the omis-sion of a creditor to sue a surety until the Statute of Limitations has run out will not discharge a co-surety, on the ground that the latter may still have contribution. But Shelton *v.* Farmer, 9 Bush, 314, contra, is better law.

(*b*) See Watts *v.* Shuttleworth, 29 L. J. Ex. 229, 234; Ex parte Agra Bank, L. R. 9 Eq. 725; Henderson *v.* Huey, 45 Ala. 275; Petty *v.* Cooke, L. R. 6 Q. B. 790; Oriental Co. *v.* Overend, L. R. 7 Ch. 142; post, §§ 498 *a*, 498 *b*.   In Dawson *v.* Lawes, Kay, 280, an official bond had been

given for faithful administration, and it was held that the surety was not discharged by the neglect of the proper parties to exercise that supervision over the official conduct of the princi-pal which by statute it was their duty to exercise.

(*c*) *Reservation of Rights.* — The text assumes that the surety's rights against his principal have for a time at least been interfered with. Tucker *v.* Laing, 2 Kay & J. 745. A creditor may however save his rights against the surety by expressly reserving them.   Pannell *v.* Mc-Mechen, 4 Har. & J. 598; Clagett *v.*

positive duty incumbent on the creditor to prosecute measures of active diligence ; and therefore mere delay on his part (at least if some other equity does not interfere), unaccompanied by any valid contract for such delay, will not amount to laches so as to discharge the surety.[1] (a)　On the other hand if the creditor has

---

[1] Wright v. Simpson, 6 Ves. 734; Heath v. Hay, 1 Y. & Jerv. 434; United

Salmon, 6 Gill & J. 314 ; Sohier v. Loring, 6 Cush. 537; Morse v. Huntington, 40 Vt. 488; Hagey v. Hill, 75 Penn. St. 108 ; Overend v. Oriental Corp. L. R. 7 II. L. 348; Nichols v. Norris, 3 Barn. & Ad. 41; Kearsley v. Cole, 16 Mees. & W. 127; Boaler v. Mayor, 19 C. B. N. s. 76; Webb v. Hewitt, 3 Kay & J. 438; Green v. Wynn, L. R. 7 Eq. 28; s. c. 4 Ch. 204.　Nor need the creditor communicate the arrangement to the surety. Webb v. Hewitt. But when the agreement to extend the time is in writing, the reservation must be embraced in it or in some writing which can be connected with it under the rule concerning parol evidence.　Hagey v. Hill, supra.

It may result from such an arrangement that the principal debtor may get little benefit out of it; for by the agreement the creditor may call upon the surety for payment at the maturity of the debt, and the surety, not having assented, may thereupon sue the principal debtor.　But that is the latter's own affair; he has made the arrangement and must abide by it.　Sohier v. Loring; Hagey v. Hill; Webb v. Hewitt ; Clagett v. Salmon.　Hence the surety, not being injured, is bound by the reservation.

If however the creditor has given the principal debtor a full technical release, and not merely agreed not to sue him, or not to sue him before a stated time (that will be a question of construction), there can be no reservation of rights, as such a release is a conveyance of the creditor's property, and he has nothing left to sue upon.　See Sohier v. Loring, supra; Nicholson v.

Revill, 4 Ad. & E. 675; Kearsley v. Cole, 16 Mees. & W. 128 ; Webb v. Hewitt, supra.　And though he may have agreed only not to sue, still if he has agreed to indemnify the principal debtor from liability, the same result will of course transpire; for if on payment by the surety the surety should sue his principal, the creditor would be bound under the agreement to assume the defence.

But the agreement, though there be no reservation, must be valid to discharge the surety.　McLemore v. Powell, 12 Wheat. 554.　Even then the surety will not be discharged if the agreement was made with a stranger.　Frazer v. Jordan, 8 El. & B. 303.　Or with a principal debtor in bankruptcy.　Tiernan v. Woodruff, 5 McLean, 350.

There can of course be no reservation such as will hold the surety if the creditor has, without his consent, surrendered any security to the principal debtor to the right to which the surety on payment would be subrogated. Hagey v. Hill, 75 Penn. St. 108; Mayhew v. Boyd, 5 Md. 102.　But perhaps if the security was for a less sum than the debt, the creditor could reserve for the difference.

Many of the cases above cited are cases of bills or notes, but the rule as to arrangements with the acceptor or maker is, in regard to its effect upon indorsers, the same as in ordinary cases of principal and surety.　Sohier v. Loring, 6 Cush. 537.

(a) Unless the Statute of Limitations has run out against a co-surety of a surety who is now sued.　See supra, § 325, note (a).

any security from the debtor and he parts with it without communication with the surety, or by his gross negligence it is lost, (*a*) that will operate at least to the value of the security to discharge the surety.[1] (*b*)

327. Sureties also are entitled to come into a Court of Equity, after a debt has become due, to compel the debtor to exonerate them from their liability by paying the debt.[2] And although (as we have seen) the creditor is not bound by his general duty to active diligence in collecting the debt, yet it has been said that a surety, when the debt has become due, may come into equity and compel the creditor to sue for and collect the debt from the principal, at least if he will indemnify the creditor against the risk, delay, and expense of the suit.[3] (*c*)   But whether the surety can thus compel the creditor to sue the principal or not, he has a clear right, upon paying the debt to the principal, to be substituted in the place of the creditor as to all securities held by the latter for the debt, and to have the same benefit that he would have therein.[4] This however is not the place to consider at large the general rights and duties of persons standing in the relation of creditors, debtors, and sureties, and we shall have occasion again to advert to the subject when considering the marshalling of securities in favor of sureties.[5] (*d*)

States *v.* Kirkpatrick, 9 Wheat. R. 720; McLemore *v.* Powell, 12 Wheat. R. 554; Joslyn *v.* Smith, 3 Weston (Verm.), R. 353.

[1] Mayhew *v.* Crickett, 2 Swanst. R. 185, 191, and note (*a*); Law *v.* East India Company, 4 Ves. 833; Capel *v.* Butler, 2 Sim. & Stu. R. 457.

[2] Nisbet *v.* Smith, 2 Bro. Ch. R. 579; Lee *v.* Brook, Moseley, R. 318; Cox *v.* Tyson, 1 Turn. & Russ. R. 395.

[3] Hayes *v.* Ward, 4 John. Ch. R. 123, 131, 132; King *v.* Baldwin, 2 John. Ch. R. 554; s. c. 17 John. Rep. 384; Wright *v.* Simpson, 6 Ves. 734; Bishop *v.* Day, 13 Vt. 81.

[4] See Langthorne *v.* Swinburne, 14 Ves. 162; Wright *v.* Morley, 11 Ves. 12, 22; Hayes *v.* Ward, 4 John. Ch. R. 123.

[5] Post, §§ 499, 502, 637.

(*a*) But see Lang *v.* Brevard, 3 Strob. Eq. 59, where it was held that the neglect of the creditor to record a mortgage given by the principal debtor did not discharge the surety. See also Pickens *v.* Finney, 12 Smedes & M. 468.

(*b*) See also Schroeppell *v.* Shaw, 3 Comst. 460. Even where the security is parted with under misapprehension,

the result appears to be the same. Ex parte Wilson, 11 Ves. 410 (as to which see Scholefield *v.* Templer, Johns. 155). See also Maquoketa *v.* Willey, 35 Iowa, 232; Pleasanton's Appeal, 75 Penn. St. 344; Harriman *v.* Egbert, 36 Iowa, 270; Hayes *v.* Little, 52 Ga. 555.

(*c*) See Gilliam *v.* Esselman, 5 Sneed, 86.

(*d*) Contracts of suretyship limited

328. Let us now pass to the consideration of the third class of constructive frauds, combining in some degree the ingredients of the others, but prohibited mainly because they unconscientiously compromit or injuriously affect the private rights, interests, or duties of the parties themselves, or operate substantially as frauds upon the private rights, interests, duties, or intentions of third persons.

329. With regard to this last class much that has been already stated under the preceding head of positive or actual fraud as to unconscionable advantages, overreaching, imposition, undue influence, and fiduciary situations, may well be applied here, although certainly with diminished force, as the remarks there made did not turn exclusively upon constructive fraud.

330. To this same class may also be referred many of the cases arising under the Statute of Frauds,[1] which requires certain contracts to be in writing in order to give them validity. In the construction of that statute a general principle has been adopted that, as it is designed as a protection against fraud, it shall never be allowed to be set up as a protection and support of fraud. Hence in a variety of cases where from fraud, imposition, or mistake a contract of this sort has not been reduced to writing, but has been suffered to rest in confidence or in parol communications between the parties, Courts of Equity will en-

[1] Stat. 29 Charles 2d, ch. 3, §§ 1, 4.

by time are usually construed strictly in favor of the surety, on a question of liability where there has been a renewal or prolongation of the contract. Thus two bankers carried on business under articles of partnership, which provided that if at the end of five years (the term fixed also for the suretyship), either should wish to carry on the business and should not take the share of the other at a valuation, the assets should be realized, the debts paid, and the surplus divided. One of the partners had procured a surety to indemnify the other against all loss in respect of the partnership, and the business of the bank was continued for upwards of a year after the expiration of the term above mentioned. It was held that the surety's liability expired with the five years, at least in equity. Small v. Currie, 5 DeG. M. & G. 141. See also Watson v. Allcock, 4 DeG. M. & G. 242; Bonar v. McDonald, 3 H. L. Cas. 226; Railton v. Mathews, 10 Clark & F. 934; Chelmsford Co. v. Demarest, 7 Gray, 1; Middlesex Manuf. Co. v. Lawrence, 1 Allen, 339; Dedham Bank v. Chickering, 3 Pick. 341; Amherst Bank v. Root, 2 Met. 522; Lexington R. Co. v. Elwell, 8 Allen, 371. Subject to the rule of strict construction in favor of the surety, the whole question is of course one of interpretation. See 2 Story, Contracts, § 1123 (5th ed.), where many cases are stated.

force it against the party guilty of a breach of confidence who attempts to shelter himself behind the provisions of the statute.[1] Some instances of this sort have been already mentioned, and others again will occur in the subsequent pages.[2]

331. And here we may apply the remark that the proper jurisdiction of Courts of Equity is to take every one's act according to conscience, and not to suffer undue advantage to be taken of the strict forms of law or of positive rules.[3] Hence it is that even if there be no proof of fraud or imposition, yet, if upon the whole circumstances the contract appears to be grossly against conscience or grossly unreasonable and oppressive, Courts of Equity will sometimes interfere and grant relief,[4] although they certainly are very cautious of interfering, unless upon very strong circumstances.[5] But the mere fact that the bargain is a very hard or unreasonable one is not generally sufficient per se to induce these courts to interfere.[6] And indeed it will be found that there are very few cases not infected with positive or actual fraud in which they do interfere, except where the parties stand in some very peculiar predicament, and in some sort under the protection of the law from age, or character, or relationship.[7]

[1] See 3 Wooddes. Lect. 57, pp. 431, 432; Montecute v. Maxwell, 1 P. Will. 619, 620; 1 Eq. Abridg. 19; Attorney-Gen. v. Sitwell, 1 Younge & Coll. 583; ante, §§ 157, 161, and note.

[2] Ante, § 158; post, §§ 374, 752 to 766.

[3] Chesterfield v. Janssen, 2 Ves. 137, arguendo.

[4] Nott v. Hill, 1 Vern. R. 167, 211; s. c. 2 Vern. 26; Bearry v. Pitt, 2 Vern. 14; Chesterfield v. Janssen, 2 Ves. 145, 148, 154, 155, 158; Twistleton v. Griffith, 1 P. Will. 310; Cole v. Gibbons, 3 P. Will. 290; Bowes v. Heaps, 3 Ves. & B. 117; Gwynne v. Heaton, 1 Bro. Ch. R. 1; Collins v. Hare, 2 Bligh, R. 106, N. S.

[5] In some cases of grossly unreasonable contracts relief may be had, even at law; as in the case of a contract to pay for a horse a barleycorn a nail, doubling it every nail, and there were thirty-two nails in the shoes of the horse. James v. Morgan, 1 Lev. 111, cited 2 Ves. 155; 1 Atk. 351, 352; Whalley v. Whalley, 3 Bligh, R. 1.

[6] Willis v. Jernegan, 2 Atk. 251, 252. See 1 Fonbl. Eq. B. 1, ch. 2, § 10, and note (h); Proof v. Hines, Cas. T. Talb. 111; Ramsbottom v. Parker, 6 Madd. R. 5; 2 Swanst. R. 147, note (a), and especially under page 150, the Reporter's citation from Lord Nottingham's MSS. of the case of Berney v. Pitt, and the remarks of Lord Hardwicke on this case, in 1 Atk. R. 352, and 2 Ves. 157; Freeman v. Bishop, 2 Atk. 39.

[7] See Huguenin v. Baseley, 14 Ves. 271. And see Mr. Swanston's valuable note to Davis v. Duke of Marlborough, 2 Swanst. 147, note (a); Jeremy on Equity Jurisd. B. 3, Pt. 2, ch. 3, § 4, p. 399; Thornhill v. Evans, 2 Atk. R. 330.

332. One of the most striking cases in which the courts interfere is in favor of a very gallant but strangely improvident class
of men, who seem to have mixed up in their character qualities
of very opposite natures, and who seem from their habits to
require guardianship during the whole course of their lives; having at the same time great generosity, credulity, extravagance,
heedlessness, and bravery. Of course it will be at once understood that we here speak of common sailors in the mercantile
and naval service. Courts of Equity are always disposed to take
an indulgent consideration of their interests, and to treat them in
the same light with which young heirs and expectants are regarded. Hence it is that contracts of seamen respecting their
wages and prize-money are watched with great jealousy, and are
generally relievable whenever any inequality appears in the bargain or any undue advantage has been taken. It has been remarked by a learned judge that this title to relief arises from a
general head of equity, partly on account of the persons with
whom the transaction is had, and partly on account of the value
of the thing purchased.[1] And he added that he was warranted
in saying that they were to be viewed in as favorable a light as
young heirs are, by what has been often said in cases of this kind,
and what has been done by the Legislature itself, which has considered them as a class of men loose and unthinking, who will
almost for nothing part with what they have acquired, perhaps
with their blood.[2]

333. But the great class of cases in which relief is granted
under this third head of constructive fraud is that where the
contract or other act is substantially a fraud upon the rights,
interests, duties, or intentions of third persons. And here the
general rule is, that particular persons in contracts and other
acts shall not only transact bona fide between themselves, but

[1] Sir Thomas Clarke, in Howe v. Wheldon, 2 Ves. 516, 518; 1 Fonbl. Eq.
B. 1, ch. 2, § 12, note (k); Jeremy on Eq. Jurisd. B. 3, Pt. 2, ch. 3, § 1,
p. 401; 3 P. Will. 131, Cox's note 1; Taylor v. Rochfort, 2 Ves. 281; Baldwin
v. Rochfort, 1 Wils. R. 229. Yet it is obvious that Lord Hardwicke in Chesterfield v. Janssen, 2 Ves. 137, did not contemplate them as entitled to such
peculiar protection; for he puts their case as not relievable. 'The contracts
of sailors, selling their shares before they knew what they were, could not be
set aside here.' But see the cases in 1 Wilson, R. 229; 2 Ves. 218.

[2] Howe v. Wheldon, 2 Ves. 516. See also the admirable opinion of Lord
Stowell, in the Juliana, 2 Hagg. Adm. Rep. 504. But see Griffith v. Spratley,
1 Cox, R. 383.

shall not transact mala fide in respect to other persons who stand in such a relation to either as to be affected by the contract or the consequences of it.[1] And as the rest of mankind besides the parties contracting are concerned, the rule is properly said to be governed by public utility.[2]

334. It is upon this ground that relief has been constantly granted in what are called catching bargains with heirs, reversioners, and expectants, during the life of their parents or other ancestors.[3] Many and indeed most of these cases (as has been pointedly remarked by Lord Hardwicke) ' have been mixed cases, compounded of almost every species of fraud, there being sometimes proof of actual fraud, which is always decisive. There is always fraud presumed or inferred from the circumstances or conditions of the parties contracting, from weakness on one side and usury on the other, or extortion or advantage taken of that weakness. There has always been an appearance of fraud from the nature of the bargain, even if there be no proof of any circumvention, but merely from the intrinsic unconscionableness of the bargain. In most of these cases have concurred deceit and illusion on other persons not privy to the fraudulent agreement. The father, ancestor, or relation from whom was the expectation of the estate has been kept in the dark. The heir or expectant has been kept from disclosing his circumstances and resorting to them for advice which might have tended to his relief and also reformation. This misleads the ancestor who has been seduced to leave his estate not to his heir or family, but to a set of artful persons who have divided the spoil beforehand.'[4]

335. Strong as this language may appear, it is fully borne out by the general complexion of the cases in which relief has been afforded. Actual fraud indeed has not unfrequently been repelled.[5] But there has always been constructive fraud, the nature and circumstances of the transaction being an imposition

---

[1] Per Lord Hardwicke, in Chesterfield v. Janssen, 2 Ves. 156, 157.

[2] Chesterfield v. Janssen, 2 Ves. 156, 157; 1 Madd. Ch. Pr. 97, 98, 99, 214; 1 Eq. Abridg. 90, &c.

[3] 1 Fonbl. Eq. B. 1, ch. 2, § 12, and note (k); Jeremy on Eq. Jurisd. B. 3, Pt. 2, ch. 3, § 4, p. 397, &c.; Davis v. Duke of Marlborough, 2 Swanst. R. 147, 151, 152, 165, 174.

[4] Lord Hardwicke, in Chesterfield v. Janssen, 2 Ves. 157; Earl of Aldborough v. Frye, 7 Clark & Finn. 436.

[5] Bowes v. Heaps, 3 Ves. & Beam. 117, 119; Peacock v. Evans, 16 Ves. 512.

and deceit upon third persons who were not parties to it. The relief is founded in part upon the policy of maintaining parental and quasi parental authority and preventing the waste of family estates. It is also founded in part upon an enlarged equity flowing from the principles of natural justice; upon the equity of protecting heedless and necessitous persons against the designs of that calculating rapacity which the law constantly discountenances; of succoring the distress frequently incident to the owners of unprofitable reversions; and of guarding against the improvidence with which men are commonly disposed to sacrifice the future to the present, especially when young, rash, and dissolute.[1] (a)

336. Indeed in cases of this sort Courts of Equity have extended a degree of protection to the parties approaching to an incapacity to bind themselves absolutely by any contract, and, as it were, reducing them to the situation of infants in order to guard them against the effects of their own conduct.[2] Hence it is that in all cases of this sort it is incumbent upon the party dealing with the heir, or expectant, or reversioner, to establish not merely that there is no fraud, but (as the phrase is) to make good the bargain; that is, to show that a fair and adequate consideration has been paid.[3] For in cases of this sort (contrary to the general rule) mere inadequacy of price or compensation

---

[1] See Davis v. Duke of Marlborough, 2 Swanston, 147, 148, the Reporter's note; Twistleton v. Griffith, 1 P. Will. 310; Cole v. Gibbons, 1 P. Will. 293; Baugh v. Price, 1 Wils. R. 320; 2 Ves. 144, 155; Barnardiston v. Lingood, 2 Atk. 135, 136; Bowes v. Heaps, 3 Ves. & Beam. 117, 119, 120; Walmesley v. Booth, 2 Atk. 27, 28; 1 Madd. Ch. Pr. 97, 98, 99.

[2] Gwynne v. Heaton, 1 Bro. Ch. R. 1, 9; Peacock v. Evans, 16 Ves. 512, 514.

[3] Earl of Aldborough v. Frye, 7 Clark & Finn. 436, 456. In this case Lord Cottenham said: 'It appears to be established by several cases, that where a party deals with an expectant heir, the onus is upon him to show that he gave a fair price.'

(a) See Butler v. Duncan, 47 Mich. 94; Godfray v. Godfray, 12 Jur. N. S. 397, in the Privy Council. The relief is grantable not only in the case of an heir; it may equally be given in the case of a younger son in England who has no expectancy except as founded upon his father's position; as where money has been loaned to a younger son without thought of repayment by him, but on the credit of such general expectancy and in the hope of extorting money from the father to prevent having his son made a bankrupt. Nevill v. Snelling, 15 Ch. D. 679.

is sufficient to set aside the contract.[1] (a)   The relief is granted upon the general principle of mischief to the public, without requiring any particular evidence of imposition, unless the contract is shown to be above all exception.[2]   But it is not necessary in cases of this sort to establish in evidence that the full value of the reversionary interest or other expectancy has been given according to the ordinary tables for calculations of this sort.   It will be sufficient to make the purchase unimpeachable, if a fair price or the fair market price be given therefor at the time of the dealing.[3]

337. The doctrine applies, as we have seen, not merely to heirs dealing with their expectancies, but to reversioners and remainder-men dealing with property already vested in them but of which the enjoyment is future, and is therefore apt to be underestimated by the giddy, the necessitous, the improvident, and the young.[4]   According however to the decisions, age does not seem to make much difference as to the protection afforded to expectant heirs; since the aim of the rule is chiefly directed to prevent deceit and imposition upon parents and other ancestors.[5]   And in regard to reversioners and remainder-men, if they are

---

[1] Peacock v. Evans, 16 Ves. 512, 514; Gowland v. De Faria, 17 Ves. 20; Bernal v. Donegal, 1 Bligh (N. s.), 594; Hincksman v. Smith, 3 Russ. R. 433; Earl of Aldborough v. Frye, 7 Clark & Finn. 436.

[2] Walmesley v. Booth, 2 Atk. 28; 1 Madd. Ch. Pr. 97, 98; Sir John Strange, in Chesterfield v. Janssen, 2 Ves. 149; Gwynne v. Heaton, 1 Bro. Ch. R. 1, 9; Hincksman v. Smith, 3 Russ. R. 433; Ryle v. Brown and Swindell, 1 M'Clel. R. 519; s. c. 13 Price, R. 758; Earl of Aldborough v. Frye, 7 Clark & Finn. 436, 456.

[3] Headen v. Rosher, M'Clel. & Younge, R. 89; Potts v. Curtis, 1 Younge, R. 543; Earl of Aldborough v. Frye, 7 Clark & Finn. 436. 458 to 461.

[4] Gowland v. De Faria, 17 Ves. 20; Peacock v. Evans, 16 Ves. 512; Mr. Swanston's note, 2 Swanston, 147, 148; 1 Fonbl. Eq. B. 1, ch. 2, § 12, note (k).   But see Nichols v. Gould, 2 Ves. 422.

[5] Davis v. Duke of Marlborough, 2 Swanst. R. 151; 1 Fonbl. Eq. B. 1, ch. 2, § 12, note (k); Ormond v. Fitzroy, 3 P. Will. 131; Wiseman v. Beake, 2 Vern. R. 121.

(a) Bacon v. Bonham, 33 N. J. Eq. 614; Edwards v. Browne, 2 Colly. 100; Boothby v. Boothby, 15 Beav. 212; St. Albyn v. Harding, 27 Beav. 11.   Slight inadequacy is enough to justify interference. Foster v. Roberts, 7 Jur. N. s. 400; s. c. 29 Beav. 467; Jones v. Ricketts, 8 Jur. N. s. 1198; s. c. 31 Beav. 130; Perfect v. Lane, 30 Beav. 197; Nesbitt v. Berridge, 9 Jur. N. s. 1044; s. c. 32 Beav. 282; Clark v. Malpas, 31 Beav. 80; Baker v. Monk, 10 Jur. N. s. 624; s. c. 33 Beav. 419; Douglas v. Culverwell, 3 Giff. 251, affd. 6 Law T. N. s. 272.

at the time necessitous, and laboring under pecuniary distress and embarrassment, an equally indulgent protection will also be afforded to them.[1] (a)

338. The ground of the interposition of Courts of Equity in cases of reversioners and remainder-men has been commented on by a late learned judge with great clearness. 'At law and in equity also,' says he, 'generally speaking, a man who has a power of disposition over his property, whether he sells to relieve

---

[1] Ibid.; Wood v. Abrey, 3 Madd. R. 418, 422; Chesterfield v. Janssen, 2 Ves. 157, 158; 1 Atk. 353; Gwynne v. Heaton, 1 Bro. Ch. R. 1, 9.

(a) It is declared to be the imperative duty of the purchaser of a reversion from an expectant heir to preserve evidence of the bona fides of the transaction, and that the sale was for a full consideration, on pain of having the same set aside. Salter v. Bradshaw, 5 Jur. N. S. 831; s. c. 26 Beav. 161. See also Lowry v. Spear, 7 Bush, 451; Bowes v. Heaps, 3 Ves. & B. 117; Edwards v. Burt, 2 DeG. M. & G. 55; Hannah v. Hodson, 5 Law T. N. S. 42. And this rule has been applied to a charge as well as to sales, in one case where the heir was of full age and perfectly understood the nature and extent of the transaction. Bromley v. Smith, 5 Jur. N. S. 833; s. c. 28 Beav. 644. The rule applies also to the case of a lease. Grosvenor v. Sherratt, 28 Beav. 659. And to a mortgage. Tottenham v. Emmet, 14 Week. R. 3. But a person entitled to a present income out of which an annuity is payable is not within the rule. Webster v. Cook, L. R. 2 Ch. 542. And equity has refused to set aside the sale of a legacy of fixed amount payable at a fixed time, though made several years before it was due, and though the legatee was a dissipated, improvident, and weak-minded young man, and the price inadequate. Parmelee v. Cameron, 41 N. Y. 392.

The sale of reversionary and the like interests for the purposes of real family settlements appears to be regarded with little or no suspicion.

Talbot v. Staniforth, 1 Johns. & H. 484; s. c. 7 Jur. N. S. 961, and 8 Jur. N. S. 757; Jenner v. Jenner, 2 DeG. F. & J. 359. See Firmin v. Pulham, 2 DeG. & S. 99; Willoughby v. Brideoke, 13 Week. R. 515; Shafts v. Adams, 4 Giff. 492; s. c. 10 Jur. N. S. 121. But to establish the validity of a transaction, not otherwise valid, on the ground that it is a family arrangement, the facts should be fully disclosed whether asked for or not. Greenwood v. Greenwood, 2 DeG. J. & S. 28.

If a creditor obtain security for a debt by a conveyance from the debtor's son, it is held to be incumbent upon him to show that the son understood the transaction, and that he did not execute the instrument by reason of any undue influence from the father. Berdoe v. Dawson, 11 Jur. N. S. 254; s. c. 34 Beav. 603. And in Chambers v. Crabbe, 11 Jur. N. S. 277; s. c. 34 Beav. 457, an assignment by a daughter for the benefit of her mother, the daughter at the time contemplating marriage, and the conveyance being made without the knowledge of the intended husband, was set aside both on the ground of undue influence and of fraud upon the husband's marital rights. But the sale will not be set aside if not unfair. Potts v. Surr, 34 Beav. 543. See also Rhodes v. Bate, 11 Jur. N. S. 803; s. c. L. R. 1 Ch. 252; Williams v. Williams, 2 Drew. & S. 378.

his necessities or to provide for the convenience of his family, cannot avoid his contract upon the mere ground of inadequacy of price.   A Court of Equity however will relieve expectant heirs and reversioners from disadvantageous bargains.   In the earlier cases it was held necessary to show that undue advantage was actually taken of the situation of such persons.   But in more modern times it has been considered not only that those who were dealing for their expectations, but those who were dealing for vested remainders also, were so exposed to imposition and hard terms, and so much in the power of those with whom they contracted, that it was a fit rule of policy to impose upon all who deal with expectant heirs and reversioners the onus of proving that they had paid a fair price, and otherwise to undo their bargains and compel a reconveyance of the property purchased.[1] (a) The principle and the policy of the rule may both be equally questionable.   Sellers of reversions are not necessarily in the power of those with whom they contract, and are not necessarily exposed to imposition and hard terms.   And persons who sell their expectations and reversions from the pressure of distress are thrown by the rule into the hands of those who are likely to take advantage of their situation, for no person can securely deal with them.   The principle of the rule cannot however be applied to sales of reversions by auction.[2]   There being no treaty between

[1] S. P. Bowtree v. Watson, 3 Mylne & Keen, 340; Newton v. Hunt, 5 Sim. R. 511.

[2] Sir John Leach, in Shelley v. Nash, 3 Madd. 232.   And see Peacock v. Evans, 16 Ves. 514, 515; 1 Madd. Ch. Pr. 98, 99.   Mr. Swanston is of opinion that though the principle of the relief afforded to reversioners by its generality seems to extend to every description of persons, dealing for or with a reversionary interest, yet it may be doubted whether, in order to constitute a title to relief, the reversioner must not also combine the character of heir.   He has collected and compared the cases.   Mr. Fonblanque manifestly does not contemplate any such limitation of the doctrine.   He says: ' The real object which the rule proposes, being to restrain the anticipation of expectancies, which must, from its very nature, furnish to designing men an opportunity to practise upon the inexperience or passion of a dissipated man, its operation is not confined to heirs, but extends to all persons the pressure of whose wants may be considered as obstructing the exercise of that judgment which might otherwise regulate their dealings.'   1 Fonbl. Eq. B. 1, ch. 4, § 12, note (k).   In Wood v. Abrey, 3 Madd. Rep. 423, the Vice-Chancellor said: ' The policy of this rule as to reversions may be well doubted; and if the cases were looked into it might be found that the rule

(a) Edwards v. Burt, 2 DeG. M. & G. 55.

the vendor and the purchaser, there can be no opportunity for fraud or imposition on the part of the purchaser. The vendor is in no sense in the power of the purchaser. The sale at auction is evidence of the market price.' This language however, correct as it may be in its application to the case before the court, where the purchaser had no knowledge of the vendor or his circumstances, or even knew his name, until after the purchase at public auction he applied for an abstract of the title, must not be interpreted to extend to all cases of sales at public auction; and especially where there had been a previous treaty in negotiation between the vendor and the purchaser, or a private sale, and the embarrassment and distress of the vendor is fully known, and the public auction is resorted to by the parties, either by design or by management, to cover up the transaction or to disguise its true character from the public. To make the sale and the purchase of the reversion valid under any circumstances, it should clearly appear that the auction is free, fair, and with the ordinary precautions.[1] The reason is plain. Where the sale at public auction is free, fair, and with the ordinary precautions, the fair market price is presumed to be obtained. But if the sale at public auction be obtained under circumstances which establish clearly that the fair market value has not been obtained, and that reasonable precautions and advertisements have not been used for this purpose, and that the parties have connived in such a manner as to make the sale appear to be a public and a free sale when it is in fact a mere cover of a private arrangement, then no such inference can arise in favor of the bona fides of the auction.[2]

339. The whole doctrine of Courts of Equity with respect to expectant heirs and reversioners, and others in a like' predicament, assumes that the one party is defenceless and is exposed to the demands of the other under the pressure of necessity. It assumes also that there is a direct or implied fraud upon the parent or other ancestor who from ignorance of the transaction is misled into a false confidence in the disposition of his property.

was *originally* referred only to expectant heirs and not to reversioners.' See also Jeremy on Eq. Jurisd. B. 3, Pt. 2, ch. 3, § 4, pp. 398, 399; Hincksman *v.* Smith, 3 Russell, R. 433. See also Newton *v.* Hunt, 5 Sim. R. 511.

[1] Ibid.; post, § 347; Earl of Aldborough *v.* Frye, 7 Clark & Finn. 436, 456, 460, 461, 466.

[2] Ibid.

Hence it should seem that one material qualification of the doctrine is the existence of such ignorance. If therefore the transaction has been fully made known at the time to the parent or other person standing in loco parentis, (a) as for example to the person from whom the spes successionis is entertained, or after the expiration of whose present estate the reversionary interest is to become vested in possession, and it is not objected to by him, the extraordinary protection generally afforded in cases of this sort by Courts of Equity will be withdrawn. A fortiori, it will be withdrawn if the transaction is expressly sanctioned or adopted by such parent, or other person standing in loco parentis.[1]

---

[1] King *v.* Hamlet, 4 Sim. R. 182; s. c. 2 Mylne & Keen, 473, 474. The judgment of Lord Brougham in this case, on this point, is very able, and deserves a thorough examination. His lordship on this occasion said: ' Two propositions I take to be incontestable as applicable to the doctrines of this court upon the subject of an expectant heir dealing with his expectancy and as governing more especially the present question. First, that the extraordinary protection given in the general case must be withdrawn if it shall appear that the transaction was known to the father or other person standing in loco parentis, — the person, for example, from whom the spes successionis was entertained, or after whom the reversionary interest was to become vested in possession, — even although such parent or other person took no active part in the negotiation; provided the transaction was not opposed by him, and so carried through in spite of him. Secondly, that if the heir flies off from the transaction and becomes opposed to him with whom he has been dealing and repudiates the whole bargain, he must not in any respect act upon it so as to alter the situation of the other party or his property; at least that if he does so, the proof lies upon him of showing that he did so under the continuing pressure of the same distress which gave rise to the original dealing. Still more fatal to his claim of relief will it be if the father, or person in loco parentis, shall be found to have concurred in this adoption of the repudiated contract. Either of these propositions would be decisive of the present question, if they are well founded in law and if the facts allow of their application to it. I shall examine each of them in both respects. The whole doctrine with respect to an expectant heir assumes that the one party is defenceless, and exposed, unprotected, to the demands of the other, under the pressure of necessity. It would be monstrous to treat the contracts of a person of mature age as the acts of an infant, when his parent was aware of his proceedings and did nothing to prevent them. The parent might thus lie by and suffer his son to obtain the assistance which he ought himself to have rendered; and then only stand forward to aid him in rescinding engagements which he had allowed him to make and to profit by. If all the cases be examined from the time of Lord Nottingham downwards, no trace will be found in any one of them of the father's or other ancestor's privity. On the contrary wherever the subject is touched upon his ignorance is always assumed as part of the case; and its

---

(a) See Jenkins *v.* Stetson, 9 Allen, 128; McBee *v.* Myers, 4 Bush, 356.

And it has been strongly said, that it would be monstrous to treat the contracts of a person of mature age as the acts of an infant, when his parent was aware of his proceedings and did nothing to prevent them. The parent might thus lie by and suffer his son to obtain the assistance which he ought himself to have rendered, and then only stand forward to aid him in rescinding engagements which he had allowed him to make and to profit by.[1]

340. The other qualification of the doctrine is not less important. The contract must be made under the pressure of some necessity; for the main ground of the doctrine is the pressure upon the heir, or the distress of the party dealing with his expectancies, who is therefore under strong temptations to make undue sacrifices of his future interests.[2] Both of these qualifications need not indeed in all cases and under all circumstances concur to justify relief. It may be sufficient that either of them forms so essential an ingredient in the case as to give rise to a just presumption of constructive fraud.[3]

---

being so seldom mentioned either way shows clearly that the privity of the father or ancestor never was contemplated. It is however several times adverted to in a manner demonstrative of the principle. In Cole v. Gibbons (3 P. Wms. 290) the ground of this whole equity is said to be the policy of the law to prevent the heir being seduced from a dependence upon the ancestor who probably would have relieved him. In the same spirit Lord Cowper, in Twistleton v. Griffith (1 P. Wms. 310), had before stated, as one effect of the law, its tendency, by cutting off relief at the hands of strangers, to make the heir disclose his difficulties at home. So in The Earl of Chesterfield v. Janssen (1 Atk. 339), Mr. Justice Burnett treats such transactions as things done behind the father's back, and as it were a fraud upon him; a view of the subject also adopted by Lord Hardwicke in the same case (1 Atk. 333, 334). It is as well to mention these cases, because there has been no decision upon the point; but it is quite a clear one, and only new because the facts never afforded a case for decision, the proposition having apparently never been questioned.'

[1] King v. Hamlet, 2 Mylne & Keen, 473, 474; s. c. 4 Sim. R. 185.

[2] King v. Hamlet, 4 Sim. R. 182; s. c. 2 Mylne & Keen, 473, 474.

[3] Earl of Portmore v. Taylor, 4 Sim. R. 182; Davis v. Duke of Marlborough, 2 Swanst. 139, 154. See also King v. Hamlet, 2 Mylne & Keen, 473, 474, 480. Lord Brougham on this occasion, addressing himself to this point, said: ' The whole ground of the doctrine is the pressure upon the heir, or the distress of the party dealing with his expectancies. While he continues under that pressure the law (as Lord Thurlow said in Gwynne v. Heaton, 1 Bro. C. C. 1) treats him as an infant. But the infancy is determined when the pressure is removed. The protection which Sir William Grant well describes in Peacock v. Evans (16 Ves. 512) as approaching nearly to incapacity of

341. The doctrine of Courts of Equity upon this subject, if it has not been directly borrowed from, does in no small degree follow out the policy of the Roman law in regard to heirs and expectants. By the Macedonian Decree (so called from the name of the usurer who gave occasion to it) all obligations of sons, contracted by the loan of money while they were living in subjection to the paternal authority and jurisdiction, were declared null without distinction. And they were not allowed to be valid even after the death of the father; not so much out of favor to the son, as out of odium to the creditor who had made an unlawful loan, which was vicious in its origin as well as in its example. 'Verba Senatusconsulti Macedoniani hæc sunt, &c. Placere, ne cui, qui filiofamilias mutuam pecuniam dedisset, etiam post mortem parentis ejus, cujus in potestate fuisset, actio petitioque daretur; ut scirent, qui pessimo exemplo fænerarent, nullius posse filiifamilias bonum nomen, expectata patris morte, fieri.'[1] Upon this decree Lord Hardwicke has remarked that the Senate and law-makers in Rome were not so weak as not to know that a law to restrain prodigality, to prevent a son's running in debt in the life of his father, would be vain in many cases. Yet they made laws to this purpose; namely, the Macedonian Decree already mentioned, happy if they could in some degree prevent it: 'Est aliquod prodire tenus.'[2]

342. It is upon similar principles that post obit bonds and other securities of a like nature are set aside when made by

contracting, must cease when the exigency of the case is at an end. When the expectant heir has himself thrown off the trammels which necessity had imposed on him, or rather had induced him to fetter himself withal, and has placed himself in an adverse attitude towards the other party, of whom he had become really independent, he must no longer be treated differently from other persons. From the rule to which all are subject he cannot be exempt, — the rule which forbids a party to repudiate a dealing of which he voluntarily and freely is availing himself. Least of all shall he be permitted to use for his own benefit, or, which is the same thing, to make away with, or in any manner place out of his reach, for his present benefit, the property of another, and then to repudiate the contract by which that property came into his possession. To hold that he was entitled to do this after the pressure of his circumstances had been removed, and merely because he owed the possession originally to the pressure of former difficulties, would be an extravagant stretch of the doctrines of this court.'

[1] Dig. Lib. 14, tit. 6, l. 1; 1 Domat, Civil Law, B. 1, tit. 6, § 4, and art. 1, 2; 1 Fonbl. Eq. B. 1, ch. 2, § 12, note (l).

[2] Chesterfield v. Janssen, 2 Ves. 158.

heirs and expectants. A post obit bond is an agreement, on the receipt of money by the obligor, to pay a larger sum, exceeding the legal rate of interest, upon the death of the person from whom he (the obligor) has some expectations, if he should survive him.[1] (a) Such bonds operate as a virtual fraud upon the bounty of the ancestor, and disappoint his intentions generally by design, and usually in the event.

343. A case of a very similar character is a contract by which an expectant heir, upon the present receipt of a sum of money, promises to pay over to the lender a large though an uncertain proportion of the property which might descend to him upon the death of his parent or other ancestor, if he should survive him. It is a fraud upon such parent or other ancestor, and introductive of the worst public mischiefs; for the parent or ancestor is thereby induced to submit in ignorance to the disposition which the law makes of his estate, upon the supposition that it will go to his heir, when in fact a stranger is, against his will, made the substituted heir.[2] It might be very different if there was a fair although a secret agreement between all the heirs to share the estate equally; for such an agreement would have a tendency to suppress all attempts of one or more to overreach the others, as well as to prevent all exertions of undue influence.[3] (b)

[1] Boynton v. Hubbard, 7 Mass. R. 119; Chesterfield v. Janssen, 2 Ves. 157; 1 Atk. R. 352; Fox v. Wright, 6 Madd. R. 111; Wharton v. May, 5 Ves. 27; Cushing v. Townshend, 19 Ves. 628; Earl of Aldborough v. Frye, 7 Clark & Finn. 436.

[2] Boynton v. Hubbard, 7 Mass. R. 112.

[3] Beckley v. Newland, 2 P. Will. 182; Wethered v. Wethered, 2 Sim. R. 183; Harwood v. Tooke, 2 Sim. R. 192; Hyde v. White, 5 Sim. R. 524. Mr. Chief Justice Parsons, in Boynton v. Hubbard (7 Mass. R. 112), expounded this whole subject with admirable fulness and force, and held that even at law such securities could be relieved against. I gladly extract the following passages from his opinion: 'Another case is, where the deceit is upon persons not parties to the contract, as a deceit on a father or other relation, to whom the affairs of an heir or expectant are not disclosed; so that they are influenced

(a) The right to relief against unconscionable interest on loans secured by mortgages of expectancies is not affected by a repeal of usury laws. Miller v. Cook, L. R. 10 Eq. 641; Tyler v. Yates, L. R. 11 Eq. 265; s. c. 6 Ch. 665.

(b) An heir expectant may covenant, with the consent of his ancestor, to convey the estate to come to him from such ancestor, a fair consideration being paid. Fitch v. Fitch, 8 Pick. 480. See Trull v. Eastman, 3 Met. 123. The familiar case of title by estoppel may also be noticed. See Bigelow, Estoppel, ch. 11 (p. 322, 3d ed.).

844. From what has been already said, it follows, as a natural inference, that contracts of this sort are not in all cases utterly

to leave their fortunes to be divided amongst a set of dangerous persons and common adventurers, in fact, although not in form. This deceit is relieved against as a public mischief, destructive of a well-regulated authority or control of persons over their children or others having expectations from them, and as encouraging extravagance, prodigality, and vice. From the forms of proceeding in Courts of Equity, it must be admitted that these principles may often be more correctly applied there than in Courts of Law. Chancery may compel a discovery of facts which a Court of Law cannot; and from facts disclosed, a chancellor, as a judge of facts, may infer other facts, whence deceit, public or private, may be irresistibly presumed. Whereas at law fraud cannot be presumed, but must be admitted or proved to a jury. But when a Court of Law has regularly the fact of fraud admitted or proved, no good reason can be assigned why relief should not be obtained there, although not always in the same way in which it may be obtained in equity. A case in which an heir or expectant is frequently relieved against his own contract is a post obit bond. This is an agreement, on the receipt of a sum of money by the obligor, to pay a larger sum, exceeding the legal rate of interest on the death of the person from whom he has some expectation, if the obligor be then living. This contract is not considered as a nullity, but it may be made on reasonable terms, in which the stipulated payment is not more than a just indemnity for the hazard. But whenever an advantage is taken of the necessity of the obligor to induce him to make this contract, he is relieved as against an unconscionable bargain, on payment of the principal and interest. This contract may be made on data whence its reasonableness may be ascertained; for the lives of the obligor and of the person on whose death the payment is to be made are subject to be valued, as is done in insurances upon lives. But the covenant declared on in the case at bar is not in the nature of a post obit contract. Another case in which an heir is relieved is when he is entitled to an estate in reversion or remainder, expectant on the death of some ancestor or relative, and he contracts to sell the same for present money. All these cases are not relieved against as fraudulent, because a reasonable and sufficient consideration may be paid, as ascertained by the annual value of the estate, and of the intervening life. But, as in post obit contracts, when an advantage is taken by the purchaser of the necessity of the seller, he will be relieved against the sale on repaying the principal and interest, and sometimes paying for reasonable repairs made by the purchaser. This relief is granted on the ground that the contract of sale was unconscionable. In unconscionable post obit contracts, Courts of Law may, when they appear, in a suit commenced upon them, to have been against conscience, give relief by directing a recovery of so much money only as shall be equal to the principal received and the interest. But in sales of remainders and reversions, by grants executed, I know of no relief that Courts of Law can give, unless the grants shall appear to have been fraudulently obtained of the grantor; in which case the fraud will vitiate and render null the grants so infected. The contract before us is not a sale of a remainder or reversion, but is different from any noticed in the Reports that have been cited. There is one case of a contract between presumptive heirs, respecting their expectancies from the same ancestor. It is the case of Beckley v. Newland. The parties had married two sisters, pre-

void ; but they are subject to all real and just equities between the parties, so that there shall be no inadequacy of price and no inequality of advantages in the bargain. If in other respects these contracts are perfectly fair, Courts of Equity will permit them to have effect as securities for the sum to which ex æquo et bono the lender is entitled ; for he who seeks equity must do equity; and therefore relief will not be granted upon such securities, except upon equitable terms.[1] (a)

sumptive heirs of Mr. Turgis. The husbands agreed that whatever should be given by Mr. Turgis should be equally divided between them. After Turgis's death the defendant, who had the greater part given to him, was compelled to execute the agreement. The reciprocal benefit of the chance was a sufficient consideration. The tendency of the agreement was to guard against undue influence over the testator; and it could not be unreasonable to covenant to do what the law would have done if Turgis had died intestate. The covenant declared on in the case at bar is an agreement by an heir, having two ancestors then living, an uncle and an aunt, that if he survive them, or either of them, he will convey to a stranger one third part of all the estate, real and personal, which shall come to him from those ancestors or either of them, by descent, distribution, or devise. And it is found by the jury that this contract was not obtained from the heir by the fraud of the purchaser. If therefore this covenant is void, it must be on the principle that it is a fraud, not on either of the parties, for that the jury have negatived, but on third persons not parties to it, productive of public mischief, and against sound public policy. If the contract had this effect, it is apparent to the court from the record, the whole contract being a part of the record. And that a contract of this nature had this effect we cannot doubt. The ancestor, having no knowledge of the existence of the contract, is induced to submit his estate to the disposition of the law, which had designated the defendant as an heir. The defendant's agreement with the plaintiff is to substitute him as a co-heir with himself to his uncle's estate. The uncle is thus made to leave a portion of his estate to Boynton, a stranger, without his knowledge, and consequently without any such intention. This Lord Hardwicke calls a deceit on the ancestor. And what is the consequence of deceits of this kind upon the public? Heirs, who ought to be under the reasonable advice and direction of their ancestor, who has no other influence over them than what arises from a fear of his displeasure, from which fear the heirs may be induced to live industriously, virtuously, and prudently, are, with the aid of money speculators, let loose from this salutary control, and may indulge in prodigality, idleness, and vice, and taking care by hypocritically preserving appearances not to alarm their ancestor, may go on trafficking with his expected bounty, making it a fund to supply the wastes of dissipation and extravagance. Certainly the policy of the law will not sanction a transaction of this kind, from a regard to the moral habits of the citizens.'

[1] Boynton v. Hubbard, 7 Mass. R. 112, 120; Curling v. Townshend, 19

(a) See Pennell v. Millar, 23 Beav. 172; Tottenham v. Emmet, 13 Week. R. 123, and 14 Week. R. 3; Benyon v. Fitch, 35 Beav. 570; Aylesford v. Morris, L. R. 8 Ch. 484.

345. And where, after the contemplated events have occurred, and the pressure of necessity has been removed, the party freely and deliberately and upon full information confirms the precedent contract or other transaction, Courts of Equity will generally hold him bound thereby ; (a) for if a man is fully informed and acts with his eyes open, he may by a new agreement bar himself from relief.[1] But if the party is still acting under the

Ves. 628; Bernal *v.* Donegal, 3 Dow, R. 133; s. c. 1 Bligh, Rep. (N. S.) 594; Wharton *v.* May, 5 Ves. 27; 1 Fonbl. Eq. B. 1, ch. 2, § 13, and note (*p*); Evans *v.* Cheshire, Belt's Supplement, 300; Crowe *v.* Ballard, 3 Bro. Ch. R. 120; Gwynne *v.* Heaton, 1 Bro. Ch. R. 1, 9, 10; Davis *v.* Duke of Marlborough, 2 Swanst. 174; Earl of Aldborough *v.* Frye, 6 Clark and Finn. 436, 462, 464.

[1] Chesterfield *v.* Janssen, 2 Ves. 125; 1 Atk. R. 354; Crowe *v.* Ballard, 3 Bro. Ch. R. 150; Coles *v.* Gibbon, 3 P. Will. 293, 294; Cole *v.* Gibson, 1 Ves. 503, 506, 507; Cann *v.* Cann, 1 P. Will. 723. Mr. Fonblanque has remarked, that Lord Hardwicke, in Chesterfield *v.* Janssen (2 Ves. 125; 1 Atk. 351), has brought together and classed all the cases upon the subject of confirmation; and the result seems to be that if the original contract be illegal or usurious, no subsequent agreement or confirmation of the party can give it validity. But if it be merely against conscience, then if the party, being fully informed of all the circumstances of it, and of the objections to it, voluntarily comes to a new agreement, he thereby bars himself of that relief which he might otherwise have had in equity. Not so if the confirmation be a continuance of the original fraud or imposition. 1 Fonbl. Eq. B. 1, ch. 2, § 13, note (*r*). See also Id. § 14, note (*v*). Whether this statement will be found fully borne out by the authorities, is perhaps not beyond doubt. Where a contract is utterly void, as from illegality, or as being contrary to good morals, or as contrary to public policy, there seems the strongest reason to say that it cannot acquire any validity from any confirmation; for the original taint attaches to it through every change. To give it efficacy would contradict two well-established maxims of the common law : ' Quod contra legem fit, pro infecto habetur.' ' Quod ab initio non valet, in tractu temporis non convalescet; et quæ malo sunt inchoata principio, vix est, ut bono peragantur exitu.' 4 Co. R. 2; Id. 31; 1 Fonbl. Eq. B. 1, ch. 4, § 11, note (*y*). But where the contract is merely voidable, it seems upon general principles capable of confirmation. The difficulty is not so much in stating that it is capable of confirmation, but under what circumstances the confirmation ought to be held conclusive. The remarks of Lord Hardwicke, in Chesterfield *v.* Janssen, 2 Ves. 158, 159; 1 Atk. R. 354; and Cole *v.* Gibson, 1 Ves. R. 506, 507, compared with those of Lord Thurlow in Crowe *v.* Ballard, 3 Bro. Ch. R. 120; s. c. 1 Ves. 219, 220; s. c. 2 Cox, R. 257, and of Lord Eldon, in Wood *v.* Downes, 18 Ves. 123, 124, 128; and of Lord Erskine, in Morse *v.* Royal, 12 Ves. 373, 374, have not wholly relieved the doctrine from difficulty. In Cole *v.* Gibson, 1 Ves. 503, 506, 507, Lord Hardwicke seemed to hold a marriage brokage bond capable of confirmation, though held void upon public policy. But in Shirley *v.* Martin, in 1779, the Court of Exchequer held that contracts avoided on account of public

(a) Bacon *v.* Bonham, 33 N. J. Eq. 614, 617.

pressure of the original transaction or the original necessity, or if he is still under the influence of the original transaction, and of the delusive opinion that it is valid and binding upon him, then, and under such circumstances, Courts of Equity will hold him not barred from relief by any such confirmation.[1] (a)

346. Similar principles will govern in cases where the heir or other expectant is relieved from his necessities and becomes opposed to the person with whom he has been dealing, and seeks to repudiate the bargain. In such cases he must not do any act by which the rights or property of the other party will be injuriously affected, after he is thus deemed to be restored to his general capacity. If he does, he becomes affected with the ordinary rule which governs in other cases, and forbids a party to repudiate a dealing, and at the same time to avail himself fully of all the rights and powers resulting therefrom, as if it were completely valid.[2]

347. Even the sale of a post obit bond at public auction will not necessarily give it validity, or free it from the imputation of being obtained under the pressure of necessity. For the circumstances may be such as to establish that the expectant is acting without any of the usual precautions to obtain a fair price, and is in great distress for money, and is really in the hands and under the control of those who choose to become bidders for the purpose of fleecing him.[3] The case is not like the case of an

inconvenience would not admit of subsequent confirmation by the party, and therefore that a marriage brokage bond was incapable of confirmation. Cited 1 Fonbl. Eq. B. 1, ch. 2, § 14, note (u); Id. ch. 4, § 10, note (s); s. c. cited 1 Ball & B. 357, 358; 3 P. W. 75, Cox's note. See also Say v. Barwick, 1 Ves. & B. 195. See Gwynne v. Heaton, 1 Bro. Ch. R. 1, and Mr. Belt's note (1), ibid. See also ante, § 263, and Newland on Contracts, ch. 25, pp. 496 to 503.

[1] Wood v. Downes, 18 Ves. 123, 124, 128; Crowe v. Ballard, 3 Bro. Ch. R. 120; s. c. 1 Ves. 214, 219, 220; s. c. 2 Cox, R. 253, 257; Taylor v. Rochfort, 2 Ves. 281; Murray v. Palmer, 2 Sch. & Lefr. 486; Roche v. O'Brien, 1 B. & Beatt. R. 338, 339, 340, 353, 354, 356; Morse v. Royal, 12 Ves. 373, 374; Gowland v. De Faria, 17 Ves. 20; Dunbar v. Tredennick, 2 Ball & B. 316, 317, 318.

[2] King v. Hamlet, 2 Mylne & Keen, R. 474, 480. See also Gwynne v. Heaton, 1 Bro. Ch. R. 1; Peacock v. Evans, 16 Ves. 512; ante, §§ 339, 340.

[3] Fox v. Wright, 6 Madd. R. 77; Earl of Aldborough v. Frye, 7 Clark & Finn. 436.

(a) As to delay in seeking relief, see Sibbering v. Balcarras, 3 DeG. & S. 735; Lord v. Jeffkins, 35 Beav. 7.

ordinary sale of a reversion at public auction, where the usual precautions are taken; for there it may be perfectly proper not to require the purchaser to show that he has given the full value.[1] Where the sale is public, and free and fair, it may be justly presumed that the fair market price is obtained, and there seems no reason to call in question its general validity; but it should be specially impeached. In sales of reversions at public auction there is not usually any opportunity, as there is upon a private treaty, for fraud and imposition upon the seller. The latter is in no just sense in the power of the purchaser. The sale by public auction is, under ordinary circumstances, evidence of the market price.[2] (a) But the sale of post obit bonds at auction carries with it generally a presumption of distress and pecuniary embarrassment; and if the ordinary precautions are thrown aside, there is a violent presumption of extravagant rashness, imprudence, or circumvention.

348. Contracts of a nature nearly resembling post obit bonds have in cases of young and expectant heirs been often relieved against upoh similar principles. Thus where tradesmen and others have sold goods to such persons at extravagant prices, and under circumstances demonstrating imposition or undue advantage, or an intention to connive at secret extravagance and profuse expenditures unknown to their parents or other ancestors, Courts of Equity have reduced the securities, and cut down the claims to their reasonable and just amount.[3]

349. Another class of constructive frauds upon the rights, interests, or duties of third persons embraces all those agreements and other acts of parties which operate directly or virtually to delay, defraud, or deceive creditors. (b) Of course we do not

---

[1] Earl of Aldborough v. Frye, 7 Clark & Finn. 436; ante, § 338.

[2] Shelly v. Nash, 3 Madd. R. 125; Fox v. Wright, 6 Madd. R. 77; Earl of Aldborough v. Frye, 7 Clark & Finn. 436, 456 to 461.

[3] Bill v. Price, 1 Vern. R. 467, and Mr. Raithby's note (1); Ibid. 1 Eq. Abr. 91, G. pl. 3; Lamplugh v. Smith, 2 Vern. 77; Witley v. Price, 2 Vern. R. 78; Brook v. Gally, 1 Atk. 34, 35, 36; Berkley v. Bishop, 1 Atk. R. 39; Gilbert, Lex Prætor, 291. But see Barney v. Beak, 2 Ch. Cas. 136; Gwynne v. Heaton, 1 Bro. Ch. R. 9, 10.

(a) Lord v. Jeffkins, 35 Beav. 7.

(b) Whether a conveyance, devise, or gift of personalty, made in good faith by A to B to hold in trust to pay the income to C (C not being a married woman), so as to prevent the creditors of C from reaching the principal, can be upheld, query. Nichols

here speak of cases of express and intentional fraud upon creditors, but of such as virtually and indirectly operate the same
mischief by abusing their confidence, misleading their judgment,
or secretly undermining their interest. It is difficult in many
cases of this sort to separate the ingredients which belong to
positive and intentional fraud from those of a mere constructive
nature which the law pronounces fraudulent upon principles of
public policy. Indeed they are often found mixed up in the
same transaction; and any attempt to distinguish between them
or to weigh them separately would be a task of little utility, and
might perhaps mislead and perplex the inquiries of students.

350. It must be a fundamental policy of all enlightened nations
to protect and subserve the rights of creditors ; and a great
anxiety to afford full relief against frauds upon them has been
manifested, not only in the civil law, but from a very early period
in the common law also. In the civil law it was declared that
whatever was done by debtors to defeat their creditors, whether
by alienation or by other disposition of their property, should be
revoked or null, as the case might require. ' Ait prætor: Quæ
fraudationis causa gesta erunt, cum eo qui fraudem non ignoraverit ; de his curatori bonorum, vel ei cui de ea re actionem
dare oportebit, intra annum, quo experiundi potestas fuerit,
actionem dabo. Idque etiam adversus ipsum, qui fraudem fecit,
servabo. Necessario prætor hoc edictum proposuit; quo edicto
consuluit creditoribus, revocando ea, quæcunque in fraudem
eorum alienata sunt.[1] Ait ergo prætor: Quæ fraudationis causa
gesta erunt. Hæc verba generalia sunt, et continent in se
omnen omnino in fraudem factam, vel alienationem vel quem-
cunque contractum. Quodcunque igitur fraudis causa factum
est, videtur his verbis revocari, qualecunque fuerit. Nam, late
ista verba patent. Sive ergo rem alienavit, sive acceptilatione vel
pacto aliquem liberavit.[2] Idem erit probandum. Et si pignora

[1] Dig. Lib. 42, tit. 8, l. 1, § 1.
[2] Dig. Lib. 42, tit. 8, l. 1, § 2; Pothier, Pand. Lib. 44, tit. 8, n. 2.

v. Levy, 5 Wall. 433, 441; Sparhawk v. Cloon, 125 Mass. 263. In these cases all the authorities are stated. Where however the effect of the deed or gift is to vest the legal title to property and a simple trust in the trustee, and the right to receive the whole in-come and the jus disponendi in the cestui que trust, the property is liable in equity for the latter's debts. Sparhawk v. Cloon, supra, distinguishing Perkins v. Hays, 3 Gray, 405, Hall v. Williams, 120 Mass. 344, and Russell v. Grinnell, 105 Mass. 425.

liberet, vel quem alium in fraudem creditorum præponat.'[1]   And the rule was not only applied to alienations, but to fraudulent debts, and indeed to every species of transaction or omission prejudicial to creditors.   'Vel ei præbuit exceptionem, sive se obligavit fraudandorum creditorum causa, sive numeravit pecuniam, vel quodcunque aliud fecit in fraudem creditorum ; palam est, edictum locum habere, &c.   Et qui aliquid fecit, ut desinat habere, quod habet, ad hoc edictum pertinet.   In fraudem facere videri etiam eum, qui non facit, quod debet facere, intelligendum est ; id est, si non utitur servitutibus.'[2]

351.   Hence all voluntary dispositions made by debtors upon the score of liberality were revocable, whether the donee knew of the prejudice intended to the creditors or not.   'Simili modo dicimus, et si cui donatum est, non esse quærendum, an sciente eo cui donatum gestum sit ; sed hoc tantum, an fraudentur creditores.'[3]   And the like rule was applied to purchasers even for a valuable consideration, if they knew the fraudulent intention at the time of their purchases, and thus became partakers of it that they might profit by it.[4]   'Quæ fraudationis causa gesta erunt, cum eo qui fraudem non ignoraverit, de his, &c., actionem dabo. Si debitor in fraudem creditorum minore pretio fundum scienti emptori vendiderit ; deinde hi, quibus de revocando eo actio datur, eum petant ; quæsitum est, an prætium restituere debent ?   Proculus existimat, omnimodi restituendum esse fundum, etiamsi pretium non solvatur ; et rescriptum est secundum Proculi sententiam.'[5]

352.   The common law adopted similar principles at an early period.   These principles however have been more fully carried into effect by the statutes of 50 Edward III., ch. 6, and 3 Henry VII., ch. 4, against fraudulent gifts of goods and chattels ; by the statute of 13 Elizabeth, ch. 5, against fraudulent conveyances of lands to defeat or delay creditors ; and by the statute of 27 Elizabeth, ch. 4, against fraudulent or voluntary conveyances of lands to defeat subsequent purchasers.   These statutes have

---

[1] Id. l. 2; 1 Domat, B. 2, tit. 10, art. 7.
[2] Dig. Lib. 42, tit. 8, l. 3, §§ 1, 2; Id. l. 4; Pothier, Pand. Lib. 42, tit. 8, n. 1 to 36; 1 Domat, B. 2, tit. 10, art. 1, pr. tot. ; Id. art. 8.
[3] Dig. Lib. 42, tit. 8, l. 6, § 11; 1 Domat, B. 2, tit. 10, art. 2.
[4] Dig. Lib. 42, tit. 8, l. 1; Pothier, Pand. Lib. 42, tit. 8, n. 1.
[5] Dig. Lib. 42, tit. 8, l. 1; Id. l. 7; 1 Domat, B. 2, tit. 10, art. 4.

always received a favorable and liberal interpretation, in all the
courts both of law and equity, in suppression of fraud.[1] Indeed
the principles and rules of the common law as now universally
known and understood are so strong against fraud in every
shape, that Lord Mansfield has remarked that the common law
would have attained every end proposed by these statutes.[2]
This is perhaps stating the matter somewhat too broadly, at least
in regard to the statute of 27 Elizabeth, ch. 4, as it is now construed ; for the latter, in favor of subsequent purchasers, applies
to cases of voluntary conveyances, whether they are fraudulent
or not.[3] Courts of Equity, from the enlarged principles upon
which they act to protect the rights and interests of creditors,
give full effect to all the provisions, and exert their jurisdiction

---

[1] Cadogan v. Kennett, Cowp. R. 439; Jeremy on Eq. Jurisd. B. 3, P. 2,
ch. 3, § 4, pp. 410, 411, 412; Newland on Contracts, ch. 23, pp. 370, 371; Com.
Dig. Covin, B. 2, 3.

[2] Ibid.; Hamilton v. Russell, 1 Cranch, 309; Com. Dig. Covin, B. 2. The
statutes of 50 Edward III., ch. 6, and 3 Henry VII., ch. 4, expressly declare
all gifts, &c. of goods and chattels, intended to defraud creditors, to be null
and void. 1 Fonbl. Eq. B. 1, ch. 4, § 12, note (c); Com. Dig. Covin, B. 2.
In Hamilton v. Russell (1 Cranch, R. 309), the Supreme Court of the United
States said, that the statute of 13 Eliz. and 27 Eliz. are considered as only
declaratory of the principles of the Common Law. See 1 Fonbl. Eq. B. 1, ch.
4, § 13, and note (d); Co. Litt. 290, b.

[3] See Buckle v. Mitchill, 18 Ves. 110; Doe v. Manning, 9 East, R. 59;
Townshend v. Windham, 2 Ves. 10, 11; Walker v. Burroughs, 1 Atk. 93, 94;
Cathcart v. Robinson, 5 Peters, R. 264.   There is a distinction made in England between the statute of 13 Eliz. ch. 5, and the statute of 27 Eliz. ch. 4,
which should be here borne in mind, though it will naturally come under consideration in a subsequent page. All voluntary conveyances are not void
against creditors, equally the same as they are against subsequent creditors.
It is necessary on the statute of 13 Eliz. to prove that the party was indebted
at the time, or immediately after the execution of the deed, or otherwise it
would be attended with bad consequences, because the statute extends to *goods*
and chattels; and such construction would defeat every provision for children
and families, though the father was not indebted at the time. Walker v.
Burroughs, 1 Atk. 93; Battersbee v. Farringdon, 1 Swanst. R. 106, 113. But
upon the statute of 27 Eliz. ch. 4, subsequent purchasers for a valuable consideration may set aside the former voluntary conveyance, though bona fide
made, even though such purchasers had full notice of such voluntary conveyance. Doe v. Routledge, Cowp. R. 711, 712; Gooch's Case, 5 Co. R. 60, 61;
Twyne's Case, 3 Co. R. 83; Doe v. Manning, 9 East, R. 59; Buckle v. Mitchill,
18 Ves. 110; Holloway v. Millard, 1 Madd. R. 227, 228, 229. The statute of
27 Eliz. ch. 4, does not apply to goods and chattels, but to lands and other
real estate only. Jones v. Croucher, 1 Sim. & Stu. 315; Atherley on Marr.
Sett. ch. 13, p. 207; post, §§ 355 to 365, and 425 to 434.

upon the same construction of these statutes which is adopted by Courts of Law.[1] (a) They go even further; and (as we shall presently see) extend their aid to many cases not reached by these statutes. (b)

353. And in the first place let us consider the nature and operation of the statute of 13 Elizabeth, ch. 5, as to creditors, which has been universally adopted in America as the basis of our jurisprudence on the same subject. The object of the Legislature evidently was to protect creditors from those frauds which are frequently practised by debtors under the pretence of discharging a moral obligation; that is, under the pretence of making suitable provisions for wives, children, and other relations. Independently of the statute, no one can reasonably doubt that a gift or conveyance, which has neither a good nor a meritorious consideration to support it, ought not to be valid against creditors; for every man is bound to be just before he is generous;[2] and the very fact that he makes a voluntary gift or conveyance to mere strangers to the prejudice of his creditors affords a conclusive ground that it is fraudulent. The statute, while it seems to protect the legal rights of creditors against the frauds of their debtors, anxiously excepts from such imputation the bona fide discharge of moral duties. It does not therefore declare all vol-

[1] Ibid.
[2] Copis v. Middleton, 2 Madd. R. 428; Partridge v. Gopp, 1 Eden, R. 166, 167, 168; s. c. Ambler, R. 598, 599.

(a) Waddell v. Lanier, 62 Ala. 347; Flewellen v. Crane, 58 Ala. 627. It is not necessary for the creditor first to exhaust his legal remedies. Fellows v. Lewis, 65 Ala. 343; Pharis v. Leachman, 20 Ala. 662; Bibb v. Freeman, 59 Ala. 612; Case v. Beauregard, 101 U. S. 688, 690; Thurmond v. Reese, 3 Ga. 449; Cornell v. Radway, 22 Wis. 260; Saunderson v. Stockdale, 11 Md. 563. But a deficiency of legal assets should be shown. Halfman v. Ellison, 51 Ala. 543; Ellis v. State Bank, 30 Ala. 478. The creditor need not have a lien to subject land fraudulently conveyed. McAnally v. O'Neal, 56 Ala. 299.

(b) An executor or an administrator of an insolvent estate can maintain a bill in equity to set aside a conveyance made by his testator or intestate in fraud of his creditors. Parker v. Flagg, 127 Mass. 28; Gilson v. Hutchinson, 120 Mass. 27; Welsh v. Welsh, 105 Mass. 229. Of course an assignee in bankruptcy can by statute set aside fraudulent conveyances of the debtor. Kent v. Riley, L. R. 14 Eq. 190; Bartholomew v. McKinstry, 2 Allen, 448; post, § 371. Whether an assignee can, independently of statute, sue in equity to recover property fraudulently conveyed, was made a question but was not decided in Verselius v. Verselius, 9 Blatchf. C. C. 189.

untary conveyances to be void, but only all fraudulent conveyances to be void.[1]   And whether a conveyance be fraudulent or
not, is declared to depend upon its being made 'upon good consideration and bona fide.'[2]   It is not sufficient that it be upon
good consideration or bona fide. It must be both. And therefore if a conveyance or gift be defective in either particular,
although it is valid between the parties and their representatives,
yet it is utterly void as to creditors.

354. This leads us to the inquiry, what are deemed good considerations in the contemplation of the statute. A good consideration is sometimes used in the sense of a consideration which
is valid in point of law, and then it includes a meritorious as well
as a valuable consideration.[3]   But it is more frequently used in
a sense contradistinguished from valuable, and then it imports a
consideration of blood or natural affection ; as when a man grants
an estate to a near relation merely founded upon motives of generosity, prudence, and natural duty. A valuable consideration
is such as money, marriage, or the like, which the law esteems
as an equivalent given for the grant ; and it is therefore founded
upon motives of justice.[4]   Deeds made upon a good consideration only are considered as merely voluntary ; those made upon
a valuable consideration are treated as compensatory. The
words 'good consideration,' in the statute may be properly construed to include both descriptions ; for it cannot be doubted
that it meant to protect conveyances made bona fide and for a

---

[1] 1 Fonbl. Eq. B. 1, ch. 4, § 12, note (a); Doe v. Routledge, Cowp. R.
708; Cadogan v. Kennett, Cowp. R. 432, 434; Holloway v. Millard, 1 Madd.
R. 227; Sagitary v. Hide, 2 Vern. 44.   Many of the succeeding remarks upon
this subject I have taken, almost literally, from Mr. Fonblanque's very able
notes; and I desire this general acknowledgment to be taken as an expression
of my very great obligations to him in every part of my work. 1 Fonbl. Eq.
B. 1, ch. 4, § 12, and note (a). The word 'voluntary' is not to be found
either in the statute of 13 Elizabeth, ch. 5, or in the statute of 27 Elizabeth,
ch. 4.   Holloway v. Millard, 1 Madd. R. 227, 228.   A voluntary conveyance
to a stranger, made bona fide by a party not indebted at the time, would be
good against subsequent creditors.   Holloway v. Millard, 1 Madd. R. 227, 228;
Walker v. Burroughs, 1 Atk. 93.

[2] Ibid. ; Bacon, Abridg. Fraud, C.

[3] Hodgson v. Butts, 3 Cranch, 140; Copis v. Middleton, 2 Madd. R. 430;
Twyne's case, 3 Co. R. 81; Taylor v. Jones, 2 Atk. 601; Newland on Con-
tracts, ch. 23, p. 386; Partridge v. Gopp, Ambler, R. 598, 599; s. c. 1 Eden,
R. 167, 168; Atherley on Marr. Sett. ch. 13, pp. 191, 192.

[4] 2 Black. Comm. 297; 1 Fonbl. Eq. B. 1, ch. 4, § 12, note (a).

valuable consideration, as well as those made bona fide upon the consideration of blood or affection.[1]

355. In regard to voluntary conveyances they are unquestionably protected by the statute in all cases where they do not break in upon the legal rights of creditors. But when they break in upon such rights, and so far as they have that effect, they are not permitted to avail against those rights. If a man therefore who is indebted conveys property to his wife or children, such a conveyance is, or at least may be, within the statute; for although the consideration is good as between the parties, yet it is not in contemplation of law bona fide; for it is inconsistent with the good faith which a debtor owes to his creditors, to withdraw his property voluntarily from the satisfaction of their claims;[2] (a) and no man has a right to prefer the claims of affection to those of justice. This doctrine however (as we shall presently see) requires or at least may admit of some qualification in relation to existing creditors where the circumstances of the indebtment and the conveyance repel any possible imputation of fraud; as where the conveyance is of a small property by a person of great wealth, and his debts bear a very small proportion to his actual means.

356. But at all events the same doctrine does not apply to a man not indebted at the time, or in favor of subsequent creditors.

---

[1] Doe v. Routledge, Cowp. R. 708, 710, 711, 712; Copis v. Middleton, 2 Madd. R. 430, Hodgson v. Butts, 3 Cranch, R. 140; Twyne's case, 3 Co. R. 81.

[2] 1 Fonbl. Eq. B. 1, ch. 4, § 12, note (a); Twyne's case, 3 Co. R. 81; Townshend v. Windham, 2 Ves. 10, 11; Doe v. Routledge, Cowp. R. 711; Russell v. Hammond, 1 Atk. 15, 16; Tynham v. Mullens, 1 Madd. R. 119; Holloway v. Millard, 1 Madd. R. 227, 228; Bayard v. Hoffman, 4 John. Ch. R. 450; Reade v. Livingston, 3 John. Ch. R. 481; Taylor v. Jones, 2 Atk. 600, 601; Townshend v. Windham, 2 Ves. 10; Copis v. Middleton, 2 Madd. R. 425. See Seward v. Jackson, 5 Cowen, R. 406; Wickes v. Clarke, 8 Paige, R. 160, 165.

(a) See post, § 369; Sayre v. Fredericks, 1 C. E. Green, 205; Kane v. Roberts, 40 Md. 590; Patten v. Casey, 57 Mo. 118; In re Johnson, 20 Ch. D. 389. The difference between a voluntary conveyance and a conveyance based on a good consideration with regard to the rights of creditors is, that in the case of a voluntary conveyance it is enough for the creditor to show an intent to defraud on the part of the grantor alone. Laughton v. Harden, 68 Maine, 208. In the other case fraud in both parties to the conveyance must be shown. In re Johnson, supra; Beurmann v. Van Buren, 44 Mich. 496; 2 Kent, 441, note (13th ed.). Compare note to § 428, post.

There is nothing inequitable or unjust in a man's making a voluntary conveyance or gift, either to a wife or to a child or even to a stranger, if it is not at the time prejudicial to the rights of any other persons or in furtherance of any meditated design of future fraud or injury to other persons.[1] (a) If indeed there is any design of fraud or collusion, or intent to deceive third persons in such conveyances, although the party be not then indebted, the conveyance will be held utterly void as to subsequent (b) as well as to present creditors, for it is not bona fide.[2]

---

[1] 1 Fonbl. Eq. B. 1, ch. 4, § 12, note (a); Townshend v. Windham, 2 Ves. 11; Walker v. Burroughs, 1 Atk. 93; Bac. Abridg. Fraud, C.; Doe v. Routledge, Cowp. R. 710, 711; Russell v. Hammond, 1 Atk. 15, 16; Holloway v. Millard, 1 Madd. R. 227, 228; Battersbee v. Farringdon, 1 Swanst. R. 106, 113; Reade v. Livingston, 3 John. Ch. R. 481.

[2] Stillman v. Ashdown, 2 Atk. 481; Reade v. Livingston, 3 John. Ch. R. 481; Richardson v. Smallwood, Jac. R. 552. As to subsequent creditors, it cannot be presumed that a voluntary conveyance is fraudulent, unless the party at the time is deeply indebted. Lord Alvanley, in Lush v. Wilkinson (5 Ves. 387), said: ' A single debt will not do. Every man must be indebted for the common bills of his house, though he pays them every week. It must depend upon this, whether he was in insolvent circumstances at the time.' Mr. Chancellor Kent, in Reade v. Livingston (3 John. Ch. R. 498), said: ' Such a loose dictum, one would suppose, was not of much weight, as there is no preceding case which gives the least countenance to it.' But Lord Alvanley probably meant no more than this; that, as to subsequent creditors, there could scarcely arise a presumption that the conveyance was intentionally fraudulent (without which such subsequent creditors could have no case for relief), unless the party were deeply indebted at the time, and contemplated a fraud upon his creditors. In this view there is much force in his lordship's remarks. Indeed this seems to be the view of the matter entertained by Mr. Chancellor Kent in the same case. Ibid. 301. See also the remarks of Sir William Grant, in Kidney v. Coussmaker, 12 Ves. 155, and Sir Thomas Plumer, in Holloway v. Millard, 1 Madd. R. 414. See the Jurist, Jan. 6, 1844, p. 461.

(a) Mattingly v. Nye, 8 Wall. 370. See also McLane v. Johnson, 43 Vt. 48; infra, § 372, and note.

(b) The better view is that the conveyance is void as to subsequent creditors only where there was an intent to hinder, delay, or defeat them. Infra, § 360, note (a). Limited by this suggestion, one cannot convey property subject to a secret trust in one's favor, though for value, as against the rights of creditors. Moore v. Wood, 100 Ill. 451; Lukin v. Aird, 6 Wall. 78; Griffin v. First National Bank, 74 Ill. 259; Annis v. Bonar, 86 Ill. 128; Jones v. King, Ib. 225; Power v. Alston, 93 Ill. 587; Robinson v. Stewart, 10 N. Y. 195; Macomber v. Peck, 39 Iowa, 354. It matters not what the actual purpose or intent of the vendor may be in such a case. Moore v. Wood; Lukin v. Aird; Phelps v. Curts, 80 Ill. 112; Power v. Alston, supra.

357. It has been justly remarked that the distinction between cases where the party is indebted, and those where he is not indebted, is drawn from considerations too obvious to require illustration from cases. For if a man indebted were allowed to divest himself of his property in favor of his wife or his children, his creditors would be defrauded. But if a man not indebted, and not meaning to commit a fraud, could not make an effective settlement in favor of such objects because by possibility he might afterwards become indebted, it would destroy those family provisions which are under certain restrictions a benefit to the public as well as to the individual objects of them.[1]

358. In regard to voluntary conveyances there is an intermediate case touching creditors which requires consideration. Suppose a party possessed of a large estate and indebted at the same time to a considerable amount, but his debts bearing a small proportion to his actual property, should make a settlement or other voluntary conveyance in favor of his wife or children of a part of his estate, which should still leave a large surplus in his own hands beyond the assets necessary to pay his debts, and afterwards at a distance of time he should lose or spend so much of his property as not to leave enough to discharge such debts. The question would then arise whether in regard to such creditors the settlement or other conveyance would be void or not. To such a case it is somewhat difficult to apply the preceding reasoning so as to avoid the settlement or other conveyance, because there is no pretence to say that upon the posture of the facts any actual fraud could be intended, or that the creditors were prejudiced except by their own voluntary delay.

359. Upon this question a learned judge (Mr. Chancellor Kent) has pronounced an opinion which, from his acknowledged ability and sagacity in sifting the authorities, is entitled to very great weight. His language is: 'The conclusion to be drawn from the cases is, that if the party is indebted at the time of the voluntary settlement it is presumed to be fraudulent in respect to such debts (that is, those antecedently due), and no circumstance will permit those debts to be affected by the settlement or repel the legal presumption of fraud. The presumption of law in this case does not depend upon the amount of the debts, or the extent of the property in settlement, or the circum-

---

[1] 1 Fonbl. Eq. B. 1, ch. 4, § 12, note.

stances of the party.   There is no such line of distinction set up
or traced in any of the cases.   The attempt would be embarrassing if not dangerous to the rights of creditors, and prove an
inlet to fraud.   The law has therefore wisely disabled the debtor
from making any voluntary settlement of his estate to stand in
the way of existing debts.   This is the clear and uniform doctrine of the cases.' [1]

360. This doctrine is certainly strictissimi juris, and assumes
as a principle of law that the mere indebtment of a party constitutes per se conclusive evidence of fraud in a voluntary conveyance in all cases where the creditors to whom he is then
indebted are concerned.[2]   Nay, it seems to go farther; for upon

---

[1] Mr. Chancellor Kent, in Reade v. Livingston, 3 John. Ch. R. 500, 501.
See also 2 Sch. & Lefr. 714; Fitzer v. Fitzer, 2 Atk. 511, 513; Taylor v.
Jones, 2 Atk. 602; Bayard v. Hoffman, 4 John. Ch. R. 450; Richardson v.
Smallwood, Jac. R. 552.   But see contra, Verplanck v. Strong, 12 John. R.
536, and Jackson v. Town, 4 Cowen, R. 603, 604.   See Seward v. Jackson, 8
Cowen, R. 406; Wickes v. Clarke, 8 Paige, R. 161, 165.   That there is very
great weight in this reasoning cannot be questioned.   That it is, upon principle, entirely satisfactory as the true exposition of the statute of 13 Elizabeth,
ch. 5, or of the common law as to creditors, may admit of some diversity of
judgment.   Lord Mansfield has justly remarked, in Cadogan v. Kennett,
Cowp. 434, upon the statute of 13 Elizabeth: ' Such a construction is not to
be made in support of creditors as will make third persons sufferers.   Therefore the statute does not mitigate against any transaction bona fide made, and
where there is *no imagination* of fraud.   And so is the common law.'   ' A fair,
voluntary conveyance may be good against creditors, notwithstanding its being
voluntary.   The circumstance of a man being indebted at the time of his
making a voluntary conveyance is an *argument* of fraud.   The question in
every case therefore is, whether the act done is a bona fide transaction, or
whether a trick or contrivance to defeat creditors.'   If this language contains
a true exposition of the law on this subject, then the question of fraud or not is
open in all cases where a man is indebted as a matter of *fact;* and the law
does not absolutely pronounce that the indebtment per se makes the settlement fraudulent.   Lord Mansfield used language to a like effect in Doe v.
Routledge, Cowp. R. 708, 709, 710, 711.   The doctrine (as we have seen) in
Hinde's Lessee v. Longworth (11 Wheat. R. 199) stands upon grounds analogous to those of Lord Mansfield, and is not easily reconcilable with that in
Reade v. Livingston, 3 John. Ch. R. 500, 501.   See also Holloway v. Millard,
1 Madd. R. 414; Jones v. Boulter, 1 Cox, R. 288, 294, 295.   In Richardson v.
Smallwood (Jac. Rep. 552), the subject was considerably discussed by the
Master of the Rolls; but from his reasoning I should not draw any other conclusion than that an indebtment at the time was a circumstance presumptive
of a fraudulent intent.

[2] In Townshend v. Windham (2 Ves. 10, 11), Lord Hardwicke said : ' I
know no case on the statute of 13 Eliz., where a man, indebted at the time,
makes a voluntary conveyance to a child, without consideration, and dies

the same reasoning subsequent creditors have been allowed to participate in the same relief, even though as to them alone without such antecedent debts there could be no relief.[1] (a) The doctrine was certainly not understood by Lord Alvanley as going to this extent, for he put the case upon the proof of fraud arising from previous insolvency.[2]

361. Where the conveyance is intentionally made to defraud creditors, it seems perfectly reasonable that it should be held void as to all subsequent as well as to all prior creditors on account

indebted, but that it shall be considered as a part of his estate for the benefit of his creditors,' &c. 'A man actually indebted and conveying voluntarily, always means it to be in fraud of creditors, as I take it.' Belt's Supp. pp. 243, 247. But this language, though so very general, ought not, on that very account, to have more than general truth ascribed to it, where the indebtment is of a nature and extent that makes it presumptive of fraud, or the conveyance is a direct and immediate interference with the rights of creditors. See Richardson v. Smallwood, Jac. Rep. 552.

[1] Reade v. Livingston, 3 John. Ch. R. 498, 499; Walker v. Burroughs, 1 Atk. 94; 1 Madd. Ch. Pr. 220, 221.

[2] Lush v. Wilkinson, 5 Ves. 387; s. c. cited in Kidney v. Coussmaker, 12 Ves. 150, 155. See also Copis v. Middleton, 2 Madd. R. 430; Reade v. Livingston, 3 John. Ch. R. 501; Stephens v. Olive, 2 Bro. Ch. R. 90.

(a) In England subsequent creditors may avoid a conveyance for fraud if existing creditors could. Freeman v. Pope, L. R. 5 Ch. 538. This is true also to some extent in America. Redfield v. Buck, 35 Conn. 328; McLane v. Johnson, 43 Vt. 48. But the more general rule in this country is that subsequent creditors cannot object unless there was an intent to hinder, delay, or defraud *them* Davidson v. Lanier, 51 Ala. 318; Miner v. Jackson, 101 Ill. 550; Harlan v. Maglaughlin, 90 Penn. St. 293; Belford v. Crane, 1 C. E. Green, 265; Matthai v. Heather, 57 Md. 483; Kane v. Roberts, 40 Md. 590; Carter v. Grimshaw, 49 N. H. 100; Baker v. Gilman, 52 Barb. 26; Savage v. Murphy, 34 N. Y. 508; Laughton v. Harden, 68 Maine, 208. See infra, § 362; and see Ex parte Russell, 19 Ch. D. 588; Ware v. Gardner, L. R. 7 Eq. 317, among English cases of the like nature in point of fact. But the intent of the grantor alone to hinder such creditors is enough. Laughton v. Harden.

On the other hand it has been declared that a voluntary conveyance cannot be avoided by subsequent creditors if it would be good against existing creditors. Thacher v. Phinney, 7 Allen, 147, 150, citing Sexton v. Wheaton, 8 Wheat. 229; Norton v. Norton, 5 Cush. 524, 529. But that may be doubted. Case v. Phelps, 39 N. Y. 164; 2 Kent, 441, note (13th ed.).

For other cases in which settlements affecting subsequent creditors have been considered, see Vance v. Smith, 2 Heisk. 343; Irion v. Mills, 41 Texas, 310; Pike v. Miles, 23 Wis. 164; Townsend v. Marquard, 45 Penn. St. 198; Lyman v. Cessford, 15 Iowa, 229; Holmes v. Clark, 48 Barb. 237; Ogden v. Prentice, 33 Barb. 160; Childs v. Connor, 38 N. Y. Sup. Ct. 471; Therasson v. Hickok, 37 Vt. 454.

of ill faith.[1] But where the conveyance is bona fide made, and under circumstances demonstrative of the non-existence of any intention to defraud any creditor, there seems some difficulty in perceiving how the subsequent creditors can make out any right as against the voluntary grantees through the equity of the antecedent creditors.[2] Mr. Chancellor Kent, in the case above referred to, after having remarked that 'there is no doubt in any case as to the safety and security of the then existing creditors,' proceeded to state : 'No voluntary post-nuptial settlement

---

[1] See Reade v. Livingston, 3 John. Ch. R. 499, 501; 1 Hovend. Supp. to Vesey, jr., p. 124 (7); Richardson v. Smallwood, Jac. Rep. 552; Jeremy on Eq. Jurisd. B. 3, Pt. 2, ch. 3, § 4, p. 413; Newland on Contracts, ch. 33, p. 389.

[2] See Holloway v. Millard, 2 Madd. R. 419; Walker v. Burroughs, 1 Atk. R. 94. In Taylor v. Jones (2 Atk. 600), the Master of the Rolls manifestly proceeded upon the ground that the conveyance was fraudulent in fact. In Stephens v. Olive (2 Bro. Ch. R. 92), where there were prior debts, but secured by mortgage, Lord Kenyon held the settlement good. See also George v. Milbanke, 9 Ves. 194, that a settlement containing a provision for payment of debts would be good against all future creditors. Lord Eldon there said: 'In general cases, prima facie a voluntary settlement will be taken to be fraudulent.' But this supposes that it is not conclusive of fraud, but that it is open to be rebutted. In Kidney v. Coussmaker (12 Ves. 136, 155), Sir William Grant said: 'Though there has been much controversy and a variety of decisions upon the question whether such a settlement (a voluntary settlement) is fraudulent as to any creditors except such as were creditors at the time, I am disposed to follow the latest decision, that of Montague v. Lord Sandwich, which is, that the settlement is fraudulent only as against such creditors as were creditors at the time.' Montague v. Lord Sandwich is nowhere reported at large. It was decided in 1797, by Lord Rosslyn, and is referred to in 5 Ves. 386, and 12 Ves. 148. Mr. Chancellor Kent has said that in this case 'Lord Rosslyn declared a settlement void as to creditors prior to its date. There was no question of insolvency made; but it was clearly held by Lord Rosslyn in this case (see 12 Ves. 156, note), that if the settlement be affected, as fraudulent against such prior creditors, the subject is thrown into assets, and all subsequent creditors are let in.' He manifestly founds this remark upon the Reporter's note (a) in 12 Ves. 156. But I have not been able to ascertain that Lord Rosslyn gave any such relief in this case to subsequent creditors. The note in 5 Ves. 586, and 12 Ves. 148, would rather lead my mind to an opposite conclusion, that he gave relief only to *prior* creditors pro tanto. Mr. Atherley (Marr. Sett. ch. 13, p. 213, note 1) has expressed an unqualified dissent from this supposed opinion of Lord Rosslyn, and in my judgment with very great reason. Where the settlement is set aside as an intentional fraud upon creditors, there is strong reason for holding it so as to subsequent creditors, and to let them into the full benefit of the property. Richardson v. Smallwood, Jac. Rep. 532. See also Holloway v. Millard, 1 Madd. R. 414. But see Walker v. Burroughs, 1 Atk. 94, on this point.

was ever permitted to affect them.   And the cases seem to agree that the *subsequent* creditors are let in only in particular cases, as where the settlement was made in contemplation of future debts, (*a*) or where it is requisite to interfere and set aside the settlement in favor of the prior creditors, or where the subsequent creditor can impeach the settlement as fraudulent by reason of the prior indebtment.'[1]   And he finally arrived at the conclusion that 'fraud in a voluntary settlement was an inference of law, and ought to be so, so far as it concerned existing debts, but that as to subsequent debts there is no such necessary legal presumption, and there must be proof of fraud in fact; and the indebtment at the time, though not amounting to insolvency, must be such as to warrant that conclusion.'[2]

362. The same subject has undergone repeated discussions in the Supreme Court of the United States.   The doctrine established in that court is, that a voluntary conveyance made by a person not indebted at the time in favor of his wife or children, cannot be impeached by subsequent creditors upon the mere ground of its being voluntary.   It must be shown to have been fraudulent, or made with a view to future debts.[3] (*b*)   And on the other hand the mere fact of indebtment at the time does not per se constitute a substantive ground to avoid a voluntary conveyance for fraud even in regard to prior creditors.   The question whether it is fraudulent or not is to be ascertained, not from

---

[1] Reade *v*. Livingston, 3 John. Ch. R. 497, 501.   See Richardson *v*. Smallwood, Jac. Rep. 552.   See on the point whether a subsequent creditor can set aside a post-nuptial settlement, a learned dissertation in the English Jurist for January, 1844, No. 365, pp. 461, 462.   In Ede *v*. Knowles, 2 Younge & Coll. N. R. 172, 178, Mr. Vice-Chancellor Bruce said: 'The plaintiff does not allege by his bill that he was a creditor at the time of the settlement.   I apprehend that a deed can only be set aside as fraudulent against creditors at the instance of a person who was a creditor at the time, though when it shall have been set aside subsequent creditors may be let in.'

[2] Reade *v*. Livingston, 3 John. Ch. R. 497, 501.   See Richardson *v*. Smallwood, Jac. Rep. 552.

[3] Sexton *v*. Wheaton, 8 Wheat. R. 229, 230; Hinde's Lessee *v*. Longworth, 11 Wheat. R. 199; Bennett *v*. Bedford Bank, 11 Mass. R. 421.

(*a*) See Ware *v*. Gardner, L. R. 7 Eq. 317; § 362.

(*b*) Supra, § 360, and note.   See Ware *v*. Gardner, L. R. 7 Eq. 317; McLaughlin *v*. Bank of Potomac, 7 How. 220; Offutt *v*. King, 1 McArth. 312; Sparkman *v*. Place, 5 Ben. 184; Summers *v*. Hoover, 42 Ind. 153; Ricketts *v*. McCully, 7 Heisk. 712; In re Cornwall, 9 Blatchf. C. C. 116.

the mere fact of indebtment at the time alone, but from all the circumstances of the case. And if the circumstances do not establish fraud, then the voluntary conveyance is deemed to be above all exception. The language of the court upon the occasion alluded to was as follows: 'A deed from a parent to a child for the consideration of love and affection is not absolutely void as against creditors. It may be so under circumstances. But the mere fact of being indebted to a small amount would not make the deed fraudulent if it could be shown that the grantor was in prosperous circumstances and unembarrassed, and that the gift to a child was a reasonable provision according to his state and condition in life, and leaving enough for the payment of the debts of the grantor. The want of a valuable consideration may be a badge of fraud; but it is only presumptive and not conclusive evidence of it, and may be met and rebutted by evidence on the other side.'[1] And this language (it should be remembered) was used in a case where the conveyance was sought to be set aside by persons claiming as judgment creditors upon antecedent debts.[2]

[1] Hinde's Lessee v. Longworth, 11 Wheat. R. 199. See also Verplank v. Sterry, 12 John. R. 536, 554, 556, 557; Partridge v. Gopp, Ambler, R. 597, 598; s. c. 1 Eden, R. 167, 168, 169; Gilmore v. North Am. Land Co., Peters, C. R. 461.

[2] The doctrine of the Supreme Court seems an entire coincidence with that held by Lord Mansfield, in Cadogan v. Kennett, Cowp. R. 432, 434, and Doe v. Routledge, Cowp. R. 705, 710, 711, 712. See also Lush v. Wilkinson, 5 Ves. 387; Holloway v. Millard, 1 Madd. R. 414; Kidney v. Coussmaker, 12 Ves. 155; Sagitary v. Hide, 2 Vern. 44. It approaches very nearly to the doctrine held in the Supreme Court of the United States as to the construction of the statute of 27th of Elizabeth, as to subsequent purchasers; for in the other case the voluntary conveyance is not held absolutely void, but only the burthen of proof to repel fraud is thrown upon the claimants under it. Cathcart v. Robinson, 5 Peters, R. 277, 280, 281. See also Verplank v. Sterry, 12 John. R. 536, 554, 556, 557, 558. In this last case Mr. Justice Spencer, in delivering his opinion in the Court of Errors, held the doctrine maintained in the Supreme Court of the United States, as to creditors, in the broadest terms. 'If,' said he, 'the person making a settlement is insolvent, or in doubtful circumstances, the settlement comes within the statute (of 13th of Elizabeth, ch. 5). But if the grantor be not indebted to such a degree as that the settlement will deprive the creditors of an ample fund for the payment of their debts, the consideration of natural love and affection will support the deed, although a voluntary one, against his creditors; for, in the language of the decisions it is free from the imputation of fraud.' Ibid. 557. Mr. Newland maintains the same opinion with great strength. Newland on Contracts, ch. 23, pp. 384, 385. Mr. Fonblanque has remarked that, 'If a conveyance

362 *a.* The same doctrine seems now well established in England. (*a*)   In a recent case, where the very point was before the court,[1] Lord Langdale said : ' There has been a little exaggeration in the arguments on both sides as to the principle on which the court acts in such cases as these ; on one side it has been assumed that the existence of any debts at the time of the execution of the deed would be such evidence of a fraudulent intention as to induce the court to set aside a voluntary conveyance, and oblige the court to do so under the statute of Elizabeth.   I cannot think the real and just construction of the statute warrants that proposition, because there is scarcely any man who can avoid being

or gift be of the whole or of the greater part of the grantor's property, such conveyance or gift would be fraudulent; for no man can voluntarily divest himself of all or the most of what he has, without being aware that future creditors will probably suffer by it.   1 Fonbl. Eq. B. 1, ch. 4, § 12, note (*a*).

[1] Townsend *v.* Westacott, 2 Beav. R. 340, 345.

(*a*) ' With regard to creditors being so at the time, it is established that it is not necessary to show from anything actually said or done by the party that he had the express design by the deed to defeat creditors; but if he includes in it property to such an amount that, having regard to the state of his property, and to the amount of his liabilities, its effect might probably be to delay or defeat creditors, — if the court is satisfied of that, — the deed is within the meaning of the statute.' Jenkyn *v.* Vaughan, 3 Drew. 419, Kindersley, V. C., quoted with approval in Crossley *v.* Elworthy, L. R. 12 Eq. 158.   See also Freeman *v.* Pope, L. R. 5 Ch. 538 (qualifying Spirett *v.* Willows, 3 DeG. J. & S. 293) ; Kent *v.* Riley, L. R. 14 Eq. 190; Cornish *v.* Clark, Ib. 184.

If insolvency follow shortly after the settlement, the fact must be satisfactorily explained or the settlement will be deemed fraudulent.   Crossley *v.* Elworthy, supra; Mackay *v.* Douglas, L. R. 14 Eq. 106.   And where the settler is about to embark in hazardous business, it is not it seems sufficient in England to justify the settlement against creditors who become such in the course of that business that he was then solvent, and that the settlement covered but a small part of his property.   Mackay *v.* Douglas, supra; Ex parte Russell, 19 Ch. D. 588, 598. But see Kent *v.* Riley, L. R. 14 Eq. 190 ; Babcock *v.* Eckline, 24 N. Y. 623.   To make a settlement on the eve of embarking in trade affords however only presumptive evidence of fraud.   Mackay *v.* Douglas.   See Tanguery *v.* Bowles, L. R. 14 Eq. 51; Cornish *v.* Clark, Ib. 184; Kent *v.* Riley, Ib. 190.

A mere surety is within the statute as well as an absolute debtor.   The case must be looked at as if the surety's undertaking had already become fixed by the failure of his principal to pay.   Nor will the fact that the surety can show that his principal was able to pay the debt when the suretyship was undertaken justify a voluntary settlement of all the surety's estate.   In re Ridler, 22 Ch. D. 74.

A settlement of leaseholds may equally be within the statute.   In re Ridler, 22 Ch. D. 74; Price *v.* Jenkins, 5 Ch. D. 619.   See Ex parte Hillman, 10 Ch. D. 622; Ex parte Dohle, 26 Week. R. 407.

indebted to some amount; he may intend to pay every debt as soon as it is contracted and constantly use his best endeavors to have ample means to do so, and yet may be frequently, if not always, indebted in some small sum; there may be a withholding of claims contrary to his intention by which he is kept indebted in spite of himself; it would be idle to allege this as the least foundation for assuming fraud or any bad intention. On the other hand it is said that something amounting to insolvency must be proved, to set aside a voluntary conveyance; this too is inconsistent with the principle of the act and with the judgments of the most eminent judges. The evidence as to Westacott's property when he executed the settlement I cannot rely on; it is brought forward many years after the witnesses had known it, and they speak to the value of the property without taking into consideration any charges that might be upon it; and I am not in a situation of knowing whether there were any charges upon it.'

363. The same doctrine has been asserted by the Supreme Court of Connecticut in a recent case which hinged exclusively upon the same point. It was there laid down as the unanimous opinion of the court, and there is much persuasiveness as well as reasonableness and equity, in the doctrine that ' Where there is no actual fraudulent intent, and a voluntary conveyance is made to a child in consideration of love and affection, if the grantor is in prosperous circumstances, unembarrassed, and not considerably indebted, and the gift is a reasonable provision for the child according to his state and condition in life, comprehending but a small portion of his estate, leaving ample funds unencumbered for the payment of his debts, then such conveyance will be valid against conveyances (debts) existing at the time. But though there be no fraudulent intent, yet if the grantor was considerably indebted and embarrassed at the time, and on the eve of bankruptcy, or if the value of the gift be unreasonable considering the condition in life of the grantor, disproportioned to his property, and leaving a scanty provision for the payment of his debts, then such conveyance will be void as to creditors.' [1]

---

[1] Salmon v. Bennett, 1 Connect. Rep. 525, 548 to 551; S. P. Newland on Contracts, ch. 23, pp. 384, 385. Mr. Chancellor Kent, in commenting on this case, says: ' I have not been able to find the case in which a mere voluntary conveyance to a wife or child has been plainly or directly held good against

364. The same doctrine has been expressly held on different occasions by the judges of the Supreme Court of New York; and

the creditor at the time. The cases appear to me to be, upon the point, uniformly in favor of the creditor.' (Reade v. Livingston, 3 John. Ch. R. 504.) Mr. Atherley (Marr. Sett. ch. 13, pp. 212 to 219) maintains the same doctrine. He holds that if the party is in debt at the time of settlement, it is void as to subsequent as well as to prior creditors; and this without any reference to the amount of the debts. See note to Bigelow's Dig. (2d edition), p. 200, title, Conveyance. On the other hand it may be asserted with some confidence that there is no English case which pointedly decides that such a conveyance is void merely from the circumstance that the party was indebted at the time, if the debts bore no proportion to his assets, and there was no presumption of meditated fraud. The cases cited by Mr. Chancellor Kent do not appear to me to reach the point, at least not in a form free from difficulty and obscurity. The case of St. Amand v. The Countess of Jersey, 1 Comyn, R. 255, is quite obscurely reported; but it may be gathered from that report that the grantor was deeply indebted at the time, and probably there was a strong presumption of fraud in fact. The case of Fitzer v. Fitzer, 2 Atk. R. 511, was the case of a subsequent creditor having an assignment under the insolvent act of 2 Geo. II. ch. 2, to compel an execution of the trusts of a deed of separation in favor of a wife. It was not the case of a voluntary conveyance held void. In Taylor v. Jones, 2 Atk. 600, 602, the reasoning of the Master of the Rolls certainly goes to the maintenance of the doctrine. But the judgment seems ultimately to have turned upon the point that the conveyance was fraudulent, and there was a trust in it in favor of the grantor *for life*. Some part of the doctrine of the Master of the Rolls would not now be held maintainable. The doctrine of Lord Hardwicke, in Russell v. Hammond, 1 Atk. 35, by no means warrants so general a conclusion. His Lordship's language in Walker v. Burroughs, 1 Atk. 39, though broad and sweeping, does not come up to it; and the case turned on the Statute of Bankruptcy, 21 Jac. I. ch. 15. Townshend v. Windham, 2 Ves. 1, 10, 11, was the case of the execution of a power; and Lord Hardwicke held the property assets for the payment of the debts of existing creditors. The question did not arise whether the debtor had other estate at the time sufficient to pay his debts; and Lord Hardwicke treated the case as an intentional execution of the power to defraud creditors. On the other hand the case of Stephens v. Olive, 2 Bro. Ch. R. 90, shows that the fact of indebtment is not sufficient to set aside the conveyance if the debt is actually secured by mortgage. Now it is somewhat difficult to distinguish between the case of a specific security for debts and a general security founded upon an ample fortune in the grantor. Each operates, if at all, to repel the same imputation of fraudulent intent; and if the law makes the mere fact of indebtment per se a fraud as to existing creditors, the security in either case cannot control the presumption. The doctrine too of Lord Alvanley in Lush v. Wilkinson, 5 Ves. 383, trenches upon the conclusiveness of the presumption. And notwithstanding Mr. Chancellor Kent's doubts on this case in Reade v. Livingston, 3 John. Ch. R. 497, 498, it has been repeatedly recognized in later cases. 12 Ves. 150, 155; 2 Madd. R. 430. It must therefore be admitted that there is some difficulty in reconciling the language of the English cases, although the cases themselves may be all distinguishable from each other. The question really resolves itself into this, whether a voluntary

in the latest case on this subject it has been expressly affirmed
that neither a creditor nor a purchaser can impeach a conveyance, bona fide made, founded on natural love and affection, and
free from the imputation of fraud, and where the grantor had,
independent of the property granted, an ample fund to satisfy
his creditors. This qualification however was then annexed to
the doctrine, that if a fraudulent use is made of such a settlement, it may be carried back to the time when the fraud was
commenced.[1] (a)

365. Under this apparent diversity of judgment it would ill
become the commentator to interpose his own views as to the
comparative weight of the respective judicial opinions. It may
probably be found in the future, as it has been in the past, that
professional opinions will continue somewhat divided upon the
subject, until it shall have undergone a more searching judicial

conveyance is void against creditors because it ultimately operates to defeat
the debts of existing creditors, or whether it is void only when from the circumstances the presumption fairly arises that it either was intended to defraud
or did necessarily defraud such creditors. Sir Thomas Plumer, in Holloway v.
Millard, 1 Madd. R. 417, 419, manifestly treated the statute of 13th of Eliz.
as only applying to fraudulent conveyances. 'This conveyance is not one
of that description (i. e. to defraud creditors). It is not fraudulent merely
because it is voluntary. A voluntary conveyance may be made of real or
personal property without any consideration whatever, and cannot be avoided
by subsequent creditors, unless it be of the description mentioned in the
statute, &c. Its being voluntary is prima facie evidence' (he does not say
conclusive), 'where the party is *loaded* with debt at the time, of an intent to
defeat and defraud his creditors; but if unindebted his disposition is good.'
He afterwards added, — 'A voluntary disposition, even in favor of a child,
is not good, if the party is indebted at the time.' But this must be taken in
connection with his preceding remarks as applying to a case of being *loaded*
with debts. See also Copis v. Middleton, 2 Madd. R. 426, 428, 430. In
Jones v. Boulter (1 Cox, R. 288, 294), Lord Ch. B. Skinner said: 'There is
no mention in the act (Stat. 13 Eliz.) of voluntary conveyances; and the
question has always been whether in the transaction there has been fraud or
covin. *Here were creditors at the time*, and this is said always to have been
a badge of fraud. It is true that this circumstance is always strong evidence
of fraud. *But if there are other circumstances in the case, that alone will not be
sufficient.*' Eyre, B. is still more explicit. He said: 'The 13th of Elizabeth
is a wholesome law, plainly penned, and I wonder how artificial reason could
puzzle it. An artificial construction has entangled courts of justice, namely,
that a voluntary conveyance of a person indebted at the time is to be deemed
fraudulent.' See also 1 Fonbl. Eq. B. 1, ch. 4, § 12, note (a).

[1] Jackson v. Town, 4 Cowp. R. 604; Verplank v. Sterry, 12 John. R. 536.
See also Huston's Admr. v. Cantril, 11 Leigh, R. 136.

(a) See Laid v. Scott, 5 Heisk. 314.

examination, not upon authority merely, but upon principle. If the question were now entirely freed from the bearing of dicta and opinions in earlier times, there is much reason to believe that it would settle down into the proposition (certainly most conformable to the language of the statute of 13th of Eliz.) that mere indebtment would not per se establish that a voluntary conveyance was void, even as to existing creditors, unless the other circumstances of the case justly created a presumption of fraud actual or constructive, from the condition, state, and rank of the parties, and the direct tendency of the conveyance to impair the rights of creditors.[1] (a) In the latest English case touching this subject it was unequivocally held that a voluntary deed made in consideration of love and affection is not necessa-

[1] See Jones v. Boulter, 1 Cox, R. 288, 294, 295; Stephens v. Olive, 2 Bro. Ch. R. 90. See also 1 Fonbl. Eq. B. 1, ch. 4, § 12, note (a); Jeremy on Eq. Jurisd. B. 3, Pt. 2, ch. 3, § 4, pp. 412, 413; Twyne's case, 3 Co. R. 81 b.; Newland on Contr. ch. 23, pp. 383, 384, 385, where the learned author asserts the opinion intimated in the text in a positive manner, and maintains it by very cogent reasoning. Mr. Chancellor Kent, in his learned opinion already noticed (3 John. Ch. R. 506), has traced out some of the analogies between the English law and the continental law on this subject, and I gladly refer the learned reader to his citations. Voet has discussed the subject in his Commentaries, 1 Voet, ad Pand. Lib. 39, tit. 5, § 20; Pothier, in his Traité des Donations entre Vifs, § 2; and Grenier, in his Traité des Donations, Tom. 1, Partie 1, ch. 2, § 2, p. 253, &c. Voet holds that the donee is liable to the existing but not to the future debts of the donor, when he is donee of all or of the major part of the donor's property; 'utrum donatis omnibus bonis, aut majore eorum parte.' Pothier says that the donee of particular things is not bound to pay the existing debts of the donor unless he knows that the donor was insolvent at the time, or that he will not have sufficient left to pay his creditors, and the donation is in fraud of his creditors. But those who are technically called 'universal donees,' donataires universels (which embrace not only donees of the whole property of the donor, but of the whole of a particular kind, as movables, &c.), are liable for the existing debts of the donor but not for his future debts.

(a) See Gridley v. Watson, 53 Ill. 186; Johnson v. West, 43 Ala. 689; Pomeroy v. Bailey, 43 N. H. 118; Thacher v. Phinney, 7 Allen, 146; Winchester v. Charter, 12 Allen, 606; s. c. 97 Mass. 140, and 102 Mass. 272; Lerow v. Wilmarth, 9 Allen, 382; Babcock v. Eckler, 24 N. Y. 623; Stevens v. Robinson, 72 Maine, 381; Spence v. Dunlap, 6 Lea, 457; Churchill v. Wells, 7 Coldw. 364; Carpenter v. Carpenter, 25 N. J. Eq. 194; Rumbolds v. Parr, 51 Mo. 592; Kuhn v. Stansfield, 28 Md. 210; Boone v. Hardie, 83 N. Car. 470; Westmoreland v. Powell, 59 Ga. 259. These cases are to the effect that the question of fraud is a question of fact on all the circumstances. See however Fink v. Denny, 75 Va. 663; Morrison v. Clark, 55 Tex. 437; Gear v. Schrel, 57 Iowa, 666; Kerrigan v. Rantigan, 43 Conn. 17. And see 2 Kent, 441, notes (13th ed.).

rily void as against the creditors of the grantor upon the common law or the statute of Elizabeth, but that it must be shown from the actual circumstances that the deed was fraudulent and necessarily tended to delay or defeat creditors.[1] (a)

366. There is another qualification of the doctrine respecting the rights of creditors which deserves attention in this place, not only from its practical importance in regard to the jurisdiction of Courts of Equity, but also from the fact that it has given rise to some diversity of judicial opinion. The point intended to be suggested is this: whether in order to make a conveyance void as against existing creditors it is indispensable that it should make a transfer of property which could be taken in execution by the creditors or compulsorily applied to the payment of the debts of the grantor, or whether the rule equally applies to the conveyance of any property whatsoever of the grantor, although not directly so applicable to the discharge of debts.

367. The English doctrine upon this subject, after various discussions, has at length settled down in favor of the former proposition; namely, that in order to make a voluntary conveyance void as to creditors, either existing or subsequent, it is indispensable that it should transfer property which would be liable to be taken in execution for the payment of debts. The reasoning by which this doctrine is established is, in substance, that the Statute of 13th of Elizabeth did not intend to enlarge the remedies of creditors, or to subject any property to execution which was not already, in law or equity, subject to the rights of creditors; that a voluntary conveyance of property not so subject could not be injurious to creditors, nor within the purview of the statute, because it would not withdraw any fund from their power which the law had not already withdrawn from it. And that would be a strange anomaly to declare that to be a fraud upon creditors which in no respect varied their rights or remedies. (b)

---

[1] Gale v. Williamson, 8 Mees. & Welsb. R. 405, 409, 410, 411.

(a) See Cornish v. Clark, L. R. 14 Eq. 184, where the children in whose favor a father had made a voluntary distribution knew that it would interfere with the claims of creditors. The distribution was held void. As to laches of the creditor see Cranson v. Smith, 47 Mich. 189.

(b) See Castle v. Palmer, 6 Allen, 401, 404; Silloway v. Brown, 12 Allen, 30, 33; Winchester v. Guddy, 72 N. Car. 115; Fellows v. Lewis, 65 Ala. 343; Lishy v. Perry, 6 Bush, 515; Cox v. Wilder, 2 Dill. 45.

Hence it has been decided that a voluntary settlement of stock, or of choses in action, or of copyholds, or of any other property not liable to execution, is good, whatever may be the state and condition of the party as to debts.[1]

368. Mr. Chancellor Kent, in a very elaborate argument, has discussed the same subject, and doubted the soundness of the reasoning by which that doctrine is attempted to be established. He maintains that in cases of fraudulent alienations of this sort Courts of Equity ought to interfere and grant remedial justice, whether the property could be reached by an execution at law or not; for otherwise a debtor under shelter of it might convert all his property into stock and settle it upon his family in defiance of his creditors and to the utter subversion of justice. And he further insists that the cases antecedent to the time of Lord Thurlow, and especially in the time of Lord Hardwicke and Lord Northington, do sustain his own doctrine.[2]

[1] See Dundas v. Dutens, 1 Ves. jr. 196; s. c. 2 Cox, R. 196; McCarthy v. Gould, 1 B. & Beatt. 390; Grogan v. Cooke, 2 B. & Beatt. 233; Caillard v. Estwick, 1 Anst. R. 381; Nantes v. Conork, 9 Ves. 188, 189; Rider v. Kidder, 10 Ves. 368; Guy v. Pearkes, 18 Ves. 196, 197; Cochrane v. Chambers, 1825; MSS. cited in Mr. Blunt's note to Horn v. Horn, Ambler, R. 79; Matthews v. Feaver, 1 Cox, R. 278.

[2] Bayard v. Hoffman, 4 John. Ch. R. 452 to 459; Edgell v. Haywood, 3 Atk. 352. See also Mitf. Pl. by Jeremy, 115, and 1 Jac. & Walk. 371; M'Durmut v. Strong, 4 John. Ch. R. 687; Spader v. Davis, 5 John. Ch. R. 280; s. c. 20 John. R. 554. The cases cited by Mr. Chancellor Kent go very far to establish the doctrine which he contends for. Taylor v. Jones (2 Atk. R. 600) is a decision of the Master of the Rolls directly in point. The case of King v. Dupine, cited in Mr. Saunders's note to 2 Atk. 603, note 2, and reported 3 Atk. R. 192, 200, is strong the same way; and so is Horn v. Horn, Ambl. R. 79. Upon this latter case Lord Thurlow is reported to have said : ' The opinion in Horn v. Horn is so anomalous and unfounded, that forty such opinions would not satisfy me. It would be preposterous and absurd to set aside an agreement, which, if set aside, leaves the stock in the name of a person where you could not touch it.' Grogan v. Cooke, 2 B. & Beatt. 233. In Partridge v. Gopp, Ambl. R. 596, s. c. 1 Eden, R. 163, Lord Chancellor Northington made the donees of £500 each refund in favor of creditors. But he seems to have been impressed with the opinion that the transaction was fraudulent, or, to use his own words, that the transaction smelt of craft and experiment. The transaction was secret; and, ' Dona clandestina sunt semper suspiciosa.' Twyne's Case, 3 Co. R. 81. Whatever may be the true doctrine on this subject, a distinction may perhaps exist between cases where a party indebted actually converts his existing *tangible property* into stock to defraud creditors, and cases where he becomes possessed of stock without indebtment at the time, or, if indebted, without having obtained it by the conversion of any other tangible property. Where tangible property is converted into stock to defraud

369. But whatever may be the true doctrine as to these critical and nice questions, it is certain that a conveyance, even if
for a valuable consideration, is not under the statute of 13th of
Elizabeth valid in point of law from that circumstance alone.   It
must also be bona fide; for if it be made with intent to defraud
or defeat creditors, it will be void although there may in the
strictest sense be a valuable, nay an adequate consideration.
This doctrine was laid down in Twyne's Case (3 Co. R. 81), and
it has ever since been steadily adhered to.[1]   Cases have repeatedly been decided in which persons have given a full and fair
price for goods, and where the possession has been actually
changed; yet, being done for the purpose of defeating creditors,
the transaction has been held fraudulent and therefore set
aside.[2] (a)   Thus where a person with knowledge of a decree
against the defendant bought the house and goods belonging to
him and gave a full price for them, the court said that the purchase being with a manifest view to defeat the creditor was
fraudulent, and, notwithstanding the valuable consideration, void.[3]
So if a man should know of a judgment and execution, and with
a view to defeat it should purchase the debtor's goods, it would
be void, because the purpose is iniquitous.[4] (b)

existing creditors, there may be a solid ground to follow the fund, however
altered.

[1] Newland on Contr. ch. 23, pp. 370, 371; 1 Fonbl. Eq. B. 1, ch. 4, § 12,
note (a); Cadogan v. Kennett, Cowp. R. 434; Worseley v. De Mattos, 1 Burr.
474, 475.

[2] Cadogan v. Kennett, Cowp. R. 434; Bridge v. Eggleston, 14 Mass. R.
245; Harrison v. Trustees of Phillips Academy, 12 Mass. R. 456.

[3] Ibid.; Worseley v. De Mattos, 1 Burr. 474, 475.

[4] Ibid.

(a) Supra, § 355, and note; Clements v. Moore, 6 Wall. 299, 312; In re
Johnson, 20 Ch. D. 389, 393; Holmes
v. Penney, 3 Kay & J. 90; Wadsworth
v. Williams, 100 Mass. 126; Chapel v.
Clapp, 29 Iowa, 191; Schaferman v.
O'Brien, 28 Md. 565; Tompkins v.
Sprout, 55 Cal. 31; Robinson v. Holt,
39 N. H. 557. See Harrison v. Ja-
quess, 29 Ind. 208; Pulliam v. New-
berry, 41 Ala. 168; Carny v. Palmer,
2 Coldw. 35; Stein v. Herman, 23 Wis.
132.

    As to partial considerations, see

Mead v. Combs, 4 C. E. Green, 112;
Cunningham v. Dwyer, 28 Md. 299.
Fraudulent purpose in the grantor
alone is enough to avoid a voluntary
conveyance; secus in the case of a
conveyance for value. Ante, § 355,
note (a).

    (b) But if the purchase was made
in good faith, without intent to defeat
the creditor, it may be upheld. Wood
v. Dixie, 7 Q. B. 892; Hale v. Saloon
Omnibus Co., 4 Drew. 492; Darvill v.
Terry, 6 Hurl. & N. 807. See Hill v.
Ahern, 135 Mass. 158; Ricker v. Ham,

370. But cases of this sort are carefully to be distinguished from others where a sale or assignment or other conveyance merely amounts to giving a preference in payment to another creditor, or where the assignment or conveyance is made for the benefit of all creditors; for such a preference (*a*) or such a general assignment or conveyance (*b*) is not treated as mala fide,

14 Mass. 137; Clapp *v.* Leatherbee, 18 Pick. 131. The insolvent may e. g. sell to get money to pay his debts. In re Coleman, L. R. 1 Ch. 128; Kent *v.* Riley, L. R. 14 Eq. 190; Lowry *v.* Howard, 35 Ind. 170.

(*a*) York Bank *v.* Carter, 38 Penn. St. 446; Davidson *v.* Lanier, 51 Ala. 318; Wilkerson *v.* Cheatham, 45 Ala. 337; Heidingsfelder *v.* Slade, 60 Ga. 396 ; Lampson *v.* Arnold, 19 Iowa, 479; Gormbel *v.* Arnett, 100 Ill. 34; Hessing *v.* McCloskey, 37 Ill. 341; Mayfield *v.* Kilgour, 31 Md. 240; Carpenter *v.* Muren, 42 Barb. 300. And if a creditor has sought out and discovered through the courts concealed property of his debtor, he is *entitled* of right to a preference over other creditors in regard to such property. Rappleye *v.* International Bank, 93 Ill. 396. Preference to a bona fide creditor is not invalid because of intent participated in by such creditor to defeat other creditors. Banfield *v.* Whipple, 14 Allen, 13. See Gray *v.* St. John, 35 Ill. 222 ; Walden *v.* Murdock, 23 Cal. 540; Young *v.* Dumas, 39 Ala. 60; Chase *v.* Walters, 28 Iowa, 460; Bear's Estate, 60 Penn. St. 430. The motive of preference is immaterial. Crawford *v.* Austin, 34 Md. 49. But it must not be a mere cover for benefit to the debtor. Banfield *v.* Whipple, supra. A reservation of the surplus however is proper. Beach *v.* Bestor, 47 Ill. 521. And a husband indebted to his wife may treat her as a preferred creditor. Davidson *v.* Lanier, 51 Ala. 318; infra, § 372. But see Kuhn *v.* Stansfield, 28 Md. 210.

But some courts hold that if the transaction is intended by the debtor to hinder or delay other existing creditors, and the preferred creditor is in any way aware of a purpose to that effect, the preference may be upset by them. Foster *v.* Grigsby, 1 Bush, 86. So a general assignment is probably void against a particular creditor whom it was the special motive of the assignment to hinder. Stickney *v.* Crane, 35 Vt. 89.

Under the English Bankrupt Act a preference made without pressure, and in contemplation of bankruptcy, is fraudulent. Ex parte Craven, L. R. 10 Eq. 648. As to pressure see Ex parte Tempest, L. R. 6 Ch. 70. The preference need not be the sole motive of the act, to make it fraudulent in England. Ex parte Hill, 23 Ch. D. 695. But it should be the dominant one, it seems. Ib. That is enough at any rate. Ib.

The transfer by way of preference may be of the debtor's entire estate. Alton *v.* Harrison, L. R. 4 Ch. 622; Hobbs *v.* Davis, 50 Ga. 213; Thornton *v.* Tandy, 39 Texas, 544.

The right of an executor or administrator to retain for a debt due to him from the decedent, so far as it exists, is of course a right of preference. See post, note at end of § 579.

(*b*) See Lee *v.* Green, 35 Eng. L. & E. 261 ; Wolverhampton Bank *v.* Marston, 7 Hurl. & N. 148; Johnson *v.* Osenton, L. R. 4 Ex. 107. But see Dalton *v.* Currier, 40 N. H. 237, where a general assignment for creditors to save the property from attachments, not made under the statute but depending upon common-law principles for its validity, was held void against the attachment laws. See also Ed-

but as merely doing what the law admits to be rightful. A sale, assignment, or other conveyance is not necessarily fraudulent because it may operate to the prejudice of a particular creditor.[1] But secret preferences made to induce particular creditors to sign a general assignment, and unknown to the other creditors who execute the assignment, are treated as frauds upon such creditors.[2]

371. It may be added that although voluntary conveyances are or may be void as to existing creditors, they are perfect and effectual as between the parties, and cannot be set aside by the grantor if he should become dissatisfied with the transaction.[3] (a) It is his own folly to have made such a conveyance. They are not only valid as to the grantor, but also as to his heirs and all other persons claiming under him in privity of estate with notice of the fraud.[4] (b)   A conveyance of this sort (it has been said with great truth and force) is void only as against creditors, and then only to the extent in which it may be necessary to deal with the conveyed estate for their satisfaction. To this extent and to this only it is treated as if it had not been made. To every other purpose it is good. Satisfy the creditors and the conveyance stands.[5] (c)   But the assignees of a bankrupt or an insolvent

---

[1] Holbird v. Anderson, 5 T. R. 235; Pickstork v. Lyster, 3 M. & Selw. R. 371.

[2] Post, § 378.

[3] Petre v. Espinasse, 2 Mylne & Keen, 496; Bill v. Cureton, Id. 510, 530.

[4] Randall v. Phillips, 3 Mason, R. 378.

[5] Sir W. Grant, in Curtis v. Price, 12 Ves. 103; Worseley v. De Mattos, 1 Burr. 474; 1 Madd. Ch. Pr. 222, 223; 1 Fonbl. Eq. B. 1, ch. 4, § 12, note (a);

---

wards v. Mitchell, 1 Gray, 239; Stanfield v. Simmons, 12 Gray, 442. But see Adams v. Blodgett, 2 Woodb. & M. 233. Such assignments are against the policy of the Bankrupt Act and invalid. In re Pierce, 3 Bank. Reg. 61; In re Spicer, Ib. 127; In re Catlin, Ib. 134.

(a) Dunaway v. Robertson, 95 Ill. 419, holding this to be true though the conveyance (having been recorded) had not been delivered. Between the parties a naked declaration of *trust* by the grantee in favor of the grantor may be enforced. Ownes v.

Ownes, 8 C. E. Green, 60; Harvey v. Varney, 98 Mass. 118. And see supra, § 298.

(b) A creditor of a decedent's estate may have a sale of such estate set aside for fraud though he was a party to judicial proceedings which authorized the sale, if he was not a party to the fraud and was ignorant of it at the time of the sale. Johnson v. Waters, 111 U. S. 640.

(c) Scholey v. Worcester, 4 Hun, 302; Dietrich v. Koch, 35 Wis. 618; Harman v. Harman, 63 Ill. 572; O'Neil v. Chandler, 42 Ind. 471; Clemens v.

debtor are entitled to the same rights and stand in the same predicament as the creditors themselves, and are deemed to represent them.[1] (a)

372. The circumstances under which a conveyance will be deemed purely voluntary, or will be deemed affected by a consideration valuable in itself or in furtherance of an equitable obligation, are very important to be considered; but they more properly belong to a distinct treatise upon the nature and validity of settlements. It may not however be useless to remark in this place, that a settlement made upon a wife after marriage is not to be treated as wholly voluntary where it is done in performance of a duty which a Court of Equity would enforce. (b) Thus if a man should contract a marriage by stealth with a young lady having a considerable fortune in the hands of trustees, and he should afterwards make a suitable settlement upon her in consideration of that fortune, the settlement would not be set aside in favor of the creditors of the husband, since a Court of Equity would not suffer him to take possession of her fortune without making a suitable settlement upon her.[2] (c) It has been said that

---

Jeremy on Eq. Jurisd. B. 3, Pt. 2, ch. 3, § 4; Malin v. Garnsey, 16 John. R. 189; Reichart v. Castelor, 5 Binn. 109; Drinkwater v. Drinkwater, 4 Mass. R. 354.

[1] Doe v. Ball, 11 Mees. & Welsb. 531, 533.

[2] Post, §§ 1372, 1373, 1377, 1415; Moor v. Rycault, Prec. Ch. 22, and other

---

Clemens, 28 Wis. 637; Noble v. Noble, 26 Ark. 317.

If a creditor is a party to such a deed, or acquiesces in one, he cannot afterwards avoid it, nor can any one claiming under him with notice or as a volunteer. Olliver v. King, 8 DeG. M. & G. 110; Baldwin v. Cawthorne, 19 Ves. 164; Steel v. Brown, 1 Taunt. 381; Ex parte Harvey, 27 Eng. L. & E. 272. As to acquiescence by the creditor, see Rapelee v. Stewart, 27 N. Y. 310; Richards v. White, 7 Minn. 345; Phillips v. Wooster, 36 N. Y. 412; French v. Mehan, 56 Penn. St. 286. One who purchases the equity of redemption on foreclosure sale must in like manner accept the mortgage, and must on redeeming pay what is justly due. Russell v. Dudley, 3 Met.

147; Taylor v. Dean, 7 Allen, 251. Secus if an assignee of an insolvent clearly manifests an intention to avoid the mortgage, and sells all his interest in the estate. Freeland v. Freeland, 102 Mass. 475.

(a) See ante, § 322, note; Bartholomew v. McKinstry, 2 Allen, 448; Verselius v. Verselius, 9 Blatchf. C. C. 189. So of executors and administrators. Parker v. Flagg, 127 Mass. 28; Welsh v. Welsh, 105 Mass. 229.

(b) See Davidson v. Lanier, 51 Ala. 318. But see Kuhn v. Stansfield, 28 Md. 210, infra.

(c) A settlement upon an intended wife, for her support and that of the children of the marriage, where the wife has already advanced considerable sums of money to the husband in

a post-nuptial voluntary agreement by a father to make a provision for a child will be specifically enforced in equity, as founded in moral duty.[1] But this doctrine, although it has the support of highly respectable authorities, seems now entirely overthrown.[2]

373. In like manner what circumstances connected with voluntary or valuable conveyances are badges of fraud or raise presumptions of intentional bad faith, though very important ingredients in the exercise of equitable jurisdiction, fall rather

cases cited in 1 Fonbl. Eq. B. 1, ch. 4, § 12, and note (b); Id. ch. 2, § 6, note (k); Jones v. Marsh, Cas. T. Talb. 64; Wheeler v. Caryl, Amb. R. 121; Jewson v. Moulton, 2 Atk. 417; Middlecome v. Marlow, 2 Atk. 519; Ward v. Shallet, 2 Ves. 16; Ramsden v. Hylton, 2 Ves. 304; Arundel v. Phipps, 10 Ves. 139; Russell v. Hammond, 1 Atk. 13; Wickes v. Clarke, 8 Paige, R. 161.

[1] Ellis v. Nimmo, Lloyd & Goold, R. 333. Post, §§ 706, 706, a; 787, 793 b; 973. See also that a voluntary assignment of a bond is a conclusive title to the assignee against the estate of the assignor, Fortescue v. Barnett, 3 M. & Keen, 36, 42, 43; ante, § 176; post, § 433, note (1); Jefferys v. Jefferys, 1 Craig & Phillips, 138, 141.

[2] See Holloway v. Headington, 8 Sim. R. 324, 325; and Jefferys v. Jefferys, 1 Craig & Phillips, 138, 141; post, §§ 433, 706, 706 a; 787, 793, 973.

contemplation of the marriage, is valid against the husband's creditors though the husband was then in very embarrassed circumstances to the knowledge of the wife, and was declared a bankrupt not long afterwards for an act subsequent to the marriage. Frazer v. Thompson, 5 Jur. N. S. 669; s. c. 1 Giff. 49. But it was here intimated that the case might be different if the ceremony has been resorted to as a mere pretence and cloak for fraud. Except in such a case as that it was said that there was no case in which any settlement of property made before and in consideration of marriage had been set aside on the ground of the insolvency or embarrassed circumstances of the husband, or as a fraud upon creditors on a subsequent bankruptcy. Campion v. Cotton, 17 Ves. 268. The case of Colombine v. Penhall, 1 Smale & G. 228, was referred to as within the exception.

Where however a husband voluntarily executed a bill of sale of his property to secure to his wife a sum of money constituting her separate estate, which he had received and invested in his business with her knowledge and consent, and without any promise at the time to refund the same, it was held in Kuhn v. Stansfield, 28 Md. 210, that the conveyance was void as to existing creditors, the husband having no other property to satisfy their claims. See Gardner v. Short, 4 C. E. Green, 341; Smith v. Vreeland, 1 C. E. Green, 198. But see Davidson v. Lanier, 51 Ala. 318.

In another case a trader sold his stock in trade, and as part of the consideration secured an annuity during the joint lives of himself and wife, equal to one fourth the profits, and a contingent annuity to the wife if she survived him equal to one sixth of the profits. The trader died, and on a creditors' bill it was held that the annuity to the wife was invalid, though the rest of the transaction was not attacked. French v. French, 6 DeG. M. & G. 95.

within the scope of treatises on evidence than of discussions touching jurisdiction.[1] It may however be generally stated that whatever would at law be deemed badges of fraud or presumptions of ill faith will be fully acted upon in Courts of Equity. But on the other hand it is by no means to be deemed a logical conclusion that because a transaction could not be reached at law as fraudulent, therefore it would be equally safe against the scrutiny of a Court of Equity ; for a Court of Equity requires a scrupulous good faith in transactions which the law might not repudiate. It acts upon conscience, and does not content itself with the narrower views of legal remedial justice.[2]

374. The question has been much discussed how far a settlement made after marriage in pursuance of an asserted parol agreement before marriage is valid, as against creditors in cases affected by the Statute of Frauds.   There is no doubt that such a settlement made in pursuance of a prior valid written agreement would be completely effectual against creditors. (a)   But the difficulty is, whether such a settlement executed in pursuance of a parol contract obligatory in foro conscientiæ ought to be protected when made, although it might not be capable of being enforced if not made.   It is certain that the mere performance of a moral duty even of the most meritorious nature has not been deemed sufficient to protect a voluntary conveyance, even in favor of a deeply injured party to whom it is designed to be a compensation for injustice and deceit.[3]   And hence the difficulty is increased of giving effect to a contract which in its own character, although founded upon an intrinsic valuable consideration, is yet in contemplation of law deemed to be a nudum pactum. There have been some struggles in Courts of Equity to maintain the efficacy of such a post-nuptial settlement against creditors, where it purported to be founded upon a parol agreement before marriage recited in the settlement.   But the strong inclination

[1] See 1 Eq. Abridg. 148 E.; 3 Stark on Evid. Pt. 4, pp. 615 to 622; Twyne's case, 3 Co. R. 80.

[2] See 1 Fonbl. Eq. B. 1, ch. 2, § 8, notes; Id. ch. 3, § 4; Id. ch. 4, §§ 12, 13, and notes.

[3] Gilham v. Locke, 9 Ves. 612; Lady Cox's case, 3 P. Will. 339; Priest v. Parrot, 2 Ves. 160.

(a) Concerning the sufficiency of a memorandum under the English statute see Skelton v. Cole, 1 DeG. & J. 587.

of these courts now seems to be to consider such a settlement
incapable of support from any evidence of a parol contract, since
it is in effect an attempt to supersede the Statute of Frauds, and
to let in all the mischiefs against which that statute was intended to guard the public generally, and especially to guard
creditors.[1] (a)

[1] See Atherley on Marr. Sett. ch. 9, p. 149. According to Mr. Cox's
Report of Dundas v. Dutens (2 Cox, R. 235), Lord Thurlow actually held
such a settlement valid, asserting that it could not be deemed fraudulent, and
that the cases, though they had gone a great way in treating settlements after
marriage as fraudulent, had never gone to such a length as that. Mr. Cox
having been of counsel in that case, his report is probably accurate. The point
is not quite so strongly stated in the report of the same case in 1 Ves. jr. 196.
But Lord Thurlow is there made in effect to say: ' If the husband made an
agreement before marriage that he would settle, and then in fraud of the
agreement got married, that he would be bound by the agreement; and he
thought there was a case in point; that it would be a kind of fraud against
which the court would relieve. If there was a *parol* agreement for a settlement upon marriage, after marriage a suit upon the ground of part performance would not do, because the statute is expressed in that manner. And he
then asked the question whether there was any case where in the settlement
the parties recite an agreement before marriage in which it has been considered as within the statute.' The distinction between cases of fraud and
a mere reliance upon a parol agreement for a settlement before marriage, and
in consideration thereof, is expressly taken in Lady Montacute v. Maxwell
(1 P. Will. 619, 620); s. c. Prec. in Ch. 526; 1 Str. R. 236; 1 Eq. Cas. Abr.
p. 19, pl. 4, where the Lord Chancellor said: ' In cases of fraud equity should
relieve even against the words of the statute, &c. But where there is no fraud,
only relying upon the honor, word, or promise of the defendant, the statute
making these promises void, equity will not interfere.' 1 Ves. jr. 199 note (a).
Post, § 768. This may be correct in cases of parol promises in consideration
of marriages, for the Statute of Frauds (29 Car. 2, ch. 3, § 4) expressly declares that no action shall be brought whereby ' to charge any person upon an
agreement made in consideration of marriage,' unless the agreement shall be
in writing and signed by the party to be charged therewith; for in such a
case it seems to have been held that the marriage is not a part-performance
to take the case out of the statute. See Montacute v. Maxwell, Ibid.; Dundas
v. Dutens, 1 Ves. jr. 196; s. c. 2 Cox, R. 235; Redding v. Wilkes, 3 Bro. Ch.
R. 400, 401; Taylor v. Buck, 1 Ves. R. 297, 298. All this seems perfectly
correct. But suppose the party to have fulfilled his parol promise after marriage, ought a Court of Equity to disturb the settlement in favor of creditors?
The marriage in such a case is not the less a valuable consideration because
a parol promise was relied on; and if relied on as valid, and the marriage is
had on the faith thereof, is not the non-fulfilment of it a fraud upon the other
party, whether intentional or not? Mr. Chancellor Kent, in Reade v. Livingston (3 John. Ch. R. 481), after reviewing the authorities, has come to a conclusion unfavorable to the validity of such a settlement. Sir William Grant,

(a) See Warden v. Jones, 2 DeG. & J. 76.

375. The same policy of affording protection to the rights of creditors pervades the provisions of the statute of 3d and 4th of William & Mary, ch. 14, respecting devises in fraud of creditors, and of the statutes made in the American States in pari materia.[1] There is an apparent anomaly in Equity Jurisprudence upon this subject not easily reconcilable with sound principles. The statute of William & Mary is confined to fraudulent devises, and therefore fraudulent conveyances, whether voluntary or not, are not reached by it. And hence it has been adjudged in England that if a man makes a conveyance of lands in his lifetime in order to defraud his creditors and dies, his bond creditors have no right to set aside the conveyance, for the statute (it is said) was only designed to secure such creditors against any imposition which might be supposed in a man's last sickness. But if he gave away his effects in his lifetime, this prevented the descent of so much to the heir, and consequently took away their remedy against the heir, who was liable only in respect to land descended. And as a bond is no lien whatever on lands in the hands of the obligor, much less can it be so when they are given away to a stranger.[2] This doctrine has been strongly questioned, and at the time when it was promulgated gave great dissatisfaction.[3] And hence we may see the reason why voluntary conveyances of lands cannot be set aside except by creditors who have reduced their debts to judgment before the death of the party; for until that time they constitute no lien on the land.[4]

376. In America however the policy of the Legislature has taken a much wider and more effectual range to attain its objects. Generally, if not universally, lands and other heredita-

in Randall v. Morgan (12 Ves. 67), seemed to think the question not settled. An anonymous case in Preced. in Ch. 101, is in favor of such a settlement. See also Ramsden v. Hylton, 2 Ves. 308, the remarks of Lord Hardwicke. See also Lavender v. Blackstone, 2 Lev. R. 146, 147; 1 Vent. 194; Guchenback v. Rose, 4 Watts & Serg. 546.

[1] See 1 Roberts on Wills, ch. 1, § 20; Jeremy on Eq. Jurisd. B. 3, Pt. 2, ch. 3, § 4, pp. 415, 416; 1 Fonbl. Eq. B. 1, ch. 4, § 14, note (i).

[2] Parslow v. Weaden, 1 Eq. Abridg. 14, Pl. 7; 1 Fonbl. Eq. B. 1, ch. 4, §§ 12, 14, and note (l).

[3] Ibid.; and Jones v. Marsh, Cas. T. Talb. 64.

[4] 1 Fonbl. Eq. B. 1, ch. 4, § 12; Gilb. Lex Prætoria, pp. 293, 294; Colman v. Croker, 1 Ves. jr. 160. See Bean v. Smith, 2 Mason, R. 282 to 285. See Mitf. Pl. Eq. by Jeremy, 126, 127; Jackson v. Caldwell, 1 Cowen, R. 622.

ments are with us made assets for the payment of debts as
auxiliary to the personal property of the deceased. And if the
party in his lifetime has fraudulently conveyed his estate with a
view to defeat his creditors upon his decease, the real assets are
subject to the same disposition as if no such conveyance had
been made.[1] The French law seems to have proceeded upon a
policy equally broad and salutary, and has enabled creditors in
cases of insolvency to rescind alienations either voluntary or in
fraud of their rights.[2]

377. These cases of interposition in favor of creditors being
founded upon the provisions of positive statutes, a question was
made at an early day whether they were exclusively cognizable
at law, or could be carried into effect also in equity. The
jurisdiction of Courts of Equity is now firmly established, for it
extends to cases of fraud whether provided against by statute or
not. And indeed the remedial justice of a Court in Equity, in
many cases arising under these statutes, is the only effectual one
which can be administered, as that of Courts of Law must often
fail from the want of adequate powers to reach or redress the
mischief.[3] (a)

378. There are other cases of constructive frauds against
creditors which the wholesome moral justice of the law has
equally discredited and denounced. We refer to that not un-
frequent class of cases in which upon the failure or insolvency of
their debtors some creditors have by secret compositions obtained
undue advantages, and thus decoyed other innocent and unsuspecting creditors into signing deeds of composition which they
supposed to be founded upon the basis of entire equality and
reciprocity among all the creditors, when in fact there was a
designed or actual imposition upon all but the favored few. The
purport of a composition or trust deed in cases of insolvency
usually is that the property of the debtor shall be assigned to

[1] See Drinkwater v. Drinkwater, 4 Mass. R. 354; Wildbridge v. Paterson,
15 Mass. R. 148.

[2] Pothier on Oblig. n. 153.

[3] Jeremy on Equity Jurisd. B. 3, Pt. 2, ch. 3, § 4, pp. 408, 409; Id. ch. 4;
1 Fonbl. Eq. B. 1, ch. 4, § 12, and note (c); Id. § 14, notes (i) and (k); 1
Eq. Abridg. 149, E. 6; White v. Hussey, Preced. Ch. 14.

(a) See Bartholomew v. McKinstry, 2 Allen, 448; Welsh v. Welsh, 105
Mass. 229; ante, § 352, and note.

trustees and shall be collected and distributed by them among the creditors according to the order and terms prescribed in the deed itself. And in consideration of the assignment, the creditors who become parties generally agree to release all their debts beyond what the funds will satisfy. Now it is obvious that in all transactions of this sort the utmost good faith is required ; and the very circumstance that other creditors of known reputation and standing have already become parties to the deed, will operate as a strong inducement to others to act in the same way. But if the signatures of such prior creditors have been procured by secret arrangements with them more favorable to them than the general terms of the composition deed warrant, those creditors really act, as has been said by a very significant although a homely figure, as decoy ducks upon the rest. They hold out false colors to draw in others to their loss or ruin.

379. In modern times the doctrine has been acted upon in Courts of Law as it has long been in Courts of Equity, that such secret arrangements are utterly void and ought not to be enforced even against the assenting debtor or his sureties or his friends.[1] There is great wisdom and deep policy in the doctrine ; and it is found in the best of all protective policy, that which acts by way of precaution rather than by mere remedial justice ; for it has a strong tendency to suppress all frauds upon the general creditors by making the cunning contrivers the victims of their own illicit and clandestine agreements. The relief is granted, not for the sake of the debtor, for no deceit or oppression may have been practised upon him, but for the sake of honest and humane and unsuspecting creditors. And hence the relief is granted equally whether the debtor has been induced to agree to the secret bargain by the threats or oppression of the favored creditors, or whether he has been a mere volunteer, offering his services and aiding in the intended deception. Such secret bargains are not only deemed incapable of being enforced or confirmed, but even money paid under them is recoverable back, as it has been obtained against the clear principles of public policy.[2]

[1] Chesterfield v. Janssen, 1 Atk. 352; 1 Ves. 155, 156; 3 P. Will. 131, Cox's note; Spurrett v. Spiller, 1 Atk. 105; Jackman v. Mitchell, 13 Ves. 581; Smith v. Bromley, Doug. 696, note; Jones v. Barkley. Id. 695, note; Cockshott v. Bennett, 2 T. Rep. 763; Jackson v. Lomas, 4 T. R. 166; Fawcett v. Gee, 3 Anst. 910.

[2] Smith v. Bromley, Doug. R. 696, note; Jones v. Barkley, Id. 695, note;

And it is wholly immaterial whether such secret bargains give to the favored creditors a larger sum, or an additional security or advantage, or only misrepresent some important fact; for the effect upon other creditors is precisely the same in each of these cases. They are misled into an act to which they might not otherwise have assented.[1]

380. For the like reasons any agreement made by an insolvent debtor with his assignee by which the estate of the insolvent is to be held in trust by the assignee to secure certain benefits for himself and his family, such as to pay certain annuities to himself and his wife out of the rents or proceeds of the property assigned, and to apply the surplus to the extinction of a debt due to the assignee, will be held void, and will be rescinded upon the ground of public policy whenever it comes before a Court of Equity, even though the suit happen to be at the instance of the insolvent himself. For it is a contrivance in fraud of creditors to which the assignee, who is or ought to be a trustee for them, is a party.[2]

381. In concluding this discussion so far as it regards creditors, it is proper to be remarked that although voluntary and other

Jackman v. Mitchell, 13 Ves. 581; Ex parte Sadler and Jackson, 15 Ves. 55; Mawson v. Stork, 6 Ves. 300; Yeomans v. Chatterton, 9 John. R. 294; Wiggin v. Bush, 12 John. R. 306.

[1] Ibid.; Eastabrook v. Scott, 3 Ves. 456; Constantine v. Blache, 1 Cox, 287; 1 Fonbl. Eq. B. 1, ch. 4, § 11, note (x); Cullingworth v. Lloyd, 2 Beav. R. 385, and the learned note of the Reporter, p. 390; Leicester v. Rose, 4 East R. 372. In Cullingworth v. Lloyd, Lord Langdale said: ' It must be observed that Edmund Grundy was winding up the business under a power of attorney, which enabled him to pay the debts by an equal pound rate; but it does not appear that there was any general meeting of the creditors or any agreement entered into by the creditors generally. The advertisements however show a proposition to the creditors at large to pay them all a composition on certain terms; and although every creditor was at liberty to refuse the composition, it is established by a series of decisions that a creditor cannot ostensibly accept such composition and sign the deed which expresses his acceptance of the terms, and at the same time stipulate for or secure to himself a peculiar and separate advantage which is not expressed upon the deed; and in the case of Leicester v. Rose (4 East, R. 372) it is stated by Mr. Justice Le Blanc that in the consideration of cases of this nature it is not material whether the agreement be entered into at a meeting of all the creditors assembled for the purpose, or impliedly by their affixing their signatures to the same deed carried round or produced to each separately, and signed by them; those who by executing the deed hold out that they come in under the general agreement are not permitted to stipulate for a further partial benefit to themselves.'

[2] McNeill v. Cahill, 2 Bligh, R. 228, Old Series.

conveyances in fraud of creditors are thus declared to be utterly void, yet they are so far only as the original parties and their privies and others claiming under them who have notice of the fraud are concerned. For bona fide purchasers for a valuable consideration, without notice of the fraudulent or voluntary grant, are of such high consideration that they will be protected, as well at law as in equity, in their purchases.[1] (a) It would be plainly inequitable that a party who has bona fide paid his money upon the faith of a good title should be defeated by any creditor of the original grantor who has no superior equity, since it would be impossible for him to guard himself against such latent frauds. The policy of the law therefore which favors the security of titles as conducive to the public good would be subverted if a creditor having no lien upon the property should yet be permitted to avail himself of the priority of his debt to defeat such a bona fide purchaser. Where the parties are equally meritorious and equally innocent, the known maxim of Courts of Equity is: 'Qui prior est in tempore, potior est in jure;' he is to be preferred who has acquired the first title.[2] This point however will naturally present itself in other aspects, when we come to the consideration of the general protection afforded by Courts of Equity to purchasers standing in such a predicament.

382. Other underhand agreements which operate as a fraud upon third persons may easily be suggested to which the same remedial justice has been applied. Thus where a father upon the marriage of his daughter entered into a covenant that upon his death he would leave her certain tenements, and that he would also by his will give and leave her a full and equal share with her brother and sister of all his personal estate, and he afterwards during his life transferred to his son a very large portion of his personal property, consisting of public stock, but retained the dividends for his life, it was held that the transfer was void, as a fraud upon the marriage articles; and the son was compelled

---

[1] Ante, §§ 64 c, 108, 139, 165; post, §§ 409, 434, 436.

[2] See Dame Burg's case, Moore, R. 602; Woodcock's case, 33, H. 6, 14; Predgers v. Langham, 1 Sid. R. 133; Wilson and Wormal's case, Godbolt, R. 161; Bean v. Smith, 1 Mason, R. 272 to 282; Anderson v. Roberts, 18 John. R. 513; Fletcher v. Peck, 6 Cranch, 133, 134; Daubeney v. Cockburn, 1 Meriv. 638, 639; Ledyard v. Butler, 9 Paige, R. 132.

(a) See Hubbell v. Currier, 10 Allen, 333.

to account for the same.[1] (a)   Covenants of this nature are proper in themselves, and ought to be honorably observed. They ought not to be, and indeed are not, construed to prohibit the father from making during his lifetime any dispositions of his personal property among his children more favorable to one than another.   But they do prohibit him from doing any acts which are designed to defeat and defraud the covenant.   He may if he pleases make a gift bona fide to a child ; but then it must be an absolute and unqualified gift which surrenders all his own interest, and not a mere reversionary gift which saves the income to himself during his own life.[2]

383. So if a friend should advance money to purchase goods for another, or to relieve another from the pressure of his necessities, and the other parties interested should enter into a private agreement over and beyond that with which the friend is made acquainted, such an agreement will be void at law as well as in equity ; for the friend is drawn in to make the advance by false colors held out to him, and under a supposition that he is acquainted with all the facts.[3]   So the guaranty of the payment of a debt procured from a friend upon the suppression by the parties of material circumstances is a virtual fraud upon him, and avoids the contract.[4]

384. Another class of constructive frauds of a large extent, and over which Courts of Equity exercise an exclusive and very salutary jurisdiction, consists of those where a man designedly or knowingly produces a false impression upon another, who is thereby drawn into some act or contract injurious to his own rights or interests.[5]   This subject has been partly treated before ; but it should be again brought under our notice in this connection.[6]   No man can reasonably doubt that if a party by the wilful

[1] Jones v. Martin, 3 Anst. R. 882; s. c. 5 Ves. 265. See also Randall v. Willis, 5 Ves. 261; 8 Brown, Parl. R. 242, by Tomlins; McNeill v. Cahill, 2 Bligh, R. 228. See Stocker v. Stocker, 4 Mylne & Craig, R. 95.

[2] Ibid.

[3] Jackson v. Duchaise, 3 T. R. 551.

[4] Pidcock v. Bishop, 3 B. & Cressw. 605; Smith v. Bank of Scotland, 1 Dow, Parl. R. 272; ante, § 215.

[5] Com. Dig. Chancery, 4 W. 28; Bean v. Smith, 2 Mason, R. 285, 286; 1 Madd. Ch. Pr. 256, 257; ante, § 191, &c.

[6] Ante, §§ 192 to 204.

(a) For a case of fraud on marital rights see McKeogh v. McKeogh, 4 L. R. Ir. Eq. 338.

suggestion of a falsehood, is the cause of prejudice to another who has a right to a full and correct representation of the fact, his claim ought in conscience to be postponed to that of the person whose confidence was induced by his representation. And there can be no real difference between an express representation and one that is naturally or necessarily implied from the circumstances.[1] (a)   The wholesome maxim of the law upon this subject is, that a party who enables another to commit a fraud is answerable for the consequences;[2] and the maxim so often cited, ' Fraus est celare fraudem,' is, with proper limitations in its application, a rule of general justice.

385. In many cases a man may innocently be silent; for, as has often been observed, ' Aliud est tacere, aliud celare.'   But in other cases a man is bound to speak out; and his very silence becomes as expressive as if he had openly consented to what is said or done, and had become a party to the transaction.[3] (b)

---

[1] 1 Fonbl. Eq. B. 1, ch. 3, § 4, notes (m) and (n); Sugden on Vendors, ch. 16.

[2] Bac. Max. 16.

[3] 1 Fonbl. Eq. B. 1, ch. 3, § 4, and notes (m) and (n); Savage v. Foster, 9 Madd. R. 35; Com. Dig. Chancery, 4 I. 3, 4 W. 28; Hanning v. Ferrers, 1 Eq. Abridg. 356, pl. 10; ante, §§ 204 to 220.

(a) See ante, pp. 204, 205, note on Misrepresentation.

(b) *Equitable Estoppel.* — The subject here introduced by the author, equitable estoppels, is made the occasion of some notes of cases near the end of this work, by the late Chief Justice Redfield. Ch. XLIV.

The doctrine of equitable estoppel, called also estoppel by conduct, though probably originating in equity (Evans v. Bicknell, 6 Ves. 174, 182), finds even more frequent expression in Courts of Law. This has been true ever since the decision in England in the well-known case of Pickard v. Sears, 6 Ad. & E. 469; though that was by no means the first case at law in which the doctrine was applied. Mildway v. Smith, 2 Wms. Saund. 343; Graves v. Key, 3 Barn. & Ad. 318, note; Heane v. Rogers, 9 Barn. & C. 586; Stephens v. Baird, 9 Cowen,

274; Welland Canal Co. v. Hathaway, 8 Wend. 480.

Equitable estoppel is merely the converse of the action of deceit, of which Pasley v. Freeman, 3 T. R. 51, is the typical example. See ante, p. 204, note. The same features enter into the estoppel that belong to the action for damages. The property held by the person claiming the benefit of the estoppel represents the damages in an action of deceit; that property can be held or not in accordance with rules of the same nature as those which govern the question whether an action of deceit for the misrepresentation might or might not be maintained if the situation were one for such an action. There must have been (1) a false representation, actual or implied, by the party to be estopped, made (2) with knowledge by him, actual or implied, of its falsity, to the

Thus if a man having a title to an estate which is offered for sale, and knowing his title, stands by and encourages the sale or does not forbid it, and thereby another person is induced to purchase the estate under the supposition that the title is good, the former, so standing by and being silent, will be bound by the sale; and neither he nor his privies will be at liberty to dispute the validity of the purchase.[1] So if a man should stand by and

---

[1] Ibid.; Storrs v. Barker, 6 John. Ch. R. 166, 169 to 172; Wendell v. Van Rensselaer, 1 John Ch. R. 354. Courts of law now act upon the same enlightened principles in regard to personal property, in the transfer of which no technical formalities usually intervene to prevent the application of them. Thus where it appeared that certain goods of the plaintiff were seized on an execution against a third person (in whose possession they were), and sold to the defendant, and the plaintiff made no objection to the sale, though he had

---

person claiming the benefit of the estoppel, or to some one under whom such person claims, that person (3) being ignorant of the facts and believing the representation to be true, and it must have been made (4) with intention, actual or implied, that the representation should be acted upon, and followed (5) by action upon the same with a material change of position. Stevens v. Dennett, 51 N. H. 324; People v. Brown, 67 Ill. 435; Martin v. Zellerbach, 38 Cal. 300, 315; Turnipseed v. Hudson, 50 Miss. 429; Bigelow, Estoppel, 484 (3d ed.).

The doctrine, like that of the action for damages, rests on the ground of fraud in the person to be estopped, or on his negligence in a situation where negligence was a breach of his duty towards the person whose action he has changed. See Slim v. Croucher, 1 DeG. F. & J. 518; s. c. 2 Giff. 37, as to negligence. It is apprehended that no estoppel can arise against a person whose conduct has been perfectly innocent; unless indeed there has been a warranty by him, such as the warranty of genuineness of the signature of the drawer of a bill by an acceptance thereof, which (with some qualifications) has the effect to preclude the acceptor from alleging a want of genuineness of such signature. Price v. Neal, 3 Burr. 1354; Ellis v. Ohio Life Ins. Co., 4 Ohio St. 628; National Bank v. Bangs, 106 Mass. 441; Bigelow, Estoppel, 437 et seq. (3d ed.). It may be doubted indeed if cases of warranty are proper cases of estoppel at all; but even these cases rest on the ground that the warranting party was, under the circumstances, bound to know the facts; as a prudent or careful man, he ought to have known them. Price v. Neal, supra. That a perfectly innocent misrepresentation as is here meant will not work an estoppel, see infra, § 386; Blake Crusher Co. v. New Haven, 46 Conn. 473; Gray v. Agnew, 95 Ill. 315; Follansbee v. Parker, 70 Ill. 11; Decorah Mill Co. v. Greer, 49 Iowa, 490; Hager v. Burlington, 42 Iowa, 661; Wright v. Newton, 130 Mass. 552; Charlestown v. County Commissioners, 109 Mass. 270; Hudson v. Densmore, 68 Ind. 391; Bell v. Elliott, 5 Blackf. 113; Smith v. Hutchinson, 61 Mo. 83. As to this and the further case of facts which ought to have been known see Bigelow, Estoppel, 519 et seq. (3d ed.), and ante, pp. 209, 210. And as to the estoppel of infants and married women, see infra, note at end of this section.

see another person as grantor execute a deed of conveyance of land belonging to himself, and knowing the facts should sign his name as a witness, he would in equity be bound by the conveyance.[1] (a)　So if a party having a title to an estate should stand by and allow an innocent purchaser to expend money upon the estate without giving him notice, he would not be permitted by a Court of Equity to assert that title against such purchaser, at least not without fully indemnifying him for all his expenditures.[2] The same rule has been applied, both at law and in equity, where the owner of chattels with a full knowledge of his own title has permitted another person to deal with these chattels as his own in his transactions with third persons who have bargained and acted in the confidence that the chattels were the property of the person with whom they dealt; (b) for in cases where one of two innocent persons must suffer a loss, and a fortiori in cases where one has misled the other, he who is the cause or occasion of that confidence by which the loss has been caused or occasioned ought to bear it.[3]　Indeed cases of this sort are viewed

full notice of it; it was held that the facts ought to be left to the jury to consider whether he had not assented to the sale and ceased to be owner of the property.　On this occasion Lord Denman, in delivering the opinion of the court, said: 'The rule of law is clear that, where one by his words or conduct wilfully causes another to believe in the existence of a certain state of things, and induces him to act on that belief, so as to alter his own previous position, the former is concluded from averring against the latter a different state of things as existing at the same time; and the plaintiff might have parted with his interest in the property by verbal gift or sale without any of those formalities that throw technical obstacles in the way of legal evidence.　And we think his conduct, in standing by and giving a sort of sanction to the proceedings under the execution, was a fact of such a nature that the opinion of the jury ought, in conformity to Heane v. Rogers (9 B. & Cressw. 586), and Graves v. Key (3 Barn. & Adol. 318, note (a),) to have been taken, whether he had not in point of fact ceased to be the owner.'　Pickard v. Sears, 6 Adolph. & Ellis, R. 474.

[1] Teasdale v. Teasdale, Sel. Cas. Ch. 59; 1 Fonbl. Eq. B. 5, ch. 3, § 4, note (m).

[2] See Cawdor v. Lewis, 1 Younge & Coll. 427; post, § 388.

[3] Nicholson v. Hooper, 4 Mylne & Craig, R. 179; Pickard v. Sears, 6 Adolph. & Ellis, 474, supra.

(a) Hale v. Skinner, 117 Mass. 474; Stevens v. Dennett, 51 N. H. 324.　See infra, § 390.

(b) Howland v. Woodruff, 60 N. Y. 73; Anderson v. Armistead, 69 Ill. 452; Stewart v. Munford, 91 Ill. 58; Bobbitt v. Shryer, 70 Ind. 513; Angell v. Johnson, 51 Iowa, 625; Morris v. Shannon, 12 Bush, 89; Chapman v. Pingree, 67 Maine, 198; Sebright v. Moore, 33 Mich. 92; Ford v. Loomis, ib. 121; Redman v. Graham, 80 N. Car. 231; Rumball v. Metropolitan Bank, 2 Q. B. D. 194.

with so much disfavor by Courts of Equity, that neither infancy nor coverture will constitute any excuse for the party guilty of the concealment or misrepresentation ; for neither infants nor femes covert are privileged to practise deceptions or cheats on other innocent persons.[1] (a)

[1] 1 Fonbl. Eq. B. 1, ch. 3, § 4; Savage v Foster, 9 Mod. R. 35; Evroy v. Nichols, 2 Eq. Abridg. 489; Clare v. Earl of Bedford, cited 2 Vern. 150, 151; Becket v. Cordley, 1 Bro. Ch. R. 357; Sugden on Vendors, ch. 16, p. 262, 9th ed.; post, § 387 to 390. See Bright v. Boyd, 1 Story, Cir. R. 478.

(a) This is rather too broadly stated. An infant is not liable in damages for a fraudulent representation that he is of age. Johnson v. Pye, 1 Sid. 258; s. c. 1 Keb. 913; Bartlett v. Wells, 1 Best & S. 836; Merriam v. Cunningham, 11 Cush. 40; Burley v. Russell, 10 N. H. 184; Conrad v. Lane, 26 Minn. 389. But see Kilgore v. Jordan, 17 Texas, 341. Nor is a married woman liable for a fraudulent representation that she is single. Liverpool Assoc. v. Fairhurst, 9 Ex. 422; Wright v. Leonard, 11 C. B. N. S. 258; Keen v. Coleman, 39 Penn. St. 299; Klein v. Caldwell, 91 Penn. St. 140.

Whether an infant or a married woman may be estopped in any case is not agreed. Neither, according to American authority, can be estopped by covenants or other contracts. Lowell v. Daniels, 2 Gray, 161, 168; Bemis v. Call, 10 Allen, 512, 517; Merriam v. Boston R. Co., 117 Mass. 241, 244; Unfried v. Heberer, 63 Ind. 67. But see Nelson v. Stocker, infra. And the same cases deny the application of the doctrine of estoppel to infants and to married women (not made sui juris) altogether. But there are many cases both at law and in equity in which the contrary is held, where there is no relation of contract between the parties to the estoppel in question. Sugden, Vendors, 743 (14th ed.); Overton v. Banister, 3 Hare, 503; Esron v. Nicholas, 1 DeG. & S. 118; Hall v. Timmons, 2 Rich. Eq.

120; Carpenter v. Carpenter, 10 C. E. Green, 194; Patterson v. Lawrence, 90 Ill. 174; Connolly v. Branstler, 3 Bush, 702; Rusk v. Fenton, 14 Bush, 490; Davis v. Zimmerman, 40 Mich. 24; Jones v. Kearney, 1 Dru. & War. 134; In re Lush, L. R. 4 Ch. 591; Nelson v. Stocker, 5 Jur. N. S. 262; s. c. 28 L. J. Ch. 751; Whittington v. Wright, 9 Ga. 23; Thompson v. Simpson, 2 Jones & L. 110. See also Stokeman v. Dawson, 1 DeG. & S. 90; Telegraph Co. v. Davenport, 97 U. S. 369; Bigelow, Estoppel, 513–517 (3d ed.). This appears to be the better view. There is just as good reason for applying the doctrine of estoppel against a person not sui juris, where to do so would not be equivalent to enforcing a contract made with such an one, as there is for allowing an action for trespass or trover. Indeed there was little authority for the broad dicta in Lowell v. Daniels, supra.

The estoppel has in England been applied to cases of contract. Nelson v. Stocker, supra. In the case cited an infant in contemplation of marriage represented himself to be of age (in ignorance as he claimed), and entered into a covenant by way of settlement upon his intended wife to pay to trustees named the agreed value of stock in business belonging to her, for her separate use and that of her children by a former marriage. He took possession of the stock and continued the business some years

386. In order however to justify the application of this cogent moral principle, it is indispensable that the party so standing by and concealing his rights should be fully apprized of them and should by his conduct or gross negligence encourage or influence the purchase; for if he is wholly ignorant of his rights, or the purchaser knows them, (a) or if his acts or silence or negligence do not mislead, or in any manner affect the transaction, there can be no just inference of actual or constructive fraud on his part.[1]

387. There are indeed cases where even ignorance of title will not excuse a party; for if he actually misleads the purchaser by his own representations although innocently, the maxim is justly applied to him, that where one of two innocent persons must suffer, he shall suffer who by his own acts occasioned the confidence and the loss.[2] Thus where a tenant in tail under a settlement encouraged a stranger to purchase an annuity charged on the land by his father's will from a younger brother, and said that he believed his brother had a good title, he was compelled to make good the annuity, notwithstanding his ignorance of his own title under the settlement, and of the annuity's being invalid; for under the circumstances of the case there was negligence on his part in not instituting proper inquiries, he having heard that there had been a settlement.[3] (b) So where a mother who was a tenant in tail, and absolute owner of a term of years,

---

[1] See 2 Hovend. on Frauds, ch. 22, p. 184.

[2] See Neville v. Wilkinson, 1 Bro. Ch. R. 546; 3 P. Will. 74, Mr. Cox's note; Scott v. Scott, 1 Cox, R. 378, 379, 380; Evans v. Bicknell, 6 Ves. 173, 182, 183, 184; Pearson v. Morgan, 2 Bro. Ch. R. 388; Com. Dig. Chancery, 4 W. 28.

[3] Hobbs v. Norton, 1 Vern. R. 136; 1 Eq. Abridg. 356, Pl. 8.

---

after he became of age, when his wife died. The trustees now required performance of the covenants, which he refused on the ground that he was an infant when the settlement was made. The court however refused to allow the defence, though partly on the ground of ratification. So too a married woman has been held bound by an election under a decree against her husband in a suit by her next friend, on the ground that the con- trary doctrine would enable her to turn her disability to a fraudulent advantage. Barrow v. Barrow, 4 Kay & J. 409.

(a) Supra, § 385, note.

(b) See also Slim v. Croucher, 1 DeG. F. & J. 518; s. c. 2 Giff. 37. But forgetfulness of title was held excusable under the circumstances, in Spencer v. Carr, 45 N. Y. 406. See Bigelow, Estoppel, 532–536 (3d ed.).

was present at a treaty for her son's marriage, and heard her son
declare that the term was to come to him after the death of the
mother, and she became a witness to a deed whereby the son
took upon himself to settle the reversion of the term expectant
on his mother's death upon the issue of the marriage, and the
mother did not insist upon more than a life estate therein, she
was held bound to make good the title, notwithstanding it was
insisted that she was ignorant that as tenant in tail she had an
absolute power to dispose of it.[1]

388. Another case illustrative of the same doctrine may be
put, arising from the expenditure of money upon another man's
estate through inadvertence or a mistake of title.[2] As for instance if a man supposing he has an absolute title to an estate
should build upon the land with the knowledge of the real owner,
who should stand by and suffer the erections to proceed without
giving any notice of his own claim, he would not be permitted
to avail himself of such improvements without paying a full
compensation therefor; for in conscience he was bound to disclose the defect of title to the builder.[3] Nay, a Court of Equity
might under circumstances go further, and oblige the real owner
to permit the person making such improvements on the ground
to enjoy it quietly and without disturbance.[4] (a)

---

[1] Hudson v. Cheyney, 2 Vern. R. 150; Storrs v. Barker, 6 John. Ch. R.
166, 168, 173, 174.   See also Beverley v. Beverley, 2 Vern. 133; Redman v.
Redman, 1 Vern. 347; Scott v. Scott, 1 Cox, R. 366, 378; Raw v. Potts, 2 Vern.
239; Savage v. Foster, 9 Mod. 35; 1 Madd. Ch. Pr. 210, 211; Bac. Abridg. I,
Fraud, B.; Raw v. Potts, Prec. Ch. 35; Brinckerhoff v. Lansing, 4 John. Ch.
R. 65, 70.

[2] Com. Dig. Chancery, 4, I. 3; ante, § 385; post, §§ 799 a, 799 b, 1237,
1238, 1239.

[3] Pillage v. Armitage, 12 Ves. 84, 85.   See Wells v. Banister, 4 Mass. R.
514; Bright v. Boyd, 1 Story, Cir. R. 478.

[4] East India Company v. Vincent, 2 Atk. 83; Davor v. Spurrier, 7 Ves.
231, 235; Jackson v. Cator, 5 Ves. 688; Storrs v. Barker, 6 John. Ch. R. 168,
169; Shannon v. Bradstreet, 1 Sch. & Lefr. 73.   The civil law carried its doctrine in cases of this sort much further; for in all cases where improvements
were bona fide made upon any estate by a purchaser or other person innocently, and under a belief that he was the true owner of the estate, he was
entitled to a compensation for the benefit actually conferred upon the estate.

(a) On the other hand one who
buys land from one not the owner,
with notice of the equities of the real
owner, is not entitled to payment for
improvements made without the express or implied consent of such
owner. Witt v. Grand Gros, 55 Wis.
376.

389. And upon the like principle if a person having a conveyance of land keeps it secret for several years, and knowingly suffers third persons afterwards to purchase parts of the same premises from his grantor, who remains in possession and is the reputed owner, and to expend money on the land without notice of his claim, he will not be permitted afterwards to assert his legal title against such innocent and bona fide purchasers. To allow him to assert his title under such circumstances would be to countenance fraud and injustice; and the conscience of the party is bound by an equitable estoppel, for in such a case it is emphatically true: 'Qui tacet, consentire videtur; qui potest et debet vetare, jubet si non vetat.'[1]

390. A more common case illustrative of the same doctrine is where a person having an incumbrance or security upon an estate suffers the owner to procure additional money upon the estate by way of lien or mortgage, concealing his prior incumbrance or security. In such a case he will be postponed to the second incumbrancer; for it would be inequitable to allow him to profit by his own wrong in concealing his claim, and thus lending encouragement to the new loan.[2] Thus if a prior mortgagee who knows that another person is about to lend money on the mortgaged property should deny that he had a mortgage, or should assert that it was satisfied, he would be postponed to the second mortgagee, who should lend his money on the faith of the representations so made.[3] So if a prior mortgagee whose mortgage is not registered should be a witness to a subsequent mortgage or conveyance of the same property, knowing the contents of the deed, and should not disclose his prior incumbrance, he

See Bright v. Boyd, 1 Story, Cir. R. 478, 494, 495, 496; post, §§ 799 a, 799 b, 1237, 1238, 1239.

[1] Wendell v. Van Rensselaer, 1 John. Ch. R. 354; 2 Inst. 146, 305; Branch's Max. 181, 182; Hanning v. Ferrers, 1 Eq. Abridg. 357; Storrs v. Barker, 6 John. Ch. R. 166, 168; Bright v. Boyd, 1 Story, Cir. R. 478; ante, § 385.

[2] Draper v. Borlau, 2 Vern. 370; Clare v. Earl of Bedford, cited 2 Vern. R. 150, 151; Mocatta v. Murgatroyd, 1 P. Will. 393, 394; Berrisford v. Milward, 2 Atk. 49; Beckett v. Cordley, 1 Bro. Ch. R. 353, 357; Evans v. Bicknell, 6 Ves. 173, 182, 183; Pearson v. Morgan, 2 Bro. Ch. R. 385, 388; Plumb v. Fluitt, 2 Anst. R. 432; 1 Fonbl. Eq. B. 1, ch. 3, § 4, note (u); Sugden on Vendors, ch. 16; Lee v. Munroe, 7 Cranch, 368.

[3] Lee v. Munroe, 7 Cranch, 366, 368.

would be postponed or barred of his title.[1] (*a*) Such transactions may well explain the maxim : ' Fraus est celare fraudem.' (*b*)

391. In all this class of cases the doctrine proceeds upon the ground of constructive fraud, or of gross negligence, which in effect implies fraud. And therefore where the circumstances of the case repel any such inference, although there may be some degree of negligence, yet Courts of Equity will not grant relief.[2] It has accordingly been laid down by a very learned judge that the cases on this subject go to this result only, that there must be positive fraud or concealment or negligence, so gross as to amount to constructive fraud.[3] And if the intention be fraudulent, although not exactly pointing to the object accomplished, yet the party will be bound to the same extent as if it had been exactly so pointed.[4]

392. Upon the same principles if a trustee should permit the title deeds of the estate to go out of his possession for the purpose of fraud, and intending to defraud one person he should defraud another, Courts of Equity will grant relief against him.[5] So if a bond should be given upon an intended marriage and to aid it, and the marriage with that person should afterwards go off, and another marriage should take place upon the credit of that bond, the bond would bind the party in the same way as it would if the original marriage had taken effect.[6]

393. What circumstances will amount to undue concealment

---

[1] Brinckerhoff *v.* Lansing, 4 John. Ch. R. 65.

[2] Tourle *v.* Rand, 2 Bro. Ch. R. 652; 1 Madd. Ch. Pr. 256, 257.

[3] Evans *v.* Bicknell, 6 Ves. 190, 191, 192; Merewether *v.* Shaw, 2 Cox, R. 124; Sugden on Vendors, ch. 16, pp. 262, &c. (9th edit.).

[4] Evans *v.* Bicknell, 6 Ves. 191, 192; Beckett *v.* Cordley, 1 Bro. Ch. R. 357; 1 Fonbl. Eq. B. 1, ch. 3, § 4; Plumb *v.* Fluitt, 2 Anst. 432, 440.

[5] Evans *v.* Bicknell, 6 Ves. 174, 191; Clifford *v.* Brooke, 12 Ves. 132.

[6] See Evans *v.* Bicknell, 6 Ves. 191.

(*a*) See supra, § 385.

(*b*) In like manner where a creditor puts the evidence of a lien of his into the debtor's hands, to enable the debtor to represent that it has been extinguished and gain further credit, the lien will be postponed to such credit if obtained. Perry-Herrick *v.* Attwood, 2 De G. & J. 21. This of course assumes that the party whose action has been affected had no notice of the facts. Comp. Young *v.* Cason, 48 Mo. 259. See also Taylor *v.* Great Indian Ry. Co., 5 Jur. N. S. 1087, where a person who had purchased shares of stock was held to have been affected with notice of fraud perpetrated by the selling broker by having seen the transfers in blank.

or to misrepresentation in cases of this sort is a point more fit for a treatise of evidence than for one of mere jurisdiction. But it has been held that a first mortgagee's merely allowing the mortgagor to have the title deeds, or a first mortgagee's witnessing a second mortgage deed, but not knowing the contents, or even concealing from a second mortgagee information of a prior mortgage when he made application therefor, the intention of the party applying to lend money not being made known, are not of themselves sufficient to affect the first mortgagee with constructive fraud.[1] There must be other ingredients to give color and body to these circumstances; for they may be compatible with entire innocence of intention and object.[2] Nothing but a voluntary, distinct, and unjustifiable concurrence on the part of the first mortgagee, in the mortgagor's retaining the title deeds, is now deemed a sufficient reason for postponing his priority. And in regard to the other acts above stated, they must

---

[1] Jeremy on Eq. Jurisd. B. 1, ch. 2, § 2, pp. 193, 194, 195; 1 Madd. Ch. Pr. 429 to 431; Id. 256; Plumb v. Fluitt, 2 Anst. R. 432; Breknell v. Evans, 6 Ves. R. 174; Cothay v. Sydenham, 2 Bro. Ch. R. 391; West v. Reid, 2 Hare, R. 249, 259. In this last case Mr. Vice-Chancellor Wigram said: ' In short let the doctrine of constructive notice be extended to all cases (it is in fact more confined, Plumb v. Fluitt, Breknell v. Evans, Cothay v. Sydenham and other cases), but let it be extended to all cases in which the purchaser has notice that the property is affected, or has notice of facts raising a presumption that it is so, and the doctrine is reasonable, though it may sometimes operate with severity. But once transgress the limits which that statement of the rule imposes, — once admit that a purchaser is to be affected with constructive notice of the contents of instruments not necessary to nor presumptively connected with the title, only because by possibility they *may* affect it (for that may be predicated of almost any instrument), and it is impossible, in sound reasoning, to stop short of the conclusion that every purchaser is affected with constructive notice of the contents of every instrument of the mere existence of which he has notice, — a purchaser must be presumed to investigate the title of the property he purchases, and may therefore be presumed to have examined every instrument forming a link, directly or by inference, in that title; and that presumption I take to be the foundation of the whole doctrine. But it is impossible to presume that a purchaser examines instruments not directly nor presumptively connected with the title, because they may by possibility affect it.' See Jackson v. Rowe, 2 Sim. & Stu. 472; Hodgson v. Dean, 2 Sim. & Stu. 221; and see also Jones v. Smith (per Lord Chancellor, on appeal), 7 Jur. 431.

[2] See 1 Fonbl. Eq. B. 1, ch. 3, § 4, and notes (*m*) and (*n*); Evans v. Bicknell, 6 Ves. 172, 182, 190, 191, 192; Ibbotson v. Rhodes, 2 Vern. R. 554; Plumb v. Fluitt, 2 Anst. R. 432; Barrett v. Weston, 12 Ves. 133; Berry v. Mutual Ins. Co., 2 John. Ch. R. 603, 608; Tourle v. Rand, 2 Bro. Ch. R. 650, and Mr. Belt's note; Peter v. Russell, 2 Vern. 726, and Mr. Raithby's note (1).

be done under circumstances which show a like concurrence and co-operation in some deceit upon the second mortgagee.[1]

394. It is curious to trace how nearly the Roman law approaches that of England on this subject; thus demonstrating that if they had not a common origin, at least each is derived from that strong sense of justice which must pervade all enlightened communities. It is an acknowledged principle of the Roman Jurisprudence, that a creditor who consents to the sale, donation, or other alienation of the property of his debtor which is pledged or mortgaged for his debt, cannot assert his title against the purchaser unless he reserves it; for his loss of title cannot under such circumstances be asserted to be to his prejudice, since it is by his consent; and otherwise the purchaser would be deceived into the bargain. 'Creditor, qui permittit rem venire, pignus dimittit.'[2] 'Si consensit venditioni creditor, liberatur hypotheca.'[3] 'Si in venditione pignoris consenserit creditor, vel ut debitor hanc rem permutet, vel donet, vel in dotem det, dicendum erit pignus liberari, nisi salva causa pignoris sui consensit, vel venditioni, vel cæteris.'[4] But as to what shall be deemed a consent the Roman law is very guarded. For it is there said that we are not to take for a consent of the creditor, to an alienation of the pledge, the knowledge which he may have of it; nor the silence which he may keep after he knows it; as if he knows that his debtor is about selling a house which is mortgaged to him, and he says nothing about it. But in order to deprive him of his right, it is necessary that it should appear by some act that he knows what is doing to his prejudice and consents to it; or that there is some ground to charge him with dishonesty for not having declared his right when he was under an obligation to do it, by which the purchaser was misled. Thus if upon the alienation the debtor declares that the property is not incumbered, and the creditor knowingly signs the contract as a party or witness, thereby rendering himself an accomplice in the false affirmation, he will be bound by the alienation. But the mere signature of the creditor as a witness to a contract

---

[1] 1 Fonbl. Eq. B. 1, ch. 3, § 4, note (n); Peter v. Russell, 2 Vern. 726, and Mr. Raithby's note (1); 1 Madd. Ch. Pr. 256, 257.

[2] Dig. Lib. 50, tit. 17, l. 158.

[3] Dig. Lib. 20, tit. 6, l. 7; Pothier, Pand. Lib. 20, tit. 6, art. 2, n. 21.

[4] Dig. Lib. 20, l. 4, § 1.

of alienation will not of itself bind him, unless there are circumstances to show that he knew the contents, and acted dis-
ingenuously and dishonestly by the purchaser.[1] 'Non videtur
consensisse creditor, si, sciente eo, debitor rem vendiderit, cum
ideo passus est venire, quod sciebat, ubique pignus sibi durare.
Sed si subscripserit forte in tabulis emptionis, consensisse videtur,
nisi manifeste appareat deceptum esse.'[2]

395. Another class of constructive frauds consists of those
where a person purchases with full notice of the legal or equitable title of other persons to the same property. In such cases
he will not be permitted to protect himself against such claims,
but his own title will be postponed, and made subservient to
theirs.[3] It would be gross injustice to allow him to defeat the
just rights of others by his own iniquitous bargain. He becomes
by such conduct particeps criminis with the fraudulent grantor;
and the rule of equity as well as of law is, 'Dolus et fraus nemini
patrocinari debent.'[4] And in all such cases of purchases with
notice Courts of Equity will hold the purchaser a trustee for
the benefit of the persons whose rights he has thus sought to
defraud or defeat.[5] Thus if title deeds should be deposited as a
security for money (which would operate as an equitable mortgage), and a creditor knowing the facts should subsequently
take a mortgage of the same property, he would be postponed
to the equitable mortgage of the prior creditor, and the notice
would raise a trust in him to the amount of such equitable mort-

[1] 1 Domat, B. 3, tit. 1, § 7, art. 15, and Strahan's note.

[2] Dig. Lib. 20, tit. 6, l. 8, § 15; Pothier, Pand. Lib. 20, tit. 6, art. 2,
n. 26, 27.

[3] Com. Dig. Chancery, 4 O. 1; Sugden on Vendors, ch. 16, §§ 5, 10; ch. 17,
§§ 1, 2. An admitted exception (which is more fully adverted to in a subsequent note) is the case of a dowress. A person purchasing with a notice of
her title may yet by getting in a prior legal title or term protect himself
against her title. This is an anomaly; but it is now so firmly established that
it cannot be shaken. See Swannock v. Lefford, Ambler, R. 6, and Mr. Blunt's
note, and the note of Lord Hardwicke's judgment in Co. Litt. 208 a; Radnor
v. Vanderberdy, Show. Parl. Cas. 69; Maundrell v. Maundrell, 10 Ves. 271,
272; Winn v. Williams, 5 Ves. 130; Male v. Smith, Jacob, R. 497; ante,
§ 57 a; post, § 410, note.

[4] 2 Fonbl. Eq. B. 2, ch. 6, § 3; 3 Co. R. 78.

[5] Ibid.; 1 Fonbl. Eq. B. 2, ch. 6, § 2; Murray v. Ballou, 1 John. Ch. R.
566; Murray v. Finster, 2 John. Ch. R. 158; Maundrell v. Maundrell, 10
Ves. 260, 261, 270.

gage.[1] (a)   So if a mortgagee with notice of a trust should get
a conveyance from the trustee in order to protect his mortgage,
he would not be allowed to derive any benefit from it; but he
would be held to be subject to the original trust in the same
manner as the trustee.   For it has been significantly said, that
although a purchaser may buy an incumbrance, or lay hold on
any plank to protect himself, yet he shall not protect himself by
the taking of a conveyance from a trustee with notice of the
trust; for he thereby becomes a trustee, and he must not, to get
a plank to save himself, be guilty of a breach of trust.[2]

396. The same principle applies to cases of a contract to sell
lands or to grant leases thereof.   If a subsequent purchaser has
notice of the contract, he is liable to the same equity, and stands
in the same place, and is bound to do the same acts, which the
person who contracted and whom he represents would be bound
to do.[3]

397. It is upon the same ground that in countries where the
registration of conveyances is required in order to make them
perfect titles against subsequent purchasers, if a subsequent purchaser has notice at the time of his purchase of any prior unregistered conveyance, he shall not be permitted to avail himself of
his title against that prior conveyance.[4] (b)   This has been long
the settled doctrine in Courts of Equity; and it is often applied
in America, although not in England, in Courts of Law, as a just

[1] Birch v. Ellames, 2 Anst. 427; Plumb v. Fluitt, 2 Anst. R. 433.

[2] Saunders v. Dehaw, 2 Vern. R. 271; 2 Fonbl. Eq. B. 2, ch. 6, § 2; post,
§§ 413, 414, 421.   See also Foster v. Blackstone, 1 Mylne & Keen, 297; Timson
v. Ramsbottom, 2 Keen, R. 35.

[3] Taylor v. Stibbert, 2 Ves. jr. 438; Davis v. Earl of Strathmore, 16 Ves.
419, 428, 429; Underwood v. Courtown, 2 Sch. & Lefr. 64; Macreath v. Symmons, 15 Ves. 350; Jeremy on Eq. Jurisd. B. 1, ch. 2, § 2, p. 192, &c.; Com.
Dig. Chancery, 4 C. 1.

[4] Sugden on Vendors, ch. 16, §§ 5, 10; ch. 17, §§ 1, 2; 1 Fonbl. Eq. B. 1,
ch. 1, § 3, note (h); 1 Madd. Ch. Pr. 260; Bushnell v. Bushnell, 1 Sch. &
Lefr. 99 to 103; Eyre v. Dolphin, 2 B. & Beatt. 302; Blades v. Blades, 1 Eq.
Abridg. 358; Worseley v. De Mattos, 1 Burr. 474, 475; Forbes v. Dennister,
1 Bro. Par. Cas. 425; Sheldon v. Coxe, 2 Eden, R. 224; Le Neve v. Le Neve,
3 Atk. 646; s. c. 1 Ves. 64; Amb. R. 436; Chandos v. Brownlow, 2 Ridg.
Parl. R. 428; Bean v. Smith, 2 Mason, R. 285; Coppinger v. Fernyhough, 2
Bro. Ch. R. 291; Sugden on Vendors, ch. 16.

(a) See Agra Bank v. Barry, 6 Ir.   H. 685; Rolland v. Hart, L. R. 6 Ch.
L. R. Eq. 128.   678.
(b) Benham v. Keane, 1 Johns. &

exposition of the Registry Acts.[1] The object of all acts of this sort is, to secure subsequent purchasers and mortgagees against prior secret conveyances and incumbrances. But where such purchasers and mortgagees have notice of any prior conveyance, it is impossible to hold that it is a secret conveyance by which they are prejudiced. On the other hand the neglect to register a prior conveyance is often a matter of mistake or of overweening confidence in the grantor; and it would be a manifest fraud to allow him to avail himself of the power by any connivance with others to defeat such prior conveyance.[2] The ground of the doctrine is (as Lord Hardwicke has remarked) plainly this : ' That the taking of a legal estate after notice of a prior right makes a person a mala fide purchaser ; and not that he is not a purchaser for a valuable consideration in every other respect. This is a species of fraud and dolus malus itself ; for he knew the first purchaser had the clear right of the estate ; and after knowing that, he takes away the right of another person by getting the legal title.[3] And this exactly agrees with the definition of the civil law of dolus malus.' [4] ' Now if a person does not stop his hand but gets the legal estate when he knows the equity was in another, machinatur ad circumveniendum.' [5]

398. This doctrine, as to postponing registered to unregistered conveyances upon the ground of notice, has broken in upon the policy of the Registration Acts in no small degree ; for a registered conveyance stands upon a different footing from an ordinary conveyance. It has indeed been greatly doubted whether courts ought ever to have suffered the question of notice to be agitated as against a party who has duly registered his conveyance. But they have said that fraud shall not be permitted to prevail. There is however this qualification upon the doc-

[1] Doe d. Robinson v. Alsop, 5 B. & Ald. 142; Norcross v. Widgery, 2 Mass. R. 506; Bigelow's Dig. Conveyance, P. and note; Jackson v. Sharp, 9 John. R. 163; Jackson v. Burgott, 10 John. R. 457; Jackson v. West, 10 John. R. 466; Johnson's Dig. Deed, VIII.; Farnsworth v. Childs, 4 Mass. R. 637. See, as to the Registry Acts, 4 Kent, Comm. Lect. 58, pp. 168 to 194, 4th edit.

[2] Le Neve v. Le Neve, 3 Atk. 646; 1 Ves. 64; Ambler, 436, and Blunt's note, ibid.; Belt's Suppl. 50; Bushnell v. Bushnell, 1 Sch. & Lefr. 98, 99, 100, 101, 102; Eyre v. Dolphin, 2 Ball & Beatt. 299, 300, 302; 1 Madd. Ch. Pr. 260, 261; Toulman v. Steere, 3 Meriv. R. 209, 224.

[3] Le Neve v. Le Neve, 3 Atk. 646, and cases before cited.

[4] Dig. Lib. 4, tit. 3, l. 2; Id. Lib. 2, tit. 14, § 9.

[5] Ibid.

trine, that it shall be available only in cases where the notice is so clearly proved as to make it fraudulent in the purchaser to take and register a conveyance in prejudice to the known title of the other party.[1]

399. What shall constitute notice, in cases of subsequent purchasers, is a point of some nicety, and resolves itself sometimes into matter of fact, and sometimes into matter of law.[2] (a) Notice may be either actual and positive, or it may be implied and constructive.[3] Actual notice requires no definition; for in that case knowledge of the fact is brought directly home to the party. Constructive notice is in its nature no more than evidence of notice the presumption of which is so violent that the court will not even allow of its being controverted.[4] (b)

400. An illustration of this doctrine of constructive notice is,

[1] Wyatt v. Barwell, 19 Ves. 439; Sugden on Vendors, ch. 16, §§ 5, 10. There are some cases in which notice does not affect a purchaser. Thus where an estate is limited to such uses as A shall appoint, and a judgment is obtained against him, and he then appoints the estate to B, who has notice of the judgment, B will, notwithstanding the notice, take the estate free from the lien of the judgment; for he takes under the deed of appointment and of course by a title prior to the judgment. Skeeles v. Shearley, 8 Sim. 156, 157; s. c. 3 Mylne & Craig, 112. See, as to the effect of this notice by an assignee of an equitable interest, to the legal holder of the property to give priority of right over prior assignees who have given no notice, Timson v. Ramsbottom, 2 Keen, R. 35; Foster v. Blackstone, 1 Mylne & Keen, R. 297; post, § 421 a, § 1035 a. (c)

[2] Com. Dig. Chancery, 4 C. 2. See Day v. Dunham, 2 John. Ch. R. 190; Jones v. Smith, 1 Hare, R. 43; post, §§ 1035, 1047, 1057.

[3] Sugden on Vendors, ch. 17, §§ 1, 2. In a treatise like the present it is impracticable to do more than to glance at topics of this nature. The learned reader will find full information on the subject in treatises which profess to examine it at large. See Sugden on Vendors, ch. 16 and 17 (9th edit.); Newland on Contracts, ch. 36, pp. 504 to 516.

[4] Plumb v. Fluitt, 2 Anst. R. 438, Per Eyre, C. B; 4 Kent, Comm. Lect. 58, pp. 179, 180 (4th edit.). See also Jones v. Smith, 1 Hare, R. 43; Meux v.

(a) The burden of proof is on him who asserts notice. Bartlett v. Varner, 56 Ala. 580.

(b) Hewitt v. Loosemore, 9 Hare, 449; Rogers v. Jones, 8 N. H. 264; Griffith v. Griffith, 1 Hoff. 153; Ogilvie v. Jeaffreson, 6 Jur. N. S. 970; Gibson v. Ingo, 6 Hare, 112; Farrow v. Rees, 4 Beav. 18; Taylor v. Baker, 5 Price, 306; Penny v. Watts, 1 Macn.

& G. 150; Kennedy v. Green, 3 Mylne & K. 718; Warren v. Sweet, 31 N. H. 332; Cambridge Bank v. Delano, 48 N. Y. 326; Acer v. Wescott, 46 N. Y. 384; Woodworth v. Paige, 5 Ohio St. 70.

(c) Chadwick v. Turner, L. R. 1 Ch. 310; Rolland v. Hart, L. R. 6 Ch. 678.

where the party has possession or knowledge of a deed, under which he claims his title, and it recites another deed which shows a title in some other person; there the court will presume him to have notice of the contents of the latter deed, and will not permit him to introduce evidence to disprove it.[1] (b)

Bell, 1 Hare, R. 73. In Jones v. Smith, 1 Hare, R. 43, Mr. Vice-Chancellor Wigram examined the cases as to constructive notice very largely, and upon that occasion said: 'It is indeed scarcely possible to declare, a priori, what shall be deemed constructive notice, because unquestionably that which would not affect one man may be abundantly sufficient to affect another. But I believe I may with sufficient accuracy for my present purpose, and without danger, assert that the cases in which constructive notice has been established resolve themselves into two classes: First, cases in which the party charged has had actual notice that the property in dispute was in fact charged, incumbered, or in some way affected, and the court has thereupon bound him with constructive notice of facts and instruments to a knowledge of which he would have been led by an inquiry after the charge, incumbrance, or other circumstance affecting the property of which he had actual notice; and secondly, cases in which the court has been satisfied from the evidence before it that the party charged had designedly abstained from inquiry from the very purpose of avoiding notice. How reluctantly the court has applied and within what strict limits it has confined the latter class of cases, I shall presently consider. The proposition of law upon which the former class of cases proceeds is not that the party charged had notice of a fact or instrument which in truth related to the subject in dispute without his knowing that such was the case, but that he had actual notice that it did so relate. The proposition of law upon which this second class proceeds is not that the party charged had incautiously neglected to make inquiries, but that he had designedly abstained from such inquiries for the purpose of avoiding knowledge, — a purpose which, if proved, would clearly show that he had a suspicion of the truth and a fraudulent determination not to learn it. If, in short, there is not actual notice that the property is in some way affected, and no fraudulent turning away from a knowledge of the facts which the res gestæ would suggest to a prudent mind; if mere want of caution, as distinguished from fraudulent and wilful blindness, is all that can be imputed to the purchaser, — then the doctrine of constructive notice will not apply; there the purchaser will in equity be considered, as in fact he is, a bona fide purchaser without notice. This is clearly Sir Edward Sugden's opinion (Vend. & Purch. Vol. 3, pp. 471, 472, Ed. 10); and with that sanction I have no hesitation in saying it is mine also.' (a)

[1] Ibid.; Cuyler v. Brandt, 2 Cain. Cas. in Err. 326; 2 Fonbl. Eq. B. 2, ch. 6, § 3, note (m); Eyre v. Dolphin, 2 B. & Beatt. 301, 302.

(a) Affirmed on appeal. 1 Phil. 244. See Kettlewell v. Watson, 21 Ch. D. 685, 706, where Fry, J., says that the notice derived from shutting one's eyes to facts is attributable to a design not to know any more, and is therefore an indication that the person knew that of which he desired to avoid the evidence.

(b) A person is of course supposed to know the contents of instruments executed or held by himself. Rogers v. Place, 35 Ind. 577; Bacon v. Markley, 46 Ind. 116; New Albany R. Co.

And generally it may be stated as a rule on this subject that where a purchaser cannot make out a title but by a deed which leads him to another fact, he shall be presumed to have knowledge of that fact.[1](a)   So the purchaser is in like manner sup-

---

[1] 2 Fonbl. Eq. B. 3, ch. 3, § 1, note (b); Mertins v. Jolliffe, Ambler, R. 311, 314; Marr v. Bennett, 2 Ch. Cas. 246; Sugden on Vendors, ch. 16; 2 Fonbl. Eq. B. 2, ch. 6, § 3, and note (m); Com. Dig. Chancery, 4 C. 2.   This doctrine however is to be received with some qualifications.   For if a man purchases an estate under a deed which happens to relate also to other lands not comprised in that purchase, and afterwards he purchases the other lands, to which an apparent title is made, independent of that deed, the former notice of the deed will not itself affect him in the second transaction; for he was not bound to carry in his recollection those parts of a deed which had no relation to the particular purchase he was then about to make, nor to take notice of more of the deed than affected his then purchase.   Hamilton v. Royal, 2 Sch. & Lefr. 327.   In short he is bound to take notice of those things only in the deed which affect his present purchase, not any future purchase.   Mertins v. Jolliffe, Ambler, R. 311.

---

v. Fields, 10 Ind. 187; Russell v. Branham, 8 Blackf. 277; Starr v. Bennett, 5 Hill, 303; Hawkins v. Hawkins, 50 Cal. 558.   This is said to be true of documents referred to in such instruments, though the contents are misrecited.   McGavock v. Drery, 1 Cold. 265.   But that needs qualification.   One who can read only with difficulty may rely upon the reading of the instrument by the opposite party, and perhaps even upon a statement of its contents.   See Keller v. Equitable Ins. Co., 28 Ind. 170.   The same would a fortiori be true if a relation of confidence existed between the parties.

(a) Upon the general doctrine of notice see Kennedy v. Green, 3 Mylne & K. 699; Jones v. Williams, 24 Beav. 47; Ware v. Egmont, 4 DeG. M. & G. 460; Willis v. Vallette, 4 Met. (Ky.) 186; Tiernan v. Thurman, 14 B. Mon. 279; Shorter v. Frazer, 64 Ala. 74.   Some special illustrations of the rule and its limitations may be given.

Upon an agreement to sell part of the vendor's land the vendor and purchaser entered into mutual covenants prohibiting building, except in a speci-

fied manner, on the unsold part.   It was held that a subsequent owner of the unsold part, claiming through the grantor by means of deeds one of which referred to the deed containing the prohibitory clause, but not to the clause, was bound in equity by the prohibition.   Coles v. Sims, 5 DeG. M. & G. 1.   But though a deed disclosing a trust is in a party's chain of title, and would have to be shown in defence of an action at law, the defence of purchaser without notice will avail in equity where knowledge was fraudulently withheld.   Pitcher v. Rawlins, L. R. 7 Ch. 259; s. c. 11 Eq. 53.

In a case before Vice-Chancellor Wood it appeared that a purchaser of shares was induced to make the purchase by representations in the prospectus which were false and fraudulent; but though the prospectus referred to the articles of association, where the truth appeared, it was held that the purchaser was not bound to go 'upon an errand of inquiry whether the statements were correct or not.'   Smith v. Reese Mining Co., 12 Jur. N. s. 616; s. c. L. R. 2 Eq. 264; L. R. 2 Ch. 604;

posed to have knowledge of the instrument under which the party with whom he contracts, as executor, or trustee, or ap-

L. R. 4 H. L. 64. But see an intimation to the contrary by Lord Romilly in the case of Ex parte Briggs, 12 Jur. N. s. 322; s. c. L. R. 1 Eq. 483. In Jones v. Williams, 24 Beav. 47, the Master of the Rolls says of the much-quoted case of Kennedy v. Green, 3 Mylne & K. 699 : ' It is always the first case cited in all causes depending on questions of notice; but in truth it rarely has any application to any one of them.'

The rule in regard to the consequences of abstaining from inquiry after actual knowledge of a fact does not depend upon the existence of a fraudulent motive, such as wilfully refusing to pursue inquiry or shutting one's eyes to the result. What Wigram, V. C., says in Jones v. Smith, 1 Hare, 43, as quoted by the author, supra, with the similar statements of Fry, J., in Kettlewell v. Watson, 21 Ch. D. 685, 706, does not apply, as Vice-Chancellor Wigram shows, to the case of actual knowledge of a fact which if pursued would lead to knowledge of the fact in question. If a man is put upon inquiry he must inquire; and it will be no excuse for him that his failure was due merely to heedlessness or to stupidity. But if he makes reasonable inquiry, and is deterred or put off the track by a false answer, he will be excused if it be such as might delude a man of average intelligence, as where the party is told by the person putting him on inquiry that a deed has no effect upon the particular property about which he is dealing. Williams v. Williams, 17 Ch. D. 437, 442. See Wilson v. Hart, L. R. 1 Ch. 463; Jones v. Smith, 1 Hare, 43; s. c. 1 Phil. 244. But see Patman v. Harland, 17 Ch. D. 353, 356, explaining Carter v. Williams, L. R. 9 Eq. 678. The party however can seldom say that if he had inquired, he would have got a false answer. Jones v. Williams,

24 Beav. 47; Ware v. Egmont, 4 DeG. M. & G. 460. But where it is reasonably certain that inquiry would lead to nothing, it seems that the party is not to be treated as having notice by failing to inquire. Carter v. Williams, supra; Patman v. Harland, supra.

So too if the fact upon which the supposed notice is founded would not naturally lead, upon inquiry on the part of a prudent man, to the particular fact in question, it is apprehended that the doctrine of constructive notice will not apply; see e. g. Bassett v. Daniels, 136 Mass. 547; and this too though the fact is clear and definite, — something more than rumor or idle talk. Thus a party should not be charged with notice of an advertisement in a newspaper, under ordinary circumstances, in the absence of statutory provision, merely because he is a subscriber to or a regular reader of the newspaper. Watkins v. Peck, 13 N. H. 360; Clark v. Ricker, 14 N. H. 44; Lincoln v. Wright, 23 Penn. St. 76. But see King v. Paterson R. Co., 5 Dutch. 82. The rule as to such a case may clearly be varied by circumstances ; but it cannot be applied where it would be unreasonable. Indeed in any case the question whether the doctrine of notice applies must depend upon all the facts taken together, in connection with the subject-matter, the situation of the parties, means of knowledge, and any other circumstances bearing upon the supposed necessity of inquiry. Strong v. Jackson, 123 Mass. 60.

See further as to the rule of notice Briggs v. Taylor, 28 Vt. 180 (where the subject is considered at length); Wormald v. Maitland, 35 L. J. Ch. 69; Briggs v. Rice, 130 Mass. 50; Warren v. Swett, 31 N. H. 332; Cambridge Bank v. Delano, 48 N. Y. 326; Baynard v. Norris, 3 Gill, 468;

pointee, derives his power.[1] (a) Indeed the doctrine is still
broader; for whatever is sufficient to put a party upon inquiry
(that is, whatever has a reasonable certainty as to time, place,
circumstances, and persons), is, in equity, held to be good notice
to bind him.[2] (b) Thus notice of a lease will be notice of its
contents.[3] So if a person should purchase an estate from the
owner, knowing it to be in the possession of tenants, he is
bound to inquire into the estate which these tenants have; and
therefore he is affected with notice of all the facts as to
their estates.[4] (c)

[1] 2 Fonbl. Eq. B. 2, ch. 6, § 3, note (m); Id. B. 3, ch. 3, § 1, note (b);
Mead v. Lord Orrery, 3 Atk. 238; Draper's Company v. Yardloy, 2 Vern. R.
662; Daniel v. Kent, 1 Vern. R. 319; Jackson v. Nealy, 10 John. R. 374;
Sugden on Vendors, ch. 17, § 2.

[2] 2 Fonbl. Eq. B. 2, ch. 6, § 3, and note (m); B. 3, ch. 3, § 1, and note
(b); Smith v. Low, 1 Atk. 490; Ferrars v. Cherry, 2 Vern. R. 384; Daniels
v. Davison, 16 Ves. 250; Howarth v. Deem, 1 Eden, R. 351, and Mr. Eden's
note, ib. ; Sterry v. Arden, 1 John. Ch. R. 267; Surman v. Barlow, 2 Eden,
R. 167; Parker v. Brooke, 9 Ves. 583; Green v. Slayter, 4 John. Ch. R. 38;
Eyre v. Dolphin, 2 B. & Beatt. 301, 302; Com. Dig. Chancery, 4 C. 2.

[3] Hall v. Smith, 14 Ves. 426.

[4] Taylor v. Stibbert, 2 Ves. jr., 440; Daniels v. Davison, 16 Ves. 249, 252;
Smith v. Low, 1 Atk. 489; Allen v. Anthony, 1 Meriv. R. 262; 2 Fonbl. Eq.
B. 2, ch. 6, § 3, and note (m); Meux v. Maltby, 2 Swanst. 281; Chesterman

---

Dahl v. Page, 2 Green, Ch. 143 ; Russell v. Ranson, 76 Ill. 167; Watt v.
Scofield, Ib. 261; Dickey v. Lyon, 19
Iowa, 544; ante, p. 215, note on Misrepresentation; Bigelow, Fraud, 288–
300. The doctrine of course is not
confined to the case of notice of the
contents of a document, as the cases
cited show. See note at end of the
present section; also Watt v. Scofield,
supra; Willis v. Vallette, 4 Met. (Ky.)
186; Attorney-Gen. v. Smith, 31 Mich.
359; Connihan v. Thompson, 111 Mass.
270; Fielden v. Slater, L. R. 7 Eq.
523; Carter v. Williams, L. R. 9 Eq. 678.

(a) One who takes as a pledge
stock standing in the name of ' A. B.
Trustee ' must ascertain the nature
and limitations of the trust at his
peril. Shaw v. Spencer, 100 Mass.
382; Comp. Ashton v. Atlantic Bank,
3 Allen, 217; 2 Perry, Trusts, §§ 814,
815.

(b) See Coy v. Coy, 15 Minn.
119.

(c) And where a person buys property with a visible state of things
which could not legally exist without
the property being subject to some
burden, he is taken to have notice of
the extent and nature of that burden.
Allen v. Seckham, 11 Ch. D. 790, 795,
Brett, L. J. See further Hendricks v.
Kelly, 64 Ala. 388 ; Seager v. Cooley,
44 Mich. 14 ; Daily v. Kastell, 56 Wis.
444; Baynard v. Norris, 3 Gill. 468;
Dahl v. Page, 2 Green, Ch. 143;
James v. Lichfield, L. R. 9 Eq. 51.
A tenant is held fixed with notice of
all covenants of his landlord. Feilden
v. Slater, L. R. 7 Eq. 523. But see
Carter v. Williams, L. R. 9 Eq. 678.
The condition of the premises may be
notice of a right of way. Davies v.
Sears, L. R. 7 Eq. 427.

400. *a.* But in a great variety of cases it must necessarily be matter of no inconsiderable doubt and difficulty to decide what circumstances are sufficient to put a party upon inquiry. Vague and indeterminate rumor or suspicion is quite too loose and inconvenient in practice to be admitted to be sufficient.[1] (*a*) But there will be found almost infinite gradations of presumption between such rumor or suspicion and that certainty as to facts which no mind could hesitate to pronounce enough to call for further inquiry, and to put the party upon his diligence. No general rule can therefore be laid down to govern such cases. Each must depend upon its own circumstances.[2] There is no case which goes the length of saying that a failure of the utmost circumspection shall have the same effect of postponing a party as if he were guilty of fraud, or wilful neglect, or had

v. Gardner, 5 John. Ch. R. 29; Hanbury *v.* Litchfield, 2 Mylne & Keen, 629, 632, 633. In this last case the Master of the Rolls (Sir C. C. Pepys) said: ‘ It is true that where a tenant is in possession of the premises a purchaser has implied notice of the nature of his title. But if at the time of his purchase the tenant in possession is not the original lessee but merely holds under a derivative lease, and has no knowledge of the covenant contained in the original lease, it has never been construed want of due diligence in the purchaser, which is to fix him with implied notice, if he does not pursue his inquiries through every derivative lessee until he arrives at the person entitled to the original lease, which can alone convey to him information of the covenant.’ See also Flagg *v.* Mann, 2 Sumner, R. 486, 554, 555.

[1] Sugden on Vendors, ch. 17; Wildgrove *v.* Wayland, Godb. R. 147; Jolland *v.* Stainbridge, 3 Ves. 478.

[2] See 2 Fonbl. Eq. B. 3, ch. 3, § 1, note (*b*); Eyre *v.* Dolphin, 2 B. & Beatt. 301; Hine *v.* Dodd, 2 Atk. 275. See Jones *v.* Smith, The English Jurist, May 27, 1845, p. 431; Flagg *v.* Mann, 2 Sumner, R. 489, 549, 560.

(*a*) Maul *v.* Rider, 59 Penn. St. 167; Richardson *v.* Smith, 11 Allen, 134; Colquitt *v.* Thomas, 8 Ga. 258; James *v.* Drake, 3 Sneed, 340. It is not necessary however that notice should come from a party to the transaction or from his agent. It is enough if it is of a kind to create belief. Rawbone's Bequest, 3 Kay & J. 300. Smith *v.* Smith, 2 Cromp. & M. 231; Lloyd *v.* Banks, L. R. 3 Ch. 488; s. c. 4 Eq. 222; In re Tichener, 35 Beav. 317; Martel *v.* Somers, 26 Texas, 551. But see In re Brown, L. R. 5 Eq. 88. It is said that general reputation and belief to the knowledge of a person should put him upon inquiry. James *v.* Drake, 3 Sneed, 340.

As to the time at which one must receive notice to affect him in equity, it is in general sufficient if it be received before he has parted with his money or placed himself in a position where he cannot resist the payment, as where the rights of third persons have intervened. Collinson *v.* Lister, 20 Beav. 356; s. c. 7 DeG. M. & G. 634; Bennett *v.* Titherington, 6 Bush, 192; Wells *v.* Morrow, 38 Ala. 125; Wilson *v.* Hunter, 30 Ind. 466.

positive notice.[1]   And although a mistake of law upon the construction of a deed or contract will not alone discharge a purchaser from the legal effects of notice of such deed or contract,
yet there may be a case of such doubtful equity, under the circumstances, that it ought not to be enforced against such a
purchaser.[2]   The mere fact that the assignees of an insolvent
debtor have made a sale of the estate at auction, under circumstances of negligence on their part, will not affect the purchaser with notice, as such circumstances are collateral to the
question of title.   Even if before he takes the conveyance he
have notice of such circumstances, yet if he have purchased
bona fide, his title is not necessarily voidable. (a)   But the
question must depend in a great measure upon this, whether
the conduct of the assignee be such a gross and palpable breach
of duty as ought justly to avoid the sale.[3] (b)

401. How far the registration of a conveyance in countries
where such registration is authorized and required by law
shall operate as constructive notice to subsequent purchasers
by mere presumption of law, independent of any actual notice,
has been much discussed both in England and in America.   It
is not doubted in either country that a prior conveyance, duly
registered, operates to give full effect to the legal and equitable
estate conveyed thereby, against subsequent conveyances of the
same legal and equitable estate.[4]   But the question becomes
important as to other collateral effects, such as defeating the
right of tacking of mortgages, and other incidentally accruing
equities between the different purchasers.   For if the mere registry in such cases, without actual knowledge of the convey-

[1] Plumb v. Fluitt, 2 Anst. R. 433, 440.   See Dey v. Dunham, 2 John. Ch.
R. 190, 191.

[2] Cordwill v. Mackrill, 2 Eden, R. 344, 348; Parker v. Brooke, 9 Ves. 583,
588; 2 Fonbl. Eq. B. 2, ch. 6, § 3, and note; Bovey v. Smith, 1 Vern. 144,
149; Walker v. Smallwood, Amb. R. 676.

[3] Borell v. Dunn, 2 Hare, R. 450 to 455.

[4] Wrightson v. Hudson, 2 Eq. Abr. 609, Pl. 7.

(a) Compare Hill v. Ahern, 135
Mass. 158; Ricker v. Ham, 14 Mass.
137; Clapp v. Leatherbee, 18 Pick.
131.   In the first of these cases this
distinction is taken on a question of
priority of mortgages; the test applied
being whether the later one was taken
by the plaintiff as a real and not as a
feigned mortgage.

(b) Attorney-Gen. v. Stephens, 6
DeG. M. & G. 111, 148; Montefiore v.
Browne, 7 H. L. Cas. 241, 269.

ance, operates as constructive notice, it shuts out many of those equities which otherwise might have an obligatory priority.[1] It has been truly remarked that there is a material difference between actual notice and the operation of the Registry Acts. Actual notice may bind the conscience of the parties; the operation of the Registry Acts may bind their title, but not their conscience.[2]

402. In England the doctrine seems at length to be settled that the mere registration of a conveyance shall not be deemed constructive notice to subsequent purchasers, but that actual notice must be brought home to the party, amounting to fraud.[3](a) The subject certainly is attended with no inconsiderable difficulty. Some learned judges have expressed a doubt whether Courts of Equity ought not to have said that in all cases of a public registry which is a known depository for conveyances, a subsequent purchaser ought to search or be bound by notice of the registry in the same way as he would be by a decree in equity or by a judgment at law.[4] Other learned judges have intimated a different opinion; assigning as a reason, that if the registration of the conveyance should be held constructive notice, it must be notice of all that is contained in the conveyance and then subsequent purchasers would be bound to inquire after the contents, the inconveniences of which cannot but be deemed exceedingly great.[5] The question seems first to have arisen in a case of the tacking of mortgages about the year 1730; and it was then decided by Lord Chancellor King that the mere registration of a second mortgage did not prevent a prior mortgagor from tacking a third mortgage when he had no actual notice of the existence of the second mortgage.[6] This decision has ever since been steadily adhered to,

[1] Newland on Contracts, ch. 36, p. 508.

[2] Underwood v. Courtown, 2 Sch. & Lefr. 66. See Latouche v. Dunsany, 1 Sch. & Lefr. 137; Dey v. Dunham, 2 John. Ch. R. 190, 191.

[3] Wyatt v. Barwell, 19 Ves. 435; Jolland v. Stainbridge, 3 Ves. 477; Com. Dig. Chancery, 4 C. 1.

[4] Morecock v. Dickens, Amb. R. 480; Hine v. Dodd, 2 Atk. 275; Parkhurst v. Alexander, 1 John. Ch. R. 399; Sugden on Vendors, ch. 16, 17.

[5] Latouche v. Dunsany, 1 Sch. & Lefr. 157; Underwood v. Courtown, 2 Sch. & Lefr. 64, 66; Pentland v. Stokes, 2 B. & Beatt. 75.

[6] Bedford v. Backhouse, 2 Eq Abridg. 615, Pl. 12; S. P. Wrightson v. Hudson, 2 Eq. Abridg. 609, Pl 7; Cator v. Cooley, 1 Cox, R. 182; Wiseman v. Westland, 1 Y. & Jerv. 117.

(a) See now 45 & 46 Vict. ch. 39, § 3.

perhaps more from its having become a rule of property than from a sense of its intrinsic propriety.

403. In America however the doctrine has been differently settled ; and it is uniformly held that the registration of a conveyance operates as constructive notice to all subsequent purchasers of any estate legal or equitable in the same property.[1] The reasoning upon which this doctrine is founded is the obvious policy of the Registry Acts, the duty of the party purchasing under such circumstances to search for prior incumbrances, the means of which search are within his power, and the danger (so forcibly alluded to by Lord Hardwicke) of letting in parol proof of notice or want of notice of the actual existence of the conveyance.[2] The American doctrine certainly has the advantage of certainty and universality of application ; and it imposes upon subsequent purchasers a reasonable degree of diligence only in examining their titles to estates.[3]

404. But this doctrine as to the registration of deeds being constructive notice to all subsequent purchasers is not to be understood of all deeds and conveyances which may be de facto registered, but of such only as are authorized and required by law to be registered, and are duly registered in compliance with law. If they are not authorized or required to be registered, or the registry itself is not in compliance with the law, the act of registration is treated as a mere nullity ; and then the subsequent purchaser is affected only by such actual notice as would amount to a fraud.[4] (b)

---

[1] Parkhurst v. Alexander, 1 John. Ch. R. 394.

[2] Hine v. Dodd, 2 Atk. 275.

[3] Johnson v. Strong, 2 John. R. 510; Frost v. Beekman, 1 John. Ch. R. 288, 299; s. c. 18 John. R. 544; Parkhurst v. Alexander, 1 John. Ch. R. 394. The better opinion also seems to be that the registration of an equitable mortgage or title or incumbrance is notice to a subsequent purchaser as much as if it were a legal security or title. Parkhurst v. Alexander, 1 John. Ch. R. 398, 399, and the cases there cited.(a)

[4] Ibid.; Underwood v. Courtown, 2 Sch. & Lefr. 68; Latouche v. Dunsany, 1 Sch. & Lefr. 157; Astor v. Wells, 4 Wheat. R. 466; Frost v. Beekman, 1 John. Ch. R. 300; Lessee of Heister v. Fortner, 2 Binn. R. 40; Farmer's Loan Trust Co. v. Maltby, 8 Paige, R. 361.

(a) Digman v. McCollum, 47 Mo. 372.

(b) So of the registration of an unacknowledged or defectively acknowledged deed, where acknowledgment is a statutory prerequisite to recording. Stevens v. Hampton, 46 Mo. 404 ; Bishop v. Schneider, Ib. 472 ; Wood

405. It is upon similar grounds that every man is presumed to be attentive to what passes in the courts of justice of the State or sovereignty where he resides. And therefore a purchase made of property actually in litigation, pendente lite, for a valuable consideration and without any express or implied notice in point of fact, affects the purchaser in the same manner as if he had such notice, and he will accordingly be bound by the judgment or decree in the suit.[1] (a)

[1] Com. Dig. Chancery, 4 C. 3 and 4; 2 Fonbl. Eq. B. 2, ch. 6, § 3, note (n); Sorrell v. Carpenter, 2 P. Will. 482; Worsley v. Earl of Scarborough, 3 Atk. 392; Bishop of Winchester v. Paine, 11 Ves. 194; Garth v. Ward, 2 Atk. 175; Mead v. Lord Orrery, 3 Atk. 242; Gaskeld v. Durdin, 2 B. & Beatt. 169; Moore v. Macnamara, 2 B. & Beatt. 186; Murray v. Ballou, 1 John. Ch. R. 566.

v. Cochrane, 39 Vt. 544; Polk v. Cosgrove, 4 Biss. 437. So of a deed not sealed. Racouillat v. Sansevain, 32 Cal. 376; Racouillat v. Rene, Ib. 450. See St. John v. Conger, 40 Ill. 535. The record of a deed from a grantor whose title deed is not on record is not constructive notice to subsequent purchasers from the record owner. Ely v. Wilcox, 20 Wis. 523. See Maul v. Rider, 59 Penn. St. 167. So also a mortgagee is not affected by the subsequent recording of deeds by his mortgagor. George v. Wood, 9 Allen, 80; Cooper v. Bigley, 13 Mich. 463; Ely v. Wilcox, supra. Indeed the record of an instrument is notice, not to all the world, but only to those who are bound to search for it. Maul v. Rider, supra. Misdescription of premises in some particulars however does not destroy the effect of recording as notice. Partridge v. Smith, 2 Biss. 133.

One who has purchased land at void judicial sale may still be entitled to claim for improvements made by him, notwithstanding the fact that the probate records would have shown that the sale was not legal, if he was not a party to or connected with the probate suit, and did not know or have ground to suspect that the sale would not be legal. Cole v. Johnson,

53 Miss. 94; Canal Bank v. Hudson, 111 U. S. 66, 80. See Green v. Biddle, 8 Wheat. 1, 79.

(a) See Tilton v. Cofield, 93 U. S. 163; Lewis v. Mew, 1 Strobh. Eq. 180; Price v. White, 1 Bail. Eq. 244; Haven v. Adams, 8 Allen, 363; Allen v. Morris, 5 Vroom, 159; McPherson v. Housel, 2 Beasl. 301; Davis v. Christian, 15 Gratt. 1; Hall v. Jack, 32 Md. 253; Porter v. Barclay, 18 Ohio St. 546; Allen v. Atchison, 26 Texas, 616; August v. Seeskind, 6 Cold. 166; In re Barned's Banking Co., L. R. 2 Ch. 171. Mere service of subpœna is not lis pendens if the case goes no further; but when the bill or declaration is filed, the rule of lis pendens relates to the service of the writ. Sugden, Vendors, 534 (Perkins's ed.). And filing a bill without subpœna is lis pendens. Drew v. Norbury, 9 Ir. Eq. 171, 176; Leitch v. Wells, 48 N. Y. 585.

In accordance with the author's rule during the pendency of a suit in equity for a specific estate in land any interest a third person may acquire in it without sanction of court will be bound by the decree, regardless of his prior right or title. Thus a claimant, no matter how good his title, shall not by his own act acquire possession, held adversely by the defendant in a suit to subject the prop-

406. Ordinarily it is true that the decree of a court binds only the parties and their privies in representation or estate. But he who purchases during the pendency of a suit is held bound by the decree that may be made against the person from whom he derives title. The litigating parties are exempted from taking any notice of the title so acquired, and such purchaser need not be made a party to the suit.[1] Where there is a real and fair purchase without any notice, the rule may operate very hardly.[2] But it is a rule founded upon a great public policy; for otherwise alienations made during a suit might defeat its whole purpose, and there would be no end to litigation.[3] And hence arises the maxim, 'Pendente lite, nihil innovetur;' the effect of which is, not to annul the conveyance, but only to render it subservient to the rights of the parties in the litigation.[4] As to the rights of these parties, the conveyance is treated as if it never had any existence, and it does not vary them.[5] (a) A lis pendens however being only a general notice of an equity to all the world, it does not affect any particular person with a fraud, unless such person had also special notice of the title in dispute in the suit.[6] If therefore the right to relief in equity depends upon any supposed co-operation in a fraud, it is indispensable to establish an express or direct notice of the fraudulent act. And although, as we have

[1] Bishop of Winchester v. Paine, 11 Ves. 197; Metcalf v. Pulvertoft, 2 V. & Beam. 205.

[2] 2 P. Will. 483; Story on Equity Plead. §§ 156, 351; 2 Story on Equity Jurisp. § 908.

[3] Co. Litt. 224, b; Metcalf v. Pulvertoft, 2 V. & Beam. 199; Gaskeld v. Durdin, 2 B. & Beatt. 169.   [4] Ibid.

[5] Ibid.; Bishop of Winchester v. Paine, 11 Ves. 197; Murray v. Ballou, 1 John. Ch. R. 566; Murray v. Finster, 2 John. Ch. R. 155.

[6] Mead v. Lord Orrery, 3 Atk. 242, 243; 2 Fonbl. Eq. B. 2, ch. 6, § 3, note (n); Id. B. 3, § 1, note (b).

erty to the payment of his debts, so as to compel the plaintiff to bring another suit. Chapman v. Gibbs, 51 Ala. 502; Creighton v. Paine, 2 Ala. 158; Kershaw v. Thompson, 4 Johns. Ch. 609; Murray v. Ballou, 1 Johns. Ch. 566.

An injunction may be had to restrain a sale, though the purchaser would take pendente lite. London Banking Co. v. Lewis, 21 Ch. D. 490 (C. A.); Spiller v. Spiller, 3 Swab. 556.

(a) It matters not, it seems, that lands in suit are located in another county than that of the litigation. Wickliffe v. Breckenridge, 1 Bush, 427. As to the duration of the incapacity by virtue of lis pendens, see Dudley v. Witter, 46 Ala. 664. And see 2 & 3 Vict. ch. 11, § 7; 30 & 31 Vict. ch. 47, § 2.

seen, a registered deed will be postponed to a prior unregistered deed where the second purchaser had actual notice of the first purchase, yet the doctrine has never been carried to the extent of making a lis pendens constructive notice of the prior unregistered deed, but actual notice is required.[1] (a)

407. In general a decree is not constructive notice to any persons who are not parties or privies to it, and therefore other persons are not presumed to have notice of its contents. But a person who is not a party to a decree, if he has actual notice of it will be bound by it, and if he pays money in opposition to it, he will be compelled to pay it again.[2] And a purchaser having notice of a judgment will be bound by it, although it has not been docketed so as to secure the priority of lien and satisfaction attached to judgments.[3] (b)

408. To constitute constructive notice it is not indispensable that it should be brought home to the party himself. It is sufficient if it is brought home to the agent, attorney, or counsel of the party; for in such cases the law presumes notice in the principal, since it would be a breach of trust in the former not to communicate the knowledge to the latter.[4] (c)   But in all these

[1] Wyatt v. Barwell, 19 Ves. 439.

[2] 2 Fonbl. Eq. B. 2, ch. 6, § 3, note (n); Harvey v. Montague, 1 Vern. R. 57; Sugden on Vendors, ch. 17, §§ 1, 2.

[3] Davis v. Earl of Strathmore, 16 Ves. 419.

[4] Com. Dig. Chancery, 4 C. 5 and 6; 2 Fonbl. Eq. B. 2, ch. 6, § 4; Sheldon v. Cox, 2 Eden, R. 224, 228; Jennings v. Moore, 2 Vern. R. 609; Sugden on Vendors, ch. 17; Astor v. Wells, 4 Wheat. R. 466.

(a) The doctrine of lis pendens is not applied to the injury of rights previously acquired, as by a mortgage. See e. g. Wiggin v. Heywood, 118 Mass. 514.

(b) But see now 27 & 28 Vict. ch. 112.

(c) The presumption of communication does not, according to some cases, arise where the agent's or partner's interest is opposed to communication, as where he has obtained knowledge by his own fraud. See Williamson v. Barbour, 9 Ch. D. 529, 535; Cave v. Cave, 15 Ch. D. 639; Kettlewell v. Watson, 21 Ch. D. 685, 705; Wilde v. Gibson, 1 H. L. Cas. 605; Dillaway v. Butler, 135 Mass. 479. But see the same cases for qualification of the rule; and see especially Ogilvie v. Jeaffreson, 6 Jur. N. S. 970. In other cases it has been held immaterial that it was against the agent's interest to communicate to his principal. Espin v. Pemberton, 5 Jur. N. S. 157; s. c. 28 L. J. Ch. 311. Still where the agent would have to communicate his own fraud, notice to the principal can hardly be imputed. Kennedy v. Green, 3 Mylne & K. 699; In re European Bank, L. R. 5 Ch. 358. See also Hunt v. Elmes, 7 Jur. N. S. 200. The rule of care and watchfulness both on the particular occasion and in the selection of the agent is

cases notice to bind the principal should be notice in the same transaction or negotiation; for if the agent, attorney, or counsel was employed in the same thing by another person or in another business or affair and at another time, since which he may have forgotten the facts, it would be unjust to charge his present principal on account of such a defect of memory.[1] (a). It was significantly observed by Lord Hardwicke that if this rule were not adhered to, it would make the titles of purchasers and mortgagees depend altogether upon the memory of their counsellors and agents, and oblige them to apply to persons of less eminence as counsel, as being less likely to have notice of former transactions.[2] (b)

408 a. Although the general rule that notice to the agent is notice to the principal is well established, yet there are some nice cases which may arise in the application of the rule. Thus for example suppose the case of a corporation acting by a board of directors, or trustees, or other officers or agents, the question may arise whether notice to one of the board of facts unknown to all the others will bind the corporation, or whether the notice should be offered to the board itself or a majority of them. The authorities on this point do not seem entirely in harmony.[3] (c)

[1] Com. Dig. Chancery, 4 C. 5 and 6, and cases before cited; Fitzgerald v. Falconberg, Fitz Gibb. R. 211.

[2] Warwick v. Warwick, 3 Atk. 294; Worsley v. Earl of Scarborough, 3 Atk. 392; Lowther v. Carlton, 2 Atk. 242, 392. But notice to a solicitor in one transaction, which is closely followed by and connected with another, so as clearly to give rise to a presumption that the prior transaction was present in his mind, and that he could not have forgotten it, is constructive notice to his client. A fortiori, if it is clear that at the time of the second transaction the first was fully in his mind. Hargraves v. Rothwell, 2 Keen, R. 154, 159.

[3] See Story on Agency, §§ 140 a, 140 b; Commercial Bank v. Cunningham, 24 Pick. R. 278.

declared in Ogilvie v. Jeaffreson, supra. See Hart v. Farmers' Bank, 33 Vt. 272. By this rule if the principal employ an agent known by him to have an interest against making communication, he will be bound by notice to the agent; secus if the principal was not at fault.

(a) McCormick v. Wheeler, 36 Ill. 114. See however Wythes v. Labouchere, 3 DeG. & J. 593; Ogilvie v. Jeaffreson, 6 Jur. N. s. 970.

(b) Jones v. Bamford, 21 Iowa, 217. Compare Saffron Building Soc. v. Rayner, 14 Ch. D. 406. So where both parties employ the same counsel. Rolland v. Hart, L. R. 6 Ch. 678; 1 Perry, Trusts, § 222.

(c) See Whelan v. McCreary, 64 Ala. 319, 329; Tirrell v. Branch Bank of Mobile, 12 Ala. 502; Porter v. Bank of Rutland, 19 Vt. 410; In re European Bank, L. R. 5 Ch. 358; Perry v. Porter, 124 Mass. 338.

409. The doctrine which has been already stated in regard to the effect of notice is strictly applicable to every purchaser whose title comes into his hands affected with such notice. But it in no manner affects any such title derived from another person, in whose hands it stood free from any such taint. Thus a purchaser with notice may protect himself by purchasing the title of another bona fide purchaser for a valuable consideration without notice; for otherwise such bona fide purchaser would not enjoy the full benefit of his own unexceptionable title.[1] (a)　Indeed he would be deprived of the marketable value of such a title, since it would be necessary to have public notoriety given to the existence of a prior incumbrance, and no buyer could be found, or none except at a depreciation equal to the value of the incumbrance. For a similar reason if a person who has notice sells to another who has no notice and is a bona fide purchaser for a valuable consideration, the latter may protect his title although it was affected with the equity arising from notice in the hands of the person from whom he derived it; for otherwise no man would be safe in any purchase, but would be liable to have his own title defeated by secret equities of which he could have no possible means of making a discovery.

410. This doctrine in both of its branches has been settled for nearly a century and a half in England; and it arose in a case in which A purchased an estate with notice of an incumbrance, and then sold it to B who had no notice, and B afterwards sold it to C who had notice; and the question was whether the incumbrance bound the estate in the hands of C. The then Master of the Rolls thought that although the equity of the incumbrance was gone while the estate was in the hands of B, yet it was revived upon the sale to C. But the Lord Keeper reversed the decision; and held that the estate in the hands of C was discharged of the incumbrance notwithstanding the notice of A and C.[2]　This doctrine has ever since been adhered to as an indis-

---

[1] 1 Fonbl. Eq. B. 2, ch. 6, § 2, note (i); Mitf. Plead. by Jeremy (1827), p. 278 (4th edit.); Com. Dig. Chancery, 4 A. 10; 4 I. 3; 4 I. 4; 4 I. 11.

[2] Harrison v. Forth, Prec. Ch. 61; s. c. 1 Eq. Abridg. Notice, A. 6, p. 331.

(a) See Perry, Trusts, § 222; Bartlett v. Verner, 56 Ala. 580; Horton v. Smith, 8 Ala. 73; Daniel v. Sorrels, 9 Ala. 436.

pensable muniment of title.[1] (a)   And it is wholly immaterial
of what nature the equity is, whether it is a lien, or an incumbrance, or a trust, or any other claim ; for a bona fide purchase
of an estate for a valuable consideration purges away the equity
from the estate in the hands of all persons who may derive title
under it, with the exception of the original party, whose conscience stands bound by the violation of his trust and meditated
fraud.   But if the estate becomes revested in him, the original
equity will re-attach to it in his hands.[2] (b)

[1] 2 Fonbl. Eq. B. 2, ch. 6, § 2, note (i); Brandlyn v. Ord, 1 West, R. 512;
s. c. 1 Atk. 571; Lowther v. Carlton, 2 Atk. 242; Ferrars v. Cherry, 2 Vern.
383; Mertins v. Jolliffe, Ambl. R. 313; Sweet v. Southcote, 2 Bro. Ch. R. 66; Mc-
Queen v. Farquhar, 11 Ves. 477, 478; Bracken v. Miller, 4 Watts & Serg. 102.

[2] 2 Fonbl. Eq. B. 2, ch. 6, § 2, note (i), and cases before cited; and Kennedy v. Daly, 1 Sch. & Lefr. 379; Bumpus v. Plattner, 1 John. Ch. R. 219;
Jackson v. Henry, 10 John. R. 185; Jackson v. Given, 8 John. R. 573;
Demarest v. Wyncoop, 3 John. Ch. R. 147; Alexander v. Pendleton, 8 Cranch,
R. 462; Ingram v. Pelham, Ambl. R. 153; Fitzsimmons v. Ogden, 7 Cranch,
218.   The rule adopted in equity in favor of bona fide purchasers without
notice not to grant any relief against them is founded, as we have seen, upon
a general principle of public policy. Wallwyn v. Lee, 9 Ves. R. 24. It is
not however absolutely universal, for it has been broken in upon in two
classes of cases. In the first place it is not allowed in favor of a judgment
creditor, who has no notice of the plaintiff's equity. This appears to proceed
upon the principle that such judgment creditor shall be deemed entitled
merely to the same rights as the debtor had, as he comes in under him, and
not through him; and upon no new consideration like a purchaser. Burgh v.
Burgh, Rep. Temp. Finch. 28. In the second place it is not allowed in favor
of a bona fide purchaser without notice against the claims of a dowress as
such. Williams v. Lambe, 3 Brown, Ch. Rep. 264. This last exception is
apparently anomalous, and has been established upon the distinction that the
protection of a bona fide purchaser does not apply against a party plaintiff seeking relief upon the ground of a legal title (such as dower is), but only against
a party plaintiff seeking relief upon an equitable title. The propriety of the distinction has been greatly questioned. It has been impugned by Lord Rosslyn
in Jerrard v. Saunders (2 Ves. jr. 454). The cases of Burlare v. Cook (2 Freem.
R. 24) and Parker v. Blythmore (2 Eq. Abridg. 79, pl. 1) are against it. Rogers
v. Leele (2 Freeman, R. 84), and the above case of Williams v. Lambe are in
its favor. Mr. Sugden doubts the correctness of the distinction. Sugden on

(a) Bell v. Twilight, 18 N. H.
159, 164; Webster v. Van Steen-
bergh, 46 Barb. 211. See Cromwell
v. Sac, 96 U. S. 51; Bigelow's Bills
and Notes, 439. It seems that a tenant in common with notice cannot
avail himself of his co-tenant's want
of notice, on deriving title from him
by partition. Blatchley v. Osborn, 33

Conn. 226. In New Jersey an assignee
of a mortgage takes subject to equities, though without notice. Conover
v. Van Mater, 3 C. E. Green, 481.
Contra in Massachusetts. Welch v.
Priest, 8 Allen, 165.

(b) See Ely v. Wilcox, 26 Wis.
91; Church v. Rutland, 64 Penn. St.
432.

411. Indeed purchasers of this sort are so much favored in equity that it may be stated to be a doctrine now generally established, that a bona fide purchaser for a valuable consideration without notice of any defect in his title at the time of his purchase may lawfully buy in any statute, mortgage, or other incumbrance upon the same estate for his protection. (a) If he can defend himself by any of them at law, his adversary will have no help in equity to set these incumbrances aside; for equity will not disarm such a purchaser, but will act upon the wise policy of the common law, to protect and quiet lawful possessions and strengthen such titles.[1] We shall have occasion hereafter in various cases to see the application of this doctrine.

412. And this naturally leads us to the consideration of the equitable doctrine of tacking, as it is technically called; that is, uniting securities given at different times so as to prevent any intermediate purchasers from claiming a title to redeem or otherwise to discharge one lien which is prior, without redeeming or discharging the other liens also which are subsequent to his own title.[2] (b) Thus if a third mortgagee without notice of a second mortgage should purchase in the first mortgage by which he would acquire the legal title, the second mortgagee would not be

---

Vendors, ch. 18, sub finem (9th edit.).   On the other hand Mr. Belt maintains its correctness. Belt's note (1) to 3 Brown, Ch. R. 264. So does Mr. Beames (Beam. Pl. Eq. 244, 245). and Mr. Roper also in his work on Husband and Wife, Vol. 1, 446, 447. Mr. Hovenden, in his note to 2 Freem. R. 24, acquiesces in it. See also Medlicott v. O'Donel, 1 B. & Beatt. 171. See also Mitf. Plead. Eq. by Jeremy, p. 274, note (d) (4th edit.). The same distinction was expressly affirmed in Collins v. Archer, 1 Russ. & Mylne, 292. There is a peculiarity in the case of a dowress which operates against her, and upon this point of notice is proper to be mentioned. Though notice of the title will protect every other interest in the inheritance, it will not protect hers. Maundrell v. Maundrell, 10 Ves. 271, 272; Wynn v. Williams, 5 Ves. 130; Mole v. Smith, Jacob, R. 497; Swannock v. Lifford, Ambl. R. 6; s. c. Co. Litt. 208 a, Butler's note (105); Radner v. Vanderbendy, Show. Parl. Cas. 69; ante, § 57 a; post, §§ 434, 437, 630, 631.

[1] 2 Fonbl. Eq. B. 3, ch. 2, § 3; Com. Dig. Chancery, 4 A. 10; 4 I. 3; 4 I. 11; 4 W. 29.

[2] Jeremy on Equity Jurisd. B. 1, ch 2, § 1, pp. 188 to 191.

(a) Gjerness v. Mathews, 27 Minn. 320. But an equitable incumbrancer cannot, after receiving notice of a prior incumbrance, obtain priority over it by getting in a legal estate from a bare trustee. Harpham v. Shacklock, 19 Ch. D. 207.

(b) Spencer v. Pearson, 24 Beav. 266. As to consolidation of mortgages, see In re Raggett, 16 Ch. D. 117, in editor's note to § 1023, post.

permitted to redeem the first mortgage without redeeming the third mortgage also; for in such a case equity tacks both mortgages together in his favor. And in such a case it will make no difference that the third mortgagee at the time of purchasing the first mortgage had notice of the second mortgage; for he is still entitled to the same protection.[1] (a)

413. There is certainly great apparent hardship in this rule, for it seems most conformable to natural justice that each mortgagee should in such a case be paid according to the order and priority of his incumbrances.[2] The general reasoning by which this doctrine is maintained is this: 'In æquali jure melior est conditio possidentis.' Where the equity is equal, the law shall prevail; and he that hath only a title in equity shall not prevail against a title by law and equity in another.[3] But however correct this reasoning may be when rightly applied, its applicability to the case stated may reasonably be doubted. It is assuming the whole case to say that the right is equal and the equity is equal. The second mortgagee has a prior right and at least an equal equity; and then the rule seems justly to apply, that where the equities are equal, that title which is prior in time shall prevail: 'Qui prior est in tempore, potior est in jure.' [4]

---

[1] 2 Fonbl. Eq. B. 3, ch. 2, § 2, and notes (b), (c); Com. Dig. Chancery, 4 A. 10; Marsh v. Lee, 2 Vent. R. 337, 338; s. c. 1 Ch. Cas. 162; Maundrell v. Maundrell, 10 Ves. 260, 270; Morret v. Parke, 2 Atk. 53, 54; Matthews v. Cartwright, 2 Atk. 347; Robinson v. Davison, 1 Bro. Ch. R. 63; Newland on Contracts, ch. 36, p. 515: Sugden on Vendors, ch. 16, 17; Powell on Mortgages, Vol. 2, p. 454, Mr. Coventry's note (A).

[2] Brace v. Duchess of Marlborough, 2 P. Will. 492; Lowthian v. Hasel, 3 Bro. Ch R. 163.

[3] Jeremy on Equity Jurisd. B. 1, ch. 2, § 1, pp. 188 to 192 (4th edit.); 2 Fonbl. Eq. B. 3, ch. 3, § 1, and notes.

[4] Mr. Chancellor Kent in his learned Commentaries has expressed a strong disapprobation of the doctrine of tacking. 'There is,' says he, 'no natural equity in tacking, and when it supersedes a prior incumbrance it works manifest injustice. By acquiring a still more antecedent incumbrance, the junior party acquires, by substitution, the rights of the first incumbrancer over the purchased security, and he justly acquires nothing more. The doctrine of tacking is founded on the assumption of a principle which is not true in point of fact; for as between A, whose deed is honestly acquired and recorded to-day, and B, whose deed is with equal honesty acquired and recorded to-morrow, the equities upon the estate are not equal. He who has been fairly prior in point of time has the better equity, for he is prior in point of right.' 4 Kent, Comm. Lect. 58, pp. 178, 179 (4th edit.).

(a) Wormald v. Maitland, 35 L. J. Ch. 69.

414. It has been significantly said that it is a plank gained by the third mortgagee in a shipwreck, 'tabula in naufragio.'[1] But independently of the inapplicability of the figure, which can justly apply only to cases of extreme hazard to life and not to mere seizures of property, it is obvious that no man can have a right in consequence of a shipwreck to convert another man's property to his own use, or to acquire an exclusive right against a prior owner. The best apology for the actual enforcement of the rule is, that it has been long established, and that it ought not now to be departed from, since it has become a rule of property.

415. Lord Hardwicke has given the following account of the origin and foundation of the doctrine: 'As to the equity of this court, that a third incumbrancer having taken his security or mortgage without notice of the second incumbrance, and then being puisne, taking in the first incumbrance shall squeeze out and have satisfaction before the second; that equity is certainly established in general, and was so in Marsh v. Lee by a very solemn determination by Lord Hale, who gave it the term of the creditor's 'tabula in naufragio.' That is the leading case. Perhaps it might be going a good way at first, but it has been followed ever since, and I believe was rightly settled only on this foundation by the particular constitution of the law of this country. It could not happen in any other country but this, because the jurisdiction of law and equity is administered here in different courts, and creates different kinds of rights in estates. And therefore as Courts of Equity break in upon the common law where necessity and conscience require it, still they allow superior force and strength to a legal title to estates; and therefore where there is a legal title and equity on one side, this court never thought fit that by reason of a prior equity against a man who had a legal title that man should be hurt; and this, by reason of that force, this court necessarily and rightly allows to the common law and to legal titles. But if this had happened in any other country, it could never have made a question; for if the law and equity are administered by the same jurisdiction, the rule, "Qui prior est in tempore, potior est in jure," must hold.'[2]

[1] Marsh v. Lee, 2 Vent. 337; Wortley v. Birkhead, 2 Ves. 574; Brace v. Duchess of Marlborough, 2 P. Will. 491.　See post, § 421 a.

[2] Wortley v. Birkhead, 2 Ves. 573.　The same quotation is in 2 Fonbl. Eq. 304, B. 3, ch. 2, § 2, in note (e).　Mr. Coventry, in his valuable notes to Powell on Mortgages (Vol. 2, p. 454, note), supposes that the English law on this

416. Indeed so little has this doctrine of tacking to commend itself, that it has stopped far short of the analogies which would seem to justify its application ; and it has been confined to cases

subject is sanctioned by the civil law. In this view of the matter he is entirely mistaken. The civil law admits no such principle as tacking; the general rule is, 'Qui prior est in tempore, potior est in jure.' There are two acknowledged exceptions: one, where the first incumbrancer consents to the second pledge, so as to give a priority; another is, where the second pledge is for money to preserve the property. The doctrine of the civil law, referred to by Mr. Coventry, simply gives to a third mortgagee, paying off a first mortgage, the same priority, by way of substitution, which the first mortgagee had. It does not change the rights of the third mortgagee as to his own mortgage. So the doctrine is stated in the Pandects (incorrectly referred to by Mr. Coventry), and so is the doctrine of Domat in the passages cited. See Dig. Lib. 20, tit. 4, 1. 16; 1 Domat, B. 3, tit. 1, § 3, art. 7, and Id. § 6, art. 6, 7; Pothier, Pand, Lib. 20, tit. 4, § 1, n. 1 to 32, and especially n. 10, 11, Cod. Lib. 8, tit. 18, l. 1, 5. The language of the civil law in the principal passage cited is: ' Plane, cum tertius creditor primum de sua pecunia dimisit, in locum ejus substituitur in ea quantitate quam superiori exsolvit.' Dig. Lib. 20, tit. 4, 1. 16. In Fonblanque's equity (2 Fonbl. B. 3, ch. 1, § 9, p. 272) it is said in the text: ' By the civil law the mortgage is properly a security only for the debt itself for which it was given, and the consequences of it, as the principal sum and interest, and the costs and damages laid out in preserving it.' The passage on which reliance is had for this purpose is the Dig. Lib. 13, tit. 7, 1. 8, § 5. ' Cum pignus ex pactione venire potest, non solum ob sortem non solutam venire poterit, sed ob cætera quoque, veluti usuras, et quæ in id impensa sunt.' Mr. Brown, in his Treatise on the Civil Law (Vol. 1, B. 2, ch 4, p. 202), deduces the conclusion that Mr. Fonblanque intended to say that it did not involve such effects as that the heir of a mortgagor, also indebted by a bond to the mortgagee, should not redeem without also paying the bond debt, and such like provisions known to our Courts of Equity. In this Mr. Brown thinks Mr. Fonblanque is incorrect; and he relies on the text of the Code (Cod. Lib. 8, tit. 27, l. 1): ' At si in possessione fueris constitutus, nisi ea quoque pecunia tibi a debitore reddatur vel offeratur, quæ sine pignore debetur, eam restituere propter exceptionem doli mali non cogeris. Jure enim contendis, debitores eam solam pecuniam cujus nomine ea pignora obligaverunt, offerentes audiri non oportere, nisi pro illa etiam satisfecerint quam mutuam simpliciter acceperunt. Quod in secundo creditore locum non habet; nec enim necessitas ei imponitur chirographarium etiam debitum priori creditori offerre.' It is apparent that this passage merely respects the right of a mortgagee to tack, as against his own debtor, a second loan, without security, when his debtor seeks to redeem. (a) It does not touch the case of tacking so as to cut out an intermediate incumbrancer. Domat supports the text of Fonblanque (1 Domat, B. 1, tit. 1, § 3, art. 4, 7, 8). That by the civil law there can be a tacking of debts so as to cut out an intermediate incumbrance seems contrary to the Dig. Lib. 20, tit. 4, 1. 20; Pothier, Pand. Lib. 20, tit. 4, n. 10. See 2 Story on Eq. Jurisp. § 1010, note, where this subject is examined more at large. But see 1 Brown, Civil Law, 208, and 4 Kent, Comm. Lect. 58, p. 136, note (a); Id. 175, 176 (4th edit.).

(a) That is, it is consolidation. See In re Raggett, 16 Ch. D. 117, Cotton, L. J.

where the party in whose favor it is allowed is originally a bona fide purchaser of an interest in the land for a valuable consideration. Thus if a puisne creditor by judgment, or statute, or recognizance, should buy in a prior mortgage, he would not be allowed to tack his judgment to such a mortgage so as to cut out a mesne mortgagee.[1] (a) The reason is said to be that a creditor can in no just sense be called a purchaser, for he does not advance his money upon the immediate credit of the land, and by his judgment he does not acquire any right in the land. He has neither jus in re nor jus ad rem, but a mere lien upon the land which may or may not afterwards be enforced upon it.[2] But if instead of being a judgment creditor he were a third mortgagee and should then purchase in a prior judgment, statute, or recognizance, in such case he would be entitled to tack both together. The reason for the diversity is, that in the latter case he did originally lend his money upon the credit of the land, but in the former he did not, but was only a general creditor trusting to the general assets of his debtor.[3]

417. The same principle applies to a first mortgagee lending to the mortgagor a further sum upon a statute or judgment. In such a case he will be entitled to retain against the mesne mortgagee till both his mortgage and statute or judgment are paid, for he lent his money originally upon the credit of the land ; and it may well be presumed that he lent the further sum upon the statute or judgment upon the same security, although it passed no present interest in the land, but gave a lien only.[4]

[1] 2 Fonbl. Eq. B. 3, ch. 3, § 1, note (a); Id. B. 3, ch. 1, § 9, and note (n); Brace v. Duchess of Marlborough, 2 P. Will. 492 to 495; Anon. 2 Ves. 262; Morret v. Paske, 2 Atk. 52, 53; Ex parte Knott, 11 Ves. 617; Belchier v. Butler, 1 Eden, R. 522, and Mr. Eden's note. But see Wright v. Pilling, Prec. Ch. 499.

[2] Ibid.; Averall v. Wade, Lloyd & Goold's Rep. 252, 262.

[3] Ibid.; Higgen v. Lyddal, 1 Cas. Ch. 149; Mackreth v. Symmons, 15 Ves. 354.

[4] Ibid.; Shepherd v. Titley, 2 Atk. 352; Ex parte Knott, 11 Ves. 617. A fortiori the same principle applies to the first mortgagee's lending on a second mortgage; for in such case he positively lends on the credit of the land, and will be allowed to tack against a mesne incumbrancer. Morret c. Paske, 2 Atk. 53, 54. And even sums subsequently lent on notes, if distinctly agreed at the time to be on the security of the mortgaged property, will be allowed to be tacked. Matthews v. Cartwright, 2 Atk. 347; 2 Story on Eq. Jurisp. § 1010, note.

(a) See Brecon v. Seymour, 26 Beav. 548.

418. And yet such a prior mortgagee having a bond debt has never been permitted to tack it against any intervening incumbrancers of a superior nature between his bond and mortgage, nor against other specialty creditors, nor even against the mortgagor himself, but only against his heir, to avoid circuity of action.[1] (a)   The reason given is, that the bond debt, except in the hands of the heir, is not a charge on the land, and tacking takes place only when the party holds both securities in the same right.   For if a prior mortgagee takes an assignment of a third mortgage as a trustee only for another person, he will not be allowed to tack two mortgages together to the prejudice of intervening incumbrancers.[2]   Neither is a mortgagee permitted to tack where the equity of redemption belongs to different persons when the mortgagee's title to both estates occurs.[3] (b)

419. It cannot be denied that some of these distinctions are extremely thin, and stand upon very artificial and unsatisfactory reasoning.   The account of the matter given by Lord Hardwicke[4] is probably the true one.   But it is a little difficult to

[1] Parvis v. Corbet, 3 Atk. 556; Lowthian v. Hasel, 3 Brown, Ch. R. 163; Morret v. Paske, 2 Atk. 52, 53; Shuttleworth v. Laycock, 1 Vern. 245; Coleman v. Winch, 1 P. Will. 775; Price v. Fastnedge, Ambler, R. 685, and Mr. Blunt's note; Houghton v. Troughton, 1 Ves. 86; Heams v. Bance, 3 Atk. 630; Jones v. Smith, 2 Ves. jr., 376; Adams v. Claxton, 6 Ves. 229; 2 Fonbl. Eq. B. 3, ch. 1, § 11; Id. § 9, note (u).   In the Roman law rules somewhat different prevailed.   While, as we have seen, tacking was not allowed against intermediate incumbrancers, the creditor himself was, as against his debtor, allowed to tack a subsequent debt contracted by his debtor after the mortgage.   Ante, § 415, note, and post, § 420; 2 Story on Eq. Jurisp. § 1010, and note.   See also 1 Brown, Civil Law, 202, and note 5; Id. 20, 8; 4 Kent, Comm. Lect. 58, p. 136, and note; Id. 175, 176 (2d and 3d edit.).

[2] Morret v. Paske, 2 Atk. 53; 2 Fonbl. Eq. B. 3, ch. 1, § 9, and note (u).

[3] White v. Hillacre, 5 Younge & Coll. 597, 609.

[4] Wortley v. Birkhead, 2 Ves. 574; ante, § 415, p. 443.   See Berry v. Mutual Ins. Co., 2 John. Ch. R. 603, 608.   Lord Rosslyn, in Jones v. Smith (2 Ves. jr., 377), said: 'Why a bond is not upon the same footing I do not know.   It is impossible to say why a bond may not be tacked to a mortgage, as well as one mortgage to another.'   The asserted ground doubtless is, that a bond debt is no lien on the land, whereas a mortgage and judgment are.   This may be still more distinctly shown by the rule that a mortgagee of a copyhold estate cannot tack a judgment to his mortgage; the reason is, that a judgment does not

(a) Where there is a further advance on a parol agreement that the same shall be secured by the existing mortgage, equity will not aid the mortgagor, or one having no better title, to redeem without repaying such advance. Stone v. Lane, 10 Allen, 74.

(b) See Mills v. Jennings, 13 Ch. D. 638, and Harter v. Coleman, 19 Ch. D. 630, in editor's note to § 1023, post.

perceive how the foundation could support such a superstructure, or rather why the intelligible equity of the case upon the principles of natural justice should not be rigorously applied to it. Courts of Equity have found no difficulty in applying it where the puisne incumbrancer has bought in a prior equitable incumbrance; for in such cases they have declared that where the puisne incumbrancer has not obtained the legal title, or where the legal title is vested in a trustee, or where he takes in autre droit, the incumbrances shall be paid in the order of their priority in point of time, according to the maxim above mentioned.[1] The reasonable principle is here adopted, that he who has the better right to call for the legal title or for its protection shall prevail.[2]

420. The civil law has proceeded upon a far more intelligible and just doctrine on this subject. It wholly repudiates the doctrine of tacking, and gives the fullest effect to the maxim, 'Qui prior est in tempore, potior est in jure;' excluding it only in cases of fraud or of consent, or of a superior equity.[3]

421. But whatever may be thought as to the foundation of the doctrine of tacking in Courts of Equity, it is now firmly established. It is however to be taken with this most important

affect or bind copyhold estates. Heir of Carmore v. Park, 6 Vin. Abridg. p. 222, pl. 6; cited 2 Fonbl. Eq B. 3, ch. 1, § 9, and note (u); Jeremy on Eq. Jurisd. B. 1, ch. 2, § 1, pp. 190, 191.

[1] Brace v. Duchess of Marlborough, 2 P. Will. 495; Ex parte Knott, 11 Ves. 618; Berry v. Mutual Ins. Co., 2 John. Ch. R. 608; Frere v. Moore, 8 Price, R. 475; Barrett v. Weston, 12 Ves. 130; Price v. Fastnedge, Ambler, R. 685, and Mr. Blunt's note; Jeremy on Eq. Jurisd. B. 1, ch. 2, §§ 1, 2, pp. 191, 193, 194; 1 Fonbl. Eq. B. 1, ch. 4, § 25, and note (e); Pomfret v. Windsor, 2 Ves. 472, 486; Brandly v. Ord, 1 Atk. 571.

[2] Ibid.; Medlicott v. O'Donel, 1 B. & Beatt. 171; 2 Fonbl. Eq. B. 2, ch. 6, § 2. In America the doctrine of tacking is never allowed as against mesne incumbrances which are duly registered; for the plain reason that the Registry Acts are held not only to be constructive notice, but the acts themselves, in effect, declare the priority to be fixed by the registration. Grant v. Bissett, 1 Caines' Cas. in Err. 112; Frost v. Beekman, 1 John. Ch. R. 298, 299; Parkhurst v. Alexander, 1 John. Ch. R. 398, 399; St. Andrew's Church v. Tomkins, 7 John. Ch. R. 14.(a) The same doctrine exists in other registry countries. Latouche v. Lord Dunsany, 1 Sch. & Lefr. 137, 157. As to tacking in cases of personal property, see 2 Story, Eq. Jurisp. §§ 1034, 1035.

[3] See Dig. Lib. 20, tit. 4, l. 16; Pothier, Pand. Lib. 20, tit. 4, § 1, n. 1 to 32; 1 Domat. B. 3, tit. 1, § 6, art. 6; ante, § 415, p. 401, note; § 418, note (1); 2 Story on Eq. Jurisp. § 1010, and note.

(a) Chandler v. Dyer, 37 Vt. 345.

qualification, that the party who seeks to avail himself of it is a
bona fide purchaser without notice of the prior incumbrance
at the time when he took his original security; for if he then
had such notice, he has not the slightest claim to the protection
or assistance of a Court of Equity, and he will not be allowed
by purchasing in such prior incumbrance to tack his own tainted
mortgage or other title to the latter.[1]

421 *a*. Questions bearing a close analogy to that of tacking
have also arisen, involving equities between parties asserting
adverse rights.   Thus for example where a mortgagee took a
mortgage and a covenant from sureties to pay the mortgage
money, and afterwards he advanced an additional sum to the
mortgagor and took a second mortgage therefor on the premises,
and subsequently he brought his action against the sureties and
recovered the amount of the first mortgage debt from them, but
he refused to give up the first mortgage or to assign it to the
sureties without being paid the second advance, and they brought
a suit against him to compel an assignment to them of the first
mortgage, the question arose whether they had a right to an
assignment of the first mortgage without paying the second
advance.   It was held that they had no priority, and before
they could compel an assignment they must pay the second
advance.[2] (*a*)

421 *b*. There are other cases standing indeed upon a firmer
ground than that of the mere right of tacking, where a subsequent assignee or incumbrancer of equitable property may acquire a priority over an elder assignee or incumbrancer of the
same property by his exercise of superior diligence and doing
acts which will give him a better claim or protection in equity.[3]

---

[1] 2 Fonbl. Eq. B. 3, ch. 3, § 1, note (*b*); Id. B. 2, ch. 6, § 2, and note (*i*);
Brace *v.* Duchess of Marlborough, 2 P. Will. 491, 495; Sugden on Vendors,
ch. 16, 17; Green *v.* Slater, 4 John. Ch. R. 38; Toulman *v.* Steere, 3 Meriv.
R. 210; Powell on Mortgages, by Coventry, Vol. 2, p. 454, note A.; Com. Dig.
Chancery, 4 A. 10, 4 I. 3, 4 I. 4, 4 W. 28; 4 Kent, Comm. Lect. 58, pp. 176 to
179 (4th edit.); post, § 434; Redfearn *v.* Ferrier, 1 Dow, R. 50.   But see
Davis *v.* Austin, 1 Ves. jr. 228; Johnson *v.* Brown, 2 Younge & Coll. N. R.
268.

[2] Williams *v.* Owens, The (English) Jurist, 30 Dec. 1843, p. 1145; post,
§§ 499, 499 *a*.

[3] Foster *v.* Blackstone, 1 Mylne & Keen, 297; Timson *v.* Ramsbottom, 2
Keen, R. 35; ante, 399, note.

(*a*) But see Smith *v.* Day, 23 Vt. 656.

Thus for example a second incumbrancer upon equitable property, who has given notice of his title to the trustees of the
property, will be preferred to a prior incumbrancer who has
omitted to give the like notice of his title to the trustees; for the
notice is an effectual protection against any subsequent dealing
on the part of the trustees.[1] (a)   So a second assignee of the

---

[1] Ibid.; ante, § 399, note; post, §§ 1035 a, 1047, 1057; Etty v. Bridges, 2
Younge & Coll. 488, 492.   In this case Mr. Vice-Chancellor Bruce said: 'That
notice should be given to the trustee of a fund upon dealing with an equitable
interest in it is not, I apprehend, so much a rule as an example, or instance,
or effect of a rule.   In Dearle v. Hall (3 Russ. R. 1) we find Lord Lyndhurst
thus expressing himself: "In cases like the present, the act of giving the
trustee notice is, in a certain degree, taking possession of the fund; it is going
as far towards equitable possession as it is possible to go; for after notice given,
the trustee of a fund becomes a trustee for the assignee who has given him
notice."   Sir Thomas Plumer's previous observations in the same case, which
occur between the 20th and the 28th pages of the same volume are, with more
minuteness of detail, to the same effect.   The opinions of the judges in Ryall
v. Rowles (1 Ves. R. 348, 1 Atk. R. 165), of which that of Mr. Justice Burnett
has been reported from his note-book by Mr. Bligh (9 Bligh, N. S. 578), contain recognitions of the same principle.   So the opinion in Foster v. Cockerell
(9 Bligh, R. N. S. 332), of Lord Lyndhurst, upon advising the House of Lords
to affirm Sir John Leach's decision in Foster v. Blackstone (1 Mylne & Keen,
R. 297), in which case the latter learned judge had before thus expressed himself: "A better equity is, where a second incumbrancer, without notice, takes
a protection against a subsequent incumbrancer which the prior incumbrancer
has neglected to take.   Thus a declaration of trust of an outstanding term
accompanied by delivery of the deeds creating and continuing the term, gives
a better equity than the mere declaration of trust to a prior incumbrancer."
These authorities, though not the only authorities, are, I apprehend, more than
sufficient to show the rule to be that to perfect a transaction of the description now in question the purchaser or incumbrancer must, if he cannot acquire
possession, go as near it as he can, — as the circumstances of the case will permit, — must in a sense, if the expression may be used, set his mark upon the
property, or do everything reasonably practicable to prevent it from being
dealt with in fraud of an innocent purchaser afterwards.   The law has held
that generally where there are trustees this is done sufficiently, upon dealing
with an equitable interest in the fund, by giving them notice; because, although
the notice does not necessarily prevent such a fraud, it renders its commission

---

(a) So a mortgagee of a life insurance policy, who gives notice even
after the death of the assured, will be
preferred to an assignee in bankruptcy
who has not given notice.   In re Russell, L. R. 15 Eq. 26; Stuart v. Cockerell, L. R. 8 Eq. 607.   But see Ex
parte Caldwell, L. R. 13 Eq. 188.   Of
course one who has a contract for the
purchase of land may assign it, and
the assignee by giving notice to trustees who hold the legal title will be
entitled to performance.   Shaw v. Foster, L. R. 5 H. L. 321; s. c. 5 Ch. 604.
But notice of intent to assign is not
enough.   Ib.; Ponder v. Scott, 44 Ala.
241.   And see Smith v. Gibson, 15
Minn. 89.

interest of the assignor in the residuary estate of a testator who has given notice to the executors thereof will be preferred to a prior assignee who has given no such notice.[1] So it is said to be a better equity where a second incumbrancer takes a protection against a subsequent incumbrancer, which the prior incumbrancer neglected to take. Thus a declaration of trust of an outstanding term, accompanied by a delivery of the deeds creating and continuing the term, will give a better equity than a mere declaration of trust taken by a prior incumbrancer.[2]

421 c. A different doctrine is maintained in some of the States of America; for it is there held that as between different assignees of a chose in action he who is first in time is first in right, notwithstanding he has given no notice to the debtor or the subsequent assignee. The debtor will however be protected if he has made payment to the second assignee before notice of the prior assignment.[3]

422. Another instance of the application of this wholesome doctrine of constructive fraud arising from notice may be seen in the dealings with executors and other persons holding a fiduciary character, and third persons colluding with them in violation of their trust. Thus purchases from executors of the personal property of their testator are ordinarily obligatory and valid notwithstanding they may be affected with some peculiar trusts or equities in the hands of the executors. For the pur-

---

much less likely, and gives an increased probability, or an increased chance of redress, if the fraud shall be committed, supposing reasonable diligence to be used; inasmuch as not only will the trustees, if asked, be likely to give the information of the notice, but if they shall fail to do so, they may be liable to make good the loss. It is obvious however that unfairness or forgetfulness, or negligence on a trustee's part, or his death or infirmity, may render the notice, as a prevention of fraud, useless.'

[1] Timson v. Ramsbottom, 2 Keen, R. 35; post, §§ 1035 a, 1047, 1057.

[2] Foster v. Blackstone, 1 Mylne & Keen, 297. But it will not create a prior equity in a subsequent incumbrancer, that he claims by a legal title and the prior incumbrancer claims by an equitable title; for if notice has been duly given by the latter, his title will prevail. Ibid. It is now also settled that an inquiry of the legal holder of equitable property as to the state of the title is not necessary to give effect to a notice by a subsequent assignee, so as to entitle him to a priority over a prior assignee who has given no notice. Timson v. Ramsbottom, 2 Keen, R. 35.

[3] Muir v. Schenck, 3 Hill, R. 228. See Story on Conflict of Laws, §§ 328, 330. See also Murray v. Lichburn, 2 John. Ch. Cas. 441, 443; post, § 1039; Redfearn v. Ferrier, 1 Dow, R. 550; Davis v. Austin, 1 Ves. jr., R. 228; Story on Conflict of Laws, §§ 395, 396; James v. Morey, 2 Cowen, R. 246.

chaser cannot be presumed to know that the sale may not be required in order to discharge the debts of the testator, for which they are legally bound before all other claims.[1] But if the purchaser knows that the executor is wasting and turning the testator's estate into money the more easily to run away with it, or for any other unlawful purpose, he will be deemed particeps criminis, and his purchase set aside as fraudulent.[2] (a)

423. The reason for this diversity of doctrine has been fully stated by Sir William Grant. 'It is true,' said he, 'that executors are, in equity, mere trustees for the performance of the will; yet in many respects and for many purposes third persons are entitled to consider them absolute owners. The mere circumstance that they are executors will not vitiate any transaction with them, for the power of disposition is generally incident, being frequently necessary; and a stranger shall not be put to examine whether in the particular instance that power has been discreetly exercised. But from that proposition that a third person is not bound to look to the trust in every respect and for

---

[1] 2 Fonbl. Eq. B. 2, ch. 6, 2, and notes (k) and (l); Humble v. Bill, 2 Vern. R. 444; Ewer v. Corbet, 2 P. Will. 148; McLeod v. Drummond, 14 Ves. 359; s. c. 17 Ves. 154, 155; Hill v. Simpson, 7 Ves. 166; Scott v. Tyler, 2 Dick. 712, 725; Newland on Contracts, ch. 36, pp. 512, 513, 514; Com. Dig. Chancery, 4 W. 29; Rayner v. Pearsall, 3 John. Ch. R. 578. This doctrine was overthrown in the case of Humble v. Bill (or Savage), upon appeal to the House of Lords. 1 Bro. Parl. Cas. 71. It was however reasserted in Ewer v. Corbet, 2 P. Will. 148; Nugent v. Clifford, 1 Atk. 463; Elliot v. Merryman, 2 Atk. 42; Ithell v. Beane, 1 Ves. R. 215; Mead v. Lord Orrery, 3 Atk. 235; Dickinson v. Lockyer, 4 Ves. 36; Hill v. Simpson, 7 Ves. 152; Taylor v. Hawkins, 8 Ves. 209; McLeod v. Drummond, 14 Ves. 352; s. c. 17 Ves. 153. In this last case the whole of the authorities were examined at large by Lord Eldon, and commented on with his usual acuteness. See also Andrews v. Wrigley, 4 Bro. Ch. R. 125.

[2] Worseley v. De Mattos, 1 Burr. 475; Ewer v. Corbet, 2 P. Will. 148; Mead v. Lord Orrery, 3 Atk. 235, 237; Benfield v. Solomons, 9 Ves. 86, 87; Hill v. Simpson, 7 Ves. 152; McLeod v. Drummond, 14 Ves. 359; s. c. 17 Ves. 153; Newland on Contracts, ch. 36, p. 513; 1 Madd. Ch. Pr. 228, 229, 230; Drohan v. Drohan, 1 Ball & Beatt. 185; Com. Dig. Chancery, 4 W. 28; Scott v. Tyler, 2 Bro. Ch. R. 431; 2 Dick. 712, 725; Bonney v. Ridgard, cited 2 Bro. Ch. R. 438; 4 Bro. Ch. R. 130; Scott v. Nesbit, 2 Bro. Ch. R. 641; s. c. 2 Cox, R. 183.

(a) So if the sale was made under circumstances such that the purchaser as a prudent man must have known that it was for the executor's own benefit. Walker v. Taylor, 4 Law T. N. S. 845; Shaw v. Spencer, 100 Mass. 382, 393; 2 Perry, Trusts, §§ 814, 815.

every purpose, it does not follow that dealing with the executor
for the assets he may equally look upon him as absolute owner,
and wholly overlook his character as trustee, when he knows the
executor is applying the assets to a purpose wholly foreign to his
trust.   No decision necessarily leads to such a consequence.'[1]
The same doctrine is applied to the cases of executors or administrators colluding with the debtors to the estate either to retain
or to waste the assets; for in such cases the creditors will be
allowed to sue the debtors directly in equity, making the executor or administrator also a party to the bill, although ordinarily
the executor or administrator only can sue for the debts due to
the deceased.[2]   So in cases of collusion between a mortgagor and
mortgagee, a creditor or annuitant of the mortgagor may have
a right to redeem and to call for an account, although ordinarily
such a right belongs only to the mortgagor and his heirs and
privies in estate.[3]   Indeed the doctrine may be even more generally stated, that he who has voluntarily concurred in the commission of a fraud by another shall never be permitted to obtain
a profit thereby against those who have been thus defrauded.

424. It seems at one time to have been thought that no person
but a creditor or a specific legatee of the property could question
the validity of a disposition made of assets by an executor, however fraudulent it might be.   But that doctrine is so repugnant
to true principles, that it could scarcely be maintained whenever
it came to be thoroughly sifted.[4]   It is now well understood that
pecuniary and residuary legatees may question the validity of
such a disposition; and indeed residuary legatees stand upon a
stronger ground than pecuniary legatees generally; for in a sense
they have a lien on the fund and may go into equity to enforce
it upon the fund.[5]

[1] Hill v. Simpson, 7 Ves. 166.
[2] Holland v. Prior, 1 Mylne & Keen, 240; Newland v. Champion, 1 Ves.
106; Doran v. Simpson, 4 Ves. 651; Alsager v. Rowley, 6 Ves. 748; Beckley v.
Dorrington, West, R. 169; post, § 581, note, § 828; Story on Equity Pleadings,
§§ 178, 514; Burroughs v. Elton, 11 Ves. 29; Benfield v. Solomons, 9 Ves. 86.
[3] White v. Parnther, 1 Knapp, 179, 229; Troughton v. Binkes, 6 Ves. 572.
[4] Mead v. Lord Orrery, 3 Atk. 235; 14 Ves. 361; 17 Ves. 169.
[5] Hill v. Simpson, 7 Ves. 152; McLeod v. Drummond, 14 Ves. 359; s. c.
17 Ves. 169; Bonney v. Ridgard, cited 2 Bro. Ch. R. 438; 4 Bro. Ch. R. 130;
17 Ves. 165.   Mr. Maddock (1 Madd. Ch. Pr. 230) states, that ' Residuary
and general legatees, and, as it seems, co-executors, are never permitted to
question the disposition which the executors have made of the assets.   But

425. The last class of cases which it is proposed to consider under the present head of Constructive Fraud is that of voluntary conveyances of real estate in regard to subsequent purchasers.[1] This class is founded in a great measure, if not altogether, upon the provisions of the statute of 27th of Eliz. ch. 4, which has been already alluded to. The object of that statute was to give full protection to subsequent purchasers from the grantor against mere volunteers under prior conveyances. As between the parties themselves such conveyances are positively binding and cannot be disturbed; for the statute does not reach such cases.[2]

426. It was for a long period of time a much-litigated question in England, whether the effect of the statute was to avoid all voluntary conveyances (that is, all such as were made merely in consideration of natural love or affection, or were mere gifts), although made bona fide in favor of all subsequent purchasers with or without notice, or whether it applied only to conveyances made with a fraudulent intent and to purchasers without notice. After no inconsiderable diversity of judicial opinion the doctrine has at length been established in England (whether in conformity to the language or intent of the statute is exceedingly questionable) that all such conveyances are void as to subsequent purchasers, whether they are purchasers with or without notice, although the original conveyance was bona fide, and without the slightest admixture of intentional fraud, upon the ground that the statute in every such case infers fraud, and will not suffer the presumption to be gainsaid.[3] (b)   The doctrine however is

creditors and specific and pecuniary legatees may follow either legal or equitable assets into the hands of third persons to whom fraud is imputable.' It appears to me that the cases above cited, and especially that of McLeod v. Drummond, 14 Ves. 353, s. c. 17 Ves. 153, establish a different conclusion.

[1] The statute does not extend to conveyances of personal property, but only to conveyances of real property. Jones v. Croucher, 1 Sim. & Stu. R. 315.(a)

[2] Petre v. Espinasse, 2 Mylne & Keen, 496; Bill v. Claxton, Id. 503, 510.

[3] Doe v. Manning, 9 East, R. 58; Pulvertoft v. Pulvertoft, 18 Ves. 84, 86,

(a) See Bohn v. Headley, 7 Har. & J. 257; Jones v. Hall, 5 Jones, Eq. 26.

(b) See Dolphin v. Aylward, L. R. 4 H. L. 486, that a voluntary settlement cannot be defeated by the settlor's suffering a judgment. And see Pelham v. Aldrich, 8 Gray, 515. It seems too that one who has made a voluntary conveyance cannot compel a subsequent purchaser to take the title. Peter v. Nicolls, L. R. 11 Eq. 391. A voluntary conveyance made without power of revocation will be set aside if it is not clear that the settlor intended it to be irrevocable. Hall v. Hall, L. R. 14 Eq. 365.

admitted to be full of difficulties ; and it has been confirmed, rather upon the pressure of authorities and the vast extent to which titles have been acquired and held under it, than upon any notion that it has a firm foundation in reason and a just construction of the statute. The rule ' stare decisis ' has here been applied to give repose and security to titles fairly acquired, upon the faith of judicial decisions.[1]

427. In America a like diversity of judicial opinion has been exhibited. Mr. Chancellor Kent has held the English doctrine obligatory, as the true result of the authorities. But at the same time he is strongly inclined to the opinion that where the purchaser has had actual (and not merely constructive) notice, it ought not to prevail.[2] When the same case in which this opinion was declared came before the Court of Errors of New York, Mr. Chief Justice Spencer delivered an elaborate opinion against the English doctrine, and asserted that no voluntary conveyance not originally fraudulent was within the statute. The Court of Errors on that occasion left the question open for future decision.[3] But the doctrine of Mr. Chief Justice Spencer has

---

111; Buckle v. Mitchell, 18 Ves. 100; Com. Dig. Chancery, 4 C. 7; Sterry v. Arden, 1 John. Ch. R. 261, 267 to 271; Com. Dig. Covin, B. 3, 4; Sugden on Vendors, ch. 16, § 1, art. 1, 2. The elaborate judgment of Lord Ellenborough, in Doe v. Manning (9 East, R. 58), contains a large survey of the authorities, to which the learned reader is referred. See also 1 Madd. Ch. Pr. 421 to 427; 1 Fonbl. Eq. B. 1, ch. 4, § 3, and notes (f) and (g); Jeremy on Eq. Jurisd. B. 1, ch. 2, § 1, pp. 188 to 192; Newland on Contracts, ch. 34, p. 391; 2 Hovenden on Frauds, ch. 18, p. 73, &c.; Belt's Suppt. to Vesey, 25, 26; Atherley on Marr. Sett. ch. 13, pp. 187, &c., 193, 194; Jeremy on Eq. Jurisd. B. 3, Pt. 2, ch. 3, § 4, pp. 408 to 411; Pulvertoft v. Pulvertoft, 18 Ves. 84, 86, 111; Doe v. Routledge, Cowper, R. 711, 712. Mr. Fonblanque has assailed the doctrine that a purchaser with notice should still be entitled to prevail against the bona fide voluntary conveyance, with great force of reasoning. He asserts that it amounts to an encouragement on the part of the purchaser of a breach of that respect which is morally due to the fair claims of others; and that it may render the provisions of a statute, intended by the Legislature to be preventive of fraud, the most effectual instrument of accomplishing it. 1 Fonbl. Eq. B. 1, ch. 4, § 13, note (g). To which it may be added that it affords a temptation, nay, a premium and justification, on the part of the grantor, to violate those obligations which his own voluntary conveyance imports, and which, in conscience and sound morals, he is bound to hold sacred.

[1] Ibid.

[2] Sterry v. Arden, 1 John. Ch. R. 261, 270, 271; s. c. 12 John. R. 536.

[3] Sterry v. Arden, 12 John. R. 536, 554 to 559.

been asserted in the Supreme Court of the same State at a later period.[1]

428. The question does not seem positively to have been adjudged in Massachusetts. But in an important case of a voluntary conveyance (which was adjudged to be intentionally fraudulent) the court said: 'That deed conveyed his (the grantor's) title to the plaintiff as against the grantor and *every other person*, unless it was *fraudulent* at the time of its execution; in which case it was void against creditors and subsequent purchasers.'[2] From this language it is certainly a just inference that voluntary conveyances, bona fide made, are in that State valid against subsequent purchasers. (a)

429. The Supreme Court of the United States have come to the same conclusion; and it may be fit here to state the grounds of that opinion as given by the Chief Justice in delivering the judgment of the court. 'The statute of Elizabeth is in force in this District [of Columbia]. The rule which has been uniformly

---

[1] Jackson v. Town, 4 Cowen, R. 603, 604. See Seward v. Jackson, 8 Cowen, R. 406; Wilkes v. Clarke, 8 Paige, R. 165.

[2] Ricker v. Ham, 14 Mass. R. 139. And see Mr. Bigelow's note, Big. Dig. Conveyance, p. 200.

(a) The point is now settled in Massachusetts as stated in the text. Beal v. Warren, 2 Gray, 446, where the authorities are examined. Putnam v. Story, 132 Mass. 205, 212; Trafton v. Hawes, 102 Mass. 533, 541; 4 Kent, 463, note. Beal v. Warren decided that a gift when the grantor was not indebted, made in good faith, and without intent to defraud future creditors or subsequent purchasers, is good against a subsequent purchaser for value *with notice*. See also Stone v. Hackett, 12 Gray, 227; Trafton v. Hawes, supra; Black v. Thornton, 31 Ga. 641; Duhme v. Young, 3 Bush, 343; Enders v. Williams, 1 Met. (Ky.) 347 (distinguishing between a voluntary conveyance to children and one to a stranger); Howard v. Snelling, 32 Ga. 195; Aiken v. Bruen, 21 Ind. 137; Chaffin v. Kimball, 23 Ill. 36. Whether the same rule applies to cases of intended fraud on the part of the grantor is not agreed. In Wyman v. Brown, 50 Maine, 139, it is held that conveyances so made are not good against subsequent purchasers for value, though with notice. Contra, Stevens v. Morse, 47 N. H. 532; Gregory v. Haworth, 25 Cal. 653. The question whether the fraudulent conveyance was for value or not may in such a case be deemed material. Coppage v. Barnett, 34 Miss. 621. See Wyman v. Brown, supra. Comp. ante, § 355, note.

It is clear that a purchaser for value without notice may avoid an actually fraudulent conveyance though for value, and a fortiori if voluntary. See Beal v. Warren, supra; Trafton v. Hawes, supra; Pelham v. Aldrich, 8 Gray, 515; Reynolds v. Vilas, 8 Wis. 471; Gardner v. Cole, 21 Iowa, 205; Howard v. Snelling, 32 Ga. 195.

observed by this court in construing statutes is, to adopt the construction made by the courts of the country by whose Legislature
the statute was enacted.   This rule may be susceptible of some
modification when applied to British statutes which are adopted
in any of these States.   By adopting them they become our own
as entirely as if they had been enacted by the Legislature of the
State.   The received construction in England at the time they
were admitted to operate in this country, indeed to the time of
our separation from the British Empire, may very properly be
considered as accompanying the statutes themselves and forming
an integral part of them.   But however we may respect subsequent decisions (and certainly they are entitled to great respect),
we do not admit their absolute authority.   If the English courts
vary their construction of a statute which is common to the two
countries, we do not hold ourselves bound to fluctuate with
them.

431. ' At the commencement of the American Revolution the
construction of the statute of 27th of Elizabeth seems not to
have been settled.   The leaning of the courts towards the opinion
that every voluntary settlement should be deemed void as to a
subsequent purchaser was very strong, and few cases are to be
found in which such a conveyance has been sustained.   But
these decisions seem to have been made on the principle that
such subsequent sale furnished a strong presumption of a fraudulent intent, which threw on the person claiming under the
settlement the burthen of proving it from the settlement itself,
or from extrinsic circumstances, to be made in good faith, rather
than as furnishing conclusive evidence not to be repelled by any
circumstances whatever.

431. ' There is some contrariety and some ambiguity in the
old cases on the subject.   But this court conceives that the
modern decisions establishing the absolute conclusiveness of a
subsequent sale to fix fraud on a family settlement made without valuable consideration — fraud not to be repelled by any
circumstances whatever — go beyond the construction which
prevailed at the American Revolution, and ought not to be
followed.

432. ' The universally received doctrine of that day unquestionably went as far as this.   A subsequent sale without notice,
by a person who had made a settlement not on a valuable con-

sideration, was presumptive evidence of fraud, which threw on those claiming under such settlement the burthen of proving that it was made bona fide. This principle therefore, according to the uniform course of this court, must be adopted in construing the statute of 27th of Elizabeth, as it applies to this case.'[1]

433. The doctrine as to subsequent conveyances of the grantor avoiding prior voluntary conveyances applies in England only to purchasers strictly and properly so called; for as between voluntary conveyances the first prevails, unless the last be for the payment of debts which indeed can scarcely under such circumstances be called voluntary.[2] (a) The doctrine is also to be understood with this qualification, that the first conveyance is bona fide; for if it is fraudulent the second will prevail.[3] But then in cases between different volunteers a Court of Equity will generally not interfere, but will leave the parties where it finds them as to title. It will not aid one against another, neither will it enforce a voluntary contract.[4] (b) It has been said that

[1] Cathcart v. Robinson, 5 Peters, 280.

[2] 1 Fonbl. Eq. B. 1, ch. 4, § 12; Id. B. 1, ch. 5, § 2, and note (h); Jeremy on Equity Jurisd. B. 2, ch. 3, p. 283, § 25; Atherley on Marr. Sett. ch. 13, p. 185; Goodwin v. Goodwin, 1 Ch. Rep. 92 [173]; Clavering v. Clavering, 2 Vern. R. 473; s. c. Prec. Ch. 235; s. c. 1 Bro. Parl. Cas. 122; Villiers v. Beaumont, 1 Vern. 100; Allen v. Arne, 1 Vern. 365; Earl of Bath and Montague's case, 3 Ch. Cas. 88, 89, 93; Chadwill v. Dollman, 2 Vern. 530, 531; Boughton v. Boughton, 1 Atk. 625; Worral v. Worral, 3 Meriv. 256, 269; Sear v. Ashwell, 3 Swanst. 411, note.

[3] Naldred v. Gilham, 1 P. Will. 580, 581; Colton v. King, 2 P. Will. 359 ; Cecil v. Butcher, 2 Jac. & Walk. 573 to 578; 1 Fonbl. Eq. B. 1, ch. 4, § 25; Viers v. Montgomery, 4 Cranch, 177; ante, § 426.

[4] Pulvertoft v. Pulvertoft, 18 Ves. 91, 93, 99; Coleman v. Sarrel, 1 Ves. jr. 52, 54; Ellison v. Ellison, 6 Ves. 656; Antrobus v. Smith, 12 Ves. 39; Ex parte Pye, 18 Ves. 140; Minturn v. Seymour, 4 John. Ch. R. 500; Atherley on Marr. Sett. ch. 13, p. 186; Id. ch. 5, pp. 125, 131 to 145; 1 Fonbl. Eq. B. 1, ch. 4, § 25, and notes (e) and (i); Id. B. 1, ch. 5, § 2, and note (h), § 3; Ex parte Pye, 18 Ves. 149. This doctrine however is to be understood with proper qualifications. If there be a voluntary contract, inter vivos, and some-

(a) Doe d. Richards v. Lewis, 5 Eng. L. & E. 400. See also Ledyard v. Butler, 9 Paige, 132; Ridgway v. Underwood, 4 Wash. 129.

(b) Young v. Young, 80 N. Y. 422. As e. g. a voluntary contract for the creation of a trust so long as it remains executory. Secus if it has become executed by a conveyance in trust.

Stone v. Hackett, 12 Gray, 227; Kekewich v. Manning, 1 DeG. M. & G. 176. In Otis v. Beckwith, 49 Ill. 121, a voluntary assignment of a policy of life assurance in trust in favor of children was upheld against the administrator of the assured though the policy and assignment had been retained by the assured assignor.

there are exceptions, and that they stand upon special grounds ; such as the interference of Courts of Equity in favor of settle-

thing remains to be done to give it effect, as for example if there be a voluntary contract to transfer stock, and the stock is not transferred, a Court of Equity will not enforce the transfer.   But if the stock is actually transferred, then a Court of Equity will enforce all the rights growing out of the transfer against anybody.   Ellison *v.* Ellison, 6 Ves. 662 ; Coleman *v.* Sarrel, 1 Ves. jr. 50 ; Pulvertoft *v.* Pulvertoft, 18 Ves. 91, 93, 99.   So in the case of a voluntary assignment of a bond, even where the bond is not delivered, but is kept in possession of the assignor, a Court of Equity, in the administration of the assets of the assignor, would consider the bond as a debt due to the assignee, no further act remaining to be done by the assignor.   There is a plain distinction between an assignment of stock where the stock has not been transferred, and an assignment of a bond.   In the former case the material act (the transfer) remains to be done by the grantor; and nothing is in fact done which will entitle the assignee to the aid of the court until the stock is transferred; whereas the court will admit the assignee of a bond as a creditor.   Upon this ground where A made a voluntary assignment of a policy upon his own life to trustees for the benefit of his sister and her children if they should outlive him, and he delivered the deed of assignment to one of the trustees, but he kept the policy in his own possession, and afterwards surrendered the policy to the office for a valuable consideration, and afterwards a bill was brought against A by the surviving trustee in the deed to have the policy replaced, it was decreed accordingly.   The court said that the gift of the policy was complete without a delivery; that no act remained to be done by the grantor to complete the title of the trustees; and therefore it was not a case where the court was called upon to assist a volunteer   Fortescue *v.* Barnett, 3 Mylne & Keen, 36.   On the other hand if something remains to be done to give effect to the voluntary act or contract, a Court of Equity will not interfere to aid the party.   Thus where a testator had indorsed upon the back of a bond of his debtor, ' I do hereby forgive the said A. B. the sum of £700, part of the within sum of £1200, for which he is indebted to me,' and afterwards died, and a suit was brought against the debtor at law for the full amount of the bond, and a bill was brought by him against the executor for an injunction to restrain further proceedings in the action on payment of all the sums due on the bond except the £700, the court refused to interfere, saying that the plaintiff gave no consideration for the alleged release, and that as the plaintiff was a mere volunteer he had no right to come into equity for relief. In truth there was no technical valid release at law, and the court was asked to supply this defect.   Tuffnell *v.* Constable, 8 Sim. R. 69.   See Flower *v.* Marten, 2 Mylne & Craig, 459, 474, 475; post, §§ 706, 706 *a.*   Upon similar grounds where an obligee of a bond, five days before her death, signed a memorandum not under seal, which was indorsed on the bond, and which purported to be an assignment of the bond without any consideration, and at the same time delivered the bond to the assignee, it was held by the Lord Chancellor that the circumstances of the case did not constitute it a donatio mortis causa, because it was unconditional; and that the gift was incomplete as an absolute gift; and as it was without consideration, it could not be enforced by the assignee.   Edward *v.* Jones, 1 Mylne & Craig, 226 ; s. c. 7 Sim. R. 325.   See Antrobus *v.* Smith, 12 Ves. R. 39.   See also Duffield *v.* Elwes,

ments upon a wife and children for whom the party is under a natural and moral obligation to provide.[1] (*a*) But although the doctrine in favor of such exceptions has been maintained by highly respectable authority, yet it must be now deemed entirely overthrown by the weight of more recent adjudications in which it has been declared that the court will not execute a voluntary contract, and that the principle of the court to withhold its assistance from a volunteer applies equally whether he seeks to have the benefit of a contract, a covenant, or a settlement.[2] (*b*)

[1] Bligh, R. 493, 529, 530, N. S., where Lord Eldon said: ' The principle which is applied in the decision of this case is the principle upon which Courts of Equity refuse to complete voluntary conveyances. No Court of Equity will compel a completion of them, and throughout the whole of what I have now read the donor is considered as a party who may refuse to complete the intent he has expressed. But I think that is a misapprehension ; because nothing can be more clear than that this donatio mortis causa must be a gift made by a donor in contemplation of the conceived approach of death ; that the title is not complete till he is actually dead; and that the question therefore never can be what the donor can be compelled to do, but what the donee, in the case of a donatio mortis causa, can call upon the representatives, real or personal, of that donor to do. The question is this, whether the act of the donor being, as far as the act of the donor itself is to be viewed, complete, the persons who represent that donor in respect of personalty, the executor, and in respect of realty, the heir-at-law, are not bound to complete that which as far as the act of the donor is concerned in the question was incomplete. In other words where it is the gift of a personal chattel, or the gift of a deed, which is the subject of the donatio mortis causa, whether after the death of the individual who made that gift the executor is not to be considered a trustee for the donee; and whether, on the other hand, if it be a gift affecting the real interest, — and I distinguish now between a security upon land and the land itself, — whether if it be a gift of such an interest in law the heir at law of the testator is not, by virtue of the operation of the trust, which is created, not by indenture but a bequest, arising from operation of law, a trustee for that donee. I apprehend that really the question does not turn at all upon what the donor could do or what the donor could not do. But if it was a good donatio mortis causa, what the donee of that donor could call upon the representatives of the donor to do after the death of that donor.'

[1] 1 Fonbl. Eq. B. 1, ch. 4, § 25, and note (*c*); Id. B. 1, ch. 5, § 2; Atherley on Marr. Sett. ch. 3, pp. 131 to 139; 1 Fonbl. Eq. B. 4, ch. 1, § 7, and note (*r*); Ellis v. Nimmo, Lloyd & Goold, R. 348. But see contra Holloway v. Headington, 8 Simons, R. 325, and Jefferys v. Jefferys, 1 Craig & Phillips, 138, 140 ; in both which cases Ellis *v.* Nimmo seems shaken, if not entirely overthrown. See ante, §§ 95, 169; post, §§ 706, 706 *a*, 787 *a*, 793 *b*, 973, 987, 1040 *b*.

[2] Lord Cottenham in Jefferys v. Jefferys, 1 Craig & Phillips, R. 138, 141; S. P. Holloway v. Headington, 8 Simons, R. 325. See also post, §§ 706, 706 *a*,

(*a*) See Otis *v.* Beckwith, 49 Ill. 121. Gale, 6 Ch. D. 144, 148; Price *v.* Jen-
(*b*) See post, § 987. But see Gale *v.* kins, 4 Ch. D. 483; s. c. 5 Ch. D. 219.

434. But although voluntary conveyances and covenous conveyances may thus, although good between the parties, be set aside and held void as to creditors and purchasers and others whom they may injure in their rights and interests, yet we are not to understand that Courts of Equity grant this relief and interpose in favor of the latter under all circumstances. On the contrary they never do interpose at all where the property has been conveyed by the voluntary and covenous grantee to a bona fide purchaser for a valuable consideration without notice. Such a person is a favorite in the eyes of Courts of Equity, and is always protected (as has been already intimated) against claims of this sort.[1] Indeed in every just sense his equity is equal to that of any other person, whether he be a creditor or a purchaser of the grantor; and where the equity is equal we have seen that the rule applies, 'potior est conditio possidentis.'[2] And where there is a bona fide purchaser from the voluntary or fraudulent grantor, and another from the voluntary or fraudulent grantee, the grantees will have preference according to the priority of their respective titles.[3] (a)

787, 793 b, 973, 987; Tuffnell v. Constable, 8 Sim. R. 69; Meek v. Kettlewell, before Lord Lyndhurst in the (English) Jurist, 23 Dec. 1843, p. 1121.

[1] Com. Dig. Chancery, 4 I. 3, 4 I. 11, 4 W. 29; ante, § 381; Atherley on Marr. Sett. ch. 5, p. 128; ch. 14, p. 238; 2 Fonbl. Eq. B. 3, ch. 3, § 1, and notes; Id. B. 2, ch. 6, § 2; Com. Dig. Covin, B. 3, 4; Chancery, 4 I. 3, 4 I. 4, 4 W. 29; Sugden on Vendors, ch. 16, § 10; Prodgers v. Langham, 1 Sid. R. 123; Parr v. Eliason, 1 East, 92, 95; Sterry v. Arden, 1 John. Ch. R. 261, 271; s. c. 12 John. R. 536; Roberts v. Anderson, 3 John. Ch. R. 377, 378; s. c. 18 John. R. 513; Bean v. Smith, 2 Mason, R. 278, 279, 280; Gore v. Brazier, 3 Mass. R. 541; State of Connecticut v. Bradish, 14 Mass. R. 296; Trull v. Bigelow, 16 Mass. R. 406; ante, §§ 64 c, 108, 139, 381, 409.

[2] 2 Fonbl. Eq. B. 3, § 1; Id. B. 2, ch. 6, § 2; 1 Fonbl. B. 1, ch. 4, § 25; Fletcher v. Peck, 6 Cranch, 87, 133; ante, § 298.

[3] Anderson v. Roberts, 18 John. R. 513; s. c. 3 John. Ch. R. 377, 378; Sands v. Hildreth, 14 John. R. 498. But see Preston v. Croput, 1 Connect. R. 527, note; Sugden on Vendors, ch. 16, § 10.

(a) Another limitation to the general doctrine concerning the Stat. 27 Eliz. has been laid down, to wit, that in order that a subsequent conveyance to a purchaser for value should have the effect to defeat a prior voluntary conveyance, it is necessary that both conveyances should be made by the same person. Hence where a voluntary conveyance had been made by an ancestor in his lifetime, and afterwards his devisee conveyed the same property to a bona fide purchaser for value, it was held that the first conveyance was valid. The court declared that the principle upon which a voluntary conveyance was invalid against subsequent purchasers for value was that

435. The civil law proceeded upon the same enlightened policy. In the case of alienations of movables and immovables bona fide purchasers for a valuable consideration having no knowledge of any fraudulent intent of the grantor or debtor were protected. Ait prætor: 'Quæ fraudationis causa gesta erunt, cum eo qui fraudem non ignoraverit, actionem dabo.'[1]   Upon this there follows this comment: 'Hoc Edictum eum coercet, qui sciens eum in fraudem creditorum hoc facere, suscepit, quod in fraudem creditorum fiebat. Quare, si quid in fraudem creditorum factum sit, si tamen is, qui cepit, ignoravit, cessare videntur verba Edicti.'[2]   And the very case is afterwards put of a bona fide purchaser from a fraudulent grantee, the validity of whose purchase is unequivocally affirmed. 'Is qui a debitore cujus bona possessa sunt, sciens rem emit, iterum alii bona fide ementi vendidit; quæsitum sit, an secundus emptor conveniri potest? Sed verior est Sabini sententia, bona fide emptorem non teneri; quia dolus ei duntaxat nocere debeat, qui eum admisit; quemadmodum diximus, non teneri eum, si ab ipso debitore ignorans emerit. Is autem qui dolo malo emit bona fide autem ementi vendidit, in solidum pretium rei, quod accepit, tenebitur.'[3]   The same doctrine is fully recognized by Voet.[4]   And its intrinsic justice is so persuasive and satisfactory, that whether derived from Roman sources or not it would have been truly surprising not to have found it embodied in the jurisprudence of England.[5]

436. Indeed the principle is more broad and comprehensive;

---

[1] Dig. Lib. 42, tit. 8, l. 1.

[2] Dig. Lib. 42, tit. 8, l. 6, § 8; 1 Domat, B. 2, tit. 10, § 1, art. 3.

[3] Dig. Lib. 42, tit. 8, l. 9; Pothier, Pand. Lib. 42, tit. 8, art. 3, § 25.

[4] 2 Voet, Comm. Lib. 42, tit. 8, § 10, p. 195.

[5] Wilson v. Wormal, Godb. 161; Bean v. Smith, 2 Mason, 279 to 281; Anderson v. Roberts, 18 John. R. 513.

by the second sale the vendor so entirely repudiated the former conveyance as to make it conclusive that the intention to sell existed when he made the voluntary conveyance, and that it was made to defeat the subsequent purchaser (a principle, it should be added, probably false in fact in most cases); which principle could not apply where the two conveyances were by different persons. Doe d. Newman v. Rusham, 17 Q. B. 723; s. c. 9 Eng. L. & E. 410, overruling Jones v. Whittaker, 1 Longf. & T. (Ir.) 14. See Bell v. McCawley, 29 Ga. 355. But a purchaser for value from the administrator of a person who had made a voluntary conveyance may, it is held, avoid the former deed under the statute. Clapp v. Leatherbee, 18 Pick. 131.

and although not absolutely universal (for we have seen that there are anomalies in the case of judgment creditors and the case of dower),[1] yet it is generally true, and applies to cases of every sort where an equity is sought to be enforced against a bona fide purchaser of the legal estate without notice, or even against a bona fide purchaser not having the legal estate, where he has a better right or title to call for the legal estate than the other party.[2] It applies therefore to cases of accident and mistake as well as to cases of fraud, which, however remediable between the original parties, are not relievable as against such purchasers under such circumstances.[3]

437. We have thus gone over the principal grounds upon which Courts of Equity grant relief in matters of accident, mistake, and fraud. In all these cases (to recur to a train of remark already suggested) it may be truly asserted that the remedy and relief administered in Courts of Equity are in general more complete, adequate, and perfect than they can be at common law. The remedy is more complete, adequate, and perfect, because equity uses instruments and proofs not accessible at law, such as an injunction operating to prevent future injustice, and a bill of discovery addressing itself to the conscience of the party in matters of proof. The relief also is more complete, adequate, and perfect, inasmuch as it adapts itself to the special circumstances of each particular case, adjusting all cross equities, and bringing all the parties in interest before the court so as to prevent multiplicity of suits and interminable litigation.[4] Courts of Law on the other hand cannot do more than pronounce a positive judgment in a set formulary for the plaintiff or for the

[1] See ante, §§ 57 a, 108, 381, 410, note; post, §§ 630, 631; 1 Fonbl. Eq. B. 1, ch. 1, § 3, note, p. 22; 2 Fonbl. Eq. B. 2, ch. 6, § 2, notes (h) and (i); Id. B. 3, ch. 3, § 1, note (a); Id. B. 6, ch. 3, § 3, note (i); 1 Fonbl. Eq. B. 1, ch. 1, § 7, note (u); Id. B. 1, ch. 1, § 3, note (f), p. 22; Id. B. 1, ch. 5, § 4; Jeremy on Eq. Jurisd. B. 2, ch. 3, p. 283; Mitford, Pl. Eq. by Jeremy, 274, note (d).

[2] 2 Fonbl. Eq. B. 2, ch. 6, § 2, and note (h); 1 Fonbl. Eq. B. 1, ch. 4, § 25, and note (e); Id. B. 1, ch. 1, § 7; Sugden on Vendors, ch. 16; 2 Chance on Powers, ch. 23, § 1, art. 2859 to 2863; Pomfret v. Windsor, 2 Ves. 472, 486; Medlicott v. O'Donel, 1 B. & Beatt. 171; Ex parte Knott, 11 Ves. 618; Brace v. Duchess of Marlborough, 2 P. Will. 495; ante, §§ 64 c, 108, 139, 381, 409, 411.

[3] Ante, §§ 64 c, 108, 381, 409, 410, 434; post, §§ 630, 631.

[4] See Mitf. Pl. Eq. by Jeremy, pp. 111, 112, 113.

defendant, without professing or attempting to qualify that judgment according to the relative equities of the parties. Thus if a deed is fraudulently obtained without consideration, or for an inadequate consideration, or if by fraud, accident, or mistake a deed is framed contrary to the intention of the parties in their contract on the subject, the forms of proceeding in the Courts of Common Law will not admit of such an investigation of the matter in those courts as will enable them to do justice. The parties claiming under the deed have therefore an advantage in proceeding in a Court of Common Law which it is against conscience they should use. Courts of Equity will (as we have seen) on this very ground interfere to restrain proceedings at law until the matter has been properly investigated. And if it finally appears that the deed has been improperly obtained, or that it is contrary to the intention of the parties in their contract, these courts will in the first case compel a delivery and cancellation of the deed, or order it to be deposited with an officer of the court, and will further direct a reconveyance of the property if it has been so conveyed that a reconveyance may be necessary. In the second case they will either rectify the deed according to the intention of the parties, or they will restrain the use of it in the points in which it has been framed contrary to, or it has gone beyond, their intention in the original contract.[1]

438. In like manner Courts of Equity will (as we have seen) aid defective securities under like circumstances. They will also interfere not only to relieve against instruments which create rights, but against those which destroy rights, such as a release fraudulently or improperly obtained.[2] (a) And finally they will not only prevent the unfair use of any advantage in proceeding in a court of ordinary jurisdiction gained by fraud, accident, or mistake, but they will also, if the consequences of the advantage have been actually obtained, restore the injured party to his rights.[3]

439. The flexibility of Courts of Equity too in adapting their

[1] Mitf. Pl. Eq. by Jeremy, 128, 129; Id. 112, 113.
[2] Mitf. Pl. Eq. by Jeremy, 129, 130.
[3] Id. 131.

(a) For a statement of the principles upon which equity takes jurisdiction in such cases see Rolfe v. Gregory, 4 DeG. J. & S. 579; 1 Perry, Trusts, § 166.

decrees to the actual relief required by the parties, in which
their proceedings form so marked a contrast to the proceedings
at the common law, is illustrated in a striking manner in cases
of accident, mistake, and fraud. If a decree were in all cases required to be given in a prescribed form, the remedial justice
would necessarily be very imperfect, and often wholly beside
the real merits of the case. Accident, mistake, and fraud are
of an infinite variety in form, character, and circumstances, and
are incapable of being adjusted by any single and uniform rule.
Of each of them one might say, 'Mille trahit varios adverso
sole colores.' The beautiful character or pervading excellence,
if one may so say, of Equity Jurisprudence is, that it varies its
adjustments and proportions so as to meet the very form and
pressure of each particular case in all its complex habitudes.
Thus (to present a summary of what has been already stated)
if conveyances or other instruments are fraudulently or improperly obtained, they are decreed to be given up and cancelled.[1]
If they are money securities on which the money has been paid,
the money is decreed to be paid back. If they are deeds or
other muniments of title detained from the rightful party, they
are decreed to be delivered up.[2] If they are deeds suppressed
or spoliated, the party is decreed to hold the same rights as if
they were in his possession and power.[3] If there has been any
undue concealment or misrepresentation or specific promise col-
lusively broken, the injured party is placed in the same situation,
and the other party is compelled to do the same acts as if all
had been transacted with the utmost good faith.[4] If the party
says nothing, but by his expressive silence misleads another
to his injury, he is compellable to make good the loss; and his
own title, if the case requires it, is made subservient to that of
the confiding purchaser.[5] If the party by fraud or misrepresentation induces another to do an act injurious to a third person

[1] See 1 Madd. Ch. Pr. 208, 211, 212, 261; Mitf. Pl. Eq. by Jeremy, 127,
128, 132.

[2] Mitf. Pl. Eq. by Jeremy, 124.

[3] Mitf. Pl. Eq. 117, 118; Jeremy on Eq. Jurisd. B. 3, Pt. 2, ch. 3, §§ 1, 385,
&c.; 1 Madd. Ch. Pr. 211, 258.

[4] 1 Madd. Ch. Pr. 209, 210; 1 Fonbl. Eq. B. 1, ch. 3, § 4, and notes.

[5] 1 Madd. Ch. Pr. 211; 1 Fonbl. Eq. B. 1, ch. 3, § 4, and notes (*m*)
and (*n*).

he is made responsible for it.[1]   If by fraud or misrepresentation he prevents acts from being done, equity treats the case as to him as if it were done, and makes him a trustee for the other.[2] If a will is revoked by a fraudulent deed, the revocation is treated as a nullity.[3]   If a devisee obtains a devise by fraud, he is treated as a trustee of the injured parties.[4]   In all these and many other cases which might be mentioned Courts of Equity undo what has been done if wrong, and do what has been left undone if right.

440. We may conclude this head by calling the attention of the reader to the remark (which has been necessarily intro- duced in another place) that Courts of Equity will exercise a concurrent jurisdiction with Courts of Law in all matters of fraud, excepting only of fraud in obtaining a will, which if of real estate is constantly referred to a Court of Law to decide it, in the shape of an issue of devisavit, vel non, (a) and which if of personal estate is in England cognizable in the Spiritual or Ecclesiastical Courts.[5] (b)   But even in this case the bill may be retained to abide the decision in the proper court, and relief be decreed according to the event.[6]   No other excepted case is known to exist; and it is not easy to discern the grounds upon which this exception stands in point of reason or principle, al- though it is clearly settled by authority.[7]   But where the fraud

---

[1] 3 P. Will. 131, note; Jeremy on Eq. Jurisd. B. 3, ch. 2, § 1, pp. 388, 389.

[2] 1 Madd. Ch. Pr. 552; 1 Jac. & Walk. 96 ; 11 Ves. 638.

[3] 1 Fonbl. Eq. B. 1, ch. 1, § 3, note (f), p. 13; Id. B. 1, ch. 2, § 13, note (q). But see Ambler, R. 215; 3 Bro. Ch. R. 156, note; 7 Ves. 373, 374.

[4] 1 Fonbl. Eq. B. 1, ch. 1, § 3, note (f), p. 13; 2 Fonbl. B. 4, Pt. 1, ch. 1, § 3, and note (g); Mitf. Eq. Pl. by Jeremy, 257.

[5] Ante, §§ 184, 238; Allen v. Macpherson, 5 Beav. R. 469; s. c. on appeal, 1 Phillips, Ch. R. 133.

[6] See ante, § 184, note; and Gaines & Wife v. Chew, 2 Howard, Sup. Ct. R. 619, 645.

[7] Ante, §§ 184, 238, 252, 254; 1 Fonbl. Eq. B. 1, ch. 1, § 3, note (f), p. 13; 2 Fonbl. Eq. B. 4, Pt. 1, ch. 1, § 3, and note (e); Kerrick v. Bransby, 3 Brown, Parl. Cas. 358; 7 Bro. Parl. Cas. by Tomlins, p. 437. See Wild v. Hobson, 2 Ves. & B. 108; Mitf. Pl. Eq. by Jeremy, 257; Barnesly v. Powel, 1 Ves. 284; Id. 119; 1 Madd. Ch. Pr. 206; Jones v. Jones, 7 Price, R. 663; Allen v. Macpherson, 1 Phill. Ch. R. 133.

(a) See Broderick's Will, 21 Wall. 503; Ellis v. Davis, 109 U. S. 485, 494; Gould v. Gould, 3 Story, 516, 537; Archer v. Meadows, 33 Wis. 167; Meluish v. Milton, 3 Ch. D. 27.

(b) Now the Court of Probate.

does not go to the whole will, but only to some particular clause, or where the fraud is in unduly obtaining the consent of the next of kin to the probate, Courts of Equity will lay hold of these circumstances to declare the executor a trustee for the next of kin.[1]

[1] Mitf. Eq. Pl. by Jeremy, 257; Barnesly v. Powel, 1 Ves. 284; Tucker v. Phipps, 3 Atk. R. 360; Allen v. Macpherson, 1 Phill. Ch. R. 133. In this last case many of the former decisions are collected in which Courts of Equity have granted relief in cases of fraud in wills. See the opinion cited at large, ante, § 184, note; and also the other authorities cited in the same note.

CHAPTER VIII.

ACCOUNT.

441. HAVING disposed of these three great heads of concurrent equitable jurisdiction in matters of accident, mistake, and fraud, the undisputed possession of which has belonged to Courts of Equity from the earliest period which can be traced out in our juridical annals, we may now pass to others of a different and less extensive character. We allude to the heads where the jurisdiction, although it may attach upon any or all of the grounds above mentioned, is not necessarily dependent upon them, and in fact is exercised in a variety of cases where they do not apply, upon another distinct ground; namely, that the subject-matter is per se within the scope of equitable jurisdiction. Among these are Matters of Account, and as incident thereto Matters of Apportionment, Contribution, and Average; Liens, Rents and Profits; Tithes, and Moduses, and Waste; Matters of Administration, Legacies, and Marshalling of Assets; Confusion of Boundaries; Matters of Dower; Marshalling of Securities; Matters of Partition; Matters of Partnership; and, lastly, Matters of Rent so far as they are not embraced in the preceding head of Account.

442. Let us begin with matters of ACCOUNT. One of the most ancient forms of action at the common law is the action of account. But the modes of proceeding in that action, although aided from time to time by statutable provisions, were found so very dilatory, inconvenient, and unsatisfactory, that as soon as Courts of Equity began to assume jurisdiction in matters of account, as they did at a very early period, the remedy at law began to decline; and although some efforts have been made in modern times to resuscitate it, it has in England fallen into almost total

disuse.[1] Courts of Equity have for a long time exercised a general
jurisdiction in all cases of mutual accounts, upon the ground of
the inadequacy of the remedy at law, and have extended the
remedy to a vast variety of cases (such as to implied and constructive trusts) to which the remedy at law never was applied.[2] So
that now the jurisdiction extends not only to cases of an equitable nature, but to many cases where the form of the account is
purely legal, and the items constituting the account are founded
on obligations purely legal. Upon such legal obligations however suits, although not in the form of actions of account, yet
in the form of assumpsit, covenant, and debt, are still daily
prosecuted in the Courts of Common Law,[3] and legal defences
are there brought forward. But even in these cases, as the courts
possess no authority to stop the ordinary progress of such suits
for the purpose of subjecting the matters in dispute to the investigation of a more convenient tribunal than a jury, unless the
parties agree to a voluntary arrangement for this purpose the
cause often proceeds to trial in a manner wholly unsuitable to
its real merits.[4] (a)

[1] In Godfrey v. Saunders (3 Wilson, R. 73, 113, 117), which is one of the
few modern actions of account in England, Lord Chief Justice Wilmot said
(p. 117), 'I am glad to see this action of account is revived in this court.'
Mr. Gwillim, in his edition of Bac. Abridg. title, Accompt, p. 31, note (a),
seemed to think that the action of account did not deserve the character
usually given of it. But the Parliamentary Commissioners, in their second
report on the common law (8 March, 1830, pp. 9, 25, 26), have no scruple to
admit its inconvenience and dilatoriness, and that it has gone into disuse. See
also Buller, N. P. 217; 2 Reeves, Hist. of the Law, 73, 178, 337; 3 Reeves,
Hist. L. 388; 4 Reeves, Hist. L. 378; Crousillat v. McCall, 5 Binn. 433; 3
Black. Comm. 164.

[2] See Corporation of Carlisle v. Wilson, 13 Ves. 275; 1 Fonbl. Eq. B. 1,
ch. 1, § 3, note (f), pp. 13, 14; Bac. Abridg. Accompt B.

[3] It was at one time doubted whether an action of assumpsit would lie for
the balance of an account where there are items on both sides. But it is now
fully established that however numerous the items may be, still if there
appears anything due on one side, an action of assumpsit will lie for the balance. Tomkins v. Willshear, 5 Taunt. R. 431; s. c. 1 Marsh, R. 115, and the
cases there cited; 2 Saund. 127, Williams's note (d). The use of the old
action of account is there said to be where the plaintiff wants an account and
cannot give evidence of his right without it. Ibid.

[4] 2 Parl. Common Law Rep. 1830, pp. 25, 26; Wilkin v. Wilkin, Salk. 9;

(a) The decision as to the proper
tribunal is governed largely by the
question of convenience in taking the
accounts. Shepard v. Brown, 4 Giff.
208. Compare Jones v. Newhall, 115
Mass. 244, 251; editor's note to § 33,
ante, near end.

443. The difficulties in the modes of proceeding in actions of account, and the convenience of the modes of proceeding in suits in equity, to attain the ends of substantial justice, are stated in an elementary work of solid reputation, with great clearness and force. The language of the learned author is as follows: ' The proceedings in this action being difficult, dilatory, and expensive, it is now seldom used, especially if the party have other remedy, as debt, covenant, case, or if the demand be of consequence and the matter of an intricate nature; for in such case it is more advisable to resort to a Court of Equity, where matters of accompt are more commodiously adjusted and determined more advantageously for both parties, — the plaintiff being entitled to a discovery of books, papers, and the defendant's oath; and on the other hand the defendant being allowed to discount the sums paid or expended by him, to discharge himself of sums under forty shillings by his own oath, and if by answer or other writing he charges himself, by the same to discharge himself, which will be good if there be no other evidence. Further all reasonable allowances are made to him; and if after the accompt is stated anything be due to him upon the balance, he is entitled to a decree in his favor.' [1]

444. To expound and justify the truth of these remarks, it may be well to take a short review of the old action of account, and to see to what narrow boundaries it was confined and by what embarrassments it was surrounded.

445. At the common law an action of account lay only in cases where there was either a privity in deed by the consent of the party as against a bailiff or receiver appointed by the party, or a privity in law, ex provisione legis, as against a guardian in socage.[2] An exception indeed, or rather an extension of the rule, was for the benefit of trade and the advancement of commerce

---

3 Black. Comm. 184. The Parliamentary Commissioners, in their second report on the common law (8 March, 1830, p. 26), proposed to invest the Courts of Common Law with power to refer such accounts to auditors in such cases; a suggestion which has since been adopted, as indeed it had been adopted before in some of the American States. See Duncan v. Logan, 3 John. Ch. R. 361; Act of Massachusetts, 20th Feb. 1818, ch. 142.

[1] Bac. Abridg. Accompt. See also 1 Eq. Abridg. p. 5, note (a); Anon. 1 Vern. 283; Wicherly v. Wicherly, 1 Vern. 470; Marshfield v. Weston, 2 Vern. 176.

[2] Co. Litt. 90 b; Id. 172 a; 2 Fonbl. Eq. B. 2, ch. 7, § 6, and note; Bac. Abridg. Accompt A.; Com. Dig. Accompt A. 1; 2 Inst. 379.

allowed in favor of and between merchants ; and therefore by the law merchant, one naming himself a merchant might have an account against another naming him a merchant, and charge him as receiver.[1] But in truth in almost every supposable case of this sort there was an established privity of contract. With this exception however (if such it be) the action was strictly confined to bailiffs, receivers, and guardians in socage.[2] So strictly was this privity of contract construed, that the action did not lie by or against executors and administrators. The statute of 13th of Edw. III. ch. 23, gave it to the executors of a merchant; the statute of 25th of Edw. III. ch. 5, gave it to the executors of executors ; and the statute of 31st of Edw. III. ch. 11, to administrators.[3] But it was not until the statute of 3d and 4th of Anne, ch. 16, that it lay against executors and administrators of guardians, bailiffs, and receivers.[4]

446. But in all cases of this latter sort, although there was no remedy at the common law, yet a bill in equity might be maintained for an account against the personal representatives of guardians, bailiffs, and receivers; and such was the usual remedy prior to the remedial statute of Anne.[5] And no action of account lay at the common law against wrong-doers ;[6] or by one joint tenant or tenant in common or his executors or administrators against the other as bailiff for receiving more than his share, or against his executors or administrators, unless there was some special contract between them whereby the one made the other his bailiff; for the relation itself was held not to create any privity of contract by operation of law.[7] This defect was afterwards cured by the statute of 3d and 4th of Anne, ch. 16.[8] The

[1] Co. Litt. 172 a; Earl of Devonshire's Case, 11 Co. R. 89.

[2] Buller's N. P. 127; 1 Eq. Abridg. 5, note (a) ; 2 Fonbl. Eq. B. 2, ch. 7, § 6, and note (n); Co. Litt. 172 a; 2 Inst. 379; Sargent v. Parsons, 12 Mass. R. 149.

[3] Co. Litt. 90 b; 2 Fonbl. Eq. B. 2, ch. 7, § 6, and note (n).

[4] Ibid. ; Bull. N. P. 127; Earl of Devonshire's Case, 11 Co. R. 89.

[5] 2 Fonbl. Eq. B. 2, ch. 7, § 6, note (n); 1 Eq. Abridg. 5, note (a).

[6] Bac. Abridg. Accompt B. We shall presently see that Courts of Equity frequently administer relief in cases of account against wrong-doers. See Bac. Abridg. Accompt B.; Bosanquet v. Dashwood, Cas. T. Talb. 38, 41.

[7] Co. Litt. 172, and Harg. note (8); Co. Litt. 186 a, 119 b, and Harg. note (83); Wheeler v. Horne, Willes, R. 208; 2 Fonbl. Eq. B. 2, ch. 7, § 6, note (n); Bac. Abridg. Accompt A.; 1 Saund. R. 216, Williams's note.

[8] Ibid.; 3 Black. Comm. 164.

common law was strict as to who was to be accounted a bailiff or receiver; for a bailiff was understood to be one who had the administration and charge of lands, goods, and chattels, to make the best benefit for the owner, and against whom therefore an action of account would lie for the profits which he had made, or might by his industry or care have reasonably made, his reasonable charges and expenses being deducted.[1] A receiver was one who received money to the use of another to render an account; but upon his account he was not allowed his expenses and charges, except in the case of merchant receivers. And this exception was provided (as it was said) by the law of the land in favor of merchants and for the advancement of trade and traffic.[2] So that it will be at once perceived from these cases (and many others might be mentioned)[3] that the remedy at the common law was very narrow; and although it was afterwards enlarged, that would not of itself displace the jurisdiction originally vested in Courts of Equity.

446 *a*. In the next place as to the modes of proceeding in actions of account. At the common law, before either the statute of Marlebridge, ch. 23, or of Westminster 2d, ch. 11, there were two methods of proceedings against an accountant : one by which the party to whom he was accountable might by consent of the accountant either take the account himself or assign an auditor or auditors to take it, and then have his action of debt for the arrearages; or in more modern times an action on the case, or insimul computassent. And the accountant, if aggrieved, might have his writ of ex parte talis, to re-examine the account in the Exchequer. The other proceeding of the plaintiff was, in the first instance, by way of a writ of account. The process by which this latter remedy might be made more effectual is particularly described in the statute of Marlebridge and the statute of Westminster 2d, upon which it is unnecessary to dwell.[4]

447. In the action of account there are two distinct courses of proceeding. In the first place the party may interpose any

---

[1] Co. Litt. 172 *a*; 2 Fonbl. Eq. B. 2, ch. 7, § 6, and note (*n*).

[2] Co. Litt. 172 *a*.

[3] See Bac. Abridg. Accompt B., C.; Com. Dig. Accompt A., B., D.; 3 Reeves, Hist. Law, 337, 338, 339; 3 Reeves, Hist. Law, 75; 4 Reeves, Hist. Law, 388.

[4] Com. Dig. Accompt A. and note (*a*); 3 Reeves, Hist. Law, 75, 76.

matter in abatement or bar of the proceeding, and if he fails in it then there is an interlocutory judgment that he shall account (quod computet) before auditors.[1] After this judgment is entered it is the duty of the court to assign auditors, who are armed with authority to convene the parties before them de die in diem, at any time or place they shall appoint, until the accounting is determined. The time by which the account is to be settled is prefixed by the court. But if the account be of a long or confused nature, the court will, upon the application of the parties, enlarge the time. In taking the account the auditors in an action of account at the common law could not administer an oath except in one or two particular cases. But under the statute of 3d and 4th Anne, ch. 16, the auditors are empowered to administer an oath and examine the parties touching the matters in question in cases within that act.[2]

448. If in the progress of the cause before the auditors when the items are successively brought under review, any controversy should arise before the auditors as to charging or discharging any items, the parties have a right, if the points involve matters of fact, to make up and join issues upon such items respectively; and if the points involve matters in law, they have a right in like manner to put in and join demurrers upon each distinct item. These issues, when so made up, are to be certified by the auditors to the court; and then the matters of law will be decided by the court, and the matters of fact will be directed to be tried by a jury, after which the accounts are to be settled by the auditors according to the results of these trials. From this circumstance the proceedings before the auditors are often tedious, expensive, and inconvenient.[3] And indeed as different points both of fact and law may arise in different stages of the suit, and in different examinations before the auditors as well after as before such issues have been joined and tried, it ought not to be surprising that the cause should be procrastinated for a great length of time by its transition from one tribunal to another, for the various purposes

---

[1] 3 Black. Comm. 164; O'Conner v. Spaight, 1 Sch. & Lefr. 309.

[2] Co. Litt. 199, and Harg. note (83); Wheeler v. Horne, Willes, R. 208, 210; 1 Selwyn, N. P. 6; Buller, N. P. 127; Bac. Abridg. Wager of Law, C.

[3] Ex parte Bax, 2 Ves. 388; Bac. Abridg. Accompt F.; Bull. N. P. 127, 128; Crousillat v. McCall, 5 Binn. 433; Com. Dig. Accompt E. 11; Yelverton, R. 202, Metcalf's note (1).

incident to a due settlement of its merits. And besides these difficulties there are many actions of account in which the defendant may wage his law, and thus escape from answering his adversary's claim.[1]

449. This summary view of the modes of proceeding in the action of account is sufficient to show that it was a very unfit instrument to ascertain and adjust the real merits of long, complicated, and cross accounts. In the first place it was inapplicable to a vast variety of cases of equitable claims, of constructive trusts, of fraudulent contrivances, and of tortious misconduct.[2] In the next place there was a want of due power to draw out the proper proofs from the party's own conscience, so that if evidence aliunde was unattainable, there was and there could be no effective redress.[3] And it has been well observed by Mr. Justice Blackstone that, notwithstanding all the legislative provisions in aid of the common-law action of account, 'It is found by experience that the most ready and effectual way to settle these matters of account is by a bill in a Court of Equity, where a discovery may be had on the defendant's oath, without relying merely on the evidence which the plaintiff may be able to produce.'[4]

---

[1] Com. Dig. Pleader, 2 W. 45; Co. Litt. 90 *b*; Ib. 295 *b*; 2 Saund. Rep. 65 *a*; Archer's Case, Cro. Eliz. 579; Bac. Abridg. Wager of Law, D., G.

[2] See 1 Fonbl. B. 1, ch. 1, § 3, note (*f*), pp. 13, 14; 2 Fonbl. Eq. B. 2, ch. 7, § 67.

[3] Mr. Chancellor Kent, in Duncan *v.* Lyon (3 John. Ch. R. 361), said: 'I have not been able to find any good reason why that action [account] has so totally fallen into disuse,' assigning as a ground of his remark, that 'in that action the auditors have all the requisite powers; for they can compel the parties to account and be examined under oath.' If what is stated in the text be correct, it is manifest that the action of account, as administered in England, cannot be admitted to be an equivalent for a Court of Equity. It is perhaps uncertain whether the learned Chancellor did not mean to confine his remarks to the actual state of the action in New York. See on this point the opinion of the same learned judge in Ludlow *v.* Simond, 2 Cain. Cas. Err. 52, 53.

[4] 3 Black. Comm. 164; ante, § 67. Lord Redesdale, in Attorney-Gen. *v.* Mayor, &c. of Dublin, 1 Bligh, R. N. S. 336, 337, gives a summary statement of the old action of account, and of the reasons of its discontinuance. He said: 'There has not been in this case a sufficient investigation of the ancient law and practice on the subject of account. It seems to have been conceived that the common law had provided sufficient means for calling to account all persons liable to account. But it was found by experience that the writ of account was a very imperfect and inefficient mode of proceeding. In the case of an individual there can be no doubt that if a person had received the rents

450. Courts of Equity in suits of this nature proceed in many respects in analogy to what is done at law. The cause is referred to a master (acting as an auditor), before whom the account is taken ; and he is armed with the fullest powers not only to examine the parties on oath, but to make all the inquiries by testimony under oath, and by documents and books and vouchers, to be produced by the parties, which are necessary for the due administration of justice. And when his report is made to the court, any objections which have been made before the master, and any exceptions taken to his report, may be re-examined by the court at the instance of the parties, and the whole case is moulded as ex æquo et bono may be required.[1] The court may besides bring all the proper parties in interest before it, where there are different parties concerned in interest ; and if any doubt arises upon any particular demand, it may direct the same to be ascertained by an issue and verdict at law.[2] So that there cannot be any real doubt that the remedy in equity in cases of account is generally more complete and adequate than it is or can be at law.[3]

of an estate belonging to a minor for which he would be accountable, the law provided a writ to call such person to account, and to compel payment of what should be found due upon the account. Yet it is every day's practice, although the common law has provided this remedy, for Courts of Equity to take upon themselves the investigation of accounts on behalf of infants suing by their next friends. The writ of account at common law did not exclude but rather was superseded by the jurisdiction of the Courts of Equity on this subject; because the proceeding in equity was found to be the more convenient mode of calling parties to account, — partly on account of the difficulty attending the process under the old writ of account, but chiefly from the advantage of compelling the party to account upon oath, according to the practice of Courts of Equity. There is on this subject a writ in the Register (Reg. Brev. p. 138), which recites that the King had been given to understand that his predecessors had granted certain rates on all merchandise brought into a town, to be applied to the walling of the town, and the inhabitants having complained that the rates collected had not been duly applied, the writ proceeds in the nature of a commission for taking the account. Under such circumstances an information at this moment would lie at the suit of the Attorney-General for taking such account. The practice of proceeding by information rather than by the writ of account has prevailed in consequence of the difficulty of proceeding under the writ. That persons under such circumstances should be rendered accountable by virtue of the writ, is said to be according to the law and custom of England.'

[1] Ex parte Bax, 2 Ves. 388.

[2] 1 Eq. Abridg. A., p. 5, note (a).

[3] See Mitford on Eq. Pl. by Jeremy, 120; Corporation of Carlisle v. Wilson, 13 Ves. 278, 279 ; ante, § 67.

451. This has accordingly been considered in modern times as the true foundation of the jurisdiction.[1] Mr. Justice Blackstone has indeed placed it upon the sole ground of the right of Courts of Equity to compel a discovery. 'For want,' said he, ' of this discovery at law, the Courts of Equity have acquired a concurrent jurisdiction with every other court in matters of account.'[2] But this although a strong yet is not the sole ground of the jurisdiction. The whole machinery of Courts of Equity is better adapted to the purpose of an account in general, and in many cases independent of the searching power of discovery, and supposing a Court of Law to possess it, it would be impossible for the latter to do entire justice between the parties ; for equitable rights and claims not cognizable at law are often involved in the contest.[3] Lord Redesdale has justly said that in a complicated account a Court of Law would be incompetent to examine it at Nisi Prius with all the necessary accuracy.[4] This is the principle on which Courts of Equity constantly act by taking cognizance of matters which though cognizable at law are yet so involved with a complex account that it cannot be properly taken at law ; (a) and until the result of the account is known, the justice of the case cannot appear.[5] Matters of account, he has added, may indeed be made the subject of an action ; but an account of this sort is not a proper subject for this mode of proceeding. The old mode of proceeding upon the writ of account shows it. The only judg-

[1] Jeremy on Eq. Jurisd. B. 3, Pt. 2, ch. 5, p. 504; Mitf. Eq. Pl. by Jeremy, 120; Ludlow v. Simond, 2 Cain. Cas. Err. 38, 52; Rathbone v. Warren, 10 John. R. 595, 596; Post v. Kimberly, 9 John. R. 493; Duncan v. Lyon, 3 John. Ch. R. 361.

[2] 3 Black. Comm. 437.   See also 1 Fonbl. Eq. B. 1, ch. 1, § 3, note (f), p. 12.   Mr. Fonblanque too seems to consider that the greater portion of the concurrent jurisdiction of Courts of Equity stands upon a similar ground; for he says that the Courts of Equity having acquired cognizance of the suit, for the purposes of discovery, will entertain it for the purpose of relief in most cases of fraud, account, accident, and relief.   1 Fonbl. Eq. B. 1, ch. 1, § 3, note (f), p. 12.   This might justify the jurisdiction, but it does not appear to me to include the whole ground on which it is maintainable.   Mr. Justice Blackstone also traces to the same compulsive power of discovery the jurisdiction of Courts of Equity in all matters of fraud.   3 Black. Comm. 439. This, as the original or sole ground for the jurisdiction in matters of fraud, admits of still more question.   [3] Ante, § 67.

[4] O'Conner v. Spaight, 1 Sch. & Lefr. 309.   See White v. Williams, 8 Ves. 193; Mitf. Eq. Pl. by Jeremy, 119, 120.

[5] O'Conner v. Spaight, 1 Sch. & Lefr. 309; Id. 205; Mitf. Eq. Pl. by Jeremy, 120; Jeremy on Eq. Jurisd. B. 3, Pt. 2, ch. 5, p. 504.

(a) See Harrington v. Churchward, 6 Jur. N. s. 576.

ment was that the party should account; and then the account was taken by the auditors. The court never went into it.[1]

452. It is not improbable that originally in cases of account which might be cognizable at law, Courts of Equity interfered upon the special ground of accident, mistake, or fraud. If so, the ground was very soon enlarged, and embraced mixed cases not governed by these matters. The courts soon arrived at the conclusion that the true principle upon which they should entertain suits for an account in matters cognizable at law was, that either a Court of Law could not give any remedy at all, or not so complete a remedy as Courts of Equity. And the moment this principle was adopted in its just extent, the concurrent jurisdiction became almost universal, and reached almost instantaneously its present boundaries.[2]

453. In virtue of this general jurisdiction in matters of account Courts of Equity exercise a very ample authority over matters apparently not very closely connected with it; but which naturally if not necessarily attach to such a jurisdiction. Mr. Justice Blackstone has said: ' As incident to accounts, they take a concurrent cognizance of the administration of personal assets; consequently of debts, legacies, the distribution of the residue, and the conduct of executors and administrators. As incident to accounts they also take the concurrent jurisdiction of tithes and all questions relating thereto, of all dealings in partnership, and many other mercantile transactions; and so of bailiffs, factors, and receivers. It would be endless to point out all the several avenues in human affairs, and in this commercial age, which lead to or end in accounts.' [3] But it is far from being admitted that the sole origin of equity jurisdiction on these subjects arises from this source. It is one, but not the sole source. In many of these cases, as well as in others which will hereafter be considered, in which accounts may be taken as incidents to the relief granted, there are other distinct if not independent sources of jurisdiction; and especially one source which is the peculiar attribute of Courts of Equity, — the jurisdiction over trusts not merely express, but implied and constructive.[4]

---

[1] Ibid.; Cooper, Eq. Pl. 134.

[2] Ante, § 67; Corporation of Carlisle v. Wilson, 13 Ves. 278.

[3] 3 Black. Comm. 437.

[4] Jeremy on Eq. Jurisd. B. 3, Pt. 2, ch. 5, pp. 522, 523, 543; 1 Fonbl. Eq. B. 1, ch. 1, § 3, note (f); 2 Fonbl. Eq. B. 2, ch. 7, § 6, and notes.

454. One of the most difficult questions arising under this head (and which has been incidentally discussed in another place)[1] is to ascertain whether there are any, and if any, what are the true boundaries of equity jurisdiction in such matters of account as are cognizable at law. We say cognizable at law ; for wherever the account stands upon equitable claims, or has equitable trusts attached to it, there is no doubt that the jurisdiction is absolutely universal and without exception, since the party is remediless at law.[2]

455. But in cases where there is a remedy at law there is no small confusion and difficulty in the authorities. The jurisdiction in matters of this sort has been asserted to be maintainable upon two grounds, distinct in their own nature and yet often running into each other.[3] In the first place it has been asserted that where in a matter of account the party seeks a discovery of facts and these appear upon his bill to be material to his right of recovery, there, if the answer does in fact make a discovery of such material facts (for it would be no ground of jurisdiction if the discovery failed),[4] the court having once a rightful jurisdiction of the cause ought to proceed to give relief in order to avoid

[1] Ante, § 67.
[2] Jeremy on Eq. Jurisd. B. 3, Pt. 2, ch. 5, pp. 504, 505, 506.
[3] See ante, §§ 64 to 69, and note to § 69; Corporation of Carlisle v. Wilson, 13 Ves. 278, 279. Lord Chancellor Erskine, in Corporation of Carlisle v. Wilson, 13 Ves. 278, 279, maintained the concurrent jurisdiction of Courts of Equity in matters of account to a very broad extent. He said: ' The principle upon which Courts of Equity originally entertained suits for an account, where the party had a legal title, is, that though he might support a suit at law, a Court of Law either cannot give a remedy or cannot give so complete a remedy as a Court of Equity; and by degrees Courts of Equity assumed a concurrent jurisdiction in cases of account; for it cannot be maintained that this court interferes only when no remedy can be had at law. The contrary is notorious.' ' The proposition asserted against this bill is, that this court ought to refuse to interfere by directing an account, if an action for money had and received, or an indebitatus assumpsit, can be maintained. That proposition cannot be maintained,' &c. ' The proposition is not that an account may be decreed in every case where an action for money had and received, or indebitatus assumpsit, may be brought (and certainly indebitatus assumpsit lies for tolls); but that, where the subject cannot be so well investigated in those actions, this court exercises a sound discretion in decreeing an account.' See what was said by Mr. Vice-Chancellor Wigram in Pearce v. Cresswick, 2 Hare, R. 286, 293, cited ante, § 64 k, note.
[4] Ante, §§ 71, 74; Russell v. Clarke's Ex'rs, 7 Cranch, 69 ; Dinwiddie v. Bailey, 6 Ves. 140, 141.

multiplicity of suits.[1] And this plain ground is asserted by the
learned author of the Treatise of Equity in a passage already
cited; and it has been often maintained in the English Courts
of Equity.[2] But (as we have already seen)[3] there are other authorities in the English courts which conflict with this doctrine,
and which, without attempting to lay down any rule for a practical discrimination as to cases within and cases without the jurisdiction, seem to deliver over the subject to interminable doubts.[4]

456. The doctrine now generally (perhaps not universally)
held in America is (as we have seen),[5] that in all cases where a
Court of Equity has jurisdiction for discovery, and the discovery
is effectual, that becomes a sufficient foundation upon which the
court may proceed to grant full relief.   In other words where
the court has legitimately acquired jurisdiction over the cause
for the purpose of discovery it will, to prevent multiplicity of
suits, entertain the suit also for relief.[6] (a)

[1] Ryle v. Haggie, 1 Jac. & Walk. 237.

[2] 1 Fonbl. Eq. B. 1, ch. 1, § 3, note (f); ante, §§ 64, 66; 2 Fonbl. Eq.
B. 6, ch. 3, § 6; Lee v. Alston, 1 Bro. Ch. R. 195, 196; Barker v. Dacie, 6 Ves.
688; Corporation of Carlisle v. Wilson, 13 Ves. 278, 279.

[3] Ante, §§ 64 k, 65, 66; 1 Fonbl. Eq. B. 1, ch. 3, note (f); note (r); Parker
v. Dee, 2 Ch. Cas. 200, 201; 1 Eq. Abridg. A., p. 5; 2 Eq. Abridg. A., p. 4;
Ryle v. Haggie, 1 Jac. & Walk. 237.

[4] See ante, §§ 64 to 69, and note to § 69. Many of the cases on this
head have been already commented on at large in note 1 to § 69.   The difficulty of reconciling the authorities is very great.   Is there any distinction
between cases of account founded in privity, and those founded in tort (such
as a waste, &c.)?

[5] Ante, §§ 67, 71, 74; Middletown Bank v. Russ, 3 Connect. R. 135.

[6] See ante, §§ 64 to 69, 71; Armstrong v. Gilchrist, 2 John. Cas. 424;
Rathbone v. Warren, 10 John. R. 587; King v. Baldwin, 17 John. R. 384;
Ludlow v. Simond, 2 Cain. Cas. Err. 1, 38, 39, 51, 52; Stanley v. Cramer,
4 Cowen, R. 727, 728.   In Fowle v. Lawrason, 5 Peters, Sup. Ct. R. 495, Mr.
Chief Justice Marshall, in delivering the opinion of the court, said: 'That a
Court of Chancery has jurisdiction in matters of account cannot be questioned,
nor can it be doubted that this jurisdiction is often beneficially exercised; but
it cannot be admitted that a Court of Equity may take cognizance of every
action, for goods, wares, and merchandise sold and delivered, or of money
advanced, where partial payments have been made, or of every contract,
express or implied, consisting of various items, on which different sums of
money have become due and different payments have been made.   Although
the line may not be drawn with absolute precision, yet it may be safely affirmed
that a Court of Chancery cannot draw to itself every transaction between individuals in which an account between parties is to be adjusted.   In all cases in

(a) See Russell v. Madden, 95 Ill. 485; ante, pp. 78–81, note.

457. Another and more general ground has been asserted for the jurisdiction; and that is, not that there is not a remedy at law, but that the remedy is more complete and adequate in equity, and besides that it prevents a multiplicity of suits. This is indeed a very broad and general ground of jurisdiction; and especially as applied to cases founded in privity of contract, where it is contemplated that the matter should give rise to an account.[1] (a)　Upon this ground Lord Hardwicke expressed himself in favor of the jurisdiction generally in a case then before him, saying, 'It is a matter of contract and account and consequently a proper subject for the jurisdiction of this court.'[2]　And this is manifestly the doctrine maintained by Lord Redesdale, who said that in matters of account, 'A Court of Equity will entertain jurisdiction of a suit, though a remedy might perhaps be had in the Courts of Common Law. The ground upon which Courts of Equity first interfered in these cases seems to have been the difficulty of proceeding to the full extent of justice in the Courts of Common Law.'　And in a note it is added, 'Perhaps in some of these cases the jurisdiction was first assumed to prevent multiplicity of suits.'[3] (b)　He subsequently said: 'The

which an action of account would be the proper remedy at law, and in all cases where a trustee is a party, the jurisdiction of a Court of Equity is undoubted. It is the appropriate tribunal. But in transactions not of this peculiar character, great complexity ought to exist in the accounts, or some difficulty at law should interpose, some discovery should be required, in order to induce a Court of Chancery to exercise jurisdiction. 1 Madd. Chan. 86; 6 Ves. 136; 9 Ves. 437. In the case at bar these difficulties do not occur. The plaintiff sues on a contract by which real property is leased to the defendant, and admits himself to be in full possession of all the testimony he requires to support his action. The defendant opposes to this claim, as an offset, a sum of money due to him for goods sold and delivered, and for money advanced, no item of which is alleged to be contested. We cannot think such a case proper for a Court of Chancery.'

[1] Jeremy on Eq. Jurisd. B. 3, Pt. 2, ch. 5; Barker v. Dacie, 6 Ves. 688; 3 Black. Comm. 437.

[2] Billon v. Hyde, 1 Atk. 127, 128.

[3] Mitford on Eq. Pl. by Jeremy, 119, 120; Barker v. Dacie, 6 Ves. 688; Mackenzie v. Johnston, 4 Madd. R. 374.

(a) See Shepard v. Brown, 4 Giff. 208; Smith v. Laveaux, 2 DeG. J. & S. 1; Flockton v. Peake, 12 Week. R. 562; Dabbs v. Nugent, 11 Jur. N. s. 943; Birmingham Gas Co. v. Ratcliffe, L. R. 6 Ex. 224; Badger v. McNamara, 123 Mass. 117.

(b) See White v. Hampton, 10 Iowa, 238; Wilson v. Riddle, 48 Ga. 609; Biddle v. Ranney, 52 Mo. 153.

Courts of Equity having gone the length of assuming jurisdiction in a variety of complicated cases of account, &c., seem by degrees to have been considered as having on these subjects a concurrent jurisdiction with the Courts of Common Law in cases where no difficulty could have attended the proceedings in those courts.' [1] In cases of mutual (*a*) accounts founded in privity of contract this doctrine is, in the English courts, acted upon in the most ample manner in our day without any limitation,[2] as it certainly is fully maintained in America.[3] (*b*)

458. Courts of Equity will also entertain jurisdiction in matters of account not only when there are mutual accounts, but also when the accounts to be examined are on one side only, and a discovery is wanted in aid of the account and is obtained.[4] (*c*)

[1] Mitf. Eq. Pl. by Jeremy, 123. See also O'Conner *v.* Spaight, 1 Sch. & Lefr. 309; Barker *v.* Dacie, 6 Ves. 688; Corporation of Carlisle *v.* Wilson, 13 Ves. 276; Coop. Eq. Pl. Introd. 31; Duke of Leeds *v.* Radnor, 2 Bro. Ch. R. 338, 518.

[2] Dinwiddie *v.* Bailey, 6 Ves. 140, 141; 2 Parl. Rep. of Common Law Commissioners, 1830, p. 26; Courtenay *v.* Godshall, 9 Ves. 473.

[3] Armstrong *v.* Gilchrist, 2 John. Cas. 424; Rathbone *v.* Warren, 10 John. R. 587; King *v.* Baldwin, 17 John. R 384; Ludlow *v.* Simond, 2 Cain. Cas. Err. 1, 38, 39, 51, 52; Post *v.* Kimberly, 9 John. R. 493; Hawley *v.* Cramer, 4 Cowen, R. 727, 728; 2 Parl. Report of the Common Law Commissioners, 1830, p. 26; Porter *v.* Spencer, 2 John. Ch. R. 171.

[4] Barker *v.* Dacie, 6 Ves. 687, 688; Frietas *v.* Don Santos, 1 Y. & Jerv. 574; Courtenay *v.* Godshall, 9 Ves. 473; Mackenzie *v.* Johnston, 4 Madd. R. 374; Massey *v.* Banner, 4 Madd. R. 416, 417; Ludlow *v.* Simond, 2 Cain. Cas. Err. 1, 38, 52; Post *v.* Kimberly, 9 John. R. 470, 493. The Vice-Chancellor (Sir John Leach) has held generally that in all cases of agency a bill will lie in equity for an account by the principal against his agent. Mackenzie *v.* Johnston, 4 Madd. R. 374; Massey *v.* Banner, 4 Madd. R. 416. The ground seems to be, though not explicitly stated by him, that there being a necessity for a discovery, the relief is consequent on that; and that it would be most unreasonable that he should pay his agent for a discovery, and then be turned round to a suit at law, which would be the case if he could not have relief on his bill. The case of Hoare *v.* Contencin (1 Bro. Ch. R. 27) is distinguishable; for there the bill was to recover back money lent, and no discovery seemed necessary. Lord Thurlow there said: 'As to an account, this is only of a repayment of money, and that the money for which the teas sold should be deducted. As it

(*a*) See Haywood *v.* Hutchins, 65 N. Car. 574 (as to disconnected accounts of both parties); Frue *v.* Loring, 120 Mass. 507.

(*b*) Mere complication of accounts, without any relation of trust, is enough to give equity jurisdiction. Kimberley *v.* Dick, L. R. 13 Eq. 1; Watford Ry. Co. *v.* London Ry. Co., L. R. 8 Eq. 231; Seymour *v.* Long Dock Co., 5 C. E. Green, 396.

(*c*) Dallas *v.* Timberlake, 54 Ala. 403.

But in such a case if no discovery is asked or required by the frame of the bill, the jurisdiction will not be maintainable.[1]   And a fortiori where there are no mutual demands but a single matter on one side, and no discovery is required, a Court of Equity will not entertain jurisdiction of the suit, although there may be payments on the other side which may be set off; for in such a case there is not only a complete remedy at law, but there is nothing requiring the peculiar aid of equity to ascertain or adjust the claim.[2]   To found the jurisdiction in cases of a claim of this sort there should be a series of transactions on one side and of payments on the other.

458 a. So it has been said that 'if there be a bill for an account in respect of particular items or any number of particular items, and the plaintiff fails in sustaining the demand upon those particular items, and the bill happens to contain a general vague charge that there are voluminous and intricate accounts between the parties, and which charge is inserted merely as a pretext for the purpose of bringing the case within the jurisdiction of a Court of Equity, the court in so vague and uncertain a case will disregard that general allegation, will consider it as struck out of the bill, and not allow it to protect the bill against a demurrer for want of equity.' [3]

stood originally therefore the bill could not have been supported.'   In Frietas v. Don Santos (1 Y. & Jerv. 574) the Court of Exchequer said: 'It is the settled practice at this time that if a bill be filed for a discovery the relief is made ancillary to it; and the party must stand or fall by the discovery, &c.   It is not every account which will entitle a Court of Equity to interfere.   It must be such an account as cannot be taken, justly and fairly, in a Court of Law.' The same doctrine was asserted in King v. Rossett (2 Y. & Jerv. 33), which was a bill by a principal against his agent for discovery and relief.   Lord Chief Baron Comyns, in his invaluable Digest (Chancery, 2 A.), lays down the principle broadly upon his own authority that 'chancery will oblige any one to give an account for money by him received.'

[1] Dinwiddie v. Bailey, 6 Ves. 136; Frietas v. Don Santos, 1 Y. & Jerv. 574; King v. Rossett, 2 Y. & Jerv. 33; Cooper, Eq. Pl. 134; but see Mackenzie v. Johnston, 4 Madd. R. 374; Massey v. Banner, 4 Madd. R. 416; Com. Dig. Chancery, 2 A.

[2] Wells v. Cooper, cited in Dinwiddie v. Bailey, 6 Ves. 139; Foster v. Spencer, 2 John. Ch. R. 171; Moses v. Lewis, 12 Price, R. 502; King v. Rossett, 2 Y. & Jerv. 33; 1 Madd. Ch. Pr. 70, 71.

[3] Darthez v. Clemens, 6 Beav. R. 165, 169.   On this occasion Lord Langdale said: ' It therefore comes to this, Does this bill contain such vague and general statements, — statements put in merely as a pretext for transferring the jurisdiction from the Court of Law to this court?   If the account can be fairly

459. So that on the whole it may be laid down as a general
doctrine that in matters of account growing out of privity of
contract Courts of Equity have a general jurisdiction where
there are mutual accounts (and a fortiori where these accounts
are complicated), (a) and also where the accounts are on one
side, but a discovery is sought and is material to the relief.[1]
And on the other hand where the accounts are all on one side
and no discovery is sought or required, and also where there is
a single matter on the side of the plaintiff seeking relief, and
mere set-offs on the other side and no discovery is sought or required, — in all such cases Courts of Equity will decline taking
jurisdiction of the cause.[2] (b)   The reason is, that no peculiar
remedial process or functions of a Court of Equity are required ;
and if under such circumstances the court were to entertain the
suit, it would merely administer the same functions in the same
way as a Court of Law would in the suit.   In short it would act
as a Court of Law.

459 a. In matters of account where several debts are due by
the debtor to the creditor, it often becomes material to ascertain to what debt a particular payment made by the debtor is to
be applied.   This is called in our law the appropriation of
payments.   It is called in the foreign law the imputation of

taken in a Court of Common Law, this court will not interfere, even in the
case of merchants' accounts consisting of mutual dealings; but in this case I
am persuaded not only that the accounts between these parties could not be
advantageously taken in a Court of Law, but that they could not be taken at
all there.   Everybody knows how an action upon such an account would necessarily end; it would end in the account being taken in this court or by a
reference.'

[1] Mackenzie v. Johnston, 4 Madd. R. 374; Massey v. Banner, 4 Madd. R.
416, 417; Pendleton v. Wambersie, 4 Cranch, R. 73.

[2] See ante, § 458, and cases there cited.   But see Com. Dig. Chancery,
2 A.

(a) Boyd v. Lewis, 42 Ga. 626;
Southampton Dock Co. v. Southampton Board, L. R. 11 Eq. 254.

(b) Frue v. Loring, 120 Mass. 507;
Appeal of Passyunk Build. Assoc. 83
Penn. St. 441; Smith v. Laveaux, 2
DeG. J. & S. 1; Scott v. Liverpool,
5 Jur. N. s. 105.   But as to this last
case see Jurist, March 26, 1859.   It
is there shown that jurisdiction rests
on one of the three following grounds:
(1) Mutual accounts; (2) Dealing so
complicated that they cannot properly be adjusted in a court of law;
(3) The existence of a fiduciary relation between the parties.   See Badger
v. McNamara, 123 Mass. 117; Avery
v. Ware, 58 Ala. 475; Knotts v. Tar-
ver, 8 Ala. 743.

payments,[1] a phrase apparently borrowed from the Roman law, where the doctrine of the appropriation of payments is carefully examined and the leading distinctions applicable to it amply discussed.[2]   The doctrine may of course find a place wherever there exist separate and independent debts between the parties ; (a) but it is chiefly in cases of running accounts between debtor and creditor, where various payments have been made and various credits have been given at different times, that its application is felt in its full force and importance, especially where the dealings have been with a firm, as for example with bankers, and one or more of the partners have deceased and the customer still continues his dealings with the new firm or the survivors of the old firm, and moneys have been paid in and drawn out from time to time.[3]   The same question also often occurs in cases of public officers, where they have given different bonds at different times with different sureties for the faithful performance of their duties, and moneys have been received by them at different periods embracing one or more of the bonds.   How in such cases, where running accounts are kept of debts and payments, of credits and receipts, are the payments, made at different times before and after the change of the firm or the change of sureties, to be appropriated?   This in former times was a matter of no inconsiderable embarrassment and difficulty.   At present the following propositions may be deemed well settled.   In the first place in the case of running accounts between parties where there are various items of debt on one side and various items of credit on the other side occurring at different times, and no special appropriation of the payments is made by either party, the successive payments or credits are to be applied to the discharge of the items of debit antecedently due in the order of time in which they stand in the account ; or in other words each item of payment or credit is applied in extinguishment of the earliest items of debt standing in the account, until the whole payment

---

[1] Pothier on Oblig. by Evans, n. 528; Id. n. 561 (Fr. edit. 1824).

[2] Pothier, Pand. lib. 46, tit. 3, n. 89 to n. 103.

[3] Bank of Scotland v. Christie, 8 Clark & Finnell. R. 214.

(a) The holder of collateral security with power to convert it into money must apply the proceeds of any sale thereof to the debt which it secures. Cilley v. Fenton, 130 Mass. 323.   See Carr v. Hodge, Ib. 55, 58; Fowley v. Palmer, 5 Gray, 549.

or credit is exhausted.[1] (a) In the next place where there are no running accounts between the parties, and the debtor himself makes no special appropriation of any payment, there the creditor is generally at liberty to apply that payment to any one or more of the debts which the debtor owes him, whether it be upon an account or otherwise.[2] (b)

459 b. The doctrine here stated proceeds partly upon the presumed intention of the parties and partly upon a rule which has been assumed in our law, that the debtor has a right to appropriate any payments which he makes, to whatever debt due to his creditor he may choose to apply it. If the debtor omits to make any such appropriation, then the creditor has a right to appropriate the payment to such debts due to him by the debtor as he may choose. And if neither party has made any appro-

---

[1] Clayton's Case, 1 Meriv. R. 572, 604, 608; Devaynes v. Noble, 1 Meriv. R. 585; Bodenham v. Purchase, 2 Barn. & Ald. 39; Simson v. Cooke, 1 Bing. R. 452; Simson v. Ingham, 2 Barn. & Cressw. 65; Pemberton v. Oakes, 4 Russ. R. 154; Bank of Scotland v. Christie, 3 Clark & Finn. R. 214, 229; United States v. Kirkpatrick, 9 Wheat. 720, 737, 738; United States v. Wardwell, 5 Mason, R. 82, 87; McDowell v. The Blackstone Canal Co., 5 Mason, R. 11; The Postmaster-General v. Furber, 4 Mason, R. 333, 335; Gass v. Stinson, 3 Sumner, R. 99, 110, 111, 112; Williams v. Griffith, 5 Mees. & Welsb. 300; Campbell v. Hodgson, Gow. R. 74; Hall v. Wood, 14 East, R. 243, n.; Thompson v. Brown, Mood. & Malk. 40; Taylor v. Kymer, 3 Barn. & Adolph. 320, 333; Copland v. Tentman, 1 West (H. of L.), R. 364; s. c. 7 Clark & Finnell.

[2] Lysaght v. Walker, 3 Bligh, R. (N. s.) 1, 28; Bosanquet v. Wray, 6 Taunt. R. 597; Brooke v. Enderby, 2 Brod. & Bing. R. 10; post, § 459 g.

(a) See Crompton v. Pratt, 105 Mass. 255; Hill v. Robbins, 22 Mich. 475.

(b) A creditor has no right to apply a general payment to any item of account which is illegal, as a claim for usurious interest, or a charge for articles sold contrary to law; though if the debtor himself apply the payment to an illegal demand knowingly, he cannot afterwards revoke it. Caldwell v. Wentworth, 14 N. H. 431; Bancroft v. Dumas, 21 Vt. 456; Parchman v. McKinney, 12 Smedes & M. 631; Ayer v. Hawkins, 19 Vt. 26; Rohan v. Hanson, 11 Cush. 44. But a payment may be applied by the creditor to a debt barred by limitation.

Ramsay v. Warner, 97 Mass. 8; Jackson v. Burke, 1 Dill. 311. Or to a debt within the Statute of Frauds. Haynes v. Nice, 100 Mass. 327. See Philpott v. Jones, 4 Nev. & M. 14; s. c. 2 Ad. & E. 41; Rohan v. Hanson, supra; Mills v. Fowkes, 5 Bing. N. C. 455; s. c. 7 Scott, 444. It is enough that the demand itself is of a lawful nature. See Haynes v. Nice, supra.

Equity has no jurisdiction, on behalf of a single creditor who has not recovered a judgment against his debtor, and whose debtor has ceased to exist, to apply to the payment of his debt property of the debtor in the hands of a third person. Thornton v. Marginal Ry. Co., 123 Mass. 32.

priation thereof, then the law will make the appropriation according to its own notion of the equity and justice of the case, and so that it may be most beneficial to both the parties.[1]   In this view the appropriation of payments upon running accounts as above stated seems most consonant to the intentions and interests of both of the parties, and is full of equity and justice.[2]

459 c. The Roman law proceeded in a great measure, if not altogether, upon similar principles.   But according to that law the election was to be made at the time of payment as well in the case of the creditor as in that of the debtor: 'In re præsenti, hoc est statim atque solutum est, — cæterum postea non permittitur.'[3]   If neither applied the payment, the law made the appropriation according to certain rules of presumption depending on the nature of the debts or the priority in which they were incurred.   And as it was the actual intention of the debtor that would in the first instance have governed, so it was his presumable intention that was first resorted to as the rule by which the application was to be determined.   In the absence therefore of any express declaration by either the inquiry was, What application would be most beneficial to the debtor ?   The payment was consequently applied to the most burdensome debt, — to one that carried interest rather than to that which carried none ; to one secured by a penalty rather than to that which rested on a simple stipulation ; and if the debts were equal, then to that which had been first contracted.   'In his vero quæ

[1] U. States v. January & Pattleson, 7 Cranch, R. 572; U. States v. Kirkpatrick, 9 Wheat. R. 720, 737; U. States v. Wardwell, 5 Mason, R. 82; Postmaster-General v. Furber, 4 Mason, R. 333; Gass v. Stinson, 3 Sumner, R. 99, 110 to 112; post, § 459 d; Smith v. Lloyd, 11 Leigh, R. 512; Seymour v. Van Slyck, 8 Wend. R. 403; U. States v. Eckford's Ex'ors, 1 Howard, Sup. Ct. R. 250; s. c. 17 Peters, R. 251; 2 Greenleaf on Evid. §§ 530 to 535.

[2] Ibid.   As to what circumstances will amount to an appropriation or not, see Taylor v. Kymer, 3 Barn. & Adolph. 320, 333, 334; Marryatts v. White, 2 Starkie, R. 101; Goddard v. Hodges, 1 Crompt. & Mees. 33; Wright v. Laing, 3 Barn. & Cressw. 165 ; Birch v. Talbott, 2 Starkie, R. 74 ; Simson v. Ingham, 2 Barn. & Cressw. 65.

[3] Dig. Lib. 46, tit. 3, l. 5.   The text of the Roman law on this whole subject will be found in the American Law Magazine for April, 1843 (Philad.), pp. 36, 37, 38, with a learned dissertation on the whole subject.   Mr. Chief Justice Gibson has contested the leading doctrines of that article, whether satisfactorily or not, it will be for the profession to decide.   But it may be affirmed without scruple that whoever studies the subject the most profoundly will be very likely to find that all the difficulties are not as easily solved as he, upon a slight examination, might be led to suppose.

præsenti die debentur, constat quotiens indistincte quid solvitur, in graviorem causam videri solutum. Si autem nulla prægravet, — id est, si omnia nomina similia fuerint, — in antiquiorem.'[1] Pothier, in his edition of the Pandects, has collected together all the texts of the Roman law on this subject;[2] and he has summed up the general results in his Treatise on Obligations.[3]

[1] Dig. Lib. 46, tit. 3, Qu. 5; Clayton's case, 1 Meriv. R. 604, 605.

[2] Pothier, Pand. lib. 46, tit. 3, art. 1, n. 89 to 99. The doctrine of the Roman law is still more fully shown and compared with the common-law decisions in a very able note to the case of Pattison v. Hull, 9 Cowen, R. 773 to 777, to which I gladly refer.

[3] Pothier, Oblig. by Evans, n. 528 to 535; Id. n. 561 to n. 572 (French, 2d edit. 1829); Gass v. Stinson, 3 Sumner, R. 98, 111. It may not be without use to insert here the leading rules stated by Pothier: 'First Rule. The debtor has the power of declaring on account of what debt he intends to apply the sum which he pays. The reason which Ulpian gives is evident, "possumus enim certam legem dicere, ei quod solvimus." According to our rule, although regularly the interest should be paid before the principal, yet if the debtor of the principal and interest, upon paying a sum of money, has declared that he paid on account of the principal, the creditor who has agreed to receive it cannot afterwards contest such application. Second Rule. If the debtor, at the time of paying, makes no application, the creditor to whom the money is due, for different causes, may make the application by the acquittance which he gives. It is requisite, 1st, that this application be made at the instant; 2d, that it be equitable. Third Rule. When the application has neither been made by the debtor nor by the creditor, it ought to be made to that debt which the debtor at the time had the most interest to discharge. The application should rather be made to a debt which is not contested than to one that is; rather to a debt which was due at the time of payment than to one which was not. Among several debts which are due the application ought rather to be made to the debt for which the debtor was liable to be imprisoned than to debts merely civil, in respect of which process could only issue against his effects. Among civil debts the application should rather be made to those which produce interest than to those which do not. The application ought rather to be made to an hypothecatory debt than to another. The application ought rather to be made to the debt for which the debtor had given sureties than to those which he owed singly. The reason is that in discharging it he discharges himself from two creditors, — from his principal creditor, and from his surety, whom he is obliged to indemnify. Now a debtor has more interest to be acquitted against two than against a single creditor. The application ought rather to be made for a debt of which the person who has paid was principal debtor, than to those which he owed as surety for other persons. Fourth Rule. If the debts are of an equal nature, and such that the debtor had no interest in acquitting one rather than the other, the application should be made to that of the longest standing. Observe, that of two debts contracted the same day, but with different terms, which are both expired, the debt of which the term was the shorter, and consequently which expired sooner, is understood to be the more ancient. Fifth Rule. If the different debts are of

459 *d.* Now the whole of this doctrine of the Roman law turns upon the intention of the debtor, either express, implied, or presumed : express, when he has directed the application of the payment, as in all cases he had a right to do ; implied, when he knowingly has allowed the creditor to make a particular application at the time of payment without objection ; presumed, when in the absence of any such special appropriation it is most for his benefit to apply it to a particular debt.   And notwithstanding there are contradictory and conflicting authorities on this subject in the English and American courts, one should think that the doctrine of the Roman law is or at least ought to be held, and may well be held, to be the true doctrine to govern in our courts.   There is a great weight of common-law authority in its favor ; and in the conflict of judicial opinion that rule may fairly be adopted which is most rational, convenient, and consonant to the presumed intention of the parties.   If the creditor has a right in any case to elect to what debt to appropriate an indefinite payment, it seems proper that he should have it only when it is utterly indifferent to the debtor to which it is applied, and then perhaps his consent that the creditor may apply it as he pleases may fairly be presumed.[1] (*a*)

the same date, and in other respects equal, the application should be made proportionately to each.   Sixth Rule.   In debts which are of a nature to produce interest, the application is made to the interest before the principal. This holds good even if the acquittance imported that the sum was paid to the account of the principal and interest, "in sortem et usuras."   The clause is understood in this sense, that the sum is received to the account of the principal after the interest is satisfied.   Observe, that if the sum paid exceeds what is due for interest, the remainder is applied to the principal, even if the application had been expressly made to the interest without mentioning the principal.'

[1] Ante, § 459 *b*; 459 *d*; Gass *v.* Stinson, 3 Sumner, R. 98, 111; Pattison *v.*

(*a*) Sometimes the interests of third persons, such as other creditors, are so concerned as to require protection against the creditor to whom the payment has been made.   Thompson *v.* Hudson, L. R. 6 Ch. 320.   Thus if a mortgagee of one who dies insolvent should, on foreclosure, find a surplus in his hands, he could not retain the same and apply it to simple contract debts owed him by the mortgagor; he must pay such surplus over to the representative of the mortgagor for distribution among all the creditors. Talbot *v.* Frere, 9 Ch. D. 569, Jessel, M. R. denying Spalding *v.* Thompson, 26 Beav. 637; In re Haselfoot, L. R. 13 Eq. 327; Ex parte National Bank, L. R. 14 Eq. 507.   This is not properly a case of appropriation of payments, but the result would no doubt be the same if it were, unless the debt to which the surplus was to be applied was a specialty debt.

459 *e.* Be this however as it may, in the actual application of the doctrine to cases of partnership where a change of the firm has occurred by a dissolution by death or otherwise, the rule is that the estate of the deceased or retiring partner is liable only to the extent of the balance due to any creditor at the time of the dissolution; and that if the creditor continues to keep a running account with the survivors or the new firm, and sums are paid to them by the creditor, and sums are drawn on their firm and paid by them and are charged and credited to the general account, and blended together as a common fund without any distinction between the sums due to the creditor by the old firm and the new, — in such a case the sums paid to the creditor are deemed to be paid upon the general blended account and go to extinguish, pro tanto, the balance of the old firm in the order of the earliest items thereof. 'In such a case,' it has been said by a very able judge, 'there is no room for any other appropriation than that which arises from the order in which the receipts and payments take place and are carried into the account. Presumably it is the sum first paid in that is first drawn out. It is the first item on the debit side of the account that is discharged or reduced by the first item on the credit side. The appropriation is made by the very act of setting the two items against each other. Upon that principle all accounts current are settled, and particularly cash accounts. When there has been a continuation of dealings, in what way can it be ascertained whether the specific balance due on a given day has, or has not, been discharged, but by examining whether payments to the amount of that balance appear by the account to have been made? You are not to take the account backwards and strike the balance at the head instead of the foot of it. A man's banker breaks, owing him on the whole account a balance of £1000. It would surprise one to hear the customer say: "I have been fortunate enough to draw out all that I paid in during the last four years; but there is £1000, which I paid

---

Hull, 9 Cowen, R. 747, 765 to 773; Clayton's case, 1 Meriv. R. 605, 606, 607, 608. But see Hall *v.* Wood, 14 East, 243, n; Kirby *v.* Duke of Marlborough, 2 Maule & Selw. 19; Marryatts *v.* White, 2 Starkie, R. 101; Peters *v.* Anderson, 5 Taunt. R. 596; Bosanquet *v.* Wray, 6 Taunt. R. 597; Shaw *v.* Picton, 4 Barn. & Cressw. 715. See an elaborate article on the question of the Appropriation of Payments in the American Law Magazine (Philadelphia), No. 1, for April, 1843, pp. 31 to 52.

in five years ago, that I hold myself never to have drawn out; and therefore if I can find anybody who was answerable for the debts of the banking-house such as they stood five years ago, I have a right to say that it is that specific sum which is still due to me, and not the £1000 that I paid in last week."[1] (a)

459 f. On the other hand if under the like circumstances moneys have been received by the new firm and drawn out by the creditor from time to time, and upon the whole the original balance due to the creditor has been increased but never at any time been diminished in the hands of the firm, — in such a case the items of payment made by the new firm are still to be applied to the extinguishment of the balance of the old firm, and will discharge the share of the deceased or retiring partner to that extent, but no further; for in such a case the general rule as to running accounts is applied with its full force.[2] A fortiori where payments have been made and no new sums have been deposited by the creditor with the new firm, the payments will be applied in extinguishment, pro tanto, of the balance due by the old firm in the order of the items thereof.[3]

459 g. The cases which we have hitherto been considering are cases of running accounts; and under such circumstances the rule will apply equally to cases where a part of the debt is secured by a guaranty or by sureties, as well as where there are no such parties.[4] But where there are no such running accounts, if no special appropriation is made by the debtor, the creditor may,

[1] Sir William Grant, in Clayton's Case, 1 Meriv. R. 608, 609; Johnes's Case, 1 Meriv. R. 619; Smith v. Wigley, 3 Moore & Scott, 174; Sterndale v. Hankinson, 1 Simons, R. 393; Bodenham v. Purchas, 2 Barn. & Ald. 39; Pemberton v. Oakes, 4 Russ. R. 154; Bank of Scotland v. Christie, 8 Clark & Finn., R. 214, 227, 228.

[2] Palmer's Case, 1 Meriv. R. 623, 624; Sleech's Case, 1 Meriv. R. 538; Bodenham v. Purchas, 2 Barn. & Ald. 39.   See In re Mason, 3 Mont. Deac. & De Gex, R. 490; Law Magazine, May, 1845, p. 184.

[3] Sleech's Case, 1 Meriv. R. 538, &c.

[4] United States v. Kirkpatrick, 9 Wheat. R. 720, 737, 738; United States v. Wardwell, 5 Mason, R. 82, 87; Postmaster-General v. Furber, 4 Mason, R. 333, 335. But see United States v. Eckford's Ex'ors, 1 Howard, Sup. Ct. R. 250; s. c. 17 Peters, R. 251; United States v. January, 7 Cranch, 572.

(a) So where the first deposit is a trust fund, but more than the amount thereof has been drawn out, the balance in bank cannot be followed as such fund. Brown v. Adams, L. R. 4 Ch. 764.

as we have seen,[1] apply the money to any demand which he has against the debtor, whether it be a balance of an old account or of a new account; for in such a case the interest of third persons is not concerned, and the case of running accounts constitutes as it were an implied appropriation by the parties to the account generally.[2] And payments made generally by a debtor to his creditor may be applied by the creditor to a balance due to the creditor, although other debts have since been incurred upon which the debtor has given a bond with a surety for security thereof.[3] By the Scotch law a creditor having several debts due from the same debtor has a right to ascribe a payment made indefinitely and without appropriation by his debtor to whichever debt he may see fit to apply it, and is entitled to make this appropriation and election even at the latest hour.[4] The rule of our law seems (as we have seen) more qualified, and to omit the right of election of the creditor to a reasonable period after the payment, or to cases where the appropriation may be presumed to be indifferent to the debtor.[5]

460. In cases of account not founded in any such privity of contract, but founded upon relations and duties required by law or upon torts and constructive trusts for which equitable redress is sought, it is more difficult to trace out a distinct line where the legal remedy ends and the equitable jurisdiction begins.

461. In our subsequent examination of this branch of jurisdiction it certainly would not be going beyond its just boundaries to include within it all subjects which arise from the two

[1] Ante, § 459 a.

[2] Lysaght v. Walker, 5 Bligh, R. (N. S.) 1, 28; Bosanquet v. Wray, 6 Taunt. R. 597; Brooke v. Enderby, 2 Brod. & Bing. R. 70. In United States v. January, 7 Cranch, R. 572, it seems to have been thought by a majority of the court that 'the rule adopted in ordinary cases is not applicable to a case where different sureties under different obligators are in interest.' But that case was one of a public officer who had given bonds at different times. The case is very obscurely reported, but its true bearing is stated in a note to United States v. Wardwell, 5 Mason, R. 87. It is true that the case of United States v. January has been recognized as good law in United States v. Eckford's Ex'ors, 1 How. Sup. Ct. R. 250, 261. But there were peculiar circumstances in this last case; and United States v. Kirkpatrick expressly recognizes the general doctrine of appropriation.

[3] Kirby v. Duke of Marlborough, 2 M. & Selw. 18; Williams v. Rawlinson, 3 Bing. R. 71.

[4] Campbell v. Dent, 2 Moore, Priv. Coun. R. 292.

[5] Ante, §§ 459 a, 459 b.

great sources already indicated and terminate in matters of account; namely, first, such as have their foundation in contract or quasi contract; and secondly, such as have their foundation in trusts actual or constructive, or in torts affecting property. But as many cases included under one head are often connected with principles belonging to the other, and as the jurisdiction of Courts of Equity is often exercised upon various grounds not completely embraced in either, or upon mixed considerations, it will be more convenient, and perhaps not less philosophical, to treat the various topics under their own appropriate heads, without any nice discrimination between them. We may thus bring together in this place such topics only as do not seem to belong to more enlarged subjects, or such as do not require any elaborate discussion, or such as peculiarly furnish matter of illustration of the general principles which regulate the jurisdiction.

462. Let us then in the first place bring together some cases arising ex contractu, or quasi ex contractu, and involving accounts. And here one of the most general heads is that of AGENCY, where one person is employed to transact the business of another for a recompense or compensation. The most important agencies of this sort which fall under the cognizance of Courts of Equity are those of attorneys, factors, bailiffs, consignees, receivers, and stewards.[1] In most agencies of this sort there are mutual accounts between the parties; or if the account is on one side, as the relation naturally gives rise to great personal confidence between the parties, it rarely happens that the principal is able in cases of controversy to establish his rights or to

[1] Jeremy on Eq. Jurisd. B. 3, Pt. 2, ch. 5, pp. 513 to 515. In general a bill will not lie by an agent against his principal for an account unless some special ground is laid, as the incapacity to get proof unless by discovery. Dinwiddie v. Bailey (6 Ves. 136). But in the case of stewards a discovery from his principal is ordinarily necessary for the reasons stated by Lord Eldon in the same case (6 Ves. 141): 'The nature of this dealing is that money is paid in confidence without vouchers, embracing a great variety of accounts with the tenants; and nine times in ten it is impossible that justice can be done to the steward,' without going into equity for an account against his principal. See Middleditch v. Sharland, 5 Ves. 87; Moses v. Lewis, 12 Price, R. 502. In this last case the court refused to entertain jurisdiction for an account, it appearing that the whole matter was a set-off or other defence at law. The court admitted the general jurisdiction of Courts of Equity in matters of account, but denied that it was applicable to cases of this sort. Id. 510. See also Frietas v. Don Santos, 1 Y. & Jerv. 574.

ascertain the true state of the accounts without resorting to a discovery from the agent. Indeed in cases of factorage and consignments and general receipts and disbursements of money by receivers and stewards it can scarcely be possible, if the relation has long subsisted, that very intricate and perp'exing accounts should not have arisen where, independently of a discovery, the remedy of the principal would be utterly nugatory or grossly defective. It would be rare that specific sales and purchases, and the charges growing out of them, could be ascertained and traced out with any reasonable certainty ; and still more rare that every receipt and disbursement could be verified by direct and positive evidence. The rules of law in all such agencies require that the agent should keep regular accounts of all his transactions, with suitable vouchers.[1] (a) And it is obvious that if he can suppress all means of access to his books of account and vouchers, the principal would be utterly without redress, except by the searching power of a bill of discovery and the close inspection of all books under the authority and guidance of a Master in Chancery. Besides, agents are not only responsible for a due account of all the property of their principals, but also for all profits which they have clandestinely obtained by any improper use of that property. And the only adequate means of reaching such profits must be by such a bill of discovery.[2] In cases of fraud also it is almost impracticable to thread all the intricacies of its combinations except by searching the conscience of the party and examining his books and vouchers; neither of which can be done by the Courts of Common Law.[3] (b)

[1] Pearce v. Green, 1 Jac. & Walk. 135; Ormond v. Hutchinson, 13 Ves. 53.

[2] East India Company v. Henchman, 1 Ves. jr. 289; Massey v. Davies, 2 Ves. jr., R. 318; Borr v. Vandall, 1 Ch. Cas. 30.

[3] Earl of Hardwicke v. Vernon, 14 Ves. 510.

(a) Zettelle v. Myers, 19 Gratt. 62; Makepiece v. Rogers, 11 Jur. N. s. 314; s. c. 34 L. J. Ch. 396. Secus where the relation is only that of servant. Rich v. Austin, 40 Vt. 416. And see Hunter v. Belcher, 9 L. T. N. s. 501.

(b) Thornton v. Thornton, 31 Gratt. 212. See Turner v. Burkinshaw, L. R. 2 Ch. 488, where fraud was charged upon the plaintiff's steward and confidential agent in transactions running through a period of nearly twenty years, with accounts rendered for ten years regularly, then not at all for five years, and then yearly for the rest of the time. The court held that there had been no fraud.

Whether the bare relation of prin-

463. In agencies also of a single nature, such as a single consignment, or the delivery of money to be laid out in the purchase of an estate or of a cargo of goods, or to be paid over to a third person, although a suit at law may be often maintainable, yet if the thing lie in privity of contract and personal confidence, the aid of a Court of Equity is often indispensable for the attainment of justice. (a) Even when not indispensable it may often be exceedingly convenient and effectual, and prevent a multiplicity of suits. The party in such cases often has an election of remedy. This doctrine was expounded with great clearness and force by Lord Chief Justice Willes, in delivering the opinion of the court in a celebrated case. Speaking of the propriety of sometimes resorting to a suit at law, he said: 'Though a bill in equity may be proper in several of these cases, yet an action at law will lie likewise. As if I pay money to another to lay out in the purchase of a particular estate or any other thing, I may either bring a bill against him considering him as a trustee, and praying that he may lay out the money in that specific thing, or I may bring an action against him as for so much money had and received for my use. Courts of Equity always retain such bills when they are brought under the notion of a trust; and therefore in this very case (a consignment to a factor for sale) they have

cipal and agent will entitle the principal to call for an account is not clear. The contrary appears from Barry v. Stevens, 31 Beav. 258. But in Makepiece v. Rogers, 11 Jur. N. S. 314; s. c. 34 L. J. Ch. 396, Lord Justice Turner in the Court of Appeal declares that there is no authority for saying that a bill will not lie at any time by a principal against an agent for an account; and he declared that there was nothing to the contrary in Phillips v. Phillips, 9 Hare, 471. See also Hunter v. Belcher, 9 L. T. N. S. 501, where the plaintiff was held entitled to an account against his agent, a commercial traveller, only from the time of requiring the agent to keep an account.

An agent cannot maintain a bill for an account upon the mere ground of being entitled to commissions.

Smith v. Leveaux, 1 Hem. & M. 123; s. c. 2 DeG. J. & S. 1. Nor can one who is merely entitled to a royalty on sales of patented articles for that reason have an account in equity. Moxon v. Bright, L. R. 4 Ch. 292. But if the party's compensation is measured by profits, the rule is otherwise. Pratt v. Tuttle, 136 Mass. 233; Badger v. McNamara, 123 Mass. 117; Hargrave v. Conroy, 4 C. E. Green, 281. If the inquiry into profits is collateral, there may be no jurisdiction unless discovery is sought. Haskins v. Burr, 106 Mass. 48.

An administrator of a principal may call the latter's general agent to account in equity. Simmons v. Simmons, 33 Gratt. 451.

(a) See Navulshaw v. Brownrigg, 1 Sim. N. S. 573; Coquillard v. Suydam, 8 Blackf. 24.

often given relief where the party might have had his remedy at law if he had thought proper to proceed in that way.' [1]

464. Perhaps the doctrine here laid down, although generally true, is a little too broadly stated. The true source of jurisdiction in such cases is not the mere notion of a virtual trust, for then equity jurisdiction would cover every case of bailment. But it is the necessity of reaching the facts by a discovery; and having jurisdiction for such a purpose, the court, to avoid multiplicity of suits, will proceed to administer the proper relief.[2] (a) And hence it is that in the case of a single consignment to a factor for sale a Court of Equity will, under the head of discovery, entertain the suit for relief as well as discovery; there being accounts and disbursements involved which, generally speaking, cannot be so thoroughly investigated at law,[3] although (as we have seen) a Court of Equity is cautious of entertaining suits upon a single transaction where there are not mutual accounts.[4] Nay, so far has the doctrine been carried, that even though the case may appear as a matter of account to be perfectly remediable at law, yet if the parties have gone on to a hearing of the merits of the cause without any preliminary objection being taken to the jurisdiction of the court upon this ground, the court will not then suffer it to prevail, but will administer suitable relief.[5]

465. Cases of account between trustees and cestuis que trust may properly be deemed confidential agencies, and are peculiarly within the appropriate jurisdiction of Courts of Equity.[6] The same general rules apply here as in other cases of agency. A

---

[1] Scott v. Surman, Willes, R. 405.

[2] Ante, § 71; 3 Black. Comm. 437; Ludlow v. Simond, 2 Cain. Cas. in Err. 1, 38, 52; Mackenzie v. Johnston, 4 Madd. R. 374; Pearce v. Green, 1 Jac. & Walk. 135.

[3] Ludlow v. Simond, 2 Cain. Err. 1. 38. 52; Post v. Kimberly, 9 John. R. 493; Mackenzie v. Johnston, 4 Madd. R. 374.

[4] Porter v. Spencer, 2 John. Ch. R. 171; Wells v. Cooper, cited 6 Ves. 136; ante, § 458.

[5] Post v. Kimberly, 9 John. R. 493.

[6] Jeremy on Eq. Jurisd. B. 3, Pt. 2, ch. 5, pp. 522, 523.

(a) Where a pledge is held as general security, and the account contains several items, the pledgor may maintain a bill for account. Conyngham's Appeal, 57 Penn. St. 474. See Durant v. Einstein, 5 Rob. (N. Y.) 423.

trustee is never permitted to make any profit to himself in any of the concerns of his trust.[1]   On the other hand he is not liable

[1] Docker *v.* Somes, 2 Mylne & Keen, 664.   In this case it was decided that if a trustee mixes trust funds with his private moneys, and employs both in a trade or adventure of his own, the cestui que trust may, if he prefers it, insist upon having a proportionate share of the profits, instead of interest on the amount of the trust funds so employed.   On this occasion Lord Brougham delivered an elaborate judgment, from which I have made the following extracts, as they strikingly exemplify the doctrine of the text.   His Lordship said: 'Wherever a trustee, or one standing in the relation of a trustee, violates his duty, and deals with the trust estate for his own behoof, the rule is that he shall account to the cestui que trust for all the gain which he has made.   Thus if trust money is laid out in buying and selling land, and a profit made by the transaction, that shall go, not to the trustee who has so applied the money, but to the cestui que trust, whose money has been thus applied.   In like manner (and cases of this kind are more numerous), where a trustee or executor has used the fund committed to his care in stock speculations, though the loss, if any, must fall upon himself, yet for every farthing of profit he may make, he shall be accountable to the trust estate.   So if he lay out the trust money in a commercial adventure, as in buying or fitting out a vessel for a voyage, or put it in the trade of another person, from which he is to derive a certain stipulated profit, — although I will not say that this has been decided, I hold it to be quite clear that he must account for the profits received by the adventure or from the concern.   In all these cases it is easy to tell what the gains are; the fund is kept distinct from the trustee's other moneys, and whatever he gets, he must account for and pay over.   It is so much fruit, so much increase on the estate or chattel of another, and must follow the ownership of the property, and go to the proprietor.   So it is also where one not expressly a trustee has bought or trafficked with another's money.   The law raises a trust by implication, clothing him, though a stranger, with the fiduciary character, for the purpose of making him accountable.   If a person has purchased land in his own name with my money, there is a resulting trust for me; if he has invested my money in any other speculation, without my consent, he is held a trustee for my benefit.   And so an attorney, guardian, or other person, standing in a like situation to another, gains not for himself, but for the client, or infant, or other party, whose confidence has been abused.   Such being the undeniable principle of equity, such the rule by which breach of trust is discouraged and punished, — discouraged, by intercepting its gains, and thus frustrating the intentions that caused it; punished, by charging all losses on the wrong-doer, while no profit can ever accrue to him, — can the court consistently draw the line, as the cases would seem to draw it, and except from the general rule those instances where the risk of the malversation is most imminent; those instances where the trustee is most likely to misappropriate; namely, those in which he uses the trust funds in his own traffic?   At first sight this seems grossly absurd, and some reflection is required to understand how the court could ever, even in appearance, countenance such an anomaly. The reason which has induced judges to be satisfied with allowing interest only I take to have been this.   They could not easily sever the profits attributable to the trust money from those belonging to the whole capital stock; and the process became still more difficult where a great proportion of the

for any loss which occurs in the discharge of his duties, unless
he has been guilty of negligence, malversation, or fraud.[1]   The

gains proceeded from skill or labor employed upon the capital. In cases of
separate appropriation there was no such difficulty, as where land or stock
had been bought, and then sold again at a profit.   And here accordingly there
was no hesitation in at once making the trustee account for the whole gains he
had made. But where, having engaged in some trade himself, he had invested
the trust money in that trade along with his own, there was so much difficulty
in severing the profits which might be supposed to come from the money
misapplied, from those which came from the rest of the capital embarked,
that it was deemed more convenient to take another course, and instead of
endeavoring to ascertain what profit had been really made, to fix upon certain
rates of interest as the supposed measure or representative of the profits, and
assign that to the trust estate. This principle is undoubtedly attended with
one advantage; it avoids the necessity of an investigation of more or less
nicety in each individual case, and it thus attains one of the important benefits resulting from all general rules. But mark what sacrifices of justice and
expediency are made for this convenience. All trust estates receive the same
compensation, whatever risks they may have run during the period of their
misappropriation; all profit equally, whatever may be the real gain derived
by the trustee from his breach of duty; nor can any amount of profit made
be reached by the court, or even the most moderate rate of mercantile profit,
that is, the legal rate of interest, be exceeded, whatever the actual gains may
have been, unless by the very clumsy and arbitrary method of allowing rests,
in other words, compound interest; and this without the least regard to the
profits actually realized.   For in the most remarkable case in which this
method has been resorted to, Raphael v. Boehm (which indeed is always cited
to be doubted, if not disapproved), the compound interest was given with a
view to the culpability of the trustee's conduct, and not upon any estimate
of the profits he had made by it.   But the principal objection which I have
to the rule is founded upon its tendency to cripple the just power of this
court, in by far the most wholesome and indeed necessary exercise of its
functions, and the encouragement thus held out to fraud and breach of trust.
What avails it towards preventing such malversations, that the contrivers of
sordid injustice feel the power of the court only where they are clumsy enough
to keep the gains of their dishonesty severed from the rest of their stores?   It
is in vain they are told of the court's arm being long enough to reach them
and strong enough to hold them, if they know that a certain delicacy of touch
is required, without which the hand might as well be paralyzed or shrunk up.
The distinction, I will not say sanctioned, but pointed at, by the negative
authority of the cases, proclaims to executors and trustees that they have only
to invest the trust money in the speculations, and expose it to the hazards of
their own commerce, and be charged 5 per cent on it; and then they may
pocket 15 or 20 per cent by a successful adventure.   Surely the supposed difficulty of ascertaining the real gain made by the misapplication is as nothing
compared with the mischiefs likely to arise from admitting this rule, or rather

[1] Wilkinson v. Stafford, 1 Ves. jr. 32, 41, 42; Shepherd v. Towgood, 1
Turn. & R. 379; Adair v. Shaw, 1 Sch. & Lefr. R. 272; Caffrey v. Darby, 6
Ves. 488.

same doctrine is applicable to cases of guardians and wards, and other relations of a similar nature.[1]

466. Cases of account between tenants in common, (a) between joint-tenants, between partners, (b) between part-owners of ships, (c) and between owners of ships and the masters, fall under the like considerations. They all involve peculiar agencies, like those of bailiffs or managers of property, and require the same operative power of discovery and the same interposition of equity.[2] Indeed in all cases of such joint interests, where one party receives all the profits, he is bound to account to the other parties in interest for their respective shares, deducting the proper charges and expenses, whether he acts expressly by their authority as bailiff, or only by implication as manager without dissent jure domini over the property.[3] (d)

this exception to one of the most general rules of equitable jurisdiction. Even if cases were more likely to occur than I can think they are, of inextricable difficulties in pursuing such inquiries, I should still deem this the lesser evil by far, and be prepared to embrace it. Mr. Solicitor-General put a case of a very plausible aspect, with the view of deterring the court from taking the course which all principle points out. He feigned the instance of an apothecary buying drugs with £100 of trust money, and earning £1000 a year by selling them to his patients; and so he might have taken the case of trust money laid out in purchasing a piece of steel or skein of silk, and these being worked up into goods of the finest fabric, Birmingham trinkets, or Brussels lace, where the work exceeds by 10,000 times the material in value. But such instances in truth prove nothing, for they are cases not of profits upon stock, but of skilful labor very highly paid; and no reasonable person would ever dream of charging a trustee, whose skill, thus bestowed, had so enormously augmented the value of the capital, as if he had only obtained from it a profit; although the refinements of the civil law would certainly bear us out even in charging all gains accruing upon those goods as in the nature of accretions belonging to the true owners of the chattels.' See Wedderburn v. Wedderburn, 4 Mylne & Craig, 41.

[1] See Jeremy on Eq. Jurisd. B. 3, Pt. 2, ch. 5, pp. 543, 544, 545; Id. pp. 522, 523.

[2] See Abbott on Shipp. B. 1, ch. 3, §§ 4, 10, 11, 12; Doddington v. Hallet, 1 Ves. 497; Ex parte Young, 2 Ves. & Beam. 242; Com. Dig. Chan. 3 V. 6, 2 A. 1; Drury v. Drury, 1 Ch. Rep. 49; Strelly v. Winson, 1 Vern. R. 297.

[3] Strelly v. Winson, 1 Vern. 297; Horn v. Gilpin, Ambl. R. 255; Pulteney v. Warren, 6 Ves. 73, 78.

(a) Leach v. Beattie, 33 Vt. 195; Darden v. Cowper, 7 Jones, 210; Picot v. Colombet, 12 Cal. 414.

(b) Near v. Lowe, 49 Mich. 482; Gordon v. Gordon, Ib. 501; Harrison v. Dewey, 46 Mich. 173.

(c) McLellan v. Osborne, 51 Maine, 118; Dyckman v. Valiente, 42 N. Y. 549.

(d) Field v. Craig, 8 Allen, 357.

466 *a*. Trustees, directors of private companies, and other persons standing in a similar situation are not only not allowed to make any profit out of their offices, but it is prima facie a breach of trust on their part to take upon themselves the management of any part of the concern for a compensation or profit by way of commission, or brokerage, or salary. Thus for example a director of a company created to employ steamships for the benefit of the company cannot assume to himself with the consent of the other directors the situation of a ship's husband, so as to charge the ship's company for such a compensation as a stranger acting in the same office might.[1]

---

[1] Benson *v.* Heathorn, 1 Younge & Coll. N. R. 326, 340, 341. In this case Mr. Vice-Chancellor Knight said: 'The next point relates to the commissions and the discounts. It may be right, and probably is fair, to assume, for the purpose of the argument, that all these charges and allowances to Mr. Heathorn were such as would have been according to usage, and proper in the case of a stranger. His position however was very different. He was one of six directors of this company, to whom exclusively the entire management of its affairs was entrusted. I say exclusively, because, as is obviously necessary in companies of this description, the shareholders in general were prohibited from interfering. These six directors, being so entrusted, receive among them from the funds of the company, as a remuneration for their trouble in being the exclusively acting partners in this concern, a sum of no less than £650 per annum, capable, as I read the deed, of increase, but not liable to diminution; this sum they are to divide between themselves as they think fit. Now it is obvious that persons so circumstanced were under an obligation to the shareholders at large to use their best exertions in all matters which related to the affairs of the company for the welfare of the concern thus entrusted, not gratuitously, to their charge. I apprehend that, without any special provision for the purpose, it was by law an implied and inherent term in the engagement that they should not make any other profit to themselves of that trust or employment, and should not acquire to themselves, while they remained directors, an interest adverse to their duty. The main or only business of this company consisted in acquiring, managing, and working steam-vessels. It may have been that a ship's husband was necessary. It is the defendants' case, or the case at least of Mr. Heathorn, that a ship's husband was necessary. This is denied on the part of the plaintiffs, who say that the directors might very well have performed such duty as the management of the vessels required, without the interposition of a ship's husband. On that I give no opinion; but if a ship's husband was necessary, it is obvious he would become the responsible servant of the directors in an onerous office,—that he would become an accounting party to them, and that his conduct as well as his accounts, however respectable he might be, would require a constant and vigilant superintendence and control. That constant and vigilant superintendence and control one and all of the directors had, for value, contracted to give; and what is done? One of these very directors becomes himself the person whose conduct and accounts it is his duty to superintend, to check,

467. In many cases of frauds by an agent a Court of Common Law cannot administer effectual remedies ; as for instance it can-

and to watch: at once, therefore, to put the case at the very lowest, and in a manner most favorable to Mr. Heathorn, paralyzing him as a director in this respect, and leaving the company, as far as these important matters were concerned, under the protection of but five, while they believed themselves to be under the protection of six. But it does not rest there. The five remaining directors were placed in the difficult and invidious position of having to check and control the accounts of one of their own body with whom they were associated on equal terms in the management of every other part of the affairs of the concern. It has been nevertheless, with an appearance of seriousness, treated as an arguable question whether I can allow this gentleman to receive profits, however reasonable in amount, if they had been claimed by another person, which he has made by this employment, in which he ought never to have embarked. If the court were to do so, if the court were to allow to a person so circumstanced that which might fairly be allowed to a stranger, it would obviously afford the strongest encouragement to a departure from what is the right and regular course in every similar establishment. A party would take a situation of this nature with the certainty of having a fair remuneration, and with the probable advantage of retaining what was unfair. It is mainly this danger, the danger of the commission of fraud in a manner and under circumstances which, in the great majority of instances, must preclude detection, that in the case of trustees and all parties whose character and responsibilities are similar (for there is no magic in the word), induces the court (not only for the sake of justice in the individual case, but for the protection of the public generally, and with a view to assert and vindicate the obligation of plain and direct dealing between man and man in all cases, but especially in those where one man is trusted by another) to adhere strictly to the rule that no profit of any description shall be made by a person so circumstanced, — saying to the person complaining that he has thus employed his time and skill without remuneration, that he has elected so to treat the matter ; that he has had his reward, for he has had the possibility, nay, the probability, of retaining to himself that which he never ought to have retained ; that he has been willing to run the risk and cannot complain if he happens to lose the stake. It is on this principle that Lord Eldon proceeded in the cases so familiar to us all, of purchases by trustees. It is only an instance of the application of the rule, not the rule itself. In those cases Lord Eldon said (I allude particularly to Ex parte Lacey (6 Ves. 627), which occurred soon after Lord Eldon first received the seal) : " The rule is founded on this; that though you may see in a particular case that he has not made advantage, it is utterly impossible to examine upon satisfactory evidence in the power of the court — by which I mean, in the power of the parties in ninety-nine cases out of a hundred — whether he has made advantage or not." If in the present case Mr. Heathorn had openly and directly brought forward the matter before the body of shareholders generally, I consider it possible, if not probable, that he would have been allowed to receive, and would now have been entitled to retain, all the sums in question paid for commission. He has not elected to take that open and straightforward course ; he has chosen that the matter should be undisclosed, and he must abide the inevitable result.'

not give damages against his estate for a loss arising from his torts when such torts die with the person; and a fortiori the rule will apply to Courts of Equity which do not entertain suits for damages. But where the tort arises in the course of an agency from a fraud of the agent and respects property, Courts of Equity will treat the loss sustained as a debt against his estate.[1]

468. Courts of Equity adopt very enlarged views in regard to the rights and duties of agents; and in all cases where the duty of keeping regular accounts and vouchers is imposed upon them, they will take care that the omission to do so shall not be used as a means of escaping responsibility or of obtaining undue recompense. If therefore an agent does not under such circumstances keep regular accounts and vouchers, he will not be allowed the compensation which otherwise would belong to his agency.[2] Upon similar grounds, as an agent is bound to keep the property of his principal distinct from his own, if he mixes it up with his own the whole will be taken both at law and in equity to be the property of the principal until the agent puts the subject-matter under such circumstances that it may be distinguished as satisfactorily as it might have been before the unauthorized mixture on his part.[3] In other words the agent is put to the necessity of showing clearly what part of the property belongs to him; and so far as he is unable to do this, it is treated as the property of his principal.[4] Courts of Equity do not in these cases proceed upon the notion that strict justice is done between the parties, but upon the ground that it is the only justice that can be done, and that it would be inequitable to suffer the fraud or negligence of the agent to prejudice the rights of his principal.[5]

[1] Lord Hardwicke v. Vernon, 4 Ves. 418; Bishop of Winchester v. Knight, 1 P. Will. 406. But see Jesus College v. Bloom, Ambler, R. 55. In many cases of tort a remedy would lie at law against the personal representative of the party, as for instance where a tenant has tortiously dug ore and sold it during his lifetime; if the ore or the proceeds of it come to the possession of his administrator or executor, or he has assets, a suit will lie at law for the same. 1 P. Will. 407. See Jesus College v. Bloom, Ambler, R. 54; Hambley v. Trott, Cowp. R. 374.

[2] White v. Lady Lincoln, 8 Ves. 363; S. P. 15 Ves. 441.

[3] Lufton v. White, 15 Ves. 436, 440.

[4] Panton v. Panton, cited 15 Ves. 440; Chadworth v. Edwards, 8 Ves. 46.

[5] Lufton v. White, 15 Ves. 441; post, § 623.

469. Another head is that of APPORTIONMENT, CONTRIBUTION, and GENERAL AVERAGE, which are in some measure blended together and require and terminate in Accounts. In most of these cases a discovery is indispensable for the purposes of justice; and where this does not occur, there are other distinct grounds for the exercise of equity jurisdiction in order to avoid circuity and multiplicity of actions. Some cases of this nature spring from contract; others again from a legal duty independent of contract; and others again from the principles of natural justice confirming the known maxim of the law, ' Qui sentit commodum, sentire debet et onus.' The two latter may therefore properly be classed among obligations resulting quasi ex contractu.[1] This will abundantly appear in the sequel of these Commentaries.[2]

470. And first as to APPORTIONMENT and CONTRIBUTION, which may conveniently be treated together. Lord Coke has remarked that the word Apportionment ' cometh of the word Portio, quasi Partio, which signifieth a part of the whole, and apportion signifieth a division of a rent, common, &c., or a making of it into parts.'[3] It is sometimes used to denote the distribution of a common fund or entire subject among all those who have a title to a portion of it.[4] Sometimes indeed in a more loose but an analogous sense it is used to denote the contribution which is to be made by different persons having distinct rights towards the discharge of a common burthen or charge to be borne by all of them. In respect then to apportionment in its

---

[1] Deering v. Earl of Winchelsea, 1 Cox, R. 318; s. c. 2 Bos. & Pull. 270.

[2] Mr. Chancellor Kent has in several of his judgments treated the subject of Contribution, and insisted strongly that it is not necessarily founded upon contract, but upon principles of natural justice, independent of contract. See Cheeseborough v. Millard, 1 John. Ch. R. 409; Stearns v. Cooper, 1 John. Ch. R. 425; Campbell v. Mesier, 4 John. Ch. R. 334. In this opinion he is not only fully borne out by the doctrines of the English law (Deering v. Earl of Winchelsea, 1 Cox, R. 318; s. c. 2 Bos. & Pull. 270), but by the Roman and foreign law, which he has, with his usual ability and learning, commented upon. And he has applied it to the case of an old party wall which divided two estates, and was necessary to be rebuilt and was rebuilt by the owner of one, who claimed contribution from the other and had a decree in his favor. There is a most persuasive course of reasoning used to support this judgment; but it is mainly rested upon principles of equity derived from the civil and foreign law. See Campbell v. Mesier, 4 John. Ch. R. 334; s. c. 6 John. R. 21.

[3] Co. Litt. 147 b.

[4] Ex parte Smyth, 1 Swanst. R. 338, 339, the Reporter's note.

application to contracts in general it is the known and familiar principle of the common law that an entire contract is not apportionable. The reason seems to be that as the contract is founded upon a consideration dependent upon the entire perform- ance of the act, and if from any cause it is not wholly performed, the casus fœderis does not arise, and the law will not make provi- sions for exigencies which the parties have neglected to provide for themselves. Under such circumstances it is deemed wholly im- material to the rights of the other party whether the non-per- formance has arisen from the design or negligence of the party bound to perform it, or to inevitable casualty or accident. In each case the contract has not been completely executed.[1] The same rule is applied to cases where the payment is to be made under a contract upon the occurrence of a certain event or upon certain conditions. In the application of this doctrine of the common law, Courts of Equity have generally, but not univer- sally, adopted the maxim, 'æquitas sequitur legem.'[2] Whether rightly or wrongly, it is now too late to inquire; although as a new question there is much doubt whether in so adopting the maxim they have not in many cases deserted the principles of natural justice and equity, as well as the analogies by which they were governed in other instances in which they have granted relief.[3] We have already had occasion to cite cases in which this rigid doctrine as to non-apportionment has been applied.[4] There are however some exceptions to the rule both at law and in equity, which we shall presently have occasion to consider, and some in which Courts of Equity have granted relief where it would at least be denied at law.[5]

471. Some cases of apportionment in equity arising under con- tract or quasi contract have already been mentioned under the head of Accident.[6] But at the common law the cases are few in which an apportionment under contracts is allowed, the gen- eral doctrine being against it unless specially stipulated by the

---

[1] Paradine v. Jane, Aleyn, R. 26, 27; Story on Bailments, § 36; Ex parte Smyth, 1 Swanst. R. 338, 339, the Reporter's note, and cases cited; Ibid. 1 Fonbl. Eq. B. 1, ch. 5, § 9, notes (m) to (r).

[2] Post, §§ 474, 480 to 483.

[3] Ibid.

[4] Ante, §§ 101 to 104.

[5] Post, §§ 472, 473, 479.

[6] Ante, § 93.

parties.(a) Thus for instance where a person was appointed collector of rents for another, and was to receive £100 per annum for his services, and he died at the end of three quarters of the year while in the service, it was held that his executor could not recover £75 for the three quarters' service, upon the ground that the contract was entire, and there could be no apportionment; for the maxim of the law is, 'Annua nec debitum judex non separat ipsum.'[1] So where the mate of a ship engaged for a voyage at thirty guineas for the voyage, and died during the voyage, it was held that at law there could be no apportionment of the wages.[2]

471 a. In its familiar practical applications the principle that an entire contract cannot be apportioned seems founded on reasoning of this nature, — that the subject of the contract being a complex event constituted by the performance of various acts, the imperfect completion of the event by the performance of some only of those acts (as service during a portion of the specified period, navigation to an extent less than the voyage undertaken) cannot by virtue of that contract of which it is not the subject afford a title to the whole or to any part of the stipulated benefit. Whatever be the origin or the policy of the principle, it has unquestionably been established as a general rule from the earliest period of our judicial history.[3]

[1] Co. Litt. 150 a; Countess of Plymouth v. Throgmorton, 1 Salk. 65; 3 Mod. R. 153.

[2] Cutter v. Powell, 6 T. R. 320. See also Appleby v. Dodd, 8 East, R. 300; Jesse v. Roy, 1 Cromp. Jerv. & Rosc. 316, 329, 339.

[3] Ex parte Smyth, 1 Swanst. R. p. 338, note. 'The following are some of the authorities by which it is enforced or qualified: Bro. Abr. Apportion, pl. 7, 13, 22, 26; Id. Contract, pl. 8, 16, 30, 31, 35; Id. Laborers, pl. 48, 10 H. 6, 23, 3 Vin. Abr. 8, 9; Finch, Law, lib. 2, c. 18; Countess of Plymouth

(a) So in regard to dividends on shares. Dexter v. Phillips, 121 Mass. 178; Granger v. Bassett, 98 Mass. 462; Clive v. Clive, Kay, 600; In re Maxwell, 1 Hem. & M. 610. And of interest coupons on United States bonds. Sargent v. Sargent, 103 Mass. 297; Dexter v. Phillips, supra. Interest on promissory notes however, given for money lent, whether or not secured by mortgage or pledge, is apportionable between the days on which payment is due. Dexter v. Phillips, 121 Mass. 178. This case contains a general consideration of the subject and authorities thereon. The question of apportionment of a written contract often turns upon construction. See e. g. Gale v. Nourse, 15 Gray, 300; Thompson v. Saco Water Power Co., 114 Mass. 159. In these cases the contracts had been terminated by the defendant under provisions therein.

472. Courts of Equity to a considerable extent act, as we have seen, upon this maxim of the common law in regard to contracts. But where equitable circumstances intervene they will grant redress. Thus if an apprentice fee of a specific sum be given, and the master afterwards becomes bankrupt, equity will, as we have seen, decree an apportionment.[1] So where an attorney while he lay ill received the sum of 120 guineas for a clerk who was placed with him, and he died within three weeks afterwards, the court decreed a return of 100 guineas, notwithstanding the articles provided that in case of the attorney's death £60 only should be returned.[2] This case, upon the statement in the report, is certainly open to the objection taken to it by Lord Kenyon, who said that it carried the jurisdiction of the court as far as it could be,[3] for it overturned the maxim, ' Modus et conventio vincunt legem.' But in truth the case (according to the Register's Book) seems to have been very correctly decided; for in the pleadings it was stated that the plaintiff at the time was unwilling to sign the articles, or to pay the 120 guineas, until the attorney had declared that in case he should not live to go abroad, the 120 guineas should be returned to him, and that he was only troubled with a cold, and hoped to be abroad in two or three days, and thereupon the plaintiff signed the articles.[4] This allegation was in all probability proved, and was the very turning-point of the case. If so, the case stands upon a plain ground of equity, — that of mutual mistake or misrepresentation or unconscientious advantage.

---

v. Throgmorton, 1 Salk. 65; Tyrie v. Fletcher, Cowp. 666; Robinson v. Bland, 2 Burr. 1077, 1 Bl. 234; Loraine v. Thomlinson, Doug. 585; Bermon v. Woodbridge, Doug. 781; Rothwell v. Cook, 1 B. & P. 172; Meyer v. Gregson, Marsh. on Insurance, 658; Chater v. Becket, 7 T. R. 201; Cook v. Jennings, 7 T. R. 381; Cuttler v. Powell, 6 T. R. 320; Wiggins v. Ingleton, Lord Raym. 1211; Cook v. Tombs, 2 Anstr. 420; Lea v. Barber, 2 Anstr. 425, n; Mulloy v. Backer, 5 East, 316; Liddard v. Lopes, 10 East, 526; How v. Synge, 15 East, 440; Fuller v. Abbott, 4 Taunt. 105; Stevenson v. Snow, 3 Burr. 1237; Long v. Allen, Marsh. on Insurance, 660; Park on Insurance, 529; Ritchie v. Atkinson, 10 East, 295; Waddington v. Oliver, 2 N. R. 61; and see Abbott's Law of Merchant Ships, p. 292, et seq.'

[1] Ante, § 93; Hale v. Webb, 2 Bro. Ch. R. 78; Ex parte Sandby, 1 Atk. 149.

[2] Newton v. Rowse, 1 Vern. 460. and Raithby's note (2).

[3] Hale v. Webb, 2 Bro. Ch. R. 80; 1 Fonbl. Eq. B. 1, ch. 5, § 8, note (g).

[4] Mr. Raithby's note to 1 Vern. 460. Ante, § 93.

473. Other cases of apprentice fees may exemplify the same salutary interposition of Courts of Equity. Thus where an apprentice had been discharged from service in consequence of the misconduct of the master, it was decreed that the indentures of apprenticeship should be delivered up, and a part of the apprentice fee paid back.[1] So where the master undertook, in consideration of the apprentice fee, to do certain acts during the apprenticeship which by his death were left undone and could not be performed, an apportionment of the apprentice fee was decreed.[2]

474. These are cases where an apportionment might not always be reached at the common law, but yet which belong to the recognized principles of equity. But on the other hand where an apprentice fee has been paid and the apprenticeship has been dissolved at the request of the friends of the apprentice, but without any default in the master and without any agreement for a return of any part of the fee, there a Court of Equity will not interfere; for there is no equity attaching itself to the transaction, and the contract does not import any return.[3]

475. In regard to rents the general rule at the common law leaned strongly against any apportionment thereof. (a)   Hence it was well established that in case of the death of a tenant for life in the interval between two periods at each of which a portion of rent becomes due from the lessee, no rent could be recovered for the occupation since the first of those periods.[4]   The rule seems to have been rested on two propositions: 1st, that an entire contract cannot be apportioned; 2d, that under a lease with a periodical reservation of rent the contract for the payment of such portion is distinct and entire.[5]   Hence it followed that on the determination of a lease by the death of the lessor before

[1] Lockley v. Eldridge, Rep. Temp. Finch, 128.   See Therman v. Abell, 2 Vern. 64.

[2] Savin v. Bowdin, Rep. Temp. Finch, 396.

[3] Hall v. Webb, 2 Bro. Ch. R. 78.

[4] Ex parte Smyth, 1 Swanst. R. 338, and note.

[5] Ibid.

(a) As where rent is payable at the end of each month or quarter. Dexter v. Phillips, 121 Mass. 178; Sohier v. Eldredge, 103 Mass. 345; In re Markby, 4 Mylne & C. 484; Brown v. Amyot, 3 Hare, 173; In re Clulow, 3 Kay & J. 689. See upon this subject of apportioning rent the note at end of § 482.

the day appointed for payment of the rent, the event on the completion of which the payment was stipulated, namely, occupation of the lands during the period stipulated, never occurring, no rent became payable, and in respect of time apportionment was not in any case permitted.[1]

475 a. Some exceptions and some qualifications were however in certain cases and under certain circumstances incorporated into the common law at an early period, in respect to rent growing out of real estate where there was a division or severance of the land from which the rent issued. In other cases the rent was held to be wholly extinguished. (a) A few examples of each sort may perhaps be usefully introduced in this place; but the full examination of the whole subject properly belongs to another department of the law.[2] Thus for instance if a man had a rent charge and purchased a part of the land out of which it issued, the whole rent charge was extinguished.[3] But if a part of the land came to him by operation of law, as by descent, then the rent charge was apportionable; that is, the tenant and the heir were to pay according to the value of the lands respectively held by them, and of course the part apportionable on the heir was extinguished.[4] But a rent service was in both cases apportionable.[5] (b) So if a lessor granted part of a reversion to a

---

[1] Ibid.; Clun's case, 10 Co. R. 127.

[2] Co. Litt. 148 a; Com. Dig. Suspension, R. 6, D. 4; 1 Fonbl. Eq. B. 1, ch. 5, § 9, and notes; Bac. Abridg. Rent, M; Com. Dig. Chancery, 4 N. 5, 2 E.; Ex parte Smyth, 1 Swanst. R. 338, 339, the Reporter's note.

[3] Co. Litt. 147 b, 148 a, 148 b; Bac. Abr. Rent, M.; Com. Dig. Suspension, C. See also Averall v. Wade, 1 Lloyd and Goold, R. 252, and the Reporter's note, pp. 264, 265. But see 1 Swanst. R. 338. note (a). Mr. Swanston, in his note (a) to Ex parte Smyth, 1 Swanst. R. 338, says: 'Apportionment frequently denotes, not division, but distribution; and in its ordinary technical sense the distribution of one subject in proportion to another previously distributed.' There is some reason to question the accuracy of this statement. Apportionment does not refer to a distribution of one subject in proportion to another 'previously distributed,' but a distribution of a claim or charge among persons having different interests or shares in proportion to their interest or shares in the subject-matter to which it attaches.

[4] Co. Litt. 149 b; Bac. Abridg. Rent, M.; Com. Dig. Suspension, C.

[5] Ibid.; Com. Dig. Suspension, E.

(a) If the act claimed to be an extinguishment was done in mistake, equity may apportion. Van Rensselaer v. Chadwick, 22 N. Y. 32.

(b) Voegtly v. Pittsburgh R. Co., 2 Grant, 243. See note to § 482, at end.

stranger, the rent was to be apportioned.[1] On the other hand if part of the land out of which a rent charge issued was evicted by a title paramount, the rent was apportioned.[2] So although a rent charge is in its nature entire and against common right, yet if it descended to co-parceners by this rule of law the rent was apportioned between them, and the tenant was subject to several distresses for the rent, and partition might be made before seisin of the rent.[3] (a) So a rent service incident to the reversion might be apportionable by a grant of a part of the reversion.[4]

475 *b*. 'In some cases a rent charge may be apportioned by the act of the party ; as if the grantee releases part of his rent to the tenant of the land, such release does not extinguish the whole rent. So if the grantee gives part of it to a stranger and the tenant attorns, such grant shall not extinguish the residue which the grantee never parted with, because such release or disposition makes no alteration in the original grant, nor defeats the intention of it as the purchase of part of the land does ; for the whole rent is still issuable out of the whole land, according to the original intention of the grant. Besides since the law allowed of such sorts of grants and thereby established such sort of property, it would have been unreasonable and severe to hinder the proprietor to make a proper distribution of it for the promotion of his children, or to provide for the contingencies of his family, which were in his view. The objection that has been made to these sorts of apportionments or divisions of rent charges is this ; that the tenant thereby would be exposed to several suits and distresses for a thing which in its original creation was entire, and recoverable upon one avowry.'[5]

475 *c*. And the question may also arise, ' Whether the tenant shall pay the whole rent though part of the thing demised be lost and of no profit to him, or though the use of the whole be for some time intercepted or taken away without his default. And

---

[1] Co. Litt. 148 *a*; Com. Dig. Suspension, E. ; Ewer *v*. Moyle, Cro. Eliz. 771; Bac. Abr. Rent, M. 1.

[2] Com. Dig. Suspension, E. ; Co. Litt. 147 *b*; Bac. Abr. Rent, M. 1, 2.

[3] Co. Litt. 164 *b*.

[4] Bac. Abridg. Rent, M. 1.

[5] Bac. Abridg. Rent, M. 1.

(a) See Conger *v*. McLaury, 41 N. Y. 219; editor's note at end of § 482.

here it seems extremely reasonable that if the use of the thing be entirely lost or taken away from the tenant, the rent ought to be abated or apportioned, because the title to the rent is founded upon this presumption, that the tenant enjoys the thing during the contract; and therefore if part of the land be surrounded or covered with the sea, this being the act of God the tenant shall not suffer by it, because the tenant without his default wants the enjoyment of part of the thing which was the consideration of his paying the rent; nor has the lessor reason to complain, because if the land had been in his own hands he must have lost the benefit of so much as the sea had covered.'[1]

476. However reasonable an apportionment may seem to be in the case last suggested, upon the ground that the tenant had not, by reason of inevitable casualty, enjoyed the full benefit of the lands demised to him, the same principle was not at the common law carried out in favor of the lessor, in case the lease by inevitable casualty determined before the entire rent was due. For in such a case the rule was inflexibly applied, that the rent should not be apportioned. If therefore the lease be determined by the death of the lessor (he having but a life estate in the land demised) before the day appointed for the payment of the rent, the event on which that payment was stipulated, namely, the occupation of the land demised during the period specified, no rent whatsoever was payable by the tenant, even although he had occupied the land up to a single day of the time when the rent would have become due; for no apportionment in respect to time was in any case admitted by the common law. The executor of the deceased was not entitled to any rent, because the contract was not completely performed; the remainder-man or reversioner was not entitled, because the rent was not due in his time.[2]   And

---

[1] Bac. Abridg. Rent, M. 2. The passage is here given as it stands in Bacon's Abridgment. But whether the doctrine therein stated would now be supported, may perhaps admit of a doubt. See ante, §§ 101 to 104.

[2] Clun's Case, 10 Co. R. 127. The principal reason there given is, 'Because the rent reserved is to be raised out of the profits of the land, and is not due until the profits are taken by the lessee: for these words "reddendo inde," or "reservando inde," is as much as to say that the lessee shall pay so much of the issues and profits at such days to the lessor; for "reddere inde nihil aliud est quam acceptum restituere, seu reddere est quasi retro dare," and "redditus dicitur a reddendo, quia retro it, sc." to the lessor, donor, &c., "sicut provent' a proveniendo;" and "obventus ab obveniendo." And that is the reason that the rent so reserved is not due or payable before the day of payment incurred,

this severe doctrine of the common law, artificial and unjust as it seems to be, was, as we shall presently see, scrupulously followed in equity. It was to cure this manifest defect that the statute of 11 Geo. 2 (ch. 19, § 15) was passed; and the like remedial justice has been still more amply provided for by the statute of 4 and 5 Will. 4, ch. 22. (*a*)

477. On the other hand cases may easily be stated where apportionment of a common charge, or, more properly speaking, where contribution towards a common charge, seems indispensable for the purposes of justice, and accordingly has been declared by the common law in the nature of an apportionment towards the discharge of a common burthen. Thus if a man owning several acres of land is bound in a judgment, or statute, or recognizance, operating as a lien on the land, and afterwards he aliens one acre to A, another to B, and another to C, &c.; there, if one alienee is compelled, in order to save his land, to pay the judgment, statute, or recognizance, he will be entitled to contribution from the other alienees.[1] (*b*) The same principle will apply in the like case where the land descends to parceners who make partition, and then one is compelled to pay the whole

because it is to be rendered and restored out of the issues and profits; and that is the reason that if the land is evicted, or if the lease determines before the legal time of payment, no rent shall be paid, for there shall never be an apportionment in respect of part of the time, as there shall be upon an eviction of part of the land; and therefore if tenant for life makes a lease for years, rendering rent at the feast of Easter, and the lessee occupies for three quarters of the year, and in the last quarter before the feast of Easter, the tenant for life dies, here shall be no apportionment of the rent for three quarters of the year, because no rent was due till the feast of Easter, and no apportionment shall be in respect of time; but in the same case if part of the land had been evicted before the feast of Easter, and the feast of Easter occurred in the life of the lessor, there shall be an apportionment of the rent, but not in respect of the time which well continued, but in respect that parcel of the land leased is evicted.' 1 Fonbl. Eq. B. 1, ch. 5, § 90, note (*o*); Ex parte Smyth, 1 Swanst. R. 338, and the Reporter's note; Bissett on Estates for Life, ch. 11, pp. 268 to 272.

[1] Harbert's Case, 3 Co. R. 12, 13; Viner's Abridg. Contribution and Average, A. pl. 4, 6, 8, 9, 12, 25, 27. See also American Law Mag. for April, 1844, art. 5, pp. 64 to 82. But see post, § 1233 *a*, where the subject is discussed in another connection, and the authorities are shown to be not in harmony on the subject.

(*a*) See now 33 & 34 Vict. ch. 35.
(*b*) There is a corresponding right to come in and share in the benefit of redemption, by contributing. Seymour *v.* Davis, 35 Conn. 264.

charge; contribution will lie against the other parceners.[1] The same doctrine will apply to co-feoffees of the land or of different parts of the land.[2] In all these cases (and others might be mentioned) a writ of contribution would lie at the common law or in virtue of the statute of Marlebridge.[3]

478. But there are many difficulties in proceeding in cases where an apportionment or contribution is allowed at the com-

[1] Ibid.; Viner's Abridg. Contribution and Average, A. pl. 6, 7, 9, 22, 23, 24.

[2] Ibid.; Harbert's Case, 3 Co. R. 12; Deering v. Earl of Winchelsea, 1 Cox, R. 321; s. c. 2 Bos. & Pull. 276; ante, § 499, and note.

[3] See Harbert's Case, 3 Co. R. 12; Deering v. Earl of Winchelsea, 1 Cox, R. 321; s. c. 2 Bos. & Pull. 270; Co. Litt. 165 a; Fitzherbert Nat. Brev. 16. Lord Chief Baron Eyre, in one of his most luminous judgments, has expounded the general grounds of the doctrine of contribution, as known at the common law as well as in equity, in a manner so clear that it will be better to quote his own language than to risk impairing its force by any abridgment. 'If we take a view,' said he, 'of the cases, both in law and equity, we shall find that contribution is bottomed and fixed on general principles of justice, and does not spring from contract; though contract may qualify it, as in Swain v. Wall, 1 Ch. Rep. 149. In the Register, p. 176 (b), there are two writs of contribution, one inter co-hæredes, the other inter co-feoffatos. These are founded on the statute of Marlebridge. The great object of the statute is to protect the inheritance from more suits than are necessary. Though contribution is a part of the provision of the statute, yet, in Fitz. N. B. 338, there is a writ of contribution at common law amongst tenants in common, as for a mill falling to decay. In the same page Fitzherbert takes notice of contribution between co-heirs and co-feoffees; and as between co-feoffees, he supposes there shall be no contribution without an agreement. And the words of the writ countenance such an idea; for the words are "ex eorum assensu;" and yet this seems to contravene the express provision of the statute. As to co-heirs the statute is express; it does not say so as to co-feoffees, but it gives contribution in the same manner. In Sir William Harbert's Case, 3 Co. 11 (b), many cases of contribution are put; and the reason given in the books is that in æquali jure the law requires equality. One shall not bear the burden in ease of the rest; and the law is grounded in great equity. Contract is never mentioned. Now the doctrine of equality operates more effectually in this court than in a Court of Law. The difficulty in Coke's cases was, how to make them contribute. They were put to their audita querela, or scire facias. In equity there is a string of cases in 1 Eq. Cas. Abr. tit. "Contribution and Average." Another case occurs in Hargrave's Law Tracts on the right of the king on the prisage of wine. The king is entitled to one tun before the mast, and one tun behind; and in that case a right of contribution accrues; for the king may take by his prerogative any two tuns of wine he thinks fit, by which one man might suffer solely. But the contribution is given, of course, on general principles, which govern all these cases.' Deering v. Earl of Winchelsea, 1 Cox, R. 321; s. c. 2 Bos. & Pull. 270, 271, 272; Lord Redesdale in Stirling v. Forrester, 3 Bligh, R. 596, o. s.

mon law ; for where the parties are numerous, as each is liable to contribute only for his own portion, separate actions and verdicts may become necessary against each. And thus a multiplicity of suits may take place, and no judgment in one suit will be conclusive in regard to the amount of contribution in a suit against another person. The like difficulty may arise in cases where an apportionment is to be made under a contract for the payment of money or rent where the parties are numerous and the circumstances complicated. Whereas in equity all parties can at once be brought before the court in a single suit, and the decree apportioning the rent will thus be conclusive upon all the parties in interest.[1]

479. But the ground of equity jurisdiction, in cases of apportionment of rent and other charges and claims, does not arise solely from the defective nature of the remedy at common law, where such a remedy exists. It extends to a great variety of cases where no remedy at all exists in law, and yet where, ex æquo et bono, the party is entitled to relief.[2] Thus for instance where a plaintiff was lessee of divers lands upon which an entire rent was reserved, and afterwards the inhabitants of the town where part of the lands lay claimed a right of common in part of the lands so let, and upon a trial succeeded in establishing their right, — in this case there could be no apportionment of the rent at law, because, although a right of common was recovered, there was no eviction of the land. But it was not doubted that in equity a bill was maintainable for an apportionment if a suitable case for relief were made out.[3] So where by an ancient composition a rent is payable in lieu of tithes, and the lands come into the seisin and possession of divers grantees, the composition will be apportioned among them in equity, though there may be no redress at law.[4] So where money is to be laid out in land, if the party who is entitled to the land in fee when purchased dies before it is purchased, the money being in the mean time secured on a mortgage and the interest made payable half-yearly, the interest will be apportioned in equity between the heir and the

[1] Post, §§ 483 to 488.

[2] Ante, §§ 472, 473.

[3] Com. Dig. Chancery, 2 E., 4 N. 5; Jew v. Thirkenell, 1 Ch. Cas. 31; s. c. 3 Ch. Rep. 11.

[4] Com. Dig. Chancery, 4 N. 5, cites Saville, R. 5. See Aynsley v. Woodsworth, 2 V. and Beam. 331.

administrator of the party so entitled, if he dies before the half-yearly payment is due.[1] So where portions are payable to daughters at eighteen or marriage, and, until the portions are due, maintenance is to be allowed, payable half-yearly at specific times, if one of the daughters should come of age in an intermediate period, the maintenance will be apportioned in equity.[2]

480. But still there are many cases in which Courts of Equity have refused to allow an apportionment of rent and other charges, acting (it must be admitted) not upon the principles which ordinarily govern them, but upon the notion of a strict obedience to the analogies of the law.   Thus where a purchaser of an interest in New South Sea Annuities from a husband during his life, remainder to other persons (which had been originally secured upon a mortgage, but by order of the court had been transferred to government securities), insisted in a petition in equity that notwithstanding the husband died before the Christmas half-year became due, yet he was entitled to be paid proportionally for the time the husband lived, Lord Hardwicke said that if it had continued a mortgage the purchaser would have been entitled to the demand he now made, because there interest accrues every day for the forbearance of the principal, though notwithstanding it is usual in mortgages to make it payable half-yearly; but that South Sea Annuities are considered as mere annuities, and therefore the purchaser is no more entitled than he would be in case of a common annuity payable half-yearly where the annuitant, in whose place he stands, dies before the half-year is completed.[3] (a)   This is certainly correct reasoning

[1] Edwards v. Countess of Warwick, 2 P. W. 176.

[2] Hay v. Palmer, 2 P. Will. 501.   See also ante, §§ 472, 473.

[3] Pearly v. Smith, 3 Atk. 261; 1 Fonbl. Eq. B. 1, ch. 5, § 9, note (o); Jeremy on Eq. Jurisd. B. 3, Pt. 2, ch. 5, pp. 520, 521, 522.

(a) A life annuity was held apportionable in In re Lackawanna Canal Co., 37 N. J. Eq. 26. So in Heath v. Nugent, 29 Beav. 226, and in Wilkins v. Rotherham, 27 Ch. D. 703, under statute; and see Blight v. Blight, 51 Penn. St. 420. But if the annuity is not clearly intended for the daily support of the beneficiary, it cannot in absence of statute be apportioned. Phillips v. Dexter, 121 Mass. 178, 180, and cases cited. Under a statute providing for the apportionment of 'income' given until a certain event, dividends of profits declared after the event have been held apportionable. Granger v. Bassett, 98 Mass. 462. See Jones v. Ogle, L. R. 14 Eq. 419. The English Apportionment Act applies not only to cases where the life estate is held under an instrument

upon the course of the authorities; and yet it is difficult to see why, in reason, interest payable half-yearly should stand distinguished from an annuity payable half-yearly. Why, in such case, may not portions of the annuity be deemed in equity to accrue daily as much as interest, when the latter is, like the former, payable only half-yearly? The same principle has been adopted in cases where money is to be laid out in land upon a settlement, and in the mean time to be invested in government securities; if the tenant for life dies in the middle of the half-year, the reversioner is entitled to the whole dividend and there is no apportionment, although there would be if the money were laid out on mortgage.[1]

[1] Sherrard v. Sherrard, 3 Atk. 502; Rashleigh v. Master, 3 Bro. Ch. R. 99, 101; Webb v. Shaftesbury, 11 Ves. 361; Wilson v. Harman, Ambl. R. 279; s. c. 2 Ves. 672; 1 Fonbl. Eq. B. 1, ch. 5, § 9, note (o); Hay v. Palmer, 2 P. Will. 502, and Mr. Cox's note. See also ante, § 479. Mr. Swanston, in his learned note to the case of Ex parte Smyth, 1 Swanst. R. 338, 348, says: 'The rule of law which refuses apportionment of rent in respect of time is applicable to all periodical payments becoming due at fixed intervals, not to sums accruing de die in diem. Annuities therefore (3 Atk. 261; 2 Bl. 1016) and dividends on money in the funds are not apportionable. Rashleigh v. Master, 3 Bro. C. C. 101; Wilson v. Harman, 2 Ves. 672; Ambl. 279; Pearly v. Smith, 3 Atk. 260; Sherrard v. Sherrard, 3 Atk. 502. But interest, whether the principal is secured by mortgage (Wilson v. Harman; Sherrard v. Sherrard) or by bond, notwithstanding that it is expressly made payable half-yearly (Banner v. Lowe, 13 Ves. 135), may be apportioned; for though reserved at fixed periods it becomes due de die in diem for forbearance of the principal, which the creditor is entitled to recall at pleasure. Thus a sum of money which it was covenanted in marriage-articles should be invested in lands, having been lent on mortgage at the death of the person entitled to an estate tail in the land, the interest was apportioned in favor of his administratrix. Edwards v. Countess of Warwick, 2 P. Will. 176; 1 Bro. P. C. ed. Toml. 207. In strictness these are not cases of apportionment (2 P. W. ed. Cox, 503, n. 1); they are not instances of the distribution of one entire subject among individuals entitled each to a part, but the appropriation of distinct subjects to the respective owners. A remarkable exception to the general rule has been

made after the act, but also to cases of leases made after the act under a settlement made before the act. Llewellyn v. Rous, L. R. 2 Eq. 27. See Heasman v. Pearse, L. R. 8 Eq. 599. Secus as to dividends of invested proceeds, when lands settled before the act were taken under the Lands Clauses Act. In re Lawton, L. R. 3 Eq. 469.

A trust to accumulate rents till A becomes twenty-one, when he is to be let into possession, falls within the English act. Wheeler v. Tootel, L. R. 3 Eq. 571. See Clive v. Clive, L. R. 7 Ch. 433; Donaldson v. Donaldson, L. R. 10 Eq. 635. The act does not apply to payments made under order of court. Jodrell v. Jodrell, L. R. 7 Eq. 461.

481. So where a tenant for life made a lease of the estate for years, rendering rent quarter-yearly, and died before the end of the quarter, an apportionment of the rent was denied in equity.[1](a) Upon this occasion the Lord Chancellor said : ' There are several remedial statutes relating to rents,[2] but this is a casus omissus.

introduced in the instance of annuities for the maintenance of infants (Hay v. Palmer, 2 P. W. 501; Rhenish v. Martin, 1746, MS.), or of married women living separate from their husbands (Howel v. Hanforth, 2 Bl. 1016; 2 Schoales & Lefr. 303) ; an exception supported by the necessity of the case and the consequent presumption of intention (2 Bl. 1017; 2 P. W. 503), and therefore not extending to an annuity for the separate use of a married woman living with her husband and maintained by him. Anderson v. Dwyer, 1 Schoales & Lefr. 301. An annuity payable quarterly, secured by the bond of a testator whose will charged his real in aid of his personal estate, being, under an order of the Court of Chancery, directed to be paid half-yearly at Midsummer and Christmas, and the annuitant having died between Lady-day and Midsummer, her representative was declared entitled to the arrears due at Lady-day. Webb v. Lady Shaftesbury, 11 Ves. 361.'

[1] Jenner v. Morgan, 1 P. Will. R. 392; ante, § 476.

[2] Before the statute of 11 Geo. 2, ch. 19, § 15, if a tenant for life died before the rent day, the intermediate rent was lost. That statute has cured many hardships of the common law on this subject, but not all. Paget v. Gee, Ambler, R. 198; s. c. Id. App. p. 807 (Mr. Blunt's edition); Wykham v. Wykham, 3 Taunt. R. 331. The recent statute of 4 & 5 Will.' ch. 22, has extended the like remedial justice to other analogous cases. Ante, § 476. It declares that all rent reserved and made payable in leases, which determine on the death of the person making them or on the death of the life or lives for which such person was entitled to the lands demised, shall be within the provisions of the statute of 11 Geo. 2, ch. 19. It also declares that all rent-service reserved in any lease by a tenant in fee, or for any life interest, or by any lease granted under any power, and all rent-charge and other rents, annuities, pensions, dividends, moduses, compositions, and all other payments of every other description, made payable or coming due at a fixed period, shall be apportioned so, and in such manner, that on the death of any person interested therein, &c. &c., or on the determination by any other means whatsoever of the interest of any such person, he or she, and his or her executors, administrators, and assigns, shall be entitled to a proportion of such rents and other payments. In the construction of this statute it has been held that it applies to cases in which the interest of the person interested in such rents and payments is terminated by his death or by the death of another person; but that it does not apply to the case of a tenant in fee, nor provide for apportionment of rent between the real and personal representatives of such person whose interest is not terminated by his death. Brown v. Amyott, 3 Hare, R. 173. See also

(a) The same is true of a tenant pur autre vie. Mills v. Trumper, L. R. 4 Ch. 320. So where the whole annual tax is assessed to the life tenant, and he dies within the year, and the tax is paid by his executors, apportionment will be refused. Holmes v. Taber, 9 Allen, 246. See further Marshall v. Moseley, 21 N. Y. 280.

The law does not apportion rent in point of time, and I do not know that equity ever did it.[1] This is an accident which the judgment creditor (the plaintiff) might have guarded against by receiving the rent weekly, so that it is his fault and becomes a gift in law to the tenant.'[2] And yet if the tenant had actually paid the whole rent to the remainder-man, including this period, from a conscientious sense of duty, the party might, under such circumstances, have been entitled to his share pro rata. At least in the case where a tenant in tail made a lease, but not according to the statute, and died without issue between the days of payment, and afterwards the remainder-man received the whole rents, Lord Hardwicke decreed that the executors of the tenant were entitled against him to an apportionment, although in strictness the tenant could not have been compelled to pay it.[3]

482. The distinction between this case and the former case is extremely thin, and the reasons given for it are rather ingenious and subtile than satisfactory. If it would not be unconscientious for the tenant to withhold the rent because the executor of the tenant for life had no equity, it is difficult to perceive that there can spring up any equity against the remainder-man unless the tenant paid the rent with an express understanding that there should be an apportionment, which can hardly be pretended to have been proved in the cases on this point.[4] It would have been perhaps more consonant to the general principles of Courts of Equity to have decided that, as the tenant held his lease upon the terms of a compensatory contract, it was against conscience

Ex parte Smyth, 1 Swanston, R. 337, 338, and Mr. Swanston's learned note, ibid., where the principal cases are commented on at large. 1 Fonbl. Eq. B. 1, ch. 5, § 9, and notes; Jeremy on Eq. Jurisd. B. 3, Pt. 2, ch. 5, pp. 519, 520, 521, 522.

[1] In Meeley v. Webber, cited 2 Eq. Abridg. 704, where a parson leased his tithes at a rent payable at Michaelmas, and died in September, the court decreed an apportionment. There is much good sense in the decision. See also Aynsley v. Woodsworth, 2 V. & Beam. R. 331.

[2] Jenner v. Morgan, 1 P. Will. 392. See Jeremy on Eq. Jurisd. B. 3, Pt. 2, ch. 5, pp. 519, 520, 521.

[3] Paget v. Gee, Ambler, R. 198; s. c. App. (Mr. Blunt's edition), p. 807; Ex parte Smyth, 1 Swanst. R. 337, and note; Id. 355, 356; Aynsley v. Woodsworth, 2 V. & Beam. 331; Jeremy on Eq. Jurisd. B. 3, Pt. 2, ch. 5, p. 520.

[4] See Hawkins v. Kelly, 8 Ves. 308 to 312; Ex parte Smyth, 1 Swanst. R. 346, 347, 348, note.

that he should be at liberty to treat the rent, under any circumstances of an involuntary departure from the terms of the lease, as a gift; [1] and that as the parties had omitted to provide in their contract for the exigency, equity would presume an intention of the parties to treat the rent as accruing, pro tanto, from day to day, and as a 'debitum in præsenti solvendum in futuro.' Lord Hardwicke, on one occasion, in discussing a question of apportionment, after quoting the maxim, 'æquitas sequitur legem,' added: 'When the court finds the rules of law right, it will follow them; but then it will likewise go beyond them.' [2] (a)

---

[1] See Vernon v. Vernon, 2 Bro. Ch. R. 659, 662. Lord Thurlow seems to have proceeded upon a principle somewhat like this in Vernon v. Vernon (2 Bro. Ch. R. 659, 662), holding that where a person was a tenant from year to year, or a tenant at will under a tenant in tail, the demises being determinable at his death, and he dying before the half-year expired, the rent should be apportioned between the representatives of the tenant in tail and the remainderman. His Lordship said that 'the tenant holding from year to year, or period to period, from a guardian, without lease or covenant, cannot be allowed to raise an implication in his own favor that he should hold without paying rent to anybody.' See Hawkins v. Kelly, 8 Ves. 312; Ex parte Smyth, 1 Swanston, R. 337, and ibid., Mr. Swanston's learned note; Clarkson v. Earl of Scarborough, cited 1 Swanston, R. 354, note (a).

[2] Paget v. Gee, Ambler, R. App. p. 810 (Mr. Blunt's edition).

(a) *Apportionment of Rent.* — The necessity for an apportionment of rent, apart from contract or statute, may arise under any of the following circumstances: (1) By division of the reversion, (2) by division of the leasehold premises, or (3) in certain cases by termination of the tenancy between rent days.

The first case may arise by the death of the lessor and the descent of the reversion upon his heirs. The rent must then be apportioned and paid to each of the heirs accordingly. Cole v. Patterson, 25 Wend. 456; Crosby v. Loop, 13 Ill. 625, 627; Bank of Pennsylvania v. Wise, 3 Watts, 404. And this as well in the case of a rent-charge. Cruger v. McLaury, 41 N. Y. 219, 223. It may also arise and be attended with the same result where the lessor grants or devises part of the land to one person, or the whole to several. Crosby v. Loop, supra; Bank of Pennsylvania v. Wise, supra; Reed v. Ward, 22 Penn. St. 144; Linton v. Hart, 25 Penn. St. 193. (As to rent-charges see infra.) And it matters not that the conveyance is involuntary. Nellis v. Lathrop, 22 Wend. 121; Buffum v. Deane, 4 Gray, 385. If however the rent be indivisible by nature, as where it is to be a specific article not severable, the result would probably be an extinguishment. See Van Rensselaer v. Bradley, 3 Denio, 135, 142.

If in a case of descent of the reversion to several, one of the heirs should enter wrongfully, before partition of the reversion, upon part of the demised estate, the tenant would be discharged from liability entirely, because the law will not apportion in favor of a wrongdoer. Reed v. Ward, 22 Penn. St. 144. Otherwise after partition; the

483. But a far more important and beneficial exercise of equity jurisdiction in cases of apportionment and contribution is

wrongful entry would then affect only the part entered upon. Ib.; Linton v. Hart, 25 Penn. St. 193.

The reversion may be divided in another way; the tenant himself may acquire part of it either by descent or by purchase, and have apportionment. Voegtly v. Pittsburgh R. Co., 2 Grant, 243 ; Ingersoll v. Sergeant, 1 Whart. 337 ; Van Rensselaer v. Gifford, 24 Barb. 349. Thus where the tenant buys at sheriff's sale part of the landlord's reversion, he may demand an apportionment of the rent. Nellis v. Lathrop, 22 Wend. 121. See also Ingersoll v. Sergeant, 1 Whart. 337; Van Rensselaer v. Bradley, 3 Denio, 135 ; Coke, Litt. 149 a; Bruerton's Case, 6 Coke, 1 b.

Much question however has been made concerning the effect of a release by the landlord to the tenant of part of the reversion, — whether the act does not amount to an entire extinguishment of the claim to rent ; though it is clear that if the estate of the landlord was not a rent-charge, the effect of the release in ordinary cases would be to give rise to a right of apportionment, and not to extinguish the right to rent altogether. Or if the lease is held by tenants in common who have had partition, a release to one will not extinguish the liability of the rest. Van Rensselaer v. Gifford, 24 Barb. 349. See Van Rensselaer v. Chadwick, ib. 333; s. c. 22 N. Y. 32.

At common law a rent-charge could not be apportioned after a release of part by the grantee of the rent. (It is not so now in England. Booth v. Smith, 14 Q. B. D. 318, on Lord St. Leonard's Act, 22 and 23 Vict. ch. 35, § 10.) This was one of the consequences attached to an estate which was considered dangerous to feudal institutions. A rent-charge was a grant by one seised in fee, in tail, or

for life of rent out of his estate, with right to distrain for non-payment. Litt. § 218. It was always treated as contrary to ' common right,' because the tenant, by creating the charge, diminished by so much his ability to perform the services due by him to his lord. No relation of tenure was created; no enjoyment of an estate was connected with it. It was so unlike a feudal estate that an eviction would not discharge the debtor from liability. Ingersoll v. Sergeant, 1 Whart. 337, 342 ; Franciscus v. Reigart, 4 Watts, 98, 116.

The courts, in sympathy with the feudal tenures, improved every opportunity to discourage the creation of rent-charges, declaring the estate at an end whenever any act of the grantee of the rent was done which could possibly be construed into a release or an extinguishment of the charge. When e. g. the grantee released part of the land from the payment of rent, this was construed into a release of the whole, on the principle that the whole rent was due from every part of the land. Ingersoll v. Sergeant, 1 Whart. 337, 352 ; Van Rensselaer v. Chadwick, 22 N. Y. 32. The argument (which has been repeated by counsel in other cases cited in this note) is clearly unsound, as may be seen by supposing an estate rented ' on shares ' of the products. It would be absurd to say that the whole of the landlord's share was due from every part of the land. Rent is due by reason of enjoyment.

There was another kind of estate that came to be treated as a rent-charge after the Stat. of Quia emptores, to which the consequence just mentioned did not attach before the statute. That estate arose where a man made a gift in fee or for life, reserving rent. This was a feudal

where incumbrances, fines, and other charges on real estate are
required to be paid off or are actually paid off by some of the

tenure, and before the statute was a
rent-service, when not a fee-farm. It
remains such still, where, as in Pennsylvania, that statute is not in force,
and a release of part is not deemed an
extinguishment of the whole. On the
contrary the case is one for apportionment. Ingersoll v. Sergeant, 1 Whart.
337, 347; Voegtly v. Pittsburgh R.
Co., 2 Grant, 243. Of this kind of
estate are the ground rents of Philadelphia. Ingersoll v. Sergeant, supra;
Voegtly v. Pittsburgh R. Co., supra;
Kennedy v. Elliott, 9 Watts, 258, 262.
See Franciscus v. Reigart, 4 Watts,
98, 116. But in New York, where the
Stat. of Quia emptores has been declared to be in force, rent reserved
upon a conveyance in fee is held to be
a rent-charge and not a rent-service;
and a release of part of the land from
the rent, by act of the party entitled
thereto, would in that State probably
extinguish the whole rent. See Van
Rensselaer v. Chadwick, 22 N. Y. 32.

It is apprehended that this would
not be generally true in this country.
It is probably safe to say that, except
in New York and possibly some others
of the colonies which became States,
even if a rent in fee were *granted* out
of an estate, so as to make a true rent-
charge, release of part of the land from
the burden would not be treated as a
release of the whole, but would merely
work an apportionment. A fortiori
would this be true where, apart from
the operation of the Stat. of Quia
emptores, the rent would be rent-
service, or where it would be fee-farm.
Ingersoll v. Sergeant, 1 Whart. 337.

But even under the common law
of England and of New York a rent-
charge is not incapable of apportionment; extinguishment of the rent can
occur only by act of the party entitled
to it. Descent of the land charged, upon
the heirs of the tenant, with partition

and interchange of conveyances, concurred in by the owner of the rent, and
then followed by release of one of the
parcels to the tenant thereof, will not
extinguish the rent due from the other
tenant. Van Rensselaer v. Chadwick,
22 N. Y. 32; Cruger v. McLaury, 41
N. Y. 219 (as to descent and partition).
Indeed a *condition* in a rent-charge,
though not apportionable by act of
the tenant, unless that act is wrongful, or by the act of the parties (Cruger v. McLaury; Dumpor's Case, 4
Coke, 119 b, 120 a), may be apportioned by act of law severing the reversion. Dumpor's Case, 4 Coke, 120 b,
and note, where some qualification of
the rule is stated. And by the Stat.
32 Hen. 8, ch. 34, a grantee of part
of the estate of the *reversion* may take
advantage of a condition. Cruger v.
McLaury, at p. 226; Smith, Real and
Personal Property, 55, n. Perhaps it
would be more accurate to say of such
cases that the condition is multiplied,
though the rent is divided; for commonly a condition is by nature indivisible. Compare Van Rensselaer v.
Bradley, infra.

The second case for apportionment
— division of the leasehold premises
— occurs oftenest perhaps where the
lessee has assigned part of a lease with
covenants running with the land.
Thus in an action of covenant or debt
against the assignee, or upon avowry
in replevin by the assignee, while he
cannot set up the severance of the
leasehold in bar of the whole demand
for rent, he can avail himself of the
fact for the purpose of an apportionment. Stevenson v. Lombard, 2 East,
575; Merceron v. Dowson, 5 Barn. &
C. 479, 483; Wollaston v. Hakewill,
3 Man. & G. 297; Astor v. Miller, 2
Paige, 68, 78; Touchstone, 199; Coke,
Litt. 385 a; Van Horne v. Crain, 1
Paige, 455; Demainville v. Mann, 32

parties in interest.[1] (a)   This subject has already come incidentally under our notice,[2] but it requires a more ample examination

[1] Com. Dig. Chancery, 2 J., 2 S.; 1 Fonbl. Eq. B. 1, ch. 5, § 9, and notes;
Ritson v. Brumlow, 1 Ch. Rep. 91; Cheeseborough v. Millard, 1 John. Ch. R.
409; Scribner v. Hitchcock, 4 John. Ch. R. 530; Averall v. Wade, Lloyd &
Goold, R. 252, and the Reporter's note, 264, 265, 266.

[2] Ante, § 477.

N. Y. 197; Van Rensselaer v. Gallup,
5 Denio, 454, 461; Van Rensselaer v.
Bradley, 3 Denio, 135.   Damages for
want of repair will also be apportioned
in such a case.   Merceron v. Dowson,
supra; Wollaston v. Hakewill, supra.
But if the rent is indivisible in kind,
it now multiplies by the number of
tenants.   Van Rensselaer v. Bradley,
3 Denio, 135, 142; Ingersoll v. Sergeant, 1 Whart. 337.   And of course
if the party has become a sub-tenant
instead of an assignee, there will be
no apportionment.   Van Rensselaer v.
Gallup, 5 Denio, 454.

A division of the leasehold may
also occur by partition between tenants in common; and this too gives,
or at least by concurrence on the part
of the lessor may give, ground against
the reversioner for an apportionment
on the terms of the partition-adjust-
ment.   Van Rensselaer v. Chadwick,
24 Barb. 333; s. c. 22 N. Y. 32.   It
may be that there is a case for apportionment in favor of co-tenants without partition, when they are in actual
possession together in several parts;
but if only one of them has possession,
he cannot have the rent apportioned.
Demainville v. Mann, 32 N. Y. 197,
where the lease had been assigned by
the lessee to tenants in common, one,
the defendant, being now alone in
possession.

The leasehold premises may also be
divided by the landlord's re-acquiring
part of the demised estate; and this

too furnishes ground for apportionment, assuming that the rent is of a
kind capable of being severed.   Van
Rensselaer v. Bradley, 3 Denio, 135,
142.   But where tenants in common
have made partition, purchase of the
interest of one will have no effect upon
the obligation of the rest.   Van
Rensselaer v. Gifford, 24 Barb. 349,
where the landlord purchased the interest of one of the parceners at execution sale.   This assumes of course
that the rent has been apportioned
between the co-tenants; if it has not,
and each is still liable in solido, the
release of one part will reduce the rent
due from the others.   Van Rensselaer
v. Chadwick, 24 Barb. 333, 336.

The premises again may be divided
so as to raise a case for apportionment
by an eviction of the tenant from part
of the land subject to rent by a third
person under title paramount.   Lansing v. Van Alstyne, 2 Wend. 561;
Poston v. Jones, 2 Ired. Eq. 350;
Manville v. Gay, 1 Wis. 250, 257.
Secus if no rent issue from the part
out of which the tenant has been
evicted.   Saunderson v. Harrison,
Cro. Jac. 679.

Another case of division with the
same result occurs where part of the
demised premises is taken under the
law of eminent domain.   Kingsland v.
Clark, 24 Mo. 24; Biddle v. Hussman,
23 Mo. 597; Gillespie v. Thomas, 15
Wend. 464.   This is because the rent
passes with the reversion, as an inci-

(a) See Lipscom v. Lipscom, L. R.
7 Eq. 501; Ley v. Ley, L. R. 6 Eq.
174; Caldwell v. Cresswell, L. R. 6

Ch. 278; Bradford v. Brownjohn,
L. R. 3 Ch. 711.

in this place.   In most cases of this sort there is no remedy at law from the extreme uncertainty of ascertaining the relative

dent thereto, to him who takes the land.

If however in the case of a fee-farm rent — that is, where the owner of an estate holds from another subject to the payment of a certain rent in fee — part of the land out of which the rent issues is taken for public purposes, and compensation made to the owner of the estate in full, he will not be entitled to apportionment unless he pays or offers to pay to the one entitled to the rent his proper proportion of the sum received.   Cuthbert *v.* Kuhn, 3 Whart. 357; Voegtly *v.* Pittsburgh R. Co., 2 Grant, 243; Workman *v.* Mifflin, 30 Penn. St. 362.

The third case, where the lease has been legally determined between rent days, is seen where the lease has been rescinded, as for fraud on the part of the lessee.   An implied obligation will now arise, it should seem, against the tenant to pay for use and occupation during the whole period of enjoyment, when the rescission has been made at a proper time, and not with a view to oppress the tenant.   The obligation arises on the ground that the special contract is out of the way under circumstances such as to raise a just claim to rent for the period of occupancy.   See Zule *v.* Zule, 24 Wend. 76.

This principle, it seems, will extend generally to cases in which, by reason of the wrongful conduct of the tenant between rent days, the landlord has become entitled, either by the terms of the lease or by law, to terminate the tenancy, and has terminated it. See Cruger *v.* McLaury, 41 N. Y. 219, 226.   Thus if a tenant at will or at sufferance should commit waste between rent days, and the landlord should thereupon put an end to the tenancy, it would be consistent with law as well as with justice to permit

him to claim rent down to that time. Dumpor's Case, 4 Coke, 119 *b*, 120 *b*. If a wrongful act, intermediate rent days, on the part of the landlord, justifying the tenant in throwing up the lease prevents, as it does prevent, the landlord from demanding apportionment, then by parity of reasoning a wrongful intermediate act of the tenant, justifying the landlord in terminating the tenancy, should give him a right to apportionment.   Indeed if a tenant hold over after his term, on a parol agreement that either party may give notice of the termination of the tenancy, the rent may be apportioned.   May *v.* Rice, 108 Mass. 150. See also Gale *v.* Nourse, 15 Gray, 300; Thompson *v.* Saco Water Power Co., 114 Mass. 159, — cases of construction of contracts terminated by the defendant.

Whether the taking the whole of the leased premises for public purposes between rent days would give the lessor a right to rent down to the day of taking, or only to the last rent day, query?   If the *lessor* has put an end to the tenancy at such a time, he clearly cannot demand apportionment, except in such a case as that mentioned in the last paragraph, unless there has been a valid agreement for it; he can claim only to the last rent day.   Zule *v.* Zule, 24 Wend. 76.   And the same appears to be true though the tenancy was determined by the act of God. Ib.   Thus if a tenant for life demise a term, and then die before the rent becomes due, his administrator cannot have apportionment.   Gee *v.* Gee, 2 Dev. & B. Eq. 103, 113.   Supra, §§ 475, 481.   For the like rule in the case of annuities payable on fixed days see Wiggin *v.* Swett, 6 Met. 194, 201.   But now see Mass. Pub. Stats. ch. 136, § 25, as to such cases. Haraden *v.* Larrabee, 113 Mass. 430.

proportions which different persons, having interests of a very different nature, quality, and duration, in the subject-matter, ought to pay. And where there is a remedy it is inconvenient and imperfect, because it involves multiplicity of suits and opens the whole matter for contestation anew in every successive litigation.[1]

484. The subject may be illustrated by one of the most common cases, that of an apportionment and contribution towards a mortgage upon an estate where the interest is required to be kept down or the incumbrance to be paid. Let us suppose a case where different parcels of land are included in the same mortgage, and these different parcels are afterwards sold to different purchasers, each holding in fee and severalty the parcel sold to himself. In such a case each purchaser is bound to contribute to the discharge of the common burden or charge in proportion to the value which his parcel bears to the whole included in the mortgage.[2] (a) But to ascertain the relative values of each is a matter of great nicety and difficulty; and unless all the different purchasers are joined in a single suit, as they can be in equity, although not at law, the most serious embarrassments may arise in fixing the proportion of each purchaser and in making it conclusive upon all others.

485. So if there are different persons having different interests

---

[1] Ante, §§ 477, 478.

[2] Cheeseborough v. Millard, 1 John. Ch. R. 409, 415; Stevens v. Cooper, 1 John. Ch. R. 425; Harris v. Ingledew, 3 P. Will. 98, 99; Harbert's Case, 3 Co. R. 14; Taylor v. Porter, 7 Mass. R. 355.

The case of Ripley v. Wightman, 4 McCord, 447, which holds that if a house, rented for a year, is made untenantable by a storm during the term, the rent is to be apportioned, seems to be opposed to the current of authority; though as a new question apportionment would seem reasonable in all such cases. It is held that there can be no apportionment on account of fire where the rent is payable and paid in advance, even though there is a covenant to *deduct* rent proportionally in case of part destruction; such not being a covenant to pay back rent received. Cross v. Button, 4 Wis. 468.

(a) But see § 1233 a, post. The rule that where two properties subject to one common charge are given to two persons they must contribute, applies only where the two properties are equally charged. Thus the rule does not apply where one of the properties is primarily charged, in exoneration of the other. In re Dunlop, 21 Ch. D. 583 (C. A.); Bute v. Cunynghame, 2 Russ. 275, 299. See Averall v. Wade, Lloyd & G. 252.

in an estate under mortgage, as for instance parceners,[1] tenants for life or in tail, remainder-men, tenants in dower or for a term of years, or for other limited interests, it is obvious that the question of apportionment and contribution in redeeming the mortgage, as well as in payment of interest, may involve most important and intricate inquiries; and, to do entire justice, it may be indispensable that all the parties in interest should actually be brought before the court. Now in a suit at the common law this is absolutely impossible; for no persons can be made parties except those whose interest is joint and of the same nature and character, and is immediate and vested in possession. So that a resort to a Court of Equity, where all these interests can be brought before the court and definitely ascertained and disposed of, is indispensable. If to this we add that in most cases of mortgage an account of what has been paid upon the mortgage, either by direct payments or by perception of the rents and profits of the estate, is necessary to be taken, we shall at once see that the machinery of a Court of Common Law is very ill adapted to any such purpose. But if we add further to all this that there may be mesne incumbrances and other cross equities between some of the parties, all of which are required to be adjusted in order to arrive at a just result and to attain the full end of the law by closing up all future litigation, we shall not fail to be convinced that the only appropriate, adequate, and effectual remedy must be administered in equity. Indeed from its very nature, as we shall have occasion to see fully hereafter, the jurisdiction over mortgages belongs peculiarly and exclusively to Courts of Equity. And wherever, as is the case in some of the American States, an attempt has been made to engraft the remedy of redemption upon the ordinary processes of Courts of Law, it has been found to be inconvenient, embarrassing, and in complicated cases impracticable.

486. Very delicate and often very intricate questions arise in the adjustment of the rights and duties of the different parties in interest in the inheritance. In the first place in regard to the paying off of incumbrances. If a tenant in tail in possession pays off an incumbrance, it will ordinarily be treated as extinguished; and the remainder-man cannot be called upon for contribution unless the tenant in tail has kept alive the incumbrance,

[1] Stirling v. Forrester, 3 Bligh, R. 590, 596.

or preserved the benefit of it to himself by some suitable assignment, or has done some other act or thing which imports a positive
intention to hold himself out as a creditor of the estate in lieu of
the mortgagee. The reason for this doctrine is, that a tenant in
tail can, if he pleases, by fine or recovery, become the absolute
owner of the estate ; and therefore his discharge of incumbrances
is treated as made in the character of owner unless he clearly
shows that he intends to discharge them and become a creditor
thereby.[1] But the like doctrine does not apply to a tenant in
tail in remainder whose estate may be altogether defeated by the
birth of issue of another person ; for it must be inferred that such
a tenant in tail, in paying off an incumbrance without an assignment, means to keep the charge alive.[2] A fortiori, the doctrine
would not apply to the case of a tenant for life paying off an incumbrance ; for if he should pay it off without taking an assignment, he would be deemed to be a creditor to the amount paid,
upon the ground that there can be no presumption that, with his
limited interest, he could intend to exonerate the estate.[3] He cannot be presumed, prima facie, to discharge the estate from the
debt; for that would be to discharge the estate of another person
from the debt. But in both cases the presumption may be rebutted by circumstances which demonstrate a contrary intention.[4]

487. In respect to the discharge of incumbrances it was formerly a rule in equity that the tenant for life and the reversioner or remainder-man were bound to contribute towards the
payment of incumbrances in a positive proportion fixed by the
court, so that they paid a gross sum in proportion to their interests in the estate. The usual proportion was for the tenant
for life to pay one third and the remainder-man or reversioner
to pay two thirds of the charge.[5] A similar rule was applied to

---

[1] Wigsell v. Wigsell, 2 Sim. & Stu. R. 364; Jones v. Morgan, 1 Bro. Ch.
R. 206; Kirkham v. Smith, 1 Ves. 258; Amesbury v. Brown, 1 Ves. 477;
Shrewsbury v. Shrewsbury, 3 Bro. Ch. R. 120; s. c. 1 Ves. jr. 227; St. Paul
v. Viscount Dudley and Ward, 15 Ves. 173; Faulkner v. Daniel, 3 Hare, R.
199, 217.

[2] Wigsell v. Wigsell, 2 Sim. & Stu. R. 364.

[3] Saville v. Saville, 2 Atk. 463, 464; Jones v. Morgan, 1 Bro. Ch. R. 218;
Shrewsbury v. Shrewsbury, 1 Ves. jr. 233; s. c. 3 Bro. Ch. R. 120; Ex parte
Digby, Jacob, R. 235.

[4] Jones v. Morgan, 1 Bro. Ch. R. 218, 219 ; St. Paul v. Viscount Dudley
and Ward, 15 Ves. 173; Redington v. Redington, 1 B. & Beatt. R. 141, 142.

[5] Powell on Mortg. ch. 11, p. 311; Ballett v. Sprainger, Prec. Ch. 62;

cases of fines paid upon the renewal of leases.[1] But the rule is now in both cases entirely exploded in England, and a far more reasonable rule is adopted. It is this: that the tenant shall contribute beyond the interest in proportion to the benefit he derives from the liquidation of the debt, and the consequent cessation of annual payments of interest during his life (which of course will depend much upon his age and the computation of the value of his life); and it will be referred to a Master to ascertain and report what proportion of the capital sum due, the tenant for life ought upon this basis to pay, and what ought to be borne by the remainder-man or reversioner.[2] If the estate is sold to discharge incumbrances (as the incumbrancer may insist that it shall be), in such a case the surplus beyond what is necessary to discharge the incumbrances is to be applied as follows: the income thereof is to go to the tenant for life during his life, and then the whole capital is to be paid over to the remainder-man or reversioner.[3] (a)

488. In regard to the interest due upon mortgages and other incumbrances the question often arises, by whom and in what manner it is to be paid. And here the general rule is that a

Shrewsbury (County of) v. Earl of Shrewsbury, 1 Ves. jr. 233; Rives v. Rives, Prec. Ch. 21; 1 Fonbl. Eq. B. 1, ch. 5, § 9, note (a), 3d ed.; Faulkner v. Daniel, 3 Hare, R. 199, 217.

[1] White v. White, 4 Ves. 33; Verney v. Verney, 1 Ves. 428; s. c. Amb. R. 88; Nightingale v. Lawson, 1 Bro. Ch. R. 440.

[2] See 1 Powell on Mortg. ch. 11, pp. 311, 312, Mr. Coventry's note, M.; Penrhyn v. Hughes, 5 Ves. 107; White v. White, 4 Ves. 33, 9 Ves. 554; Allan v. Backhouse, 2 Ves. & B. 70, 79.

[3] Penrhyn v. Hughes, 5 Ves. 107; White v. White, 4 Ves. 33; 3 Powell on Mortg. ch. 19, p. 922, Mr. Coventry's note, H.; Id. 1043, note, O.; Lloyd v. Johnes, 9 Ves. 37; Foster v. Hilliard, 1 Story, R. 77. Many cases may occur of far more complicated adjustments than are here stated; but in a treatise like the present little more than the general rules can be indicated. See Rives v. Rives, Prec. Ch. 21; 1 Fonbl. Eq. B. 1, ch. 5, § 9, and note. See also Gibson v. Crehore, 5 Pick. R. 146. The converse case of that stated in the text will readily occur to the learned reader; namely, where mortgage money or a mortgage is devised to a tenant for life with a remainder over, and the mortgage money is paid by the mortgagor. The old rule used to be to divide it between the tenant for life and the remainder-man in the proportion of one third and two thirds. But it would probably now be governed by the same rules as those in the text. 3 Powell on Mortg. 1043, Mr. Coventry's note, O.

(a) See Thomas v. Thomas, 2 C. E. Green, 356, 359.

tenant for life of an equity of redemption is bound to keep down and pay the interest, although he is under no obligation to pay off the principal.[1] But a tenant in tail is not bound to keep down the interest; and yet, if he does, his personal representative has no right to be allowed the sums so paid as a charge on the estate.[2] The reason of this distinction is that a tenant in tail discharging the interest is supposed to do it as owner for the benefit of the estate. He is not compellable to pay the interest, because he has the power at any time to make himself absolute owner against the remainder-man and reversioner. The latter have no equity to compel him in their favor to keep down the interest, inasmuch as if they take anything it is solely by his forbearance, and of course they must take it cum onere.[3]

488 a. Similar questions may arise as to the apportionment of the money between a tenant for life and a remainder-man in fee, who have united in a sale of the estate without providing for the manner of apportioning the purchase-money between them, and one of them has died before any apportionment has been made. In such a case how is the money to be divided ? Is the tenant for life to be deemed entitled to the income of the whole fund during his life, and then the whole fund to go to the remainder-man ? Or is the value of the estate of each party to be ascertained, calculating that of the tenant for life according to the common tables respecting the probabilities of life, and the principal of the fund to be apportioned between them accordingly ? It has been held upon deliberate consideration that the latter is the true rule applicable to such cases, upon the ground that it must be presumed in such cases of a joint sale that the parties mean to share the purchase-money according to their respec-

---

[1] Saville v. Saville, 2 Atk. 463, 464; Shrewsbury v. Shrewsbury, 1 Ves. jr. 233.

[2] Amesbury v. Brown, 1 Ves. 480, 481; Redington v. Redington, 1 Ball & B. 143; Chaplin v. Chaplin, 3 P. Will. 234, 235.

[3] Ibid.   There is an exception to the general rule that a tenant in tail is not bound to keep down the interest, which confirms rather than impugns the general rule.   If the tenant in tail is an infant, his guardian or trustee will in that case be required to keep down the interest.   The reason is that the infant of his own free will cannot bar the remainder and make himself absolute owner.   See Jeremy on Eq. Jurisd. B. 1, ch. 2, § 1, p. 187; Sergeson v. Sealey, 2 Atk. 416, and Mr. Saunders's note (1), ibid.; Amesbury v. Brown, 1 Ves. 479, 480, 481; Bertie v. Lord Abingdon, 3 Meriv. R. 560.

tive interests in the estate at the time of the sale, and not merely to substitute one fund for another.[1]

489. These remarks may suffice to show (for it is not our purpose to bring the minute distinctions upon these important subjects under a full review)[2] the beneficial operation of Courts of Equity in apportionments and contributions upon this confessedly intricate subject; and also how utterly inadequate a Court of Common Law would be to do complete justice in a vast variety of cases which may easily be suggested. Without some proceedings in the nature of an account before a Master, there would be no suitable elements upon which any court of justice could dispose of the merits of such cases so as to suppress future litigation, or to administer to the conflicting rights of different parties.

490. Another class of cases which still more fully illustrates the importance and value of this branch of equity jurisdiction is that of GENERAL AVERAGE, a subject of daily occurrence in maritime and commercial operations. General Average, in the sense of the maritime law, means a general contribution that is to be made by all parties in interest towards a loss or expense which is voluntarily sustained or incurred for the benefit of all.[3] The principle upon which this contribution is founded is not the result of contract, but has its origin in the plain dictates of natural law.[4] It has been more immediately derived to us from the positive declarations of the Roman law, which borrowed it from the more ancient text of the Rhodian Jurisprudence. Thus the Rhodian law in cases of jettison declared that, ' If goods are thrown overboard in order to lighten a ship, the loss incurred for the sake of all shall be made good by the contribution of all. " Lege Rhodia," says the Digest, " cavetur, utsi levandæ navis gratia jactus mercium factus est, omnium contributione sarciatur,

---

[1] Foster v. Hilliard, 1 Story, R. 77, where the subject was discussed at large. See also Brent v. Brent, 1 Vern. R. 69; Thynn v. Duvall, 2 Vern. R. 117; Houghton v. Hapgood, 13 Pick. R. 154. But see Penrhyn v. Hughes, 5 Ves. 99, 107.

[2] See 1 Bridgman's Digest, Average and Contribution, I., II.; 1 Chitty, Eq. Dig. Apportionment.

[3] Abbott on Shipp. Pt. 3, ch. 8, § 1, p. 342; Moore's Rep. 297; Viner's Abridg. Contribution and Average, A. pl. 1, 2, 26.

[4] Id.; Deering v. Earl of Winchelsea, 1 Cox, R. 318, 323; s. c. 2 Bos. & Pull. 270, 274; Stirling v. Forrester, 3 Bligh, R. 590, 596.

quod pro omnibus datum est." ' [1] But the principle is by no means confined to cases of jettison; but it is applied to all other sacrifices of property, sums paid, and expenses voluntarily incurred in the course of maritime voyages for the common benefit of all persons concerned in the adventure. The principle has indeed been confined to a sacrifice of property, and the contribution confined to the property saved thereby; although it certainly might have gone further and have required a corresponding apportionment of the loss or sacrifice of property upon all persons whose lives have been preserved thereby, upon the same common sense of danger and purchase of safety alluded to by Juvenal, when in a similar case his friend desired his life to be saved by a sacrifice of his property: ' Fundite quæ mea sunt, etiam pulcherrima.'

491. General Average being then, as has been already stated, not confined to cases of jettison, but extending to other losses and expenditures for the common benefit, it may readily be perceived how difficult it would be for a Court of Law to apportion and adjust the amount which is to be paid by each distinct interest which is involved in the common calamity and expenditure. Take for instance the common case of a general ship or packet trading between Liverpool and New York, and having on board various shipments of goods not unfrequently exceeding a hundred in number, consigned to different persons as owners or consignees; and suppose a case of general average to arise during the voyage, and the loss or expenditure to be apportioned among all these various shippers according to their respective interests and the amount which the whole cargo is to contribute to the reimbursement thereof. By the general rule of the maritime law in all cases of general average, the ship, the freight for the voyage, and the cargo on board are to contribute to such reimbursement according to their relative values. ⌐ The first step in the process of general average is to ascertain the amount of the loss for which contribution is to be made; as for instance in the case of jettison, the value of the property thrown overboard or sacrificed for the common preservation. The value is generally indefinite and unascertained, and from its very nature rarely admits of an exact and fixed computation. The same remark applies to the case of ascertainment of the value of the contribu-

[1] Dig. Lib. 14, tit. 2, l. 1.

tory interests, — the ship, the freight, and the cargo. These are generally differently estimated by different persons, and rarely admit of a positive and indisputable estimation in price or value. Now as the owners of the ship and the freight and the cargo may be and generally are, in the supposed case, different persons having a separate interest, and often an adverse interest to each other, it is obvious that unless all the persons in interest can be made parties in one common suit, so as to have the whole adjustment made at once and made binding upon all of them, infinite embarrassments must arise in ascertaining and apportioning the general average. In a proceeding at the common law every party having a sole and distinct interest must be separately sued;[1] and as the verdict and judgment in one case will not only not be conclusive, but not even be admissible evidence in another suit, as it is res inter alios acta, and as the amount to be recovered must in each case depend upon the value of all the interests to be affected, which of course might be differently estimated by different juries, it is manifest that the grossest injustice or the most oppressive litigation might take place in all cases of general average on board of general ships. A Court of Equity having authority to bring all the parties before it and to refer the whole matter to a Master to take an account and to adjust the whole apportionment at once, affords a safe, convenient, and expeditious remedy. And it is accordingly the customary mode of remedy in all cases where a controversy arises and a Court of Equity exists in the place capable of administering the remedy.[2]

492. Another class of cases to illustrate the beneficial effects of Equity Jurisdiction over matters of account is that of CON-TRIBUTION BETWEEN SURETIES who are bound for the same principal, and upon his default one of them is compelled to pay the money or to perform any other obligation for which they all became bound.[3] In cases of this sort the surety who has paid the whole is entitled to receive contribution from all the others for what he has done in relieving them from a common burden.[4] (a)

---

[1] Abbott on Shipp. Pt. 3, ch. 8, § 17.

[2] Abbott on Shipp. Pt. 3, ch. 8, § 17; Shepherd v. Wright, Shower, Parl. Cas. 18; Hallett v. Bousfield, 18 Ves. 190, 196.

[3] Com. Dig. Chancery, 4 D. 6.

[4] Layer v. Nelson, 1 Vern. 456. On the subject of contribution there is a

(a) A surety may pay before judgment, but if he does, he must show that he was bound to pay. Fishback v. Weaver, 34 Ark. 569.

493. The claim certainly has its foundation in the clearest principles of natural justice ; for as all are equally bound and are equally relieved, it seems but just that in such a case all should contribute in proportion towards a benefit obtained by all, upon the maxim, ' Qui sentit commodum, sentire debet et onus.' [1] And the doctrine has an equal foundation in morals, since no one ought to profit by another man's loss where he himself has incurred a like responsibility. Any other rule would put it in the power of the creditor to select his own victim, and upon motives of mere caprice or favoritism to make a common burden a most gross personal oppression. It would be against equity for the creditor to exact or receive payment from one and to permit or by his conduct to cause the other debtors to be exempt from payment. And the creditor is always bound in conscience, although he is seldom bound by contract, as far as he is able, to put the party paying the debt upon the same footing with those who are equally bound.[2] It can be no matter of surprise therefore to find that Courts of Equity at a very early period adopted and acted upon this salutary doctrine as equally well founded in equity and morality.[3] The ground of relief does not therefore stand upon any notion of mutual contract express or implied, between the sureties to indemnify each other in proportion (as has sometimes been argued), but it arises from principles of equity independent of contract.[4] (a)   If the doctrine were other-

valuable note of the Reporters to the case of Averall v. Wade, Lloyd & Goold, Rep. 264 to 266; Spencer v. Parry, 3 Adolph. & Ell. 331; Davies v. Humphreys, 6 Maule & Selw. 153; Cowell v. Edwards, 2 Bos. & Pull. 268; Brown v. Lee, 6 Barn. & Cres. 689; Kemp v. Finden, 12 Mees. & Welsb. 421.

[1] See Shelley's Case, 1 Co. Rep. 99; Deering v. Earl of Winchelsea, 1 Cox, R. 318, 322; s. c. 2 Bos. & Pull. 270, 274; Craythorne v. Swinburne, 14 Ves. 159; Rogers v. Mackenzie, 4 Ves. 752.

[2] Stirling v. Forrester, 3 Bligh, Rep. 590, 591.

[3] Com. Dig. Chancery, 4 D. 6, S. 2; Peter v. Rich, 1 Ch. R. 34; Morgan v. Seymour, 1 Ch. R. 121; Stirling v. Forrester, 3 Bligh, R. 590, 591.

[4] Deering v. Earl of Winchelsea, 1 Cox, R. 318; s. c. 2 Bos. & Pull. 270; Ex parte Gifford, 6 Ves. 805; Craythorne v. Swinburne, 14 Ves. 159; Stirling v. Forrester, 3 Bligh, R. 590, 596; Campbell v. Mesier, 4 John. Ch. R. 334, 338; Onge v. Truelock, 2 Molloy, R. 31, 42; Copis v. Middleton, 1 Turn. & Russ. 224; Hodgson v. Shaw, 3 Mylne & Keen, 191. In Stirling v. Forrester, 3 Bligh, R. 496, Lord Redesdale said: ' The decision in Deering v. Lord Winchelsea (1 Cox, 318; 2 Bos. & Pull. 270) proceeded on a principle of law which must exist in all countries, that where several persons are debtors all shall be

(a) Chipman v. Morrill, 20 Cal. 130.

wise, a surety would be utterly without relief; because (as we shall presently see) he has not either in equity or at law any title to compel the obligee to assign over the bond to him upon his making payment or otherwise discharging the obligation.[1]

494. In the Roman law analogous principles existed, although from the different arrangements of that system they were developed under very different modifications. By that law sureties

---

equal. The doctrine is illustrated in that case by the practice in questions of average, &c., where there is no express contract, but equity distributes the loss equally. On the prisage of wines it is immaterial whose wines are taken; all must contribute equally. So it is where goods are thrown overboard for the safety of the ship. The owners of the goods saved by that act must contribute proportionally to the loss. The duty of contribution extends to all persons who are within the scope of the equitable obligation.' Post, § 495, note 2. But see Johnson v. Johnson, 11 Mass. R. 359; Taylor v. Savage, 12 Mass. R. 98.

[1] Gammon v. Stone, 1 Ves. 339; Woffington v. Sparks, 2 Ves. 569, 570. But see Morgan v. Seymour, 1 Ch. R. 120, and Ex parte Crisp, 1 Atk. 135; Copis v. Middleton, 1 Turn. & Russ. R. 224; Hodgson v. Shaw, 3 Mylne & Keen, 189; Dowbiggin v. Bourne, 2 Younge & Coll. 471; Reed v. Norris, 2 Mylne & Craig, 361. Mr. Chancellor Kent, in Cheeseborough v. Millard (1 John. Ch. R. 413) seems to have thought that a surety paying off a debt is entitled to a cession or assignment of the debt to enable him to have satisfaction from the principal and his co-sureties. He relied on the cases in 1 Ch. R. 20, and 1 Atk. 35; but he did not cite the cases in 1 Ves. 339, and 2 Ves. 569, 570. However the point was not decided by him. See also Avery v. Petten, 7 John. Ch. R. 211, where the same learned chancellor acted upon the ground that an assignment might be decreed; but upon very satisfactory grounds he refused it in that case. His grounds however seem equally applicable against any assignment in any case where all the parties in interest are not before the court; and if they are, there seems no necessity for the assignment, since there may be a direct decree for contribution without it. It is one thing to decide that a surety is entitled, on payment, to have an assignment of the debt, and quite another to decide that he is entitled to be subrogated or substituted, as to other equities and securities, in the place of the creditor against the debtor and his co-sureties. See King v. Baldwin, 2 John. Ch. R. 560; Hayes v. Ward, 4 John. Ch. R. 123. See also Himes v. Keller, 3 Watts & Serg. 401; Bowditch v. Green, 3 Metc. R. 310; Powell's Ex'ors v. White, 11 Leigh, R. 309. In Stirling v. Forrester, 3 Bligh, R. 590, 591, Lord Redesdale said: ' If several persons are indebted, and one makes payment, the creditor is bound in conscience, if not by contract, to give the party paying the debt all his remedies against the other debtors.' Mr. Theobald, in his Treatise on Principal and Surety, ch. 10, § 270, has by mistake attributed a remark of Sir Samuel Romilly, arguendo, to the Lord Chancellor. It bears on this very point, and therefore the error should be corrected. See post, §§ 499 to 502, and notes, ibid.; and Wright v. Morley, 11 Ves. 12, 22; Butcher v. Churchill, 14 Ves. 568, 575, 576; post, §§ 635, 636.

were liable indeed for the whole debt due to the creditor; but this liability was subject to three modifications. In the first place the creditor was generally bound to proceed by process of discussion (as it is now called), in the first instance against the principal debtor, to obtain satisfaction out of his effects before he could resort to the sureties. In the next place, in a suit against one surety, although each surety was bound for the whole debt after the discussion of the principal debtor, yet the surety in such suit had a right to have the debt apportioned among all the solvent sureties on the same obligation, so that he should be compellable to pay his own share only; and this was called the benefit of division.[1] But if a surety should pay the whole debt without insisting upon the benefit of division, then he had no right of recourse over against his co-sureties unless (which is the third case) upon the payment he procured himself to be substituted to the original debt (which he might insist on) by a cession thereof from the creditor; in which case he might insist upon a payment of a proper proportion from each of his co-sureties.[2] And in case of the insolvency of either of the sureties the share of the insolvent was to be apportioned upon all the solvent sureties pro rata.[3] The same principles in a great measure, but not in all cases, now regulate the same subject among the continental nations of Europe whose jurisprudence is derived from the civil law.[4]

[1] 1 Domat, B. 3, tit. 4, § 2, art. 1, 6; Pothier on Oblig. by Evans, n. 407; Pothier, Pand. Lib. 46, tit. 1, § 5, art. 1, n. 41 to 45; Id. art. 3, n. 51 to 61; Cheeseborough v. Millard, 1 John. Ch. R. 414; Hayes v. Ward, 4 John. Ch. R. 131, 132; post, § 636, note.

[2] 1 Domat, B. 3, tit. 4, § 4, art. 1; Pothier on Oblig. by Evans, n. 407, 519, 520, 521 (556, 557, 558, of the French editions); Pothier, Pand. Lib. 46, tit. 1, art. 2, n. 45 to 51.

[3] 1 Domat, B. 3, tit. 4, art. 2; Pothier on Oblig. by Evans, n. 407, 415, 418, 419, 420, 421, 445, 518, 519, 520, 521 (555 to 559, of French editions); Id. 282; Pothier, Pand. Lib. 46, tit. 1, art. 2, n. 45 to 51; Dig. Lib. 46, tit. 1, l. 26; Cod. Lib. 8, tit. 14, l. 2. See also 1 Bell, Comm. B. 3, Pt. 1, ch. 3, § 3, art. 283 to 286; Ersk. Inst. B. 3, tit. 3, art. 61 to 74; 1 Domat, B. 3, tit. 1, § 3, art. 6, and Domat's note; post, § 635.

[4] Merlin, Repert. art. Discussion; Id. Division; Pothier on Oblig. by Evans, Pt. 2, ch. 6, art. 2, n. 407, 415, 416; Id. Pt. 2, ch. 3, art. 8, n. 280; Id. Pt. 3, ch. 1, art. 6, § 2, n. 519 to 524 (556 to 559, of the French editions); 1 Domat, B. 3, tit. 1, § 3, art. 6, and Domat's note, ibid.; Cod. Lib. 8, tit. 14, l. 2. The same principle in regard to the necessity of the creditor's discussing the principal debtor before resorting to the surety, has been adopted in most

495. Originally it seems to have been questioned whether contribution between sureties, unless founded upon some positive contract between them incurring such liability, was a matter capable of being enforced at law.   But there is now no doubt that it may be enforced at law as well as in equity, although no such contract exists.[1] (a)   And it matters not, in case of a debt, whether the sureties are jointly and severally bound, or only severally; or whether their suretyship arises under the same obligation or

countries deriving their jurisprudence from the civil law; but it is not universally adopted.   It prevails in France, Holland, and Scotland, but not (as it seems) generally in Germany.   See Mr. Chancellor Kent's learned opinion in Hayes v. Ward, 4 John. Ch. R. 130 to 135, where he cites the foreign authorities on this point.   These authorities fully justify his statement.   The following extract from that opinion may be acceptable : ' According to the Roman law in use before the time of Justinian, the creditor, as with us, could apply to the surety before applying to the principal.   " Jure nostro est potestas creditori, relicto reo, eligendi fidejussores " (Code, Lib. 8, tit. 41, § 5); and the same law was declared in another imperial ordinance (Code, Lib. 8, tit. 41, § 19).   But Justinian, in one of his Novels (Nov. 4, c. 1, entitled " Ut Creditores primo loco conveniant principalem "), allowed to sureties the exception of discussion, or beneficium ordinis, by which they could require that before they were sued the principal debtor should, at their expense, be prosecuted to judgment and execution.   It is a dilatory exception, and puts off the action of the creditor against the surety until the remedy against the principal debtor has been sufficiently exhausted.   This provision in the Novels has not been followed in the states and cities of Germany, except in Pomerania (Heinecc. Elem. Jur. Germ. lib. 2, tit. 16, §§ 449, 450, 451, 465); but it has been adopted in those other countries in Europe, as France, Holland, Scotland, &c., which follow the rules of the civil law (Pothier, Trait. des Oblig. No. 407–414; Code Napoléon, No. 2021, 2, 3; Voet, Com. ad Pand. tit. De Fidejussoribus, 46, 1, 14–20; Hub. Prælec. lib. 3, tit. 21, § 6; Ersk. Inst. 504, § 61).   A rule of such general adoption shows that there is nothing in it inconsistent with the relative rights and duties of principal and surety, and that it accords with a common sense of justice and the natural equity of mankind.'   It may be well here to state that I generally cite Pothier on Obligations from Mr. Evans's edition.   It is important to remark that after n. 456, in Evans's edition, the subsequent numbers differ from the common French editions, owing to Pothier having, in his later editions, inserted between that number and number 457 a new section containing thirty-five numbers, so that No. 457, in Evans's edition, stands, in the common editions of Pothier, No. 493.   See Mr. Evans's note (a) to Pothier on Oblig. Pt. 2, ch. 6, § 9, p. 306.   This explanation may be useful to the reader, to prevent mistakes or supposed mistakes in the references usually made in English and American works to Pothier.   Post, §§ 635 to 640.

[1] See Kemp v. Finden, 12 Mees. & Welsb. 421.

(a) See Cooper v. Evans, L. R. 4 Eq. 45.

instrument, or under divers obligations or instruments, (*a*) if all the instruments are for the same identical debt.[1] (*b*)

496. But still the jurisdiction now assumed in Courts of Law upon this subject in no manner affects that originally and intrinsically belonging to equity.[2] (*c*) Indeed there are many cases in which the relief is more complete and effectual in equity than it can be at law ; as for instance where an account and discovery are wanted, or where there are numerous parties in inter-

---

[1] Deering *v*. Earl of Winchelsea, 1 Cox, R. 318; s. c. 2 Bos. & Pull. 270; 1 Saund. R. 264 (*a*), Mr. Williams's note (*c*); Craythorne *v*. Swinburne, 14 Ves. 159, 169. In Stirling *v*. Forrester (3 Bligh, R. 590, o. s.), Lord Redesdale said: 'The principle established in the case of Deering *v*. Lord Winchelsea is universal, that the right and duty of contribution is founded in doctrines of equity. It does not depend upon contract. If several persons are indebted and one makes the payment, the creditor is bound in conscience, if not by contract, to give to the party paying the debt all his remedies against the other debtors. The cases of average in equity rest upon the same principle. It would be against equity for the creditor to exact or receive payment from one, and to permit, or by his conduct to cause, the other debtors to be exempt from payment. He is bound, seldom by contract, but always in conscience, as far as he is able, to put the party paying the debt upon the same footing with those who are equally bound. That was the principle of decision in Deering *v*. Lord Winchelsea; and in that case there was no evidence of contract as in this. So in the case of land descending to coparceners subject to a debt, if the creditor proceeds against one of the coparceners, the others must contribute. If the creditor discharges one of the coparceners, he cannot proceed for the whole debt against the others; at the most they are only bound to pay their proportions.' His Lordship afterwards, in pronouncing judgment, added the words which have been already cited in § 493, note. See also post, § 498, in what cases no contribution is allowed.

[2] Wright *v*. Hunter, 5 Ves. 792.

(*a*) Armitage *v*. Pulver, 37 N. Y. 494; Whiting *v*. Burke, L. R. 6 Ch. 342. See however § 498, post; Coope *v*. Twynam, Turn. & R. 426; Keller *v*. Williams, 10 Bush, 216; Hartwell *v*. Smith, 15 Ohio St. 200, that this is true only where the sureties stand in æquali jure.

(*b*) It matters not whether the sureties have had communication with each other. Norton *v*. Coons, 2 Seld. 33. A surety is not ordinarily entitled to call upon his co-surety for contribution until he has paid more than his proportion of the debt, even though the co-surety has not been required by the creditor to pay anything, provided the co-surety has not been released by the creditor. Ex parte Snowdon, 17 Ch. D. 44; Davies *v*. Humphreys, 6 Mees. & W. 153, 168. Nor can a surety, in the absence of contract, require surrender from his principal of collaterals before payment of all the debts to secure which they were given. Farebrother *v*. Wodehouse, 23 Beav. 18.

(*c*) Broughton *v*. Wimberley, 65 Ala. 549; Couch *v*. Terry, 12 Ala. 225; Buckner *v*. Stewart, 34 Ala. 529; Cooper *v*. Evans, L. R. 4 Eq. 45.

est which would occasion a multiplicity of suits.[1] In some cases
the remedy at law is now utterly inadequate.   As if there are
several sureties and one is insolvent and another pays the debt,
he can at law recover from the other solvent sureties only the
same share as he could if all were solvent. Thus if there are
four sureties and one is insolvent, a solvent surety who pays the
whole debt can recover only one fourth part thereof (and not a
third part) against the other two solvent sureties.[2] But in a
Court of Equity he will be entitled to recover one third part of
the debt against each of them ; for in equity the insolvent's
share is apportioned among all the other solvent sureties.[3] (a)

497. And upon the like grounds if one of the sureties dies,
the remedy at law lies only against the surviving parties ; whereas
in equity it may be enforced against the representative of the
deceased party, and he may be compelled to contribute his share
to the surviving surety who shall pay the whole debt.[4]   Where
there are several distinct bonds with different penalties and a
surety upon one bond pays the whole, the contribution between
the sureties is in proportion to the penalties of their respective
bonds.   But as between the sureties to the same bond the general rule is that of equality of burden inter sese.[5]

498. These are cases of contribution of a simple and distinct

---

[1] Craythorne v. Swinburne, 14 Ves. 159; Cornell v. Edwards, 2 Bos. &
Pull. 268; Wright v. Hunter, 5 Ves. 792.

[2] Cornell v. Edwards, 2 Bos. & Pull. 268; Brown v. Lee, 6 B. & Cressw.
697.   See also Rogers v. Mackenzie, 4 Ves. 752; Wright v. Hunter, 5 Ves.
792.

[3] Peter v. Rich, 1 Ch. Rep. 34; Cornell v. Edwards, 2 Bos. & Pull. 268;
Hale v. Harrison, 1 Ch. Cas. 246; Deering v. Earl of Winchelsea, 2 Bos. &
Pull. 270; s. c. 1 Cox, R. 318.   But see Swain v. Wall, 1 Ch. Rep. 149, 150,
151.   See also Pothier on Oblig. n. 275, 281, 282, 428, 521 (n. 556, of the
French editions), the same principles.

[4] Primrose v. Bromley, 1 Atk. 89.

[5] See Deering v. Earl of Winchelsea, 1 Cox, R. 318; s. c. 2 Bos. & Pull.
270.

(a) See Armitage v. Pulver, 37 N. Y. 494.   Courts of Law in some of the States follow the rule in equity. Mills v. Hyde, 19 Vt. 59; Henderson v. McDuffee, 5 N. H. 38; Chitty, Contracts, 584 (Perkins), and note. See also Jones v. Blanton, 6 Ired. Eq. 116; Aiken v. Peay, 5 Strob. 15; Johnson v. Vaughn, 65 Ill. 425; Whiting v. Burke, L. R. 10 Eq. 539; s. c. 6 Ch. 342.   If the cause of action is barred against one surety, he cannot be compelled to contribute. Shelton v. Farmer, 9 Bush, 314.   But see Camp v. Bostwick, 20 Ohio St. 337; ante, § 325.

character. But in cases of suretyship others of a very complicated nature may arise from counter equities between some or all
of the parties, resulting from contract, or from equities between
themselves, or from peculiar transactions regarding third persons.[1]
Thus for instance although the general rule is that there shall
be a contribution between sureties by the rule of equality, that
may be modified by express contract between them ; and in such
a case Courts of Equity will be governed by the terms of such
contract in giving or refusing contribution.[2] In like manner
there may arise by implication, from the very nature of the transaction, an exemption of one surety from becoming liable to contribution in favor of another. Thus if one surety should not
upon his own mere motion, but at the express solicitation of his
co-surety, become a party to the instrument, and such co-surety
should afterwards be compelled to pay the whole debt, — in such
a case he would not be entitled to contribution unless it clearly
appeared that there was no intention to vary the general right of
contribution in the understanding of the parties.[3] (a) So if different sureties should be bound by different instruments for equal
portions of the debt of the same principal, and it clearly appeared
that the suretyship of each was a separate and distinct transaction, there would be no right of contribution of one against the
other.[4] (b) So if there should be separate bonds given with
different sureties, and one bond is intended to be subsidiary to
and a security for the other in case of a default in payment of
the latter, and not to be a primary concurrent security, — in such

[1] See Hyde v. Tracey, 2 Day, Cas. 422; Ransom v. Keyes, 9 Cowen, R.
128.
[2] Swain v. Wall, 1 Ch. R. 149; Craythorne v. Swinburne, 14 Ves. 159, 169;
Deering v. Earl of Winchelsea, 1 Cox, R. 318; s. c. 2 Bos. & Pull. 270.
[3] Turner v. Davies, 2 Esp. R. 478; Mayhew v. Crickett, 2 Swanst. R. 193;
Taylor v. Savage, 12 Mass. R. 98, 102.
[4] Coope v. Twynam, 1 Turn. & Russ. 426. It would be different if it
should appear that it was the same transaction split into different parts by the
agreement of all the parties. Ibid.

(a) Cutter v. Emery, 37 N. H. 567;
Hartwell v. Smith, 15 Ohio St. 200.
See also Bagott v. Mullen, 32 Ind.
332; Hendrick v. Whittemore, 105
Mass. 23; Tucker v. Campbell, 27
Mich. 497.

(b) See Keller v. Williams, 10
Bush, 216; Armitage v. Pulver, 37
N. Y. 494; Hartwell v. Smith, 15
Ohio St. 200.

a case the sureties in the second bond would not be compellable to aid those in the first bond by any contribution.[1](a)

498 a. A question of another sort has arisen : How far and under what circumstances the discharge of one surety by the creditor would operate as a discharge of the other sureties from their liability. It seems now clearly established at law that a release or discharge of one surety by the creditor will operate as a discharge of all the other sureties, (b) even though it may be founded on a mere mistake of law.[2] But it may be doubtful whether the same rule will be allowed universally to prevail in equity. Thus if a creditor has accepted a composition from one surety and discharged him, it has been thought that he might still recover against another surety his full proportion of the original debt without deducting the composition paid, if it did not exceed the proportion for which the surety was originally liable. In other words each surety, notwithstanding such discharge, might be held liable in equity to pay his share of the original debt, treating each as liable for his equal or pro rata proportion upon an equitable apportionment of it.[3] (c)

[1] Craythorne v. Swinburne, 14 Ves. 159.   See Cooke v. ———, 2 Freem. R. 97.

[2] Nicholson v. Revell, 4 Adolph. & Ellis, 675; s. c. 6 Nev. & Mann. R. 200; ante, § 112.

[3] In Ex parte Gifford (6 Ves. 805), Lord Eldon held that a discharge of one surety did not discharge the other sureties; and that as each surety was bound to contribute his share towards the general payment, no one could recover over against another who had been discharged, unless for the excess paid by him beyond his due proportion.   The creditor might therefore accept a

(a) But see a special case in Whiting v. Burke, L. R. 10 Eq. 539; s. c. 6 Ch. 342, where contribution was allowed.

(b) But not if the creditor reserve his rights against the surety not discharged   Ante, § 325, editor's note at end.

It has sometimes been held that the holder of a bill of exchange accepted for accommodation of the drawee, if taken for value and without notice, may discharge the drawee notwithstanding the fact that after taking the paper he received notice of the nature of the acceptance. Ex parte Graham,

5 DeG. M. & G. 356; Farmers' Bank v. Rathbone, 26 Vt. 19.   But this probably is not good law. Oriental Co. v. Overend, L. R. 7 Ch. 142.   Clearly if the fact is known to the creditor on taking the bill, he must deal with the parties according to their real, and not according to their apparent, relation to each other.   Davies v. Stainbank, 6 DeG. M. & G. 679; Wythes v. Labouchere, 3 DeG. & J. 593.

(c) But see Evans v. Bremridge, 2 Kay & J. 174, 183, where it is said that the dicta in Ex parte Gifford, 6 Ves. 805, referred to by the author, have not been followed.

498 *b*. Indeed circumstances may exist under which even a release of the principal might not release the surety from the

composition from one surety, and still proceed against another to recover his full proportion of the original debt without deducting the composition paid, if it did not exceed the proportion for which the surety was originally liable. Mr. Theobald, in his Treatise on Principal and Surety (ch. 11, § 283, note (*i*), p. 267), thinks this decision could not have been made, and that it is misreported. I see no reason to question either the accuracy of the report or the soundness of the doctrine. If the discharge of one surety is not the discharge of another, it seems difficult to see how the sum paid by one surety shall take away the obligation of another to pay his proportion of the original debt, if upon the discharge the right to proceed against such surety for his proportion was expressly or by implication reserved to the extent of that proportion. This seems to have been the ground of Lord Eldon's decision. In Stirling *v.* Forrester (3 Bligh, R. 591), Lord Redesdale said : ' If the creditor discharges one of the coparceners, he cannot proceed for his whole debt against the others; at the most they are only bound for their proportions.' The same principle would apply to co-sureties; and indeed Stirling *v.* Forrester (3 Bligh, R. 591, 596) seems mainly to have been decided upon this ground. The distinction is between a discharge of the principal and a discharge of the surety; between a part payment by a surety and a part payment by the principal. In the recent case of Nicholson *v.* Revill (4 Adolph. & Ellis, 675; s. c. 6 Nev. & Mann. 192, 200), the Court of King's Bench decided that the creditor's discharge of one debtor on a joint and several note was in law a discharge of all the debtors. Lord Denman, in delivering the judgment of the court, said : ' This view cannot perhaps be made entirely consistent with all that is said by Lord Eldon in the case Ex parte Gifford, where his Lordship dismissed a petition to expunge the proof of a surety against the estate of a co-surety. But the principle to which we have adverted was not presented to his mind in its simple form, and the point certainly did not undergo much consideration. For some of the expressions employed would seem to lay it down that a joint debtee might release one of his debtors, and yet by using some language of reservation in the agreement between himself and such debtor keep his remedy entire against the others, even without consulting them. If Lord Eldon used any language which could be so interpreted, we must conclude that he either did not guard himself so cautiously as he intended, or that he did not lend that degree of attention to the legal doctrine connected with the case before him which he was accustomed to afford. We do not find that any other authority clashes with our present judgment, which must be in favor of the defendant.' It is however to be remembered that his Lordship was here dealing with the question at law; but it by no means follows that because a security is extinguished at law, therefore it is extinguished in equity, if it is the clear intention of the parties that it shall not be extinguished. See 2 Story on Eq. Jurisp. §§ 1370, 1372. Pothier adopts very much the same principles and reasoning as Lord Eldon; asserting that the release of the creditor of one debtor would liberate all the others if the creditor meant thereby to extinguish the debt, but not if the creditor meant to reserve his rights against the other co-debtors for their proportions. 1 Pothier on Oblig. by Evans, n. 275, 278, 279, 280, 281; Id. n. 521 [556]. Pothier has also treated the point of a discharge of one surety ; and he holds that a discharge of one surety discharges the other sure-

debt where it was clear, from the whole transaction, that it was intended that the surety should remain bound. Thus where, before the release to the principal, the surety had paid part of the debt and given a security (an acceptance) for the remainder, it was held that it was not a release of the surety in the absence of all evidence to establish the contrary intent.[1] (a)

499. Sureties are not only entitled to contribution from each other for moneys paid in discharge of their joint liabilities for the principal, but they are also entitled to the benefit of all securities which have been taken by any one of them to indemnify himself against such liabilities.[2] (b)   Courts of Equity have gone further in their favor, and held them entitled, upon payment of the debt

---

ties for such proportion of the debt as upon payment of the whole debt they could have had recourse to him for. Pothier on Oblig. by Evans, n. 275, 277, 280, 281, 428, 429, 445, 519, 520, 521, 521 B., 523 [n. 556–560, of the French editions]. The rule of the Civil Law is the same. ' Si ex duobus, qui apud te fidejusserant in *viginti*, alter, ne ab eo peteres, *quinque* tibi deberit, vel promiserit; nec alter liberabitur. Et si ab altero *quindecim* petere institueris, nulla exceptione (cedendarum actionum) summoveris. Reliqua autem *quinque*, si a priori fidejussore petere institueris, doli mali exceptione summoveris.' Dig. Lib. 46, tit. 1, l. 15, § 1; Pothier, Pand. Lib. 46, tit. 1, n. 47.

[1] Hall *v.* Hutchens, 3 Mylne & Keen, 426.

[2] See Theobald on Principal and Surety, ch. 11, § 283; Swain *v.* Wall, 1 Ch. Rep. 149. But see Bowditch *v.* Green, 3 Metc. R. 360; Himes *v.* Keller, 3 Watts & Serg. R. 401; Commercial Bank of Lake Erie *v.* Western Reserve Bank, 11 Ohio (Stanton) R. 444; Wiggin *v.* Dorr, 3 Sumner, R. 410.

(a) In Pearl *v.* Deacon, 1 DeG. & J. 461, it was held that a landlord, having a note with surety for money loaned his tenant, and also a security for this and other money afterwards loaned, in the way of a mortgage on the tenant's furniture, released the surety by taking the furniture under a distress for rent in arrear. Kinnaird *v.* Webster, 10 Ch. D. 139, 144.

(b) Steel *v.* Dixon, 17 Ch. D. 825, 831; Guild *v.* Butler, 127 Mass. 386; Newton *v.* Chorlton, 10 Hare, 646; Forbes *v.* Jackson, 19 Ch. D. 615, 620; Wooldridge *v.* Norris, L. R. 6 Eq. 410; Fishback *v.* Weaver, 34 Ark. 569, 580; Gilbert *v.* Neely, 35 Ark. 24; Miller *v.* Sawyer, 30 Vt. 412; Hall *v.* Robinson, 8 Ired. 56; Leary *v.*

Cheshire, 3 Jones, Eq. 170; McCune *v.* Belt, 45 Mo. 174; Aldrich *v.* Hapgood, 39 Vt. 617; Furnold *v.* Bank of Missouri, 44 Mo. 336. This right of subrogation arises without contract but may be defeated by contract. Fishback *v.* Weaver, supra. But a stranger cannot claim subrogation. Young *v* Morgan, 89 Ill. 199; Webster's Appeal, 86 Penn. St. 409. The creditor must not with knowledge that one of the debtors is a surety surrender securities to the principal debtor. Guild *v.* Butler, supra. In some cases the surety may, before he has paid anything, look to the indemnity provided for him. Wooldridge *v.* Norris, supra.

due by their principal to the creditor, to have the full benefit of all the collateral securities both of a legal and an equitable nature which the creditor has taken as an additional pledge for his debt.[1] (a)   Thus for example if at the time when the bond of the principal and surety is given a mortgage also is made by the principal to the creditor as an additional security for the debt, there, if the surety pays the debt, he will be entitled to have an assignment of that mortgage and to stand in the place of the mortgagee. (b)   And as the mortgagor cannot get back his estate again without a reconveyance, that assignment and security will remain a valid and effectual security in favor of the surety notwithstanding the bond is paid.[2]   This indeed is but an illustra-

---

[1] Craythorne v. Swinburne, 14 Ves. 159; Wright v. Morley, 11 Ves. 12, 22; Copis v. Middleton, 1 Turn. & Russ. R. 224; Jones v. Davis, 4 Russ. R. 277; Dowbiggin v. Bourne, 1 Younge, R. 111; s. c. 2 Younge & Coll. 462, 470; Hodgson v. Shaw, 3 Mylne & Keen, 183; Reed v. Norris, 2 M. & Craig, R. 361; ante, § 327; Ex parte Rushworth, 10 Ves. 409, 420, 422; Mayhew v. Crickett, 2 Swanst. R. 191; Wade v. Coope, 2 Sim. R. 155. But see Bowditch v. Green, 3 Metc. R. 360, contra. But a surety for a part of a debt is not entitled to the benefit of a security given by the debtor to the creditor at a different time for another part of the debt. Wade v. Coope, 2 Simons, R. 155. (c)

[2] Ante, § 421 a; Williams v. Owen, The (English) Jurist, 30 Dec. 1843, p. 1145, and the learned note of the Reporter, pp. 1146, 1147; Copis v. Middleton, 1 Turn. & Russ. 224, 229, 231; Dowbiggin v. Bourne, 2 Younge & Coll. 471, 472. Lord Brougham, in the case of Hodgson v. Shaw, 3 Mylne & Keen, 190, 191, 192, puts this doctrine in a strong light. ' The rule here,' says he, ' is undoubted, and it is one founded on the plainest principles of natural reason and justice, that the surety paying off a debt shall stand in the place of the

---

(a) It was formerly supposed that the surety's right extended only to securities held by the creditor at the date of the contract. Farebrother v. Wodehouse, 23 Beav. 18; Williams v. Owen, 13 Sim. 597; Newton v. Chorlton, 10 Hare, 646. But it is now held that the surety is entitled to the benefit of after-acquired securities. Forbes v. Jackson, 19 Ch. D. 615; Lake v. Brutton, 8 DeG. M. & G. 441; Pledge v. Buss, Johns. 663. See also Mayhew v. Crickett, 2 Swab. 185; Hall v. Cushman, 16 N. H. 462. But the surety would not be entitled to the benefit of future securities given on advances not covered by his own engagement; though such a state of things would not affect his right to the securities which without the new advances he would be entitled to. Forbes v. Jackson, 19 Ch. D. 615, 621. After ratable payment by the sureties whatever an individual surety recovers from the principal he may hold without division among them all. For an exception see Harrison v. Phillips, 46 Mo. 520.

(b) Gedye v. Matson, 25 Beav. 310.

(c) Secus if he pay the whole debt. Wilcox v. Fairhaven Bank, 7 Allen, 270. See York v. Landis, 65 N. Car. 535; Berthold v. Berthold, 46 Mo. 557.

tion of a much broader doctrine established by Courts of Equity; which is that a creditor shall not, by his own election of the fund out of which he will receive payment, prejudice the rights which other persons are entitled to; but they shall either be substituted to his rights, or they may compel him to seek satisfaction out of the fund to which they cannot resort.[1] (a)   It is often exemplified in cases where a party having two funds to resort to for payment of his debt elects to proceed against one, and thereby disappoints another party who can resort to that fund only.   In such a case the disappointed party is substituted in the place of the electing creditor, or the latter is compelled to resort in the first instance to that fund which will not interfere with the rights of the other.[2] (b)

creditor and have all the rights which he has for the purpose of obtaining his reimbursement. It is hardly possible to put this right of substitution too high; and the right results more from equity than from contract or quasi contract, unless in so far as the known equity may be supposed to be imported into any transaction, and so to raise a contract by implication. The doctrine of the court in this respect was luminously expounded in the argument of Sir Samuel Romilly in Craythorne v. Swinburne (14 Ves. 159); and Lord Eldon, in giving judgment in that case, sanctioned the exposition by his full approval. " A surety," to use the language of Sir S. Romilly's reply, " will be entitled to every remedy which the creditor has against the principal debtor, to enforce every security and all means of payment; to stand in the place of the creditor, not only through the medium of contract, but even by means of securities entered into without the knowledge of the surety, having a right to have those securities transferred to him, though there was no stipulation for that, and to avail himself of all those securities against the debtor.' "   See also Boultby v. Stubbs, 16 Ves. R. 20; Stokes v. Mendon, 3 Swanst. R. 130, note; Mayhew v. Crickett, 2 Swanst. R. 185, 190, note; Beckett v. Booth, 1 Eq. Abridg. 595.

[1] Wright v. Morley, 11 Ves. 12; Ex parte Gifford, 6 Ves. 805, 807. See Rumbold v. Rumbold, 3 Ves. 63; Mayhew v. Crickett, 2 Swanst. R. 186, 191; Miller v. Ord, 2 Binn. 382; Cheeseborough v. Millard, 1 John. Ch. R. 409, 412; Stevens v. Cooper, 1 John. Ch. R. 430; Lawrence v. Cornell, 4 John. Ch. R. 545; King v. Baldwin, 2 John. Ch. R. 554; Hayes v. Ward, 4 John. Ch. R. 123; Clason v. Morris, 10 John. R. 524; Evertson v. Booth, 19 John. R. 486; Averall v. Wade, Lloyd & Goold, R. 252; ante, §§ 324, 326, 493; post, § 502; Stirling v. Forrester, 3 Bligh, R. 590, 591; post, §§ 633 to 640; Selby v. Selby, 4 Russ. R. 336; Gwynne v. Edwards, 2 Russ. R. 289 n; Bute v. Cunynghame, 2 Russ. R. 275; post, §§ 558, 559, 560 to 568; Boazman v. Johnson, 3 Sim. R. 377.

[2] Sagittary v. Hyde, 1 Vern. 455, and Mr. Raithby's note; Mills v. Eden,

(a) The rules as to a surety's right to securities on payment of the debt seem to apply to indorsers as such of negotiable paper. Duncan v. North Wales Bank, 6 App. Cas. 1, reversing 11 Ch. D. 88.

(b) Heyman v. Dubois, L. R. 13 Eq. 158. When a creditor has two

499 *a*. The principle seems in former times to have been carried further by Courts of Equity, and to have authorized the surety to insist upon an assignment, not merely of collateral securities properly speaking, but of collateral incidents and dependent rights growing out of the original debt. Thus where the principal in a bond had been sued, and gave bail, and judgment was obtained against the principal and also against the bail by the creditor, and afterwards the sureties on the original bond (who had counter bonds) were compelled to pay it, and then brought their bill in equity to have the benefit of the judgment of the creditor against the bail by having it assigned to them, it was decreed by the court accordingly. So that although the bail were themselves but sureties, as between themselves and the principal debtor, yet coming in the room of the principal debtor as to the creditor, it was held that they likewise came in the room of the principal debtor as to the sureties on the original bond.[1] (*a*) This decision consequently established that the original sureties had precisely the same rights that the creditor had, and were to stand in his place. The original sureties had no direct contract or engagement by which the bail were bound to them; but only a claim against the bail, through the medium of the creditor, to all whose rights, and the power of enforcing them, they were held to be entitled.[2] This decision has been much questioned; and although it may be distinguishable in its circumstances from others on which we shall have occasion to comment, yet it must

10 Mod. R. 488; Aldrich *v.* Cooper, 8 Ves. 388; Trimmer *v.* Bayne, 9 Ves. 209; Robinson *v.* Wilson, 2 Madd. R. 437; Cheeseborough *v.* Millard, 1 John. Ch. R. 412, 413; King *v.* Baldwin, 2 John. Ch. R. 554; Hayes *v.* Ward, 4 John. Ch. R. 123; 1 Madd. Ch. Pr. 202, 203; post, §§ 558, 559, 633, 634, 635, 636, 1028.

[1] Parsons *v.* Briddock, 2 Vern. R. 608; Wright *v.* Morley, 11 Ves. 22.
[2] Wright *v.* Morley, 11 Ves. 22.

securities from his debtor for different debts, the fact that one of the securities may be insufficient to meet the debt for which it is held will not justify the creditor in taking the other security before default in respect of the debt to which that belongs. Cummins *v.* Fletcher, 14 Ch. D. 699 (C. A.), explaining Selby *v.* Pomfret, 1 Johns. & H. 339. The case of Beevor *v.* Luck, L. R. 4 Eq. 537, in which it was held that a security given by a partner for his own private debt could be consolidated with a security given by two or more partners for a partnership debt, was denied. Further as to consolidation see editor's note to § 1023, post.

(*a*) Schnitzel's Appeal, 49 Penn. St. 23.

now be deemed to be much shaken in point of authority.[1] But however this may be, it seems certain that a surety upon a second bond given as collateral security for the original bond has a right, upon payment of his own bond, to be substituted to the original creditor as to the first bond, and to have an assignment thereof as an independent subsisting obligation for the debt.[2]

499 b. Another point of more extensive importance in practice is, whether a surety, who pays off the debt of the principal, for which he is bound, is entitled to require the creditor, upon such payment, to make an assignment to him of the debt and of the instrument by which it is evidenced. It seems formerly to have been thought that he had such a right; and the general language of some of the authorities, that the surety is in such cases entitled to every remedy which the creditor had against the principal, was supposed fully to justify and support this conclusion.[3] But the doctrine is now fully established that the surety has no such right to be enforced in equity, and that he cannot insist upon any such assignment.(a) The ground is, that by the payment of

---

[1] Hodgson *v.* Shaw, 3 Mylne & Keen, 189. But see Wright *v.* Morley, 11 Ves. 22; Dowbiggin *v.* Bourne, 1 Younge, R. 111, 114, 115; s. c. 2 Younge & Coll. 462, 472, 473.

[2] Hodgson *v.* Shaw, 3 Mylne & Keen, 183, 193; ante, § 493, note; Cheeseborough *v.* Millard, 1 John. Ch. R. 413; Avery *v.* Petten, 7 John. Ch. R. 211. See Himes *v.* Keller, 3 Watts & Serg. 401.

[3] Ex parte Crispe, 1 Atk. 135; Parsons *v.* Briddock, 2 Vern. R. 608; Wright *v.* Morley, 11 Ves. 12, 21, 22; Dowbiggin *v.* Bourne, 1 Younge, R. 111; s. c. 2 Younge & Coll. 464; Butcher *v.* Churchill, 14 Ves. 567, 575, 576; Ex parte Rushforth, 10 Ves. 409, 414; Robinson *v.* Wilson, 2 Madd. R. 464; Craythorne *v.* Swinburne, 14 Ves. 160, 162. See also Hodgson *v.* Shaw, 3 Mylne & Keen, 183, 185; Hotham *v.* Stone, 1 Turner & Russ. R. 226, note.

(a) It is more generally held in this country that though the debt is paid by the surety, he will still be entitled to treat the same, with all the securities behind it, as existing in equity for the purpose of relief to himself. See Lewis *v.* Palmer, 28 N. Y. 271; Lathrop's Appeal, 1 Barr, 512; Powell *v.* White, 11 Leigh, 309; Speiglemyer *v.* Crawford, 6 Paige, 254; Rodgers *v.* McCluer, 4 Gratt. 81; McCleary *v.* Beirne, 10 Leigh, 395; Perkins *v.* Kershaw, 1 Hill, Ch. 344; Watkins *v.* Worthington, 2 Bland, 509; Tinsley *v.* Anderson, 3 Call, 329; Burns *v.* Huntington Bank, 1 Penn. 395; Fleming *v.* Beaver, 2 Rawle, 132; Dempsey *v.* Bush, 18 Ohio St. 376; Wilson *v.* Stewart, 26 Ohio St. 504; Craft *v.* Moore, 9 Watts, 417; Cuyler *v.* Ensworth, 6 Paige, 32; Matthews *v.* Aiken, 1 Const. 595; Ellsworth *v.* Lockwood, 42 N. Y. 89; York *v.* Landis, 65 N. Car. 535; Berthold *v.* Berthold, 46 Mo. 557. By the English Mercantile Law Amendment Act, 19

the debt the title derived under the instrument has become extinguished and functus officio, and therefore an assignment thereof would be utterly useless; and if the surety should afterwards sue for the debt at law in the name of the creditor, the principal might plead such payment in bar of the action.[1] In such a case it would make no difference in the right of the surety to sue that, upon payment of the debt, he had procured an assignment thereof to be made to a third person instead of to himself for his benefit.[2] Neither would it make any difference that several judgments had been obtained by the creditor against the principal and surety, and that the latter had paid the debt on the judgment against him, and then sought an assignment to be made of the judgment against the principal; for the judgment would be effectually extinguished by such payment, and the surety would not be permitted to avail himself of it against the principal.[3]

499 c. The error of the contrary opinion, if indeed upon the principles of enlarged equity any there be, seems to have arisen from confounding the right of the surety on payment of the debt to be substituted for the creditor, and to have an assignment of any independent collateral securities, with the supposed right to have the original debt assigned. Such independent collateral

[1] Woffington v. Shaw, 2 Ves. 569; Gammon v. Stone, 1 Ves. 339; Copis v. Middleton, 1 Turn. & Russ. 224, 229; Jones v. Davids, 4 Russ. R. 297; Hodgson v. Shaw, 3 Mylne & Keen, 183; Hudson v. Stalwood, Cas. Temp. Hard. 133; Armitage v. Baldwin, 5 Beav. R. 278.

[2] See Reed v. Norris, 2 Mylne & Craig, 361; Jones v. Davids, 4 Russ. R. 277; Copis v. Middleton, 1 Turn. & Russ. 224, 229. But see Butcher v. Churchill, 14 Ves. 568, 575, 576.

[3] Dowbiggin v. Bourne, 2 Younge & Coll. 464. But see Hill v. Kelly, 1 Ridg. L. & Schoales, R. 265.

& 20 Vict. ch. 97, the surety is entitled to an assignment on paying the debt. In re Cochran's Estate, L. R. 5 Eq. 209. But it is held that a surety who pays a judgment is not entitled to treat it as existent. Hull v. Sherwood, 59 Mo. 172. See Holmes v. Day, 108 Mass. 563, where however there was no suretyship proper. And compare Milligan's Appeal, 104 Penn. St. 503. Between joint debtors payment of the judgment is an extinguishment of the same towards all. Holmes v. Day.

It will be observed that the doctrine of Lord Eldon, in Copis v. Middleton (see author's note, supra), applies at most only to cases in which payment of the debt would per se *destroy* the security, without further action; if the security does not at once return functus officio to the hands of the principal debtor, as where it is a mortgage by him, or a fortiori where it is the instrument of a third person, the rule would not apply.

securities may well be required to be assigned by the creditor in
favor of the surety ; because in many cases the principal would
not be entitled to have a re-transfer thereof from the surety, without paying him the sums advanced by him to the creditor as a
matter of equity between the parties. But the assignment of the
debt itself, which had been already paid, would be a mere nullity
in equity as well as at law, since it could not have, in the hands
of the surety, any subsisting obligation.[1]

[1] This whole subject is examined in a masterly manner by Lord Eldon, in
Copis *v.* Middleton, 1 Turn. & Russ. R. 224, 229, 231, and by Lord Brougham
in Hodgson *v.* Shaw, 3 Mylne & Keen, 183. In a former case Lord Eldon
said: ' It is a general rule that in equity a surety is entitled to the benefit of
all the securities which the creditor has against the principal. But then the
nature of those securities must be considered. When there is a bond merely,
if an action was brought upon the bond, it would appear upon oyer of the bond
that the debt was extinguished. The general rule therefore must be qualified
by considering it to apply to such securities as continue to exist, and do not get
back, upon payment, to the person of the principal debtor. In the case for
instance where in addition to the bond there is a mortgage with a covenant on
the part of the principal debtor to pay the money, the surety paying the money
would be entitled to say: I have lost the benefit of the bond; but the creditor
has a mortgage, and I have a right to the benefit of the mortgaged estate,
which has not got back to the debtor.' Lord Brougham, speaking on the
same subject, said: ' The rule here is undoubted, and it is one founded on the
plainest principles of natural reason and justice, that the surety, paying off a
debt, shall stand in the place of the creditor, and have all the rights which he
has, for the purpose of obtaining his reimbursement. It is hardly possible to
put this right of substitution too high; and the right results more from equity
than from contract or quasi contract; unless in so far as the known equity may
be supposed to be imported into any transaction, and so to raise a contract
by implication. The doctrine of the court, in this respect, was luminously
expounded in the argument of Sir Samuel Romilly in Craythorne *v.* Swinburne; and Lord Eldon, in giving judgment in that case, sanctioned the
exposition by his full approval. " A surety," to use the language of Sir Samuel Romilly's reply, " will be entitled to every remedy which the creditor has
against the principal debtor, to enforce every security and all means of payment; to stand in the place of the creditor, not only through the medium of
contract, but even by means of securities entered into without the knowledge
of the surety; having a right to have those securities transferred to him,
though there was no stipulation for that, and to avail himself of all those securities against the debtor." I have purposely taken this statement of the right,
because it is there placed as high as it ever can be placed; and yet it is quite
consistent with the principle of Copis *v.* Middleton. Thus the surety paying
is entitled to every remedy which the creditor has. But can the creditor be
said to have any specialty after the bond is gone by payment? The surety
may enforce any security against the debtor which the creditor has; but by
the supposition there is no security to enforce, for the payment has extinguished it. He has a right to have all the securities transferred to him; but

499 *d*. Upon reasoning somewhat analogous to that, the supposed error of which we have been considering, it was formerly held that if a surety upon a bond debt should discharge it, he would be entitled to be considered as substituted for the original creditor as a specialty creditor of his principal; and consequently, in the marshalling of the assets of the principal, he would, as to the debt so paid, have a priority over simple contract creditors.[1]

there are, in the case supposed, none to transfer. They are absolutely gone. He may avail himself of all those securities against the debtor, but his own act of payment has left none of which he can take advantage.' See also Dowbiggin *v.* Bourne, 2 Younge & Coll. 462, 471. It is observable that the whole of this reasoning proceeds upon the ground that by the payment by the surety the original debt is extinguished. Now that is precisely what the Roman law (as we shall presently see) denied; and it treated the transaction between the surety and the creditor according to the presumed intention of the parties to be not so much a payment as a sale of the debt. 1 Domat, B. 3, tit. 1, § 6, art. 1; post, § 500, and §§ 635, 636, 637. It is not wonderful that Courts of Equity, with this enlarged doctrine in their view, which is in entire conformity to the intention of the parties as well as to the demands of justice, should have struggled to adopt it into the Equity Jurisprudence of England. The opposing doctrine is founded more on technical rules than on any solid reasoning founded in general equity. In truth Courts of Equity in many cases do adopt it and act upon it; as in cases where they give the right of substitution to particular parties, where there are two funds, out of one of which a creditor has insisted upon receiving satisfaction to the disappointment of the parties who have no claim upon the other fund. Ante, § 499; post, §§ 633 to 640. Whether it might not have been as wise for Courts of Equity to have followed out the Roman law to its full extent, instead of adopting a modified rule, which stops, or may stop, short of some of the purposes of reciprocal justice, it is now too late to inquire, and therefore the discussion would be useless. See Cheeseborough *v.* Millard, 1 John. Ch. R. 409, 412, 413, 414; ante, § 493, note. Sir William Grant, in Butcher *v.* Churchill (14 Ves. 568, 575, 576), seems to have proceeded upon the principle of the Roman law, in holding that the assignment of a bond to a surety who had compounded the debt with the creditor and taken the assignment ought to be upheld in equity, however it might be at law, for the purpose of securing to him the amount he had paid on the bond and interest. But see Armitage *v.* Baldwin, 5 Beav. R. 278, where the surety paid the debt due to the creditor after the creditor had obtained judgment for it against the principal debtor, and also another judgment against his bail in that action, and upon such payment the surety took an assignment from the creditor of both judgments, — Lord Langdale thought that as the bill alleged that the surety had ' duly paid and satisfied the original judgment,' he could not maintain a bill against the bail on the judgment against him to charge the estate of the bail. But his Lordship suggested that the plaintiff might, by a proper proceeding, ultimately succeed in establishing a right against the estate of the bail.

[1] Hotham *v.* Stone, 1 Turn. & Russ. R. 226, note; Robinson *v.* Wilson, 2 Madd. R. 464; Wright *v.* Morley, 11 Ves. 22; Powell's Ex'ors *v.* White, 11 Leigh, R. 309, fully approves this same doctrine.

But upon this point also a different doctrine is now established; and it is held that a surety so paying a bond debt will be treated, in marshalling assets, as a mere simple contract creditor.[1] (a) The ground of this doctrine is, that the surety is not subrogated to the rights of the creditor in such a case (whether he has procured an assignment of the bond when paid or not); but he is in fact as well as in law to be deemed only as having paid money for the principal upon the footing of an implied contract of indemnity subsisting between them.[2] Yet there are many cases in

[1] Copis v. Middleton, 1 Turn. & Russ. 224, 229, 231; Jones v. Davids, 4 Russ. R. 277; Hodgson v. Shaw, 3 Mylne & Keen, 183.

[2] Ibid. Lord Eldon, in Copis v. Middleton, 1 Turn. & Russ. 228, said: ' I take the present case to be simply this. Upon loans of money to A, joint bonds were given by A and B, B being surety for A; two of the bonds were paid off by B in the lifetime of A: now, if one of two joint obligors, being a surety, pays off the debt in the lifetime of the principal, he is at law merely a simple contract creditor of the principal; and if the principal lives for twenty years after the payment of the debt, he continues during all that time to be at law a simple contract creditor only. Then the question is, Whether, by the death of the principal, he is to be converted in a Court of Equity into a specialty creditor against his assets. With respect to the bond paid off after the death of the principal the questions are: Whether, inasmuch as at the death of the principal, there was money due upon the bond, there was an equity on the part of the surety to compel the creditor to go in against the assets of the principal; and Whether, there having been no interposition for that purpose, the right of the surety to stand in the place of the creditor can now be maintained. When it is considered that this was a joint bond, and that no action at law could be maintained except against the surety, the surviving debtor, it is a strong proposition to say that the surviving debtor is to be considered in equity as a specialty creditor against the assets of the deceased debtor.' And again, in pp. 230, 231, 232, he said: ' The facts of this case are simply these. Two individuals gave a bond, the one as principal, and the other as surety; no other assurance was executed at the time; no mortgage was made to secure the debt; no counterbond was given by the principal to the surety; and the question to be decided is, Whether the surety, having paid the bond after it was due, is a simple contract, or a specialty, creditor. I understand it to have been the opinion of the Master, an opinion founded on one or two cases which have been stated, that the surety was to be considered as a specialty creditor, to stand in the place of the person whom he

(a) Contra in most of the States. See Eppes v. Randolph, 2 Call, 125; Tinsley v. Anderson, 3 Call, 329; West v. Belches, 5 Munf. 187; McMahon v. Fawcett, 2 Rand. 514; Watts v. Kinney, 3 Leigh, 272; Wheatley v. Calhoun, 12 Leigh, 264; Litterdale v. Robinson, 2 Brock. 159; s. c. 12 Wheat. 594; Pride v. Boyce, Rice, Eq. 276; Schultz v. Carter, 1 Speer, Eq. 534; Croft v. Moore, 9 Watts, 451; Lathrop's Appeal, 1 Barr, 512; Enders v. Brune, 4 Rand. 438; Grider v. Payne, 9 Dana, 188; Dias v. Bouchaud, 3 Edw. Ch. 485; United States v. Hunter, 5 Mason, 62.

which a surety, paying a debt, will be entitled to stand in the
place of the creditor or to obtain the full benefit of all the pro-

paid. That doctrine appears to me to be contrary to all that has been settled
during the whole time I have been in this court. Everything that was
arranged in bankruptcy before the late statute, enabling the surety to prove
everything determined before, appears to me to have authorized the court to
consider it quite clear, that if there was nothing in the case beyond
what I have stated, the surety, having paid the bond, could be nothing
more than a simple contract creditor in respect of that payment. The
bond was not assigned to anybody in consideration of a sum of money
paid, which was one way we used to manage these things; there was no
counter bond given, which was another way in which we used to manage these
things; so that if the surety paid one bond he became instantly a specialty
creditor by virtue of the other bond. If any suit was now instituted, I apprehend the payment of the bond would show that the bond was gone. There
has been a case cited, where upon the general ground that a surety is entitled
to the benefit of all securities which the creditor has against the principal, it
seems to have been thought that the surety was entitled to be as it were a
bond creditor, by virtue of the bond. I take it to be exceedingly clear, if, at
the time a bond is given, a mortgage is also made for securing the debt, the
surety, if he pays the bond, has a right to stand in the place of the mortgagee; and as the mortgagor cannot get back his estate again without a conveyance, that security remains a valid and effectual security, notwithstanding
the bond debt is paid. But if there is nothing but the bond, my notion is that,
as the law says that bond is discharged by the payment of what was due upon
it, the bond is gone and cannot be set up.' Lord Brougham, in Hodgson v.
Shaw, 3 Mylne & Keen, 190, 191, 192, still more elaborately expounded the
doctrine. 'When,' said he, 'a person pays off a bond in which he is either
co-obligor or bound subsidiarié, he has, at law, an action against the principal
for money paid to his use, and he can have nothing more. The joint obligation towards the creditor is held to give to the principal notice of the payment, and also to prove his consent or authority to the making that payment.
This is necessary for enabling any man who pays another's debt to come
against that other; because a person cannot make himself the creditor of
another by volunteering to discharge his obligations. But beyond this claim,
which is on simple contract merely, there exists none against the principal by
the surety who pays his debt; nor, when the matter is closely viewed, ought
there to exist any other. The obligation by specialty is incurred, not towards
the surety, even in the event of his paying, but only towards the obligee.
And there is no natural reason why, because I bind myself under seal to pay
another person's debt, the creditor requiring a security of that high nature, I
should therefore have as high a security against the principal debtor. If I had
chosen to demand it, I might have taken a similar obligation when I became
so bound. And if I omitted to do so, I can only be considered as possessing
the rights which arise from having paid money for him, which I had voluntarily, and without consideration, undertaken to pay. The case standing thus
at law, do considerations of equity make any alteration in its aspect?' His
Lordship then proceeded to state what is contained in the passage already cited,
ante, § 499 c, note 1, p. 520, and then added: 'Living the principal debtor,
the surety could only bring indebitatus assumpsit for the money he had paid to

ceedings of the creditor against the principal. Thus for example if the creditor, in case of the bankruptcy of the principal,
has proved his debt before the commissioners, and then the
surety pays the debt, the latter will be entitled to the dividends
declared on his estate, and the creditor will be held to be his
trustee for this purpose.[1] (a) So the surety may compel the
creditor to go in and prove his debt before the commissioners;
and then, if he pays the whole debt, the creditor will in like
manner become a trustee of the dividends for him.[2] In cases of
this sort Courts of Equity seem to be regulated by the same principles which govern their interference in favor of sureties to compel creditors to proceed in the first instance against the principal
for the recovery of their debts.[3] (b)

that principal's use. The death of that debtor cannot clothe him with a
higher title. Living the debtor, the creditor could not have assigned the bond
on payment by the surety; for there was no longer anything to assign. The
death of the debtor cannot surely operate a revivor of the specialty, enable the
creditor to assign it or the court to hold it assigned in equity, and empower
the surety to sue upon it the executors or administrators of him who, had he
chanced to survive, never could have been sued except upon the money counts
in an action of assumpsit. Observe the consequence that would have followed
from any other principles, while the law of debtor and creditor continued, as
it was till the recent alteration, and when landed estates were not real assets
for payment of simple contract debts. If the principal debtor continued alive,
the surety could not in any way touch his real estates, except through the
medium of a judgment. But if he happened to die, his real estates became
assets, although the law had never been changed. There can be no doubt
therefore with respect to the principle of Copis v. Middleton; and Lord Eldon
expressed himself without any hesitation in that case, though pressed with the
authority of Sir William Grant in Hotham v. Stone, upon which he remarked
that the case had been appealed and compromised without coming to an argument.' But see in America the case of Powell's Ex'ors v. White, 11 Leigh,
R. 309, which upholds the old doctrine.

[1] Ex parte Rushforth, 10 Ves. 409; Wright v. Morley, 11 Ves. 12, 22, 23;
Watkins v. Flanagan, 3 Russ. R. 421; Ex parte Houston, 2 G. & Jamieson,
36; Ex parte Gee, 1 G. & Jamieson, 330.

[2] Ex parte Rushforth, 10 Ves. 409, 414; Wright v. Simpson, 6 Ves. 734.

[3] Ante, § 327; post, § 639.

(a) If the surety has paid but part
of the debt proved, the dividends will
be apportioned accordingly. Hobson
v. Bass, L. R. 6 Ch. 792. See Gray
v. Seckham, L. R. 7 Ch. 680. A
surety will be restrained from strip-
ping himself of his property so as to
throw the burden of the debt on a
co-surety. Bowen v. Hoskins, 45
Miss. 183.

(b) A surety for the purchase-
price of land on payment of the debt
will be subrogated to the vendor's
lien on the land for the unpaid money.
Eddy v. Traver, 6 Paige, 521; Welch
v. Parran, 2 Gill, 320; Magruder v.

500. Upon this subject a far more liberal and comprehensive doctrine pervades the Roman law. Not only is the surety by that law entitled in such cases to the benefit of all the collateral securities taken by the creditor, but he is also entitled to be substituted, as to the very debt itself, to the creditor by way of cession or assignment. And upon such cession or assignment upon payment of the debt by the surety, the debt is, in favor of the surety, treated not so much as paid, as sold; not as extinguished, but as transferred with all its original obligatory force against the principal.[1] 'Fidejussoribus succurri solet, ut stipulator compellatur ei, qui solidum solvere paratus est, vendere cæterorum nomina. Cum is, qui et reum et fidejussores habens, ab uno ex fidejussoribus accepta pecunia, præstat actiones; poterit quidem dici, nullas jam esse, cum suum perceperit, et perceptione omnes liberati sunt. Sed non ita est; non enim in solutum accepit, sed quodammodo nomen debitoris vendidit. Et ideo habet actiones, quia tenetur ad id ipsum, ut præstet actiones.'[2] Here we have the doctrine distinctly put, the objection to it stated, and the ground upon which its solution depends, affirmed. The reasoning may seem a little artificial, but it has a deep foundation in natural justice. The same doctrine stands in substance approved in all the countries which derive their jurisprudence from the civil law.[3]

---

[1] Pothier on Oblig. by Evans, n. 275, 280, 281, 428, 429, 430, 519, 520, 521, 522 [n. 556, 557, 558, 559, of the French editions].

[2] Dig. Lib. 46, tit. 1, l. 17, 36; Pothier, Pand. Lib. 46, tit. 1. n. 46; ante, §§ 327, 494; post, §§ 635 to 638; 1 Domat, B. 3, tit. 1, § 3, art. 6, 7; Id. § 6, art. 6, 7; Pothier on Oblig. by Evans, n. 275, 280, 281, 428, 429, 430, 519, 520, 521, 522 [n. 556, 557, 558, 559, of the French editions].

[3] Voet, ad Pand. lib. 46, tit. 1, §§ 27, 29, 30; Pothier on Oblig. by Evans, n. 275, 280, 281, 427, 428, 429, 430, 519, 520, 522 [n. 555, 556, 557, of the French editions]; Huber, Prælect. Inst. Lib. 3, tit. 21, n. 8; 1 Bell, Comm.

Peter, 11 Gill & J. 219; Kleiser v. Scott, 6 Dana, 137; Burk v. Chishman, 3 B. Mon. 50; In re McGill, 6 Barr, 504; Davidson v. Carroll, 20 La. An. 199; Tuck v. Calvert, 33 Md. 209. If a creditor who is also a surety takes security both for the debt due him and for his liability as surety, he will be entitled to have his own debt paid first in full before applying any portion of the security for the benefit of his co-sureties. Brown v. Ray, 18 N. H. 102; Hess's Estate, 69 Penn. St. 272; Field v. Hamilton, 45 Vt. 35; Magee v. Leggett, 48 Miss. 139; Allison v. Sutherlin, 50 Mo. 274. In some States it must be shown that the principal is insolvent before a surety who has paid can require his co-surety to share the burden with him. Bolling v. Doneghy, 1 Duv. 220.

501. The Roman law carried its doctrines yet further in furtherance of the great principles of equity. It held the creditor bound not to deprive himself of the power to cede his rights and securities to the surety who should pay him the debt; and if by any voluntary and unnecessary act of his own such a cession became impracticable, the surety might, by what was technically called ' exceptio cedendarum actionum,' bar the creditor of so much of his demand as the surety might have received by a cession or assignment of his liens and rights of action against the principal debtor. 'Si creditor a debitore culpa sua causa ceciderit, prope est, ut actione mandati nihil a mandatore consequi debeat ; cum ipsius vitio acciderit, ne mandatori possit actionibus cedere.' [1] But this qualification should be added, that a mere omission by the creditor to collect the debt due of the hypothecated property, so that it is lost by his laches, will not discharge the sureties ; but the creditor must be guilty of some wrongful act, as by a release or fraudulent surrender of the pledge, in order to discharge the surety.[2]

502. The same doctrine has been in some measure transfused

B. 3, Pt. 1, ch. 3, § 3, p. 264, &c., art. 283, 4th edit.; Ersk. Inst. B. 3, tit. 3, art. 68; 1 Kaimes, Eq. 122, 124.

[1] Dig. Lib. 46, tit. 2, l. 95, § 11; Pothier, Pand. Lib. 46, tit. 1, n. 46, 47; Pothier on Oblig. by Evans, n. 275, 280, 428, 429, 430, 519, 520, 521, 521 B., 522 [n. 555, 556, 557, 558, 559, 560, of the French editions]; Cheeseborough v. Millard, 1 John. Ch. R. 414; Stevens v. Cooper, 1 John. Ch. R. 430, 431; Hayes v. Ward, 4 John. Ch. R. 130.   In this last case Mr. Chancellor Kent said: ' According to the doctrine of the civil law, the surety may, " per exceptionem cedendarum actionum," bar the creditor of so much of his demand as the surety might have received by an assignment of his lien and right of action against the principal debtor; provided the creditor had by his own unnecessary or improper act deprived the surety of that resource.   The surety by his very character and relation of surety has an interest that the mortgage taken from the principal debtor should be dealt with in good faith, and held in trust not only for the creditor's security but for the surety's indemnity. A mortgage so taken by the creditor is taken and held in trust as well for the secondary interest of the surety as for the more direct and immediate benefit of the creditor; and the latter must do no wilful act either to poison it in the first instance or to destroy or cancel it afterwards.   These are general principles founded in equity, and are contained in the doctrines laid down in Pothier's Treatise on Obligations, No. 496, 519, 520, to which reference has been made in the former decisions of this court.' See also post, §§ 635, 636. The case of Macdonald v. Bell, 3 Moore, Privy Council, Rep. 315, 332, fully recognizes the same doctrine.

[2] Macdonald v. Bell, 3 Moore, Privy Council, Rep. 315, 332.

into the English law in an analogous form ; not indeed by requiring an assignment or cession of the debt to be made, but
by putting the surety paying the debt (*a*) under some circumstances in the place of the creditor.[1]   And if the creditor should
knowingly have done any act to deprive the surety of this benefit, the surety as against him would be entitled to the same
equity as if the act had not been done.[2] (*b*)   On the other hand
if a surety has a counter bond or security from the principal, the
creditor will be entitled to the benefit of it, and may in equity
reach such security to satisfy his debt.[3] (*c*)

[1] Robinson *v.* Wilson, 2 Madd. 437.   In the case of a Crown debtor, a
surety is substituted to the prerogative of the Crown in regard to the debt,
and then is admitted to use the Crown remedies.   The King *v.* Bennet, Wight-
wick, R. 2 to 6 ; ante, §§ 499 to 499 *d*, and notes.

[2] Hayes *v.* Ward, 4 John. Ch. R. 130 ; Cheeseborough *v.* Millard, 1 John.
Ch. R. 413, 414 ; Stevens *v.* Cooper, 1 John. Ch. R. 430 ; Miller *v.* Ord, 2 Binn.
382 ; Aldrich *v.* Cooper, 8 Ves. 388, 391, 395 ;   Ex parte Rushforth, 10 Ves.
409 ; Wright *v.* Morley, 11 Ves. 22.

[3] 1 Eq. Abridg. p. 93, K. 5.   See also Com. Dig. Chancery, 4 D. 6.

(*a*) The surety must ordinarily
have paid the whole debt before he
can have subrogation.   McConnell *v.*
Beattie, 34 Ark. 113. See Pool *v.*
Doster, 59 Miss. 258. But not always.
Wooldridge *v.* Norris, L. R. 6 Eq. 410.

(*b*) See Hoysradt *v.* Holland, 50
N. H. 433.

(*c*) New Bedford Sav. Inst. *v.* Fairhaven Bank, 9 Allen, 175, 178 ; Kelly
v. Herrick, 131 Mass. 373 ; Eastman
v. Foster, 8 Met. 19 ; Rice *v.* Dewey,
13 Gray, 47 ; Lane *v.* Stacey, 8 Allen,
41 ; Paris *v.* Hulett, 26 Vt. 308 ; Saffold *v.* Wade, 51 Ala. 214 ; Chamberlain *v.* St. Paul R. Co. 92 U. S. 299,
306 ; Brown *v.* Ray, 18 N. H. 102 ;
Carpenter *v.* Bowen, 42 Miss. 28 ;
post, § 638.   And see Jones *v.* Quini-
piack Bank, 29 Conn. 25 (holding a
qualified doctrine).   Thus securities
given by a former guardian to indemnify his sureties in case they should
be compelled to pay debts of his to the
ward's estate, may be sold, and the
proceeds applied by a later guardian
to the payment of such debt, where the
former guardian has become insolvent

and a portion only of the debt has
been paid by the sureties.   The sureties hold such property in trust for the
creditors. Kelly *v.* Herrick, 131 Mass.
373.

Nor can the sureties come in as
general creditors of the principal and
be reimbursed out of the collateral
securities for their partial payments.
The creditors must first be paid in
full.   Kelly *v.* Herrick, supra ; Ohio
Ins. Co. *v.* Ledyard, 8 Ala. 866 ; Ten
Eyck *v.* Holmes, 3 Sandf. Ch. 428 ;
Clark *v.* Ely, 2 Sandf. Ch. 166.   The
creditor need not exhaust his legal
remedies before being entitled to the
securities. Saffold *v.* Wade, 51 Ala.
214.   But the security in question
must have been given by the principal
debtor ; a creditor is not entitled to be
subrogated to a security given by one
of two co-sureties to the other.   Hampton *v.* Phipps, 108 U. S. 260.

In some States a distinction is made
between securities given by the principal debtor to his surety as a personal
indemnity to him and securities given
for debt.   In the first case it is held

503. There are many other cases of contribution in which the jurisdiction of Courts of Equity is required to be exercised in order to accomplish the purposes of justice. Thus for instance in cases of a deficiency of assets to pay all debts and legacies, if any of the legatees have been paid more than their proportion before all the debts are ascertained, they may be compelled to refund and contribute in favor of the unpaid debts, at the instance of creditors, at the instance of other legatees, and in many cases, although not universally, at the instance of the executor himself.[1] (a)

504. In like manner contribution lies between partners for any excess which has been paid by one partner beyond his share

[1] Ante, §§ 90, 92; Jeremy on Eq. Jurisd. B. 3, Pt. 2, ch. 2, p. 364; Id. B. 3, Pt. 2, ch. 5, p. 518; Noel v. Robinson, 1 Vern. 94, and Mr. Raithby's notes, ibid.; Walcott v. Hall, 2 Bro. Ch. R. 305; Anon. 1 P. Will. 495, and Mr. Cox's note; Newman v. Barton, 2 Vern. 265, and Mr. Raithby's note; Edwards v. Freeman, 2 P. Will. 447; Hardwick v. Wynd, 1 Anst. 112; Davis v. Davis, 1 Dick. R. 32; Jewson v. Grant, 3 Swanst. R. 659; Com. Dig. Chancery, 3 V. 6. See also, on the subject of contribution, the Reporters' note to Averall v. Wade, Lloyd & Goold, Rep. 264; ante, § 492.

that there can be no resort to the security except as a means to indemnify the surety according to the terms of the instrument creating it; in the second case the security is available by the creditor as a trust for the payment of his demand. Pool v. Doster, 59 Miss. 258. This distinction is not generally taken.

If a surety make a new and an independent arrangement with the creditor in regard to the security for the debt, and put himself in the situation of a principal debtor, he cannot complain of the creditor for treating him to a certain extent in that light. An example occurs where a surety, after judgment against him, makes an arrangement with the creditor, without regard to the principal debtor, for a stay of execution, so long as he shall keep up certain policies for securing the debt, and afterwards the creditor, having taken the principal debtor in execution, discharges him without payment. Reade v. Lowndes, 23 Beav. 361.

Again if the surety has been fully indemnified by the principal, he will not be released by any new contract made with the principal debtor; the surety being now treated as a virtual co-principal. Smith v. Steele, 25 Vt. 427. And if a surety so indemnified should procure the assignment of the debt to a third person for his benefit, equity would restrain any suit by such person against a co-surety. Silvey v. Dowell, 53 Ill 260. Of course the fully indemnified surety may be compelled, by his co-surety on payment, to pay the debt. Parham v. Green, 64 N. Car. 436.

(a) If one of several heirs contribute out of the estate descended more than his proportion to pay debts of the ancestor, he will be subrogated to the rights of the creditor against his co-heirs so far as may be necessary for equality. Winston v. McAlpine, 65 Ala. 377; Stallworth v. Preslar, 34 Ala. 505.

against the other partners, if upon a winding up of the partnership affairs such a balance appears in his favor; or if upon a dissolution he has been compelled to pay any sum for which he ought to be indemnified. The cases in which a recovery can be had at law by way of contribution between partners are very few, and stand upon special circumstances. The usual and indeed almost the only effectual remedy is in equity, where an account of all the partnership transactions can be taken ; and the remedy to ascertain and adjust the balance is, in a just sense, plain, adequate, and complete.[1] It is under the same circumstances that an action of account at the common law lies ; but that, as we have already seen, is in most cases a very cumbersome, inconvenient, and tardy remedy. The same remark applies to an action of covenant on sealed articles of partnership or an action of assumpsit upon unsealed articles where there have been any breaches of the articles ; for there may be many breaches of them during the continuance of the partnership which scarcely admit of adequate redress in this way.[2] This subject will however hereafter present itself in a more enlarged form.[3]

505. Contribution also lies between joint tenants, tenants in common, and part owners of ships and other chattels for all charges and expenditures incurred for the common benefit. But it seems unnecessary to dwell upon these cases and others of a like nature, as they embrace nothing more than a plain application of principles already fully expounded.[4] (a) We may conclude this head with the remark that the remedial justice of Courts of Equity in all cases of apportionment and contribution is so complete and so flexible in its adaptation to all the par-

---

[1] See Collyer on Partnership, ch. 8, §§ 2, 4, pp. 143, 157, 162; Gow on Partn. ch. 2, §§ 3, 4, pp. 92 to 141. See Wright v. Hunter, 1 East, R. 20; Wells v. Hubbell's Administrators, 2 John. Ch. R. 397; Wright v. Hunter, 5 Ves. 792.

[2] See Duncan v. Lyon, 3 John. Ch. R. 362; Neven v. Speckerman, 12 John. R. 401; Gow on Partn. ch. 2, § 3, p. 92; Dunham v. Gillis, 8 Mass. R. 462.

[3] Post, §§ 650 to 683; Story on Partn. §§ 219 to 242.

[4] Com. Dig. Chancery, 3 V. 6; Rogers v. Mackenzie, 4 Ves. 752; Lingard v. Bromley, 1 V. & Beam. 114.

(a) As to contribution between cestuis que trust, see Gardner v. Diedricks, 41 Ill. 158. Between tenants in common, see Calvert v. Aldrich, 99 Mass. 74; Husband v. Aldrich, 135 Mass. 317.

ticular circumstances and equities, that it has in a great measure superseded all efforts to obtain redress in any other tribunals.

506. LIENS also give rise to matters of account, and although this is not the sole or indeed the necessary ground of the interference of Courts of Equity, yet directly or incidentally it becomes a most important ingredient in the remedial justice administered by them in cases of this sort. The subject as a general head of equity jurisdiction will more properly fall under discussion in another place. But a few considerations touching matters of account involved in it may be here glanced at. A lien is not in strictness either a jus in re or a jus ad rem, but it is simply a right to possess and retain property until some charge attaching to it is paid or discharged.[1] It generally exists in favor of artisans and others who have bestowed labor and services upon the property in its repair, improvement, and preservation.[2] It has also an existence in many other cases by the usages of trade; and in maritime transactions, as in cases of salvage and general average.[3] It is often created and sustained in equity where it is unknown at law, as in cases of the sale of lands where a lien exists for the unpaid purchase-money.[4] It is not confined to cases of mere labor and services on the very property, or connected therewith, but it often is by the usage of trade extended to cases of a general balance of accounts in favor of factors and others.[5] Now it is obvious that most of these cases must give rise to matters of account; and as no suit is maintainable at law for the property by the owner until the lien is discharged, and as the nature and amount of the lien often are involved in great uncertainty, a resort to a Court of Equity to ascertain and adjust the account seems in many cases absolutely indispensable for the purposes of justice; since if a tender were made at law it would be at the peril of the owner; and if it was

[1] Brace v. Duchess of Marlborough, 2 P. Will. 491; Gilman v. Brown, 1 Mason, R. 221; Ex parte Heywood, 2 Rose, R. 355, 357; post, §§ 1215, 1216.

[2] Abbott on Shipping, Pt. 2, ch. 3, §§ 1, 17; Chase v. Westmore, 5 M. & Selw. 180.

[3] Abbott on Shipping, Pt. 2, ch. 3, §§ 1, 17; Pt. 3, ch. 3, § 11; Id. ch. 10, §§ 1, 2.

[4] Sugden on Vendors, ch. 12, § 1, p. 541 (7th edit.); Id. ch. 12, § 1, vol. 2, p. 57 (9th edit.).

[5] Paley on Agency, ch. 2, § 3; Kruger v. Wilcocks, Ambler, R. 252, and Mr. Blunt's note; Green v. Farmer, 4 Burr. 2218.

less than the amount due, he would inevitably be cast in the suit and be put to the necessity of a new litigation under more favorable circumstances. So in many cases where a lien exists upon various parcels of land, some parts of which have been afterwards sold to different purchasers, and the lien is sought to be enforced upon the lands of the purchaser, it may often become necessary to ascertain what parcels ought primarily to be subjected to the lien in exoneration of others; and a bill for this purpose, as well as for an account of the amount of the incumbrance, may be indispensable for the purposes of justice.[1] Cases of pledges present a similar illustration whenever they involve indefinite and unascertained charges and accounts.

507. Let us in the next place bring together some few cases involving accounts which may arise either from privity of contract or relation, or from adverse or conflicting interests.

508. Under this head the jurisdiction of Courts of Equity in regard to RENTS AND PROFITS may properly be considered. A great variety of cases of this sort resolve themselves into matters of account, not only when they arise from privity of contract, but also when they arise from adverse claims and titles asserted by different persons.[2] Between landlord and tenant accounts often extend over a number of years where there are any special terms or stipulations in the lease requiring expenditures on one side and allowances on the other. In such cases, where there are any controverted claims, a resort to Courts of Equity is often necessary to a due adjustment of the respective rights of each party.[3]

509. Mr. Fonblanque asserts that Courts of Equity when resorted to for the purpose of an account of mesne profits will in many cases consult the principle of convenience, and will therefore sometimes decree it where the party has not already established his right at law.[4] To some extent, as in cases of shareholders in real property of a peculiar nature (such as shareholders in the New River Water-works in England), he is borne

---

[1] Skeel v. Spraker, 8 Paige, R. 182; Patty v. Pease, 8 Paige, R. 277; post, §§ 634 a, 1233 a, where the marshalling of securities and priority as to contributions is more fully considered.

[2] See 1 Fonbl. Eq. B. 1, ch. 3, § 3, and note (k); Id. B. 1, ch. 1; Id. B. 1, ch. 1, § 3, note (f); Bac. Abridg. Accompt, B.

[3] O'Conner v. Spaight, 1 Sch. & Lefr. 305. See The King v. The Free Fishers of Whitstable, 7 East, R. 353, 356.

[4] 1 Fonbl. Eq. B. 1, ch. 3, § 3, note (k).

out by authority. But there is great reason to question whether the doctrine is generally admissible as a rule in equity resulting from mere convenience.[1] It seems rather to result from the peculiar character of the property where there are many proprietors in the nature of partners having a common title to the profits, and therefore the whole becomes appropriately a matter of account.[2]

510. But another class of cases is still more frequent, arising from tortious or adverse claims and titles.[3] Thus where a judgment creditor or a conusee of a recognizance or other statute security has had his execution levied upon the real estate of the judgment debtor or conusor, it may often be necessary to take an account of the rents and profits in order to ascertain whether, and when, the debt has been satisfied by a perception of those rents and profits.[4] At law the tenant under an elegit is not bound to answer in account except for the extended value. But in Courts of Equity, as the elegit is a mere security for the debt, the tenant will be compelled to account for the rents and profits which he has actually received, deducting of course all reasonable charges.[5]

511. It is observable that in these cases of elegit there exists a privity in law, and there is an implied trust between the parties. In the ordinary cases of mesne profits, where a clear remedy exists at law, Courts of Equity will not interfere, but will leave the party to his remedy at law. Some special circumstances are therefore necessary to draw into activity the remedial interference of a Court of Equity;[6] and when these exist it will interfere, not only in cases arising under contract, but in cases arising under direct or constructive torts. Thus for instance if a man intrudes

---

[1] Townsend v. Ash, 3 Atk. 336. See Pulteney v. Warren, 6 Ves. 91, 92; Norton v. Frecker, 1 Atk. 524, 525.

[2] Adley v. Whitstable Comp. 17 Ves. 324; Lorimer v. Lorimer, 5 Madd. R. 369.

[3] Bac. Abridg. Accompt, B.   The gradual development of equity jurisdiction in cases of tort and mesne profits arising under contracts, trusts, and torts, is well stated in Bac. Abridg. Accompt, B.

[4] Yates v. Hambley, 2 Atk. 362, 363; Owen v. Griffith, Ambl. R. 520; s. c. 1 Ves. 250.

[5] Owen v. Griffith, 1 Ves. 250; Yates v. Hambley, 2 Atk. 362, 363. See 3 Black. Comm. 418 to 420; Taylor v. Earl of Abingdon, Doug. R. 472; Com. Dig. Execution, C. 14.

[6] Tilley v. Bridges, Prec. Ch. 252; 1 Eq. Abridg. 285.

upon an infant's lands and takes the profits, he is compellable to account for them, and will be treated as a guardian or trustee for the infant.[1] And this is but following out the rule of law in the like case; for so greatly does the law favor infants, that if a stranger enters into and occupies an infant's lands, he is compellable at law to render an account of the rents and profits, and will be chargeable as guardian or bailiff.[2]

512. Other cases may be easily put where a like remedial justice is administered in equity. (*a*) But in all these cases it will be found that there is some peculiar equitable ground for interference, such as fraud or accident or mistake, the want of a discovery, some impediment at law, the existence of a constructive trust, or the necessity of interposing to prevent multiplicity of suits.[3] It is perfectly clear that if there is a trust estate, and the cestui que trust comes into equity upon his title to recover the estate, he will be decreed to have the further relief of an account of the rents and profits.[4] So in the case of bond creditors who come in for a distribution of assets, they may have an account of rents and profits against the heir in equity; for it is clear that they have an equity, and yet they are without remedy at law.[5] So in

[1] Newburgh *v.* Bickerstaffe, 1 Vern. 295; Carey *v.* Bertie, 2 Vern. 342; Hutton *v.* Simpson, 2 Vern. 724; Lockey *v.* Lockey, Prec. Ch. 518, 129; 1 Eq. Abridg. 7, Pl. 10, 11; Id. 280, A.; Bennet *v.* Whitehead, 2 P. Will. 644; 1 Fonbl. Eq. B. 1, ch. 3, § 3, and note (*k*); Dormer *v.* Fortescue, 3 Atk. 129, 130.

[2] Littleton, § 124; Co. Litt. 89 *b*, 90 *a*; Pulteney *v.* Warren, 6 Ves. 88, 89; Com. Dig. Accompt, A. 2; Dormer *v.* Fortescue, 3 Atk. 129, 130; Curtis *v.* Curtis, 2 Bro. Ch. 628, 632; Townsend *v.* Ash, 3 Atk. 337.

[3] Ibid.; and Sayer *v.* Pierce, 1 Ves. 232; Curtis *v.* Curtis, 2 Bro. Ch. R. 628, 632, 633; Tilley *v.* Bridges, Prec. Ch. 252.

[4] Dormer *v.* Fortescue, 3 Atk. 129; Coventry *v.* Hall, 2 Ch. Rep. 259.

[5] Curtis *v.* Curtis, 2 Bro. Ch. R. 628, 629, 633.

(*a*) For example the case of a mortgagee in possession who must account for net rents and profits. Post, vol. 2, § 1016; Scruggs *v.* Memphis R. Co., 108 U. S. 368; Shepard *v.* Jones, 21 Ch. D. 469; Mayer *v.* Murray, 8 Ch. D. 424. The case of a deed set aside for actual fraud practised on the grantor may furnish another example. See Hack *v.* Norris, 46 Mich. 587. A purchaser who before completion of the purchase exercises acts of ownership over the land to be purchased must pay interest on the price pending delay in the completion of the sale, and this though the delay is caused by the vendor, and the land is not occupied, so that he does not derive rents or profits from it. Ballard *v.* Shutt, 15 Ch. D. 122. See Rhys *v.* Dare Ry. Co., L. R. 19 Eq. 93; Fludyer *v.* Cocker, 12 Ves. 25; Attorney-Gen. *v.* Christ Church, 13 Sim. 214.

the case of dower (of which more will presently be said) ; if the widow is entitled to dower and her claim is merely upon a legal title, but she cannot ascertain the lands out of which she is dowable, and comes into equity for discovery and relief, she will be entitled to an account of the rents and profits upon having her title established.[1]   So if an heir or devisee is compelled to come into equity for a discovery of title deeds and the ascertainment of his title, or to put aside some impediments to his recovery, there he will be entitled to an account of the rents and profits.[2]

513. Another case illustrative of the same doctrine as connected with torts, is where a recovery has been had in an ejectment brought to recover lands, and afterwards the plaintiff is prevented from enforcing his judgment by an injunction obtained on a bill brought by the tenant, who dies before the bill is finally disposed of.   In such a case at law the remedy by an action of trespass for the mesne profits is gone by the death of the tenant, as actions of tort do not survive at law.   But a Court of Equity will, in such a case, entertain a bill for an account of the mesne profits in favor of the plaintiff in ejectment, against the personal representatives of the tenant ; for it is inequitable that his estate should receive the benefit and profits of the property of another person.   It would be a reproach to equity if a man who has taken the property of another and disposed of it in his lifetime should, by his death, throw the proceeds into his own assets and leave the injured party remediless.[3]   It is true that the death of the tenant cannot be treated as the case of an accident against which a Court of Equity will relieve.[4]   But there seems the most manifest justice in holding that where property or its proceeds has come to the use of a party, the mere fact that the title has originated in a tort should not prevent the party and his personal representatives from rendering an account thereof.   And in truth this is but following out the principles now adopted in Courts of Law, where the action for a tort dies with the person, but the right of

---

[1] Ibid.; Curtis v. Curtis, 2 Brown, Ch. R. 620; 1 Fonbl. Eq. B. 1, ch. 3, § 3, note (k).

[2] Dormer v. Fortescue, 3 Atk. 124; Coventry v. Hall, 2 Ch. Rep. 259; Bennet v. Whitehead, 2 P. Will. 644; Pulteney v. Warren, 6 Ves. 88, 89.

[3] Bishop of Winchester v. Knight, 1 P. Will. 407; Lansdowne v. Lansdowne, 1 Madd. R. 116.

[4] Pulteney v. Warren, 6 Ves. 88; Garth v. Cotton, 3 Atk. 755; s. c. 1 Ves. 524; Id. 546.

property in the thing or its proceeds survives against the personal representatives.[1]

514. There is also another distinct ground which, although not always followed out by the Courts of Equity in England, is of itself sufficient to maintain the jurisdiction; and that is, that in these cases a discovery is sought, and if it is effectual, then, to prevent multiplicity of suits, the court ought to decree at once the payment of the mesne profits which have been thus ascertained.[2] But a definite and very satisfactory ground to maintain the jurisdiction in such cases is, that it is inequitable that a party who suspends the just operation of a suit or judgment by an injunction should thereby deprive the other party of his rights and profits belonging to the suit or judgment, if the merits turn out to be ultimately in favor of the latter. He ought, under such circumstances, to be compelled to put the plaintiff in the original suit in the same situation as if no such injunction had intervened.[3]

515. Cases of WASTE by tenants and other persons afford another illustration of the same doctrine.[4] (a)   Thus where one

---

[1] Hambley v. Trott, Cowp. R. 371; Lansdowne v. Lansdowne, 1 Madd. R. 116. There are recent statutes both in England and America which alter the common law in this respect; but this change has not taken away the original jurisdiction in equity.

[2] See Jesus College v. Bloom, 3 Atk. 262; s. c. Ambler, R. 54; Whitfield v. Bewit, 2 P. Will. 240; s. c. 3 P. Will. 267; Dormer v. Fortescue, 2 Atk. 282; s. c. 3 Atk. 124; Townsend v. Ash, 3 Atk. 336, 337.

[3] Pulteney v. Warren, 6 Ves. 88, 92.

[4] We here speak of legal waste; for, if the waste be equitable only, of

---

(a) Where timber is of a growth or in a state to make it good husbandry to cut it, this it seems may be done by a tenant without incurring liability, at least in this country. Drown v. Smith, 52 Maine, 141; Bond v. Lockwood, 33 Ill. 212. As to the law of England see Seagram v. Knight, L. R. 2 Ch. 628; s. c. 3 Eq. 398; Higginbotham v. Hawkins, L. R. 7 Ch. 676; Gent v. Harrison, Johns. 517; Harcourt v. White, 6 Jur. N. S. 1087. And what shall be done with the same after it has been cut may raise a question for equity. As timber is not annual profit of the estate, it cannot be appropriated, or at any rate consumed further than is necessary,

by the life tenant. It should be sold and the price invested in favor of the remainder-man, the annual interest being made payable to the tenant during the continuance of his estate, and then to the remainder-man. See Gent v. Harrison, Johns. 517. If the money is not invested, the proceeds are held in trust for the benefit of the inheritance, and equity will enforce the trust and require an account. Phillips v. Allen, 5 Allen, 85.

Equity may enjoin waste after a decree for partition. Bailey v. Hobson, L. R. 5 Ch. 180. And it may stay waste during the suit for partition. Coffin v. Loper, 25 N. J. Eq. 443.

held customary lands of a manor and opened a copper mine in
the lands and dug the ore and sold great quantities of it in his
lifetime, and then died and his heir continued digging and disposing of the ore in like manner, upon a bill brought against the
executor for an account and against the heir also for an account,
it was decided that the bill was maintainable both against the
executor and the heir. Lord Cowper seems to have entertained
the jurisdiction upon general principles, and especially upon the
ground that the tenant was a sort of fiduciary of the lord; and
it was against conscience that he should shelter himself or his
representative from responsibility for a breach of trust in a Court
of Equity.[1]

516. This case has been supposed to have been decided upon
the ground that, as to the executor, there was no remedy at law;
and that, as to the heir, there was some fraud or concealment,
and a necessity for a discovery; or that, as to him, an injunction
was sought. Without some one of these ingredients it would be
difficult to maintain the case in its apparent extent, for there
would otherwise be a complete and perfect remedy at law. And
in the later commentaries upon this case this has been the dis-
tinctive ground upon which its authority has been admitted.[2]
Lord Hardwicke seems to have thought that it being the case of
a mine might distinguish it from other cases of waste, as the digging of mines is a sort of trade; and then it would fall within the
general doctrine as to an account in matters of trade [3]

517. Cases of waste by the cutting down of timber by tenants
have given rise to questions of the same sort in regard to jurisdiction. In some of the cases upon this subject it seems to have
been maintained that, although the remedy for waste is ordinarily at law, yet if a discovery is wanted, that alone, if it turns
out to be important and is obtained, will carry the ulterior juris-

course a remedy lies in equity. Lansdowne v. Lansdowne, 1 Madd. R. 116;
Marquis of Ormond v. Kynersley, 5 Madd. R. 369.(a) An injunction to
stay waste will lie in favor of one tenant in common against another. Hawley v. Clowes, 2 John. Ch. R. 122.

[1] Bishop of Winchester v. Knight, 1 P. Will. 407; s. c. 2 Eq. Abridg. 226.

[2] Pulteney v. Warren, 6 Ves. 89, 90; Jesus College v. Bloom, 3 Atk. 262;
s. c. Ambler, R. 54.

[3] Jesus College v. Bloom, 3 Atk. 262; s. c. Ambler, R. 54; Story v. Lord
Windsor, 2 Atk. 630; Sayer v. Pierce, 1 Ves. 232.

(a) But see Kingham v. Lee, 15 Sim. 396, as to Marquis of Ormond
v. Kynersley.

diction to account in order to prevent multiplicity of suits;[1] a ground the sufficiency of which it seems difficult to resist upon general principles.[2] But other decisions, and those which are relied on as constituting the established doctrine of the court, are differently qualified, and seem to require, in order to maintain the jurisdiction for an account, that there should be a prayer for an injunction to prevent future waste.[3] (a)

518. Lord Hardwicke upon one occasion expounded this ground of jurisdiction very clearly (although he does not seem himself afterwards to have been satisfied with so limiting it[4]), and said: ' Waste is a loss for which there is a proper remedy by action. In a Court of Law the party is not necessitated to bring an action of waste, but he may bring trover. (b) These are the remedies, and therefore there is no ground of equity to come into this court. For satisfaction of damages is not the proper ground for the court to admit of these sorts of bills, but the staying of waste ; because the court presumes, when a man has done waste, he may do the same again, and therefore will suffer the lessor or rever- sioner, when he brings his bill for an injunction to stay waste, to pray at the same time for an account of the waste done. And it is upon this ground, to prevent multiplicity of suits, that this court will decree an account of waste done, at the same time with an injunction. Just like the case of a bill for a discovery of assets ; an account may be prayed for at the same time. And though originally the bill was only brought for a discovery of assets, yet to prevent a multiplicity of suits the court will direct an account to be taken.'[5] Now if this reasoning be well founded

[1] Whitfield v. Bewit, 2 P. Will. 240; Garth v. Cotton, 3 Atk. 756; s. c. 1 Ves. 524, 546; Lee v. Alston, 1 Bro. Ch. R. 194; Eden on Injunct. ch. 9, p. 206, &c.

[2] See Barker v. Dacie, 6 Ves. 688; Jeremy on Eq. Jurisd. B. 3, Pt. 2, ch. 5, p. 510.

[3] See Pulteney v. Warren, 6 Ves. 89, 90; Gherson v. Eyre, 9 Ves. 89; Richards v. Noble, 3 Meriv. R. 673. But see Lansdowne v. Lansdowne, 1 Madd. R. 116; Eden on Injunct. ch. 9, p. 206, &c.

[4] See Garth v. Cotton, 3 Atk. 756; s. c. 1 Ves. 524, 546.

[5] Jesus College v. Bloom, Ambler, R. 54; s. c. 3 Atk. 262; Pulteney v. Warren, 6 Ves. 89; Bishop v. Church, 2 Ves. 104; Yates v. Hambley, 2 Atk. 362; Watson v. Hunter, 5 John. Ch. R. 169; Smith v. Cooke, 3 Atk. 381. It may be said that on a bill for a discovery of assets an account is necessary

(a) Higginbotham v. Hawkins, L. R. 7 Ch. 676. See Birch-Wolfe v. Birch, L. R. 9 Eq. 683.

(b) Or an action for money had and received if the timber is sold. Gent v. Harrison, Johns. 517.

either in itself or upon the analogy of the case put of assets, it
goes clearly to show that where discovery is sought and is obtained, there also, to prevent multiplicity of suits, an account
ought to be decreed without the additional ingredient of an injunction to stay future waste. And Lord Thurlow seems to have
acted upon this ground.[1] (a)

to ascertain the assets; and when taken, the court ought to proceed to decree
satisfaction in order to prevent multiplicity of suits. But precisely the same
thing may occur on a bill for an account of waste. Before the waste can be
ascertained it may be indispensable to have an account; and when taken, the
court ought to proceed to decree satisfaction. In Jesus College v. Bloom,
(Ambl. R. 54), the term was gone by an assignment to another tenant, and
no injunction was asked as to future waste.

[1] Lee v. Alston, 1 Bro. Ch. R. 194, 195; s. c. 1 Ves. jr. 78. See also
Eden on Injunct. ch. 9, p. 206, &c., 1 Fonbl. Eq. B. 1, ch. 1, § 3, note (ƒ).

(a) It seems clear that there may
be cases of waste over which equity
will assume jurisdiction on a bill for
an account though there be no prayer
for injunction against future waste.
But the jurisdiction in such a case is
founded, it seems, on the demand for
an account; and it may be denied
where the bill does not make a proper
case for an account in accordance with
the general principles of equity relating
to that subject. It seems that if the
bill fail in this respect, it will not help
the case that at one stage of the wrong
the situation was such as to have jus-
tified an injunction at that time. In
Morris v. Morris, 3 DeG. & J. 323,
a tenant for life without impeachment
for waste pulled down the mansion
house of the estate and built a better,
in a more desirable situation, upon the
premises. Those entitled in remainder filed a bill for an account of waste;
but on proof that the bulk of the
materials of the old house had been
used in building the new, and no evidence that any of the old materials
had been sold, the bill was held to
have been properly dismissed. But
the opinion was expressed that if the
materials of the old house had been
sold, a bill for an account would have
been proper. See also Morris v.

Morris, 15 Sim. 505; Leeds v. Amherst, 2 Phil. 117; Micklethwait v.
Micklethwait, 1 DeG. & J. 504.

That an injunction is maintainable
to restrain equitable waste — waste
which a prudent man would not commit in the management of his own
estate — is clear, though the tenant is
' not impeachable of waste,' which
means legal waste. Turner v. Wright,
Johns. 740; s. c. 6 Jur. N. s 809;
Ib. 647; Gent v. Harrison, Johns. 517;
Baker v. Sebright, 13 Ch D. 179;
Micklethwait v. Micklethwait, 1 DeG.
& J. 504. The reason is that the
tenant is using his legal powers unfairly. Baker v. Sebright Whether
such proceeding may be had over un-
permitted legal waste is not so clear.
See the first two cases just cited, and
see Jurist, July 12, 1860, where,
doubting Turner v. Wright, supra, it
is maintained that there is no distinction in principle between legal and
equitable waste concerning the right
of equity to interfere by injunction,
and that a tenant for life should be
restrained from committing either.

Equity will enjoin waste by a
mortgagor if alleged to be such as will
impair the security. Coker v. Whit-
lock, 54 Ala. 180; King v. Smith, 2
Hare, 244.

519. In regard to TITHES also, and incidentally to MODUSES and other compositions, Courts of Equity in England exercise an extensive jurisdiction of an analogous nature.[1] There is a very ancient jurisdiction in the Court of Exchequer in the matter of tithes. Lord Nottingham is said to have stated that the jurisdiction in the Exchequer over tithes by bill in equity is not earlier than the reign of Henry VIII., and that it took its rise from the statute of augmentations in his reign (33 Hen. VIII. ch. 39).[2] But other persons assert that it had a more early origin; and in respect to extra-parochial tithes, which are a part of the ancient inheritance of the Crown, they insist that suits for tithes must always have fallen within the compass of the direct and substantial jurisdiction of the Court of Exchequer, as a Court of Revenue, and that the proper jurisdiction of tithes belongs there.[3] Be this as it may, the jurisdiction of the Court of Chancery over the same subject seems to have been of a much later origin, or at least to have been matter of doubt and controversy to a much later period, the jurisdiction not having been firmly established until after the restoration of Charles II.[4] The Court of Chancery has ever since been held to have a concurrent jurisdiction with the Court of Exchequer.[5] This concurrent jurisdiction in both courts is now generally considered to be merely incidental and collateral, arising from the general equitable jurisdiction of these courts in matters of account and in compelling a discovery.[6] And therefore wherever the right to tithes is clearly established, an account is consequential; for it would be otherwise impossible to give full effect to that right unless upon a discovery and account.[7] If the right is disputed, it must be first ascertained at law before an account will be decreed.[8] Indeed it may be truly

---

[1] Com. Dig. Chancery, 3 C., Id. Dismes. M. 13; 2 Fonbl. Eq. B. 4, Pt. 1, ch. 1, § 1.

[2] Harg. note to Co. Litt. 159 a, note 290; Anon. 1 Freem. R. 303.

[3] Harg. note to Co. Litt. 159 a, note 290; Anon. 1 Freem. R. 303, Hardcastle v. Smithson, 3 Atk. 247.

[4] Ibid.; Anon. 1 Freem. R. 203; Anon. 2 Ch. Cas. 337; s. c. 2 Freem. R. 27; 1 Madd. Ch. Pr. 84.

[5] Bacon, Abridg. Tythes, B 6; Com. Dig. Chancery, 3 C., Id. Dismes. M. 13.

[6] 3 Black. Comm. 437; Co. Litt. 159 a, Hargrave's note, 290; Jeremy on Eq. Jurisd. B. 3, Pt. 2, ch. 5, pp. 510, 511.

[7] Foxcraft v. Parris, 5 Ves. 221; 1 Madd. Ch. Pr. 84 to 88; Jeremy on Eq. Jurisd. B. 3, Pt. 2, ch. 5, pp. 510, 511.

[8] Ibid.; Hughes v. Davies, 5 Sim. R. 349.

said that in all matters of tithes a Court of Equity is far more competent than a Court of Law to administer an appropriate remedy.[1]

520. Courts of Equity in England will not only enforce an account in cases of tithes, but they will also exercise jurisdiction to establish a modus or composition in cases where the party insisting on the modus has been disturbed by proceedings at law, or in equity, or in the Ecclesiastical Courts as to tithes, but not otherwise. The peculiarities belonging to the law of tithes, and the doctrines respecting moduses, are the less important to be dwelt on in this place because they do not in any important manner illustrate any of the general doctrines of equity; but they turn upon considerations eminently of an ecclesiastical nature, and are more suitable for a general treatise on tithes.[2]

521. Having passed under review some of the principal heads of equity jurisdiction in matters of account which do not require a very elaborate examination or belong to subjects which peculiarly illustrate the nature of it, we may conclude this examination with some few matters which appropriately belong to the head of Account, and are incident to the exercise of this remedial jurisdiction in all its forms.

522. In the first place in all bills in equity for an account both parties are deemed actors when the cause is before the court upon its merits. It is upon this ground that the party defendant, contrary to the ordinary course of equity proceedings, is entitled to orders in a cause to which a plaintiff alone is generally entitled. As for instance in such a case a defendant may have an order for a ne exeat regno even against a co-defendant.[3] So it is a general rule that no person but a plaintiff can entitle himself to a decree. But in bills for an account, if a balance is ultimately found in favor of the defendant, he is entitled to a decree for such balance against the plaintiff. And for a like reason, although a defendant cannot ordinarily revive a suit which has not proceeded

---

[1] Mitford, Pl. Eq. by Jeremy, 125; Pulteney v. Warren, 6 Ves. 89.

[2] Earl of Coventry v. Burslen, 2 Anst. R. 567, note; Gordon v. Simpkinson, 11 Ves. 509; Stawell v. Atkyns, 2 Anst. R. 564; 1 Madd. Ch. Pr. 202; Mayor of York v. Pilkington, 1 Atk. 282, 283; Warden &c. of St. Paul's v. Morris, 9 Ves. 155. See also Whaley v. Dawson, 2 Sch. & Lefr. 370, 371; Daws v. Benn, 1 Jac. & Walk. 493.

[3] Done's Case, 1 P. Will. 263.

to a decree, yet in a bill for an account, if the plaintiff dies after
an interlocutory decree to account, the defendant is entitled to
revive the suit against the personal representatives of the plaintiff.[1] And if the defendant dies, his personal representatives
may revive the suit against the plaintiff.[2] The good sense of the
doctrine seems to be that wherever a defendant may derive a
benefit from further proceedings, whether before or after a decree,
he may be said to have an interest in it, and consequently ought
to have a right to revive it.[3]

523. In the next place there are some matters of defence
either peculiarly belonging to cases of account or strikingly illustrative of some of the principles already alluded to under the
head of Accident, Mistake, or Fraud. Thus it is ordinarily a
good bar to a suit for an account, that the parties have already
in writing stated and adjusted the items of the account and
struck the balance.[4] (a) In such a case a Court of Equity will
not interfere; for under such circumstances an indebitatus assumpsit upon an insimul computassent lies at law, and there is
no ground for resorting to equity. If therefore there has been
an account stated, that may be set up by way of plea as a bar to
all discovery and relief, unless some matter is shown which calls
for the interposition of a Court of Equity.[5] But if there has
been any mistake, or omission, or accident, or fraud, or undue
advantage by which the account stated is in truth vitiated and
the balance is incorrectly fixed, a Court of Equity will not suffer
it to be conclusive upon the parties, but will allow it to be

---

[1] 1 Eq. Abridg. 3 Pl. 5; Anon. 3. Atk. 691, 692; Ludlow *v.* Simond, 2
Cain. Cas. Err. 39; Lord Stowell *v.* Cole, 2 Vern. 219, and Mr. Raithby's
note; Harwood *v.* Schmedes, 12 Ves. 316.

[2] Kent *v.* Kent, Prec. Ch. 197.

[3] Williams *v.* Cooke, 10 Ves. 406; Harwood *v.* Schmedes, 12 Ves. 311, 316.

[4] Dawson *v.* Dawson, 1 Atk. 1; Taylor *v.* Haylin, 2 Bro. Ch. R. 310; Johnson *v.* Curtis, cited 2 Bro. Ch. R. 310, Mr. Belt's note; s. c. 3 Bro. Ch. 266,
and Mr. Belt's note; Burk *v.* Brown, 2 Atk. 397, 399; Sumner *v.* Thorpe, 2
Atk. 1; Story on Equity Plead. §§ 798 to 802.

[5] Ibid.; Dawson *v.* Dawson, 1 Atk. 1; Anon. 2 Freeman, R. 62; Cham-
bers *v.* Goldwin, 9 Ves. 265, 266; Taylor *v.* Hayling, 1 Cox, R. 435; s. c. 3
Bro. Ch. R. 310; Chappedelaine *v.* Dechenaux, 4 Cranch, R. 306; Perkins *v.*
Hart, 11 Wheat. R. 237; Story on Equity Plead. §§ 798 to 802.

(a) As in the case of a fair compromise between partners. Harrison *v.*
Dewey, 46 Mich. 173.

opened and re-examined.[1] (a)   In some cases, as of gross fraud, or gross mistake, or undue advantage or imposition, made palpable to the court, it will direct the whole account to be opened and taken de novo.[2]   In other cases, where the mistake, or omission, or inaccuracy, or fraud, or imposition is not shown to affect or stain all the items of the transaction, the court will content itself with a more moderate exercise of its authority.[3]   It will allow the account to stand with liberty to the plaintiff to surcharge and falsify it; the effect of which is to leave the account in full force and vigor as a stated account, except so far as

---

[1] A settled account between client and attorney, or between other persons standing in confidential relations to each other, will be more readily opened than any others; and even it is said upon general allegations of error, without any specific errors being pointed out, where the answer admits errors. Matthews v. Wolwyn, 4 Ves. 125; Newman v. Payne, 2 Ves. jr. 199.   See also Beaumont v. Boultbee, 5 Ves. 485; Story on Equity Plead. § 800.

[2] 1 Fonbl. Eq. B. 1, ch. 1, § 3, note (f); Vernon v. Vawdry, 2 Atk. 119; Barrow v. Rhinelander, 1 John. Ch. R. 550; Piddock v. Brown, 3 P. Will. 288; Wharton v. May, 5 Ves. 27, 48, 49; Story on Equity Plead. §§ 800 to 802.

[3] Ibid.; Johnson v. Curtis, 2 Bro. Ch. R. 310, Mr. Belt's note; s. c. 3 Bro. Ch. R. 266, Mr. Belt's note.

(a) La Trobe v. Hayward, 13 Fla. 190; Shirk's Appeal, 3 Brewst. 119; Paulling v. Creagh, 54 Ala. 646; Williamson v. Barbour, 9 Ch. D. 529; Chatham v. Niles, 36 Conn. 403; Floyd v. Priester, 8 Rich. Eq. 248; Bankhead v. Alloway, 6 Cold. 56.   Where accounts are impeached and it is shown that they contain errors of considerable extent in number and amount, the court, whether the errors are due to mistake or fraud, will order the accounts to be opened though they extend over many years, and will not merely give leave to surcharge and falsify.   And if a fiduciary relation, such as principal and agent, exist, the court will make a similar order where the accounts contain a less number of errors or any fraudulent entries. Williamson v. Barbour, supra.   If an account is opened, errors on both sides may be corrected.   Floyd v. Priester, 8 Rich. Eq. 248.

For a single error, without fraud, an account will not be opened entirely, though the error is important, but liberty to surcharge and falsify will be granted. Gething v. Keighley, 9 Ch. D. 547, Jessel M. R.   But see Taylor v. Haylin, 2 Bro. C. C. 310; Coleman v. Mellersh, 2 Macn. & G. 309; Pritt v. Clay, 6 Beav. 503, where accounts were allowed to be opened for a single error.

Where both parties have equal knowledge of the facts, and precise accuracy is not contemplated, the settlement will not be opened for an unimportant error. Hamilton Woollen Co. v. Goodrich, 6 Allen, 191.   See Harrison v. Dewey, 46 Mich. 173; Hager v. Thomson, 1 Black, 80; Bankhead v. Alloway, 6 Cold. 56.   If however the parties are not on equal footing in settling the account, equity will more readily open it and often disregard it entirely; as where the subject-matter of an account grows out of the relation of attorney and client.   Kennedy v. Brown, 13 C. B. N. s. 677.

it can be impugned by the opposing party, who has the burden of proof on him to establish errors and mistakes.[1] Sometimes a still more moderate course is adopted, and the account is simply opened to contestation as to one or more items which are specially set forth in the bill of the plaintiff as being erroneous or unjustifiable ; and in all other respects it is treated as conclusive.[2] (a)

524. When upon a bill to open a stated account liberty is given to surcharge and falsify, the cause is referred to a master. The examination of the account then takes place before him, and upon his report the court finally acts ; for in matters of account it never acts directly, but only through the instrumentality of a master, by whom the whole matter is thoroughly sifted. The liberty to surcharge and falsify includes not only an examination of errors of fact, but of errors of law.[3] (b)

525. These terms, 'surcharge' and 'falsify,' have a distinct sense in the vocabulary of Courts of Equity a little removed from that which they bear in the ordinary language of common life. In the language of common life we understand 'surcharge' to import an overcharge in quantity, or price, or value, beyond what is just, correct, and reasonable. In this sense it is nearly equivalent to 'falsify ;' for every item which is not truly charged as it should be is false, and by establishing such overcharge it is falsified. But in the sense of Courts of Equity these words are used in contradistinction to each other. A surcharge is appropriately applied to the balance of the whole account, and supposes credits to be omitted which ought to be allowed. A falsification applies to some item in the debits, and supposes that the item is wholly false, or in some part erroneous. This distinction is taken notice of by Lord Hardwicke, and the words used by him are so clear that they supersede all necessity for further commentary. 'Upon a liberty to the plaintiff to surcharge and falsify,' says he, 'the onus probandi is always on the party having that liberty ; for the court takes it as a stated

---

[1] Pitt v. Cholmondeley, 2 Ves. 565, 566; Perkins v. Hart, 11 Wheat. R. 237; Story on Equity Plead. §§ 801, 802.

[2] Brownell v. Brownell, 2 Bro. Ch. R. 62, 63; Consequa v. Fanning, 3 John. Ch. R. 587; s. c. 17 John. R. 511; Twogood v. Swanston, 6 Ves. 484, 486.

[3] Roberts v. Kuffin, 2 Atk. 112.

(a) Paulling v. Creagh, 54 Ala. 646.   (b) Daniell v. Sinclair, 6 App. Cas. 181.

account and establishes it. But if any of the parties can show an omission for which credit ought to be, that is a *surcharge;* or if anything is inserted that is a wrong charge, he is at liberty to show it, and that is a *falsification.* But that must be by proof on his side. And that makes a great difference between the general cases of an open account, and where [leave is given] only to surcharge and falsify; for such must be made out.'[1]

526. What shall constitute in the sense of a Court of Equity a stated account, is in some measure dependent upon the particular circumstances of the case. An account in writing examined and signed by the parties will be deemed a stated account, notwithstanding it contains the ordinary preliminary clause that errors are excepted.[2] But in order to make an account a stated account, it is not necessary that it should be signed by the parties.[3] It is sufficient if it has been examined and accepted by both parties. And this acceptance need not be express, but may be implied from circumstances.[4] Between merchants at home, an account which has been presented and no objection made thereto after the lapse of several posts is treated under ordinary circumstances as being by acquiescence a stated account.[5] (a) Between merchants in different countries, a rule founded in similar considerations prevails. If an account has been transmitted from the one to the other, and no objection is made after several opportunities of writing have occurred, it is treated as an acquiescence in the correctness of the account transmitted, and therefore it is deemed a stated account.[6] In truth in each case the rule admits or rather requires the same general exposition. It is, that an account rendered shall be deemed an account stated from the presumed approbation or acquiescence of the parties, unless an objection is made thereto

[1] Pitt *v.* Cholmondeley, 2 Ves. 565, 566. See also Perkins *v.* Hart, 11 Wheat. R. 237, 256.

[2] See Johnson *v.* Curtis, cited 2 Brown, Ch. R. 310; 3 Brown, Ch. R. 266, and Mr. Belt's notes.

[3] Willis *v.* Jernegan, 2 Atk. 251, 252.

[4] Ibid.

[5] Sherman *v.* Sherman, 2 Vern. 276; s. c. 1 Eq. Abridg. 12, Pl. 10, 11; Irving *v.* Young, 1 Sim. & Stu. 333.

[6] Willis *v.* Jernegan, 2 Atk. 252; Tickel *v.* Short, 2 Ves. R. 239; Murray *v.* Toland, 3 John. Ch. R. 569, 575; Freeland *v.* Heron, 7 Cranch, 147.

(a) Wiggins *v.* Burkam, 10 Wall. 129.

within a reasonable time.[1] (a)   That reasonable time is to be judged of in ordinary cases by the habits of business at home and abroad; and the usual course is required to be followed, unless there are special circumstances to vary it or to excuse a departure from it. (b)

527. Upon like grounds a fortiori a settled account will be deemed conclusive between the parties, unless some fraud, mistake, omission, or inaccuracy is shown. (c)   For it would be most mischievous to allow settled accounts between the parties, especially where vouchers have been delivered up or destroyed, to be unravelled unless for urgent reasons and under circumstances of plain error which ought to be corrected.[2] (d)   And in cases of settled accounts the court will not generally open the account, but will at most only grant liberty to surcharge and falsify unless in cases of apparent fraud.[3]

528. In regard to acquiescence in stated accounts, although it amounts to an admission or presumption of their correctness, it by no means establishes the fact of their having been settled, even though the acquiescence has been for a considerable time. There must be other ingredients in the case to justify the conclusion of a settlement.[4]

529. It is too a most material ground, in all bills for an account, to ascertain whether they are brought to open and correct errors in the account recenti facto, or whether the application is

[1] Ibid.; Com. Dig. Chancery, 2 A. 3.

[2] Brownell v. Brownell, 2 Bro. Ch. R. 62; Taylor v. Haylin, 2 Bro. Ch. R. 310; Johnson v. Curtis, cited 2 Bro. Ch. R. 310; s. c. 3 Brown, Ch. R. 266, Mr. Belt's notes; Chambers v. Goldwin, 8 Ves. 837, 838; Pitt v. Cholmondeley, 2 Ves. 566.

[3] Vernon v. Vawdry, 2 Atk. 119; Chambers v. Goldwin, 8 Ves. 265, 266; Drew v. Power, 1 Sch. & Lefr. 192.

[4] Lord Clancarty v. Latouche, 1 B. & Beatt. R. 428; Irving v. Young, 1 Sim. & Stu. 333.

(a) Wiggins v. Burkam, 10 Wall. 129; Lockwood v. Thorne, 11 N. Y. 170; s. c. 18 N. Y. 285; Towsley v. Denison, 45 Barb. 490; Mansell v. Payne, 18 La. An. 124.

(b) Lockwood v. Thorne, 18 N. Y. 285.

(c) Lockwood v. Thorne, 11 N. Y. 170; s. c. 18 N. Y. 285; Harrison v. Dewey, 46 Mich. 173; Bull v. Harris, 31 Ill. 487; Sutphen v. Cushman, 35 Ill. 186; Town v. Wood, 37 Ill. 512; Dickinson v. Lewis, 34 Ala. 638; Badger v. Badger, 2 Cliff. 137. Charges of fraud should be specific. Badger v. Badger.

(d) Wier v. Tucker, L. R. 14 Eq. 25, 30.

made after a great lapse of time. In cases of this sort, where the
demand is strictly of a legal nature or might be cognizable at
law, Courts of Equity govern themselves by the same limitations
as to entertaining such suits as are prescribed by the Statute of
Limitations in regard to suits in Courts of Common Law in matters of account. If therefore the ordinary limitation of such
suits at law be six years, Courts of Equity will follow the same
period of limitation.[1] (a)   In so doing they do not act in cases
of this sort (that is, in matters of concurrent jurisdiction) so
much upon the ground of analogy to the Statute of Limitations as
positively in obedience to such statute.[2]   But where the demand
is not of a legal nature but is purely equitable, or where the bar
of the statute is inapplicable, Courts of Equity have another rule,
founded sometimes upon the analogies of the law, where such
analogy exists, and sometimes upon its own inherent doctrine
not to entertain stale or antiquated demands, and not to encourage laches and negligence.[3]   Hence in matters of account, although not barred by the Statute of Limitations, Courts of Equity
refuse to interfere, after a considerable lapse of time, from considerations of public policy, from the difficulty of doing entire
justice when the original transactions have become obscure by
time and the evidence may be lost, and from the consciousness
that the repose of titles and the security of property are mainly
promoted by a full enforcement of the maxim, ' Vigilantibus, non
dormientibus, jura subveniunt.'[4]   Under peculiar circumstances

[1] Hovenden v. Lord Annesley, 2 Sch. & Lefr. 629; Smith v. Clay, 3 Brown,
Ch. R. 639, n.

[2] Hovenden v. Lord Annesley, 2 Sch. & Lefr. 629, 630, 631; Spring v. Gray,
5 Mason, R. 527, 528; Sherwood v. Sutton, 5 Mason, R. 143, 146; ante, § 55 a.

[3] Sherman v. Sherman, 2 Vern. R. 576; s. c. 1 Eq. Abridg. 12; Bridges v.
Mitchill, Bunb. 217; s. c. Gilb. Eq. R. 217; Foster v. Hodgson, 19 Ves. 180,
184; Sturt v. Mellish, 2 Atk. 610; Pomfret v. Lord Windsor, 2 Ves. 472, 476,
477; Bond v. Hopkins, 1 Sch. & Lefr. 428; Smith v. Clay, Amb. R. 647; 3
Bro. Ch. R. 639, note; Stackhouse v. Barnston, 10 Ves. 466, 467; Moore v.
White, 6 John. Ch. R. 360; Rayner v. Pearsall, 3 John. Ch. R. 578; Ray v.
Bogart, 2 John. Cas. 432; Ellison v. Moffat, 1 John. Ch. R. 46; Sherwood
v. Sutton, 4 Mason, R. 143, 146; Robinson v. Hook, 4 Mason, R. 139, 150,
152; Piatt v. Vattier. 9 Peters, R. 405; Willison v. Watkins, 3 Peters, R. 44;
Miller v. McIntire, 6 Peters, R. 61, 66; 1 Fonbl. Eq. B. 1, ch. 4, § 27, and
notes ; Brownell v. Brownell, 2 Bro. Ch. R. 62.

[4] 1 Fonbl. Eq. B. 1, ch. 4, § 27, and notes; Jeremy on Eq. Jurisd. B. 3,

(a) Randel v. Ely, 3 Brewst. 270; German Seminary v. Keifer, 43 Mich.
105.

however, excusing or justifying the delay, Courts of Equity will not refuse their aid in furtherance of the rights of the party, since in such cases there is no pretence to insist upon laches or negligence as a ground for dismissal of the suit.[1]

Pt. 2, ch. 5, pp. 549, 550; 1 Madd. Ch. Pr. 79, 80; Holtscomb v. Rivers, 1 Ch. Cas. 127. Mr. Fonblanque's collection of principles and authorities to illustrate this doctrine is very comprehensive, and characterized by his usual acuteness and strong sense. 1 Fonbl. Eq. B. 1, ch. 4, § 27, and notes. Mr. Jeremy also upon this subject has given us a very ample and discriminating collection of authorities. Jeremy on Eq. Jurisd. B. 3, Pt. 2, ch. 5, pp. 549, 550.

[1] Lopdell v. Creagh, 1 Bligh (N. S.), 255.

CHAPTER IX.

ADMINISTRATION.

530. HAVING thus gone over some of the more important cases in which matters of account are involved as the principal and sometimes as the exclusive ground of jurisdiction, we shall now take leave of this part of the subject and proceed to the consideration of other branches of concurrent jurisdiction in equity; in which, although accounts are sometimes involved, yet the jurisdiction is derived from or essentially connected with other sources of jurisdiction, and accounts whenever taken are mere incidents to other relief.

531. And in the first place the jurisdiction of Courts of Equity in the administration of the assets of deceased persons. (a) The word assets is derived from the French word *assez*, which means sufficient, or enough; that is, sufficient or enough in the hands of the executor or administrator to make him chargeable to the creditors, legatees, and distributees of the deceased so far as the personal property of the deceased extends, which comes to the hands of the executor or administrator for administration. In an accurate and legal sense all the personal property of the deceased, which is of a salable nature and may be converted into ready money, is deemed assets.[1] But the word is not confined to such property; for all other property of the deceased which is chargeable with his debts or legacies and is applicable to that purpose is in a large sense assets.[2]

532. It has been said that the whole jurisdiction of Courts of

[1] 2 Black. Comm. 510; Toller on Executors, B. 2, ch. 1, p. 137.
[2] 2 Black. Comm. 244, 340; Toller on Executors, B. 3, ch. 8, p. 409.

(a) Equity has no jurisdiction to set up or to set aside wills. Broderick's Will, 21 Wall. 504; Meluish *v.* Milton, 3 Ch. D. 27; ante, §§ 179–185, and notes.

Equity in the administration of assets is founded on the principle that it is the duty of the court to enforce the execution of trusts; and that the executor or administrator who has the property in his hands is bound to apply that property to the payment of debts and legacies, and to apply the surplus according to the will of the testator, or, in case of intestacy, according to the Statute of Distributions. So that the sole ground on which Courts of Equity proceed in cases of this kind is to be deemed the execution of a trust.[1] (a)

533. This is certainly a very satisfactory foundation on which to rest the jurisdiction in many cases; for under many circumstances, as an execution of a trust, the subject would be properly cognizable in equity and especially if the party would not be chargeable at law, since it is the ordinary reason for a Court of Equity to grant relief that the party is remediless at law. It has also been truly said that the only thing inquired of in a Court of Equity is whether the property bound by a trust has come into the hands of persons who are either bound to execute the trust or to preserve the property for the persons entitled to it. If we advert to the cases on the subject, we shall find that trusts are enforced, not only against those persons who are rightfully possessed of trust property, as trustees, but also against all persons who come into possession of the property bound by the trust, with notice of the trust. And whoever so comes into possession is considered as bound, with respect to that special property, to the execution of the trust.[2] (b)

[1] Adair v. Shaw, 1 Sch. & Lefr. 262. See also Farrington v. Knightley, 1 P. Will. 548, 549; Rachfield v. Careless, 2 P. Will. 161; Duke of Rutland v. Duchess of Rutland, 2 P. Will. 210, 211; Elliot v. Collier, 1 Ves. 16; Anon. 1 Atk. 491; Wind v. Jekyll, 2 P. Will. 575; Nicholson v. Sherman, 1 Cas. Ch. 57; Bac. Abridg. Legacy, M.; 1 Madd. Ch. Pr. 466, 467.

[2] Ibid.

(a) As to the jurisdiction of equity to require an executor or administrator to account, see Carswell v. Spencer, 44 Ala. 204; Finger v. Finger, 64 N. Car. 183. It is held in some cases that there must be a judgment at law before filing a bill to have equitable assets applied. Harrison v. Hallum, 5 Cold. 525. But see Steere v. Hoagland, 39 Ill. 264; Ragsdale v. Holmes, 1 S. Car. 91.

(b) See Thorndike v. Hunt, 3 DeG. & J. 563; Hopper v. Conyers, 12 Jur. N. S. 328. A stranger who has received assets from an executor de son tort cannot be called to account as executor de son tort though the assets may be followed into his hands. Hill v. Curtis, L. R. 1 Eq. 90. See Rayner v. Koehler, L. R. 14 Eq. 264.

534. Certainly to no persons can these considerations more appropriately apply than to executors and administrators and those claiming under them with notice of the administration and assets. But if it were the sole ground of sustaining the jurisdiction, that it is the case of a trust cognizable in equity alone, it would follow that, instead of being a matter of concurrent jurisdiction, it would be a matter belonging to the exclusive jurisdiction of equity. For although equity does not purport to entertain jurisdiction of all trusts, some of them, such as cases of bailments, being ordinarily cognizable at law,[1] yet of such trusts as are peculiar to Courts of Equity the jurisdiction is exclusive in such courts. Now we all know that both the Courts of Common Law and the Ecclesiastical Courts have cognizance of administrations, and many suits respecting the administration of assets are daily entertained therein. Courts of Equity therefore in assuming general jurisdiction over cases of administration do indeed in some measure found themselves upon the notion of a constructive trust in the executors or administrators.[2] But the fact of there being a constructive trust is not the sole ground of jurisdiction. Other auxiliary grounds also exist, such as the necessity of taking accounts and compelling a discovery,[3] and the consideration that the remedy at law when it exists is not plain, adequate, and complete. The jurisdiction therefore now assumed by Courts of Equity to so wide an extent over all administrations and the settlement of estates, in cases of testacy and intestacy, is not (as it should seem) exclusively referable to the mere existence of a constructive trust (which is often sufficiently remediable at law), but it is referable to the mixed considerations already adverted to, each of which has a large operation in equity.[4] (a)

535. A little attention to the nature of the jurisdiction exercised in the Courts of Common Law and the Ecclesiastical Courts in cases of administrations will abundantly show the necessity of the interposition of Courts of Equity. In the first place in suits

[1] 3 Black. Comm. 431, 432; 1 Wooddeson, Lect. vii., pp. 208, 209.

[2] Bac. Abridg. Legacy, M.

[3] Com. Dig. Chancery, 2 A. 1; 3 Black. Comm. 98.

[4] See Mitford, Pl. Eq. by Jeremy, pp. 125, 126, 136.

(a) Where equity has taken jurisdiction of an administration, it may proceed to distribution and relief as in probate. Key v. Jones, 52 Ala. 238.

at common law nothing more can be done than to establish the debt of the creditor; and if there is any controversy as to the existence of the assets and a discovery is wanted, or if the assets are not of a legal nature, or if a marshalling of the assets is indispensable to a due payment of the creditor's claim, it is obvious that the remedy at law cannot be effectual. But there may be other interests injuriously affected by the judgment of a Court of Common Law in a suit by a creditor, which injury that court could not redress or prevent, but which Courts of Equity could completely redress or prevent.

536. In the next place as to the Ecclesiastical Courts. They have, it is true, an ancient jurisdiction over the probate of wills and the granting of administrations, and as incident thereto an authority to enforce the payment of legacies of personal property.[1] But by the common law, although an executor was compellable to account before the ordinary or ecclesiastical judge, and so was an administrator, yet the ordinary was to take the account as given in by the executor or administrator, and could not oblige him to prove the items of it or to swear to the truth of it.[2]

537. The statute of 31st of Edward III. ch. 11, put executors and administrators upon the same footing as to accounting for assets, but it in no manner whatsoever changed the mode of accounting by either of them.[3] A legatee might falsify the account of an executor or administrator in the Spiritual Court, as may also the next of kin, since the Statute of Distributions of 22d and 23d of Car. II., ch. 10. But a creditor of the estate could not falsify the account in the Ecclesiastical Court, for his proper remedy was held to be at the common law.[4] By the statute of 21st of Henry VIII., ch. 5, § 4, executors and administrators were bound to deliver an inventory of the effects of the deceased upon oath to the ordinary. But the inventory could

---

[1] 2 Black. Comm. 494; 3 Black. Comm. 98; Bac. Abridg. Legacies, M.; 2 Fonbl. Eq. B. 4, ch. 1, § 1, and notes; Marriott v. Marriott, 1 Str. Rep. 666.

[2] 2 Fonbl. Eq. B. 4, ch. 3, § 2, and note (d); Archbishop of Canterbury v. Wills, 1 Salk. 315.

[3] Ibid.; 2 Black. Comm. 496; 4 Burns, Eccles. Law, Wills, Distribution, Account, viii., p. 368; 2 Fonbl. Eq. B. 4, Pt. 2, ch. 3, § 2, note (d).

[4] 2 Fonbl. Eq. B. 4, Pt. 2, ch. 3, § 2, note (d); Hinton v. Parker, 8 Mod. 168; Catchside v. Ovington, 3 Burr. R. 1922; Archbishop of Canterbury v. Wills, 1 Salk. 315.

not be controverted in the Ecclesiastical Courts by a creditor, but only by a legatee.[1] Even an administration bond will not be broken by an omission to pay a creditor's debt, but it is a security merely for those who are interested in the estate.[2] Indeed before the Statute of Distributions it was a matter greatly debated whether an administrator could be compelled to make any distribution of an intestate's estate ; and for a great length of time it was held that an executor was in all cases entitled to the personal estate of his testator not disposed of by his will.[3]

538. The jurisdiction of the Ecclesiastical Courts being so manifestly defective in the case of creditors, resort was almost necessarily had to Courts of Equity to compel a discovery of assets and an account. And where a creditor did not seek a general settlement of the estate by a suit in behalf of himself and all other creditors, still he was entitled to a discovery in Courts of Equity to enable him to recover his own debt in an action at law.[4]

539. In regard to legatees also the remedy was in many cases quite as defective. No remedy lies at the common law in cases of pecuniary legacies,[5] and although (as has been stated) a remedy does lie in the Spiritual Courts, yet in a great variety of cases that remedy is insufficient and imperfect. Thus if payment of a legacy should be pleaded to a suit in the Ecclesiastical Courts, and there is but one witness of the fact (which the Ecclesiastical Courts will not admit as sufficient proof, for their law requires two), there the Temporal Courts will grant a prohibition to further proceedings.[6] So if a husband should sue for a legacy in the Ecclesiastical Courts, the Court of Chancery will prohibit him ; because the Ecclesiastical Courts cannot compel him

---

[1] Hinton v. Parker, 8 Mod. 168; Catchside v. Ovington, 3 Burr. 1922; 2 Fonbl. Eq. B. 4, Pt. 2, ch. 3, § 2. Mr. Fonblanque is in an error when he says, ' The inventory could not be controverted in the Spiritual Court.' The authorities cited by him show that it could be by a legatee but not by a creditor. 2 Fonbl. Eq. B. 4, Pt. 2, ch. 3, § 2.

[2] Archbishop of Canterbury v. Wills, 1 Salk. 315; Greenside v. Benson, 3 Atk. 248, 252; Ashley v. Baillie, 3 Ves. 268; Wallis v. Pipon, Ambler, R. 183; Archbishop of Canterbury v. House, Cowp. R. 140; Thomas v. Archbishop of Canterbury, 1 Cox, R. 399.

[3] 2 Black. Comm. 514, 515; Toller on Ex'ors, B. 3, ch. 6, p. 369.

[4] Com. Dig. Chancery, 2 C. 3; Id. 3 B. 1, 2.

[5] Decks v. Strutt, 5 Term R. 690; 2 Fonbl. Eq. B. 4, Pt. 1, ch. 1, § 2.

[6] Bacon, Abridg. Legacy, M.; 3 Black. Comm. 112.

to make any settlement on his wife in consideration of the legacy.[1] So if a legacy is due to an infant, the Court of Chancery will interfere at the instance of the executor and prevent the Spiritual Courts from proceeding, because the executor may be entitled to a bond to indemnify him, and to refund in case of a deficiency of assets.[2] Many other cases might be put of a like nature.

540. But a stronger instance may be stated. If the testator does not dispose of the residue of his estate, and yet from the circumstances of the will the executor is plainly not entitled to the residue, there he will be held liable to distribute it as a trustee for the next of kin. But the Spiritual Courts have no jurisdiction whatsoever in such a case to enforce a distribution; for trusts are not cognizable in those courts and cannot be enforced by them.[3] Even in the common case of a legacy of personal estate the legacy does not vest in the legatee until the executor assents to it; and until he assents, it would seem not to be suable in the Spiritual Courts. But Courts of Equity consider the executor to be a trustee of the legatee, and will compel him to assent to and pay the legacy as a matter of trust.[4] And if there are no legal assets to pay a legacy, although there are ample equitable assets, the Spiritual Courts cannot enforce payment of the legacy; for they have no jurisdiction over equitable assets.[5]

541. In cases of distribution of the residue of estates the remedy in the Spiritual Courts is also on other accounts exceedingly defective; for those courts do not possess any adequate means for a perfect ascertainment of all the debts; or to compel a payment of them, when ascertained, so as to fix the precise residuum; or to protect the executor or administrator in his administration according to their decree.[6] Besides, the interposition of a Court of Equity may be required for many other purposes before a

---

[1] Ibid.; 2 Fonbl. Eq. B. 4, Pt. 1, ch. 1, § 2, and note (d).

[2] Horrell v. Waldron, 1 Vern. R. 26; Noel v. Robinson, 1 Vern. R. 91. But see Anon. 1 Atk. R. 491; Hawkins v. Day, Ambler, R. 162; 2 Fonbl. Eq. B. 4, Pt. 1, ch. 1, § 2.

[3] Farrington v. Knightly, 1 P. Will. 545, 548.

[4] Wind v. Jekyll, 1 P. Will. 575.

[5] Barker v. May, 9 B. & Cressw. 489. See also Paschall v. Ketterich, Dyer, 151 b; Edwards v. Graves, Hob. R. 265; Bac. Abridg. Legacy, M.

[6] See 2 Fonbl. Eq. B. 4, Pt. 2, ch. 3, § 2, note (d); Id. B. 4, Pt. 1, ch. 1, § 2, and note (d).

final settlement and distribution of the estate ; as for instance to
compel an executor to bring the funds into court; or to give
security for the payment of debts, legacies, and distributive
shares where there is danger of insolvency or he is wasting the
assets; or where the debts, legacies, and distributive shares are
not presently payable or payment cannot be presently enforced.[1]

542. The jurisdiction of Courts of Equity to superintend the
administration of assets and decree a distribution of the residue
after payment of all debts and charges among the parties entitled either as legatees or as distributees, does not seem to
have been thoroughly established until near the close of the
reign of Charles II. The objection was then made that the
Spiritual Courts had full authority, under the Statute of Distributions, to decree a distribution of the residue. But upon a
demurrer filed to a bill for a distribution it was held by the
Lord Chancellor that there being no negative words in the Act
of Parliament (the Statute of Distributions), the jurisdiction of
the Court of Chancery was not taken away; for the remedy
in chancery was more complete and effectual than that in the
Spiritual Courts; or to use the language of the court upon that
occasion, the Spiritual Court in that case had but a lame jurisdiction.[2]   And although ordinarily in cases of concurrent jurisdiction the decree of the court first having possession of the
cause is held conclusive, yet Courts of Chancery have not held
themselves bound by decrees of the Spiritual Courts in cases of
distribution from their supposed inability to do entire justice.[3]

543. For a great length of time the usual resort has been to
the Court of Chancery to settle the administration of estates; so
that, practically speaking, in cases of any complication or difficulty it has acquired almost an exclusive jurisdiction.   In many
cases indeed besides those which have been already mentioned

[1] See 2 Fonbl. Eq. B. 4, Pt. 1, ch. 1, § 2, and note (d); Duncumban v.
Stint, 1 Ch. Cas. 121; Strange v. Harris, 3 Bro. Ch. R. 365; Blake v. Blake,
2 Sch. & Lefr. 26.

[2] Matthews v. Newby, 1 Vern. 133; Howard v. Howard, 1 Vern. 134;
Buccle v. Atleo, 2 Vern. R. 37; Gibbons v. Dawley, 2 Ch. Cas. 198; Pamplin
v. Green, 2 Ch. Cas. 95; Lord Winchelsea v. Duke of Norfolk, 2 Ch. R. 367;
2 Fonbl. Eq. B. 4, ch. 1, § 2 ; Digby v. Cornwallis, 3 Ch. R. 72; Petit v.
Smith, 1 P. Will. 7; 1 Madd. Ch. Pr. 467.

[3] See Bissell v. Axtell, 2 Vern. 47, and Mr. Raithby's note; 1 Eq. Abridg.
E., p. 136, Pl. 2, 3, 4.

it is impossible for any other court than a Court of Equity to administer full and satisfactory justice among all the parties in interest; and especially where equitable assets are to be administered or the assets are to be marshalled, as we shall abundantly see in the further progress of these Commentaries. (*a*)

544. The application for aid and relief in the administration of estates is sometimes made by the executor or administrator himself, when he finds the affairs of his testator or intestate so much involved that he cannot safely administer the estate except under the direction of a Court of Equity. In such a case it is competent for him to institute a suit against the creditors generally, for the purpose of having all their claims adjusted, and a final decree settling the order and payment of the assets.[1] (*b*) These are sometimes called Bills of Conformity (probably because the executor or administrator in such case undertakes to conform to the decree, or the creditors are compelled by the decree to conform thereto); and they are not encouraged, because they have a tendency to take away the preference which one creditor may gain over another by his legal diligence. Besides it has been said that these bills may be made use of by executors and administrators to keep creditors out of their money longer than they otherwise would be.[2] However correct these reasons may be for a refusal to interfere in ordinary cases involving no difficulty, they are not sufficient to show that the court ought not to interfere in behalf of an executor or administrator under special circumstances where injustice to himself or injury to the estate may otherwise arise.[3] (*c*)

[1] Com. Dig. Chancery, 3 G. 6; Buccle *v.* Atleo, 2 Vern. 37. See Rush *v.* Higgs, 4 Ves. jr., 638, 643; Jackson *v.* Leap, 1 Jac. & Walk. 231; 2 Fonbl. Eq. B. 4, Pt. 2, ch. 2, § 4, note (*u*).

[2] Morrice *v.* Bank of England, Cas. Temp. Talb. 224; Blackwell's case, 1 Vern. 153, 155; 1 Fonbl. Eq. B. 4, Pt. 2, ch. 2, § 3, note (*u*).

[3] Com. Dig. Chancery, 3 G. 6.

(*a*) Upon the jurisdiction of equity see Tichborne *v.* Tichborne, L. R. 2 P. & M. 41; Harding *v.* Harding, L. R. 13 Eq. 493; Adams *v.* Adams, 22 Vt. 50; Stewart *v.* Stewart, 31 Ala. 207; Seymour *v.* Seymour, 4 Johns. Ch. 409; Van Meter *v.* Sickler, 1 Stockt. 483; Clerke *v.* Johnston, 2 Stockt. 287; Fleming *v.* McKesson, 3 Jones, Eq. 316; Heward *v.* Slagle, 52 Ill. 336; Humphreys *v.* Burleson, 72 Ala. 1; McNeill *v.* McNeill, 36 Ala. 109.

(*b*) It is not enough that there are numerous claims to be settled; there must be complications that cannot be adequately dealt with at law. Bryan *v.* Hickson, 40 Ga. 405. See Irvin *v.* Bond, 41 Ga. 630; Jeter *v.* Barnard, 42 Ga. 43.

(*c*) A bill of conformity will not

545. A doubt has indeed been suggested whether a bill can be maintained against all the creditors.[1] But if the bill is brought against certain known creditors who are proceeding at law, it may be asked, What is the difficulty of proceeding in the same way as is done as to all creditors upon a bill brought by one or more creditors in behalf of themselves and all other creditors? Upon a decree for the executor or administrator to account, all the creditors are, or may be, required to present and prove their debts before the master in the first case as they are now required to do in the last case. But upon such a bill, brought by an executor or administrator, the court will not interpose by way of injunction to prohibit creditors proceeding at law, until there has been a decree against the executor or administrator to account in that suit; for otherwise the latter might without reason make it a ground of undue delay of the creditors.[2]

546. But the more ordinary case of relief sought in equity in cases of administration is by creditors. A creditor may file his bill for payment of his own debt and seek a discovery of assets for this purpose only. (a) If he does so, and the bill is sustained,

[1] Rush v. Higgs, 4 Ves. jr., 638, 643.
[2] Ibid.

lie when it appears that by due diligence in the payment of the decedent's debts there would have been enough to pay all. Weakley v. Gurley, 60 Ala. 399.

(a) Clark v. Hogle, 52 Ill. 427; Fairfield v. Fairfield, 15 Gray, 596; Carter v. Hampton, 77 Va. 631; Kennedy v. Cresswell, 101 U. S. 641, 646. Secus in North Carolina. Wilkins v. Finch, Phill. Eq. 355. And in Alabama. Scott v. Ware, 64 Ala. 174. Filing a creditor's bill, or at least service of process, gives the plaintiff a lien upon the judgment debtor's property by placing it under control of court. First National Bank v. Gage, 93 Ill. 172. And this lien survives the debtor's death and is available in the hands of his representative. Ib., Brown v. Nichols, 42 N. Y. 26. As to equitable interests and choses in action the rule appears to be that the

lien is fixed by the commencement of the suit. But in regard to chattels liable to execution at law the lien may be defeated by seizure of the goods on execution in favor of another creditor before the appointment of a receiver. First Nat. Bank v. Gage, supra; Davenport v. Kelly, 42 N. Y. 193. The lien extends only to property which the debtor had at the commencement of the suit. First Nat. Bank v. Gage.

A creditor's bill to subject his debtor's interest in property must show that all remedy at law has been exhausted. Case v. Beauregard, 101 U. S. 688; Smith v. Railroad Co., 99 U. S. 398. See Shufeldt v. Boehm, 96 Ill. 560. Generally speaking it should appear that judgment has been rendered, and execution issued and returned nulla bona. But it is enough to allege that the debtor is insolvent,

and an account is decreed to be taken, the court will, upon the
footing of such an account, proceed to make a final decree in
favor of the creditor without sending him back to law for the
recovery of his debt; for this is one of the cases in which a Court
of Equity, being once in rightful possession of a cause for a discovery and account, will proceed to a final decree upon all the
merits.[1] (a)   Upon a bill thus brought by a single creditor for
his own debt only, no general account of debts is usually directed
to be taken; but the common course is, to direct an account of
the personal estate and of that particular debt which is ordered
to be paid in the due course of administration.[2] (b)

---

[1] Attorney-Gen. v. Cornthwaite, 2 Cox, 44.   See McKay v. Green, 3 John.
Ch. R. 58; Thompson v. Brown, 4 John. R. 619, 630 to 643; Morrice v. Bank
of England, Cas. Temp. Talb. 220.

[2] Attorney-Gen. v. Cornthwaite, 2 Cox, R. 44; Morrice v. Bank of England, Cas. Temp. Talb. 217; Anon. 3 Atk. 572; Perry v. Phelips, 10 Ves. 38.
Although this is the usual course in the case of a creditor seeking an account
and payment of his own debt only, it is not therefore to be considered that

---

and that an execution would be of no
avail.   Case v. Beauregard, 101 U. S.
688, 690.   This is certainly true where
the creditor has a lien or a trust in
his favor. Ib.; Tappan v. Evans,
11 N. H. 311; Holt v. Bancroft, 30
Ala. 193.

When the property of a corporation has been divided among the stockholders before its debts are all paid,
a creditor may have a bill against an
individual stockholder to subject the
property which has fallen to him without making the rest of the stockholders parties.   Bartlett v. Drew, 57 N.Y.
587; Hatch v. Dana, 101 U. S. 205,
212; Ogilvie v. Knox Ins. Co., 22
How. 380; Montgomery R. Co. v.
Branch, 59 Ala. 139, 153; Huckabee
v. Smith, 53 Ala. 191.   See Pierce v.
Milwaukee Constr. Co., 38 Wis. 253.
And an individual stockholder who
has not paid up in full his subscription
may be proceeded against in the same
way.   Hatch v. Dana, supra, distinguishing Pollard v. Bailey, 20 Wall.
520; Terry v. Tubman, 92 U. S. 156;
Pierce v. Milwaukee Constr. Co., su-

pra; Marsh v. Burroughs, 1 Woods,
468; Wetherbee v. Baker, 35 N. J.
Eq. 501; Dalton R. Co. v. McDaniel,
56 Ga. 191.   It is not necessary that
there should have been calls to pay up
by the corporation.   Hatch v. Dana,
supra; Henry v. Railroad Co., 17 Ohio,
187.   As to the mode of proceeding to
enforce special individual liability of
stockholders, see Terry v. Little, 101
U. S. 216.

In ordinary cases the plaintiff should,
it seems, show that he has exhausted
his legal remedies against the corporation by judgment, execution, and return of nulla bona before seeking to
compel a stockholder to pay up his
subscription. Wetherbee v. Baker, 35
N. J. Eq. 501.

(a) Kennedy v. Cresswell, 101
U. S. 641, 646.

(b) Where the personalty is insufficient, permission will be given to sell
real estate.   Clark v. Hogle, 52 Ill.
427.   But see Eno v. Calder, 14 Rich.
Eq. 154.   See further Wadsworth v.
Davis, 63 N. Car. 251.

547. The more usual course however pursued in the case of creditors is for one or more creditors to file a bill (commonly called a creditor's bill) by and in behalf of him, or themselves, and all other creditors who shall come under the decree, for an account of the assets and a due settlement of the estate.[1] And this applies as well when the party suing is a creditor whose debt is payable in presenti, as when his debt is due in futuro, if it be 'debitum in presenti, solvendum in futuro,' [2] and whether he has a mortgage or not.[3] Bills of this sort have been allowed upon the mere principle that, as executors and administrators have vast powers of preference at law, Courts of Equity ought, upon the principle that equality is equity, to interpose upon the application of any creditor by such a bill to secure a distribution of the assets without preference to any one or more creditors.[4] And as a decree in equity is held of equal dignity and importance with a judgment at law, a decree upon a bill of this sort, being for the benefit of all creditors, makes them all creditors by decree upon an equality with creditors by judgment so as to exclude, from the time of such decree, all preferences in favor of the latter.[5]

548. The usual decree in the case of creditors' bills against the executor or administrator is (as it is commonly phrased) quod computet ; that is to say, it directs the master to take the accounts between the deceased and all his creditors, and to cause the creditors, upon due public notice, to come before him to prove their

---

the court itself is absolutely incompetent upon such a bill to make a more general decree in the form of a decree upon a general creditors' bill. On the contrary a case may be made out upon the answer and proofs, which might render it, if not indispensable, at least highly expedient for the purposes of justice, to adopt the latter course. See Ram on Assets, &c., ch. 24, § 2; Martin v. Martin, 1 Ves. 213, 214; Sheppard v. Kent, Prec. Ch. 190, 193 ; s. c. 2 Vern. 435; Anon. 3 Atk. 572; Perry v. Phelips, 10 Ves. 38, 40, 41 ; Rush v. Higgs, 4 Ves. 638; Thompson v. Brown, 4 John. Ch. R. 610, 630, 643, 646.

[1] See the case of The Creditors of Sir Charles Cox, 3 P. Will. 343.

[2] Whitmore v. Oxborn, 2 Younge & Coll. (N. R.) 13, 17.

[3] Greenwood v. Firth, 2 Hare, R. 241, note; Aldridge v. Westbrook, 5 Beav. R. 138; Shey v. Bennett, 2 Younge & Coll. (N. R.) 405; White v. Hillacre, 3 Younge & Coll. 597, 609, 610; Story, Eq. Pl. §§ 101, 158.

[4] Rush v. Higgs, 4 Ves. jr. 638, 643; Gilpin v. Lady Southampton, 18 Ves. 469; Martin v. Martin, 1 Ves. 210; Thompson v. Brown, 4 John. Ch. R. 619, 630, 643.

[5] Ibid.; Morrice v. Bank of England, Cas. T. Talb. 217; Perry v. Phelips, 10 Ves. 38, 39, 40; Brooks v. Reynolds, 1 Bro. Ch. R. 183; Paxton v. Douglas, 8 Ves. 520; Thompson v. Brown, 4 John. Ch. R. 619.

debts at a certain place and within a limited period; and it also directs the master to take an account of all the personal estate of the deceased in the hands of the executor or administrator, and the same to be applied in payment of the debts and other charges in a due course of administration.[1]　In all cases of this sort each creditor is entitled to appear before the master, and may there, if he chooses, contest the claim of any other creditor in the same manner as if it were an adversary suit.[2]

548 *a*. But although the usual decree is as above stated upon a bill by a creditor in behalf of himself and all other creditors, this decree is not applicable (as it seems) to cases where the executor or administrator admits assets; for he thereby admits himself liable for the payment of the debt, and in such a case the plaintiff may have a decree for the payment of his own debt only, without any decree for a general account; for the other creditors are not prejudiced by such a decree for the payment of the plaintiff's debt under such circumstances.[3]

[1] Van Heythuysen, Eq. Draft. Title, Decrees, p. 647; The Creditors of Sir Charles Cox, 3 P. Will. 343; Sheppard *v.* Kent, Prec. Ch. 190; s. c. 2 Vern. 435, Kenyon *v.* Worthington, 2 Dick. R. 668; Thompson *v.* Brown, 4 John. Ch. R. 619.

[2] Owens *v.* Dickenson, 1 Craig & Phill. 48, 56. See as to the form of a decree in an administration suit, in case all the parties interested should not be parties at the hearing, Fisk *v.* Norton, 2 Hare, R. 381.

[3] Woodgate *v.* Field, 2 Hare, R. 211, 212. Mr. Vice-Chancellor Wigram on that occasion said: 'The reason for and the principle of the usual form of decree are stated in Owens *v.* Dickenson (Cr. & Ph. 48), but that reasoning has no application where assets are admitted, for the executor thereby makes himself liable to the payment of the debt. In such a case the other creditors cannot be prejudiced by a decree for payment of the plaintiff's debt, and the object of the special form of the decree in a creditors' suit fails. I entertained no doubt upon this point, nor can I, upon inquiry, find that it was ever doubted in the other branches of the court. In effect the rule is proved by the fact that the creditor and defendant, the executor, may settle the matter pending the suit by the latter paying the debt and costs of the suit. And it has twice been decided at the Rolls, that the court will order the same thing to be done, even when the suit had proceeded to a considerable extent. If then the court would compel a creditor to accept payment of his debt when the executor offers to pay it, with the costs of suit, where is the line to be drawn beyond which the plaintiff cannot be allowed to have the exclusive benefit of his own suit? I am satisfied that in this case there ought to be a decree for immediate payment. It was objected however that in Sterndale *v.* Hankinson, Sir A. Hart said that on the filing of a creditors' bill every creditor has an inchoate right in the suit; the meaning of that expression is, that a right then commences which may indeed fail, but may also be perfected by decree, and it is not inaccurately called an inchoate right. After the decree every creditor has

549. As soon as the decree to account is made in such a suit brought in behalf of all the creditors, and not before, the executor or administrator is entitled to an injunction out of chancery to prevent any of the creditors from suing him at law or proceeding in any suits already commenced except under the direction and control of the Court of Equity where the decree is passed.[1] (a) The object of the court under such circumstances is to compel all the creditors to come in and prove their debts before the master, and to have the proper payments and discharges made under the authority of the court, so that the executor or administrator may not be harassed by multiplicity of suits, or a race of diligence be encouraged between different creditors each striving for an undue mastery and preference.[2] And this action of the court presupposes that all the legal rights of every creditor and the validity of his debt may be and indeed must be determined in equity upon the same principles as it would be at law.[3] But in order to pre-

an interest in the suit; but the question is whether the plaintiff, until decree, is not " dominus litis," so that he may deal with the suit as he pleases. There is nothing to prevent other creditors from filing bills for a like purpose; and there is nothing more common than for several suits to exist together, and the court permits them to go on together until a decree in one of them is obtained, because it is possible before the decree that the litigating creditor may stop his suit.'

[1] Morrice v. Bank of England, Cas. Temp. Talb. 217; Martin v. Martin, 1 Ves. 211, 212; Perry v. Phelips, 10 Ves. 38, 39; Brooks v. Reynolds, 1 Bro. Ch. R. 183, and Mr. Belt's note; Douglas v. Clay, 1 Dick. R. 393; Kenyon v. Worthington, 2 Dick. R. 668; Paxton v. Douglas, 8 Ves. 520; Jackson v. Leap, 1 Jac. & Walk. 231, and note; McKay v. Green, 3 John. Ch. 58; Burles v. Popplewell, 10 Sim. R. 383. See Underwood v. Hatton, 5 Beav. R. 31.

[2] Jeremy on Eq. Jurisd. B. 3, Pt. 2, ch. 5, pp. 538 to 543.

[3] Whitaker v. Wright, 2 Hare, R. 310. On this occasion Mr. Vice-Chancellor Wigram said: ' With respect to the form of a decree in a creditors' suit the court does not treat the decree as conclusive proof of the debt. It is clear that it is not so treated for all purposes, for any other creditor may challenge the debt, Owens v. Dickenson (1 Cr. & Ph. 48); and it is equally clear that in practice the executor himself is allowed to impeach it. If, in a case where the plaintiff sues on behalf of himself and all the other creditors, and the defendants, who represent the estate, do not admit assets (see Woodgate v. Field), it is objected at the hearing that the debt is not well proved, — the court tries the question only whether there is sufficient proof upon which to found a decree; and however clearly the debt may be proved in the cause, the decree decides nothing more than that the debt is sufficiently proved to entitle the plaintiff to go into the master's office; and a new case may be made in the master's office, and new evidence may be there tendered. The real question

(a) As to enjoining the executor from paying debts see Wadsworth v. Davis, 63 N. Car. 251.

vent any abuse of such bills by connivance between an executor
or administrator and a creditor, it is now a common practice to
grant an injunction only when the answer or affidavit of the executor or administrator states the amount of the assets, and upon
the terms of his bringing the assets into court or obeying such
other order of the court as the circumstances of the case may
require.[1] The same remedial justice is applied where the appli-

---

is, in what way the new case is to be tried, or what is the course to be pursued
in the master's office ? The plaintiff says that the course should be the same
as at law, and that he brings his legal rights with him into equity ; and, subject to some qualification, I cannot refuse my assent to the plaintiff's proposition. When a decree is made in a creditors' suit, under which all the creditors may come in, this court will not permit the estate to be embarrassed by
proceedings which might conflict with each other, to the prejudice of the executor or administrator, Perry v. Phelips (10 Ves. 34) ; but nothing would be
more unjust than that the court should restrain the creditor from proceeding
to enforce his rights at law, except upon the principle of allowing him to bring
his legal rights with him into the office of the court, which it substitutes for
the proceedings at law, Dornford v. Dornford (12 Ves. 127) ; Berrington v.
Evans (1 You. 276) ; and the circumstance that the creditor is also the plaintiff in the suit in equity makes no difference in that respect. The only qualifications which now occur to me of the general rule that a legal creditor brings
all his legal rights with him, are founded, first, upon the circumstance that in
certain special cases a Court of Equity in the ordinary course of administering
assets will distinguish a voluntary bond from one given for value, Lady Cox's
case (3 P. Wms. 339) ; Jones v. Powell (Eq. Cas. Abr. 84, pl. 2) ; Gilham v.
Locke (9 Ves. 612) ; Assignees of Gardiner v. Shannon (2 Sch & Lefr. 228) ;
and secondly, that in all cases this court requires an affidavit of the truth of
the debt from the creditor, which at law is not required. This affidavit is
required to extend to the consideration of a simple-contract debt, but not
to the consideration of bond or other specialty debts. The third qualification — if indeed there be any other than those which I have mentioned —
is that which is said to be introduced by the case of Rundell v. Lord Rivers
(Phillips, 88).'

[1] Gilpin v. Lady Southampton, 18 Ves. 469 ; Clarke v. Ormonde, Jac. Rep.
122, 123, 124, 125; Mitford, Eq. Pl. by Jeremy, p. 311. In Lee v. Park, 1
Keen, R. 714, 719 to 724, Lord Langdale (Master of the Rolls) went into an
elaborate examination of the doctrine on this subject, and refused to stay the
execution of a creditor who had obtained a judgment before the decree to
account in chancery. Although it is long, yet it gives so full an account of
the history, progress, and present state of the jurisdiction, that it seems
proper to be here given at large. 'It has been argued,' says he, 'that in
cases of this nature the court pays no regard to the question whether the
decree or judgment has priority in time, but considers only the quality of the
judgment, and that the judgment in this case being a judgment to recover de
bonis testatoris the executors are, as of course, entitled to restrain the judgment creditors from issuing execution. I do not accede to that argument.
The jurisdiction in these cases was first established upon questions which

cation, instead of being made by creditors, is made by legatees or trustees.[1]

arose between judgments at law and decrees in equity for payment of ascertained debts out of the assets. It was determined that such decrees and such judgments were in the administration of legal assets to be considered of equal value, and that the one which was prior in time (whether decree or judgment) should be first satisfied out of the assets. Morrice v. The Bank of England, Cas. Temp. Talb. 217; s. c. more fully, 3 Swanst. 575, and 2 Bro. P. C. 465, edit. Toml.; Martin v. Martin, 1 Ves. sen., 211. In the beginning a judgment obtained after a decree quod computet (not being a decree for payment of an ascertained sum out of the assets) was preferred. Ferrers v. Shirley, cited 10 Ves. 39. But subsequently Lord Thurlow put the jurisdiction on this, — that the court, having decreed an account of debts and assets, and ordered payment in a due course of administration, must be considered to have taken the fund into its own hands, and could not suffer its decree to be rendered nugatory by altering the course of administration, but ought to protect the executor in obeying its decrees. And he therefore granted injunctions to restrain proceedings at law after a decree quod computet. Kenyon v. Worthington, 2 Dick. 668. And as it was the practice in creditors' suits for the plaintiff, suing for himself and others, to prove his own debt prior to the hearing, there was perhaps not much difficulty in considering a decree for the administration of assets in such a suit, as in the nature of a judgment for all the creditors. But Lord Thurlow, acting on the principle to which he attributed the jurisdiction, gave the like authority to a decree quod computet which was obtained in a suit instituted by the trustees under a testator's will, and to which no creditor was a party; Brooks v. Reynolds, 1 Bro. C. C. 183. It was however contended that the creditor was not to be deprived of the benefit of a judgment which he had obtained prior to the decree; Goate v. Fryer, 2 Cox, 201; Largan v Bowen, 1 Sch. & Lefr. 296. In the case of Paxton v. Douglas (8 Ves. 520) the creditor had obtained an interlocutory judgment prior to the application for an injunction. What was the state of the proceeding at law at the date of the decree is not stated, and no question on the subject appears to have been raised. In some subsequent cases, where the decree had priority in point of time, a question was raised whether the executor by improper pleading, or by confessing judgment, did not lose his right to be protected by an injunction; and upon these cases it has been considered that if the executor so pleaded as to entitle the creditor, plaintiff at law, to a judgment to recover his demand de bonis propriis, this court could not restrain the execution; Brook v. Skinner, 2 Mer. 481, n.; Terrewest v. Featherby, 2 Mer. 480; Drewry v. Thacker, 3 Swanst. 529; Clarke v. Lord Ormonde, Jac. 108; Lord v. Wormleighton, Jac. 148. In the cases of Price v. Evans (4 Sim. 514), and Kent v. Pickering (5 Sim. 569), the vice-chancellor granted injunctions which only restrained the creditor from taking out execution against the assets of the intestate or testator. But it has been held that suffering judgment to go by default, or putting in pleas considered false, if done merely for the purpose of gaining time to apply to this court, did not deprive the executor of his right to protection. Dyer v. Kearsley, 2 Mer.

[1] Perry v. Phelips, 10 Ves. 38; Brooks v. Reynolds, 1 Bro. Ch. R. 183; Jackson v. Leap, 1 Jack. & Walker, 231, and note.

550. The considerations already mentioned apply to cases where the assets are purely of a legal nature, and no peculiar

482, n.; Fielden v. Fielden, 1 Sim. & Stu. 225.   In a useful work on the Law of Executors (Williams's Law of Executors, 1181) it has been observed that in the consideration of some of these cases some misconception seems to have prevailed respecting the effect of the executor's pleas and of the judgment against him; and considering what in the argument of this case has been called the quality of the judgment, it seems proper to notice that a judgment against an executor, whether by default or on demurrer, or upon verdict on any plea pleaded, except a general or special plene administravit, is conclusive upon him that he has assets to answer the demand; Leonard v. Simpson, 2 Bing. N. C. 176; Palmer v. Waller, 1 Mees. & Wel. 689.   If the action can only be supported against him in his character of executor, and he pleads any plea which admits that he has acted as such (except a release to himself), the judgment against him is that the plaintiff do recover the debt and costs to be levied out of the assets of the testator, if the defendant have so much; but if not, then the costs out of the defendant's own goods.   Such is the form of the judgment where the defendant has pleaded non est factum testatoris, non assumpsit, or release to the testator, although all of these pleas are held to admit assets.   But upon a subsequent deficiency of assets the executor has to pay out of his own goods, because in law the judgment is held to be a proof that he had assets to satisfy it.   Upon the sheriff's return of nulla bona the plaintiff may issue a scire facias, or bring an action of debt on the judgment, suggesting a devastavit.   In the proceedings on the scire facias the plaintiff has not to prove that the executor has property of the testator in his hands, and in the action the executor cannot plead plene administravit, but only deny the devastavit, and of that the judgment against him and the sheriff's return of nulla bona are evidence; and in this action the creditor obtains judgment to recover his demand de bonis propriis.   The case of Drewry v. Thacker (3 Swanst. 529) is, as far as I am aware, the only case in which the executor has been in any degree protected against execution upon a judgment obtained prior to the decree.   The administratrix in that case had given cognovits to Stanley and Lucas, two bond creditors, with stay of execution if payment was made by instalments at certain times.   After default had been made a decree for administration was obtained, and after the plaintiff at law had notice of the decree the sheriff took the intestate's goods in the hands of the administratrix in execution.   The vice-chancellor, Sir John Leach, ordered the sheriff to restore the goods on payment of costs; and further that if upon the administration of the estate by the court there should be a deficiency of assets to pay Stanley and Lucas in full, they were to be at liberty to proceed at law against the administratrix, as if the sheriff had returned nulla bona præter the sum received by Stanley and Lucas upon the administration of the assets in this case, she by her counsel undertaking not to dispute the suggestion of such return in the writ at law.   Now Lord Eldon very recently, before the date of this order, in the case of Terrewest v. Featherby had observed that " the creditor's judgment would be of no service to him if he were delayed here until it could be ascertained whether there were assets of the testator to answer his demand, which might not be till after all chance of recovering against the executor de bonis propriis was entirely gone."   The order of the vice-chancellor in Drewry v. Thacker did however so delay the

circumstances require the interposition of Courts of Equity except those appertaining to the necessity of taking an account,
and having a discovery and decreeing a final settlement of the
estate.   But in a great variety of cases the jurisdiction of Courts
of Equity becomes indispensable from the fact that no other
courts possess any adequate jurisdiction to reach the entire
merits or dispose of the entire merits.   This must necessarily be
the case where there are equitable assets as well as legal assets,
and also where the assets are required to be marshalled in order
to a full and perfect administration of the estate and to prevent any creditor, legatee, or distributee from being deprived of
his own proper benefit by reason of any prior claims which obstruct it.

551. And first in relation to equitable assets.   That portion
only of the assets of the deceased party is deemed legal assets
which by law is directly liable, in the hands of his executor or
administrator, to the payment of debts and legacies.[1]   It is not
within the design of these Commentaries to enter into a minute
examination of what are deemed legal assets.   But generally
speaking they are such as can be reached in the hands of an

creditor; and on a motion before Lord Eldon to discharge the order, he seems
to have found considerable difficulty in dealing with it.   He clearly considered
that if the administratrix was liable at law she was liable to a greater extent
than she was left by the vice-chancellor's order; and that there had been no
instance where the proceedings at law had been restrained after judgment de
bonis testatoris, and si non de bonis propriis of an executor, and execution
issued on a decree subsequently obtained for an administration of the assets;
and he said that his memory furnished him with the recollection of no case
in which the court had interposed, as in the vice-chancellor's order, namely,
by restraining the proceedings at law for a time, but considering those proceedings effectual for some purposes, to be carried into execution at a future
time when the fruits to be collected from them had been ascertained by the
result of certain proceedings in equity.   In the result he made no order upon
the motion before him; so that the order of the vice-chancellor was in effect
left undisturbed, but under circumstances which prevent it from being regarded as an authority.   In the subsequent case of Clarke v. Lord Ormonde
(Jac. 108), in which the point was not raised, Lord Eldon is reported to have
said that even if a creditor has got a judgment before a decree, though he
may come in and prove as such, he must not take out execution; and in reference to the conduct of the parties and perhaps to the nature of the claim there
may be such cases, but such is not the ordinary rule.'

[1] 1 Madd. Ch. Pr. 473; Ram on Assets, ch. 8, p. 143; Id. ch. 27, p. 317;
3 Wooddeson, Lect. 59, pp. 482 to 488.   See in the English Law Mag. for
Feb. 1844, p. 27, a dissertation on what constitutes the true distinction and
test between legal and equitable assets.

executor or administrator by a suit at law against him, either by a common judgment or by a judgment upon a devastavit against him personally.[1] But it is perhaps more accurate to say that legal assets are such as come into the hands and power of an executor or administrator, or such as he is entrusted with by law, virtute officii, to dispose of in the course of administration.[2] In other words whatever an executor or administrator takes qua executor or administrator, or in respect to his office, is to be considered as legal assets.[3]

552. Equitable assets are on the other hand all assets which are chargeable with the payment of debts or legacies in equity, and which do not fall under the description of legal assets. They are called equitable assets because, in obtaining payment out of them, they can be reached only by the aid and instrumentality of a Court of Equity.[4] They are also called equitable for another reason ; and that is, that the rules of distribution by which they are governed are different from those of the distribution of legal assets. In general it may be said that equitable assets are of two kinds : the first is where assets are created such by the intent of the party ; the second is where they result from the nature of the

---

[1] See Farres v. Newnham, 4 T. Rep. 621; Whale v. Booth, 4 T. Rep. 625, note; s. c. 4 Doug. R. 36. In some cases it is necessary to go into a Court of Equity to enforce payment out of what are properly legal assets. Thus for instance if there should be a lease for years, or a bond debt, or an annuity in a trustee's name, belonging to the deceased, there, although a creditor could not come at it without the aid of a Court of Equity, yet the assets would be treated as legal assets, and should be applied in the course of administration as such. Wilson v. Fielding, 2 Vern. R. 763; The case of Sir Charles Cox's Creditors, 2 P. Will. 342, 343; 2 Fonbl. Eq. B. 4, Pt. 2, ch. 2, § 1, note (*f*). So a term of years taken in the name of A, in trust for B, is legal assets, although recoverable in equity only. Ibid.; 3 P. Will. 342, 343, and Mr. Cox's note (2) ; Hartwell v. Chitters, Ambler, R. 308, and Mr. Blunt's note. By the statute of 29 Charles II., ch. 3, the trusts of an inheritance in land are liable for the payment of bond debts, which makes such trust estates legal assets, although they can be enforced only in equity. See 2 Freeman, Rep. 150, C. 130; 2 Fonbl. Eq. B. 4, Pt. 2, ch. 2, § 1, note (*f*); Moses v. Murgatroyd, 1 John. Ch. R. 119, 130.

[2] 2 Fonbl. Eq. B. 4, Pt. 2, ch. 2, § 1; Bac. Abridg. Executors and Administrators, H.; 3 Wooddes. Lect. 59, pp. 484 to 488.

[3] 2 Fonbl. Eq. B. 4, Pt. 2, ch. 2, § 1, and note (*e*); Deg v. Deg, 2 P. Will. 416, and Mr. Cox's note.

[4] 2 Fonbl. Eq. B. 4, Pt. 2, ch. 2, § 1, and notes (*e*), (*f*), (*g*); Wilson v. Fielding, 2 Vern. 763; Gott v. Atkinson, Willes, R. 523, 524; 1 Madd. Ch. Pr. 473; Ram on Assets, ch. 27, p. 317; 3 Wooddes. Lect. 59, pp. 486, 487.

estate made chargeable. Thus for instance if a testator devises land to trustees to sell for the payment of debts, the assets resulting from the execution of the trust are equitable assets upon the plain intent of the testator, notwithstanding the trustees are also made his executors; for by directing the sale to be for the payment of debts generally, he excludes all preferences, and the property would not otherwise be liable to the payment of simple contract debts.[1] The same principle applies if the testator merely charges his lands with the payment of his debts.[2] On the other hand if the estate be of an equitable nature and be chargeable with debts, the fund is to be deemed equitable assets, unless by some statute it is expressly made legal assets; for it cannot be reached except through the instrumentality of a Court of Equity.[3] And it may be laid down as a general principle that everything is considered as equitable assets which the debtor has made subject to his debts generally, and which without his act would not have been subject to the payment of his debts generally.[4]

552 a. Wherever real estate is by statute made liable for the payment of the debts of the deceased, there it constitutes legal assets.[5] But notwithstanding such provision, if the testator should by his will charge his real estate with his debt, there the real estate so charged would be equitable assets.[6] (a)

[1] Lewin v. Oakley, 2 Atk. 50; Newton v. Bennet, 1 Bro. Ch. R. 135; Silk v. Prime, 1 Bro. Ch. R. 138, note; Bailey v. Ekins, 7 Ves. 319; Shiphard v. Lutwidge, 8 Ves. 26, 30; Benson v. Leroy, 4 John. Ch. R. 651; Clay v. Willis, 1 B. & Cressw. 364; Barker v. May, 9 B. & Cressw. 489.

[2] Ibid.

[3] 2 Fonbl. Eq. B. 4, Pt. 2, ch. 2, § 1, note (g).

[4] 2 Fonbl. Eq. B. 4, Pt. 2, ch. 2, § 1, note (e); Ram on Assets, ch. 17, p. 317. In Silk v. Prime, 1 Bro. Ch. R. 138, note, Lord Camden took notice of the early cases, which had decided that where land is devised to be sold by executors qua executors, or devised to executors qua executors, to be sold for payment of debts, the assets were purely legal (Co. Litt. 112 b, 113 a); and he added: 'I can hardly now suggest a case where the assets would be legal, but where the executor has a naked power to sell qua executor.' See also Girling v. Lee, 1 Vern. R. 63, and Raithby's notes. It is questionable whether even in this latter case the assets would now be held to be legal. See Barker v. May, 9 B. & Cressw. 489, 493; Paschall v. Ketterich, Dyer, R. 151 b; Anon. Dyer, R. 264 b; Bac. Abridg. Legacy, M.; 2 Fonbl. Eq. B. 4, Pt. 2, ch. 2, § 1, note (e); Deg v. Deg, 2 P. Will. 416, Cox's note.

[5] Goodchild v. Ferrett, 5 Beav. R. 398.

[6] Charlton v. Wright, 12 Simons, R. 274.

(a) In Attorney-Gen. v. Brunning, 8 H. L. Cas. 243, 258, Lord Cranworth declared that nothing which an administrator is entitled to receive as

553. In the course of the administration of assets Courts of Equity follow the same rules in regard to legal assets which are adopted by Courts of Law, and give the same priority to the different classes of creditors which is enjoyed at law, thus maintaining a practical exposition of the maxim, 'æquitas sequitur legem.'[1] In the like manner Courts of Equity recognize and enforce all antecedent liens, claims, and charges, in rem, existing upon the property, according to their priorities, whether these charges are of a legal or of an equitable nature, and whether the assets are legal or equitable.[2]

554. But in regard to equitable assets (subject to the exception already stated) Courts of Equity, in the actual administration of them, adopt very different rules from those adopted in Courts of Law in the administration of legal assets. Thus in equity it is a general rule that equitable assets shall be distributed equally and pari passu among all the creditors without any reference to the priority or dignity of the debts; for Courts of Equity regard all debts in conscience as equal jure naturali and equally entitled to be paid; and here they follow their own favorite maxim that equality is equity: 'Æquitas est quasi æqualitas.'[3] And if the fund falls short, all the creditors are required to abate in proportion.[4] (a)

[1] See 2 Fonbl. Eq. B. 4, Pt. 2, ch. 2, §§ 1, 2; Wride v. Clarke, 1 Dick. R. 382 ; Morrice v. Bank of England, Cas. Temp. Talb. 220, 221.

[2] Freemoult v. Dedire, 1 P. Will. 429; Finch v. Earl of Winchelsea, 1 P. Will. 277, 278; Burgh v. Francis, 1 Eq. Abridg. 320, Pl. 1; Girling v. Lee, 1 Vern. 63, and Raithby's notes; Plunkett v. Penson, 2 Atk. 290; Pope v. Gwinn, 8 Ves. 28, note; Morgan v. Sherrard, 1 Vern. 273; Cole v. Warden, 1 Vern. 410, and note; Wilson v. Fielding, 2 Vern. 763, 764; Foly's Case, 2 Freem. R. 49; Wride v. Clarke, 1 Dick. R. 382; Sharpe v. Earl of Scarborough, 4 Ves. 538.

[3] Co. Litt. 24; Hixam v. Witham, 1 Cas. Ch. 248; Gott v. Atkinson, Willes, R. 521; Turner v. Turner, 1 Jac. & Walk. 45; Creditors of Sir Charles Cox, 3 P. Will. 343, 344; Deg v. Deg. 2 P. Will. 412, 416; Wride v. Clarke, 1 Dick. 382; Morrice v. Bank of England, Cas. Temp. Talb. 220; Wilson v. Paul, 8 Sim. R. 63.

[4] Hixam v. Witham, 1 Freem. R. 301; s. c. 1 Ch. Cas. 248; Deg v. Deg,

such can be equitable assets ; and he said that in considering whether assets were legal or equitable the question was not whether the estate was recoverable at law or in equity, but whether it was money which the personal representative was entitled to recover re-

gardless of any directions by the testator.

(a) Including the executor as a creditor. Bain v. Sadler, L. R. 12 Eq. 570. Nor is the rule as to equitable assets affected by the law of place. Pardo v. Bingham, L. R. 6 Eq. 485.

555. It frequently happens also that lands and other property not strictly legal assets are charged not only with the payment of debts but also with the payment of legacies. In that case all the legatees take pari passu ; and if the equitable assets (after payment of the debts) are not sufficient to pay all the legacies, the legatees are all required to abate in proportion, unless some priority is specially given by the testator to particular legatees ; for prima facie the testator must be presumed to intend that all his legacies shall be equally paid.[1] But suppose the case to be that the equitable assets are sufficient to pay all the debts, but after such payment not sufficient to pay any of the legacies, and the property is charged with the payment of both debts and legacies ; in such a conflict of rights the question must arise whether the creditors and legatees are to share in proportion pari passu, or the creditors are to enjoy a priority of satisfaction out of the equitable assets. This was formerly a matter of no inconsiderable doubt ; and it was contended, with much apparent strength of reasoning, that as both creditors and legatees in such a case take out of the fund by the bounty of the testator, and not of strict right, they ought to share in proportion pari passu. After some struggle in the Courts of Equity upon this point,[2] it is at length settled, that although as between themselves in regard to equitable assets the creditors are all equal, and are to share in proportion pari passu, yet as between them and legatees the creditors are entitled to a priority and preference, and that legatees are to take nothing until the debts are all paid.

2 P. Will. 412; Wride v. Clarke, 1 Dick. 382; Foly's Case, 2 Freem. 49; Woolstonecroft v. Long, 2 Freem. R. 175; s. c. 2 Eq. Abridg. 459; 1 Cas. Ch. 32; 3 Ch. Rep. 12. The civil law, like the common law, had different classes of debts to which it annexed different privileges or priorities, founded indeed upon principles more general and more sound than those of the common law in its classification. There were in the civil law three orders of creditors: (1) Those who go before all others and take priority among themselves, according to the distinctions of their privileges. (2) Those who have mortgages, and rank after the privileged creditors according to the dates of their respective mortgages. (3) Those who are creditors by bonds, or others, who have only personal actions (the two first have liens or privileges in rem), and who come in therefore together, and share equally in proportion to their debts. 1 Domat, B. 3, tit. 1, § 5, and especially art. 34.

[1] Brown v. Brown, 1 Keen, R. 275.

[2] See Anon. 2 Vern. 133; Hixam v. Witham, 1 Cas. Ch. 248; s. c. 1 Freem. R. 305; Walker v. Meagher, 2 P. Will. 550.

556. The ground of this decision is that it is the duty of every man to be just before he is generous; and no one can well doubt the moral obligation of every man to provide for the payment of all his debts. The presumption therefore, in the absence of all other words showing a different intent (which intent would in such a case still prevail), is, that a testator means to provide first for the discharge of his moral duties, and next for the objects of his bounty, and not to confound the one with the other. For otherwise the testator would in truth and in foro conscientiæ be disposing of another's debt, and not making gifts ultra æs alienum.[1] The good sense of this latter reasoning can scarcely escape observation. It proceeds upon the just and benignant interpretation of the intention of the party to fulfil his moral obligations in the just order which natural law would assign to them.

557. In cases where the assets are partly legal and partly equitable, Courts of Equity will not interfere to take away the legal preference of any creditors to the legal assets. But if any creditor has been partly paid out of the legal assets by insisting on his preference, and he seeks satisfaction of the residue of his debt out of the equitable assets, he will be postponed till all the other creditors not possessing such a preference have received out of such equitable assets an equal proportion of their respective debts.[2] (a) This doctrine is founded upon and flows from that which we have been already considering, that in natural justice and conscience all debts are equal, that the debtor himself is equally bound to satisfy them all,[3] and that equality is equity. When therefore a Court of Equity is called upon to assist a creditor, it has a right to insist, before relief is granted, that he who seeks equity shall do equity; that he shall not make

---

[1] Hixam v. Witham, 1 Cas. Ch. 258; s. c. 1 Freem. R. 305; Walker v. Meager, 2 P. Will. 551, 552; s. c. Moseley, R. 204; Petre v. Bruen, cited ibid.; Greaves v. Powell, 2 Vern. R. 248, and Mr. Raithby's note (2); 1 Eq. Abridg. 141, Pl. 3; Kidney v. Cousmaker, 12 Ves. 154.

[2] Sheppard v. Kent, 2 Vern. R. 435; Deg v. Deg, 3 P. Will. 417; Haslewood v. Pope, 3 P. Will. 323; Morrice v. Bank of England, Cas. Temp. Talb. 220; 2 Fonbl. Eq. B. 4, Pt. 2, ch. 2, § 1.

[3] Morrice v. Bank of England, Cas. Temp. Talb. 219, 220, 221; 2 Fonbl. Eq. B. 4, Pt. 2, ch. 2, § 1.

(a) Bain v. Sadler, L. R. 12 Eq. 570.

use of the law in his own favor to exclude equity, and at the same time insist that equity shall aid the defects of the law to the injury of equally meritorious claimants. The usual decree in cases of this sort is, that ‘If any of the creditors by specialty have exhausted (or shall exhaust) any part of the testator's personal estate in satisfaction of their debts, then they are not to come upon or receive any further satisfaction out of the testator's real estate (or other equitable assets) until the other creditors shall thereout be made up equal with them.'[1] This is sometimes called marshalling the assets.[2] But that appellation more appropriately belongs (as we shall immediately see) to another mode of equitable interference. The present is rather an exercise of equitable jurisdiction in refusing relief, unless upon the terms of doing equity.

558. In the next place, as to marshalling assets (strictly so called) in the course of administration.[3] In the sense of lexicographers, to marshal is to arrange or rank in order; and in this sense the marshalling of assets would be to arrange or rank assets in the due order of administration. This primary sense of the language has been transferred into the vocabulary of Courts of Equity, and has there received a somewhat peculiar and technical sense, although still german to its original signification. In the sense of Courts of Equity the marshalling of assets is such an arrangement of the different funds under administration as shall enable all the parties having equities thereon to receive their due proportions, notwithstanding any intervening interests, liens, or other claims of particular persons to prior satisfaction out of a portion of these funds.[4] Thus where there exist two or more funds, and there are several claimants against them, and at law one of the parties may resort to either fund for satisfaction, but the others can come upon one only, there Courts of Equity exercise the authority to marshal (as it is called) the funds, and by this means enable the parties whose remedy at law is confined to one fund only to receive due satisfaction.[5] The general

---

[1] Plunket v. Penson, 2 Atk. 294; Wride v. Clarke, 1 Dick. R. 382.

[2] See Aldrich v. Cooper, 8 Ves. 388, 394.

[3] Aldrich v. Cooper, 8 Ves. 388, 394; post, §§ 633 to 643.

[4] See 3 Wooddes. Lect. 59, p. 488, 489; post, §§ 633 to 642.

[5] 1 Madd. Ch. Pr. 499; Ram on Assets, ch. 28, § 1, p. 329; Aldrich v. Cooper, 8 Ves. 388, 398; Lanoy v. Duke of Athol, 2 Atk. 446; Attorney-Gen.

principle upon which Courts of Equity interfere in these cases is, that without such interference he who has a title to the double fund would possess an unreasonable power of defeating the claimants upon either fund by taking his satisfaction out of the other, to the exclusion of them. So that in fact it would be entirely in his election whether they should receive any satisfaction or not. Now Courts of Equity treat such an exercise of power as wholly unjust and unconscientious, and therefore will interfere, not indeed to modify or absolutely to destroy the power, but to prevent it from being made an instrument of caprice, injustice, or imposition. Equity in affording redress in such cases does little more than apply the maxim: 'Nemo ex alterius detrimento fieri debet locupletior.' [1]

559. And this principle is by no means confined to the administration of assets, but it is applied to a vast variety of other cases (as we shall hereafter see) ; as for instance to cases of two mortgages, where one covers two estates and the other but one, to cases of extents by the Crown, and indeed to cases of double securities generally.[2] It may be laid down as the general rule of the Courts of Equity in cases of this sort, that if a creditor has two funds, he shall take his satisfaction (if he may) out of that fund upon which another creditor has no lien ; and the like rule is applied to other persons standing in a similar predicament.[3]

560. But although the rule is so general, yet it is not to be understood without some qualifications. It is never applied except where it can be done without injustice to the creditor or

v. Tyndall, Ambl. R. 614; 2 Fonbl. Eq. B. 3, ch. 2, § 6; Selby v. Selby, 4 Russ. R. 336, 341. See the Reporter's Note to Phillips v. Parker, 1 Tamlyn, R. 136, 143.

[1] 2 Fonbl. Eq. B. 3, ch. 2, § 6, and note (i). See Mills v. Eden, 10 Mod. 499; ante, §§ 327, 499; post, §§ 633 to 642.

[2] 1 Madd. Ch. Pr. 202, 203; Lanoy v. Duke of Athol, 2 Atk. 446; Aldrich v. Cooper, 8 Ves. 382, 388; Kempe v. Antill, 2 Bro. Ch. R. 11; Wright v. Simpson, 6 Ves. 714; 2 Fonbl. Eq. B. 3, ch. 2, § 6; ante, §§ 327, 499; post, §§ 633, 638, 642.

[3] Lanoy v. Athol, 2 Atk. 446; Colchester v. Stamford, 2 Freem. R. 124; Lacam v. Mertins, 1 Ves. 312; Ex parte Kendall, 17 Ves. 514, 520; Aldrich v. Cooper, 8 Ves. 388, 395; Trimmer v. Bayne, 9 Ves. 210, 211; Rumbold v. Rumbold, 3 Ves. 64; Dorr v. Shaw, 4 John. Ch. R. 17; Cheeseborough v. Millard, 1 John. Ch. R. 412; Greenwood v. Taylor, 1 Russell & Mylne, 185; Gwynne v. Edwards, 2 Russ. R. 289, n.; Bute v. Cunninghame, 2 Russ. R. 275; Boazma v. Johnston, 3 Sim. R. 377; ante, §§ 327, 499; post, §§ 633, 638, 642.

other party in interest having a title to the double fund, (a) and also without injustice to the common debtor.[1] (b)   Nor is it applied in favor of persons who are not common creditors of the same common debtor, except upon some special equity.   Thus a creditor of A has no right, unless some peculiar equity intervenes, to insist that a creditor of A and B shall proceed against B's estate alone for the satisfaction of this debt, so that he may thereby receive a greater dividend from A's estate.[2]   So where a creditor is a creditor upon two estates for the same debt, he will be entitled to receive dividends to the full amount from both estates, until he has been fully satisfied for his debt; for his title in such a case is not to be made to yield in favor of either estate, or the creditors of either, to his own prejudice.[3]   It has indeed been said by Lord Hardwicke that Courts of Equity have no right to marshal the assets of a person who is alive, but only the real and personal assets of a person deceased; for the assets are not subject to the jurisdiction of equity until his death.[4]   But this language is to be understood with reference to the case in which it was spoken; for there is no doubt that there may be a marshalling of the real and personal assets of living persons under particular circumstances where peculiar equities attach upon the one or the other, although such cases are very rare.[5]

561. The rule of Courts of Equity in marshalling assets in the course of administration is, that every claimant upon the assets of a deceased person shall be satisfied, as far as such assets can, by any arrangement consistent with the nature of their respective claims, be applied in satisfaction thereof.[6]   The rule must

[1] See Earl of Clarendon v. Barham, 1 Younge & Coll. N. R. 688, 709.

[2] Ex parte Kendall, 17 Ves. 514, 520; post, §§ 642 to 645.

[3] Bense v. Cox, 6 Beav. R. 84.

[4] Lacam v. Mertins, 1 Ves 312.

[5] See Ex parte Kendall, 17 Ves. 514; Aldrich v. Cooper, 8 Ves. 388, 389, 394; Dorr v. Shaw, 4 John. Ch. R. 17; Sneed v. Lord Culpepper, 2 Eq. Abridg. 255, 260.

[6] See Clifton v. Burt, 1 P. Will. 679. Mr. Cox's valuable note (1), from which I have freely drawn; 2 Fonbl. Eq. B. 3, ch. 2, § 6; post, § 633, note.

(a) See post, § 633, note; Van Meter v. Ely, 1 Beasl. 271; Kidder v. Page, 48 N. H. 380; Emmons v. Bradley, 56 Maine, 333; Dodds v. Snyder, 44 Ill. 53.

(b) See Marr v. Lewis, 31 Ark.

203. But it seems that the debtor himself cannot ask for marshalling to save an estate, e. g. his homestead, mortgaged. White v. Polleys, 20 Wis. 503. See post, §§ 633, 640, notes.

necessarily, in its application to the actual circumstances of different cases, admit, nay must require, very different modifications of relief. It may be illustrated by the suggestion of a few cases which present its application in a clear view and show the limitations belonging to it.

562. In the first place if a specialty creditor whose debt is a lien on the real estate receive satisfaction out of the personal assets of the deceased, a simple contract creditor (who has no claim except upon those personal assets) shall in equity stand in the place of the specialty creditor against the real assets, so far as the latter shall have exhausted the personal assets in payment of his debts, and no farther.[1] But the court will not in cases of this sort extend the relief to creditors further than the nature of the contract will justify it. Therefore it must be a specialty creditor of the person whose assets are in question ; such a one as might have a remedy against both the real and personal estate of the deceased debtor or against either of them. For it is not every specialty creditor in whose place the simple contract creditors can come to affect the real assets. If the specialty creditor himself cannot affect the real estate, as if the heirs are not bound by the specialty, or if there is no personal covenant binding the party to pay, or if the creditors are not creditors of the same person and have not any demand against both funds as being the property of the same person, — in these and the like cases there is no ground for the interposition of Courts of Equity.[2]

563. On the other hand if a specialty creditor having a right to resort to two funds has not as yet received satisfaction out of either, a Court of Equity will interfere, and either throw him, for satisfaction, upon the fund which can be affected by him only to the intent that the other fund shall be clear for him who can have access to the latter only,[3] (a) or it will put the creditor to

---

[1] Anon. 2 Ch. Cas. 4; Sagittary v. Hyde, 1 Vern. 455; Neave v. Alderton, 1 Eq. Abridg. 144; Galton v. Hancock, 2 Atk. 436; Clifton v. Burt, 1 P. Will. 679, Cox's note (1); Cheeseborough v. Millard, 1 John. Ch. R. 413.

[2] Lacam v. Mertins, 1 Ves. 312, 313; Aldrich v. Cooper, 8 Ves. 388, 389, 390, 394 ; Ex parte Kendall, 17 Ves. 520.

[3] Sagittary v. Hyde, 1 Vern. 455; Lanoy v. Duke of Athol, 2 Atk. 446; Pollexfen v. Moore, 3 Atk. 272; Attorney-Gen. v. Tyndall, Ambler, R. 615. See Sproule v. Pryor, 8 Sim. 189.

(a) See post, § 633, and notes, from which it will appear that there are doubts of the soundness of this position as applied to the case of a credi-

his election between the one fund and the other. And if the creditor resorts to the fund upon which alone the other party has any security, it will decree satisfaction pro tanto to the latter out of the other fund.[1] The usual decree in such cases is, that ' In case any of the specialty creditors shall exhaust any part of the personal estate, then the simple contract creditors are to stand in their place and receive a satisfaction pro tanto out of' the real assets.[2]

564. The same principle applies to the case of a mortgagee who exhausts the personal estate in the payment of his debt. In such a case the simple contract creditors will be allowed to stand in the place of the mortgagee in regard to the real estate bound by the mortgage.[3] And where the personal assets have been so applied in discharge of a mortgage, the simple contract creditors may, in furtherance of the same principle, compel the heir to refund so much of the personal assets as have been applied to pay off the mortgage.[4]

564 a. It was formerly doubted whether the same principle applied to the case of a vendor of an estate whose unpaid purchase money was, after the death of the purchaser, paid out of his personal estate. But it is now settled that, in such a case, the simple contract creditors of the purchaser shall stand in the place of the vendor, with respect to his lien on the estate so sold, against the devisee as well as against the heir of the same estate. For the established rule being that simple contract creditors are, as against a devisee, to stand in the place of specialty creditors who have exhausted the personal assets, because the specialty creditor had the two funds of real and personal estate to resort to ; by analogy, the simple contract creditors ought to be entitled

[1] Aldrich v. Cooper, 8 Ves. 389, 394, 395; Trimmer v. Bayne, 9 Ves. 210, 211.

[2] Westfaling v. Westfaling, 3 Atk. 467; Davies v. Topp, 1 Bro. Ch. R. 526; ante, § 557.

[3] Aldrich v. Cooper, 8 Ves. 388, 395, 396; Lutkins v. Leigh, Cas. Temp. Talb. 53; Wilson v. Fielding, 2 Vern. 763; Selby v. Selby, 4 Russ. 336, 341.

[4] Wilson v. Fielding, 2 Vern. 763.

tor having two securities of varying availability. If the only remedy of the first of two mortgagees e. g. is foreclosure in equity, the only course for the second mortgagee perhaps is to redeem the first mortgage and so take the position of the prior incumbrancer. But if the first mortgagee has a power of sale, and a sale of the security not mortgaged to the other incumbrancer will suffice in all respects, then the doctrine of the text will be applied. See Warren v. Warren, 30 Vt. 530; Lloyd v. Galbraith, 32 Penn. St. 103.

to stand in the place of the vendor against the devisees, because the vendor has equally a charge upon the double fund of real and personal estate. Indeed if the charge or lien of the vendor is to be considered in the same manner as if it were secured by mortgage, or in the nature of a mortgage (as it well may be), the principle above stated would clearly apply in favor of the simple contract creditors.[1]

565. In general, legatees are entitled to the same equities where the personal estate is exhausted by specialty creditors, (a) for they would otherwise be without any means of receiving the bounty of the testator.[2] They are therefore permitted to stand in the place of the specialty creditors against the real assets descended to the heir.[3] So they are permitted in like manner to stand in the place of a mortgagee who has exhausted the personal estate in paying his mortgage.[4] And their equity will prevail, not only in cases where the mortgaged premises have descended to the heir at law, but also where they have been devised to a devisee who is to take subject to the mortgage.[5] But their equity will not generally prevail against a devisee of the real estate not mortgaged, whether he be a specific or a residuary devisee, for he also takes by the bounty of the testator; and between persons equally taking by the bounty of the testator

---

[1] Selby v. Selby, 4 Russ. R. 336, 340, 341; Trimmer v. Bayne, 9 Ves. 209. But see Pollexfen v. Moore, 3 Atk. 272, which is said in Sproule v. Pryor, 8 Sim. R. 189, to be overruled. The same rule is now applied in favor of legatees. Sproule v. Pryor, 8 Sim. R. 189. (b)

[2] Arnold v. Chapman, 1 Ves. 110; Mogg v. Hodges, 2 Ves. 51; Aldrich v. Cooper, 8 Ves. 396; Lomas v. Wright, 2 Mylne & Keen, 769, 775.

[3] Herne v. Meyrick, 1 P. Will. 201, 202; Culpepper v. Aston, 2 Ch. Cas. 117; Bowaman v. Reeve, Prec. Ch. 578; Tipping v. Tipping, 1 P. Will. 729, 730; Clifton v. Burt, 1 P. Will. 679, Cox's note; Fenhoulhet v. Passavant, 1 Dick. R. 253; Pollexfen v. Moore, 3 Atk. 272; Wythe v. Henniker, 2 Mylne & Keen, 645, 646; Selby v. Selby, 4 Russ. 336, 341; Lomas v. Wright, 2 Mylne & Keen, 769.

[4] Lutkins v. Leigh, Cas. Temp. Talb. 53; Forrester v. Leigh, Ambl. R. 171; Selby v. Selby, 4 Russ. R. 336, 341; Sproule v. Pryor, 8 Sim. R. 189.

[5] Lutkins v. Leigh, Cas. Temp. Talb. 53, 54; Forrester v. Leigh, Ambl. R. 171; Norris v. Norris, 2 Dick. R. 542; Wythe v. Henniker, 2 Mylne & Keen, 644; Selby v. Selby, 4 Russ. 336, 340, 341.

(a) Rice v. Harbeson, 63 N. Y. 493.

(b) Lilford v. Powys-Keck, L. R. 1 Eq. 347. It was there held that a pecuniary legatee could stand in the place of the vendor, with a lien for unpaid purchase-money, where realty contracted for by the testator had been paid for out of assets.

equity will not interfere, unless the testator has clearly shown
some ground of preference or priority of the one over the
other.[1] (a) So that there is a distinction between the case
where the estate is devised and there are specialty creditors, and
the case where it is devised and there is a mortgage on it. In
the latter case the legatees stand in the place of the mortgagee
if he exhausts the personal assets; in the former case they do
not stand in the place of the specialty creditors. The reason
assigned is that a specialty debt is no lien on land in the hands
of the obligor, or his heir or devisee. But a mortgage is a lien,
and an estate in the land. By a devise of land mortgaged
nothing passes but the equity of redemption, if it is a mortgage
in fee; if it is for years, the reversion and equity of redemption
pass.[2]

[1] Clifton v. Burt, 1 P. Will. 679, 680, and Cox's note; Haslewood v. Pope,
3 P. Will. 322, 324; Scott v. Scott, Ambl. R. 383; s. c. 1 Eden, R. 458; Forrester v. Leigh, Ambler, 171; Aldrich v. Cooper, 8 Ves. 396, 397. Such preference or priority may be shown in various ways. Thus if real estate is devised
for or subject to the payment of debts, if the personal estate is exhausted in
payment of debts, the legatees will stand in the place of creditors on the real
assets. 2 Fonbl. Eq. B. 3, ch. 2, § 7, note (k); Foster v. Cook, 3 Bro. Ch. R.
347; Haslewood v. Pope, 3 P. Will. 323; Aldrich v. Cooper, 8 Ves. 396, 397.
Such preference or priority may also be rebutted by circumstances. Thus it
has been said that there is no rule, that, where real and personal estate is
charged with the payment of debts, and the residue is given to a legatee or
children, the court would in such case turn the charge on the real estate, to
give the whole personal estate to the legatee. Arnold v. Chapman, 1 Ves. 110.
See also Wythe v. Henniker, 2 Mylne & Keen, 635, 644, 645;(b) Lomas v.
Wright, 2 Mylne & Keen, 769. In this last case it was held that creditors by
specialty who are mere volunteers are not entitled to compete with creditors
on simple contract for a valuable consideration. But as against the devisees
they have a right to stand in the place of the mortgagees, who have exhausted
the fund provided by the testator for the payment of debts.
[2] Forrester v. Leigh, Ambl. R. 171, 174. See also Lutkins v. Leigh, Cas.
Temp. Talb. 53; 2 Fonbl. Eq. B. 3, ch. 2, § 7, and note (k); Aldrich v.
Cooper, 8 Ves. 396, 397. This distinction between the heir and the devisee

(a) It is laid down in Hensman v.
Fryer, L. R. 3 Ch. 420, that a pecuniary legatee and a residuary devisee
must contribute ratably to the payment of debts, where the personal
estate is insufficient. But see Dugdale v. Dugdale, L. R. 14 Eq. 234, and
Collins v. Lewis, L. R. 8 Eq. 708,
where Hensman v. Fryer was commented on and not followed. A residuary devise remains specific in
England even since the Wills Act.
See Gibbens v. Eyden, L. R. 7 Eq.
371; Hensman v. Fryer, supra.
(b) This case was not followed in
Lilford v. Powys-Keck, L. R. 1 Eq.
347.

566. In like manner where lands are subjected to the payment of all debts, legatees are permitted to stand, in regard to such lands, in the place of simple contract creditors who have come upon the personal estate and exhausted it so far as to prevent a satisfaction of their legacies.[1] So where legacies given by a will are charged on real estate but legacies by a codicil are not, the former legatees will be compelled to resort to the real assets if there is a deficiency of the personal assets to satisfy both.[2] (a)

566 a. Upon analogous grounds if a specific legacy is pledged by the testator, the specific legatee is entitled to have his specific legacy redeemed ; and if the executor fail to perform that duty, the specific legatee is entitled to compensation to the amount of the legacy out of the general assets of the testator. So if a specific legacy is incumbered with a mortgage or other charge, the specific legatee is entitled to have it paid off by the executor out of the general assets of the testator ; and if that be not done, he is entitled to stand in the same situation as if the duty of the executor had been faithfully performed. Indeed the same principle applies to specific legatees as to devisees in respect to the redemption of the subject-matter of the gift out of the general assets of the testator.[3] (b)

567. The doctrine adopted in all these cases of allowing one creditor to stand in the place of another, having two funds to resort to, and electing to take satisfaction out of one to which

makes it very important in many cases to ascertain whether under a will an heir takes by descent or by purchase. See Herne v. Meyrick, 1 P. Will. 201; Scott v. Scott, 1 Eden, R. 458; s. c. Ambl. R. 383; Clifton v. Burt, 1 P. Will. 678, 679, Cox's note (1).

[1] Clifton v. Burt, 1 P. Will. 678, 679, and Cox's note; Haslewood v. Pope, 3 P. Will. 323.

[2] Hyde v. Hyde, 3 Ch. Rep. 155; Masters v. Masters, 1 P. Will. 422; Bligh v. Earl of Darnley, 2 P. Will. 620; Clifton v. Burt, 1 P. Will. 679, Cox's note; Norman v. Morrill, 4 Ves. 769.

[3] Knight v. Davis, 3 Mylne & K. 358, 361.

(a) So where an annuity is charged on real and personal estate, and other legacies are not, the legatees may require the annuity to be paid out of the real estate descended upon a deficiency of personal estate. Allen v. Allen, 3 Wall. Jr. 289.

(b) See Lewis v. Lewis, L. R. 13 Eq. 218. It is held that marshalling should not be adopted where property specifically bequeathed to several is subject to an incumbrance paramount to the testator's title, and the share of one is seized. Peeples v. Horton, 39 Miss. 406.

alone another creditor can resort, was probably transferred from the civil law into Equity Jurisprudence. It is certainly founded in principles of natural justice, and it early worked its way, under the title of substitution, into the civil law, where it was applied in a very large and liberal manner. But upon this subject we shall have occasion to speak hereafter in another place.[1]

568. There are other cases in which the marshalling of assets is in like manner enforced in Courts of Equity; as for instance in favor of the widow of a person deceased. After the death of the husband his creditors cannot take his widow's necessary apparel in satisfaction of their debts.[2] With this exception a widow's paraphernalia are generally subject to the payment of the debts of her husband.[3] But in favor of the widow, and to preserve her paraphernalia, Courts of Equity will interfere by turning creditors, entitled to proceed against real assets or funds, over to these assets and funds for satisfaction. And if the paraphernalia have been actually taken by creditors in satisfaction of their debts, the widow will be allowed to stand in their place, and the assets will be marshalled so as to give her a compensation pro tanto.[4]

569. In speaking of the marshalling of assets in cases of legacies, whether specific or residuary (when the latter are entitled to the benefit), it must be understood that the legacies are to private persons taking for their own benefit, and not legacies for charity, either directly or through the instrumentality of a trustee or legatee. In general legacies of personal property to charitable uses are valid in point of law. But since the statute of 9th George II., ch. 36, in England, legacies or bequests by will to charitable uses, payable out of real estate, or charged on real estate, or to arise from the sale of real estate, are utterly void. And Courts of Equity, following out the intent and object of the statute, have refused to interfere in favor of legatees of personal property for charity by marshalling assets for this purpose in any

---

[1] See Cheeseborough v. Millard, 1 John. Ch. R. 412, 413, and ante, § 494, on the subject of contribution between sureties. Post, §§ 635, 636, 637.

[2] 2 Black. Comm. 436; Noy's Maxims, ch. 49; Townshend v. Windham, 2 Ves. 7.

[3] Ram on Assets, ch. 10, § 1; 2 Black. Comm. 436; Toller on Executors, B. 3, ch. 8, pp. 421, 422, 423.

[4] Ram on Assets, ch. 18, pp. 353, 354, and the cases there cited; Aldrich v. Cooper, 8 Ves. 397; Incledon v. Northcote, 3 Atk. R. 438.

case whatever; as by throwing the debts or legacies on real assets for payment, or by allowing the charity legatees to stand in the place of any creditor or legatee who has exhausted the personal estate against the real assets.[1] (a)

570. Hitherto we have been speaking of marshalling assets in favor of creditors, legatees, or widows. But it is not to be understood that these are the only persons entitled to the benefit of this wholesome doctrine of Courts of Equity. Heirs at law and devisees are, in a great variety of cases, entitled to the protection of it. Thus for instance if an heir or devisee of real estate is sued by a bond creditor, he may, in many cases, be entitled to stand in the place of such specialty creditor against the personal estate of the deceased testator or intestate.[2]

571. In order more fully to comprehend the nature and limitations of this doctrine, it is necessary to state that, in the view of Courts of Equity, the personal estate of the deceased constitutes the primary and natural fund for the payment of his debts; and they will direct it to be applied in the first instance to that purpose, unless, from the will of the deceased or from some other controlling equities, it is clear that it ought not to be so applied.[3] (b) But in the order of satisfaction out of the personal estate of the deceased, if it is not sufficient for all purposes, creditors are preferred to legatees; specific legatees are preferred to the heir and devisee of the real estate charged with specialties or with the payment of debts;[4] and specific legacies are liable to be

---

[1] Ram on Assets, ch. 18, § 3, pp. 346 to 353; Mogg v. Hodges, 2 Ves. 52; Attorney-Gen. v. Tyndall, Ambl. R. 614; s. c. 2 Eden, R. 207; Clifton v. Burt, 1 P. Will. 670, Cox's note; Ridges v. Morrison, 1 Cox, R. 189; Toller on Executors, B. 3, ch. 8, p. 423; Attorney-Gen. v. Winchelsea, 3 Bro. Ch. R. 380, and Belt's note (3); Attorney-Gen. v. Hurst, 2 Cox, R. 364; post, 2 Eq. Jurisp. § 1180.

[2] Mogg v. Hodges, 2 Ves. 52; Galton v. Hancock, 2 Atk. 424, 425.

[3] See Co. Litt. 208 b, Butler's note, 106.

[4] 2 Fonbl. Eq. B. 3, ch. 2, §§ 3, 4, 5, and notes (e), (f), (g), (h); Cope v. Cope, 2 Salk. 449.

(a) But see Wigg v. Nicholl, L. R. 14 Eq. 92, where assets were marshalled according to the testator's direction so as to give the impure personalty to such of several charities named as legatees as could take it. And see Gaskins v. Rogers, L. R. 2 Eq. 284; Macdonald v. Macdonald, L. R. 14 Eq. 60; Beaumont v. Oliveira, L. R. 6 Eq. 534; s. c. 4 Ch. 309; Robinson v. Geldard, 3 Macn. & G. 735.

(b) Morse v. Bassett, 132 Mass. 502; Johnson v. Goss, 128 Mass. 433; Richardson v. Hall, 124 Mass. 228. See post, § 1248, and notes.

applied in payment of specialty debts in priority to real estate devised;[1] (a) the devisee of mortgaged premises is preferred to

[1] Cornwall v. Cornwall, 12 Sim. & Stu. 298.

(a) But see Tombs v. Roch, 2 Colly. 490; Gervis v. Gervis, 14 Sim. 654 (where Cornwall v. Cornwall is overruled); Hensman v. Fryer, L. R. 3 Ch. 420. Contra, Dugdale v. Dugdale, L. R. 14 Eq. 234 ; Collins v. Lewis, L. R. 8 Eq. 708; Farquharson v. Floyer, 3 Ch. D. 109; Tomkins v. Colthurst, 1 Ch. D. 626; Mirehouse v. Scaife, 2 Mylne & C. 695, following the older rule of the text.

The rule of the text is based on the ground that in England land is not regarded as general assets for the payment of simple contract debts, which has not been true in the United States to any considerable extent. The rule itself that specific devises are to be preferred over specific legacies never applied to specialty debts, because land might be liable to them; as to these, devises contributed ratably with specific legacies. In like manner in those States in which no distinction exists between simple contract debts and specialty debts no preference of specific devises exists. Brant v. Brant, 40 Mo. 266; Grim's Appeal, 89 Penn. St. 333; Loomis's Appeal, 10 Barr, 387; Teas's Appeal, 23 Penn. St. 223; Armstrong's Appeal, 63 Penn. St. 312; Knecht's Appeal, 71 Penn. St. 333 ; Snyder's Appeal, 75 Penn. St. 191; 2 Jarman, Wills, 622, note (Bigelow's ed.).

The general rule applicable between different kinds of legacies in regard to abatement for the payment of debts is that residuary legacies are first to be taken, then general or pecuniary legacies, then specific legacies. Alsop v. Bowers, 76 N. Car. 168. But this may be varied either by the actual or presumable intention of the testator. Thus the courts will take into account the situation of the benefici-

aries, giving a preference to those who are required to forego some benefit on accepting the gift. Such are treated in the light of purchasers, and are preferred over pure beneficiaries. A legacy to the testator's widow in lieu of dower is a case in point; in marshalling this would be preferred over a simple gift to a child of the testator. Farnum v. Bascom, 122 Mass. 282; Heath v. Dendy, 1 Russ. 543; Norcott v. Gordon, 14 Sim. 258 ; Towle v. Swasey, 106 Mass. 100. This is true though the legacies are specific, at least if the gift to the widow is also specific. Farnum v. Bascom; Towle v. Swasey. But courts do not incline to declare gifts specific; a clear intention in the will must appear to make them do so. Wilcox v. Wilcox, 13 Allen, 252, 256; Newton v. Stanley, 28 N. Y. 61.

So too near relationship may be a decisive ground of preference, with other indications in the will pointing the same way. See Richardson v. Hall, 127 Mass. 64, 66; s. c. 124 Mass. 233; Towle v. Swasey, 106 Mass. 100. For other considerations of a similar kind see King v. Gridley, 46 Conn. 555; Grim's Appeal, 89 Penn. St. 333; McFarland's Appeal, 37 Penn. St. 300; Wilson v. McKeehan, 53 Penn. St. 79. But to overcome the presumption that the testator designed to have all general legacies abate ratably in case of necessity, there must be clear evidence in the will of a different purpose. Titus v. Titus, 26 N. J. Eq. 111; Shepherd v. Guernsey, 9 Paige, 357.

The English order of application of all the several funds liable to the payment of the decedent's debts is thus stated in Jarman on Wills, 622 (5th ed.): —

the heir at law of descended estates;[1] and a fortiori the devisee of premises not mortgaged is preferred to the heir at law.[2] In case unincumbered lands and mortgaged lands are both specifically devised, but expressly after the payment of all debts, they are to contribute proportionally in discharge of the mortgage.[3] Where the equities of the legatees and devisees are equal, which (as we have seen) is sometimes the case, Courts of Equity remain neutral and silently suffer the law to prevail.[4] But where the personal assets are sufficient to pay all the debts and legacies and other charges, there the heir or devisee, who has been compelled to pay any debt or incumbrance of his ancestor or testator binding upon him, is entitled (unless there be some other equity which repels the claim) to have the debt paid out of the personal assets in preference to the residuary legatees or distributees. Thus for instance if a specialty debt or mortgage of an ancestor or testator is paid by the heir or devisee, he is entitled to have it

[1] Toller on Executors, B. 3, ch. 8, p. 418; Howell v. Price, 1 P. Will. 294, Mr. Cox's note; Cope v. Cope, 2 Salk. 449, Mr. Evans's note. Lord Hardwicke at first decided otherwise in Galton v. Hancock, 2 Atk. 424, but afterwards altered his opinion; Id. 2 Atk. 430.

[2] Chaplin v. Chaplin, 3 P. Will. 364; Davies v. Topp, 1 Bro. Ch. R. 524; Manning v. Spooner, 3 Ves. 114; Livingston v. Newkirk, 3 John. Ch. R. 319; 2 Fonbl. Eq. B. 3, ch. 2, §§ 3, 4, 5, and notes.

[3] Carter v. Barnardiston, 2 P. Will. 505; 2 Bro. Par. Cas. 1; Howell v. Price, 1 P. Will. 294, Cox's note.

[4] The whole subject was largely discussed in Davies v. Topp, 1 Bro. Ch. R. 524, Appx.; Donne v. Lewis, 2 Bro. Ch. R. 257; Manning v. Spooner, 3 Ves. 114; Galton v. Hancock, 2 Atk. 424, 430; Harwood v. Oglander, 8 Ves. 106, 124; Milnes v. Slater, 8 Ves. 294, 303; and in Mr. Cox's note to Howell v. Price, 1 P. Will. 294; and Evelyn v. Evelyn, 2 P. Will. 664; Bootle v. Blundell, 1 Meriv. R. 215 to 238; Ram on Assets, ch. 28, §§ 1 to 4, ch. 29, §§ 1 to 4. See the Reporter's note to Phillips v. Parker, 1 Tamlyn, R. 136, 143.

1. The general personal estate not expressly or by implication exempted.

2. Lands expressly devised to pay debts, whether the inheritance or a term carved out of it be so limited.

3. Estates which descend to the heir, whether acquired before or after making the will. See Hurst v. Hurst, 28 Ch. D. 159, where the estate descended to the testator's heir by reason of a forfeiture.

4. Real or personal property devised or bequeathed, either to the heir or to a stranger, charged with debts, and disposed of subject to such charge.

5. General pecuniary legacies pro rata.

6. Specific legacies and real estate devised, whether in terms specific or residuary, pro rata.

7. Real and personal property which the testator has power to appoint, and which he has appointed by will. See infra, § 577.

paid out of the personal assets in the hands of the executor, unless the testator, by express words or other manifest intention, has clearly exempted the personal assets from the payment.[1] And the personal assets are liable in such cases of mortgage even although there may not be any personal covenant for the payment of the debt or collateral bond.[2] And lands subject to or devised for the payment of debts are in like manner liable to discharge such mortgage in favor of the heir or devisee to whom the mortgaged lands may belong.[3] (a)

572. What shall constitute proof of such an intended exemption by the testator is not, in many cases, ascertainable upon abstract principles, but must depend upon circumstances. It is certain however that a devise of all the testator's real estate subject to the payment of his debts, or a devise of a particular estate subject to the payment of debts, will not alone be sufficient to exempt the personal estate.[4] (b) But on the other hand, if the real estate be directed to be sold for the payment of debts and the personal estate is expressly bequeathed to legatees, there the personal estate will, by necessary implication, be exempted.[5]

573. The doctrine of the court in all cases of this sort is founded upon the same principle, that is, to follow out the intention of the testator. The personal estate is deemed the natural and primary fund for the payment of all debts, and the testator

[1] 2 Fonbl. Eq. B. 3, ch. 2, § 1, and note (a); 1 Madd. Ch. Pr. 474, 475; Toller on Executors, B. 3, ch. 8, p. 418; Howell v. Price, 1 P. Will. 291, 294, and Cox's note (1); Cope v. Cope, 2 Salk. 449; Ancaster v. Mayor, 1 Bro. Ch. R. 454.

[2] Ibid.

[3] Bartholomew v. May, 1 Atk. 487; Tweedale v. Coventry, 1 Bro. Ch. R. 240; Howell v. Price, 1 P. Will. 294, Cox's note; Serle v. St. Eloy, 2 P. Will. 386.

[4] Ibid.; Bridgman v. Dove, 3 Atk. 201, 202; Haslewood v. Pope, 3 P. Will. 325; Inchiquin v. French, Ambl. R. 33; s. c. 1 Cox, R. 1; 1 Wils. R. 82; 1 Bro. Ch. R. 458; Lupton v. Lupton, 2 John. Ch. R. 628; Livingston v. Newkirk, 3 John. Ch. R. 319; Walker v. Jackson, 2 Atk. 625; Ancaster v. Mayor, 1 Bro. Ch. R. 454; Bootle v. Blundell, 1 Meriv. R. 194, 210.

[5] 2 Fonbl. Eq. B. 3, ch. 2, § 1, and note (a); Id. § 3, and notes (e), (a); Wainwright v. Bendlowes, 2 Vern. 718; s. c. Prec. Ch. 451; Bamfield v. Wyndham, Prec. Ch. 101; Walker v. Jackson, 2 Atk. 624, 625; Gray v. Minnethorp, 3 Ves. 103; Bootle v. Blundell, 1 Meriv. R. 194, 210, 224; Milnes v. Slater, 8 Ves. 293, 303.

(a) Andrews v. Bishop, 5 Allen, 490; Plimpton v. Fuller, 11 Allen, 139; Thomas v. Thomas, 2 C. E. Green, 356, 359; Towle v. Swasey, 106 Mass. 100. See Glass v. Dunn, 17 Ohio St. 413; editor's note at end of § 1248.

(b) See note just cited.

is presumed to act upon this legal doctrine until he shows some
other distinct and unequivocal intention. The general rule
therefore of Courts of Equity, although sometimes delivered in
one form and sometimes in another, is (as Lord Hardwicke has
expressed it), that the personal estate shall be first applied to
the payment of debts, unless there be express words or a plain
intention of the testator to exempt his personal estate or to give
his personal estate as a *specific* legacy; for he may do this, as
well as give the bulk of his real estate by way of specific legacy.[1]

574. But although the personal estate is thus deemed the general and primary fund for the payment of debts, and still remains
so notwithstanding the real estate is also collaterally chargeable,
yet the rule is otherwise, or rather is differently applied, where
the charge of the debt is principally and primarily upon the real
estate and the personal security or covenant is only collateral;
for the primary fund ought in conscience in all cases to exonerate the auxiliary fund.[2] The debt or incumbrance may be in its
nature real, or it may become so by the act of the person who has
the power of charging both the real and the personal funds; or
the land, although it be auxiliary only to the personal estate of the
original contractor of the debt or incumbrance, may yet become
the primary fund as between itself and the personal estate of
another person who may take the land either by descent or
purchase subject to the charge. In both these cases the personal
estate is charged (if at all) only as a security for the land, and
it ought to have the same measure of equity as the land is entitled to when it is pledged as a security for a personal debt.[3]

575. The first class of cases may be illustrated by the case of
a jointure or portion to be raised out of lands by the execution
of a power. In such a case, notwithstanding there may be a personal covenant or agreement to raise the jointure or portion to
the stipulated amount, yet the charge when raised is to be

[1] Walker v. Jackson, 2 Atk. 625.
[2] See Co. Litt. 208 b, Butler's note, 106; Lechmere v. Charlton, 15 Ves.
197, 198.
[3] See Earl of Clarendon v. Barham, 1 Younge & Coll. N. R. 688, 711, 712,
where Scott v. Beecher, 5 Madd. R. 96, and Lord Ilchester v. Carnarvon, 1
Beav. R. 209, are remarked on. I borrow this language, and the cases which
illustrate it, from the valuable note of Mr. Cox to Evelyn v. Evelyn, 2 P. Will.
664, note (1). See also Mr. Cox's note to Howell v. Price, 1 P. Will. 294,
note (1).

deemed a primary charge on the lands, and the personal estate of
the covenantor only security therefor. In other words although
the covenantor is the original contractor, yet the charge being in
its nature real and the covenant only an additional security, the
land will be decreed to bear the burden in exoneration of the
personal estate.[1] The same principle will apply to pecuniary
portions to be raised in favor of daughters in a marriage settlement out of lands placed in the hands of trustees for this
purpose, although there be a personal covenant also of the settler
to have the portion thus raised.[2]

576. The second class of cases may be illustrated by the common case of a mortgage created by an ancestor and the mortgaged estate descending upon his heir. There although the
heir should become personally bound to pay the mortgage, yet
his personal estate would not be liable to be charged in favor of
any person who should derive title by descent under him to the
mortgaged premises subject to the mortgage. For the debt was
not originally contracted by him, and it was as to him primarily
chargeable on the land; and even his covenant to pay the mortgage would only be considered as a security for the debt.[3] (a)

[1] Coventry v. Coventry, 9 Mod. 13; s. c. 2 P. Will. 222; 2 Fonbl. Eq. B.
3, ch. 2, § 2, note (b).

[2] Edwards v. Freeman, 2 P. Will. 435; Evelyn v. Evelyn, 2 P. Will. 664,
Mr. Cox's note (1); Ward v. Dudley & Ward, 2 Bro. Ch R. 316; s. c. 1 Cox,
R. 438; Wilson v. Darlington, 1 Cox, R. 172; Duke of Ancaster v. Mayor, 1
Bro. Ch. R. 454, 464, and Belt's note (2); Bassett v. Percival, 1 Cox, R. 268;
2 Fonbl. Eq. B. 3, ch. 2, § 2, note (b). See Lechmere v. Charlton, 15 Ves.
197, 198.

[3] Cope v. Cope, 2 Salk. 449; Evelyn v. Evelyn, 2 P. Will. 664, and Mr.
Cox's note (1), and also his note (1) to Howell v. Price, 1 P. Will. 294; Leman
v. Newnham, 1 Ves. 51; Lacam v. Mertins, 1 Ves. 312; Ancaster v. Mayor, 1
Bro. Ch. R. 454, 464, and Belt's note (2); Lawson v. Hudson, 1 Bro. Ch. R.
58, and Mr. Belt's note.   Earl of Clarendon v. Barham, 1 Younge & Coll.
N. R. 688, 711, 712.   In this case Mr. Vice-Chancellor Bruce said: 'I have,
I think, only farther to consider whether the Island estate as it now stands is
the prior or the secondary fund for the payment of the Island mortgage debt.
To the discharge of an ordinary debt due from Mr. Joseph Foster Barham his
personal estate ought, I apprehend, in the ordinary course to be first applied.
It has been contended however by the plaintiffs that with regard to the sum
secured on the Island estate this cannot be, and that to the payment of that
sum the Island estate must primarily be applied. The first reason assigned
for this is that there is evidence in the cause showing (as the plaintiffs insist)
that in point of fact Mr. John Barham intended that, as between the person-

(a) Hewes v. Dehon, 3 Gray, 205, 208; post, § 1248.

Therefore where land descended to the wife, subject to a mortgage made by her father, and on an assignment of the mortgage

alty and the mortgaged realty liable to this debt, the latter should be the prior fund to be applied. I am unable however to discover any such evidence. It is true that in my opinion there was an absence of intention on his part that any part of the capital of his mother's fortune should be considered as either satisfied or extinguished. But this does not appear to me to amount to anything for the present purpose. He could not, as to the other persons interested in Lady Caroline's fortune, without their consent (a consent neither asked nor obtained, nor probably thought of) relieve any portion of his father's assets from the liability under which the whole of those assets was to make good that fortune, and I do not see any ground whatever for saying that he ever in fact indicated any wish or design that any one part should wholly or partially indemnify any other part of the assets in respect of it. The other assigned reason is that, independently of any proof of actual intention, the united characters of acting executor and sole residuary legatee, as well as heir and devisee of his father, having rendered Mr. John Barham solely and equally interested in the whole of the funds from which the fortune was due, it is a necessary consequence that the portion of those funds specifically pledged, though not exclusively liable for its payment, must bear the burthen of the pledge without indemnity or contribution. The necessity of such a consequence is not obvious to my apprehension. The general rule is that a pledge or security for a debt, though having its full operation in favor of the creditor, does not take away the character of debt, and neither excludes him from any other remedy nor changes or affects the mode in which, as between those who take the debtor's property subject to his debts, that property is to be applied. Generally with regard to such a question the case is dealt with as if the pledge or security did not exist. I do not forget the distinctions or exceptions established or recognized in Lutkins v. Leigh (Ca. temp. Talb. 53); Halliwell v. Tanner (1 Russ. & M. 633), Wythe v. Henniker (2 Myl. & K. 635), and the authorities to which reference is there made, distinctions or exceptions proving the rule, but otherwise seeming to me to have no place in the present case. If the mere fact of the union of interests were material, it would have had its operation and effect though Mr. John Barham had died within an hour of his father's death, ignorant of it. In that case there might have arisen, and as matters are there may arise, an absolute necessity for deciding which is the first fund for paying an unsecured specialty debt due from Mr. Joseph Foster Barham. Suppose such a creditor in existence: it would be contrary to all principle to hold that his caprice or election should decide between real estate now belonging to one person, and personal estate now belonging to another, which of the two is finally to bear the burden. The court must decide in such a case. And on what ground could it be held that the personal estate ought not, as between that and the real estate, to be first applied? What could have taken place in the event that I have supposed, — what has in fact taken place to change the ordinary course as to such an unsecured debt? In my opinion nothing. If so, in the absence of proof of actual intention, why should the mortgage or pledge make any difference? Yet if the plaintiffs' contention is right, they would in the event of the mortgagees recovering, as it is admitted that they are entitled to recover, their debt against the general personal estate of Joseph Foster Barham, be entitled to stand in the mortgagee's place against, or be indemni-

the husband covenanted to pay the money to the assignee, it was
decreed that the husband's personal estate should not exonerate

fied by, the Island estate.   The foundation of such a state of things in principle I am unable to see.   Agreeing entirely with the doctrine laid down in
Bagot v. Oughton (1 P. W. 347) and Evelyn v. Evelyn (2 P. W. 659), which
has been recognized in many other cases (particularly one in this family,
Barham v. Lord Thanet, 3 M. & K. 607), I do not see any clear and irresistible reason for not holding that an executor, who, being also sole residuary
legatee, has received more personal estate than enough to pay all the funeral
and testamentary expenses, and debts and liabilities of every description, as
well as legacies, becomes himself substantially debtor to the creditors of the
testator.   And whether such an executor is sole executor or survived by a co-
executor, I apprehend that the doctrine of Lord Chief Baron Gilbert, Lex
Præt. 315, equally applies in principle.   The case also of Lord Belvedere
v. Rochfort (5 Bro. P. C. 299) in the House of Lords (though I am aware of
what Lord Thurlow has in Tweddell v. Tweddell (2 Bro. C. C. 101), and
Lord Alvanley in Woods v. Huntingford (3 Ves. 130) said of that case) may
be thought to have at least a considerable bearing the same way, and consequently against the plaintiffs.   Lord Thurlow, who as leading counsel signed
the case for the successful party, the respondent in Lord Belvedere v. Rochfort, appears to have considered that the House of Lords held, but ought not
to have held, that the mortgage debt in question there had been made the debt
of Robert Rochfort, the grandfather, as between his real and his personal
estate; and he is reported to have said, " In that case George had a fee-simple
in the estate, he was capable of giving it after the charges were extinguished."
But I am not at all persuaded that he dissented from the doctrine to be found
in Gilbert, and upon which doctrine the printed cases in Lord Belvedere v.
Rochfort, and the statements of Lord Thurlow and Lord Alvanley in Tweddell v. Tweddell, and Woods v. Huntingford, show, if not the certainty, at
least a very high degree of probability, that in Lord Belvedere's case both
Lord Lifford and the House of Lords meant to act and did act independently
of Lord Jocelyn's decree, and not by reason or in consequence of what Lord
Jocelyn had done.   Nor can I see that Perkyns v. Bayntun (2 P. W. 664, n.),
as to which I have examined the Registrar's book, is at variance with this doctrine.   In Perkyns v. Bayntum no account was sought of the personal estate
of Sir William Osbaldistone, who had died a quarter of a century before the
suit.   What was its amount, whether it was considerable or inconsiderable,
whether as to his personal estate in fact he died solvent or insolvent, was not
stated and does not appear.   The point in Gilbert seems not to have been
raised or touched in that case.   Upon the whole thinking the opinion of Lord
Chief Baron Gilbert well founded in principle, and corroborated, if touched,
by Lord Belvedere's case, I should, had the cases of Scott v. Beecher (5 Madd.
96), Evans v. Smithson (not reported), and Lord Ilchester v. Lord Carnarvon
(1 Beav. 209) not existed, have held and decided that the personal estate of
Joseph Foster Barham, and therefore in substance the personal estate of John
Barham, is the first fund for the payment of the mortgage on the Island
estate.   Consistently however with the opinions which appear to have been
expressed judicially by Sir John Leach, Lord Lyndhurst, and Lord Langdale
in these three cases, I apprehend that I cannot so decide.   Feeling the respect
due from me to these authorities, independently of Lord Lyndhurst's present

the mortgaged premises; for the debt was originally the father's, and the husband's covenant was only collateral security therefor.[1] So where a mortgaged estate is purchased by an ancestor subject to the mortgage, and of course so much less is paid for it as the mortgage amounts to, there, upon a descent cast if it be a fee, or upon devolution upon executors or legatees if it be a leasehold estate, the personal estate of the purchaser will not be held bound to exonerate the mortgaged premises from the mortgage; for it is not the personal debt of the purchaser.[2]

577. These illustrations may suffice to explain some of the more important doctrines of Courts of Equity upon this complicated subject of the marshalling of assets (for in a work like the present it is impossible to examine all of them minutely),[3] and to show upon what nice presumptions and curious analogies they sometimes proceed, some of which (to say the least of them) are sufficiently artificial and elaborate and subtile. The manner in

position, deferring to them. and not upon this point acting in accordance with my own opinion, I direct the insertion in the decree of a declaration that the Island estate is the first fund for the payment of the Island mortgage. The property which I have called the Island estate, subjected to this mortgage for 10,773*l.* 6*s.* 2*d.*, may possibly not be wholly real estate. It may include some personalty, — a remark which I do not mean as extending to the Island compensation-money, which as I have said I cannot hold to have been or to be ascribed or applied or applicable, otherwise than merely as part of the general mass of the general assets of Joseph Foster Barham, or general personal estate of John Barham, this being as it seems to me a consequence of the manner in which and expressed title under which he received it, and of his conduct in all respects. His father had nothing more than a life interest in the benefit of the Island mortgage. Before concluding I may observe that the reference which I have made to Evans *v.* Smithson has been occasioned by my entire reliance upon the authenticity of the information from which Mr. Tinney's statement of that case was made, and my supposition that Lord Lyndhurst's view of the law, as to a vendor's lien, agreed with that of Sir W. Grant, in Trimmer *v.* Bayne (9 Ves. 209), and of Sir L. Shadwell, in Sproule *v.* Prior (8 Sim. 189). It seems that the passage in Gilbert was brought under his Lordship's notice, but not Lord Belvedere's case, and that neither was cited before Sir J. Leach or the present Master of the Rolls.'

[1] Ibid.; Bagot *v.* Oughton, 1 P. Will. 347.

[2] Ancaster *v.* Mayor, 1 Bro. Ch. R. 454, and Mr. Belt's note (2); Tweddell *v.* Tweddell, 2 Bro. Ch. R. 101, and Mr. Belt's note; Butler *v.* Butler, 5 Ves. 534, 538; Cumberland *v.* Codrington, 3 John. Ch. R. 229; Mr. Cox's note to Howell *v.* Price, 1 P. Will. 294, and his note to Evelyn *v.* Evelyn, 2 P. Will. 664; 2 Fonbl. Eq. B. 3, ch. 2, § 2, note (*b*); 4 Kent, Comm. Lect. 65, p. 420, 421 (4th edition).

[3] See other cases, 2 Fonbl. Eq. B. 3, ch. 2, § 1, 2, 3. and notes; Harwood *v.* Oglander, 8 Ves. 106, 124; Milnes *v.* Slater, 8 Ves. 293, 303.

which assets are now generally marshalled in the payment of
debts may be arranged in the following order. First, the general personal estate is applied to the payment of debts, unless
exempted expressly or by plain implication.   Secondly, any
estate particularly devised for the payment of debts, and only
for that purpose.   Thirdly, estates descended to the heir.
Fourthly, estates specifically devised to particular devisees, although charged with the payment of debts.[1] (a)

578. This review of the jurisdiction of Courts of Equity over
the administration of assets, however imperfect and brief, is quite
sufficient to establish the truth of the remarks already stated,
that the jurisdiction is not wholly and solely dependent upon
the mere fact that there exists a constructive trust of the funds
in the hands of the personal representative requiring them to be
properly applied and distributed.   But there are other and numerous sources of jurisdiction collaterally connected with it ; such
as the necessity of a discovery, and taking accounts, and cross
equities by substitution and otherwise, existing in a great variety
of cases in very complicated forms, all of which are or may be
necessary to be examined in order to a full and due administration of the estate.   Indeed the whole topic of marshalling assets seems properly to belong rather to the peculiar doctrines of
Courts of Equity in regard to conflicting rights and equities than
to any notion of trust in the parties.

579. Before quitting this subject it may be useful to take
notice of the interposition of Courts of Equity in regard to the
administration of assets in cases where there is any alienation or
waste of them on the part of the personal representative of the
deceased.   At common law the executor or administrator is
treated for many purposes as the owner of the assets, and has a
power to dispose of and aliene them.[2]   There is no such thing

---

[1] Davies v. Topp, 1 Bro. Ch. R. 526; Donne v. Lewis, 2 Bro. Ch. R. 263;
Harwood v. Oglander, 8 Ves. 106, 124; Milnes v. Slater, 8 Ves. 293, 303;
Livingston v. Newkirk, 3 John. Ch. R. 319; 4 Kent, Comm. Lect. 65, p. 420,
421 (4th edition); 1 Madd. Ch. Pr. 474; Ram on Assets, ch. 30, p. 374; Jeremy on Eq. Jurisd. B. 3, Pt. 2, ch. 5, pp. 524, 537 to 543.
[2] Hill v. Simpson, 7 Ves. 166; McLeod v. Drummond, 14 Ves. 353; s. c.
17 Ves. 154, 168.

(a) See supra, note to § 571;   Verdier v. Verdier, 12 Rich. Eq. 138;
Thomas v. Thomas, 2 C. E. Green, 356,   Mitchell v. Mitchell, 21 Md. 244.
358; Gully v. Holloway, 63 N. Car. 84;

known as the assets in the hands of an executor being the debt-
or, or as a creditor's having a lien on them; but the person of
the executor, in respect to the assets which he has in his hands,
is treated as the debtor.[1]   At law the assets of the testator may
perhaps, at least under special circumstances, be taken in execution for the personal debt of the executor, unless indeed there
be some fraud or collusion between the execution creditor and
the executor;[2] as they certainly may also be taken in execution
for the debts of the testator.[3]   But in Courts of Equity the assets are treated as the debtor, or in other words as a trust fund
to be administered by the executor for the benefit of all persons
who are interested in it, whether they are creditors, or legatees,
or distributees, or otherwise interested, according to their relative priorities, privileges, and equities.[4] (a)

[1] Farr v. Newnham, 4 T. Rep. 621, 634; Whale v. Booth, 4 T. R. 625, note;
s. c. 4 Doug. R. 36; Nugent v. Gifford, 1 West, Rep. 496, 497; s. c. 1 Atk.
463; s. c. 2 Ves. 269. But see Hill v. Simpson, 7 Ves. 152; McLeod v.
Drummond, 14 Ves. 361; s. c. 17 Ves. 154, 168.
[2] Whale v. Booth, 4 T. R. 623, note; s. c. 4 Doug. R. 36; Farr v. Newnham, 4 T. R. 621; McLeod v. Drummond, 17 Ves. 154; Ray v. Ray, Cooper, R. 264.
[3] Ibid.; Contra, McLeod v. Drummond, 17 Ves. 154, 168.
[4] Farr v. Newnham, 4 T. R. 636, per Buller, J.; Whale v. Booth, 4 T. R.
625, note; s. c. 4 Doug. R. 36.

(a) *Retainer of an Executor.* — In
regard to retainer in administration, a
subject not considered by the author,
it is said in a well-known work:
' As an executor or administrator
among creditors of equal degree may
pay one in preference to another, so
it is another of his privileges that
he has a right to retain for his own
debt due to him from the deceased
in preference to all other creditors of
equal degree.   This remedy arises
from the mere operation of law, on the
ground that it were absurd and incon-
gruous that he should sue himself, or
that the same hand should at once pay
and receive the same debt.   And therefore he may appropriate a sufficient
part of the assets in satisfaction of his
own demand.' 2 Williams, Executors,
1043 (8th Eng. ed.).
   But this does not apply to assets
which are merely equitable; ' for in

equity all debts are equal, and a Court
of Equity will never,' it is said, ' assist
a retainer.' Ib. p. 1045. It does not
apply therefore, at least in this country, to lands devised to be sold for the
payment of debts.   Harrison v. Henderson, 7 Heisk. 315.
   The following special cases of the
right of retainer are among others
given in 2 Williams, Executors, 1045,
et seq.: For debts due to the executor
or administrator as trustee. Plumer
v. Marchant, 3 Burr. 1380 (cited 3
Ad. & E. 858); Sander v. Heathfield,
L. R. 19 Eq. 21.   See also Bain v.
Sadler, L. R. 12 Eq. 570.   And con-
versely for debts due to him as cestui
que trust. Cockroft v. Black, 2 P. Wms.
298; Franks v. Cooper, 4 Ves. 763;
Loomes v. Stotherd, 1 Sim. & S. 461;
Roskelly v. Godolphin, T. Raym. 483;
Marriot v. Thompson, Willes, 186.
An executor of an executor may also

580. Still however Courts of Equity do not supersede the principles of law upon the same subject. And therefore a sale made bona fide by the executor for a valuable consideration, even with notice of there being assets, will be held valid; so that they cannot be followed by creditors or others into the hands of the purchaser.[1] In this respect there is a manifest difference between the case of an ordinary trust where notice takes away the protection of a bona fide purchase from the party, and this peculiar sort of trust mixed up in some measure with general ownership.[2] To affect a sale or other transaction of an executor attempting to bind the assets so as to let in the claim of creditors and others who are principally interested, there must be some fraud, or collusion, or misconduct, between the parties.[3] A mere secret intention of the executor to misapply the funds unknown to the other party dealing with him, or a subsequent unconnected misapplication of them, will not affect the purchaser. He must be conusant of such intention, and designedly aid or assist in its execution.[4] But in the view of Courts

[1] Ibid.; McLeod v. Drummond, 17 Ves. 154, 155, 168; Keane v. Roberts, 4 Madd. 357.

[2] Mead v. Lord Orrery, 3 Atk. 238, 239, 240.

[3] Hill v. Simpson, 7 Ves. 152; Nugent v. Gifford, 1 Atk. 463, cited 4 Bro. Ch. R. 136, and 17 Ves. 160, 163; Andrews v. Wrigley, 4 Bro. Ch. R. 125; Mead v. Lord Orrery, 3 Atk. 235, 238, 239; McLeod v. Drummond, 14 Ves. 355; 17 Ves. 154, 168, 169, 170, 171.

[4] McLeod v. Drummond, 14 Ves. 355; s. c. 17 Ves. 154, 158, 169, 170, 171; Andrews v. Wrigley, 4 Bro. Ch. R. 125; Scott v. Tyler, 2 Bro. Ch. 431; 2 Dick. R. 724; Keane v. Roberts, 4 Madd. R. 357.

retain. Hopton v. Dryden, Prec. Ch. 180; Thomson v. Grant, 1 Russ. C. C. 540, note. So may an executor of an administrator. Weeks v. Gore, 3 P. Wms. 184. Or for a debt to his wife. Prince v. Rowson, 1 Mod. 208; 2 Mod. 51. But an executor de son tort cannot retain except in a single case provided for by Stat. of 43 Eliz. ch. 8.

It has also been held that an executor may retain the amount of a debt barred by the Statute of Limitations. Hill v. Walker, 4 Kay & J. 166. Further see Birt v. Birt, 22 Ch. D. 604; Wilson v. Coxwell, 23 Ch. D. 764; Walters v. Walters, 18 Ch. D. 182; Richmond v. White, 12 Ch. D. 361;

s. c. 10 Ch. D. 727; Crowder v. Stewart, 16 Ch. D. 300.

The subject of the right of an executor or an administrator in this country to retain is often regulated by statute. See Willey v. Thompson, 9 Met. 329; Henderson v. Ayres, 23 Texas, 96; Hubbard v. Hubbard, 16 Ind. 25; Wright v. Wright, 72 Ind. 149; Williams v. Purdy, 6 Paige, 166. In the absence of statute the English rule of retainer will probably be upheld. See Page v. Patton, 5 Peters, 303; Shields v. Alsup, 5 Lea, 508, 519; Smith v. Watson, 8 Humph. 340; Chaffin v. Chaffin, 2 Dev. & B. Eq. 255; Adams v. Adams, 22 Vt. 50.

of Equity there is a broad distinction between cases of a sale or pledge of the testator's assets for a present advance, and cases of such a sale or pledge for an antecedent debt of the executor ;[1] for in the latter case the parties must be generally understood to co-operate in a misapplication of the assets from their proper purpose, unless that inference is repelled by the circumstances.[2] (a)

581. The general doctrine now maintained by Courts of Equity upon this subject cannot be better summed up than it is by a learned judge (Sir John Leach) in an important case.[3] 'Every person,' said he, 'who acquires personal assets by a breach of trust or a devastavit by the executor is responsible to those who are entitled under the will, if he is a party to the breach of trust. Generally speaking he does not become a party to the breach of trust by buying or receiving as a pledge for money advanced to the executor at the time any part of the personal assets whether specifically given by the will or otherwise ; because this sale or pledge is held to be prima facie consistent with the duty of an executor. Generally speaking he does become a party to the breach of trust by buying or receiving in pledge any part of the personal assets not for money advanced at the time, but in satisfaction of his private debt ; because this sale or pledge is prima facie inconsistent with the duty of an executor. I preface both of these propositions with the term " generally speaking," because they both seem to admit of exceptions.' And it may be added that whenever there is a misapplication of the personal assets, and the assets or their proceeds can be traced into the hands of any persons affected with notice of such misapplication, there the trust will attach upon the property or proceeds in the hands of such persons, whatever may have been the extent of such misapplication or conversion.[4] (b)

---

[1] McLeod v. Drummond, 14 Ves. 361, 362; s. c. 17 Ves. 154, 155, 158 to 171; Hill v. Simpson, 7 Ves. 152.

[2] Ibid. See also Mr. Roscoe's learned note to Whale v. Booth, 4 Doug. R. 47, note (66).

[3] Keane v. Roberts, 4 Madd. Rep. 357, 358. See also Ram on Assets, ch. 37, § 4, p. 484; 2 Fonbl. Eq. B. 2, ch. 6, § 2, note (l); Watkins v. Cheek, 2 Sim. & Stu. 205.

[4] See Ram on Assets, ch. 37, § 4, pp. 491, 492; Adair v. Shaw, 1 Sch. &

(a) Though an executor may pledge assets for an advance, it seems that he cannot create a debt against the estate for any excess beyond the value of the pledge. Farhall v. Farhall, L. R. 7 Ch. 123.

(b) See Burwell v. Fauber, 21

582. In cases where during coverture the assets of a feme covert executrix are wasted by the husband and he then dies, no action at law lies by the creditors against the assets of the husband. But Courts of Equity will in such a case interfere and relieve the creditors upon the ground of the breach of trust in the husband, and his conversion of the assets of the wife's testator into funds in aid of his own assets.[1]

583. And here we might treat of the nature and extent of the jurisdiction which Courts of Equity will exercise in regard to the assets of foreigners, (a) collected under what is called an ancil-

Lefr. 261, 262. The same principle may be further illustrated by the cases already mentioned, where creditors and others are permitted to sue the debtors of the deceased when they collude with the executor or administrator, although they are not suable except by the executor or administrator. Lord Brougham, in Holland v. Prior, 7 Mylne & Keen, 240, said: 'Although the general principle of the court for preventing multiplicity of suits and avoiding circuity of proceeding is to bring all the parties concerned in the subject-matter before it, and to adjudicate once for all among them; and although this would lead in administering the assets of deceased persons to going beyond the personal representatives, following the estate of the deceased and taking note of his credits and consequently bringing forward his debtors; yet the practice of the court has prescribed bounds to the inquiry, and accordingly the rule is, to stop short at the personal representatives, unless where there is insolvency or where other parties stand in such relation to the deceased, or his estate, or his representative, that they may be said either to have been mixed with him and his affairs during his lifetime, or to have aided his representative after his decease, in withdrawing his estate from his creditors, or to have undertaken more directly quasi representative of him.' Ante, §§ 422 to 424; Story on Eq. Pleadings, §§ 178, 514; Newland v. Champion, 1 Ves. 106; Doran v. Simpson, 4 Ves. 651; Alsager v. Rowley, 6 Ves. 748; Beckley v. Dorington, West, Rep. 169; White v. Parnther, 1 Knapp, R. 179, 226 ; Troughton v. Binkes, 6 Ves. 572.

[1] Adair v. Shaw, 1 Sch. & Lefr. 261, 262, 263.

Gratt. 446, real estate subject to a charge.

(a) Equity may exercise jurisdiction generally over the assets of non-residents, if such assets are within its jurisdiction; as in a proper case by restraining the payment of them to the non-resident owner or claimant. Tomson v. Tomson, 31 N. J. Eq. 464; Felch v. Hooper, 119 Mass. 52 (statute). On the other hand equity will in England restrain the representatives and legatees of an estate of a resident from taking proceedings in a foreign court to administer the personalty; nor will they be allowed to take proceedings for administering the realty abroad, if by so doing the administration of the personalty in the domestic forum would be embarrassed. Hope v. Carnegie, L. R. 1 Ch. 320. See also as to jurisdiction over foreign property, Mead v. New York R. Co., 45 Conn. 199, 223; Davis v. Morriss, 76 Va. 21. In some cases equity will entertain a bill in aid of proceedings in a foreign court. Transatlantic Co. v. Pietroni, 6 Jur. N. S. 532. But not unless there is special need. Ib.; Bent v. Young, 9 Sim. 180, 190.

lary administration (because it is subordinate to the original administration), taken out in the country where the assets are locally situate. This subject however has been largely discussed in another place, in considering the conflict of the laws of different countries upon the subject of administrations of property situate therein, and therefore it will be but very briefly taken notice of here.[1] In general it may be said that where a domestic executor or administrator collects assets of the deceased in a foreign country without any letters of administration taken out or any actual administration accounted for in such foreign country, and brings them home, they will be treated as personal assets of the deceased, to be administered here under the domestic administration.[2] But where such assets have been collected abroad under a foreign administration and such administration is still open, there seems much difficulty in holding that the executor or administrator can be called upon to account for such assets under the domestic administration, unless perhaps under very peculiar circumstances; since it would constitute no just bar to proceedings under the foreign administration in the courts of the foreign country.[3] And indeed probates of wills and letters of administration are not granted in any country in respect to assets generally, but only in respect to such assets as are within the jurisdiction of the country by which the probate is established or the administration granted.[4]

584. Where there are different administrations[5] granted in different countries, those which are in their nature ancillary are, as we have seen, generally held subordinate to the original administration. (a)　But each administration is deemed so far independent of the other that property received under one can-

[1] See Story, Comment. on Conflict of Laws, ch. 13, §§ 492 to 530.

[2] Dowdale's case, 6 Co. Rep. 47, 48; s. c. Cro. Jac. 55; Attorney-Gen. v. Dimond, 1 Cromp. & Jervis, 370; Erving's case, 1 Cromp. & Jerv. R. 151; s. c. 1 Tyrw. R. 91.

[3] See Story, Comm. on Conflict of Laws, ch. 13, §§ 512 to 519. But see Attorney-Gen. v. Dimond, 1 Cromp. & Jerv. 370; Erving's Case, 1 Cromp. & Jerv. 151; 1 Tyrw. R. 191.

[4] Ibid.

[5] This and the three following sections are taken almost verbatim from Story's Conflict of Laws, §§ 518, 524, 525, 528.

(a) Shegogg v. Perkins, 34 Ark.　Miss. 569; Carr v. Lowe, 7 Heisk. 84, 117.　But see Carroll v. McPike, 53　under statutory law.

not be sued for under another, although it may at the moment be locally situate within the jurisdiction of the latter. Thus if property is received by a foreign executor or administrator abroad, and afterwards remitted here, an executor or administrator appointed here could not assert a claim to it here, either against the person in whose hands it might happen to be, or against the foreign executor or administrator. The only mode of reaching it, if necessary for the purposes of due administration here, would be to require its transmission or distribution after all claims against the foreign administration had been ascertained and settled abroad.[1] (a)

585. In relation to the mode of administering assets by executors and administrators there are in different countries very different regulations. The priority of debts, the order of payments, the marshalling of assets for this purpose, and in cases of insolvency the modes of proof as well as of distribution, differ in different countries. In some countries all debts stand in an equal rank; and in cases of insolvency the creditors are to be paid pari passu. In others there are certain classes of debts entitled to a priority of payment and therefore deemed privileged debts. Thus in England bond debts and judgment debts possess this privilege; and the like law exists in some of the States of this Union. Similar provisions may be found in the law of France in favor of particular classes of creditors. On the other hand in Massachusetts and in many other States of the Union all debts except those due to the government possess an equal rank and are payable pari passu. Let us suppose then that a debtor dies domiciled in a country where such priority of right and privilege exists, and that he has assets situate in a State where all debts stand in an equal rank, and administration is duly taken out in the place of his domicil and also in the place of the situs of the assets. What rule is to govern in the marshalling of the assets? The law of the domicil or the law of the situs? The established rule now is, that in regard to creditors the administration of the assets of deceased persons is to be governed altogether by the law of the country where the executor or administrator acts, and from which he derives his authority to collect them, and not by

---

[1] Story's Conflict of Laws, § 518.

(a) See Lynes v. Coley, 1 Redf. 407; Banta v. Moore, 2 McCart. 97, 101.

that of the domicil of the deceased.   The rule has been laid down with great clearness and force on many occasions.[1] (a)

586. The ground upon which this doctrine has been established seems entirely satisfactory.   Every nation having a right to dispose of all the property actually situate within it has (as has often been said) a right to protect itself and its citizens against the inequalities of foreign laws which are injurious to their interests. The rule of a preference or of an equality in the payment of debts, whether the one or the other course is adopted, is purely local in its nature, and can have no just claim to be admitted by any other nation which in its domestic arrangements pursues an opposite policy.   And in a conflict between our own and foreign laws the doctrine avowed by Huberus is highly reasonable, that we should prefer our own.   'In tali conflictu magis est ut jus nostrum, quam jus alienum, servemus.'[2]

587. In the course of administrations also in different countries questions often arise as to particular debts, whether they are properly and ultimately payable out of the personal estate, or whether they are chargeable upon the real estate of the deceased. (b)   In all such cases the settled rule now is that the law of the domicil of the deceased will govern in cases of intestacy, and in cases of testacy, the intention of the testator. (c)   A case illustrating this doctrine occurred in England many years ago.   A testator who lived in Holland and was seised of real estate there, and of considerable personal estate in England, devised all his real estate to one person and all his personal estate to another, whom he made his executor.   At the time of his death he owed some debts by specialty and some by simple contract in Holland, and had no assets there to satisfy those debts; but his real estate was, by the laws of Holland, made liable for the payment of simple contract debts as well as specialty debts, if there were not personal assets to answer the same.   The creditors in Holland sued the devisee and obtained a decree for the sale of the lands devised for the payment of their debts; and then the

---

[1] Story's Conflict of Laws, § 524.
[2] Ibid. § 525.

(a) See St. John v. Hodges, 9 Baxt. 334.

(b) See Rice v. Harbeson, 63 N. Y. 493.

(c) See Macdonald v. Macdonald, L. R. 14 Eq. 60; Lynch v. Paraguay, L. R. 2 P. & M. 268; Harrison v. Harrison, L. R. 8 Ch. 342.

devisee brought a suit in England against the executor (the legatee of the personalty) for reimbursement out of the personal
estate. The court decided in his favor, upon the ground that, in
Holland as in England, the personal estate was the primary fund
for the payment of debts, and should come in aid of the real estate
and be charged in the first place.[1]

588. Every ancillary administration is, upon principles of international law, made subservient to the rights of creditors, legatees, and distributees in the country where such administration is
taken out; although the distribution, as to legatees and distributees or heirs, is governed by the law of the place of the testator's or intestate's domicil. But a most important question often
arises, — What is to be done as to the residue of the assets after
discharging all the debts and other claims of the deceased due to
persons resident in the country where the ancillary administration
is taken out? Is it to be remitted to the forum of the testator's
or intestate's domicil, to be there finally settled, adjusted, and
distributed among all the claimants according to the law of the
country of the domicil of the testator or intestate? Or may creditors, legatees, and distributees of any foreign country come into
the Courts of Equity or other courts of the country granting such
ancillary administration, and there have all their respective claims
adjusted and satisfied according to the law of the testator's or intestate's domicil, or to any other law? And in cases of insolvency
or other deficiency of assets, what rules are to govern in regard
to the rights, preferences, and priorities of different classes of
claimants under the laws of different countries seeking such distribution of the residue?

589. These are questions which have given rise to very ample
discussions in various courts in the present age, and they have
been thought to be not unattended with difficulty. It seems now
however to be understood as the general result of the authorities,
that Courts of Equity of the country where the ancillary administration is granted (and other courts exercising a like jurisdiction
in cases of administrations) are not incompetent to act upon such
matters, and to decree a final distribution of the assets to and
among the various claimants having equities or rights in the funds,
whatever may be their domicil, whether it be that of the testator
or intestate, or be in some other foreign country. The question

---

[1] Story's Conflict of Laws, § 528.

whether the court, entertaining the suit for such a purpose, ought
to decree such a distribution, or to remit the property to the forum
of the domicil of the party deceased, is treated not so much as a
matter of jurisdiction, as of judicial discretion dependent upon
the particular circumstances of each case. There can be, and
ought to be, no universal rule on the subject. But every nation
is bound to lend the aid of its own judicial tribunals for the purpose of enforcing the rights of all persons having a title to the
fund, when such interference will not be productive of injustice,
or inconvenience, or conflicting equities, which may call upon
such tribunals for abstinence in the exercise of the jurisdiction.[1]

[1] Harvey *v.* Richards, 1 Mason, R. 381; Dawes *v.* Head, 3 Pick. R. 128;
Story's Conflict of Laws, ch. 13, § 513, and the cases in note (2), ibid.

CHAPTER X.

LEGACIES.

590. ANOTHER head of concurrent jurisdiction in equity is in regard to LEGACIES. This subject has been in part incidentally treated before, but it is proper to bring the subject more fully under review. It seems that originally the jurisdiction over personal legacies was claimed and exercised in the Temporal Courts of Common Law, or at least that it was a jurisdiction mixti fori, claimed and exercised in the County Court where the bishop and sheriff sat together.[1] Afterwards (at least from the reign of Henry the Third) the Spiritual or Ecclesiastical Courts obtained exclusive jurisdiction over the probate of wills of personal property; and as incident thereto they acquired jurisdiction (though not exclusive) over legacies.[2] This latter jurisdiction still continues in the Ecclesiastical Courts, though it is at present rarely exercised; a more efficient and complete jurisdiction being, as we shall presently see, exercised by Courts of Equity.[3]

591. In regard to legacies, whether pecuniary or specific, it is very clear that no suit will lie at the common law to recover them, unless the executor has assented thereto.[4] (a)   If no such

[1] Swinb. on Wills, Pt. 6, § 11, pp. 430, 431, 432; 2 Fonbl. Eq. B. 4, Pt. 1, ch. 1, § 1, and notes (a) and (b); 2 Black. Comm. 491, 492; 3 Black. Comm. 61, 95, 96; Marriott v. Marriott, 1 Str. R. 667, 669, 670; 2 Roper on Legacies, by White, ch. 25, p. 685; 1 Reeves, Hist. of the Law, 92, 308.

[2] Ibid.; 3 Black. Comm. 98; Com. Dig. Prohibition, G. 17; Bac. Abridg. Legacies, M.; Atkins v. Hill, Cowp. 287.

[3] Bac. Abridg. Legacies, M.; 2 Roper on Legacies, by White, ch. 25, § 2, p. 693; 5 Madd. R. 357.

[4] Deeks v. Strutt, 5 T. Rep. 690.

(a) Nor will an action lie in a Common-Law Court to recover a distributive share in an estate after decree of the Probate Court, unless it be upon the bond of the administrator or executor. Howard v. Brown, 11 Vt. 361.

assent has been given, the remedy is exclusively in the Ecclesiastical Courts or in the Courts of Equity. But in cases of specific legacies of goods and chattels after the executor has assented thereto the property vests immediately in the legatee, who may maintain an action at law for the recovery thereof.[1] The same rule has been attempted to be applied at law to cases of pecuniary legacies where the executor had *expressly* assented thereto; for it is agreed on all sides that the mere possession of assets without such assent will not support an action.[2] There are certainly decisions which establish that in the case of an express promise to pay a pecuniary legacy in consideration of assets, an action will lie at law for the recovery thereof.[3] But these cases seem not to have been decided upon satisfactory principles; and though they have not been directly overturned in England, they have been doubted and disapproved by judges as well as by elementary writers.[4]

592. The ground upon which these decisions have been doubted or denied is the pernicious consequences which would follow from allowing such an action at law; for Courts of Law, if compellable to entertain the jurisdiction, cannot impose any terms upon the parties. Thus for instance a suit might be maintained by a husband for a legacy given to his wife, without making any provision for her or for her family; whereas a Court of Equity would require such a provision to be made.[5]

593. But whether a pecuniary legacy is recoverable at law or not after an assent thereto by an executor, it is very certain that Courts of Equity now exercise a concurrent jurisdiction with all

[1] Doe *v.* Gay, 3 East, R. 120; Paramore *v.* Yardley, Plowd. 539; Young *v.* Holmes, 1 Str. 70; 4 Co. Rep. 28 *b.*

[2] Deeks *v.* Strutt, 5 T. R. 690; Doe *v.* Gay, 3 East, R. 120.

[3] Atkins *v.* Hill, Cowp. R. 284; Hawkes *v.* Saunders, Cowp. R. 289.

[4] See Deeks *v.* Strutt, 5 T. R. 690; Doe *v.* Gay, 3 East, R. 120; 2 Roper on Legacies, by White, ch. 25, § 2, pp. 696, 697; Bac. Abridg. Legacies, M., Gwillim's note. See also 3 Dyer, Rep. 264 *b*; Beecker *v.* Beecker, 7 John. R. 99; Farish *v.* Wilson, Peake, Rep. 73; Mayor of Southampton *v.* Greaves, 8 T. Rep. 583; 2 Madd. Ch. Pr. 1, 2, 3.

[5] Deeks *v.* Strutt, 5 T. R. 692. An action at law for a pecuniary legacy has been maintained against an executor after his assent to the legacy, in some of the courts of America. In some of the States an action at law is expressly given by statute. See Dewitt *v.* Schoonmaker, 2 John. R. 243; Beecker *v.* Beecker, 7 John. R. 99; Farwell *v.* Jacobs, 4 Mass. R. 634; Bigelow's Digest, Legacy, C.

other courts in cases of legacies, whether the executor has assented thereto or not.[1] (a)   The grounds of this jurisdiction are various.   In the first place the executor is treated as a trustee for the benefit of the legatees; and therefore as a matter of trust legacies are within the cognizance of Courts of Equity, whether the executor has assented thereto or not.   This seems a universal ground for the jurisdiction.[2]   In the next place the jurisdiction is maintainable in all cases where an account or discovery or distribution of the assets is sought upon general principles.   Indeed Lord Mansfield seems to have thought that the jurisdiction arose as an incident to discovery and account.[3]   In the next place there is in many cases the want of any adequate or complete remedy in any other court.[4]

594.   Obvious as some of these grounds are to found a general jurisdiction in equity in cases of legacies, it does not appear that the jurisdiction was familiarly exercised until a comparatively recent period.   Lord Kenyon indeed has said the jurisdiction over questions of legacies was not exercised in equity until the time of Lord Chancellor Nottingham.[5]   In this remark Lord Kenyon was probably under some slight mistake; for traces are found of an exercise of the jurisdiction as early as the time of Lord Chancellor Ellesmere, in cases where the defendant answered the bill and took no exceptions; although he appears to have entertained the opinion that the Ecclesiastical Courts were more proper to give relief in cases of legacies.[6]   But it is highly probable that the jurisdiction was not firmly established beyond controversy until Lord Nottingham's time.

595.   Indeed in many cases Courts of Equity exercise an exclusive jurisdiction in regard to legacies; as for instance where the bequest of the legacy involves the execution of trusts either express or implied; or where the trusts, engrafted on the bequest,

---

[1] Franco v. Alvares, 3 Atk. 346.

[2] 2 Roper on Legacies, by White, ch. 25, p. 685; Jeremy on Eq. Jurisd. B. 1, ch. 1, § 2, p. 104; Farrington v. Knightly, 1 P. Will. 549, 554; Wind v. Jekyl, 1 P. Will. 575; Hurst v. Beach, 5 Madd. R. 360; 2 Madd. Ch. Pract. 1, 2.

[3] Atkins v. Hill, Cowper, R. 287; 2 Madd. Ch. Pract. 1, 2.

[4] 2 Madd. Ch. Pr. 1, 2, 3; Franco v. Alvares, 3 Atk. 346.

[5] Deeks v. Strutt, 5 T. Rep. 692.

[6] 2 Madd. Ch. Pr. 1, 2.

(a) James v. Faulk, 54 Ala. 184.

are themselves to be pointed out by the court; for (as we have seen) the Spiritual Courts cannot, any more than the Temporal Common Law Courts, enforce the execution of trusts.[1] (a)

596. It is upon this account that where a testator by his will has not disposed of the surplus of his personal estate, the Spiritual Courts have no authority to decree distribution of it; for in such a case the executor is at law entitled to it; although under circumstances he may in equity be held to be a trustee for the next of kin.[2] And therefore it is that if the Spiritual Courts attempt to enforce the payment of a legacy which involves a trust, a Court of Equity will award an injunction in order to protect its own exclusive jurisdiction.[3]

597. So where the jurisdiction in the Spiritual Courts cannot

[1] 2 Roper on Legacies, by White, ch. 25, § 2, p. 693; Farrington v. Knightly, 1 P. Will. 549; Anon. 1 Atk. R. 491; Hill v. Turner, 1 Atk. 516; Attorney-Gen. v. Pyle, 1 Atk. 435.

[2] 2 Madd. Ch. Pr. 1, 2, 3; Farrington v. Knightly, 1 P. Will. 549, 550, 553, 554, and Mr. Cox's note (1); Id. 550; Petit v. Smith, 1 P. Will. 7; Hatton v. Hatton, 2 Str. R. 865; ante, §§ 536, 537. At law the appointment of an executor is deemed to be a virtual gift to him of all the surplus of the personal estate after the payment of all debts and legacies. But in equity he is considered as a mere trustee of such surplus, for the benefit of the next of kin, if from the nature and circumstances of the will a presumption arises that the testator did not intend that the executor should take such surplus to his own use. The effect of the doctrine therefore is that the legal right of the executor will prevail unless there are circumstances which repel that conclusion. Wilson v. Ivat, 2 Ves. 165; Bennett v. Batchelor, 1 Ves. jr. 67; Dawson v. Clarke, 18 Ves. 254; Haynes v. Littlefear, 1 Sim. & Stu. 496. What circumstances will be sufficient to turn the legal estate of the executor into a trust is a matter which would require a very large discussion in order to bring before the reader all the appropriate learning. It is in truth rather a matter of presumptive evidence than of equity jurisdiction. The subject is amply treated in Jeremy on Equity Jurisd. B. 1, ch. 1, § 2, pp. 122 to 135; and in 2 Roper on Legacies, by White, ch. 24, p. 579; Id. 590 to 640. It may however be generally stated that where there arises upon the face of the will a presumption that the executor is not to take the surplus for his own use, there parol evidence may be admitted on his part to repel the presumption, or on the part of the next of kin to confirm it. But if no such presumption arises on the face of the will, parol evidence is not admissible on the part of the next of kin to show that the executor was not intended to take beneficially. Ibid.; 1 Roper on Legacies, by White, ch. 6, § 2, pp. 337, 338; White v. Williams, 3 Ves. & B. 72, 73; Langham v. Sandford, 2 Meriv. R. 17, 18; Hurst v. Beach, 5 Madd. R. 360.

[3] 2 Roper on Legacies, by White, ch. 25, § 2, p. 693; Anon. 1 Atk. 591.

(a) When assumpsit will lie, and when a bill in equity, see Prescott v. More, 62 Maine, 447.

be exercised in a manner adequate to protect the just rights of all
the parties concerned in the case of a legacy, Courts of Equity
will assume an exclusive jurisdiction, and grant an injunction to
stay proceedings of the Spiritual Courts for such legacy. It was
upon this account that injunctions were formerly granted by
Courts of Equity to proceedings in the Spiritual Courts for a
legacy, where there was no offer or requirement of security to
refund it (which such courts might insist on or not)[1] in case of
a deficiency of assets. For it was said that there is a difference
between a suit for a legacy in a Court of Equity, and a suit for
a legacy in the Spiritual Courts. If in the Spiritual Courts they
would compel an executor to pay a legacy without security to
refund, there a prohibition should go. But in a Court of Equity,
though there be no provision made for refunding (which was
formerly a usual provision, but is now discontinued), yet the
common justice of the court would compel a legatee to refund.[2]

598. But there are other instances, illustrative of the same
principle of exclusive jurisdiction, of a more general character,
and dependent upon the state of the legatee. Thus if a legacy
is given to a married woman, and her husband sues therefor in the
Spiritual Court, a Court of Equity will grant an injunction ; for
the Spiritual Court has no authority (as we have seen) to require
him to make a suitable settlement on her and her family, as a
Court of Equity has ; and therefore to allow the suit in the
Spiritual Court to proceed would enable the husband to do injustice to her rights, and to defeat her equity to a settlement.[3]

599. In general it is true that in cases of concurrent jurisdiction (as of legacies) that court which is first in possession of the

---

[1] Nicholas v. Nicholas, Prec. Ch. 546, 547; 2 Fonbl. Eq. B. 4, Pt. 1, ch. 1,
§ 2; Horrell v. Waldron, 1 Vern. 26, 27; Mr. Cox's note B. to Slanning v.
Style, 3 P. Will. 337.

[2] Noel v. Robinson, 1 Vern. 93, 94; Anon. 1 Atk. 491; Hawkins v. Day,
Ambler, R. 161, 162; 2 Fonbl. Eq. B. 4, Pt. 1, ch. 1, § 2, note (d). In Anon.
1 Atk. 491, Lord Hardwicke said that the rule of the court was varied since
the case in 1 Vern. 93; for legatees are not obliged to give security to refund
upon a deficiency of assets. See ante, §§ 537, 538. In Hawkins v. Day,
Ambler, R. 162, Lord Hardwicke said: ' The rule of this court to grant pro-
hibitions in case legatees sue in the Spiritual Court and refuse to give security is out of use now. But this court will decree a legatee to refund.'

[3] Meals v. Meals, 1 Dick. R. 373; Anon. 1 Atk. 491; Hill v. Turner, 1
Atk. R. 516; Jewson v. Moulson, 2 Atk. 419, 420; Prec. Ch. 548; 2 Fonbl.
Eq. B. 4, Pt. 1, ch. 1, § 2, note (d); 2 Madd. Ch. Pr. 2; ante, §§ 539, 592.

cause is entitled to go on with it, and no other court ought to intermeddle with it. But this rule is applicable only to cases where the same remedial justice can be administered in each court, and the same protection furnished by each to the rights of the parties.[1] (a) In cases of married women it is obvious, from what has above stated, that the same remedial justice cannot be administered in each court, and therefore Courts of Equity will insist upon making it exclusive.

600. In like manner in the case of infants to whom legacies are given Courts of Equity will interfere, and exercise an exclusive jurisdiction, and prevent proceedings in the Spiritual Court by an injunction ; for Courts of Equity can give proper directions for securing and improving the fund, which the Spiritual Court cannot do. And indeed it would be proper for the executor to resort to a Court of Equity in order to procure suitable indemnity for the payment of the legacy, and security to refund in case of a deficiency of assets.[2]

601. In cases where a discovery of assets is required, or the due administration and settlement of the estate is indispensable to the rights of the legatees, as in the case of residuary legatees, it follows of course that Courts of Equity should entertain the exclusive jurisdiction, since they alone are competent to such an investigation. But this subject has been already sufficiently examined under the preceding head of the jurisdiction of Courts of Equity in cases of administrations.[3]

602. In regard to legacies charged on land Courts of Equity, for the reasons already stated, also exercise an exclusive jurisdiction ; for the Spiritual Courts have no cognizance of legacies chargeable on lands but only of purely personal legacies.[4] (b) In deciding upon the validity and interpretation of purely personal legacies Courts of Equity implicitly follow the rules of the civil law as recognized and acted on in the Spiritual Courts.[5] But

---

[1] Nicholas v. Nicholas, Prec. Ch. 546, 547.

[2] Horrell v. Waldron, 1 Vern. R. 26; Nicholas v. Nicholas, Prec. Ch. 546, 547; 2 Roper on Legacies, by White, ch. 25, § 2, p. 694; ante, §§ 539, 597.

[3] Ante, § 534.

[4] Reynish v. Martin, 3 Atk. 333.

[5] Ibid; Franco v. Alvares, 3 Atk. R. 346; Hurst v. Beach, 5 Madd. R.

(a) Sweeny v. Williams, 36 N. J. Eq. 627; Hause v. Hause, 57 Ala. 262.   (b) See Sherman v. Sherman, 4 Allen, 392.

in legacies chargeable on land they follow the rules of the common law as to the validity and interpretation thereof.[1]

603. But the beneficial operation of the jurisdiction of Courts of Equity in cases of legacies is even more apparent in some other cases, where the remedies are peculiar to such courts, and are protective of the rights and interests of legatees. Thus for instance in cases of pecuniary legacies due and payable at a future day (whether contingent or otherwise),[2] Courts of Equity will compel the executor to give security for the due payment thereof;[3] (a) or what is the modern and perhaps generally the more approved practice, will order the fund to be paid into court, even if there be not any actual waste, or danger of waste, of the estate.[4]

360; 2 Fonbl. Eq. B. 4, Pt. 1, ch. 1, § 4, and note (h). But see Cray v. Willis, 2 P. Will. 530.

[1] Reynish v. Martin, 3 Atk. 333, 334; Paschall v. Keterich, Dyer, 151 b, (5). But see Dyer, 264 b.

[2] Formerly a distinction was taken between cases of contingent and cases of absolute legacies, payable in futuro; the latter were entitled to be made secure in equity, the former were not. See Palmer v. Mason, 1 Atk. R. 505; Heath v. Perry, 3 Atk. 101, 105. But that distinction is now overruled. See Mr. Saunders's note to Heath v. Perry, 3 Atk. 105, note (1); Mr. Blunt's note to Ferrand v. Prentice, Ambler, R. 273, note (1); Johnson v. De la Creuze, cited 1 Bro. Ch. R. 105; Green v. Pigott, 1 Bro. Ch. R. 103, 105; Flight v. Cook, 2 Ves. 619; Gawler v. Standerwick, 2 Cox, R. 15, 18; Carey v. Askew, 2 Bro. Ch. R. 55; Jeremy on Eq. Jurisd. B. 3, ch. 2, § 2, pp. 351, 352; Studholme v. Hodgson, 3 P. Will. 300, 303, 304; Johnson v. Mills, 1 Ves. 282, 283; 1 Madd. Ch. Pr. 180, 181; post, §§ 844, 848.

[3] 2 Fonbl. Eq. B. 4, Pt. 1, ch. 1, § 2, note (d); Rous v. Noble, 2 Vern. 249; s. c. 1 Eq. Abridg. 238, Pl. 22; Duncumban v. Stint, 1 Cas. Ch. 121.

[4] Johnson v. Mills, 1 Ves. R. 282; Ferrand v. Prentice, Ambler, R. 273; s. c. 2 Dick. R. 569; Phipps v. Annesley, 2 Atk. R. 58; Green v. Pigott, 1 Bro. Ch. R. 104; Webber v. Webber, 1 Sim. & Stu. R. 311; Johnson v. De la Creuze, 1 Bro. Ch. R. 105; Strange v. Harris, 3 Bro. Ch. 365; Yare v. Harrison, 2 Cox, R. 377; Slanning v. Style, 3 P. Will. 336; Batten v. Earnley, 2 P. Will. 163; Jeremy on Equity Jurisd. B. 3, ch. 2, § 2, pp. 351, 352; Blake v. Blake, 2 Sch. & Lefr. 26. In Slanning v. Style, 3 P. Will. 336, it was said by Lord Talbot: 'Generally speaking, where the testator thinks fit to repose a trust, in such a case, until some breach of that trust be shown, or at least a tendency thereto, the court will continue to entrust the same hand, without calling for any other security than what the testator has required.' Yet in that very case, where an annuity was charged on the residue

(a) And this though there has been no misconduct on the part of the executor and there is no reason to apprehend any. Randle v. Carter, 62 Ala. 95.

604. Another class of cases of the same nature is where a specific legacy is given to one for life, and after his death to another; there the legatee in remainder was formerly entitled in all cases to come into a Court of Equity, and to have a decree for security from the tenant for life for the due delivery over of the legacy to the remainder-man. But the modern rule is, not to entertain such a bill unless there be some allegation and proof of waste, or of danger of waste, of the property. Without such ingredients the remainder-man is only entitled to have an inventory of the property bequeathed to him, so that he may be enabled to identify it; and when his absolute right accrues, to enforce a due delivery of it.[1] (a)

of the personal estate of the testator, he ordered assets to the amount necessary to secure it to be brought into court. But where there is any danger of loss or deterioration of the fund, Courts of Equity in all cases used to require security. Rous v. Noble, 2 Vern. 249; s. c. 1 Eq. Abridg. 238, Pl. 22. But the modern practice seems to be (as stated in the text), to have the money paid into court; though it is certainly competent for the court to adopt either course.

[1] 1 Madd. Ch. Pr. 178, 179; Bracken v. Bentley, 1 Ch. Rep. 110; Anon. 2 Freem. R. 206; Foley v. Burnell, 1 Bro. Ch. 279; Slanning v. Style, 3 P. Will. 335, 336; Hyde v. Parrat, 1 P. Will. 1; Batten v. Earnley, 2 P. Will. 163; Leeke v. Bennett, 1 Atk. 471; Bill v. Kinaston, 2 Atk. 82; Covenhoven v. Shuler, 2 Paige, R. 122, 132. This last case involved the question, What was to be done in case of a bill bequeathing to a wife the one third of the residue of the personal estate of the testator, and also the use of the residue during her widowhood; and it was held by Mr. Chancellor Walworth that the widow was bound to account for the whole personal estate; and that the two thirds of the residue of the personal estate, which was bequeathed over after the death of the wife, ought to be invested in permanent securities, and the income thereof paid to the wife during her widowhood, and after her death or marriage, to the legatees in remainder. The learned chancellor on that occasion said: ' The modern practice in such cases is only to require an inventory of the articles, specifying that they belong to the first taker for the particular period only, and afterwards to the person in remainder ; and security is not required unless there is danger that the articles may be wasted or otherwise lost to the remainder-man. Foley v. Burnell, 1 Bro. Ch. Cas. 279; Slanning v. Style, 3 P. Will. 336. Whether a gift for life of specific articles, as of hay, grain, &c., which must necessarily be consumed in the using, is to

(a) Nor where personal property is given by will to A for life and then to B absolutely, can B, as mere matter of right, require the legacy to be brought into court and invested and the testator's estate administered by the court, for the purpose of security to himself. There must be some reasonable ground for an application of the kind, such as danger to the fund. In re Braithwaite, 21 Ch. D. 121. See Phipps v. Annesley, 2 Atk. 57; Ferrand v. Prentice, Ambl. 273; Freeman v. Fairlie, 3 Mer. 29.

605. This may suffice, in this place, on the subject of the peculiar jurisdiction of Courts of Equity in cases of legacies where the relief sought and given is of a precautionary and pro-

be considered an absolute gift of the property, or whether they must be sold, and the interest or income only of the money applied to the use of the tenant for life, appears to be a question still unsettled in England. 3 Ves. 314; 3 Mer. 194. But none of these principles, in relation to specific bequests of particular articles, whether capable of a separate use for life or otherwise, are applicable to this case. Where there is a general bequest of a residue for life with a remainder over, although it includes articles of both descriptions, as well as other property, the whole must be sold and converted into money by the executor, and the proceeds must be invested in permanent securities and the interest or income only is to be paid to the legatee for life. This distinction is recognized by the Master of the Rolls in Randall *v.* Russell, 3 Mer. R. 193. He says if such articles are included in a residuary bequest for life, then they are to be sold, and the interest enjoyed by the tenant for life. This is also recognized by Roper and Preston as a settled principle of law in England. Prest. on Leg. 96; Roper on Leg. 209. See also Howe *v.* Earl of Dartmouth, 7 Ves. 137, and cases in the notes.(*a*) The case of De Witt *v.* Schoonmaker (2 John. R. 243) seems to be in collision with this principle. But Mr. Justice Tompkins, who delivered the opinion of the court there, does not appear to have noticed the distinction between the bequest of a general residue and the bequest of specific articles. He says however it was the duty of the executors on the death of the widow to have paid and delivered the personal estate to the residuary legatee. If such was their duty they were not bound to deliver the principal of the estate into her hands without requiring security that it should be preserved and paid over to the residuary legatee after her death. That case was correctly decided; for it was manifestly the intention of the testator that the property should be delivered over to the son after the death of the widow, and that he should pay the legacy to his sister. This court presumed he had received the property agreeably to the directions of the will, and the executors were held not to be liable to the legatee in a Court of Law. In the case before me the widow was not entitled to the use or possession of any specific article of the personal estate, but only to one third of the principal, and the interest or income of two thirds of the remainder of the general residue after the debts of the testator and the legacy to Mrs. Cady were paid or satisfied. The complainants are therefore entitled to an account of all the personal estate of the testator in value as it existed at the death of their father; and after deducting the legacy to Mrs. Cady, and the funeral charges and the expenses of administration, their share of the balance must be invested in permanent securities, and the income thereof paid to Lena Shuler during her life or widowhood; and the principal after her death or marriage must go to the complainants.'

(*a*) See Mills *v.* Mills, 7 Sim. 501; Fryer *v.* Butler, 8 Sim. 442; Benn *v.* Dixon, 10 Sim. 636; Cafe *v.* Bent, 5 Hare, 24, 36; Hunt *v.* Scott, 1 DeG. & S. 219; Howe *v.* Howe, 14 Jur. 359; Neville *v.* Fortescue, 16 Sim. 333; Morgan *v.* Morgan, 14 Beav. 72; s. c. 7 Eng. L. & E. 216.

tective nature.   The subject will again come under review in the consideration of bills quia timet.[1]

606. In regard to a donation mortis causa, which is a sort of amphibious gift, between a gift inter vivos and a legacy, it is not properly cognizable by the Ecclesiastical Courts ; neither does it fall regularly within an administration ; nor does it require any act of the executor to constitute a title in the donee.[2]   It is properly a gift of personal property, (a) by a party who is in peril of death, upon condition that it shall presently belong to the donee in case the donor shall die, but not otherwise.[3] (b)   To give it effect, there must be a delivery of it by the donor ; (c) and it is subject to be defeated by his subsequent personal revocation,(d) or by his recovery or escape from the impending peril of death.[4] (e)   If no event happens which revokes it, the title of the donee is deemed to be directly derived from the donor in his lifetime, and therefore in no sense is it a testamentary act.[5] (f)   And

---

[1] Post, §§ 844, 845, 846.

[2] 1 Roper, Leg. by White, ch. 1, § 2, p. 2; Thompson v. Hodgson, 2 Str. R. 777; Ward v. Turner, 2 Ves. 431; Miller v. Miller, 3 P. Will. 356 ; 3 Wooddeson, Lect. 60, p. 513; Hedges v. Hedges, Prec. Ch. 269; Gilb. Eq. R. 12 ; 2 Vern. 615.

[3] Ibid.; Wells v. Tucker, 3 Binn. R. 366, 370; Edwards v. Jones, 1 Mylne & Craig, 226 ; s. c. 7 Sim. R. 325; 1 Williams on Executors, Pt. 2, B. 2, ch. 2, § 4, pp. 544 to 554 (edit. 1838); Duffield v. Elwes, 1 Bligh, R. 530, N. s.; Lawson v. Lawson, 1 P. Will. 441; Hedges v. Hedges, Prec. Ch. 269; Gilb. Eq. Rep. 12; 2 Vern. R. 615; Tate v. Hilbert, 2 Ves. jr. 121; s. c. 4 Bro. Ch. R. 290; Miller v. Miller, 3 P. Will. 357; Irons v. Smallpiece, 2 Barn. & Ald. 552, 553.

[4] Ibid.; 1 Williams on Executors and Administrators, Pt. 2, B. 2, ch. 2, § 4, pp. 544, 545, 546, 547; Ward v. Turner, 2 Ves. 431; Jones v. Selby, Prec. Ch. 300.

[5] Ibid.   Mr. Williams, in his excellent work on the Law of Executors and

(a) Meach v. Meach, 24 Vt. 591.

(b) The intention to give must be clear.   See First National Bank v. Balcom, 35 Conn. 351; Prickett v. Prickett, 5 C. E. Green, 478.

(c) Upon this point see Ellis v. Secor, 31 Mich. 185; infra, 607 a.

(d) Parker v. Marston, 27 Maine, 196; Stevens v. Stevens, 5 Thomp. & C. 87.

(e) Further upon the nature of this gift see Nicholas v. Adams, 2 Whart. 17; Raymond v. Sellick, 10 Conn. 480; Harris v. Clark, 2 Barb. 94; Parish v. Stone, 14 Pick. 198; Miller v. Jeffries, 4 Gratt. 472; Sims v. Walker, 8 Humph. 503; Brinckerhoff v. Lawrence, 2 Sandf. 401; Dole v. Lincoln, 31 Maine, 422.

(f) Upon the proof of capacity to make such a gift, the rule differs from that applied to testamentary acts. Crum v. Thornley, 47 Ill. 192.   Failing as a will, a written instrument is not to be construed as a gift mortis causa unless all the elements of such gift are present.   McGrath v. Reynolds, 116 Mass. 566.

this is the reason why the Ecclesiastical Courts have no jurisdiction, as they can interpose only in testamentary matters. Courts of Equity however maintain a concurrent jurisdiction in all cases of such donations where the remedy at law is not adequate or complete. But in such cases the jurisdiction stands upon general grounds, and not upon any notion that a donation mortis causa is from its own nature properly cognizable therein.

606 *a*. We have had occasion to say that a donatio mortis causa is of an amphibious nature, — partaking of the character of a gift inter vivos and of a legacy. It differs from a legacy in these respects: (1) It need not be proved — nay, it cannot be proved — as a testamentary act in the Ecclesiastical Courts, for it takes effect as a gift from the delivery by the donor to the donee in his lifetime. (2) It requires no assent or other act on the part of the executor or administrator to perfect the title of the donee. The claim is not from the executor or administrator, but against him. It differs from a gift inter vivos in several respects in which it resembles a legacy: (1) It is ambulatory, incomplete, and revocable during the donor's lifetime. (2) It may be made to the wife of the donor. (3) It is liable to the debts of the donor upon a deficiency of assets.[1]

607. The notion of a donation mortis causa was originally derived into the English law from the civil law. In that law it was thus defined: ' Mortis causa donatio est, quæ propter mortis fit suspicionem; cum quis ita donat ut si quid humanitus ei contigisset, haberet is qui accepit. Sin autem supervixisset is qui donavit, reciperet; vel si eum donationis pœninuisset, aut prior decesserit is cui donatum sit.'[2] It was a long time a question among the Roman lawyers whether a donation mortis causa ought

---

Administrators, says that ' to constitute a donatio mortis causa there must be two attributes: (1) The gift must be with a view to the donor's death. (2) It must be conditioned to take effect only on the death of the donor by the existing disorder. A third essential quality is required by our law, which according to some authorities was not necessary according to the Roman and civil law; namely, (3) There must be a delivery of the subject of the donation.' 1 Williams on Executors and Administrators, Pt. 2, B. 2, ch. 2, § 4, p. 544 (edit. 1838.) See the remarks on this last point by Lord Hardwicke, in Ward *v.* Turner, 1 Ves. 439, 440, 441; Voet, ad Pand. Lib. 39, tit. 6, § 6; Tate *v.* Hilbert, 2 Ves. jr., 111, 112.

[1] 1 Williams on Executors and Administrators, Pt. 2, B. 2, ch. 2, § 4, p. 552 (edit. 1838); 1 Roper on Legacies, by White, ch. 1, § 2, pp. 2, 3 (3d edit.).

[2] Inst. Lib. 2, tit. 7, § 1.

to be reputed a gift or a legacy, inasmuch as it partakes of the nature of both (et utriusque causæ quædam habebat insignia); and Justinian finally settled that it should be deemed of the nature of legacies: 'Hæ mortis causa donationes ad exemplum legatorum redactæ sunt per omnia.'[1]

607 *a*. We have already seen that by our law there can be no valid donation mortis causa: (1) unless the gift be with a view to the donor's death; (2) unless it be conditioned to take effect only on the donor's death by his existing disorder or in his existing illness; (*a*) and (3) unless there be an actual delivery of the subject of the donation. (*b*) This last requisite has been thought by some learned judges to belong exclusively to our law, and not to have existed in the Roman law.[2] (*c*) But a more important practical question is, what may be the subject of a donatio mortis causa. There is no doubt that there may be a good donation of

---

[1] Ibid.; Tate *v.* Hilbert, 2 Ves. jr., 118, 119.   [2] See note 5, p. 607.

(*a*) See Grymes *v.* Hone, 49 N. Y. 17. A gift conditioned on the donor's death in war, for service in which he is enlisted, has been held invalid. Irish *v.* Nutting, 47 Barb. 370; Gourley *v.* Linsinbigler, 51 Penn. St. 345; Dexheimer *v.* Gautier, 5 Rob. (N. Y.) 216. Contra, Gass *v.* Simpson, 4 Cold. 288; Baker *v.* Williams, 34 Ind. 547.

(*b*) See Coleman *v.* Parker, 114 Mass. 30; McGrath *v.* Reynolds, 116 Mass. 566; Parish *v.* Stone, 14 Pick. 198, 203; Sessions *v.* Moseley, 4 Cush. 87, 92; Marshall *v.* Berry, 13 Allen, 43; Grymes *v.* Hone, 49 N. Y. 17; Huntington *v.* Gilmore, 14 Barb. 243; Hitch *v.* Davis, 3 Md. Ch. 266; Jones *v.* Deyer, 16 Ala. 221; Tate *v.* Leithead, Kay, 658; Ellis *v.* Secor, 31 Mich. 185; Rhodes *v.* Childs, 64 Penn. St. 18. Delivery to an agent to hold for the *giver* would not be enough; the delivery must be to the donee or to some one for the donee. Farquharson *v.* Cave, 2 Colly. 356, 367. See Moore *v.* Darton, 20 L. J. Ch. 626; s. c. 7 Eng. L. & E. 134; Wells *v.* Tucker, 3 Binn. 366, 370; McGillicuddy *v.* Cook, 5 Blackf. 179; Sessions *v.* Moseley, 4 Cush. 87. Delivery to one in trust for the donee will be good. Kemper *v.* Kemper, 1 Duv. 401; Baker *v.* Williams, 34 Ind. 547; Clough *v.* Clough, 117 Mass. 83. So where the chattel is already in the hands of a trustee, it may be given mortis causa without delivery. Sutherland *v.* Sutherland, 5 Bush, 591. And where money is already in the hands of the donee, a gift of the receipt will be effectual, it seems. Champney *v.* Blanchard, 39 N. Y. 111. So where a promissory note is in the hands of the donee, that is enough. Wing *v.* Merchant, 57 Maine, 383. Indeed where the donor has done everything in his power to effect a delivery, and fully intends to make a complete gift, that is enough so far as delivery is concerned. Ellis *v.* Secor, 31 Mich. 185.

A husband may make this sort of gift to his wife. Whitney *v.* Wheeler, 116 Mass. 490.

(*c*) See Bunn *v.* Markham, 7 Taunt. 224; Farquharson *v.* Cave, 2 Colly. 356; Ellis *v.* Secor, 31 Mich. 185, a striking case.

anything which has a physical existence and admits of a corporal delivery ; as for example, of jewels, gems, a bag of money, a trunk of goods, and even of things of bulk which are capable of possession by a symbolical delivery, (*a*) such as goods in a warehouse by a delivery of the key of the warehouse.[1] But the question was formerly mooted whether choses in action, bonds, and other incorporeal rights could pass by a donation mortis causa. The doctrine now established is, that not only negotiable notes and bills of exchange payable to bearer, or indorsed in blank, exchequer notes, and bank notes, may be the subjects of a donatio mortis causa, because they may, and do, in the ordinary course of business, pass by delivery, (*b*) but that bonds and mortgages

---

[1] See Ward *v.* Turner, 2 Ves. 443; 1 Williams on Executors and Administrators, Pt. 2, B. 2, ch. 2, § 4, pp. 547, 548, 549; Bunn *v.* Markham, 7 Taunt. R. 224; Miller *v.* Miller, 3 P. Will. 356. See also Rankin *v.* Weguelin, at the Rolls, 14 June, 1832, cited in Chitty on Bills, Addenda, p. 791, 8th edit. 1833; Id. p. 2, note (*a*), 9th edit. (*c*)

(*a*) ' Symbolical ' delivery as a means of getting the chattel is certainly good where it is the only practicable thing, or perhaps the most convenient thing, notwithstanding the broad dictum in McGrath *v.* Reynolds, 116 Mass. 566, 568. ' There are many articles which might be made the subjects of a donatio mortis causa in which a manual delivery . . . might be inconvenient or impracticable. We have no doubt that a trunk with its contents might be effectually given and delivered in such a case by a delivery of the key, not as a symbolical delivery of the property but because it is the means of obtaining possession.' Coleman *v.* Parker, 114 Mass. 30, 33, Ames, J.; Ward *v.* Turner, 2 Ves. Sr. 431, 433; Wing *v.* Merchant, 57 Maine, 383; Dole *v.* Lincoln, 31 Maine, 422; Bunn *v.* Markham, 7 Taunt. 224. See however as to the delivery of a key to a trunk containing stocks and bonds, Hatch *v.* Atkinson, 56 Maine, 324, and qu. as to the decision. But the key must be given to the donee or to some one for him. Coleman *v.* Parker, supra; Powell *v.* Hellicar, 29 Beav.

261; Bunn *v.* Markham, 7 Taunt. 224. Properly this is actual delivery; it may give actual possession.

(*b*) A distinction is taken by the authorities between the paper of the donor and that of a third person. That the paper of a third person may be the subject of this peculiar kind of gift is clear. Westerlo *v.* De Witt, 36 N. Y. 340 (certificate of deposit); Boutts *v.* Ellis, 21 Eng. L. & E. 337 (bank check); Bedell *v.* Carll, 33 N. Y. 581; Gourley *v.* Linsinbigler, 51 Penn. St. 345; Ashbrook *v.* Ryon, 2 Bush, 228; House *v.* Grant, 4 Lans. 296. And this though the paper, e. g. a check, is payable to the donor's order and has not been indorsed by him. Wing *v.* Merchant, 57 Maine, 383; Clement *v.* Cheesman, 27 Ch. D. 631; In re Mead, 15 Ch. D. 654; Veal *v.* Veal, 27 Beav. 303; Bates *v.* Kempton, 7 Gray, 382; Chase *v.* Ridding, 13 Gray, 418, 420; Grymes *v.* Hone, 49 N. Y. 17, 23. On the other hand it seems equally clear that the donor's own note or check, unless paid before death, cannot, as such, unsupported by a consideration, be made the subject of a valid gift mortis

(*c*) 27 Beav. 309.

may also be the subjects of a donatio mortis causa, and pass by
the delivery of the deeds and instruments by which they are created.[1] (a) Bonds have been so held upon the ground that a bond
could not be sued for at law without a profert; and that a Court
of Equity would not, after a donatio mortis causa accompanied
with a delivery of the bond to the donee, direct the latter to give
it up to the personal representative of the donor, but would hold
the title of the donee to it good.[2] And mortgaged deeds, when

[1] Ibid.; Drury v. Smith, 1 P. Will. 405; Miller v. Miller, 3 P. Will. 356.
See also Pennington v. Gittings, 2 Gill & John. R. 208; Bradley v. Hunt, 5
Gill & John. 54; Hill v. Chapman, 2 Bro. Ch. R. 612; Jones v. Selby, Prec.
Ch. 300; 1 Roper on Legacies, by White, ch. 1, § 2, pp. 13, 14, 15, 16 (3d
edit.); Ward v. Turner, 1 Ves. 441, 442.

[2] Ibid.; Gardner v. Parker, 3 Madd. R. 184; Snelgrove v. Bailey, 3 Atk.
214; Duffield v. Elwes, 1 Bligh, N. s. R. 542; Ward v. Turner, 2 Ves. 441,
442. In this last case Lord Hardwicke said: 'In Bailey v. Snelgrove, determined by me, 11th March, 1774, it was urged, where a bond was given in
prospect of death, the manner of gift was admitted, the bond was delivered,
and I held it a good donation mortis causa. It was argued that there was a
want of actual delivery there or possession, the bond being but a chose in
action, and therefore there was no delivery but of the paper. If I went too
far in that case, it is not a reason I should go farther; and I choose to stop
here. But I am of opinion that decree was right, and differs from this case;
for though it is true that a bond which is specialty is a chose in action, and
its principal value consists in the thing in action, yet some property is conveyed by the delivery; for the property is vested; and to this degree, that the
law-books say the person to whom this specialty is given may cancel, burn,
and destroy it. The consequence of which is that it puts it in his power to
destroy the obligee's power of bringing an action, because no one can bring an
action on a bond without a profert in curia. Another thing made it amount
to a delivery: that the law allows it a locality; and therefore a bond is bona
notabilia, so as to require a prerogative administration where a bond is in one
diocese and goods in another. Not that this is conclusive. This reasoning
I have gone upon is agreeable to Jenk. Cent. 109, case 9, relating to delivery
to effectuate gifts. How Jenkins applied that rule of law he mentions there
I know not, but rather apprehend he applied it to a donation mortis causa;
for if to a donation inter vivos, I doubt he went too far.' See also Wells v.
Tucker, 3 Binn. R. 366; Bradley v. Hunt, 5 Gill & John. R. 54.

causa. Starr v. Starr, 9 Ohio St. 74;
Hamor v. Moore, 8 Ohio St. 239;
Brown v. Moore, 3 Head, 671; Carr v.
Silloway, 111 Mass. 24; Harris v.
Clarke, 3 Comst. 93; Fiero v. Fiero,
5 Thomp. & C. 151; Johnson v. Spies,
5 Hun, 468; Kenestons v. Sceva, 54
Md. 24; Case v. Denison, 9 R. I. 88;
Hewitt v. Kaye, L. R. 6 Eq. 198
(check, but good if presented before
death); Second Nat. Bank v. Williams,
13 Mich. 282 (check). And it makes
no difference, it is held, that the donor's pass-book was delivered with the
check. In re Beak, L. R. 13 Eq. 489.
See Ashbrook v. Ryon, 2 Bush, 228.
But see Tillinghast v. Wheaton, 8
R. I. 536, that the delivery of a sav-
ings-bank book alone is good to pass
the deposit.
  (a) So of stocks. Grymes v. Hone,
49 N. Y. 17.

delivered, are treated but as securities for debts, and would, in the hands of the donee, be governed by the same rules. The delivery in the case of a mortgage is therefore treated, not as a complete act passing the property, but as creating a trust by operation of law in favor of the donee, which a Court of Equity will enforce in the same manner as it would the right of the donee to a bond.[1] In short in all cases in which a donatio mortis causa is carried into effect by a Court of Equity the court has not considered the interest as completely vested by the gift, but that it is so vested in the donee that the donee has a right to call on a Court of Equity for its aid, and in case of personal estate, to compel the executor or administrator of the donor to carry into effect the intention manifested by the person whom he represents; as for example if the donation be a bond, to compel the executor or administrator to allow the donee to use his name in suing the bond upon being indemnified, because it is a trust for the donee.[2] (a)

[1] Duffield v. Elwes, 1 Bligh, N. s. R. 497, 530, 534, 535, 536, 541, 542, which overrules the decision of the vice-chancellor in the same case. 1 Sim. & Stu. 243.

[2] Duffield v. Elwes, 1 Bligh, N. s. R. 497, 530, 534; Gardner v. Parker, 3 Madd. R. 184. We have already extracted in another place (ante, § 433, note 4) a part of the opinion of Lord Eldon on this subject, which it may perhaps be useful here to repeat. ' The question,' said he, ' is this: Whether the act of the donor being, as far as the act of the donor itself is to be viewed, complete, the persons who represent that donor — in respect of personalty, the executor, and in respect of realty, the heir at law — are not bound to complete that which, as far as the act of the donor is concerned in the question, was incomplete; in other words, Where it is the gift of a personal chattel or the gift of a deed which is the subject of the donatio mortis causa, whether, after the death of the individual who made that gift the executor is not to be considered a trustee for the donee; and whether on the other hand, if it be a gift affecting the real interest, — and I distinguish now between a security upon land and the land itself, — whether if it be a gift of such an interest in law, the heir at law of the testator is not, by virtue of the operation of the trust which is created, not by indenture, but a bequest arising from operation of law, a trustee for that donee.' His Lordship afterwards, in discussing the point whether a mortgage would pass by a delivery of it as a donation mortis causa, said: ' Lord Hardwicke, with respect to the bond (and it is necessary that I should take some notice of this, because there has been a change in the law which that great judge did not foresee, but which in later times and in my own time has become very familiar in the Courts of Law), — Lord Hardwicke states as one ground of his opinion in the case of the bond that it is a good gift causa mortis, because he says he who has got the bond may do what he pleases with it. He certainly disables the person who has not got the bond from bringing an action upon it; for, says Lord Hardwicke, no man ever heard, (and I have seen in the manuscript of the same Lord

607 *b*. The same doctrine is applicable to the case of a donatio mortis causa of a bond and mortgage by the mortgagee to the mortgagor consummated by the delivery of the bond and mortgage to him.   In such a case it will operate as a release or discharge of the debt if the donor should die of his existing illness. For (it has been said) if it was a gift inter vivos, the mortgagee could not get back the deeds from the mortgagor; but by operation of law a trust would be created in the mortgagee to make good a gift of the debt to the mortgagor to whom he had delivered the deeds.[1]   But however this may be, it seems clear that in the case of such a donatio mortis causa the representatives of the donor would never be permitted to enforce the mortgage or bond against the donee.[2]

607 *c*. On the other hand as by our law there must be a delivery

Hardwicke that he said no man will ever hear) that a person shall bring an action upon a bond without the profert of that bond.   But we now have got into a practice of sliding from Courts of Equity into Courts of Law the doctrine respecting lost instruments; and I take the liberty most humbly of saying, that when that doctrine was so transplanted, it was transplanted upon the idea that the thing might be as well conducted in a Court of Law as in a Court of Equity, — a doctrine which cannot be held by any person who knows what the doctrine of Courts of Equity is as to a lost instrument.   Then if the delivery of a bond would, as it is admitted (notwithstanding any change in the doctrine about profert), — if the delivery of a bond would give the debt in that bond so as to secure to the donee of that bond the debt so given by the delivery of the bond, the question is, the person having got, by the delivery of that bond, a right to call upon the executor to make his title by suing or giving him authority to sue upon the bond, what are we to do with the other securities if they are not given up?   But there is another question to which an answer is to be given: What are we to do with respect to the other securities if they are delivered?   In the one case the bond and mortgage are delivered; in the other the judgment, which is to be considered on the same ground as a specialty, is delivered.   With that the evidences of the debts are all delivered.   The instrument containing the covenant to pay is delivered. They are all delivered in such a way that the donor could never have got the deeds back again.   Then the question is, Whether, regard being had to what is the nature of a mortgage, contradistinguishing it from an estate in land, those circumstances do not as effectually give the property in the debt as if the debt was secured by a bond only?   The opinion which I have formed is, that this is a good donatio mortis causa, raising by operation of law a trust; a trust which being raised by operation of law is not within the Statute of Frauds, but a trust which a Court of Equity will execute.'

[1] Richards *v*. Symes, 2 Atk. 319; 2 Barnard. R. 90; 2 Eq. Abridg. 617; Duffield *v*. Elwes, 1 Bligh, Rep. 537, 538, 539, N. s.; Hurst *v*. Beach, 5 Madd. R. 351.

[2] Ibid.

of the thing or of the instrument which represents it in order
to make a good donatio mortis causa, if the thing is incapable
of delivery it cannot be the subject of such donation ; for, it is
said, there must be a parting with the legal power and dominion
over the thing which is evidenced only by the delivery.   Thus a
mere chose in action not subsisting in any specific instrument
cannot pass by a donatio mortis causa.   So it has been ruled that
a promissory note or bill of exchange not payable to bearer or
indorsed in blank cannot so take effect, inasmuch as no property
therein can pass by the delivery of the instrument.[1] (*a*)   So it
has been ruled that South Sea Annuity Receipts cannot be the
proper subject of a donatio mortis causa, because the delivery
thereof does not pass the property in the annuities ; and stocks
and annuities are by act of Parliament made capable of a transfer
of the legal property.[2]   But it may admit of doubt whether the
doctrine of these last cases can now, upon principle, be supported ;

[1] Miller *v.* Miller, 3 P. Will. 356, 358; Ward *v.* Turner, 2 Ves. 442, 443 ;
Pennington *v.* Gittings, 2 Gill & John. R. 208 ; Bradley *v.* Hunt, 5 Gill &
John. R. 54.

[2] Ward *v.* Turner, 2 Ves. sen., 431, 442, 443. Lord Hardwicke on this
occasion said: ' Therefore from the authority of Swinburne, and all these
cases, the consequence is that by the civil law, as received and allowed in England, and consequently by the law of England, tradition or delivery is necessary to make a good donation mortis causa; which brings it to the question,
Whether delivery of the three receipts was a sufficient delivery of the thing
given to effectuate the gift. I am of opinion it was not. It is argued that
though some delivery is necessary, yet delivery of the thing is not necessary,
but delivery of anything by way of symbol is sufficient. But I cannot agree
to that. Nor do I find any authority for that in the civil law, which required
delivery to some gifts, or in the law of England, which required delivery
throughout. Where the civil law requires it, they require actual tradition,
delivery over of the thing. So in all the cases in this court delivery of the
thing given is relied on, and not in the name of the thing, as in the delivery
of sixpence in Shargold *v.* Shargold; if it was allowed any effect, that would
have been a gift mortis causa, not as a will; but that was allowed as testamentary, proved as a will, and stood. The only case wherein such a symbol
seems to be held good is Jones *v.* Selby. But I am of opinion that amounted
to the same thing as delivery of possession of the tally, provided it was in the
trunk at the time. Therefore it was rightly compared to the cases upon 21
J. 1, Ryal *v.* Rowles and others. It never was imagined on that statute that
delivery of a mere symbol, in name of the thing, would be sufficient to take
it out of that statute; yet notwithstanding delivery of the key of bulky goods

(*a*) Contra, Veal *v.* Veal, 6 Jur.   *v.* Kempton, 7 Gray, 382; Chase *v.*
N. S. 527; s. c. 27 Beav. 303; Clem-   Ridding, 13 Gray, 418, 420; supra,
ent *v.* Cheesman, 27 Ch. D. 631; Wing   note (*b*), p. 610.
v. Marchant, 57 Maine, 383; Bates

for the ground upon which Courts of Equity now support donations mortis causa is not that a complete property in the thing
must pass by the delivery, but that it must so far pass by the delivery of the instrument as to give a title to the donee to the assistance of a Court of Equity to make the donation complete.   The
doctrine no longer prevails that where a delivery will not execute a complete gift inter vivos it cannot create a donatio mortis
causa, because it would not prevent the property from vesting in
the executor ; and as a Court of Equity will not inter vivos compel a party to complete his gift, so it will not compel the executor
to complete the gift of his testator.[1]   On the contrary the doc-

where wines, &c. are, has been allowed as delivery of the possession; because
it is the way of coming at the possession, or to make use of the thing; and
therefore the key is not a symbol, which would not do.   If so, then delivery
of these receipts amounts to so much waste-paper ; for if one purchases stock
or annuities, what avail are they after acceptance of the stock ?   It is true
they are of some avail as to the identity of the person coming to receive; but
after that is over they are nothing but waste-paper, and are seldom taken care
of afterwards.   Suppose Fly, instead of delivering over these receipts to
Mosely, had delivered over the broker's note, whom he had employed, — that
had not been a good delivery of the possession.   There is no color for it; it is no
evidence of the thing or part of the title to it.   For suppose it had been a
mortgage in question, and a separate receipt had been taken for the mortgage
money, not on the back of the deed (which was a very common way formerly,
and is frequently seen in the evidence of ancient titles), and the mortgagee
had delivered over this separate receipt for the consideration-money, that
would not have been a good delivery of the possession, nor given the mortgage
mortis causa by force of that act.   Nor does it appear to me by proof that
possession of these three receipts continued with Mosely from the time they
were given in February to the time of Fly's death; for there is a witness who
speaks that in some short time before his death Fly showed him these receipts
and said he intended them for his uncle Mosely.   Therefore I am of opinion
it would be most dangerous to allow this donation mortis causa from parol
proof of delivery of such receipts, which are not regarded or taken care of
after acceptance.   And if these annuities are called choses in action, there
is less reason to allow of it in this case than in any other chose in action; because stocks and annuities are capable of a transfer of the legal property by
act of Parliament, which might be done easily; and if the intestate had such
an aversion to make a will as supposed, he might have transferred to Mosely;
consequently this is merely legatary, and amounts to a nuncupative will, and
contrary to the Statute of Frauds, and would introduce a greater breach on
that law than ever was yet made; for if you take away the necessity of delivery of the thing given, it remains merely nuncupative.'   The decision of Lord
Eldon in Duffield v. Elwes, 1 Bligh, N. s. R. 498, very much shakes the reasoning of Lord Hardwicke on this particular point.

[1] Duffield v. Elwes, 1 Sim. & Stu. 238, overturned an appeal in 1 Bligh,
N. s. R. 498.

trine, now established by the highest authority, is (as we have seen) that Courts of Equity do not consider the interest as completely vested in the donee, but treat the delivery of the instrument as creating a trust for the donee to be enforced in equity.[1]

607 *d.* According to the civil law a donation mortis causa may be made subject to a trust or condition. ' Eorum quibus mortis causa donatum est, fidei committi quoquo tempore potest ; quod fidei commissum, hæredes, salva Falcidiæ ratione, quam in his quoque donationibus exemplo legatorum, locum habere placuit, præstabunt. Si pars donationis fidei commisso teneatur, fidei commissum quoque munere Falcidiæ fungetur. Si tamen alimenta præstari voluit, collationis totum onus in residuo donationis esse respondendum erit ex defuncti voluntate, qui de majore pecunia præstari non dubie voluit, integra.[2] Ab eo qui neque legatum neque fidei commissum neque hæreditatem vel mortis causa donationem accepit nihil per fidei commissum relinqui

---

[1] Duffield *v.* Elwes, 1 Bligh, N. S. R. 497, 530, 534. In Pennington *v.* Gittings, 2 Gill & John. R. 208, the Court of Appeals of Maryland held that a delivery of a certificate of bank stock, transferable at the bank only, personally or by attorney, indorsed in blank by the donor and delivered to the donee, could not pass as a donatio mortis causa. In Bradley *v.* Hunt, 5 Gill & John. R. 54, the same learned court decided that a promissory note or certificate of the profit, payable to the order of the donor, and delivered to the donee, was not a good donatio mortis causa. In each of these cases the court proceeded upon the same general ground that, to constitute a donatio mortis causa the gift should be full and complete at the time, passing from the donor the legal power and dominion over the thing intended to be given, and leaving nothing to be done by him or his executor to perfect it; and that in these cases the thing was not susceptible of such delivery, and the delivery of the instrument did not convey a perfect title to the thing. The court relied upon the cases of Miller *v.* Miller, 3 P. Will. 356, 358; Ward *v.* Turner, 2 Ves. 431; Tate *v.* Hilbert, 2 Ves. jr., 112, and Duffield *v.* Elwes, 1 Sim. & Stu. 239, as in point. But since the decision in 1 Bligh, N. S. R. 497, these cases can no longer be deemed satisfactory authorities. On the other hand in Wright *v.* Wright, 1 Cowen, R. 598, the Supreme Court of New York held that a promissory note of the donor himself, executed in his last illness, and delivered by the maker to the donee (the payee) in contemplation of death, was a good donatio mortis causa, although no consideration passed. And in Coutant *v.* Schuyler, 1 Paige, R. 316, Mr. Chancellor Walworth held that a promissory note of a third person was a proper subject of a donatio mortis causa, and might be delivered to a third person for the benefit of the donee. The court said that there was no real difference between the delivery of a bond and the delivery of a note, as a donatio mortis causa. Each is valid. See also Wells *v.* Tucker, 3 Binn. 366, R.

[2] Dig. Lib. 31, tit. 1, 1. 77, § 1, cited in Hambrooke *v.* Simmons, 4 Russ. R. 27.

potest.'[1]   The point does not seem to have been directly established in modern Equity Jurisprudence, but the manifest inclination of the courts is to sustain such a donation although it is
coupled with a trust or condition.[2]

608. It has been already stated that in the interpretation of
purely personal legacies Courts of Equity follow the rules of the
Spiritual Courts, and in those which are charged on lands, the
rules of the common law.[3]   But although this is generally true,
it is not to be taken for granted that Courts of Equity do, in all
cases, follow the rules of Courts of Common Law in deciding upon
the nature, extent, interpretation, and effect of legacies.   There
are some cases in which Courts of Equity act upon principles
peculiar to themselves in relation to legacies.[4]   But any attempt
to point them out in a satisfactory manner would require a general review of the whole doctrine of legacies ; a task which is
incompatible with the objects of the present Commentaries.[5]

---

[1] Cod. Lib. 6, tit. 42, l. 9, cited 4 Russ. 27.

[2] See Drury *v.* Smith, 1 P. Will. 404; Blount *v.* Burrow, 4 Bro. Ch. R. 75;
Hambrooke *v.* Simmons, 4 Russ. R. 25; 1 Williams on Executors and Administrators, Pt. 2, B. 2, ch. 2, § 4, p. 548, note (*v*), (edit. 1838).

[3] Ante, § 602; Keily *v.* Monck, 3 Ridgw. Parl. Cas. 243.

[4] See 2 Fonbl. Eq. B. 4, Pt. 1, ch. 1, §§ 4, 5, and notes (*i*) and (*l*) ; 3
Wooddes. Lect. 59, pp. 479, 480, 481; Id. 494; Jeremy on Eq. Jurisd. B. 1,
ch. 1, § 2, p. 106 ; Arnald *v.* Arnald, 1 Bro. Ch. R. 403.

[5] The whole subject of legacies is very amply discussed in Mr. Roper's
Treatise on Legacies, as newly edited by Mr. White; in 2 Fonbl. Eq. B. 4,
Pt. 1, ch. 1, 2; in Jeremy on Eq. Jurisd. B. 1, ch. 1, § 2, pp. 104 to 135, and
in Wooddeson, Lect. 60, p. 509, &c.   The most important topics are the description of the persons who are to take; when legacies are specific or not;
when they are cumulative or not ; when they lapse or merge; when there is an
ademption of them; when an abatement of them; when conditional; when
personal or chargeable on land ; when they vest; when interest is allowed ; and
lastly, the marshalling of assets in favor of them.

CHAPTER XI.

CONFUSION OF BOUNDARIES.

609. HAVING disposed of the subject of Administrations and Legacies, we shall next proceed to the consideration of another head of concurrent jurisdiction, arising from the confusion of the boundaries of land, and the confusion or entanglement of other rights and claims of an analogous nature, calling for the interposition of Courts of Equity in order to restore and ascertain and fix them.

610. In the first place in regard to CONFUSION OF BOUNDARIES. The issuing of commissions to ascertain boundaries is certainly a very ancient branch of equity jurisdiction.[1] A number of cases of this sort will be found in the earliest of the Chancery Reports. Thus in Mullineux *v.* Mullineux, in 14th Jac. 1, a commission was awarded, ' to set out lands, that lye promiscuously, to be liable for the payment of debts.' In Peckering *v.* Kimpton, 5 Car. 1,[2] a commission was awarded, ' to set out copyhold lands free from land, which lye obscured ; if the commissioners cannot sever it, then to set out so much in lieu thereof.'

611. It is not very easy to ascertain with exactness the origin of this jurisdiction.[3] It has been supposed by Lord Northington and Lord Thurlow that consent was the ground upon which it was originally exercised.[4] There are two writs in the Register concerning the adjustment of controverted boundaries, from one of which (in the opinion of Sir William Grant) it is probable that the exercise of this jurisdiction in the Court of Chancery

---

[1] Jeremy on Eq. Jurisd. B. 3, ch. 1, § 3, n 1, pp. 301, 302.

[2] Tothill, R. 39 (edit. 1649). See also Wake *v.* Conyers, 1 Eden, R. 337, note. See Co. Litt. 169 *a*; Hargrave's note 23, vii.

[3] Ibid.

[4] Speer *v.* Crawter, 2 Meriv. 417.

took its commencement.[1]   The one is the writ De Rationabilibus divisis, which properly lies where two men have lands in divers towns or hamlets, so that one is seised of the land in one town or hamlet, and the other of the land in the other town or hamlet by himself; and they do not know the boundaries of the towns or hamlets whereby to ascertain which is the land of one and which is the land of the other.   In such a case, to set the bounds certain, this writ lies for the one against the other.[2]   The other writ is De Perambulatione facienda.   This writ is sued out with the assent of both parties, where they are in doubt of the bounds of their lordships or manors, or of their towns.   And upon such assent the writ issues to the sheriff to make the perambulation and to set out the bounds and limits between them in certainty.[3] And it is added in Fitzherbert (in which he follows the rule of the Registrum Brevium) that the perambulation may be made for divers towns and in divers counties; and the parties ought to come into the chancery, and there acknowledge and grant that a perambulation be made betwixt them; and the acknowledgment shall be enrolled in the chancery; and thereupon a commission or writ shall issue forth.[4]

612. Sir William Grant further supposes that the jurisdiction having thus originated in consent, the next step would probably be to grant the commission on the application of one party who showed an equitable ground for obtaining it; such as that a tenant or copyholder had destroyed, or not preserved, the boundaries between his own property and that of his lessor or lord.(a) And to its exercise on such an equitable ground no objection has ever been made;[5] and, it may be added, no just objection can be made.

613. This account of the origin of the chancery jurisdiction seems highly probable in itself; but however satisfactory it may seem, it can scarcely be said to afford more than a reasonable conjecture, and is not a conclusive proof that such was the actual

---

[1] Ibid.; Regist. Brevium, 157 *b*.
[2] Fitzherb. Nat. Brev. 300 [128].
[3] Fitzherb. Nat. Brev. 309 [133].
[4] Ibid.; Regis. Brev. 157, and Regula. ibid.
[5] Speer *v.* Crawter, 2 Meriv. 417.

(a) It is then a case of trust.   Attorney-Gen. *v.* Stephens, 6 DeG. M. & G. 111, 132; infra, § 620, and note (a).

origin. In truth the recent discoveries made of the actual exercise of chancery jurisdiction in early times, as disclosed in the Report of the Parliamentary Commissioners, already referred to in a former part of these Commentaries, are sufficient to teach us to rely with a subdued confidence upon all such conjectural sources of jurisdiction.[1] It is very certain that in some cases the Court of Chancery has granted commissions or directed issues on no other apparent ground than that the boundaries of manors were in controversy.[2] And Lord Northington seems to have assigned a different origin to the jurisdiction from that already suggested upon one important occasion at least; namely, that parties originally came into the court for relief in cases of confusion of boundaries under the equity of preventing multiplicity of suits.[3]

614. The civil law was far more provident than ours upon the subject of boundaries. It considered that there was a tacit agreement or duty between adjacent proprietors to keep up and preserve the boundaries between their respective estates; and it enabled all persons having an interest, to bring a suit to have the boundaries between them settled; and this, whether they were tenants for years, usufructuaries, mortgagees, or other proprietors. The action was called 'actio finium regundorum'; and if the possession was also in dispute, that might be ascertained and fixed in the same suit, and indeed was incident to it.[4] Perhaps it might not have been originally unfit for Courts of Equity to have entertained the same general jurisdiction in cases of confusion of boundaries, upon the ground of enforcing a specific performance of the implied engagement or duty of the civil law. Such a broad origin or exercise of the jurisdiction has however never been claimed or exercised.

615. But whatever may have been the origin of this branch of jurisdiction, it is one which has been watched with a good deal of jealousy by Courts of Equity of late years; and there seems no inclination to favor it, unless special grounds are laid to sus-

---

[1] Ante, § 47, 48, and notes, ibid.

[2] Ibid. See Lethulier v. Castlemain, 1 Dick. R. 46; s. c. 2 Eq. Abridg. 161; Sel. Cas. Ch. 60; Metcalfe v. Beckwith, 2 P. Will. 376.

[3] Wake v. Conyers, 1 Eden, R. 334; s. c. 1 Cox, R. 360.

[4] See 1 Domat, B. 2, tit. 6, §§ 1, 2, pp. 308, 309; Co. Litt. 169 a, Hargrave's note 23; Dig. Lib. 10, tit. 1, l. 1, per tot.

tain it.   The general rule now adopted is, not to entertain jurisdiction, in cases of confusion of boundaries, upon the ground
that the boundaries are in controversy,[1] (a) but to require that
there should be some equity superinduced by the act of the parties ; (b) such as some particular circumstances of fraud ; or some
confusion, where one person has ploughed too near another;
or some gross negligence, omission, or misconduct on the part of
persons whose special duty it is to preserve or perpetuate the
boundaries.[2] (c)

616.   Where there is an ordinary legal remedy there is certainly
no ground for the interference of Courts of Equity, unless some
peculiar equity supervenes which a Court of Common Law cannot take notice of or protect.   It has been said by Lord Northington that where there is no legal remedy it does not therefore
follow that there must be an equitable remedy, unless there is
also an equitable right.   Where there is a legal right, there must
be a legal remedy ; and if there is no legal right, in many cases
there can be no equitable one.[3]   On this account he dismissed a
bill to settle the boundaries between manors, it appearing that
there was no dispute as to the right of soil and freehold on both
sides the boundary marks (which right was admitted by the bill
to be in the defendant), and that the right of seigniory alone (an
incorporeal hereditament), and not that of the soil, was in dispute.
And his Lordship on this occasion remarked that 'all the cases

---

[1] But see Lethulier v. Castlemain, 1 Dick. R. 46; s. c. 2 Eq. Abridg. 161;
Sel. Cas. in Ch. 60.

[2] Wake v. Conyers, 1 Eden, R. 331; s. c. 1 Cox, R. 360.   See Miller v.
Warmington, 1 Jac. & Walk. 473; Eden on Injunctions, ch. 16, pp. 361, 362.

[3] Ibid.

(a) Kilgannon v. Jenkinson, 51 Mich. 241; Haskell v. Allen, 23 Maine, 448; Stuart v. Coalter, 4 Rand. 74; Hale v. Darter, 5 Humph. 79; Topp v. Williams, 7 Humph. 569; Wetherbee v. Dunn, 36 Cal. 249; Norris's Appeal, 64 Penn. St. 275; Tillmes v. Marsh, 67 Penn. St. 507; O'Hara v. Strange, 11 Ir. Eq. 262 ; Ireland v. Wilson, 1 Ir. Ch. 623 ; Dickerson v. Stoll, 4 Halst. Ch. 294; DeVeney v. Gallagher, 5 C. E. Green, 33, 34.

(b) Stuart v. Coalter, supra; Norris's Appeal, supra; Tillmes v. Marsh, supra; Beatty v. Dixon, 56 Cal. 619; Wetherbee v. Dunn, 36 Cal. 249; DeVeney v. Gallagher, 5 C. E. Green, 33.   Equity may perhaps enforce an oral agreement to fix a boundary. Jamison v. Petit, 6 Bush,. 669 ; sed qu.   The necessity of discovery to ascertain and fix boundaries will give equity jurisdiction.   Brown v. Wales, 42 L. J. Ch. 45.

(c) O'Hara v. Strange, 11 Ir. Eq. 262; Speer v. Crawter. 2 Meriv. 410; Attorney-Gen. v. Stephens, 6 DeG. M. & G. 111, 133.

where the court has entertained bills for establishing boundaries
have been where the soil itself was in question, or where there
might have been a multiplicity of suits.' [1]

617. So in a case where a bill was brought by one parish
against another to ascertain the boundaries of the two parishes
in making their rates, and a number of houses had been built
upon land formerly waste, and it was doubtful to which parish
each part of the waste belonged, Lord Thurlow refused to interfere, and observed that the greatest inconvenience might arise
from doing so. For if a commission were granted, and the
bounds set out by commissioners, any other parties, on a different
ground of dispute, might equally claim another commission.
These other commissioners might make a different return; and
so, in place of settling differences, endless confusion would be
created.[2] In another report of the same case he is reported to
have said if he should entertain the bill, and direct an issue in
such a case as that, he did not see what case would be peculiar
to the Courts of Law; and he did not know how to extract a
rule from the Mayor of York v. Pilkington (1 Atk. R. 282).[3]
Where there was a common right to be tried, such a proceeding
was to be understood. The boundary between the two jurisdic-
tions was apparent. That is the case where the tenants of a
manor claim a right of common by custom, because the right of all
the tenants of the manor is tried by trying the right of one. But
in the case before him he saw no common right which the parish-
ioners had in the boundaries of the parish. It would be to try the
boundaries of all the parishes in the kingdom on account of the
poor-laws.[4] The ground of dismissing the bill seems, from these

[1] Ibid.

[2] St. Luke's v. Leonard's Parish, or Waring v. Hotham, cited by Ch. Baron
McDonald, in Atkins v. Hatton, 2 Anstr. R. 395; s. c. 2 Dick. 550.

[3] Waring v. Hotham, 1 Bro. Ch. R. 40, and Mr. Belt's note (2). The case
of the Mayor of York v. Pilkington, 1 Atk. 282, was a bill brought to quiet
the plaintiffs in a right of fishery in the river Ouse, of which they claimed the
sole fishery, against the defendants, who (as was suggested in the bill) claimed
several rights, either as lords of manors or as occupiers of the adjacent lands;
and also for a discovery and account of the fish taken. The defendants de-
murred to the bill as being matter cognizable at law only. Lord Hardwicke
at first sustained the demurrer, but afterwards overruled it. Lord Thurlow
disapproved of this final decision; and to this a part of his reasoning in 1 Bro.
Ch. R. 40, is addressed.

[4] Waring v. Hotham, or St. Luke's v. St. Leonard's Parish, 1 Bro. Ch. R.
40; s. c. 2 Dick. 550. See Metcalfe v. Beckwith, 2 P. Will. 376.

very imperfect statements of the case, to have been : first, that the proper remedy was at law ; and secondly, that no equity was superinduced, for it would not even suppress multiplicity of suits.

618. In Atkins v. Hatton (2 Anstr. R. 386) the court refused to entertain a bill brought by the rector of a parish principally for an account of tithes, and to have a commission to settle the boundaries of the parish and the glebe. The court said : ' The plaintiff here calls upon the court to grant a commission to ascertain the boundaries of the parish, upon the presumption that all the lands which shall be found within those boundaries would be tithable to him. That is indeed a prima facie inference, but by no means conclusive. And there is no instance of the court ever granting a commission in order to attain a remote consequential advantage. It is a jurisdiction which the Courts of Equity have always been very cautious of exercising.' It is observable that no special equity was here set up ; but the party desired the commission solely upon the ground of founding a possible right against some persons for tithes, upon the ground that the land which they occupied was intraparochial and tithable. This was properly a matter at law, to be ascertained by a special suit against every owner or occupant of land severally, and not against them jointly, in a bill to ascertain boundaries.

619. These cases are sufficient to show that the existence of a controverted boundary by no means constitutes a sufficient ground for the interposition of Courts of Equity to ascertain and fix that boundary. Between independent proprietors such cases would be left to the proper redress at law.[1] It is therefore necessary to maintain such a bill (as has been already stated), that some peculiar equity should be superinduced.[2] In other words there must be some equitable ground attaching itself to the controversy ; and we may therefore inquire what will constitute such a ground ? This has been in part already suggested. In the first place it may be stated that if the confusion of boundaries has been occasioned by fraud, that alone will constitute a sufficient ground for the interference of the court.[3] And if the fraud is established,

---

[1] Speer v. Crawter, 2 Meriv. R. 410, 417; Miller v. Warmington, 1 Jac. &. Walk. 472; Loker v. Rolle, 3 Ves. 4.

[2] Wake v. Conyers, 1 Eden, R. 331 ; s. c. 1 Cox, R. 360; Speer v. Crawter, 7 Meriv. R. 417, 418.

[3] This is understood to have been the ground of the decision of the House

the court will by commission ascertain the boundaries if practicable, and if not practicable, will do justice between the parties by assigning reasonable boundaries or setting out lands of equal value.[1]

620. In the next place it will be a sufficient ground for the exercise of jurisdiction that there is a relation between the parties which makes it the duty of one of them to preserve and protect the boundaries, and that by his negligence or misconduct the confusion of boundaries has arisen. Thus if through the default of a tenant (a) or a copyholder (who is under an implied obligation to preserve them) there arises a confusion of boundaries, the court will interfere as against such tenant or copyholder to ascertain and fix the boundaries.[2] But even in such cases it is further indispensable to aver and to establish by suitable proofs that the boundaries, without such assistance, cannot be found.[3] And the relation of the parties, entitling them to the redress, must also be clearly stated; for where the parties claim by adverse titles, without any superinduced equity, we have already seen that the remedy is purely at law.[4]

621. In the next place a bill in equity will lie to ascertain and fix boundaries when it will prevent a multiplicity of suits. This

of Lords, in Rouse v. Barker, 3 Bro. Ch. Rep. 180, reversing the decree of the Exchequer in the same cause. See Atkins v. Hatton, 2 Anstruth. R. 396.

[1] Speer v. Crawter, 2 Meriv. R. 418; Duke of Leeds v. Earl of Strafford, 4 Ves. 181; Grierson v. Eyre, 9 Ves. 345; Attorney-Gen. v. Fullerton, 2 Ves. & Beam. 263; Willis v. Parkinson, 2 Meriv. R. 507. The common form of a decree for a commission in a case of this nature will be found in Willis v. Parkinson, 2 Meriv. R. 506, 509; Duke of Leeds v. Strafford, 4 Ves. 186.

[2] Ibid.; Ashton v. Lord Exeter, 6 Ves. 293; Miller v. Warmington, 1 Jac. & Walk. 472; Attorney-Gen. v. Fullerton, 2 Ves. & Beam. 263; Speer v. Crawter, 17 Ves. 216.

[3] Miller v. Warmington, 1 Jac. & Walk. 472.

[4] Ibid.

(a) The jurisdiction is based on a species of trust; it being the duty of the tenant to keep all boundaries clear between the demised premises and premises of *his own* immediately adjoining. Attorney-Gen. v. Stephens, 6 DeG. M. & G. 111, 133; Spike v. Harding, 7 Ch. D. 871; Southwell v. Thompson, 6 L. J. Ch. N. s. 196; Godfrey v. Littel, 2 Russ. & M. 630, 632; s. c. 1 Russ. & M. 59. And this duty exists throughout the term, giving equity a right to interfere at any time. Spike v. Harding, supra. In some cases relief may be granted where the confusion was due to the plaintiff or to one under whom he claims. See Hicks v. Hastings, 3 Kay & J. 701, where a testatrix, under whom the plaintiff claimed, had mixed up freehold and leasehold premises.

is an old head of equity jurisdiction, and it has been very properly applied to cases of boundaries.[1]	Indeed in many cases of this nature, as for instance where the right affects a large number of persons, such as a common right in lands, or in a waste, claimed by parishioners, commoners, and others, where the boundaries have become confused by lapse of time, accident, or mistake, the appropriate remedy to adjust such conflicting claims and to prevent expensive and interminable litigation seems properly to be in equity.[2]	And it will not constitute any objection to a bill to settle the boundaries between two estates, that they are situate in a foreign country, if in other respects the bill is from its frame properly maintainable.[3]

622. There are cases of an analogous nature (which constitute the second class of cases, arising from confusion or entanglement of other rights and claims than to lands) where a mischief, otherwise irremediable, arising from confusion of boundaries, has been redressed in Courts of Equity.	Thus where a rent is chargeable on lands and the remedy by distress is, by confusion of boundaries or otherwise, become impracticable, the jurisdiction of equity has been most beneficially exerted to adjust the rights and settle the claims of the parties.[4]

623. Other illustrations will present themselves more appropriately under other heads in the course of these Commentaries. One instance however may be mentioned in which Courts of Equity administer the most wholesome moral justice following out the principles of law; and that is, where an agent, by fraud or gross negligence, has confounded his own property with that of his principal, so that they are not distinguishable.	In such a

---

[1] Wake v. Conyers, 1 Eden, 331; s. c. 1 Cox, R. 360; Waring v. Hotham, 1 Bro. Ch. R. 40; s. c. cited 2 Anstruth. R. 395; Bouverie v. Prentice, 1 Bro. Ch. R. 200; Mayor of York v. Pilkington, 1 Atk. 282, 284.	See Whaley v. Dawson, 2 Sch. & Lefr. 370, 371.

[2] See ibid.

[3] Penn v. Lord Baltimore, 1 Ves. R. 444; Pike v. Hoare, 2 Eden, R. 182; Bayley v. Edwards, 3 Swanst. R. 703; Tulloch v. Hartley, 1 Younge & Coll. New Cas. in Chan. 114.

[4] Bowman v. Yeat, cited 1 Cas. Ch. 145, 146; Duke of Leeds v. Powell, 1 Ves. R. 171, and Belt's Supp. 98; Bouverie v. Prentice, 1 Bro. Ch. R. 200; North v. Earl of Strafford, 3 P. Will. 148, 149; Duke of Leeds v. New Radnor, 2 Bro. Ch. R. 338, 518; Mitf. Pl. Eq. 117, by Jeremy; 1 Fonbl. Eq. B. 1, ch. 3, § 3, and note (g); post, § 689.

case the whole will be treated in equity as belonging to the principal so far as it is incapable of being distinguished.[1]

---

[1] Lupton *v.* White, 15 Ves. 432; Panton *v.* Panton, cited ibid.; Chedworth *v.* Edwards, 8 Ves. 46; Hart *v.* Ten Eyck, 2 John. Ch. R. 108; 2 Black. Comm. 405; Story on Bailm. § 40; ante, § 468; 2 Black. Comm. 405; 4 Burr. R. 2349; Colburn *v.* Simms, 2 Hare, R. 554; cited at large, post, § 933, note.

CHAPTER XII.

DOWER.

624. ANOTHER head of concurrent equitable jurisdiction is in matters of DOWER. As dower is a strictly legal right, it might seem at first view that the proper remedy belonged to Courts of Common Law. The jurisdiction of Courts of Equity in matters of dower for the purpose of assisting the widow by a discovery of lands or title-deeds or for the removing of impediments to her rendering her legal title available at law has never been doubted.[1] And indeed it is extremely difficult to perceive any just ground upon which to rest an objection to it which would not apply with equal force to the remedial justice of Courts of Equity in all other cases of legal rights in a similar predicament. But the question has been made how far Courts of Equity should entertain general jurisdiction to give general relief in those cases where there appeared to be no obstacle to her legal remedy.[2] Upon this question there has in former times been no inconsiderable discussion and some diversity of judgment. But the result of the various decisions upon this subject is, that Courts of Equity will now entertain a general concurrent jurisdiction with Courts of Law in the assignment of dower in all cases.[3] (a) The ground most

---

[1] 1 Fonbl. Eq. B. 1, ch. 1, § 3, note (*f*).

[2] 1 Fonbl. Eq. B. 1, ch. 1, § 3, note (*f*); Huddlestone *v.* Huddlestone, 1 Ch. R. 38; Park on Dower, ch. 15, p. 317.

[3] Curtis *v.* Curtis, 2 Bro. Ch. R. 620; Mundy *v.* Mundy, 2 Ves. jr., 122; s. c. 4 Bro. Ch. R. 294. I am aware that Mr. Park, in his excellent Treatise

(a) Badgley *v.* Bruce, 4 Paige, 98; Hartshorne *v.* Hartshorne, 2 N. J. Eq. 349; Palmer *v.* Casperson, 17 N. J. Eq. 204; Wells *v.* Beall, 2 Gill & J. 468; Brooks *v.* Woods, 40 Ala. 538; Blain *v.* Harrison, 11 Ill. 384; Campbell *v.* Murphy, 2 Jones, Eq. 357; Blunt *v.* Gee, 5 Call, 481; Naill *v.* Maurer, 25 Md. 532.

commonly suggested for this result is, that the widow is often much embarrassed, in proceedings upon a writ of dower at the common law, to discover the titles of her deceased husband to the estates out of which she claims her dower (the title-deeds being in the hands of heirs, devisees, or trustees), to ascertain the comparative value of different estates, and to obtain a fair assignment of her third part.[1] In such cases where the title of the widow to her dower is not disputed the court proceeds directly to the assignment of dower; but if the title is disputed it is first required to be established by an issue at law or otherwise.[2]

625. There are some cases in which the remedy for dower in equity seems indispensable. At law, if the tenant dies after judgment and before damages are assessed, the widow loses her damages. And so if the widow herself dies before the damages are assessed, her personal representative cannot claim any. But a Court of Equity will in such cases entertain a bill for relief, and decree an account of rents and profits against the respective representatives of the several persons who may have been in possession of the estate since the death of the husband; provided at the time of filing the bill the legal right to damages is not gone.[3]

626. Upon principle there would not seem to be any real difficulty in maintaining the concurrent jurisdiction in Courts of Equity in all cases of dower; for a case can scarcely be supposed in which the widow may not want either a discovery of the title-deeds or of dowable lands, or some impediment to her recovery at law removed, or an account of mesne profits before the assignment of dower, or a more full ascertainment of the relative values

---

on Dower, doubts if the doctrine is maintainable to this full extent. But notwithstanding his doubts it appears to me the just result of the authorities, and maintainable upon principle. Indeed Mr. Park seems to admit that where a discovery or account is wanted, there seems no just objection to the jurisdiction. Park on Dower, ch. 15, pp. 317, 320, 325, 326, 329, 330; Strickland v. Strickland, 6 Beav. R. 77, 81.

[1] Mitf. Pl. Eq. 121, 122, 123, by Jeremy, and note (a); Jeremy on Eq. Jurisd. B. 3, Pt. 2, ch. 5, pp. 508, 509.

[2] Ibid.; Park on Dower, ch. 15, p. 329.

[3] Park on Dower, ch. 15, p. 330; Id. 309; Curtis v. Curtis, 2 Bro. Ch R. 632; Dormer v. Fortescue, 3 Atk. 130; Mordant v. Thorold, 3 Lev. R. 275; 1 Salk. 252.

of the dowable lands; and for any of these purposes (independent of cases of accident, mistake, or fraud, or other occasional equities) there seems to be a positive necessity for the assistance of a Court of Equity.[1] (a)   And if a Court of Equity has once a just possession of the cause in point of jurisdiction, there seems to be no reason why it should stop short of giving full relief instead of turning the dowress round to her ultimate remedy at law, which is often dilatory and always expensive.[2]   Dower is favored as well in law as in equity.[3]   And the mere circumstance that a discovery of any sort may be wanted to enforce the claim would, under such circumstances, seem to furnish a sufficient reason why the jurisdiction for discovery should carry the jurisdiction for relief.[4]

627. Lord Eldon has put this matter in a strong light.   After having remarked that he did not know any case in which an heir had claimed, merely as heir, an account (of mesne profits) without stating some impediment to his recovery at law, as that the defendant has the title-deeds necessary to maintain his title, that terms are in the way of his recovery at law, or other legal impediments which do or may probably prevent it, upon which probability or upon the fact the court might found its jurisdiction, he proceeded to say: ' The case of the dowress is upon a principle somewhat and not entirely analogous to that of the heir.   An indulgence has been allowed to her case upon the great difficulty

---

[1] The action of dower is now in consequence of the jurisdiction in equity being established less frequently resorted to at law than in former times. And the Parliamentary Commissioners, in their Report (2 Report of Common Law, p. 7, 1830), say: ' The necessity for a discovery to ascertain the state of the legal title before a widow can safely resolve to commence an action against any person as tenant of the freehold, and the convenience of a commission for setting out her dower under the authority of a Court of Equity, generally make it expedient that a suit in equity should be instituted.'

[2] See Park on Dower, ch. 15, p. 318.

[3] Com. Dig. Chancery, 3 E. 1, 2.

[4] See Dormer v. Fortescue, 3 Atk. 130, 131; Moor v. Black, Cas. Temp. Talb. 126; Herbert v. Wren, 7 Cranch, 370, 376; Curtis v. Curtis, 2 Bro. Ch. R. 620; Mundy v. Mundy, 2 Ves. jr., 122; s. c. 4 Bro. Ch. 294; Graham v. Graham, 1 Ves. 262; D'Arcy v. Blake, 2 Sch. & Lefr. 389, 390; Powell v. The Monson Manuf. Co., 3 Mason, R. 347.

(a) See McAllister v. McAllister, 37 Ala. 484; Boyd v. Hunter, 44 Ala. 705; Irvine v. Armistead, 46 Ala. 363; Donoghue v. Chicago, 57 Ill. 235; Ringhouse v. Keever, 49 Ill. 470; Badgley v. Bruce, 4 Paige, 98.

of determining a priori whether she could recover at law ignorant of all the circumstances, and the person against whom she seeks relief, etc., having in his possession all the information necessary to establish her rights. Therefore it is considered unconscientious in him to expose her to all that difficulty to which, if that information was fairly imparted as conscience and justice require, she could not possibly be exposed.'[1]

628. But the propriety of maintaining a general jurisdiction in equity in matters of dower is still more fully vindicated in a most elaborate opinion of Lord Alvanley, when Master of the Rolls, in a case which now constitutes the polar star of the doctrine. After adverting to the fact that dower is a mere legal demand and the widow's remedy is at law, he said: 'But then the question comes, Whether the widow cannot come either for a discovery of those facts which may enable her to proceed at law, and on an allegation of impediments thrown in her way in her proceedings at law this court has not a right to assume a jurisdiction to the extent of giving her relief for her dower; and if the alleged facts are not positively denied, to give her the full assistance of the court, she being in conscience as well as at law entitled to her dower.' He then proceeded to state the reasons why the widow should have the assistance of the court by relief as well as by recovery; insisting that the case of the widow is not distinguishable from that of an infant, where the relief would clearly be granted, and that it would be unconscientious to turn her round to a suit at law for the recovery of her dower, which must be supposed to be necessary for her to live upon when she has been compelled to resort to equity for a discovery. And he finally

---

[1] Pulteney *v.* Warren, 6 Ves. 89. See Co. Litt. 208, Butler's note (105), as to dower in case of a mortgage for a term of years. Strickland *v.* Strickland, 6 Beav. R. 77, 80. In this case Lord Langdale said: ' It was argued that if difficulties are shown to exist, and if from the nature of the case it appears to be in the power of the defendant to raise those difficulties, this court will not only restrain the defendant from raising the difficulties, but will assume the whole jurisdiction over the case; and if this were so, the plaintiff might be entitled to relief on this bill. But there is no such general rule; there are indeed some particular cases of legal right, such as dower and partition, in which the court has assumed a general jurisdiction, probably in consequence of the difficulties to which the plaintiff would be subjected in seeking to obtain complete justice at law; but in other cases the plaintiff is to show what the difficulties are, and how they impede him in a manner contrary to equity, and his bill ought to pray to be relieved from them.'

concluded by saying that the widow labors under so many disadvantages at law, that she is fully entitled to every assistance that this court can give her, not only in paving the way for her to establish her right at law, but also by giving complete relief when the right is ascertained.[1]

[1] Curtis v. Curtis, 2 Bro. Ch. R. 620, 630 to 634. The judgment of the Master of the Rolls contains so masterly a view of the doctrine, that I venture to transcribe the material passages, as they cannot be abridged without injury to their force: ' Dower therefore is a mere legal demand, and the widow's remedy is prima facie at law. But then the question comes, Whether the widow cannot come, either for a discovery of those facts which may enable her to proceed at law, and, on an allegation of impediments thrown in her way in her proceedings at law, this court has not a right to assume a jurisdiction to the extent of giving her relief for her dower, and if the alleged facts are not positively denied, to give her the full assistance of this court, she being in conscience as well as at law entitled to her dower. Her remedy at law is a writ of dower. Generally there are no damages in real actions; but so favorable was the law to this particular action that it provided a special relief for the widow by giving her damages. If the widow was disturbed in her quarantine she had a particular writ penned for her relief. As to dower, the widow at first was only entitled to have an assignment of the land by metes and bounds. Then came the statute of Merton, which showed particular anxiety for the relief of widows. And it is curious to see that the attempt now is to drive the widow to that remedy as the least advantageous, though it is very evident the statute was meant to give her an additional remedy. The deforcers of dower are (by that statute) to be in mercy, or fined at the pleasure of the king, which in those days was a very serious thing, and was meant as a real punishment to deforcers. I own I think it an odd construction of this statute, that the damages given by it are to be considered strictly as damages, that is, as vindictive damages in the breast of a jury, and not capable of ascertainment by the court, and that therefore they are to die with the person. However so it has been determined. As to what is said in Sayer's Law of Damages, that a widow shall have no damages when her dower is assigned to her in chancery, it certainly is a mistake of the meaning of Co. Litt. 33 a; for Coke is there speaking of the writ " de dote assignanda," issued by the Court of Chancery, and not a decree of a Court of Equity. In Fitzherbert's Natura Brevium the nature of the writ " de dote assignanda " appears very clear; and on this there are no damages, because there is no deforcement of the widow, who is put to no trouble, but has a summary remedy provided for her. Now as to the cases which have been cited, Hutton v. Simpson, 2 Vern. 722, does not seem to bear much upon this case. Tilley v. Bridges, Prec. Ch. 252, is also reported in 2 Vern. 519, and I have some doubt about the authority of that case; for it is more particularly stated in Vernon than in Prec. Ch.; and yet what is said in Vernon as to the injunction not preventing the entry certainly cannot be right. Duke of Bolton v. Deane, Norton v. Frecker, and other cases have been mentioned to show that there must be some fraud to give this court a jurisdiction, and that in the simple case of a widow claiming her dower no such jurisdiction exists. Dormer v. Fortescue is also brought to show that there must either be an infant concerned or some particular cir-

629. Dower, as has been already suggested, is highly favored in equity. And as was said by the Master of the Rolls (Sir

cumstances in the case to entitle this court to proceed. Now it seems difficult to distinguish the two cases of the infant and the widow. The principle in the case of the infant is, that he is thought not conusant of his rights at law sufficiently to enable him to proceed there, and therefore the Court of Equity will give him all the relief he could have at law, and something more; for on a bill by an infant for an account he will get the mesne profits, which would certainly be gone at law by the death of the party. I argue in the same manner for the widow. She comes here and says, " The law gives me dower out of the estates of my husband and the mesne profits from his death; I do not know how to proceed; for if there should turn out to be any mortgage or term of years in my way, then I must pay the costs. The defendant has all the title-deeds in his hands, and knows what the estates are; his conscience is affected, and yet, instead of putting me in possession of my rights, he turns me out of doors and keeps all the title-deeds." Now I think this argument is a strong one on the subject of fraud and concealment on the part of the heir, in not informing the widow of all that is necessary to enable her to proceed safely at law. If then she comes here for a discovery of these matters which the heir withholds from her, she shall have her complete relief in this court. If you deny her right to dower, the question must be tried at law; but when the fact is ascertained, she shall have her relief here. It must be supposed the dowress has nothing to live upon but her dower, and the mesne profits are her subsistence from the time of her husband's death; and the course of this court seems therefore to have been to assign her dower, and universally to give her an account from the death of her husband. I admit she has no costs where the heir has thrown no difficulties in her way; and if the heir admits the widow's case, he is safe. I wished to find, if I could, any instance of the widow's being turned round on such a case as this; but verily I believe there is no such instance. And indeed the case of Moor v. Black (Cas. Temp. Talb. 126) is pretty clear to show that Lord Talbot thought the widow's claim to be rightly made here, for he overruled the demurrer in that case on both points. It shows that the difficulty under which a widow labors is a reason for her coming here. Delver v. Hunter does not govern this case; for there the widow had recovered possession. Lucas v. Calcraft has also been mentioned, as showing that this court would give no other relief as to dower than such as the law would give the widow, and that the Lord Chancellor had refused to give costs in that case, because no costs were given at law. But in that case the heir had thrown no impediment in the widow's way, and therefore there were no costs on either side. Now taking it for granted that the widow, coming after the death of the heir, would not be entitled to her mesne profits, it by no means follows that when the widow is right in this court, but the heir happens to die before she has fully established her right, she is not entitled to her mesne profits; for unquestionably if the heir instead of contesting the widow's right had admitted it, she would have been entitled to her decree for mesne profits, and his having thrown an impediment in her way shall not make the difference. At the same time I must again admit that the widow's right at law is gone by the death of the party. Mordant v. Thorold is principally relied upon as to this point. It has been cited from Salkeld, tit. Dower; but it is also reported in 3 Lev. 275, and the result is stated differ-

Thomas Trevor) on one occasion, the right that a dowress has to her dower is not only a legal right and so adjudged at law, but

ently in the latter book, though the state of the case seems copied from the other; for in Levinz it is said the court inclined to that opinion, but it being a new case they would advise, and no decision was given; and it is to be observed that Levinz was himself counsel in that case. Aleworth v. Roberts, 1 Lev. 38, is mentioned in the former case; there the action was against the heir of the heir and the alienee of the heir, and not against the heir's executor; and the ground of that case was that neither the heir nor the alienee were deforcers, and the damages were not a lien upon the land; and then the distinction is taken between the cases of tithes and dower: that in the first case the damages were certain, in dower uncertain. But surely in common sense they are equally certain. If it were not for the case of Mordant v. Thorold, I really should have doubted much the construction of this statute. I should have thought that the damages given by the statute were certain, and were not arbitrary, uncertain damages, to be ascertained by the discretion of a jury. However it does seem a settled point at law, and that at law the widow could not have recovered against the executor of Thomas Curtis. This being so, it is insisted on the part of the widow that still she has a right to come here for full relief, and that she ought to be in the same situation as if the heir had admitted her claim at first (and to be sure in this case the heir has given every opposition to her claim that he possibly could) ; and that in this and many other cases this court gives a further remedy than the law will do. It is true where the law gives neither right nor remedy, however hard it may be, equity cannot assist. So in the case of damages for a personal injury which arises ex delicto, and not ex contractu, they are gone with the person. But it is not so clear in the case of a demand the recovery of which has been prevented by a difficulty unconscientiously thrown in the way of another person. There equity will give relief, and the relief it gives is beyond that which the party could obtain at law. It is the practice in equity that bond-creditors coming for a distribution of assets shall have an account of rents and profits, which they could not have at law. And yet the same argument might be used against that additional relief as has been used in this case. The law gives the creditor only the land to hold until he is satisfied. Equity goes further, and says, If the remedy at law is not sufficient, we will sell the inheritance of the estate; and if that will not do, we will direct an account of rents and profits against the heir. Dormer v. Fortescue certainly supports these ideas very strongly, though I am sure Lord Hardwicke's words must have been misconceived by Mr. Atkyns as to what he was supposed to have said in respect of the time from which the statute of 9 Henry III. gives the widow damages. But as far as one can collect Lord Hardwicke's sentiments from that case, he thought this court would expect the widow to establish her title at law, but she having so done, [this] would give her relief here as to the mesne profits. That is saying, Let the widow bring her action at law, out of form, for the purpose of determining her title to dower, and when she has done that we will give her an adequate remedy. Here I confess I agree most fully in thinking that the widow labors under so many disadvantages at law from the embarrassments of trust-terms, &c., that she is fully entitled to every assistance that this court can give her, not only in paving the way for her to establish her right at law, but also by giving complete relief when the right is ascer-

it is also a moral right to be provided for and have a maintenance and sustenance out of her husband's estate to live upon. She is therefore in the care of the law and a favorite of the law. And upon this moral law is the law of England founded as to the right of dower.[1] So much is this the case that the widow will be aided in equity for her dower against a term of years which attends the inheritance, if it is not the case of a purchaser against whom she claims.[2] (a) And if she has recovered her dower against an heir who is an infant, and there is a term to protect the inheritance which, by the neglect of his guardian, is not pleaded, the term will not be allowed in equity to be set up against her.[3]

630. Indeed so highly favored is dower that a bill for a discovery and relief has been maintained even against a purchaser for a valuable consideration without notice, who is perhaps generally as much favored as any one in Courts of Equity.[4] The ground of maintaining the bill in such a case is that the suit for dower is upon a legal title and not upon a mere equitable claim, to which only the plea of a purchase for a valuable consideration has been supposed properly to apply.[5] This decision has often

tained.' Curtis v. Curtis, 2 Bro. Ch. R. 630 to 634; Strickland v. Strickland, 6 Beav. R. 77.

[1] Dudley & Ward v. Dudley, Prec. Ch. 244; Banks v. Sutton, 2 P. Will. 703, 704. See Co. Litt. 208, Butler's note (105), when the widow is entitled to dower in case of a mortgage of the estate for years.

[2] Com. Dig. Chancery, 3 E. 1; Radnor v. Vandebendy, 1 Vern. R. 356; s. c. 2 Ch. Cas. 172; Prec. Ch. 65; 1 Eq. Abridg. 219; Dudley v. Dudley, 1 Eq. Abridg. 219; D'Arcy v. Blake, 2 Sch. & Lefr. 389, 390; Mole v. Smith, 1 Jac. 496, 497.

[3] Com. Dig. Chancery, 3 E. 1; Wray v. Williams, Prec. Ch. 151; s. c. 1 Eq. Abridg. 219; 1 P. Will. 137; 2 Vern. 378, and Mr. Cox's note; Dudley & Ward v. Dudley, Prec. Ch. 241; Banks v. Sutton, 2 P. Will. 706, 707, 708; D'Arcy v. Blake, 2 Sch. & Lefr. 389, 390; Swannock v. Lyford, Ambl. R. 6, 7; Hitchins v. Hitchins, 2 Freem. 242.

[4] Ante, §§ 64 c, 108, 139, 163, 381, 409, 434, 436.

[5] Williams v. Lambe, 3 Bro. Ch. R. 264. In Collins v. Archer, 1 Russ. & Mylne, 284, Sir John Leach, following the case of Williams v. Lambe, held that a purchaser for a valuable consideration without notice had no defence in equity against a plaintiff relying upon a legal title. But in Payne v. Compton, 2 Younge & Coll. 457, 461, Lord Abinger seems to have thought that such a purchaser would be protected in equity against any claim by the owner of the legal estate. Neither of these cases was a claim of dower by the plaintiff.

(a) See Anderson v. Pignet, L. R. Maundrell v. Maundrell, 7 Ves. 567; 8 Ch. 180, reversing 11 Eq. 32f; Wynn v. Williams, 5 Ves. 130.

been found fault with, and in some cases the doctrine of it denied. It has however been vindicated with great apparent force upon the following reasoning. It is admitted that dower is a mere legal right, and that a Court of Equity in assuming a concurrent jurisdiction with Courts of Law upon the subject professedly acts upon the legal right; for dower does not attach upon an equitable estate. In so acting the court should proceed in analogy to the law where such a plea of a purchase for a valuable consideration without notice would not be looked at; and therefore as an equitable plea it should also be inadmissible. But this analogy will not hold where the widow applies for equitable relief, as for the removal of terms out of her way, or for a discovery. In the latter cases the equitable plea of a purchase for a valuable consideration without notice cannot be resisted. In the former case the widow proceeding upon the concurrent jurisdiction of the court merely enforces a right which the defendant cannot at law resist by such a mode of defence. In the latter case she applies to the equity of the court to take away from him a defence which at law would protect him against her demand.[1]

631. Other learned minds have however arrived at a different conclusion, and have insisted that upon principle the plea of a purchase for a valuable consideration without notice is a good plea in all cases against a legal as well as against an equitable claim, and that dower constitutes no just exception from the doctrine. They put themselves upon the general principle of conscience and equity, upon which such a plea must always stand, that such a purchaser has an equal right to protection and support as any other claimant, and that he has a right to say that having bona fide and honestly paid his money no person has a right to require him to discover any facts which shall show any infirmity in his title. The general correctness of the argument cannot be doubted; and the only recognized exception seems to be that of dower, if that can be deemed a fixed exception.[2]

[1] 1 Roper on Husband and Wife, 446, 447; ante, §§ 57 *a*, 410, note, 434, 436; Williams *v.* Lambe, 3 Bro. Ch. R. 264; Collins *v.* Archer, 1 Russ. & Mylne, R. 284.

[2] The authorities are both ways. The case of Williams *v.* Lambe, 3 Bro. Ch. R. 264; Collins *v.* Archer, 1 Russ. & Mylne, 284; and Rogers *v.* Seale, 2 Freem. R. 84, are in favor of the doctrine that the plea is not good against a legal title. Against it is the decision in Burlace *v.* Cooke, 2 Freeman, R. 24; Parker *v.* Blythmore, 2 Eq. Abridg. 79, Pl. 1; Jerrard *v.* Saunders, 2 Ves. jr.

632. Generally speaking in America fewer cases occur in regard to dower, in which the aid of a Court of Equity is wanted, than in England, from the greater simplicity of our titles, and the rareness of family settlements and the general distribution of property among all the descendants in equal or in nearly equal proportions. Still however cases do occur in which a resort to equity is found to be highly convenient and sometimes indispensable. (a) Thus for instance if the lands of which dower is sought are undivided, the husband being a tenant in common, and a partition or an account or a discovery is necessary, the remedy in equity is peculiarly appropriate and easy.[1] So where the lands are in the hands of various purchasers; or their relative values are not easily ascertainable, as for instance if they have become the site of a flourishing manufacturing establishment; or if the right is affected with numerous or conflicting equities, — in such cases the jurisdiction of a Court of Equity is perhaps the only adequate remedy.[2]

454, and Payne v. Compton, 2 Younge & Coll. 457, 461; ante, § 630, note 5. Mr. Sugden, in a very late edition of his work on Vendors and Purchasers, ch. 18, pp. 762, 763 (1826), maintains that the authorities in favor of the sufficiency of the plea against a legal title preponderate, and that therefore we may venture to assert that it will protect the purchaser against a legal as well as against an equitable claim. On the other hand Mr. Beames, Mr. Belt, and Mr. Roper maintain the opposite doctrine. Beam. Pl. Eq. 234, 245; 3 Bro. Ch. R. 264, Belt's note (1); 1 Roper on Husband and Wife, 446, 447. See also Medlicott v. O'Donell, 1 Ball & Beatt. 171; Mitford, Pl. Eq. 274, by Jeremy, and note (d); 2 Fonbl. Eq. B. 2, ch. 6, § 2, note (h); 1 Fonbl. Eq. B. 1, ch. 4, § 25, and note. In a case of such conflict of learned opinions a commentator's duty is best performed by leaving the authorities for the reader's own judgment. See Park on Dower, ch. 15, pp. 327, 328, and the Reporter's note to 1 Russ. & Mylne, 289, n.

[1] Herbert v. Wren, 7 Cranch, 370, 376.

[2] Powell v. Monson Manufacturing Company, 3 Mason, 347; Id. 459.

(a) As where the husband has made a mortgage, and the widow, having released dower therein, seeks to redeem, or seeks dower in the equity of redemption. Gibson v. Crehore, 5 Pick. 146; s. c. 3 Pick. 475, 481; Messiter v. Wright, 16 Pick. 151; Smith v. Eustis, 7 Greenl. 41; Chiswell v. Morris, 1 McCart. 101; Eldridge v. Eldridge, Ib. 195; Bank of Commerce v. Owens, 31 Md. 320; McCabe v. Swap, 14 Allen, 188; Wing v. Ayer, 53 Maine, 138; Dawson v. Bank of Whitehaven, 4 Ch. D. 639; s. c. 6 Ch. D. 218. But see Meek v. Chamberlain, 8 Q. B. D. 31, distinguishing the last case.

CHAPTER XIII.

MARSHALLING OF SECURITIES.

633. ANOTHER head of concurrent jurisdiction in Courts of Equity is that of MARSHALLING SECURITIES.[1] We have already had occasion in another place to, consider the topic of marshalling assets in cases of administration, to which the present bears a very close analogy ; and also the doctrine of apportionment and contribution between sureties, to which it also has a near relation. The general principle is, that if one party has a lien (*a*) on, or interest in, two funds for a debt, and another party has a lien on, or interest in, one only of the funds for another debt; the latter has a right in equity to compel the former to resort to the other fund, in the first instance for satisfaction, if that course is necessary for the satisfaction of the claims of both parties,[2] whenever it will not trench upon the rights or operate to the prejudice of the party entitled to the double fund. (*b*)   Thus a mortgagee

---

[1] See Aldrich v. Cooper, 8 Ves. 394; Eden on Injunct. ch. 2, pp. 38, 39, 40; ante, §§ 499, 558, 559, 560; post, § 662.

[2] Lanoy v. Duke of Athol, 2 Atk. 446; Aldrich v. Cooper, 8 Ves. 388, 395, 396; Ex parte Kendall, 17 Ves. 520; Trimmer v. Bayne, 9 Ves. 209; Cheeseborough v. Millard, 1 John. Ch. 413; Averall v. Wade, Lloyd & Goold, R. 252; Gwynne v. Edwards, 2 Russ. R. 289; Attorney-Gen. v. Tyndall, Ambler, R. 614; Selby v. Selby, 4 Russ. 336, 341; Trimmer v. Bayne, 9 Ves. 209; Greenwood v. Taylor, 1 Russ. & Mylne, 185; 2 Fonbl. Eq. B. 3, ch. 2, § 6; ante, §§ 557, 558, 559, 560; post, § 642; Wiggin v. Dorr, 3 Sumner, R. 410, 414.

(*a*) Moss v. Adams, 32 Ark. 562.

(*b*) The following cases will be found to contain useful illustrations of the rule: Rice v. Harbeson, 63 N. Y. 493; Ingalls v. Morgan, 10 N. Y. 178; Wiley v. Mahood, 10 W. Va. 206; Glass v. Pullen, 6 Bush, 346; Wolf v. Smith, 36 Iowa, 454; Witte v. Clarke, 17 S. Car. 313; Sibley v. Baker, 23 Mich. 312; Applegate v. Mason, 13 Ind. 75; Warren v. Warren, 30 Vt. 530; Lyman v. Lyman, 32 Vt. 79; Gibson v. Seagrim, 20 Beav. 614 ; In re Lawder, 11 Ir. Ch. 346, 351;

who has two funds as against the other specialty creditors who have but one fund, will in the case of the death of the mortgagor,

Tidd v. Lister, 3 DeG. M. & G. 857; In re Fox, 5 Ir. Ch. 541; In re Lynch, Ir. R. 1 Eq. 396.

From the rule of the text it follows that where a creditor with security on two funds releases, with notice of another creditor's rights, one of the funds, sufficient to pay him, to which the other creditor cannot resort, the releasing creditor can have recourse only to the surplus, if any, to be realized by the junior creditor out of the doubly-charged fund. Ingalls v. Morgan, 10 N. Y. 178; Lemay v. Johnson, 35 Ark. 225, 233. Reasonable notice however of the junior creditor's rights should be fixed upon the senior creditor. Clarke v. Bancroft, 13 Iowa, 320 ; Ingalls v. Morgan, supra.

Marshalling may be required in cases of judgments Pittman's Appeal, 48 Penn. 315. See infra, § 634; In re Lawder, 11 Ir. Ch. 346, 352; In re Lynch, Ir. R. 1 Eq. 396. It may be required where mortgaged and unmortgaged personalty is taken in distress, though the tenant becomes bankrupt. Ex parte Stephenson, DeG. (Bankr.) 586. So where a pledge covers property of the pledgor and of his consignor. Broadbent v. Barlow, 3 DeG. F. & J. 570; Ex parte Alston, L. R. 4 Ch. 168. It may be invoked where a mechanics' lien exists. Hamilton v. Schwehr, 34 Md. 107. And it is applicable as well to the claims of legatees as to the mere situation of debtor and creditor. Rice v. Harbeson, 63 N. Y. 493; ante, § 565 et seq.

It is held too that marshalling may be applied where one of the estates in question is by law exempt from the claims of creditors, some of the creditors having the benefit of a waiver of the exemption and others not, as in the case of an estate embracing an exempt homestead. The non-favored creditors can for their own protection demand a marshalling. Pittman's Appeal, 48 Penn. St. 315. But on the other hand a mortgagee of the non-exempt estate could not compel the mortgagee of both the non-exempt and the exempt estates to proceed first against the exempt estate, unless the mortgage provided that that should be resorted to first. The very fact that it is exempt furnishes a reason for not proceeding against it till the non-exempt property is exhausted. Dodds v. Snyder, 44 Ill. 53. The common debtor has or may have rights in such a case that deserve protection against such marshalling. Dickson v. Chorn, 6 Clarke (Iowa), 19. Still where the debtor, in a case of exempt property, is himself seeking protection in regard to the same, if it appears that other creditors may be injured by granting the relief sought, the bill will be dismissed. White v. Polleys, 20 Wis. 503; Jones v. Dow, 18 Wis. 241. This is but a particular expression of a general rule further noticed infra.

The rule of marshalling has been applied also in favor of volunteers. Thus it has been held that a donee under a voluntary settlement with covenants against incumbrances or for quiet enjoyment may compel a subsequent mortgagee of the settled and other estates to marshal his securities. Hales v. Cox, 32 Beav. 118. See Keaton v. Miller, 38 Miss. 630. But where a voluntary settlement of one estate was made by a testator, though with a covenant for further assurance, and another estate was devised by him, both estates being previously and then subject to a charge, it was held that the settled estate must contribute, no intention to the contrary on the part of the testator being shown. Ker v. Ker, Ir. R. 4 Eq. 15,

and the administration of his assets, be compelled to resort first to the mortgage security, and will be allowed to claim against

distinguishing, on the grounds here stated, Hales v. Cox, supra. See also Dolphin v. Aylward, L. R. 4 H. L. 486, 501–503; In re Lawder, 11 Irish Ch. 346; In re Rorke, 15 Ir. Ch. 316; Hartley v. O'Flaherty, Lloyd & G. t. Plunket, 208; Stronge v. Hawkins, 4 DeG. & J. 632; Barnes v. Racster, 1 Younge & C. Ch. C. 401, 410.

Marshalling is generally restricted to cases in which there are two or more successive lien creditors of the same debtor. In the absence of agreement it will not be applied in favor of the *debtor* even then, except in special cases where the law itself extends a peculiar protection to him, as in the case of homestead above noticed. Rogers v. Meyers, 63 Ill. 72; In re Athill, 16 Ch. D. 211 (the fact that a security is spoken of as ' collateral ' to another does not make it secondary to the other); post, § 640. Nor will marshalling be applied between a mortgagee and a subsequent purchaser of the equity of redemption. Stevens v. Church, 41 Conn. 369. See Rogers v. Meyers, supra. Nor between mere attaching creditors. Shedd v. Bank of Brattleboro', 32 Vt. 709, 718. Nor can it be applied where the funds sought to be marshalled are not in existence; a call e. g. upon the stockholders of an insolvent company will not be ordered to create one of the funds. In re Professional Assur. Co., L. R. 3 Eq. 668. Nor where, as e. g. by reason of alienation of one of the funds, both funds are not in the hands of the common debtor. Lloyd v. Galbraith, 32 Penn. St. 103; McCormick's Appeal, 57 Penn. St. 54, 60. See Ayres v. Husted, 15 Conn. 504.

The rule of marshalling securities applies more certainly to cases where the single fund, being sufficient for the earlier claim, may be directly reduced to money. If this is not the case, — if e. g. there must be a process of foreclosure in the courts, — and if the doubly-charged fund is more directly available, it is very doubtful if the junior incumbrancer can require marshalling, unless that has been agreed to by the creditor in chief. See ante, § 563, note of editor. Clearly, as the text and all the authorities declare, marshalling cannot be required to the hurt of the earlier creditor. Van Meter v. Ely, 1 Beasl. 271, and cases at the head of this note. Thus it is declared that marshalling will not be ordered where the fund to which it is sought to restrict the chief creditor is of doubtful validity, or is to be reached only by setting the courts in motion. Walker v. Covar, 2 S. Car. 16; Witte v. Clarke, 17 S. Car. 313; Kidder v. Page, 48 N. H. 380; Emmons v. Bradley, 56 Maine, 333; Herriman v. Skillman, 33 Barb. 378; Dodds v. Snyder, 44 Ill. 53; Wolf v. Smith, 36 Iowa, 454. Or where the doubly-charged fund is in another jurisdiction. Denham v. Williams, 39 Ga. 312; Shedd v. Bank of Brattleboro', 32 Vt. 709, 717. Compare upon this point of prejudice to the chief creditor the difference which exists in England between the extent of proof open to a mortgagee or other secured creditor in bankruptcy and in winding up in chancery. Kellock's Case, L. R. 3 Ch. 769; Tuckley v. Thompson, 1 Johns. & H. 126; Mason v. Bogg, 2 Mylne & C. 443. It will be seen that the rule in chancery favors the rights of the secured creditor, in accordance with the engagement with the debtor, conformably with the rule here set forth in regard to marshalling. The American courts of bankruptcy follow the English chancery rule. Ex parte Talcott, 9 Bankr. Reg. 502; In re Ellerhorst, 5 Bankr.

the common fund only what the mortgage, on a sale consented to
by him, is deficient to pay.[1] So if A has a mortgage upon two
different estates for the same debt, and B has a mortgage upon
one only of the estates for another debt, B has a right to throw
A, in the first instance, for satisfaction upon the security which
he, B, cannot touch, at least where it will not prejudice A's
rights or improperly control his remedies.[2] The reason is obvious,
and has been already stated ; for by compelling A, under such
circumstances, to take satisfaction out of one of the funds, no injustice is done to him in point of security or payment. But it is
the only way by which B can receive payment. And natural
justice requires that one man should not be permitted, from wan-

---

[1] Greenwood *v.* Taylor, 1 Russ. & Mylne, 185, 187.

[2] Ibid. ; ante, §§ 499, 558, 559, 560; Barnes *v.* Racster, 1 Younge & Coll.
New R. 401; The York & Jersey Steam &c Company *v.* Associates of the
Jersey Company, Hopkins, Ch. R. 460; post, § 642; Conrad *v.* Harrison, 3
Leigh, R. 532.

Reg. 144; Downing *v.* Traders' Bank,
2 Dill. 136; Bigelow's L. C. Bills and
Notes, 665.

Not only will marshalling not be
ordered to the prejudice of the creditor
in chief, — it will not be ordered to
the prejudice of third persons having
legal or equitable rights, as a third
incumbrancer. Dolphin *v.* Aylward,
L. R. 4 H. L. 486; In re Mower,
L. R. 8 Eq. 110; Reilly *v.* Mayer, 1
Beasl. 55; White *v.* Polleys, 20 Wis.
503; Jones *v.* Dow, 18 Wis. 241;
Mechanics' Assoc. *v.* Conover, 1
McCart. 219.   See Herbert *v.* Mechanics' Assoc., 2 C. E. Green, 497;
Sibley *v.* Baker, 23 Mich. 312. Thus
it is held that a junior incumbrancer
of one of the two estates cannot turn
the chief creditor upon the other
estate, charged in favor of another
junior incumbrancer, to the latter's
hurt. Dolphin *v.* Aylward, L. R. 4
H. L. 486, 501. Between the two
junior incumbrancers the chief creditor must satisfy himself, principal,
interest, and costs, out of the two
estates ratably, according to their
respective values, leaving the surplus
proceeds of each estate to be applied
in payment of the later incumbrances
respectively. Gibson *v.* Seagrim, 20
Beav. 614, 619; In re Lawder, 11 Ir.
Ch. 346, 352; Barnes *v.* Racster, 1
Younge & C. Ch. C. 401; Semmes *v.*
Boykim, 27 Ga. 47; infra, § 634 *a*.
However in South *v.* Bloxam, 2 Hem.
& Mil. 457, securities were marshalled
against a surety, in favor of a second
mortgagee, in such a way as to deprive
the surety of his right to the costs of
his defence, which, against the principal debtor, he would have had the
right to tack to his mortgage.

In marshalling the assets of decedents the English courts will not order
a sale of an estate subject to mortgage,
free from the mortgage, without the
consent of the mortgagee. Wicken-
den *v.* Rayson, 6 DeG. M. & G. 210.
But in this country such a sale may,
it seems, be ordered in cases of insolvency, the lien being shifted to the
proceeds. Foster *v.* Ames, 1 Lowell,
313. Compare cases of partition sales,
Kilgour *v.* Crawford, 51 Ill. 249;
editor's note to § 654, infra.

tonness, or caprice, or rashness, to do an injury to another.[1]　In short we may here apply the common civil maxim, ' Sic utere tuo

[1] Lord Chancellor Sugden, in Averall v. Wade (Lloyd & Goold's Rep. 255), expressed an opinion which may be thought to imply a doubt whether the doctrine did apply to the case of two mortgages. His language was: ' The general doctrine is this. Where one creditor has a demand against two estates, and another a demand against one only, the latter is entitled to throw the former on the fund that is not common to both. This is a narrow doctrine, and cannot generally be enforced against an incumbrancer who is a mortgagee. Whatever may be the equity of the creditor with only one security, the mortgagee of both estates has a right to compel the debtor to redeem, or he may foreclose.' On the other hand Lord Hardwicke, in Lanoy v. The Duke of Athol, 2 Atk. R. 446, said: ' Suppose a person who has two real estates mortgages both to one person, and afterwards only one estate to a second mortgagee, who had no notice of the first; the court, in order to relieve the second mortgagee, have directed the first to take his satisfaction out of that estate only which is not in mortgage to the second mortgagee, if that is sufficient to satisfy the first mortgage, in order to make room for the second mortgagee, even though the estates descended to two different persons.' Lord Eldon, in Aldrich v. Cooper, 8 Ves. 388, used language leading to the same conclusion as that of Lord Hardwicke. He said: ' Suppose there was no freehold estate, but there was a copyhold estate, which the owner had subjected to a mortgage, and died. It is clear the mortgagee having two funds might, if he pleased, resort to the copyhold estate. But would this court compel him to resort to it? If so, the court marshals by the necessary consequence of its act. If the court would not compel him, is it not clear that it is purely matter of his will whether the simple contract creditors shall be paid or not? That, at least, contradicts all the authorities, that, if a party has two funds (not applying now to assets particularly), a person having an interest in one only has a right in equity to compel the former to resort to the other if that is necessary for the satisfaction of both. I never understood that, if A has two mortgages, and B has one, the right of B to throw A upon the security, which B cannot touch, depends upon the circumstance whether it is a freehold or a copyhold mortgage. It does not depend upon assets only; a species of marshalling being applied in other cases, though technically we do not apply that term except to assets. So where in bankruptcy the Crown by extent laying hold of all the property, even against creditors, the Crown has been confined to such property as would leave the securities of incumbrancers effectual. So in the case of the surety it is not by the force of the contract, but that equity upon which it is considered against conscience that the holder of the securities should use them to the prejudice of the surety; and therefore there is nothing hard in the act of the court placing the surety exactly in the situation of the creditor. So a surety may have the benefit of a mortgage of a copyhold estate exactly as of freehold. It is very difficult to reconcile this with the principle of all those cases between living persons.' And again: ' Suppose another case; two estates mortgaged to A, and one of them mortgaged to B. He has no claim under the deed upon the other estate. It may be so constructed that he could not affect that estate after the death of the mortgagor. But it is the ordinary case to say a person having two funds, shall not by his election disappoint the party having only one fund; and equity, to satisfy both, will throw him who has two funds

ut non alienum lædas ; ' and still more emphatically the Christian maxim, ' Do unto others as you would they should do to you.' [1]

upon that which can be affected by him only, to the intent that the only fund to which the other has access may remain clear to him. This has been carried to a great extent in bankruptcy; for a mortgagee whose interest in the estate was affected by an extent of the Crown has found his way, even in a question with the general creditors, to this relief; that he was held entitled to stand in the place of the Crown as to those securities which he could not affect per directum, because the Crown affected those in pledge to him. Another case may be put; that a man died, having no fund but a freehold and a copyhold estate; that they were both comprehended in a mortgage to A, and the free-hold estate only was mortgaged to B; and that B was not only a mortgagee of the freehold estate, but also a specialty creditor by a covenant or a bond. In that case as well as in this it might be said the mortgagee of both estates might, if he thought proper, apply to the freehold estate and exhaust the whole value of it. The other would then stand as a naked specialty creditor, the fund being taken out of his reach; and there is no doubt that being both a specialty creditor and a mortgagee of the freehold estate, but not having any claim as mortgagee upon the copyhold estate, the same arrangement would take place, that he in equity shall throw the prior incumbrancer upon the estate to which the other has no resort.' Mr. Powell, in his Treatise on Mort-gages (1 Powell on Mortg. 343, and Coventry & Rand's notes, Id. 1014), and Mr. Fonblanque (2 Fonbl. Eq. B. 3, ch. 2, § 6, note (*i*), seem to have taken the same view. It may perhaps be true that the doctrine propounded by Lord Chancellor Sugden was intended to be applied only to cases where there could be a sale of the mortgaged property either by the original contract or by a decree of a Court of Equity in the exercise of its appropriate jurisdiction; and not to reach cases where, as in England, the mortgagee had a right to, and might insist upon, a foreclosure (post, 2 Story, Eq. Jurispr. § 1026). But such a qualification of the doctrine is not intimated, as far as I have seen, except in the case before Lord Chancellor Sugden. In the late case of Barnes *v.* Racster (1 Younge & Coll. New Rep. 401, 403), Mr. Vice-Chancellor Bruce seems to have thought the doctrine of Mr. Sugden to be applicable to the case where, after the first mortgage of two estates, there are distinct mortgages to different persons of each estate mortgaged to the first mortgagee; and that, as between these last conflicting incumbrancers, Courts of Equity will not marshal the estates, but merely apportion the first charge between the two estates. It may be thought that a Court of Equity would be going too far by interfering with the creditor's right of foreclosure, and that it would be sufficient to give the second mortgagee a right to redeem the first mortgage. In America there has hitherto been no difficulty on the part of our Courts of Equity to give full effect to the doctrine of Lord Hardwicke in the case of two funds and two successive mortgages. Instead of a foreclosure, the usual course is, to decree a sale, as it is in Ireland; so that the main difficulty in narrowing the rights of the first mortgagee is avoided. See Cheeseborough *v.* Millard, 1 John. Ch. R. 413; Stevens *v.* Cooper, 1 John. Ch. R. 425; Evertson *v.* Booth, 19 John. R.

[1] See Cheeseborough *v.* Millard, 1 John. Ch. R. 413; Evertson *v.* Booth, 19 John. R. 486; Hayes *v.* Ward, 4 John. Ch. R. 123; Wiggin *v.* Dorr, 3 Sum-ner, R. 410.

634. The same principle applies to one judgment creditor who has a right to go upon two funds, and another judgment creditor

486; Hayes *v.* Ward, 4 John. Ch. R. 123; Campbell *v.* Macomb, 4 John. Ch. R. 534; Conrad *v.* Harrison, 3 Leigh, R. 532; 1 Powell on Mortg. 343, and notes by Coventry & Rand. But at all events it is very certain that wherever a creditor, by his election to take one of two funds to which alone another creditor has the right to resort, deprives the latter of his claim to that fund, he will be permitted in equity to stand in the place of that creditor in regard to the other fund. In Aldrich *v.* Cooper, 8 Ves. 396, Lord Eldon referred to many cases of this sort, and, among other things, said: ' The cases with respect to creditors and other classes of claimants go exactly the same length. In the cases of legatees against assets descended a legatee has not so strong a claim to this species of equity as a creditor. But the mere bounty of the testator enables the legatee to call for this species of marshalling; that, if those creditors, having a right to go to the real estate descended, will go to the personal estate, the choice of the creditors shall not determine whether the legatees shall be paid or not. That in some measure is upon the doctrine of assets, but with relation to the fact of a double fund. Both are in law liable to the creditors; and therefore by making the option to go against the one they shall not disappoint another person who the testator intended should be satisfied. That is not so strong as where it is not bounty, but the party has by his own act, in his life, made liable to the whole of the debt a copyhold estate not in law liable; and who, having also a freehold estate, must be understood to mean that the freehold estate shall be liable, according to law, to his specialty debts. The case is exactly the same with reference to the distinction taken, that, where lands are specifically devised, the legatees shall not stand in the place of the creditors against the devisees; for that is upon the supposition that there is in the will as strong an inclination of the testator in favor of a specific devisee as a pecuniary legatee; and therefore there shall be no marshalling. But if, though specifically devised, the land is made subject to all debts, that distinguishes the case; for there is a double fund, and as by that denotation of intention the creditor has a double fund, the land devised and the personal estate, he shall not disappoint the legatee. The case is also the same where, instead of the case of a mere specialty creditor, the land specifically devised is subject to a mortgage by the testator, as in Lutkins *v.* Leigh; there he shall not disappoint the legatee. So the case of paraphernalia is very strong for this proposition; that wherever there is a double fund, though this court will not restrain the party, yet he shall not so operate his payment as to disappoint another claim, whether arising by the law or by the act of the testator.' Ante, §§ 558, 559, 560 to 578. See also the Reporter's note to Averall *v.* Wade, Lloyd & Goold, Rep. 264, and especially p. 268, where they say: ' The general principle of marshalling is, that where one claimant has two funds to resort to, and another only one, the court will either compel the person having the double security to resort to that fund not liable to the demand of the other (citing 2 Atk. 446, 8 Ves. 391, 395, and 1 Russ. & Mylne, 187); or if satisfaction has been already obtained by him who has the double security out of the fund to which alone the other can resort, the court will allow the latter claimant to stand in the place of the former pro tanto.' See the note to Clifton *v.* Burt (by Cox), 1 P. Will. 679, where the principal authorities are collected. Ante, § 561, note 6.

who has a right upon one only of them, both belonging to the same debtor. The former may be compelled to apply first to the fund which cannot be reached by the second judgment; so that both judgments may be satisfied.[1] (a)   But if the first creditor has a judgment against A and B, and the second against B only, and it does not appear whether A or B ought to pay the debt due to the first creditor, nor whether any equitable right exists in B to have the debt charged on A alone, — in such a case equity will not compel the creditor first to take the land of A in satisfaction; for it is not (as we shall presently and more fully see) a case of different debts and securities against one common debtor.[2]

634 a. Another case may easily be put to illustrate the general doctrine and the exceptions to it. Suppose the mortgagor to mortgage two estates to the mortgagee, and afterwards he should mortgage one of the estates to B and the other to C, by distinct mortgages, and B and C should each have knowledge of the first mortgage, and C should also have notice of B's mortgage at the time of taking his own, and the mortgaged estates should finally turn out not to be sufficient to pay all the three mortgages, — in such a case it would seem that B would not have any right to have the estates marshalled so as to throw the whole charge upon the estate mortgaged to C, for he has no superior equity to C; and therefore the charge of the first mortgage ought to be ratably apportioned between B and C.[3]   But this must be propounded as open to some doubt, as there is a conflict in the authorities.[4] (b)

---

[1] Dorr v. Shaw, 4 John. Ch. R. 17; Averall v. Wade, Lloyd & Goold, R. 252.   In this last case Lord Chancellor Sugden decided that where a party, seised of several estates, and indebted by judgment, settled one of the estates for a valuable consideration, with a covenant against incumbrances, and subsequently acknowledged other judgments, the prior judgments should be thrown altogether upon the unsettled estates, and that the subsequent judgment creditors had no right to make the settled estate contribute.

[2] Dorr v. Shaw, 4 John. Ch. R. 17; post, §§ 642, 643.

[3] Barnes v. Racster, 1 Younge & Coll. New R. 401.

[4] Post, § 1233 a; Barnes v. Racster, 1 Younge & Coll. N. R. 401; Gouverneur v. Lynch, 2 Paige R. 300; Skeel v. Spraker, 8 Paige, R. 182; Patty v. Pease, 8 Paige, R. 277; Schryver v. Teller, 9 Paige, R. 173.

(a) See Hurd v. Eaton, 28 Ill. 122; Marshall v. Moon, 36 Ill. 321; McCormick's Appeal, 57 Penn. St. 54; Jones v. Jones, 13 Iowa, 276.

(b) The rule seems now to be settled as propounded by the author. See Gibson v. Seagrim, 20 Beav. 614, 619; and the editor's note to § 633.

635. It is not improbable that this doctrine of marshalling securities or funds, which under another form had its existence in the Roman law, and was therein called subrogation or substitution, was derived into the jurisprudence of equity from that source, as it might well be, since it is a doctrine belonging to an age of enlightened policy, and refined although natural justice. In the Roman law (as we have already seen) a surety upon a bond or security, paying it to the creditor, was entitled to a cession of the debt, and a subrogation or substitution to all the rights and actions of the creditor against the debtor ; and the security was treated, as between the surety and the debtor, as still subsisting and unextinguished.[1]　And where one creditor had any hypothecation or privilege upon property as security for a debt, and another creditor had a like subsequent security upon the same property for another debt, there the latter upon payment of the prior debt to the prior creditor was entitled to a cession of the property, and to a subrogation to all the rights and actions of the same creditor for that debt.　So the doctrine is laid down in the Digest: ' Plane, cum tertius creditor primum de sua pecunia dimisit, in locum ejus substituitur in ea quantitate quam superiori exsolvit.' [2]

636. We here see the original elements from which our present system of equitable relief is, or at least might have been, derived. The principal difference between the Roman system and ours is, that our Courts of Equity arrive directly at the same result by compelling the first creditor to resort to the fund over which he has a complete control, for satisfaction of his debt; and the Roman system substituted the second creditor to the rights of the first, by a cession thereof upon his payment of the debt.　It is true that the case of a double fund is not put in the text of the Civil law ; but it is an irresistible inference from the principles upon which it is founded.[3]

---

[1] Pothier on Oblig. by Evans, n. 275, 280, 281; Id. n. 428, 429, 430; Id. n. 556, 557, 558, 559 (n. 591, 592, 593, 594, of the French editions) ; 1 Domat, Civ. Law, B. 3, tit. 1, § 6, per tot. pp. 377, 378, 379; 2 Voet, ad Pand. Lib. 46, tit. 1, §§ 27, 28, 29, 30; ante, §§ 494, 499, 500.

[2] Dig. Lib. 20, tit. 4, l. 16, 17, l. 11, § 4, l. 12, § 9.　See also 1 Domat, B. 3, tit. 1, § 6, art. 2, 3, 4, 6, 7, 8; ante, §§ 500, 501.

[3] See Pothier on Oblig. by Evans, n. 520, 521, 522 (n. 555, 556, 557, of the French editions), B.; Hayes v. Ward, 4 John. Ch. R. 130 to 132; Cheeseborough v. Millard, 1 John. Ch. R. 414.　There are three texts of the civil law pointing to cases of hypothecations or mortgages, which bear upon the sub-

637. Lord Kaimes has put the very case, as founded in a clear and indisputable principle of natural equity. After having adverted to the cases of sureties (fidejussores) and correi debendi (debtors bound jointly and severally to the same creditor),[1] he proceeds to state : 'Another connection of the same nature with the former is that between one creditor who is infeft in two different tenements for his security, and another creditor who hath an infeftment on one of the tenements of a later date. Here the two creditors are connected by having the same debtor and a security upon the same subject. Hence it follows as in the former case that if it be the will of the preferable creditor to draw his whole payment out of that subject in which the other creditor is infeft, the latter for his relief is entitled to have the preferable security assigned to him ; which can be done upon the construction above mentioned. For the sum recovered by the preferable creditor out of the subject on which the other creditor is also infeft is justly understood to be advanced by the latter, being a sum which he was entitled to and must have drawn had not the preferable creditor intervened ; and this sum is held to be purchase-money of the conveyance. This construction preserving

---

ject. In the Code it is said: 'Non omnino succedunt in locum hypothecarii creditoris hi quorum pecunia ad creditorem transit. Hoc enim tunc observatur; cum is qui pecuniam postea dat, sub hoc pacto credat ut idem pignus ei obligetur, et in locum ejus succedat. Quod cum in persona tua factum non sit (judicatum est enim te pignora non accepisse), frustra putas tibi auxilio opus esse Constitutionis nostræ ad eam rem pertinentis.' And again: 'Si potiores creditores pecunia tua dimissi sunt, quibus obligata fuit possessio, quam emisse te dicis, ita ut pretium perveniret ad eosdem priores creditores, in jus eorum successisti; et contra eos, qui inferiores illis fuerunt, justa defensione te tueri potes.' And again: 'Si prior Respublica contraxit, fundusque ei est obligatus, tibi secundo creditori offerenti pecuniam potestas est, ut succedas etiam in jus Reipublicæ.' Cod. Lib. 8, tit. 19, l. 1, 3, 4. Pothier has expounded the sense of these passages with admirable clearness. Pothier on Oblig. by Evans, n. 521, B. (3) (n. 556 of the French editions). Domat, B. 3, tit. 1, § 3, art. 6, says: 'Although the creditor who has a mortgage, whether general or special, may exercise his right on all lands and tenements that are subject to the mortgage, and even on those which are in possession of third persons, yet it seems agreeable to equity that if he can hope to recover payment of his debt out of the other effects which remain of the debtor, he should not begin with troubling the third possessor, even although his mortgage were special; but that before he molests the third possessor, and gives occasion to the consequences of having recourse against the debtor, he ought to discuss the other effects remaining in the debtor's possession.' See also Domat's note, ibid. and Cod. Lib. 8, tit. 14, l. 2; ante, § 494, notes 1 and 2.

[1] Ersk. Instit. B. 3, tit. 3, § 74.

the preferable debt entire in the person of the second creditor entitles him to draw payment of that debt out of the other tenement.   By this equitable construction matters are restored to the same state as if the first creditor had drawn his payment out of the separate subject, leaving the other entire, for payment of the second creditor.   Utility also concurs to support this equitable claim.' [1]

638. But the interposition of Courts of Equity is not confined to cases strictly of two funds and of different mortgagees ; for it will be applied (as we have seen) in favor of sureties where the creditor has collateral securities or pledges for his debt.[2]   In such cases the court will place the surety exactly in the situation of the creditor as to such securities or pledges whenever he is called upon to pay the debt ; for it would be against conscience that the creditor should use the securities or pledges to the prejudice of the sureties, or refuse to them the benefit thereof in aid of their own responsibility.[3] (a)   And on the other hand if a principal has given any securities or other pledges to his surety, the creditor is entitled to all the benefit of such securities or pledges in the hands of the surety, to be applied in payment of his debt.[4] (b)

639. Courts of Equity do not stop here. If the debt is due, and the creditor does not choose to call upon the debtor for payment, the surety may come into equity by a bill against the cred-

---

[1] 1 Kaimes, Equity, B. 1, Pt. 1, ch. 3, § 1, pp. 122, 123.

[2] Com. Dig. Chancery, 4 D. 6; Stirling v. Forrester, 3 Bligh, R. 590, 591; ante, §§ 327, 499, 502.

[3] Aldrich v. Cooper, 8 Ves. 388, 389.   See Gammon v. Stone, 1 Ves. 339; Cheeseborough v. Millard, 1 John. Ch. R. 413; Hayes v. Ward, 4 John. Ch. R. 130, 131, 132; Clason v. Morris, 10 John. R. 524, 539; Stevens v. Cooper, 1 John. Ch. R. 430, 431; Robinson v. Wilson, 2 Madd. Ch. Rep. 569; Ex parte Rushforth, 10 Ves. 410, 414; Wright v. Morley, 11 Ves. 23; Parsons v. Ruddock, 2 Vern. 608; Ex parte Kendall, 17 Ves. 520; Wright v. Simpson, 6 Ves. 734; 2 Fonbl. Eq. B. 3, ch. 2, § 6, note (i); Stirling v. Forrester, 3 Bligh, R. 590, 591; ante, §§ 324, 326.

[4] Wright v. Morley, 11 Ves. 22; ante, §§ 327, 499, 558.

(a) Shinn v. Budd, 1 McCart. 234.

(b) See ante, § 502, and note.

Where the surety had effected an insurance upon the life of the principal debtor, with his consent, and the principal had deceased, having made the surety his executor, it was held that the insurance money, beyond what was needed to indemnify the surety, should be applied to the payment of the debt. Lea v. Hinton, 5 DeG. M. & G. 823. See also Drysdale v. Piggott, 22 Beav. 238.

itor and the debtor, and compel the latter to make payment of the
debt so as to exonerate the surety from his responsibility; for it
is unreasonable that a man should always have such a cloud hang
over him.[1] (a)   In cases of this sort there is not however (as has
been already stated) any duty of active diligence incumbent
upon the creditor. It is for the surety to move in the matter.
But if the surety requires the exercise of such diligence and there
is no risk, delay, or expense to the creditor, or a suitable indemnity is offered against the consequences of risk, delay, and expense,
it seems that the surety has a right to call upon the creditor to
do the most he can for his benefit; and if he will not, a Court of
Equity will compel him.[2]

640. But as between the debtor himself and the creditor where
the latter has a formal obligation of the debtor, and also a security or a fund to which he may resort for payment, there seems
no ground to say (at least unless some other equity intervenes)
that a Court of Equity ought to compel the creditor to resort to
such fund before he asserts his claim by a personal suit against
his debtor. Why in such case should a Court of Equity interfere
to stop the election of the creditor as to any of the remedies
which he possesses in virtue of or under his contract? There is
nothing in natural or conventional justice which requires it. It
is true that a different doctrine has been strenuously maintained
by very learned judges in a most elaborate manner.[3] But their
opinions however able have been met by a reasoning exceedingly

---

[1] Ante, §§ 327, 494; Ranelaugh v. Hayes, 1 Vern. 189, 190; 1 Eq. Abridg.
17, Pl. 6; Id. 79, Pl. 5; Wright v. Simpson, 6 Ves. 734; Antrobus v. Davidson, 3 Meriv. R. 579; King v. Baldwin, 2 John. Ch. R. 561, 562, 563; s. c.
17 John. Rep. 384; Hayes v. Ward, 4 John. Ch. R. 432; Nisbet v. Smith, 2
Bro. Ch. R. 579; Lee v. Rook, Moseley, R. 318.

[2] Wright v. Simpson, 6 Ves. 734; Nisbet v. Smith, 2 Bro. Ch. R. 579;
Cottin v. Blane, 2 Anstr. R. 544; Eden on Injunct. ch. 2, pp. 38, 39, 40; King
v. Baldwin, 2 John. Ch. R. 561, 563; s. c. 17 John. R. 384; Hayes v. Ward,
4 John. Ch. R. 123; ante, §§ 327, 499 d.

[3] See Lord Thurlow's opinion in Wright v. Nutt, 1 H. Bl. 136, 150, and
Lord Loughborough in Folliott v. Ogden, 1 H. Bl. 124. See also Averall v.
Wade, Lloyd & Goold, R. 255.

(a) Ferrer v. Barrett, 4 Jones, Eq.
455; Irick v. Black, 2 C. E. Green, 189.
A person however, under engagement
to indemnify another from loss, cannot
be compelled to make good the engagement before the damage or liability
has arisen which gives rise to the
indemnity. Hughes-Hallett v. Indian
Mines Co., 22 Ch. D. 561, overruling
Ranelaugh v. Hayes, 1 Vern. 189, cited
by the author, supra. See Phené v.
Gillan, 5 Hare, 1, 12.

cogent, if not absolutely conclusive on the other side. And at all events the settled doctrine now seems to be in conformity to the early as well as the latest decisions, that the debtor himself has no right to insist that the creditor in such a case should pretermit any of his remedies or elect between them, unless some peculiar equity springs up from other circumstances.[1] (a)

641. The civil law, as we have seen, in the case of sureties required the creditor in the first instance to pursue his remedy against the debtor. But if the surety thought himself in peril of loss by the delay of the creditor, he might compel the latter to sue the debtor and thus obtain his indemnity. 'Fidejussor,' says the Digest,[2] 'an, et prius quam solvat, agere possit, ut liberetur?   Nec tamen semper expectandum est ut solvat, aut judicio accepto condemnetur; si diu in solutione reus cessabit, aut certe bona sua dissipabit; præsertim si domi pecuniam fidejussor non habebit, qua numerata creditori, mandati actione conveniat.'   This is a very wholesome and just principle.[3]

---

[1] Holditch v. Mist, 1 P. Will. 695; Wright v. Simpson, 6 Ves. 713, 726, 728 to 738, Lord Eldon's opinion. See Hayes v. Ward, 4 John. Ch. R. 132, 133; Eden on Injunct. ch. 2, p. 38, 39, 40.

[2] Dig. Lib. 17, tit. 1, l. 38; King v. Baldwin, 2 John. Ch. R. 562; Hayes v. Ward, 4 John. Ch. R. 132, 133; ante, §§ 327, 494.

[3] Mr. Chancellor Kent in his learned opinion in Campbell v. Macomb, 4 John. Ch. R. 538, speaking upon this subject, says: 'The question on this subject, so often raised in the civil law, assumed the fact that the principal debtor was in default, " Si diu in solutione reus cessabit;" and when it is added, " aut certe bona sua dissipabit," the reference was still to the case in which the debtor had failed to pay, and was also wasting his goods. I apprehend this must be the true construction; for the only question raised by Marcellus in the text referred to (Dig. Lib. 17, 1, 38, 1) was whether the surety could seek indemnity before he had himself paid, " Fidejussor an, et prius quam solvat, agere possit, ut liberetur?" It was a very equitable provision in the civil law to afford a remedy to the surety when the debtor neglected to pay, though the creditor had not required payment, and though the surety had not actually advanced the debt. But it would not have been very just to have given the surety an action for indemnity against the debtor before the latter was in default, and when such a previous claim made no part of the original contract. The debtor, as the civil law truly observes in another place (Dig. Lib. 17, 1, 22, 1), has an interest not to be compelled to pay before the day; and yet I perceive that several writers on the civil law (Domat, Part 1, B. 3, tit. 4, sec. 3, art 3; Wood's Institutes of the Civil Law, p. 227; Brown's Lectures on the Civil Law, Vol. 1, 362) refer to this very text to prove that if the surety be in peril he may sue before the time

(a) See editor's note to § 633, ante.

642. But although Courts of Equity will thus administer relief to both parties in cases of double funds which are subject to
the same debt, and will in favor of sureties marshal the securities
for their benefit, yet this will be so done in cases where no injustice is done to the common debtor, for then other equities may
intervene. And the interposition always supposes that the par-

of payment, to be indemnified or discharged. It may be so; but these writers
refer to no other text but that already cited, and that certainly does not, by
any necessary interpretation, warrant the doctrine. Indeed it seems to preclude
it; because the remedy was intended or provided (and so it is expressed)
especially for the case of a surety who could not conveniently discharge the
debt himself, and have his regular recourse over at once by the action mandatum. It was a benevolent provision in that view, and just in no other. In
other parts of the Pandects (Dig. Lib. 17, 1, 22, 1, and Lib. 46, 1, 31) Paul
and Ulpian lay down a rule in respect to sureties in perfect accordance with
the construction I have ventured to adopt; for they say that if the surety pays
before the day he cannot have recourse over to the debtor until the day of
payment has arrived. A number of civilians who have very fully discussed
the rights and remedies of sureties under the civil law, and always with this
text of Marcellus in view, give us no intimation of such a doctrine. The
general rule of the civil law was, that the action by the surety against his
principal depended upon his having paid the creditor. (Inst. Lib. 3, 21, 6,
and Ferriere's Inst. h. t.) And the cases in which he might have recourse
over before payment were all special cases; as where judgment had already
passed against the surety, or the debtor was in failing circumstances, or such
a recourse over was part of the original contract, or the debtor had neglected
a long time, as from three to ten years, to pay, or the creditor to demand. In
all these excepted cases the surety might sue the debtor for his indemnity or
discharge. But when might he sue him? Not before the debt was due and
payable to the creditor, but before the surety had paid the creditor. The
authorities to which I now refer (Hub. Prælec. Lib. 3, tit. 21, De Fide
Jussoribus, 11; Voet, ad Pand. Lib. 46, tit. 1, 34; Pothier, Traité des Oblig.
n. 441; Ersk. Inst. B. 3, c. 65) all consider these exceptions as only providing
for the relief of the surety ante solutionem. He may sue the principal debtor
before he has actually paid the debt, and the exceptions were to relieve him
from that burden; for without one of these special causes, says the Code, there
would be no foundation before payment for the action of mandatum. (" Nulla
juris ratione, antequam satis creditori pro ea feceris, eam ad solutionem
urgeri, certum est." Code 4, 35, 10.) This plain and equitable principle, that
until the debtor is in default either in his contract with the creditor or in his
contract with the surety he is not bound to pay or indemnify, seems to pervade equally every part of the civil law. Pothier says (ubi sup. n. 442) that
if the obligation to which the surety has acceded must, from its nature, exist
a long time, as, if he was surety for the due execution of a trust, he cannot
within the time sue the principal debtor or trustee for his discharge, for he
knew, or ought to have known, the nature of the obligation he contracted.
Though where he is surety indefinitely, as for payment of an annuity, he
may after a long time, as, say ten years, demand that the principal debtor
liberate him by redeeming the annuity.'

ties seeking aid are creditors of the same common debtor; for if they are not, they are not entitled to have the funds marshalled in order to leave a larger dividend out of one fund for those who can claim only against that. This principle may be easily illustrated by supposing the case of a joint debt due to one creditor by two persons, and a several debt due by one of them to another creditor. In such a case if the joint creditor obtains a judgment against the joint debtors, and the several creditor obtains a subsequent judgment against his own several debtor, a Court of Equity will not compel the joint creditor to resort to the funds of one of the joint debtors so as to leave the second judgment in full force against the funds of the other several debtor. At least it will not do so unless it should appear that the debt, though joint in form, ought to be paid by one of the debtors only, or there should be some other supervening equity.[1] (a)

643. Another case has been put, of a similar nature, by Lord Eldon. 'We have gone this length,' said he: 'If A has a right to go upon two funds and B upon one, having both the same debtor, A shall take payment from that fund to which he can resort exclusively, that by those means of distribution both may be paid. That takes place where both are creditors of the same person and have demands against funds the property of the same person. But it was never said that if I have a demand against A and B, a creditor of B shall compel me to go against A without more, as if B himself could insist that A ought to pay in the first instance, as in the ordinary case of drawer and acceptor, or principal and surety, to the intent that all obligations arising out of these complicated relations may be satisfied. But if I have a demand against both, the creditors of B have no right to compel me to seek payment from A if not founded in some equity giving B the right for his own sake to compel me to seek payment from A.'[2]

644. Upon this ground where there was a partnership of five persons, one of whom died, and the other four partners con-

---

[1] Dorr v. Shaw, 4 John. Ch. R. 17, 20.
[2] Ex parte Kendall, 17 Ves. 520.

(a) See Ayres v. Husted, 15 Conn. Ga. 392, 400; House v. Thompson, 504, 516; Newsom v. McLendon, 6 3 Head, 512, 516; ante, § 633.

tinued the partnership and afterwards became bankrupt, and the creditors of the four surviving partners sought to have the debts of the five paid out of the assets of the deceased partner so that the dividend of the estate of the four bankrupts might be thereby increased in favor of their exclusive creditors, without showing that the assets of the deceased partner ought as between the partners to pay those debts, or that there was any other equity to justify the claim, the court refused the relief. On that occasion the Lord Chancellor said that even if it was clear that the creditors of the five partners could go against the separate assets of the deceased partner (which of course depended upon equitable circumstances, as the legal remedy was against the survivors only), yet if it was not clear that the survivors had a right to turn the creditors of the five against those assets, it did not advance the claim that without such arrangement the creditors of the four would get less. Unless the latter could establish that it is just and equitable that the estate of the deceased partner should pay in the first instance, they had no right to compel a creditor to go against that estate who had a right to resort to both funds.[1] Indeed there might exist an opposite equity, that of compelling the creditor to go first against the property of the survivors before resorting to the estate of the deceased partner.[2]

645. The ground of all these decisions is the same general doctrine already suggested, though the application of that doctrine is necessarily varied by the circumstances. Where a creditor has a right to resort to two persons who are his joint and several debtors, he is not compellable to yield up his remedy against either, since he has a right to stand upon the letter and spirit of his contract unless some supervening equity changes or modifies his rights. If each debtor is equally bound in equity and justice for the debt, as is the case of joint debtors or partners where both have had the full benefit of the debt, the interference of a Court of Equity to change the responsibility from both debtors or partners to one would seem to be utterly without any principle to support it, unless there was a duty in one of the debtors or partners to pay the debt in discharge of the other. And if this be so, a fortiori the creditors of one of the debtors or part-

---

[1] Lord Eldon in Ex parte Kendall, 17 Ves. 520.
[2] Ibid.

ners cannot be entitled to such interference for their own bene-fit; for they can in no just sense in such a case work out any right except through the equity of the debtor or partner under whom their title is derived. (*a*)

(*a*) Ayres *v.* Husted, 15 Conn. 504, 517. It is held that in equity the creditors of an insolvent partner-ship are entitled to have the partnership assets applied in satisfaction of their claims in preference to the creditors of the individual partners, though the latter creditors may have been the first to attach those assets. And as the partnership creditors have this prior lien upon partnership effects, the other creditors may compel them to exhaust the partnership effects first. For any balance remaining unpaid thereafter both classes of creditors stand upon an equal footing; and the party effecting the first lien, whether by contract or by legal process, will be allowed to maintain such priority. In the absence of any such lien equity will decree an equal distribution. Washburn *v.* Bank of Bellows Falls, 19 Vt. 278; Bardwell *v.* Perry, Ib. 292. See also Miner *v.* Pierce, 38 Vt. 610, 614; Tiffany *v.* Crawford, 1 McCart. 278; post, § 675.

CHAPTER XIV.

PARTITION.

646. ANOTHER head of concurrent jurisdiction is that of PARTI-
TION in cases of real estate, (*a*) held by joint tenants, tenants in
common, (*b*) and coparceners. It is not easy, as has been well
observed by Mr. Fonblanque, to trace back or establish the origin
of any branch of equitable jurisdiction.[1] (*c*) But the jurisdiction of Courts of Equity in cases of partition is beyond question
very ancient. It is curious enough to observe the terms of apparent indignation with which Mr. Hargrave has spoken of this
jurisdiction as if it were not only new, but a clear usurpation.
Yet he admits its existence and practical exercise as early as the
reign of Queen Elizabeth;[2] a period so remote that at least one
half of the law which is at present by way of distinction called
the common law, and regulates the rights of property and the
operation of contracts, and especially of commercial contracts,

---

[1] 1 Fonbl. Eq. B. 1, ch. 1, § 3, note (*f*); Miller *v.* Warmington, 1 Jac. &
Walk. 484.

[2] See Mr. Fonblanque's Remarks on the passage, 1 Fonbl. Eq. B. 1, ch. 1,
§ 3, note (*f*).

(*a*) A bill may be maintained, at
least in some States, for partition of
personalty. Marshal *v.* Crow, 29 Ala.
278; Crapster *v.* Griffith, 2 Bland, 5;
Hewitt's Case, 3 Bland, 184; Tinney
v. Stebbins, 28 Barb. 290. See Biggs
v. Peacock, 22 Ch. D. 284.

(*b*) Corbitt *v.* Corbitt, 1 Jones,
Eq. 114.

(*c*) Before the Stat. 4 & 5 Vict.
ch. 35, § 85, equity had no power to
direct partition of copyholds or of
customary freeholds. Horncastle *v.*

Charlesworth, 11 Sim. 315; Jope *v.*
Morshead, 6 Beav. 217; Burrell *v.* Dodd,
3 Bos. & P. 378. Though it might
decree specific performance of an
agreement to divide copyholds. Bolton *v.* Ward, 4 Hare, 350. Equity
may decree partition of a manor.
Hanbury *v.* Hussey, 14 Beav. 152.
The writ of partition was abolished
in England by Stat. 3 & 4 Will. 4,
ch. 27, § 36, leaving equity with exclusive jurisdiction.

has had its origin since that time. 'A new and compulsory mode of partition,' says Mr. Hargrave, 'has sprung up and is now fully established; namely, by decree of chancery exercising its equitable jurisdiction on a bill filed, praying for a partition, in which it is usual for the court to issue a commission for the purpose to various persons, who proceed without a jury. How far this branch of equitable jurisdiction, so trenching upon the writ of partition and wresting from a Court of Common Law its ancient exclusive jurisdiction of this subject might be traced by examining the records of chancery, I know not. But the earliest instance of a bill of partition I observe to be noticed in the printed books, is a case of the 48th Elizabeth in Tothill's Transactions of Chancery, title, Partition.[1] According to this short report of the case the court interfered from necessity in respect of the minority of one of the parties, the book expressing that on that account he could not be made a party to a writ of partition, which reason seems very inaccurate; for if Lord Coke is right, that writ doth lie against an infant, and he shall not have his age in it, and after judgment he is bound by the partition.[2] But probably in Lord Coke's time this was a rare and rather unsettled mode of compelling partition; for I observe in a case in chancery of the 6th Car. I., which was referred to the judges on a point of law between two coparceners, that the judges certified for issuing a writ of partition between them, and that the court ordered one accordingly, which I presume would scarcely have been done if the decree for partition and a commission to make it had then been a current and familiar proceeding with chancery.[3] However it appears by the language of the court in a very important cause, in which the grand question was, whether the Lord Chancellor here could hold plea of a trust of lands in Ireland, that in the reign of James II. bills of partition were become common.'[4]

647. These remarks of the learned author are open to much criticism, if it were the object of these Commentaries to indulge in such a course of discussion. It cannot however escape notice that when the learned author speaks of this branch of equitable

[1] Speke v. Walrond, &c. (a), Tothill's Trans. 155 (edit. 1649).
[2] Co. Litt. 171 b.
[3] 1 Chan. Rep. 49.
[4] Hargrave's note (2) to Co. Litt. 169 b.

jurisdiction as trenching upon the writ of partition and wresting from the Courts of Common Law their ancient *exclusive* jurisdiction over the subject he assumes the very matter in controversy. That the writ of partition is a very ancient course of proceeding at the common law is not doubted. But it by no means follows that the Courts of Common Law had an exclusive jurisdiction over the subject of partition. The contrary may fairly be deemed to have been the case, from the notorious inadequacy of that writ to attain, in many cases, the purposes of justice. Thus for instance we know that until the reign of Henry VIII. no writ of partition lay except in the case of parceners. Littleton (§ 264) expressly says: 'For such a writ lyeth by parceners only.' And to show how narrowly the whole remedial justice of this writ was construed, it was the known settled doctrine that if two coparceners be, and one should alien in fee, the remaining parcener might bring a writ of partition against the alienee, but the alienee could not have such a writ *against* the parcener. And the like diversity existed in cases of a writ of partition by or against a tenant by the curtesy.[1] Now such a case would, upon the very face of it, constitute a clear case for the interposition of a Court of Chancery, upon the ground of the total defect of any remedy at law, and yet of an unquestionable equitable right to partition. Cases of joint tenancy and tenancy in common afford equally striking illustrations. Until the statute of 31st Henry VIII., ch. 1, and 32d Henry VIII., ch. 32, no writ of partition lay at law for a joint tenant or tenant in common.[2] And yet the grossest injustice might have arisen if a Court of Chancery could not in such a case have interposed and granted relief upon the analogy to the legal remedy. The reason given at the common law against partition in such cases was more specious than solid. It was, that a joint tenancy being an estate originally created by the act or agreement of the parties, the law would not permit any one or more of the tenants to destroy the united possession without a similar universal consent. The good sense of the doctrine would rather seem to be that the joint tenancy being created by the act or agreement of the parties, in a case capable of a severance of interest the joint interest should continue (exactly as in

---

[1] Co. Litt. 175 *a*.

[2] Co. Litt. 175 *a*; 2 Black. Comm. 185; Com. Dig. Parcener, C. 6; Miller *v.* Warmington, 1 Jac. & Walk. 473; Baring *v.* Nash, 1 Ves. & B. 555.

cases of partnership) so long as, and no longer than, both parties should consent to its continuance.

648. Mr. Justice Blackstone has cited the civil law as confirmatory of the reasoning of the common law: 'Nemo enim invitus compellitur ad communionem.'[1] But that law deemed it against good morals to compel joint owners to hold a thing in common, since it could not fail to occasion strife and disagreement among them.   Hence the acknowledged rule was, 'In communione vel societate nemo compellitur invitus detineri.'[2] And therefore a decree of partition might always be insisted on, even when some of the part-owners did not desire it. 'Communi dividendo judicium ideo necessarium fuit, quod *pro socio* actio magis ad personales invicem præstationes pertinet, quam ad communium rerum divisionem.'[3] 'Etsi non omnes, qui rem communem habent, sed certi ex his dividere desiderant, hoc judicium inter eos accipi potest.'[4]

649. But independently of considerations of this sort, which might have brought many cases of partition into the Court of Chancery in very early times from the manifest defect of any remedy at law, there must have been many cases where bills for partition were properly entertainable upon the ordinary ground of a discovery wanted or of other equities intervening between the parties.[5] (a) Lord Loughborough upon one occasion said that there is no original jurisdiction in chancery in partition, which is a proceeding at the common law.[6] This may be true sub modo where the party is completely remediable at law, but not otherwise.   On another occasion his Lordship said: 'A party choosing to have a partition has the law open to him; there is no equity for it.   But the jurisdiction of this court obtained upon a principle of *convenience*.   It is not for the court to say one party shall not hold his estate as he pleases; but another person has

---

[1] Dig. Lib. 12, tit. 6, 1. 26, § 4; 2 Black. Comm. 185, note (c).
[2] Cod. Lib. 3, tit. 37, 1. 5, ult.
[3] Dig. Lib. 10, tit. 3, 1. 1; 1 Domat, Civ. Law, B. 2, tit. 5, § 2, art. 11.
[4] Dig. Lib. 10, tit. 3, 1. 8; 1 Domat, Civ. Law, B. 2, tit. 5, § 2, art. 11, pp. 303, 306; Id. B. 1, tit. 4, § 1, pp. 632, 633; Fulbeck's Parallel, B. 2, pp. 57, 58; Ersk. Instit. B. 3, tit. 3, § 56; 1 Stair's Inst. 48.
[5] See Watson v. Duke of Northumberland, 11 Ves. 155, Arguendo.
[6] Mundy v. Mundy, 2 Ves. jr., 124.

(a) As where the shares are unequal. Paddock v. Shields, 57 Miss. 340.

also the same right to enjoy his part as he pleases, and therefore to have the estate divided. The law has provided that one shall not defeat the right of the other to the divided estate. Then the only question is, Whether the legal mode of proceeding is so convenient as the means this court affords to settle the interest between them with perfect fairness and equality. It is evident that the commission is much more convenient than the writ; the valuation of these proportions is much more considered; the interests of all parties are much better attended to; and it is a work carried on for the common benefit of both.'[1]

650. This language (it must certainly be admitted) is sufficiently loose and general. But it appears to be by no means a just description of the true nature and reason of the jurisdiction of Courts of Equity in cases of partition. It is not a jurisdiction founded at all in mere convenience, but in the judicial incompetency of the Courts of Common Law to furnish a plain, complete, and adequate remedy for such cases.[2] The true ground is far more correctly stated by Lord Redesdale in his admirable treatise on Pleadings in Equity. 'In cases of partition of an estate,' says he, 'if the titles of the parties are in any degree complicated, the difficulties which have occurred in proceeding at the common law have led to applications to Courts of Equity for partitions which are effected by first ascertaining the rights of the several persons interested, and then issuing a commission to make the partition required; and upon the return of the commissioners, and confirmation of that return by the court, the partition is finally completed by mutual conveyances of the allotments made to the several parties.'[3]

[1] Calmady v. Calmady, 2 Ves. jr., 570. See also Baring v. Nash, 1 Ves. & Beam. 555.

[2] Mitford, Pl. Eq. by Jeremy, 120; Strickland v. Strickland, 6 Beav. R. 77, 31; ante, § 627, note.

[3] Mitford, Pl. Eq. by Jeremy, 120; 1 Fonbl. Eq. B. 1, ch. 1, § 3, note (f), pp. 120, 121. The commissioners do not ascertain the interests of the respective parties; but the court first ascertains the interest and the proportion of each party in the land; and then the commissioners make the allotments accordingly. Agar v. Fairfax, 17 Ves. 543. The mode of ascertainment is through the instrumentality of a master, to whom the subject is referred. Id. See also Phelps v. Green, 3 John. Ch. R. 304, 305. (a) But the court will gen-

(a) Unless the title of *both* parties is clear, equity cannot decree partition. Burhans v. Burhans, 2 Barb. Ch. 398, 404; Garret v. White, 3 Ired. Eq. 131. So the plaintiff must prove his title and show that he is entitled to parti-

651. The ground here stated is of a complication of titles as the true foundation of the jurisdiction. But it is not even here expressed with entire legal precision. However complicated the titles of the parties might be, still if they could be thoroughly investigated at law in the usual course of proceedings in the common-law courts, there would seem to be no sufficient reason for transferring the jurisdiction of such cases to the Courts of Equity. (*a*) The true expression of the doctrine should have been that Courts of Equity interfere in cases of such a complication of titles, because the remedy at law is inadequate and imperfect, without the aid of a Court of Equity to promote a discovery, or to remove obstructions to the right, or to grant some other equitable redress.[1] (*b*)   Besides, the remedy in

---

erally, where the title is denied, and has not been established at law, require it to be first established at law; and will retain the bill to await the decision. Wilkin *v.* Wilkin, 1 John. Ch. R. 117; Parker *v.* Gerrard, Ambler, R. 236 ; Phelps *v.* Green, 3 John. Ch. R. 305; Cox *v.* Smith, 4 John. Ch. R. 271, 276.

[1] See Manaton *v.* Squire, 2 Freem. 26; Agar *v.* Fairfax, 17 Ves. 551; Watson *v.* Duke of Northumberland, 11 Ves. 153; Mitford, Pl. Eq. by Jeremy, 120; 1 Fonbl. Eq. B. 1, ch. 1, § 3, note (*f*), pp. 20, 21; Jeremy on Equity Jurisd. B. 3, ch. 1, § 1, pp. 303, 304.   This is the ground of the jurisdiction as stated by Lord Eldon in Agar *v.* Fairfax (17 Ves. 551). 'This court,' said he, 'issues the commission, not under the authority of any act of Parliament, but on account of the extreme difficulty attending the process of partition at law; where the plaintiff must prove his title, as he declares, and also the titles of the defendants, and judgment is given for partition according to the respective titles so proved.   That is attended with so much difficulty, that by analogy to the jurisdiction of a Court of Equity in the case of dower a partition

---

tion against the defendant. Ramsay *v.* Bell, 3 Ired. Eq. 209; Jope *v.* Morshead, 6 Beav. 213; Arnett *v.* Bailey, 60 Ala. 435; Oliver *v.* Jernigan, 46 Ala. 41. A bill for partition cannot be made the means of trying a disputed title, but the bill may be retained to give opportunity to try the title at law. Campbell *v.* Lowe, 9 Md. 500; Slade *v.* Barlow, L. R. 7 Eq. 296; Bolton *v.* Bolton, Ib. 298, note; Giffard *v.* Williams, L. R. 5 Ch. 546, reversing 8 Eq. 494; Daniel *v.* Green, 42 Ill. 471; Hoffman *v.* Beard, 22 Mich. 59; DeWitt *v.* Ackerman, 2 C. E. Green, 215; Hay *v.* Estell, 3 C. E. Green, 251; Hassam *v.* Day, 39 Miss.

392.   See further Gourley *v.* Woodbury, 42 Vt. 395; Morenhout *v.* Higuera, 32 Cal. 289; Campau *v.* Campau, 19 Mich. 116; Riverview Cem. Co. *v.* Turner, 24 N. J. Eq. 18; Hardy *v.* Mills, 35 Wis. 141; Byers *v.* Domley, 27 Ark. 77; Chaplin *v.* Holmes, Ib. 414; Groves *v.* Groves, 3 Sneed, 187.

(*a*) See Whiting *v.* Whiting, 15 Gray, 503; Husband *v.* Aldrich, 135 Mass. 317. Secus if the titles are equitable, or if there are equities to settle. Carter *v.* Taylor, 3 Head, 30; infra, § 653.

(*b*) See Adam *v.* Briggs Iron Co., 7 Cush. 361; Husband *v.* Aldrich, 135 Mass. 317.

Courts of Equity, even in such cases, is more perfect and extensive than at law; for in equity conveyances are directed to be made by the parties in pursuance of the allotments of the commissioners, which is a mode of redress of great importance as a permanent muniment of title, and of which a Court of Law is, by its own structure, incapable.

652. This is very clearly but briefly stated in a judgment of Lord Redesdale. 'Partition at law,' said that learned judge, ' and in equity are different things. The first operates by the judgment of a Court of Law and delivering up possession in pursuance of it, which concludes all the parties to it. Partition in equity proceeds upon conveyances to be executed by the parties; and if the parties be not competent to execute the conveyances, the partition cannot be effectually had.'[1](a)   Hence if the infancy of the parties or other circumstances prevent such mutual conveyances, the decree can only extend to make the partition, give possession, and order enjoyment accordingly until effectual conveyances can be made. If the defect arise from infancy, the infant must have a day, after attaining twenty-one years, to show cause against the decree. (b)   If a contingent remainder, not barable or extinguishable, is limited to a person not in existence, the conveyance cannot be made until he comes into being and is capable, or until the contingency is determined. An executory devise may occasion a similar embarrassment. And in either of

may be obtained by bill. The plaintiff must however state upon the record his own title and the titles of the defendants; and with a view to enable the plaintiff to obtain a judgment for partition, the court will direct inquiries to ascertain who are together with him entitled to the whole subject.' The inquiries are (as we have seen) by a reference to a master. See the form of a Decree in Partition in 17 Ves. 545, 553, 554; Strickland v. Strickland, 6 Beav. R. 77, 80, 81; ante, § 627, note.

[1] Whaley v. Dawson, 2 Sch. & Lefr. 371, 372.

(a) Gay v. Parpart, 106 U. S. 679, 690.

(b) In New York it is held that an infant cannot maintain a suit in equity for partition either alone or as a joint party with an adult. Postley v. Kain, 4 Sandf. Ch. 508. See Jackson v. Edwards, 7 Paige, 386, apart from statute. As to the present rule and practice in England see 13 & 14 Vict. ch. 60, §§ 7, 30; 31 & 32 Vict. ch. 40; 39 & 40 Vict. ch. 17; Bowra v. Wright, 20 L J. Ch. 216; s. c. 3 Eng. L. & E. 190; Orger v. Spark, 9 Week. R. 180; Shepherd v. Churchill, 25 Beav. 21. In cases of lunacy, Bryant v. Stearns, 16 Ala. 302; In re Bloomar, 2 DeG. & J. 88; Moorehead v. Moorehead, 2 Ir. R. Eq. 492. Further as to partition among minors see Cocks v. Simmons, 57 Miss. 183; Shull v. Kennon, 12 Ind. 34; Thornton v. Thornton, 27 Mo. 302.

these cases a supplemental bill will be necessary to carry the original decree into execution.[1]

653. It is upon this account that Lord Hardwicke has spoken of the remedy by partition in equity as being discretionary and not a matter of right in the parties. 'Here,' said he, 'the reason' (that the plaintiff should show a title in himself and not allege generally that he is in possession of a moiety of the land) 'is because conveyances are directed and not a partition only; which makes it discretionary in this court, where a plaintiff has a legal title, [whether] they [it] will grant a partition or not; and where there are suspicious circumstances in the plaintiff's title, the court will leave him to law.'[2]   His Lordship was here speaking of legal titles; for in the same case he expressly stated that where the bill for a partition was founded on an equitable title, a Court of Equity might determine it, (a) or otherwise it would be without remedy.[3]   And indeed if there are no suspicious circumstances, but the title is clear at law, the remedy for a partition in equity is as much a matter of right as at law.[4] (b)

654. In regard to partitions there is also another distinct

[1] Mitford, Pl. Eq. by Jeremy, 120, 121; Attorney-Gen. v. Hamilton, 1 Madd. Rep. 214; Wills v. Slade, 6 Ves. 498; Com. Dig. Chancery, 4 E.; Brook v. Hertford, 3 P. Will. 518, 519; Tuckfield v. Buller, 1 Dick. R. 240; Thomas v. Gyles, 2 Vern. 232; Gaskell v. Gaskell, 6 Sim. R. 643.   See Martyn v. Perryman, 1 Rep. in Ch. 235; post, § 656 a.

[2] Cartwright v. Pulteney, 2 Atk. 380.

[3] Ibid.   It is essential to a partition in equity that the legal title should be before the court.   It would be a decisive answer that the equitable title only is before the court; for then how could the conveyances be made if any should be necessary?   See the opinion of Sir Thomas Plumer (Master of the Rolls) in Miller v. Warmington, 1 Jac. & Walk. 473.

[4] Baring v. Nash, 1 Ves. & B. 555, 556; Parker v. Gerrard, Ambler, R. 236, and Mr. Blunt's note; post, § 656.

(a) Supra, note to § 651; Campbell v. Lowe, 9 Md. 500; Lucas v. King, 2 Stockt. 277; Hosford v. Merwin, 5 Barb. 51; Leverton v. Waters, 7 Coldw. 20; Ross v. Cobb, 48 Ill. 111; Carter v. Taylor, 3 Head, 30; Williams v. Wiggand, 53 Ill. 233; Dameron v. Jameson, 71 Mo. 97, showing that the bill will be upheld though the defendant is in adverse possession if the plaintiff's title is equitable. See also as to possession Wommack v. Whitmore, 48 Mo. 448.

(b) Wiseley v. Findlay, 3 Rand. 361, 398; Smith v. Smith, 10 Paige, 473; Lucas v. King, 2 Stockt. 277. Partition of real estate will not be decreed in favor of one partner and against another on the dissolution of the partnership.   Either partner is entitled to have the whole partnership property disposed of.   Wild v. Milne, 26 Beav. 504; Crawshay v. Maule, 1 Swanst. 495, 518; Darby v. Darby, 3 Drew. 495, 501.

ground upon which the jurisdiction of Courts of Equity is maintainable, as it constitutes a part of its appropriate and peculiar
remedial justice.   It is that Courts of Equity are not restrained,
as Courts of Law are, to a mere partition or allotment of the
lands and other real estate between the parties according to their
respective interests in the same and having a regard to the true
value thereof.[1] But Courts of Equity may, with a view to the
more convenient and perfect partition or allotment of the premises, decree a pecuniary compensation to one of the parties for
owelty or equality of partition, so as to prevent any injustice or
unavoidable inequality.[2] (a)   This a Court of Common Law is

---

[1] Co. Litt. 176, *a* and *b*; Id. 168 *a*.

[2] See Calmady *v.* Calmady, 2 Ves. jr., 570; Earl of Clarendon *v.* Hornby,
1 P. Will. 446, 447; Warner *v.* Baynes, Ambler, R. 589; Wilkin *v.* Wilkin,
1 John. Ch. R. 116, 117; Phelps *v.* Green, 3 John. Ch. R. 302, 305; Larkin *v.*
Mann, 2 Paige, R. 27; Storey *v.* Johnson, 1 Younge & Coll. 538; s. c. 2
Younge & Coll. 586, 610, 611; post, § 657.

(a) This power rests only with the
court. The commissioners of partition cannot award a sum to be paid
for owelty of partition.   Mole *v.*
Mansfield, 15 Sim. 41.   It seems that
in England, before the Partition Act
of 1868, 31 & 32 Vict. ch. 40, §§ 3, 4,
Courts of Equity would, in small cases
at least, order a sale in lieu of partition when satisfied it was for the benefit of all parties, though minors or
persons out of the realm were interested. Davis *v.* Turvey, 32 Beav.
554; Hubbard *v.* Hubbard, 2 Hem. &
M. 38. Though not against the will
of a party in interest. Griffies *v.*
Griffies, 11 Week. R. 943. But since
that act sale may be ordered without
the assent of all. See Roebuck *v.*
Chadebet, L. R. 8 Eq. 127 (partition
of part and sale of part); France *v.*
France, L. R. 13 Eq. 173 (infant);
Higgs *v.* Dorkis, Ib. 280 (married
woman); Holland *v.* Holland, Ib. 406;
Pemberton *v.* Barnes, L. R. 6 Ch. 685.
See Act of 1876, 39 & 40 Vict. ch. 17;
Pitt *v.* Jones, 8 Ch. D. 548; s. c. 11
Ch. D. 28; 5 App. Cas. 651; Porter *v.*
Lopes, 7 Ch. D. 358. As to parties
out of the jurisdiction see Peters *v.*

Bacon, L. R. 8 Eq. 125; Silver *v.*
Udell, L. R. 9 Eq. 227; Hurry *v.*
Hurry, L. R. 10 Eq. 346 ; Teall *v.*
Watts, L. R. 11 Eq. 213.

In many of the States there are
statutes authorizing sale.   Haywood
v. Judson, 4 Barb. 228 (part allotted
to one, the rest to be sold and proceeds distributed); Wilson *v.* Duncan,
44 Miss. 642; Hickenbotham *v.* Black-
ledge, 54 Ill 316; Thruston *v.* Minke,
32 Md. 571; Graham *v.* Graham, 8
Bush, 334; Pockman *v.* Meatt, 49 Mo.
344; Loyd *v.* Loyd, 23 La. 231; Welsh
v. Freeman, 21 Ohio St. 402; McCall's
Appeal, 56 Penn. St. 363.   Whether
in the absence of statute equity will
order a sale where infants are concerned see Rivers *v.* Durr, 46 Ala. 418.

It seems that a sale may be ordered
with discharge of mortgages, the lien
to attach to the proceeds. See Kilgour *v.* Crawford, 51 Ill. 249; Garvin
v. Garvin, 1 S. Car. 55; Girard Ins.
Co. *v.* Farmers' Bank, 57 Penn. St.
388. Compare the case of marshalling in the editor's note to § 633, supra,
at the end. The partition may be
confined to setting off the aliquot part
of the plaintiff if the defendants do

not at liberty to do; for when a partition is awarded by such a court, the exigency of the writ is that the sheriff do cause, by a jury of twelve men, the partition to be made of the premises between the parties, regard being had to the true value thereof, without any authority to make any compensation for any inequality in any other manner.[1]

655. Cases of a different nature involving equitable compensation to which a Court of Law is utterly inadequate may easily be put; such for instance as cases where one party has laid out large sums in improvements on the estate. For although under such circumstances the money so laid out does not in strictness constitute a lien on the estate, yet a Court of Equity will not grant a partition without first directing an account and compelling the party applying for partition to make due compensation.[2] So where one tenant in common has been in the exclusive perception of the rents and profits on a bill for a partition and account, the latter will also be decreed.[3] So where one tenant in common, supposing himself to be legally entitled to the whole premises, has erected valuable buildings thereon, he will be entitled to an equitable partition of the premises, so as to give him the benefit of his improvements; or if that cannot be done, he will be entitled to a compensation for those improvements.[4] (a)

---

[1] Co. Litt. 167 d; Com. Dig. Pleader, 3 F. 4. Littleton (§ 251) has spoken of a rent-charge in cases of partition for owelty or equality in partition. But this is not in a case of compulsory partition by writ, but of a voluntary partition by deed or by parol, as the context abundantly shows. Co. Litt. 168 b; Litt. §§ 250, 252.

[2] Swan v. Swan, 8 Price, R. 518.

[3] Hill v. Fulbrook, 1 Jac. R. 574; Lorimer v. Lorimer, 5 Madd. R. 363; Storey v. Johnson, 1 Younge & Coll. 538; s. c. 2 Younge & Coll. 586.

[4] Town v. Needham, 3 Paige, R. 546, 555. See also Teal v. Woodworth, 3 Paige, R. 470.

---

not desire further partition. Hobson v. Sherwood, 4 Beav. 184. As to setting off shares of two or more together, see Peers v. Needham, 19 Beav. 316.

Further as to owelty of partition see Thomas v. Farmers' Bank, 32 Md. 57; Cooke v. Moore, 2 S. Car. 52.

(a) Equity will incidentally settle an account between co-tenants, and charge one who occupies to the exclusion of the rest with occupation rent.

Pascoe v. Swan, 27 Beav. 508. But it has been held that one co-tenant will not ordinarily be allowed for permanent improvements made with knowledge of the state of title, except as an offset to occupation rent. Teasdale v. Sanderson, 33 Beav. 534; Scott v. Guernsey, 48 N. Y. 106. But see Hall v. Piddock, 6 C. E. Green, 311, where it is held that the tenant is entitled in equity to claim for improve-

656. Indeed in a great variety of cases, especially where the property is of a very complicated nature as to rights, easements, modes of enjoyment, and interfering claims, the interposition of a Court of Equity seems indispensable for the purposes of justice. For since partition is ordinarily a matter of right, no difficulty in making a partition is allowed to prevail in equity, whatever may be the case at law, as the powers of the court are adequate to a full and just compensatory adjustment.[1] There have been cases disposed of in equity which seemed almost impracticable for allotment at law, as in the case of the Cold Bath Fields, in which Lord Hardwicke did not hesitate to act, notwithstanding the admitted difficulties.[2] Nor does it constitute any objection in equity that the partition does not or may not finally conclude the interests of all persons, as where the partition is asked only by or against a tenant for life, or where there are contingent interests to vest in persons not in esse.[3] For the court will still proceed to make partition between the parties before the court who possess competent present interests, such as a tenant for life or for years.[4] (a) But under such circumstances the partition is binding upon those parties only who are before the

[1] Ante, § 653.

[2] Warner v. Baynes, Ambler, R. 589; Turner v. Morgan, 8 Ves. 143, 144.

[3] Gaskell v. Gaskell, 6 Sim. 643.

[4] Wills v. Slade, 6 Ves. 498; Baring v. Nash, 1 Ves. & B. 555; Wotten v. Copeland, 7 John. Ch. R. 140; Gaskell v. Gaskell, 6 Sim. R. 643; Striker v. Mott, 2 Paige, R. 387, 389; Woodworth v. Campbell, 5 Paige, R. 518.

ments made in good faith, though with knowledge. In Campbell v. Campbell, 21 Mich. 438, where in a suit for partition there had been improvements, but whether they had been paid for, and by whom, and what were the rights of the parties in regard to the same, was doubtful, it was held that partition should be made regardless of such questions. See further Green v. Putnam, 1 Barb. 500; Putnam v. Ritchie, 6 Paige, 390; In re Heller, 3 Paige, 199; Conklin v. Conklin, 3 Sandf. Ch. 64. But if the erection of improvements has under the circumstances created a claim, the portion improved should be set off to the party who made them, if this can be done without injury to the rights of the rest ; if it cannot so be done, then there must be compensation. Kurtz v. Hibner, 55 Ill. 514; Dean v. O'Meara, 47 Ill. 120. See Hall v. Piddock, 6 C. E. Green, 311, 314.

The defendant co-tenant should bring any claim of his for improvements by cross-bill. Stafford v. Nutt, 39 Ind. 93; Bond v. Hill, 37 Texas, 626.

In regard to the right of a tenant in common to partition where the land is subject to a charge in favor of such party and of others, see Otway-Cave v. Otway, L. R. 2 Eq. 725.

(a) See Heaton v. Dearden, 16 Beav. 147.

court, and those whom they virtually represent;[1] and the interests of third persons are not affected.[2] And it is not an unimportant ingredient in the exercise of equity jurisdiction in cases of partition that the parties in interest may be brought before the court far more extensively than they can be by any processes known to the Courts of Law, for the purpose of doing complete justice.[3] (a)

656 a. Doubts were formerly entertained whether in a suit in equity for a partition brought only by or against a tenant for life of the estate where the remainder is to persons not in esse, a decree could be made which would be binding upon the persons in remainder. That doubt however is now removed, and the decree is held binding upon them upon the ground of a virtual representation of them by the tenant for life in such cases.[4] But if the partition is made in pursuance of an agreement between the tenant for life and the other party, under such circumstances the court will direct it to be referred to a master to inquire and state whether it will be for the future benefit of the remaindermen that the agreement should be carried into execution without any variations, or if with variations, what the variations ought to be.[5]

656 b. In suits in equity also for partition various other equitable rights and claims and adjustments will be made which are beyond the reach of Courts of Law. Thus if improvements have been made by one tenant in common, a suitable compensation will (as we have seen) be made him upon the partition, or the property on which the improvements have been made assigned to him.[6] So Courts of Equity will not only take care that the parties have an equal share and just compensation, but they will assign to the parties respectively such parts of the estate as would best

---

[1] Story on Equity Pleadings, §§ 144 to 148 ; Gaskell v. Gaskell, 6 Sim. R. 643.

[2] Agar v. Fairfax, 17 Ves. 544.

[3] Anon. 3 Swanst. R. 139, note (b).

[4] Gaskell v. Gaskell, 6 Sim. R. 643.   See also Martyn v. Perryman, 1 Ch. Rep. 235; Brook v. Hertford, 2 P. Will. 518; ante, § 653.

[5] Gaskell v. Gaskell, 6 Sim. R. 643.   [6] Ante, § 655.

(a) Where the defendant is a nonresident, the jurisdiction is statutory entirely, and the statute must be strictly complied with. Platt v. Stewart, 10 Mich. 260. Courts of one State cannot order partition of lands in another. Johnson v. Kimbro, 3 Head, 557.

accommodate them and be of most value to them with reference
to their respective situations in relation to the property before
the partition.[1] (*a*)   For in all cases of partition a Court of Equity
does not act merely in a ministerial character and in obedience
to the call of the parties who have a right to the partition, but it
founds itself upon its general jurisdiction as a Court of Equity,
and administers its relief ex æquo et bono according to its own
notions of general justice and equity between the parties.   It
will therefore by its decree adjust all the equitable rights of the
parties interested in the estate, (*b*) and will if necessary for this
purpose give special instructions to the commissioners, and
nominate the commissioners, instead of allowing them to be
nominated by the parties.[2] (*c*)

656 *c*. And Courts of Equity in making these adjustments will
not confine themselves to the mere legal rights of the original
tenants in common, but will have regard to the legal and equitable rights of all other parties interested in the estate which have
been derived from any of the original tenants in common; and
will if necessary for this purpose direct a distinct partition of
each of several portions of the estate in which the derivative
alienees have a distinct interest, in order to protect that interest.[3]
Thus where A, B, and C were tenants in common in undivided
third parts of an estate comprising Whiteacre and Blackacre,
and C had conveyed his interest in Blackacre to D and his
interest in Whiteacre to E, upon a bill filed by A and B for
partition of the whole estate the court directed that Blackacre
should be divided into three parts, and one part should be conveyed to A and B and D respectively, and that Whiteacre
should be divided into three parts, and one part should be conveyed to A and B and E respectively.   In this way, consistently with the rights of A and B, the interests of D and E
were, as in equity they ought to be, fully protected and secured.[4]

---

[1] Storey *v.* Johnson, 1 Younge & Coll. 538; s. c. 2 Younge & Coll. 586.
[2] Ibid.   [3] Ibid.
[4] Storey *v.* Johnson, 1 Younge & Coll. 538; s. c. 2 Younge & Coll. 586.

(*a*) See note to § 655, supra.

(*b*) The claims of the ancestor's
creditors may be adjusted in a suit
between heirs for partition. Gate-
wood *v.* Toomer, 14 Rich. Eq. 39.

(*c*) Haywood *v.* Judson, 4 Barb.
228. The report of the commissioners is regarded in the same light as
the verdict of a jury in a trial at law,
and will be set aside only on grounds
which would justify a new trial at law.
Livingston *v.* Clarkson, 4 Edw. 596.

657. In equity too (and it would seem that the same rule prevails at law, though this has sometimes been doubted),[1] where there are divers parcels of lands, messuages, and houses, partition need not be made of each estate separately so as to give to each party his moiety or other portion in every estate; but the whole of one estate may be allotted to one, and the whole of another estate to the other, provided that his equal share is allotted to each.[2] (a)   But it is obvious that at law such a partition can rarely be conveniently made, because the court cannot decree compensation so as to make up for any inequality which must ordinarily occur in the allotment of different estates to each party.   In equity it is in the ordinary course.[3]

658. It is upon some or all of these grounds, the necessity of a discovery of titles, the inadequacy of the remedy at law, the difficulty of making the appropriate and indispensable compensatory adjustments, the peculiar remedial processes of Courts of Equity, and their ability to clear away all intermediate obstructions against complete justice, that these courts have assumed a general concurrent jurisdiction with Courts of Law in all cases of partition. (b)   So that it is not now deemed necessary to state in the bill any peculiar ground of equitable interference ;[4] (c) and unless I am greatly misled in my judgment, this review of the true sources and objects of this concurrent jurisdiction demonstrates in the most satisfactory manner how ill founded the animadversions of Mr. Hargrave (already cited) are upon the exercise of this jurisdiction.[5]   But the most conclusive proof in its favor is, that wherever it exists it has almost entirely superseded any resort to Courts of Law to obtain a partition.   In

---

[1] See Arguendo in Earl of Clarendon v. Hornby, 1 P. Will. 446, 447; Storey v. Johnson, 1 Younge & Coll. 538; s. c. 2 Younge & Coll. 586.

[2] Earl of Clarendon v. Hornby, 1 P. Will. 446, 447.

[3] Ibid.; ante, § 654.

[4] Mitford, Plead. Eq. by Jeremy, 120; Jeremy on Eq. Jurisd. B. 3, ch. 1, § 2, pp. 304, 305; 1 Fonbl. Eq. B. 1, ch. 1, § 3; note (f), pp. 10, 21.

[5] Ante, § 646.

(a) Peers v. Needham, 19 Beav. 316.

(b) Haywood v. Judson, 4 Barb. 228.

(c) It is held in Husband v. Aldrich, 135 Mass. 317, and in Whiting v. Whiting, 15 Gray, 503, that equity has no jurisdiction in Massachusetts to decree partition between tenants in common, on the ground that by statute full relief can be had at law.   But see Hess v. Voss, 52 Ill. 472, contra. And see the editor's note to § 33, ante.

making partition however Courts of Equity generally follow the
analogies of the law, and will decree it in such cases as the
Courts of Law recognize as fit for their interference.[1] But Courts
of Equity are not therefore to be understood as limiting their
jurisdiction in partition to cases cognizable or relievable at law;
for there is no doubt that they may interfere in cases where a
writ of partition would not lie at law,[2] (*a*) as for instance in
the case where an equitable title is set up.[3] (*b*)

[1] Ibid.; Wills *v.* Slade, 6 Ves. 498; Baring *v.* Nash, 1 Ves. & B. 555.

[2] Swan *v.* Swan, 8 Price, R. 519; Woodworth *v.* Campbell, 5 Paige, 518.

[3] Cartwright *v.* Pulteney, 2 Atk. 380; Cox *v.* Smith, 4 John. Ch. R. 276.
See Miller *v.* Warmington, 1 Jac. & Walk. 473; Com. Dig. Chancery, 4 E.
Partition; ante, § 653.

(*a*) Bailey *v.* Sisson, 1 R. I. 233;
Haywood *v.* Judson, 4 Barb. 228.

(*b*) Hosford *v.* Merwin, 5 Barb. 51.
But where an estate is devised to
trustees for conversion inter alia, the
beneficiaries must in England all
agree to the partition though their
interest is vested. Biggs *v.* Peacock,
22 Ch. D. 284. See Taylor *v.* Grange,
15 Ch. D. 165; s. c. 13 Ch. D. 223;
Swaine *v.* Denby, 14 Ch. D. 326.
Partition may be decreed though the
trustees have a discretionary power of
sale. Boyd *v.* Allen, 24 Ch. D. 622.
As to costs in cases of partition, Lan-
dell *v.* Baker, L. R. 6 Eq. 268; Osborn
v. Osborn, Ib. 338 (infants); France
v. France, L. R. 13 Eq. 173; Miller
v. Marriott, L. R. 7 Eq. 1; Cannon *v.*
Johnson, L. R. 11 Eq. 90.

CHAPTER XV.

PARTNERSHIP.

659. ANOTHER head of concurrent jurisdiction arising from similar causes is in relation to PARTNERSHIP.[1] In cases of this nature where a remedy at law actually exists it is often found to be very imperfect, inconvenient, and circuitous. But in a very great variety of cases there is in fact no remedy at all at law to meet the exigency of the case. We shall in the first instance take notice of such remedies as exist at law, and then proceed to the considerations of others which are peculiar to Courts of Equity.

660. And here it may be proper to begin by a reference to that which is in its own nature preliminary to all other inquiries; to wit, the actual existence of the partnership itself. Although in many cases written articles or instruments of partnership exist as the foundation of the joint concerns, yet in many other cases the partnership itself exists merely in parol. And even in cases of written articles there are many defects and omissions which the parties have left unprovided for. (a) Now a controversy may arise in regard to the existence of the partnership between the partners themselves, or between them and third persons. (b) In each case its existence may mainly depend upon

[1] See Com. Dig. Chancery, 3 V. 6.

(a) When after the expiration of the term limited by the partnership articles the business is carried on by the partners without new articles, the old provisions will govern so far as consistent with a partnership now at will. Cox v. Willoughby, 13 Ch. D. 863.

(b) Query whether persons associated together for the purpose of procuring an act of incorporation under which to trade are to be treated before

the act is obtained as partners, so as to permit one of them to have recourse in equity against the others for a simple tort. In the cases of Holmes v. Higgins, 1 Barn. & C. 74, and Lucas v. Beach, 1 Man. & G. 417, it is held they are. See however 1 Lindl. Part. (4th ed.), 31, 32; Dole v. Wooldredge, 135 Mass. 140.

How far members of a mutual insurance company are partners, see In

the discovery to be obtained through the instrumentality of a Court of Equity. If written articles exist, they may be suppressed or concealed; if none exist, it may be impracticable to obtain due knowledge of the partnership by any competent witnesses in the ordinary course of law. But in by far the most numerous and important class of cases, that of secret and dormant partners, there may not be and indeed ordinarily will not be any adequate means at law to get at the names or numbers of the partners. In all such cases the powers of a Court of Equity will be found most effective by means of a bill of discovery to bring out all the facts, as well in controversies between the partners themselves as between them and third persons.

661. But admitting a partnership to exist, let us now proceed to consider what are the remedies at law which exist between the partners themselves. These of course are dependent upon the nature of the partnership and the grievance for which a remedy is sought. If the articles of partnership are under seal, and any violation of any of the stipulations therein contained exists, it may be and is properly remediable by an action of covenant. If there are written articles not under seal, or the partnership is by a parol agreement, the proper remedy for any breach of the stipulations is by an action of assumpsit. But, as we shall presently see, both these remedies are utterly inadequate to provide for many exigencies and injuries which may arise out of the violation of partnership rights and duties.

662. The most extensive and generally the most operative remedy at law between partners is an action of account. This is the appropriate and except under very peculiar circumstances is the only remedy at the common law for the final adjustment and settlement of partnership transactions. It is a very ancient remedy between partners, in which one naming himself a merchant may sue his partner for a reasonable account, naming him a merchant, and charging him as the receiver of the moneys of himself arising from whatever cause or contract for the common profit of both according to the law merchant.[1]

[1] Co. Litt 172 *a*; Fitz. N. B. 117 D.

re Albion Assur. Co. 16 Ch. D. 83; Winstone's Case, 12 Ch. D. 239. Further what constitutes partner- ship, see Powsey *v.* Armstrong, 18 Ch. D. 698; Steward *v.* Blakeway, L. R. 6 Eq. 479; s. c. 4 Ch. 603.

663. But it is wholly unnecessary to dwell upon the inadequacy of this remedy in cases of partnership, as all the remarks already made in respect to the dilatory, cumbrous, and inconvenient proceedings in actions of account [1] apply with augmented force to cases of partnership, where it is absolutely impossible, in many cases, to settle the concerns of the partnership without the production of the books, vouchers, and other documents belonging to the partnership, and the personal examination of the partners themselves. So intimate is the confidence and so universal the community of interest and operations between partners, that no proceedings, not including a thorough and minute discovery, can enable any court to arrive at the means of doing even reasonable justice between them. And in addition to the common difficulties in ordinary cases, the death of either partner put an end, at the common law, to any means of enforcing this remedy by account; for it being founded in privity between the parties, no suit lay by or against the personal representative of the deceased partner to compel an account.[2]

664. In a few cases indeed where there has been a covenant or promise to account, Courts of Law have attempted to approximate towards an effectual remedy in the shape of damages for a breach of the obligation. But it is manifest that even in these cases the damages must be wholly uncertain unless an account can be fully and fairly taken between the parties, for otherwise there will be no rule by which to ascertain the damages. There has too been a struggle in cases where one partner has been compelled to advance or pay money on the partnership account out of his own private funds, to give him a remedy at law for a contribution from the other partners. But it is difficult to perceive how, except under very peculiar circumstances, such a remedy will lie.[3] For it is impossible, during the continuance of the

[1] Ante, §§ 442 to 449.

[2] Ante, § 446.

[3] It is no part of the object of these Commentaries to show in minute detail the nature and extent of the legal remedies in cases of this sort. Where the partnership has been dissolved, and upon such a dissolution all the accounts of the partnership have been adjusted, as between the partners, or where one partner has purchased the property and agreed to pay all the debts, there, if the other partner is called upon to pay a partnership debt, he may be entitled at law to contribution. So where upon a dissolution of a partnership all the accounts have been adjusted and a balance struck, an action at law will lie for such balance. So where a sum of money has been received for one

partnership, without taking a general account, to say that any one partner, so called upon to advance or pay money, is on the whole a creditor of the firm to such an amount.   And if he is, how, in point of technical propriety, can he institute a remedy against his other partners alone as contradistinguished from the partnership ?   It is very certain that if he should lend the partnership a sum of money, he could not sue for it at law, for he could not sue himself; and it is not very easy to perceive a clear distinction between this and the former case.   And if it should turn out, upon taking a general account, that such partner was a debtor to the partnership, it would be unreasonable and useless to allow him to recover the very money which he must refund to the partnership ; for the maxim of common sense as well as of common justice is, ' Frustra petis quod statim alteri reddere cogeris.' [1]

665. Cases have also occurred in which suits at law have been maintained for the breach of an agreement to furnish a certain sum or stock for the partnership purposes.   In such a case the transaction is not so much a partnership transaction as an agreement to launch the partnership ; and an agreement to pay money or furnish stock for such a purpose is an individual engagement of each partner to the other.[2]   For the breach of such an agreement there seems no reasonable objection to the maintenance of

partner's separate account by the other partners, he may recover the same in an action of assumpsit as money had and received for his use.   But all these and other cases of the like nature stand upon their own special circumstances, and steer wide of the general doctrine.   There is no case in the English courts (although there may be cases in some of the American courts) where any action at law except on account has been held to lie generally to settle partnership accounts, or for a contribution by one partner against the others, for money paid by him for the use of the partnership.   The learned reader will find many of the cases collected and commented on in Mr. Collyer's valuable work on Partnership, B. 2, ch. 3, §§ 1, 2, 4, and in the notes of the able American editor, Mr. Phillips, in his edition of that work.   Mr. Gow, in his work on the same subject (ch. 2, § 3), has discussed the same subject at large; and in his last (the third) edition he has corrected some of the inadvertences into which he had fallen on this subject by relying too much upon some loose dicta in some of the authorities.   See also Holmes v. Higgins, 1 B. & Cressw. 74; Harvey v. Crickett, 5 M. & Selw. 336; Bovill v. Hammond, 6 B. & Cressw. 149.

[1] Branch's Maxims, 55.

[2] See Venning v. Leckie, 13 East, R. 7; Gale v. Leckie, 2 Stark. R. 107; Terrill v. Richards, 1 Nott & McCord, R. 20.

a suit at law. (a)   But what should be the measure of the damages must depend upon the circumstances of each particular case. No general rule can be laid down to govern all cases.   If the partnership has no specific term fixed for its continuance, in many cases the damages would be merely nominal.   If it has such a specific fixed term, the damages must necessarily be of a very uncertain nature and extent.   The whole sum agreed for the partnership stock could not be the true rule, for that would be in effect to give one partner the whole capital stock.   And on the other hand the possible profits of the partnership if carried on would not furnish a rule, because of the uncertainty of such profits and their being to arise in futuro, and the injury not being certain at the time of the breach. (b)

666. The remedial justice administered by Courts of Equity is far more complete, extensive, and various, adapting itself to the particular nature of the grievance, and granting relief in the most beneficial and effectual manner where no redress whatsoever, or very imperfect redress, could be obtained at law.   In the first place they may decree a specific performance of a contract to enter into a partnership for a specific term of time (for it would ordinarily be useless to enforce one which might be dissolved instantly at the will of either party),[1] (c) and to furnish a share of the capital stock, which a Court of Law is incapable of doing.[2] This remedy however is rarely sought, for the plain reason that few partnerships can be hoped to be successful where they begin in mutual distrust, dissatisfaction, or enmity. (d)

[1] This qualification (ordinarily) is necessary; for a specific performance may in some cases be important to establish rights under a partnership which has no fixed term for its continuance.   Mr. Swanston, in his excellent note to Crawshay v. Maule, 1 Swanst. R. 511, 512, 513, has clearly shown the propriety of the qualification.   See also Birchett v. Bolling, 5 Munf. R. 442.

[2] Anon. 2 Ves. 629, 630; Hercy v. Birch, 9 Ves. 357; Buxton v. Lister, 3 Atk. 385; Hibbert v. Hibbert, cited in Collyer on Partn. B. 2, ch. 2, § 2, p. 197; Crawshay v. Maule, 1 Swanst. 511, 512, Mr. Swanston's note; Peacock v. Peacock, 16 Ves. 49; Birchett v. Bolling, 5 Munf. R. 442.

(a) See Hill v. Palmer, 56 Wis. 123; Vance v. Blain, 18 Ohio, 532; Ellison v. Chapman, 7 Blackf. 224 : Ness v. Fisher, 5 Lans. 236.

(b) See some special cases in Watney v. Wells, L. R. 2 Ch. 250; Dinham v. Bradford, L. R. 5 Ch. 519.

(c) Somerby v. Buntin, 118 Mass. 279, 287.   But equity will secure to a partner the interest in property to which the partnership contract entitles him.   Ib.

(d) Equity will not specifically enforce a verbal contract to form a part-

667. In like manner after the commencement and during the continuation of a partnership Courts of Equity will in many cases interpose to decree a specific performance of other agreements in the articles of partnership. If for instance there be an agreement to insert the name of a partner in the firm name, so as to clothe him publicly with all the rights of acting for the partnership, and there be a studied, intentional, prolonged, and continued inattention to the application of the partner to have his name so used and inserted in the firm name, Courts of Equity will grant a specific relief by an injunction against the use of any other firm name not including his. But the remedy in such cases is strictly confined to cases of studied delay and omission, and relief will not be given for a temporary, accidental, or trivial omission.[1] So where there is an agreement not to raise money in the name or on the credit of the firm for the private use of any one partner, Courts of Equity will, from the manifest danger of injury to the firm, interpose by injunction to stop such an abuse of the credit of the firm.[2] (a)   So where there is an agreement by the partners not to engage in any other business, Courts of Equity will act by injunction to enforce it, and if profits have been made by any partner in violation of such an agreement in any other business, the profits will be decreed to belong to the partnership.[3] (b)   So if it is agreed that upon the dissolution of a partnership a certain partnership-book shall belong to one of the partners and the other shall have a copy of it, Courts of Equity will decree a specific performance.[4] (c)

---

[1] Marshall v. Colman, 2 Jac. & Walk. 266, 269.   [2] Ibid.

[3] See Somerville v. Mackay, 16 Ves. 382, 387, 389.

[4] Lingen v. Simpson, 1 Sim. & Stu. 600.   For a more full consideration of

nership for trading in land, as it seems. Mason v. Kaine, 63 Penn. St. 335. Indeed Courts of Equity now decline in general to enforce executory contracts for forming partnerships. Ib.; Stocker v. Wedderborn, 3 Kay & J. 393; Scott v. Rayment, L. R. 7 Eq. 112; Somerby v. Buntin, 118 Mass. 279, 287; Sichel v. Mosenthal, 8 Jur. N. s. 275; 30 Beav. 371; Manning v. Wadsworth, 4 Md. 59. But see England v. Curling, 8 Beav. 129; Whitworth v. Harris, 40 Miss. 483, as to

cases where such remedy is necessary for the protection of rights.

(a) See Stockdale v. Allery, 37 Penn. St. 486.

(b) See Lock v. Lyman, 4 Ir. Ch. 188; Dean v. McDowell, 8 Ch. D. 345; Tyrrell v. Bank of London, 10 H. L. Cas. 26; s. c. 8 Jur. N. s. 849; Jones v. Dexter, 130 Mass. 380; Freeman v. Freeman, 136 Mass. 260; Herrick v. Ames, 8 Bosw. 115; Love v. Carpenter, 30 Ind. 284; ante, § 323, note.

(c) Featherstonhaugh v. Turner,

668. Courts of Equity will even go further, and in case of a partnership existing during the pleasure of the parties, with no time fixed for its renunciation, will interfere (as it should seem) to qualify or restrain that renunciation unless it is done under fair and reasonable circumstances; for if a sudden dissolution is about to be made in ill faith and will work irreparable injury, Courts of Equity will, upon their ordinary jurisdiction to prevent irreparable mischief, grant an injunction against such a dissolution.[1] And this is in strict conformity to the doctrine of the civil law on the same subject. By that law a partnership, without any express agreement for its continuance, may be dissolved by either party provided the renunciation be bona fide and reasonable. 'Societas coiri potest vel in perpetuum, id est, dum vivunt, vel ad tempus, vel ex tempore, vel sub conditione. Dissociamur renunciatione, morte, capitis minutione, et egestate.'[2] But then it is afterwards added: 'Diximus dissensu solvi societatem; hoc ita est si omnes dissientiunt. Quid ergo si unus renunciet? Cassius scripsit, eum qui renunciaverit societati, a se quidem liberare socios suos, se autem ab illis non liberare. Quod utique observandum est, si dolo malo renunciatio facta sit,' etc.[3] 'Si intempestive renuncietur societati, esse pro socio actionem.'[4] And again Labeo writes: 'Si renunciaverit societati unus ex sociis eo tempore quo interfuit socii non dirimi societatem, committere eum in pro socio actione.'[5] And again in a more general form it is said: 'In societate coeunda, nihil attinet de renunciatione cavere; quia ipso jure societatis intempestiva renunciatio in æstimationem venit.'[6] The same principles are recognized in

this subject, see Story on Partnership, §§ 188 to 190; Id. §§ 204 to 215; Id. §§ 224 to 232; post, § 671; Richardson v. Bank of England, 4 Mylne & Craig, R. 165, 172, 173.

[1] See Chavany v. Van Sommer, 3 Wooddes. Lect. 416, note; s. c. cited 1 Swanst. R. 511, 512, in a note. See Id. 123; 16 Ves. 49; 17 Ves. 198, 308.

[2] Dig. Lib. 17, tit. 2, l. 1, 4.

[3] Dig. Lib. 17, tit. 2, l. 65, § 3.

[4] Dig. Lib. 17, tit. 2, l. 14.

[5] Dig. Lib. 17, tit. 2, l. 65, § 5; Id. l. 17, § 2; 1 Swanst. R. 510, 511, 512, note; Vinn. in Inst. Comm. 680, §§ 1, 2, 3.

[6] Dig. Lib. 17, tit. 2, l. 17, § 2.

25 Beav. 382. Equity will also enjoin the taking away partnership-books. Taylor v. Davis, 3 Beav. 388, note;

Greatrex v. Greatrex, 1 DeG. & S. 692.

the countries which derive their jurisprudence from the civil law.[1]

669. In like manner Courts of Equity will interfere by way of injunction to prevent a partner, during the continuation of the partnership, from doing any acts injurious thereto; as by signing or indorsing notes to the injury of the partnership, or by driving away customers, or by violating the rights of the other parties, or his duty to them, even when a dissolution is not necessarily contemplated.[2] (a)

670. These are instances (and others might be mentioned)[3] of the remedial justice of Courts of Equity in carrying into specific effect the articles of partnership where the remedy at law would be wholly illusory or inadequate. But it is not hence to be inferred that Courts of Equity will in all cases interfere to enforce a specific performance of such articles. Where the remedy at law is entirely adequate, no relief will be granted in equity. And where the stipulation, though not against the policy of the law, yet is an effort to devest the ordinary jurisdiction of the common tribunals of justice, such as an agreement, in case of any disputes, to refer the same to arbitrators, Courts of Equity will not, any more than Courts of Law, interfere to enforce that agreement, but they will leave the parties to their own good pleasure in regard to such agreements. (b) The regular administration of justice might be greatly impeded or interfered with by such stipulations if they were specifically enforced. And at all events courts of justice are presumed to be better capable of administering and enforcing the real rights of the parties than any mere private arbitrators, as well from their superior knowledge as their superior means of sifting the controversy to the very bottom.[4] (c)

[1] See 2 Bell, Comm. B. 7, ch. 3, n. 1227; Ersk. Inst. B. 3, tit. 3, § 26; 1 Stair's Inst. B. 1, tit. 16, § 4; Pothier, Traité de Société, n. 65, 149, 150, 151.

[2] See Charlton v. Poulter, 19 Ves. 148, n.; Goodman v. Whitcomb, 1 Jac. & Walk. 589; Collyer on Partn. B. 2, ch. 3, § 5.

[3] See Collyer on Partn. B. 2, ch. 3, § 5.

[4] Street v. Rigby, 6 Ves. 815, 818; Thompson v. Charnock, 8 T. R. 139; Waters v. Taylor, 15 Ves. 10; Wellington v. Mackintosh, 2 Atk. 569.

(a) Marshall v. Watson, 25 Beav. 501; England v. Curling, 8 Beav. 129; Hall v. Hall, 12 Beav. 414; Marble Co. v. Ripley, 10 Wall. 339.

(b) But see editor's note at end of § 1457.

(c) See Agar v. Macklew, 2 Sim. & S. 418; Darby v. Whitaker, 4 Drew. 134; Jackson v. Jackson, 1 Sm. & G. 184; Dinham v. Bradford, L. R. 5 Ch. 519; post, § 1457, and notes.

671. The remedial justice of Courts of Equity is not confined to cases of the nature above stated. They may not only provide for a more effectual settlement of all the accounts of the partnership after a dissolution, but they may take steps for this purpose which Courts of Law are inadequate to afford. They may perhaps interpose and decree an account where a dissolution has not taken place and is not asked for; although ordinarily they are not inclined to decree an account unless under special circumstances, if there is not an actual or contemplated dissolution so that all the affairs of the partnership may be wound up.[1]

[1] Forman v. Homfray, 2 Ves. & B. 329; Harrison v. Armitage, 4 Madd. R. 143; Russell v. Loscombe, 4 Simons, R. 8; Knowles v. Haughton, 11 Ves. 168; s. c. Collyer on Part. B. 2, ch. 3, § 3, p. 163, note (a); Waters v. Taylor, 15 Ves. 15. Lord Eldon, in Forman v. Homfray (2 Ves. & Beam. 329), thought that no account ought to be decreed unless there is also a prayer for a dissolution. But the then vice-chancellor (Sir John Leach), in Harrison v. Armitage (4 Madd. R. 143), thought otherwise. In the later case of Russell v. Loscombe (4 Simons, R. 8), the present vice-chancellor (Sir Lancelot Shadwell) agreed with Lord Eldon, and held the bill demurrable for not praying a dissolution. In Walworth v. Holt, 4 Mylne & Craig, 619, 635 to 639, Lord Cottenham reviewed the cases at large and said: 'When it is said that the court cannot give relief of this limited kind, it is, I presume, meant that the bill ought to have prayed a dissolution and a final winding up of the affairs of the company. How far this court will interfere between partners, except in cases of dissolution, has been the subject of much difference of opinion, upon which it is not my purpose to say anything beyond what is necessary for the decision of this case; but there are strong authorities for holding that to a bill praying a dissolution all the partners must be parties, and this bill alleges that they are so numerous as to make that impossible. The result therefore of these two rules would be, — the one binding the court to withhold its jurisdiction except upon bills praying a dissolution, and the other requiring that all the partners should be parties to a bill praying it, — that the door of this court would be shut in all cases in which the partners or shareholders are too numerous to be made parties, which in the present state of the transactions of mankind would be an absolute denial of justice to a large portion of the subjects of the realm in some of the most important of their affairs. This result is quite sufficient to show that such cannot be the law; for as I have said upon other occasions, I think it the duty of this court to adapt its practice and course of proceeding to the existing state of society, and not by too strict an adherence to forms and rules, established under different circumstances, to decline to administer justice and to enforce rights for which there is no other remedy. This has always been the principle of this court, though not at all times sufficiently attended to. It is the ground upon which the court has in many cases dispensed with the presence of parties who would, according to the general practice, have been necessary parties. In Cockburn v. Thomson Lord Eldon says: " A general rule established for the convenient administration of justice must not be adhered to in cases in which, consist-

672. But where such dissolution has taken place an account will not only be decreed, but, if necessary, a manager or receiver

ently with practical convenience, it is incapable of application;" and again, "The difficulty must be overcome upon this principle, that it is better to go as far as possible towards justice than to deny it altogether." If therefore it were necessary to go much further than it is, in opposition to some highly sanctioned opinions, in order to open the door of justice in this court to those who cannot obtain it elsewhere, I should not shrink from the responsibility of doing so; but in this particular case, notwithstanding the opinions to which I have referred, it will be found that there is much more of authority in support of the equity claimed by this bill than there is against it. It is true that the bill does not pray for a dissolution, and that it states the company to be still subsisting; but it does not pray for an account of partnership dealing and transactions for the purpose of obtaining the share of profits due to the plaintiffs, which seems to be the case contemplated in the opinions to which I have referred; but its object is to have the common assets realized and applied to their legitimate purpose, in order that the plaintiffs may be relieved from the responsibility to which they are exposed, and which is contrary to the provisions of their common contract and to every principle of justice. But whether the interest of the plaintiffs, in right of which they sue, arises from such responsibility or from any other cause cannot be material; the question being, Whether some partners, having an interest in the application of the partnership property, are entitled on behalf of themselves and the other partners, except the defendants, to sue such remaining partners in this court for that purpose, pending the subsistence of the partnership; and if it shall appear that such a suit may be maintained by some partners on behalf of themselves and others similarly circumstanced, against other persons, whether trustees and agents for the company, or strangers being possessed of property of the company, it may be asked, Why the same right of suit should not exist when the party in possession of such property happens also to be a partner or shareholder. In Chancey v. May, the defendants were partners. In the Widows' Case before Lord Thurlow, cited by Lord Eldon, the bill was on behalf of the plaintiffs and all others in the same interest, and sought to provide funds for a subsisting establishment. In Knowles v. Haughton, 11th July, 1805, reported in Vesey, but more fully in Collyer on the Law of Partnership, the bill prayed an account of partnership transactions, and that the partnership might be established; and the decree directed an account of the brokerage business, and to ascertain what, if anything, was due to the plaintiff in respect thereof; and the master was to inquire whether the partnership between the plaintiff and the defendant had at any time, and when, been dissolved; showing that the court did not consider the dissolution of the partnership as a preliminary necessary before directing the account. In Cockburn v. Thomson the bill prayed a dissolution; but it was filed by certain proprietors on behalf of themselves and others, and Lord Eldon overruled the objection that the others were not parties. In Hichens v. Congreve the bill was on behalf of the plaintiff and the other shareholders, against certain shareholders who were also directors, not praying a dissolution, but seeking only the repayment to the company of certain funds alleged to have been improperly abstracted from the partnership property by the defendants; and Sir Anthony Hart overruled a demurrer, and his decision was affirmed by Lord Lyndhurst. In Walburn v. Ingilby

will be appointed to close the partnership business and make sale
of the partnership property, so that a final distribution may be
made of the partnership effects.[1] (b)   This a Court of Law is

the bill did not pray a dissolution of partnership, and Lord Brougham, in
allowing the demurrer upon other grounds, stated that it could not be supported upon the ground of want of parties, because a dissolution was not
prayed.   In Taylor v. Salmon the suit was by some shareholders on behalf of
themselves and others, against Salmon, also a shareholder, to recover property
claimed by the company, which he had appropriated to himself; and the vice-
chancellor decreed for the plaintiff, which was affirmed on appeal.   The bill
did not pray a dissolution, and the company was a subsisting and continuing
partnership.   That case and Hichens v. Congreve differ from the present in
this only, that in those cases the partnerships were flourishing and likely to
continue; whereas in the present, though not dissolved, it is unable to carry
on the purposes for which it was formed, an inability to be attributed in part
to the withholding that property which this bill seeks to recover.   So far this
case approximates to those in which the partnership has been dissolved; as to
which it is admitted that this court exercises its jurisdiction.   This case also
differs from the two last-mentioned cases in this, that the difficulty in which
the plaintiffs are placed, and the consequent necessity for the assistance of this
court, is greater in this case, — no reason, certainly, for withholding that
assistance.   How far the principle upon which these cases have proceeded is
consistent with the doctrine in Russell v. Loscombe, "That in occasional
breaches of contract between partners, when they are not of so grievous a
nature as to make it impossible that the partnership should continue, the court
stands neuter," will be to be considered if the case should arise.   It is not
necessary to express any opinion as to that in the present case; but it may be
suggested that the supposed rule that the court will not direct an account of
partnership dealings and transactions, except as consequent upon a dissolution,
though true in some cases and to a certain extent, has been supposed to be more
generally applicable than it is upon authority, or ought to be upon principle.
It is however certain that this supposed rule is directly opposed to the decision
of Sir J. Leach in Harrison v. Armitage and Richards v. Davies.   Having
referred to so many cases in which suits similar to the present have been
maintained by some partners on behalf of themselves and others, it is scarcely
necessary to say anything as to the objection for want of parties; and as to
the assignees of those shareholders who have become bankrupts, those
assignees are now shareholders in their places, for the purpose of any interest
they have in the property of the company; and as such are included in the
number of those on whose behalf the suit is instituted.   A similar objection
was raised and overruled in Taylor v. Salmon as to the shares of Salmon.
Upon the authority of the cases to which I have referred, and of the principle
to which I have alluded, if it be necessary to resort to it, I am of opinion that
the demurrer cannot be supported; and that the usual order, overruling a demurrer, must be substituted for that pronounced by the vice-chancellor.'   The
point must therefore be held to be still open for further consideration.(a)

[1] See Crawshay v. Maule, 1 Swanst. R. 506, 523; Peacock v. Peacock, 16

(a) See Hall v. Hall, 3 Macn. & G.   Smith v. Jeges, 4 Beav. 503; Fair-
79; s. c. 12 Beav. 419, and 20 Beav.   thorne v. Weston, 3 Hare, 387.
139; Thomas v. Davies, 11 Beav. 29;   (b) See Richards v. Baurman, 65

incompetent to do.   The accounts are usually directed to be taken
(as has been already suggested) before a master, who examines
the parties if necessary, and requires the production of all the
books, papers, and vouchers of the partnership ; and he is armed,
from time to time, by the court, with all the powers necessary to
effectuate the objects of the reference to him.   If it is deemed
expedient and proper, the court will restrain the partners from
collecting the debts or disposing of the property of the concern,
and will direct the moneys of the firm received by any of them
to be paid into court.   In this way it adapts its remedial authority to the exigencies of each particular case.[2] (a)

673. But perhaps one of the strongest cases to illustrate the

Ves. 57, 58; Featherstonhaugh v. Fenwick, 17 Ves. 298, 308; Crawshay v.
Collins, 15 Ves. 218; Wilson v. Greenwood, 1 Swanst. R. 471; Oliver v.
Hamilton, 2 Anst. R. 453.

    [2] See Collyer on Partn. B. 2, ch. 3, § 3, and the cases there cited; Foster
v. Donald, 1 Jac. & Walk. 252, 253.

N. Car. 162; Phillips v. Trezevant,
67 N. Car. 370.

    (a) Equity in general will not ap-
point a receiver or manager at the
instance of one of the partners, in a
suit which does not seek to dissolve
the partnership.   Roberts v. Eber-
hardt, Kay, 148.   See Sheppard v.
Oxenford, Kay & J. 491, infra; Sloan
v. Moore, 37 Penn. St. 217; Garretson
v. Weaver, 3 Edw. 385; cases indi-
cating exceptions to the general rule.
Nor in a suit which does seek dissolution will a receiver be appointed
upon an interlocutory application, and
merely upon evidence that the partners do not co-operate in the management of the business, unless one has
wrongfully excluded the other from
participation therein.   Roberts v. Eber-
hardt, supra; Werner v. Leisen, 31
Wis. 169.   See Birdsall v. Colie, 2
Stockt. 63; Hall v. Hall, 3 Macn. &
G. 79; Henn v. Walsh, 2 Edw. 129;
Walker v. House, 4 Md. Ch. 39;
Madgwick v. Wimble, 6 Beav. 495.

    Among the exceptions to the rule
first stated may be noticed the case of
Sheppard v. Oxenford, supra.   There

the partnership property consisted in
mines, plant, and slaves in Brazil,
put into shares and sold in England
in the form of scrip transferable by
delivery, and the defendant and another, at a meeting of the shareholders,
had been appointed sole directors and
trustees of the property, and the associate had died and disputes had arisen.
It was held that an owner of shares
purchased in the market might maintain a bill against the defendant as
sole surviving trustee for an account
of the receipts and payments of the
debts of the association, and a division
of the profits, and for a receiver,
though the bill did not pray for a
dissolution.   The defendant had however left England after the filing of
the bill and pending the motion for a
receiver; and it was considered that
the plaintiff had an equity to have the
property secured by the appointment
of a receiver.   Sheppard v. Oxenford,
1 Kay & J. 491.   Further as to partnerships with transferable shares see
Phillips v. Blatchford, 137 Mass. 510,
a case of contribution.

beneficial operation of the jurisdiction of Courts of Equity in regard to partnership is their power to dissolve the partnership during the term for which it is stipulated. This is a peculiar remedy which Courts of Common Law are incapable of administering by the nature of their organization. Such a dissolution may be granted in the first place on account of the impracticability of carrying on the undertaking either at all or according to the stipulations of the articles.[1] (a)   In the next place it may be granted on account of the insanity (b) or permanent incapacity of one of the partners.[2]   In the next place it may be granted on account of the gross misconduct of one or more of the part-

---

[1] Baring v. Dix, 1 Cox, R. 213; Waters v. Taylor, 2 Ves. & B. 299; Barr v. Speirs, 2 Bell, Comm. 642, § 1227, note (6).

[2] Waters v. Taylor, 2 Ves. & B. 299; Sayer v. Bennet, 1 Cox, R. 107; s. c. 1 Montague on Partn. Appx. 18; Collyer on Partn. B. 2, ch. 3, § 3; Pearse v. Chamberlain, 2 Ves. 34, 35; Wrexham v. Hudleston, 1 Swanst. R. 514, note.

(a) Harrison v. Tennant, 21 Beav. 482; Slemmer's Appeal, 58 Penn. St. 168.   But dissolution will not ordinarily be decreed at a time when it would work special hardship, as at the beginning of a large operation. Richards v. Baurman, 65 N. Car. 162.

(b) In Anonymous, 2 Kay & J. 441, a motion was made for a preliminary injunction to restrain a partner who six months before, being temporarily insane, had attempted to commit suicide, from interfering in the partnership affairs. It was refused on the ground that the evidence did not show that at the time of the motion he was incompetent to conduct the business of the partnership according to the articles. And it was declared that the fact that the conduct and state of mind of the partner in question were such as at once to destroy the confidence of the other partners, and to induce customers to withdraw their custom from the firm, and that the malady was such as might have led the partner to attempt the life of one of his associates, did not show sufficient ground for granting the motion.   And a motion in a cross-suit, to restrain the de-

fendants therein from preventing the partner in question from transacting the business of the firm as a partner, was granted.

It was considered in the same case that the following propositions had been established by the authorities : 1. That actual insanity of a partner is not of itself a dissolution of the partnership; there must be a decree of dissolution.   2. That such a decree, notwithstanding proof of actual insanity before the filing of the bill, will not be made in a disputed case without further inquiry upon the point whether, at the time when the relief is sought, the party is in such a state of mind as to be able to conduct the business with the other members of the firm according to the articles.   3. That insanity existing when the relief is sought, with probability of its continuance, is ground for dissolution.   See Kirby v. Carr, 3 Younge & C. 184; Jones v. Noy, 2 Mylne & K. 125; Saddler v. Lee, 6 Beav. 324; Besch v. Frolich, 1 Phill. 172; Leaf v. Coles, 1 DeG. M. & G. 171 ; Bagshaw v. Parker, 10 Beav. 532.

ners.[1] (a)   But trifling faults and misbehavior which do not go
to the substance of the contract do not constitute a sufficient
ground to justify a decree for a dissolution.[2] (b)

674. There are other considerations which make a resort to a
Court of Equity instead of a Court of Law not only a more convenient but even an indispensable instrument for the purposes of
justice. Thus real estate may be bought and held for purposes
of the partnership and really be a part of the stock in trade.
The conveyance in such a case may be in the name of one for the
benefit of all the partners, or in the name of all as tenants in
common or as joint tenants. In case of the death of a partner
by which a dissolution takes place, the real estate may thus become severed at law from the partnership funds and vest in the

---

[1] See Marshall v. Coleman, 2 Jac. & Walk. [266] 300; Goodman v. Whitcomb, 1 Jac. & Walk. [569] 594; Chapman v. Beach, Id. [573] 594; Norway
v. Rowe, 19 Ves. 148; Waters v. Taylor, 2 Ves. & B. 304; Master v. Kirton,
3 Ves. 74; De Berenger v. Hammel, 7 Jarman, Convey. 26, cited Collyer on
Partn. B. 2, ch. 3, § 3, p. 161; Russell v. Loscombe, 4 Simons, R. 8.

[2] Goodman v. Whitcomb, 1 Jac. & Walk. [569] 592; Collyer on Partn. B.
2, ch. 3, § 3.

(a) Bluck v. Capstick, 12 Ch. D. 863; Essell v. Hayward, 6 Jur. N. S. 690 ; Hartman v. Woehr, 3 C. E. Green, 383; Seighortner v. Weissenborn, 5 C. E. Green, 172; Werner v. Leisen, 31 Wis. 169. And this though the party asking for dissolution may have committed the first wrong. Blake v. Dorgan, 1 Green (Iowa). 537. If however the plaintiff knew of the bad character of the defendant before he entered into partnership with him, he may be barred. Ambler v. Whipple, 20 Wall. 546.

Error of judgment in a partner is no ground for dissolution. Cash v. Earnshaw, 66 Ill. 402.

Dissolution may be granted for the fraud of the defendant in inducing the plaintiff to join him in partnership, with an injunction of course against the further use of the plaintiff's name. Smith v. Everett, 126 Mass. 304 ; Richards v. Todd, 127 Mass. 167 ; Rawlins v. Wickham, 3 DeG. & J. 304; Mycock v. Beatson, 13 Ch. D. 384; Rose v. Watson, 10 H. L. Cas. 672 ; Aberamen Iron Works v. Wickens, L. R. 4 Ch. 101. And equity will order the defendant to repay all sums of money the plaintiff has paid into the firm as his part of the capital stock, pay him a reasonable compensation for the time spent as partner, and indemnify him from all liability arising out of such partnership. Richards v. Todd, supra. The plaintiff also will be entitled to a lien on the surplus of the partnership assets after satisfying the partnership debts, in respect of the sum paid on entering the firm; and in respect of any surplus paid in satisfying partnership debts, he will be entitled to stand in the place of the partnership creditors to whom he has made payment. Mycock v. Beatson, supra.

As to dissolution on the ground of disputes between the partners, see Lyon v. Tweddell, 17 Ch. D. 529.

(b) Cash v. Earnshaw, 66 Ill. 402; Anderson v. Anderson, 25 Beav. 190.

surviving partner exclusively, or in the heirs of a deceased partner in common with the survivor, according to the particular
circumstances of the case. In taking an account of the partnership effects at law it is impossible for the court for the benefit of
creditors to bring such real estate into the account, or to direct
a sale of it, or to hold it a part of the partnership funds. It
must be treated in Courts of Law just as its character is according to the common law. But in a Court of Equity in such a
case the real estate is treated to all intents and purposes as a
part of the partnership funds, whatever may be the form of the
conveyance. (a) For a Court of Equity considers the real estate
to all intents and purposes as personal estate, and subjects it to
all the equitable rights and liens of the partners which would
apply to it if it were personal estate. And this doctrine not
only prevails as between the partners themselves and their creditors, but (as it should seem) as between the representatives of
the partners also. So that real estate held in fee for the partnership and as a part of its funds will upon the death of the partner
belong in equity not to the heirs at law but to the personal representatives and distributees of the deceased ; unless perhaps there
be a clear and determinate expression of the deceased partner
that it shall go to his heir at law beneficially.[1] (b)

---

[1] See Collyer on Partn. B. 2, ch. 1, § 1, pp. 68 to 76; Lake v. Craddock, 3
P. Will. 158; Elliot v. Brown, 9 Ves. 597; Thornton v. Dixon, 3 Bro. Ch. R.
199 (Belt's edition); Bell v. Phyn, 7 Ves. 453; Ripley v. Waterworth, 7 Ves.
425; Selkrig v. Davies, 2 Dow, R. 242; Townsend v. Devaynes, 1 Montague

(a) The following cases contain
illustrations of the text : Shanks v.
Klein, 104 U. S. 18; Attorney-Gen. v.
Hubbuck, 13 Q. B. D. 275; Murtagh v.
Costello, 7 L. R. Ir. 428; Goodburn v.
Stevens, 5 Gill, 1; Rice v. Barnard,
20 Vt. 479 ; Buchan v. Sumner, 2
Barb. Ch. 165; Washburn v. Bank of
Bellows Falls, 19 Vt. 278, 292; Day
v. Perkins, 2 Sandf. Ch. 359; Cox v.
McBurney, 2 Sandf. (Law) 561; Aver-
ill v. Loucks, 6 Barb. 19, 470; Uhler
v. Semple, 5 C. E. Green, 288; Scruggs
v. Blair, 44 Miss. 406 ; Stroud v.
Stroud, Phill. (N. Car.) 525; Mauck
v. Mauck, 54 Ill. 281; Cornwall v.
Cornwall, 6 Bush, 369; Bank of Louis-
ville v. Hall, 8 Bush, 672; Lime Rock
Bank v. Phetteplace, 8 R. I. 56 ; National Bank v. Sprague, 5 C. E. Green,
13; Ware v. Owens, 42 Ala. 212; Pe-
cot v. Armelin, 21 La. An. 667; His-
cock v. Phelps, 49 N. Y. 47; Deveney
v. Mahoney, 23 N. J. Eq. 247; Story,
Partnership, § 93, Gray's ed. Equity
will compel the application of partnership land to the purposes for which
it was bought. Faulds v. Yates, 57
Ill. 416.

(b) Murtagh v. Costello, 7 L. R. Ir.
428; Steward v. Blakeway, L. R. 4
Ch. 603; s. c. 6 Eq. 479; Waterer v.
Waterer, L. R. 15 Eq. 402; Shanks v.
Klein, 104 U. S. 18; Miller v. Proctor,

675. The lien also of partners upon the whole funds of the partnership for the balance finally due to them respectively seems incapable of being enforced in any other manner than by a Court of Equity through the instrumentality of a sale. Besides, the creditors of the partnership have a preference to have their debts paid out of the partnership funds before the private creditors of either of the partners. (*a*)   But this preference is at law generally disregarded ; in equity it is worked out through the equity of the partners over the whole funds.¹ (*b*)   On the other hand the separate creditors of each partner are entitled to be first paid out of the separate effects of their debtor before the partnership creditors can claim anything, (*c*) which also can be accomplished only by the aid of a Court of Equity ; for at law a joint creditor may proceed directly against the separate estate.²(*d*)

on Partn. Appx. 96 [101]; Gow on Partn. ch. 2, § 1; Randall *v.* Randall, 7 Sim. R. 271; Morris *v.* Kearsley, 2 Younge & Coll. 139; Bligh *v.* Brent, 2 Younge & Coll. 268, 288; Houghton *v.* Houghton, 11 Simons, R. 491; Hoxie *v.* Carr, 1 Sumner, R. 173.

¹ Twiss *v.* Massey, 1 Atk. 67; Ex parte Cook, P. Will. 500; Ex parte Elter, 3 Ves. 240; Ex parte Clay, 6 Ves. 833; Collyer on Partnership, B. 4, ch. 2, §§ 1, 2, 3; Campbell *v.* Mullett, 2 Swanst. 574, 575; Ex parte Ruffin, 6 Ves. 125, 126; Gray *v.* Chiswell, 9 Ves. 118; Commercial Bank *v.* Wilkins, 9 Greenl. 28.

² Ibid.; Dutton *v.* Morrison, 17 Ves. 205 to 210; Tucker *v.* Oxley, 5 Cranch, 34.

20 Ohio St. 442; Delmonico *v.* Guillaume, 2 Sandf. 366; Darby *v.* Darby, 3 Drew. 497; Cornwall *v.* Cornwall, 6 Bush, 369; Meily *v.* Wood, 71 Penn. St. 488. But it is held in Massachusetts that where, after all debts and balances between the parties are satisfied, there remains real estate of the partnership, in which the legal title of each partner corresponds to his interest or share in the partnership, equity will not interfere to convert such realty into personalty. Wilcox *v.* Wilcox, 13 Allen, 252; Shearer *v.* Shearer, 98 Mass. 107.

(*a*) See Miner *v.* Pierce, 38 Vt. 610, 614; Washburn *v.* Bank of Bellows Falls, 19 Vt. 278; Bardwell *v.* Perry, Ib. 292; ante, § 645, note.

(*b*) See Muir *v.* Leitch, 7 Barb. 341 ; Freeman *v.* Stewart, 41 Miss. 138; O'Bannon *v.* Miller, 4 Bush, 25 ;

Harman *v.* Clark, 13 Gray, 114; Allen *v.* Center Valley Co., 21 Conn. 130; Rainey *v.* Nance, 54 Ill. 29.

(*c*) Murrill *v.* Neill, 8 How. 414; Jarvis *v.* Brooks, 23 N. H. 136.   But see Cleghorn *v.* Insurance Bank, 9 Ga. 319; Grosvenor *v.* Austin, 6 Ohio, 103. And see Black's Appeal, 44 Penn. St. 503; McCormick's Appeal, 55 Penn. St. 252; Millnight *v.* Smith, 2 C. E. Green, 259; Morgan *v.* Skidmore, 55 Barb. 263; Morris *v.* Morris, 4 Gratt. 293.

(*d*) Cleghorn *v.* Insurance Bank, supra.   It has been held however, even at law, that if a joint creditor first levy execution upon the separate real estate of one partner, a private creditor may still levy upon the same estate, and bring a writ of entry against the partnership creditor. Jarvis *v.* Brooks, 23 N. H. 136.

This is another illustration of the doctrine of marshalling assets, and proceeds upon analogous principles, and it is commonly applied in cases of insolvency or bankruptcy. There are certain exceptions to the rule which confirm rather than abate its force, as they stand upon peculiar reasons.

676. In like manner in cases of partnership debts if one of the partners dies and the survivor becomes insolvent or bankrupt, the joint creditors have a right to be paid out of the estate of the deceased partner through the medium of the equities subsisting between the partners.[1] (a)   Indeed a broader principle is now established; and it is held that insolvency or bankruptcy is not necessary in order to justify the creditors of the partnership in resorting to the assets of the deceased partner, and that such creditors may in the first instance proceed against the executor or administrator of the deceased partner, leaving him to his remedy over against the surviving partners; though certainly the surviving partners in a suit in equity in such a case would be proper parties if not necessary parties to the bill.[2] (b)   The

---

[1] Collyer on Partn. B. 3, ch. 3, § 4; Cowell v. Sykes, 2 Russ. R. 191; Campbell v. Mullett, 2 Swanst. 574, 575; Ex parte Ruffin, 6 Ves. 125, 126; Ex parte Kendall, 17 Ves. 514, 526, 527; Lane v. Williams, 2 Vern. R. 277, 292; Vulliamy v. Noble, 3 Meriv. 614, 618; Gray v. Chiswell, 9 Ves. 118; Brice's Case, 1 Meriv. R. 620; Hamersley v. Lambert, 2 John. Ch. R. 509, 510; Jenkins v. De Groot, 1 Cain. Cas. Err. 122. If the right of the joint creditors is worked out altogether through the equity of the partners, it seems somewhat difficult to perceive how the separate estate of a deceased partner who is a creditor of the firm far beyond all the partnership funds, should, the joint estate being insolvent, be compellable to pay any of the joint debts beyond these funds. Yet Lord Eldon acted upon the ground of the liability of such separate estate in Gray v. Chiswell, 9 Ves. 118. If on the other hand the true doctrine be that avowed by Sir William Grant in the case of Devaynes v. Noble (1 Meriv. R. 529), afterwards affirmed by Lord Brougham (2 Russ. & Mylne, 495), that a partnership contract is several as well as joint, then there seems no ground to make any difference whatsoever in any case between joint and several creditors as to payment out of joint or separate assets. See Collyer on Partn. B. 3, ch. 3, § 4, pp. 337 to 347; Hamersley v. Lambert, 2 John. Ch. R. 509, 510. This is now the established doctrine. Wilkinson v. Henderson, 1 Mylne & Keen, 582; Thorpe v. Jackson, 2 Younge & Coll. 553, 561, 562; Story on Partn. § 312; ante, §§ 162 to 164.

[2] Wilkinson v. Henderson, 1 Mylne & Keen, 582; Devaynes v. Noble, 2

(a) Freeman v. Stewart, 41 Miss. 138. A bill in equity may be maintained by the personal representative of a deceased partner to compel an account and to discover partnership property. Denver v. Roane, 99 U. S. 355.

(b) Freeman v. Stewart, 41 Miss. 138.

doubts formerly entertained upon this subject seem to have
arisen from the general principle that the joint estate is the first
fund for the payment of the joint debts; and as the joint estate
vests in the surviving partner, the joint creditors upon equitable
considerations ought to resort to the surviving partner before
they seek satisfaction from the assets of the deceased partner.[1]
The ground of the present doctrine is that every partnership
debt is joint and several; and in all such cases resort may primarily be had for the debt to the surviving partners or to the
assets of the deceased partner.[2] Nor is this doctrine confined to
cases of partnership or to cases of a mercantile character. It
equally applies to all cases where there is a joint loan to several
persons not partners, whether it be in the course of mercantile
transactions or not; for the debt will be treated in equity as
joint and several, and in case any of the debtors die the creditor
may have relief out of his assets without claiming any relief
against the surviving joint debtors, or showing that they are
unable to pay the debt by reason of their insolvency.[3] (a)

Russ. & Mylne, 495; Thorpe v. Jackson, 2 Younge & Coll. 553; Sleech's Case,
1 Meriv. R. 539; Braithwaite v. Britain, 1 Keen, R. 219.

[1] Wilkinson v. Henderson, 1 Mylne & Keen, 582.

[2] Thorpe v. Jackson, 2 Younge & Coll. 553, 561, 562; Sleech's Case, 1 Meriv.
539.

[3] Ibid.

(a) It sometimes happens, either on
account of the form of the partnership
articles, or the manner in which the
surviving partners treat the effects of
the partnership after the decease of
one of the partners, that they are
liable to account for a share of the
profits to the personal representatives
of the deceased partner or the legal
beneficiary. In Wedderburn v. Wedderburn, 22 Beav. 84; s. c. 2 Keen,
722; 4 Mylne & C. 41, Sir John Romilly, M. R., divides the cases into the
following classes: 1. Where the surviving partners continue the trade
with the capital, composed in whole
or in part of the estate of the deceased
partner. (See Heath v. Waters, 40
Mich. 457; Ex parte Butcher, 13 Ch.
D. 465; Knox v. Gye, L. R. 5 H. L.
656; Noyes v. Crawley, 10 Ch. D. 31,
39.) The liability to account in such
a case proceeds wholly on the ground
that the profits are the product of the
capital in part, and therefore belong
to that extent to the owner of the capital. (As to the Stat. of Limitations
in such a case, see Noyes v. Crawley,
supra.) 2. Where the legal representatives of the deceased partner employ
the assets in carrying on trade for
themselves. The liability to account
in such a case proceeds upon the misconduct of the personal representatives; and the cestuis que trust are
entitled at their choice to legal interest on the amount, or to a share in the
profits. 3. Where the surviving partners are also the personal representatives of the deceased partner. The

677. In regard to partnership property another illustration of a kindred character involving the necessity of an account may be put to establish the utility and importance of equity jurisdiction. It is well known that at law an execution for the separate debt of one of the partners may be levied upon the joint property of the partnership. (*a*) In such a case however the judgment creditor can levy, not the moiety or undivided share of the judgment debtor in the property as if there were no debts of the partnership or lien on the same for the balance due to the other partner, but he can levy the interest only of the judgment debtor, if any, in the property after the payment of all debts and other charges thereon.[1] In short he can take only the same interest in the property which the judgment debtor himself would have upon the final settlement of all the accounts of the partnership. When therefore the sheriff seizes such property upon an execution, he seizes only such undivided and unascertained interest; and if he sells under the execution, the sale conveys nothing more to the vendee, who thereby becomes a tenant in common, substituted to the rights and interests of the judgment debtor in the property seized.[2] (*b*) In truth the sale does not transfer any part of the joint property to the vendee so as to entitle him to take it from the other partners, for that would be to place him in a better situation than the partner himself. But it gives him, properly speaking, a right in equity to call for an account, and thus to entitle himself to the interest of the partner in the property which shall upon such settlement be ascertained to

---

[1] West *v.* Skip, 1 Ves. 239; 2 Swanst. 526; Barker *v.* Goodair, 11 Ves. 85; Dutton *v.* Morrison, 17 Ves. 205, 206, 207; Gow on Partn. ch. 4, § 1, pp. 247, 248.

[2] West *v.* Skip, 1 Ves. 239; Chapman *v.* Koops, 3 Bos. & Pull. 289; Skip *v.* Harwood, 2 Swanst. R. 586; s. c. cited Cowp. R. 451; Dutton *v.* Morrison, 17 Ves. 205, 206; Heydon *v.* Heydon, 1 Salk. 392; Taylor *v.* Fields, 4 Ves. 396; Fox *v.* Hanbury, Cowp. R. 445; Nicoll *v.* Mumford, 4 John. Ch. R. 522; In re Wait, 1 Jac. & Walk. 587, 588, 589; Moody *v.* Payne, 2 John. Ch. R. 548.

liability to account in such a case may involve an inquiry into the misconduct of the executors, but is affected more or less by the articles of partnership. 'Without some act on his part the executor would not become a partner.' Holmes, J., in Phillips *v.* Blatchford, 137 Mass. 510, 514.

(*a*) See Cleghorn *v.* Insurance Bank, 9 Ga. 319; Jarvis *v.* Brooks, 23 N. H. 136, 141; Dow *v.* Sayward, 14 N. H. 9; Place *v.* Sweetzer, 16 Ohio, 142; Hardy *v.* Donellan, 33 Ind. 501; Story, Partnership, § 261, note, Gray's ed.

(*b*) Habershon *v.* Blurton, 1 DeG. & S. 121.

exist.[1] It is obvious, from what has been already stated, how utterly inadequate the means of a Court of Law are to take such an account. And indeed under a levy of this sort it is not easy to perceive what authority a Court of Law has to interfere at all to take an account of the partnership transactions, or by what process it can enforce it.[2] (a) In such a case therefore the proper remedy for the other partners, if nothing is due to the judgment debtor out of the partnership funds, is to file a bill in equity against the vendee of the sheriff to have the proper accounts taken.[3]

678. In cases of the seizure of the joint property for the separate debt of one of the partners a question has arisen how far a Court of Equity would interfere upon a bill for an account of the partnership to restrain the sheriff from a sale, or the vendee of the sheriff from an alienation of the property seized, until the account was taken and the share of the partner ascertained. Mr. Chancellor Kent has decided that an injunction for such a purpose ought not to issue to restrain a sale by the sheriff upon the

---

[1] Gow on Partn. ch. 4, § 1, pp. 249 to 254; In re Smith, 16 John. R. 106; Nicoll v. Mumford, 4 John. Ch. R. 522, 525; s. c. 20 John. R. 611; Shaver v. White, 6 Munf. R. 110; Murray v. Murray, 5 John. Ch. R. 70; Marquand v. New York Manuf. Company, 17 John. R. 525.

[2] See Chapman v. Koops, 3 Bos. & Pull. 389; Eddie v. Davidson, 2 Doug. R. 650; Waters v. Taylor, 2 Ves. & B. 300, 301; Dutton v. Morrison, 17 Ves. 205, 206; In re Wait, 1 Jac. & Walk. 585. The remarks of Lord Eldon on this point, in Waters v. Taylor (2 Ves. & B. 301), are very striking and important. ' If the Courts of Law,' said he, ' have followed Courts of Equity in giving execution against partnership effects, I desire to have it understood that they do not appear to me to adhere to the principle when they suppose that the interest can be sold before it has been ascertained what is the subject of sale and purchase. According to the old law, I mean before Lord Mansfield's time, the sheriff under an execution against partnership effects took the undivided share of the debtor without reference to the partnership account. But a Court of Equity would have set that right by taking the account and ascertaining what the sheriff ought to have sold. The Courts of Law however have now repeatedly laid down that they will sell the actual interest of the partner, professing to execute the equities between the parties, but forgetting that a Court of Equity ascertained previously what was to be sold. How could a Court of Law ascertain what was the interest to be sold and what the equities depending upon an account of all the concerns of the partners for years? '

[3] Chapman v. Koops, 3 Bos. & Pull. 290; Waters v. Taylor, 2 Ves. & B. 300, 301; Taylor v. Fields, 4 Ves. 396; Dutton v. Morrison, 17 Ves. 205, 206, 207; In re Wait, 1 Jac. & Walk. 588, 589; Gow on Partn. ch. 4, § 1, pp. 253, 254.

(a) Habershon v. Blurton, 1 DeG. & S. 121.

ground that no harm is done to the other partners; and the sacrifice, if any, is the loss of the judgment debtor only.[1] (a)   But
that does not seem a sufficient ground upon which such an injunction is to be denied.   If the debtor partner has or will have
upon a final adjustment of the accounts no interest in the partnership funds, and if the other partners have a lien upon the
funds not only for the debts of the partnership but for the balance ultimately due to them, it may most materially affect their
rights whether a sale takes place or not.   For it may be extremely difficult to follow the property into the hands of the
various vendees; and their lien may perhaps be displaced, or
other equities arise by intermediate bona fide sales of the property by the vendees to other purchasers without notice, and the
partners may have to sustain all the chances of any supervening
insolvencies of the immediate vendees.[2]   To prevent multiplicity
of suits and irreparable mischiefs, and to insure an unquestionable lien, it would seem perfectly proper in cases of this sort to
restrain any sale by the sheriff.   And besides it is also doing
some injustice to the judgment debtor by compelling a sale of
his interest under circumstances in which there must generally
from its uncertainty and litigious character be a very great sacrifice to his injury.   If he has no right in such a case to maintain a bill to save his own interest, it furnishes no ground why
the court should not interfere in his favor through the equities
of the other partners.   This seems (notwithstanding the doubts
suggested by Mr. Chancellor Kent) to be the true result of the
English decisions on this subject, which do not distinguish between the case of an assignee of a partner and that of an executor or administrator of a partner, or of the sheriff, or of an
assignee in bankruptcy.[3]

[1] Moody v. Payne, 2 John. Ch. R. 548, 549.
[2] See Skip v. Harwood, 2 Swanst. R. 586, 587.
[3] See Taylor v. Field, 4 Ves. 396, 397, 398; s. c. 15 Ves. 559, note;
Barker v. Goodair, 11 Ves. 85, 86, 87; Skip v. Harwood, 2 Swanst. R. 586,
587; Franklyn v. Thomas, 3 Meriv. 234; Hawkshaw v. Parkins, 2 Swanst.
548, 549; Parker v. Pistor, 3 Bos. & Pull. 288, 289; Eden on Injunct. 31;
Collyer on Partn. B. 3, ch. 6, § 10, pp. 474 to 478; 1 Madd. Ch. Pr. 112.   See

(a) See Hardy v. Donellan, 33 Ind.   Backus v. Murphy, 39 Penn. St. 397;
501; Jarvis v. Brooks, 23 N. H. 136.   Hubbard v. Curtis, 8 Iowa, 1; Thomp-
But see Miner v. Pierce, 38 Vt. 610;   son v. Frist, 15 Md. 24.

679. Another illustration of the beneficial result of equity jurisdiction in cases of partnership may be found in the not uncommon case of two firms dealing with each other where some or all of the partners in one firm are partners with other persons in the other firm.　Upon the technical principles of the common law in such cases no suit can be maintained at law in regard to any transactions or debts between the two firms ; for in such suit all the partners must join and be joined, and no person can maintain a suit against himself or against himself and others.　The objection is at law a complete bar to the action.[1]　Nay, even after the death of the partner or partners belonging to both firms no action upon any contract or mutual dealing ex contractu is maintainable by the survivors of one firm against those of the other firm ; for in a legal view there never was any subsisting contract between the firms, as a partner cannot contract with himself.[2]

680. But there is no difficulty in proceeding in Courts of Equity to a final adjustment of all the concerns of both firms in regard to each other ; for in equity it is sufficient that all parties in interest are before the court as plaintiffs or as defendants, and they need not, as at law, in such a case be on the opposite sides of the record.　In equity all contracts and dealings between such firms of a moral and legal nature are deemed obligatory, though void at law.[3]　Courts of Equity in all such cases look behind the form of the transactions to their substance, and treat the different firms for the purposes of substantial justice exactly as if they were composed of strangers, or were in fact corporate companies. (a)

681. Upon similar grounds one partner cannot at law maintain a suit against his copartners to recover the amount of money which he has paid for the partnership, since he cannot sue them without suing himself also as one of the partnership.　And if one partner in fraud of the partnership rights or credits should release an action, that release would at law be obligatory upon all the

also Brewster v. Hammet, 4 Connect R. 540.　See also In re Smith, 16 John. R. 106, and the Reporter's learned note; Gow on Partn. ch. 4, § 1, p. 252.

[1] Bosanquet v. Wray, 6 Taunt. 597; s. c. 2 Marsh. 319; Mainwaring v. Newman, 2 Bos. & Pull. 120.

[2] Ibid.　　　　　　　　　　　　　　[3] Ibid.

(a) See Haven v. Wakefield, 39 Ill. 509; Printup v. Fort, 40 Ga. 276; Chapman v. Evans, 44 Miss. 113; Hayes v. Bement, 3 Sandf. 394.

partners.   But a Court of Equity would not under such circumstances hesitate to relieve the partnership.[1] (a)

682. Courts of Equity in this respect act upon principles familiarly recognized in the civil law and in the jurisprudence of those nations which derive their law from that most extensive source. This will abundantly appear by reference to the known jurisprudence of Scotland and that of the continental nations of Europe.[2]   Indeed it would be a matter not merely of curiosity, but of solid instruction (if this were the proper place for such an examination), to trace out the strong lines of analogy between the law of partnership as understood in England, and especially as administered in equity, and that of the Roman Jurisprudence. Unexpected coincidences are everywhere to be found, while the differences are comparatively few ; and for the most part these arise rather from the different processes and forms of administering justice in different countries than from any general diversity of principles.[3]   Among other illustrations we may cite the general doctrine that the partnership property is first liable to the partnership debts ; that the right of any one partner is only to his share of the surplus ; that joint creditors have a priority or privilege of payment before separate creditors ;[4] and that the estates of deceased partners are liable to contribute towards the payment of the joint debts.[5]

683. This review of some of the more important cases in which Courts of Equity interfere in regard to partnerships does (unless my judgment greatly misleads me) establish in the most conclusive manner the utter inadequacy of Courts of Law to administer

---

[1] Ante, § 504, note; Jones v. Yates, 9 B. & Cressw. 532, 538, 539, 540.

[2] See 2 Bell, Comm. B. 7, ch. 2, § 2, art. 1214.

[3] To establish this statement the learned reader may be referred to the Digest, Lib. 17, tit. 2, Pro Socio; and Voet, Comm. ad id.; Vinnius, Comm. Inst. Lib. 3, tit. 26; 1 Domat, Civil Law, tit. Partnership, B. 1, tit. 8, per tot.; 2 Bell, Comm. B. 4, ch. 2, art. 1250 to 1263; Code Civil of France, art. 1832 to 1873; Pothier, Traité de Société, per tot.

[4] 1 Domat, B. 1, tit. 8, § 3, art. 10.

[5] 1 Domat, B. 1, tit. 8, § 6, art. 1, 2; Pothier, de Société, n. 96, 136, 161, 162.

(a) See Craig v. Hulschizer, 34 N. J. 363; Piercy v. Fynney, L. R. 12 Eq. 69.   But if one partner make advances to his associate, and an agreement is made to repay that particular sum, an action at law can be maintained.   Sprout v. Crowley, 30 Wis. 187.   See also Wells v. Carpenter, 65 Ill. 447; Hale v. Wilson, 112 Mass. 444.

justice in most cases growing out of partnerships, and the indispensable necessity of resorting to Courts of Equity for plain, complete, and adequate redress. Where a discovery, an account, a contribution, an injunction, or a dissolution (a) is sought in cases of partnership, or even where a due enforcement of partnership rights and duties and credits is required, it is impossible not to perceive that generally a resort to Courts at Law would be little more than a solemn mockery of justice. Hence it can excite no surprise that Courts of Equity now exercise a full concurrent jurisdiction with Courts of Law in all matters of partnership; and indeed it may be said that practically speaking they exercise an exclusive jurisdiction over the subject in all cases of any complexity or difficulty.

(a) Or where the partnership transactions have taken place abroad. See Hendrick v. Wood, 9 Jur. N. S. 117; Cookney v. Anderson, 8 Jur. N. S. 1220; s. c. 31 Beav. 452; 9 Jur. N. S. 736; 1 DeG. J. & S. 365; Maunder v. Lloyd, 2 Johns. & H. 718; Steele v. Stuart, 12 Week. R. 247; Norris v. Chambers, 29 Beav. 246; Harvey v. Varney, 104 Mass. 436 (that a receiver will not be appointed of partnership assets out of the jurisdiction); Desper v. Continental Co., 137 Mass. 252.

CHAPTER XVI.

MATTERS OF RENT.

684. ANOTHER head of concurrent jurisdiction of the same nature and resulting also from the imperfection of the remedy at
law is in the case of RENTS. This subject has been already
touched in other places; [1] and a few particulars only will be here
taken notice of, which have not been already fully discussed. Thus
for instance in case of a rent seck if the grantee has never had seisin
and the rent cannot be recovered at law, Courts of Equity will
decree a seisin of the rent and perhaps also that it be paid to the
party.[2] So if the deeds are lost by which a rent is created, so that
it is uncertain what kind of rent it was, [3] or if (as we have seen)
by reason of a confusion of boundaries or otherwise the lands out
of which it issues cannot be exactly ascertained, Courts of Equity
will in like manner interfere.[4] So if the remedy for the rent has
become difficult or doubtful at law, or if there is an apparent per-
plexity and uncertainty as to the title or as to the extent of the
responsibility of the party from whom it is sought, — in all such

[1] Ante, §§ 508 to 515.

[2] Francis's Maxims, 6, § 3, p. 25 (edit. 1739); Ferris *v.* Newby, cited
1 Cas. Ch. 147; Palmer *v.* Whettenhal, 1 Cas. Ch. 184; 1 Fonbl. on Equity,
B. 1, ch. 3, § 3; Com. Dig. Chancery, 4 N. 1, Rent; Thorndike *v.* Collington,
1 Cas. Ch. 79; Web *v.* Web, Moore, R. 626; Davy *v.* Davy, 1 Cas. Ch. 147.

[3] Collet *v.* Jacques, 1 Cas. Ch. 120; Cocks *v.* Foley, 1 Vern. 359; Duke of
Leeds *v.* New Radnor, 2 Bro. Ch. R. 338, 518, 519; Holder *v.* Chambury,
3 P. Will. 256; Livingston *v.* Livingston, 4 John. Ch. R. 290, 291.

[4] Ante, § 622; 1 Fonbl. Eq. B. 1, ch. 3, § 3, note (*f*); Francis's Maxims,
6, § 3, p. 25 (edit. 1739); Bowman *v.* Yeat, cited 1 Ch. Cas. 145; Davy *v.*
Davy, 1 Ch. Cas. 146, 147; Cocks *v.* Foley, 1 Vern. 359; North *v.* Earl of
Strafford, 3 P. Will. 148; Holder *v.* Chambury, 3 P. Will. 256; Com. Dig.
Chancery, 4 N. 1, Rent; Duke of Bridgewater *v.* Edwards, 4 Bro. Parl. Cas.
139; s. c. 6 Bro. Parl. Cas., by Tomlins, 368. As to the ancient remedy for
rents, see 3 Reeves's History of the Law, ch. 21, pp. 317 to 320; 3 Black.
Comm. 6; Id. 231; 2 Black. Comm. 42; Id. 288; Bacon, Abridg. Rent, A. K.

cases Courts of Equity will maintain jurisdiction and upon a due ascertainment of the right will decree the rent.[1] (a)   So if a rent is devised out of a rectory to a devisee for which he cannot have any remedy by distress or otherwise at law, Courts of Equity will decree him the rent, not only in future, but all arrears.[2]   So if a lease of an incorporeal thing is assigned, and the assignee enjoys it, he will be decreed in equity to pay the rent, although not bound at law.[3]   So if an assignee of a term rendering rent assigns over, the lessor will be entitled to relief in equity for the rent against the first assignee so long as he held the land, although he may have no remedy at law for these arrears.[4]   So the executor of a terre-tenant of lands liable for a rent charge which the terre-tenant has suffered to be in arrear, will be compellable in equity to pay the same, although the testator was not personally bound for the rent, which was recoverable only by distress; for his personal estate has been augmented by the non-payment.[5]   So a cestui que trust of a lease rendering rent will in equity be compellable to pay the rent during the time wherein he has taken the profits if his trustee (the lessee) has become insolvent.[6]   So

---

[1] Livingston v. Livingston, 4 John. Ch. R. 287, 290.   In Benson v. Baldwyn (1 Atk. R. 508), Lord Hardwicke said: ' Where a man is entitled to a rent out of lands, and through process of time the remedy at law is lost or become very difficult, this court has interfered and given relief upon the foundation only of payment of the rent for a long time, which bills are called bills founded upon the solet.   Nay, the court has gone so far as to give relief where the nature of the rent (as there are many kinds at law) has not been known so as to be set forth   But then all the terre-tenants of the lands out of which the rent issues must be brought before the court, in order for the court to make a complete decree.'   See also Collet v. Jacques, 1 Ch. Cas. 120.

[2] Com. Dig. Chancery, 4 N. 1, Rent; Thorndike v. Collington, 1 Ch. Cas. 79.

[3] Com. Dig. Chancery, 4 N. 1, Rent, which cites City of London v. Richmond, 2 Vern. 423; s. c. 1 Bro. Parl. Cas. 30 [Id. 516, Tomlins's edit.].

[4] Com. Dig. Chancery, 4 N. 1, Rent, which cites Treackle v. Coke, 1 Vern. 165; Valliant v. Dodemede, 2 Atk. 546, 548; Richmond v. City of London, 1 Bro. Parl. Cas. 30; [Id. 516, Tomlins's edit ;] s. c. 2 Vern. 422, 423.

[5] Com. Dig. Chancery, 4 N. 1, Rent, which cites Eton College v. Beauchamp, 1 Cas. Ch. 121.

[6] Clavering v. Westley, 3 P. Will. 402. (b)

(a) See Swedesborough Church v. Shivers, 1 C. E. Green, 453; Holmes v. Shepard, 49 Mo. 600.   So where rent could not be recovered at law for want of a legal title.   Fleming v. Chunn, 4 Jones, Eq. 422.

(b) As to this case however see Walters v. Northern Coal Co., 5 DeG. M. & G. 629, 646, 647.   See also Cox v. Bishop, 8 De G. M. & G. 815 ; Wright v. Pitt, L. R. 12 Eq. 408.

although a grantee of a rent shall not have a remedy in equity merely for the want of a distress, yet if the want of such distress be caused by the fraud or other default of the tenant, there he will be relieved in equity.[1] So if a rent is settled upon a woman by way of jointure, but she has no power of distress or other remedy at law, payment of the rent will be decreed in equity according to the intent of the conveyance.[2] So where a person is a grantee of an entire rent issuing out of a manor, and there are no demesne lands to distrain on, the rent will be decreed in equity.[3]

684 *a*. This jurisdiction in matters of rent is asserted upon the general principle that where there is a right there ought to be a remedy ; and if the law gives none, it ought to be administered in equity.[4] This principle is of frequent application in equity, but still it is not to be understood as of as universal application as its terms seem to import, for there are limitations upon it.   An obvious exception is where a man becomes remediless at law from his own negligence.[5] So if he should destroy his own remedy to distrain for rent and debt would not lie for the arrears of rent, he would not be relievable in equity.[6]

684 *b*. Courts of Equity have in some cases carried their remedial justice further in aid of parties entitled to rent. It is plain enough that they may well give relief where a bill for discovery and relief is filed and the discovery is essential to the plaintiff's case, and the defendant admits the right of the plaintiff to the rent ; for in such a case the relief may well be held to be consequent upon the discovery.[7] But where no special ground of this sort has been stated in the bill, and where upon the circumstances there might well have been a remedy at law, Courts of Equity have in some cases gone on to decree the rent when the defendant has by his answer admitted the plaintiff's right, and no

---

[1] Com. Dig. Chancery, 4 N. 3, Rent; Davy *v.* Davy, 1 Cas. Ch. 144, 147; Ferris *v.* Newby, cited 1 Ch. Cas. 147; Ferrers *v.* Tanner, cited 3 Ch. Cas. 91.

[2] Mitf. Eq. Pl. by Jeremy, 115, 116; Plunket *v.* Brereton, 1 Rep. in Chan. 5; Champernoon *v.* Gubbs, 2 Vern. R. 382.

[3] Duke of Leeds *v.* Powell, 1 Ves. 171.

[4] 1 Fonbl. Eq. B. 1, ch. 3, § 3, note (*f*), and cases before cited.

[5] Francis's Maxims, 6, § 3, p. 25 (edit. 1739); Vincent *v.* Beverlye, Noy, R. 82; 1 Fonbl. on Equity, B. 1, ch. 3, § 3.

[6] 1 Fonbl. Eq. B. 1, ch. 3, § 3; 1 Roll. Abridg. 375, Pl. 3.

[7] Ante, § 71; post, §§ 690, 691, 1483; Story on Eq. Plead. §§ 311, 312, 314, 315.

exception has been taken to the jurisdiction by demurrer or by answer, but simply at the hearing.[1]

684 *c.* These latter cases seem to stand upon grounds which, if not unquestionable, may at least be deemed anomalous. The general doctrine of Courts of Equity certainly is, that where the party entitled to rent has a complete remedy at law, either by an action or by distress, no suit will be entertained in equity for his relief;[2] and the cases in which a suit in equity is commonly entertained are of the kind above mentioned; namely, such as stand upon some peculiar equity between the parties, or where the remedy at law is gone without laches, or where it is inadequate or doubtful.[3] It is not enough to show that the remedy in equity may be more beneficial if the remedy at law is complete and adequate,[4] or even to show that the remedy at law by distress is gone if there be no fraud or default in the tenant.[5]

[1] Duke of Leeds *v.* New Radnor, 2 Bro. Ch. R. 338, 518; North *v.* Earl of Strafford, 3 P. Will. 184; Holder *v.* Chambury, 3 P. Will. 256; Livingston *v.* Livingston, 4 John. Ch. R. 287, 291, 292.

[2] Com. Dig. Chancery, 4 N. 3, Rent; Palmer *v.* Whettenhal, 1 Cas. Ch. 184; Francis's Maxims, 6, § 3, p. 25 (edit. 1739), marg. note; Champernoon *v.* Gubbs, 2 Vern. 382; Fairfax *v.* Derby, 2 Vern. 613; Holder *v.* Chambury, 3 P. Will. 256; Duke of Leeds *v.* New Radnor, 2 Bro. Ch. R. 338, and Mr. Belt's note, Id. 519; Bouverie *v.* Prentice, 1 Bro. Ch. R. 200.

[3] Ante, § 684. Mr. Fonblanque, in commenting on the case of the Duke of Leeds *v.* New Radnor, 2 Bro. Ch. R. 338, 519, has said: ' The case of the Duke of Leeds *v.* Corporation of New Radnor may in its first impression be thought to have been relievable at law; for though, for the purpose of making it the subject of equitable jurisdiction, the bill alleged that the lands in question had undergone various alterations in their boundaries, yet the defendants by their answer denied that any alteration whatever had taken place in such particulars, and insisted that the plaintiff's remedy was at law. And Lord Kenyon, then Master of the Rolls, appears to have been of such opinion, but he retained the bill for a year. Lord Thurlow, C., however conceived the legal remedy to be doubtful, and was of opinion that the defendants having admitted the plaintiff's right, and the bill having been retained, had done away the objection pressed against the jurisdiction of the court. It may be material to observe that his lordship's opinion went upon the grounds of an admission of the right and the previous retaking of the bill. As to the admission of the right, if it stood alone, that probably would not be thought a sufficient circumstance to give to a Court of Equity cognizance of a matter not properly within its jurisdiction; and with respect to the bill having been retained for a year, the same circumstance occurred in Ryan *v.* Macmath, 3 Bro. Rep. 15, notwithstanding which the suit was dismissed for want of equity. See also Curtis *v.* Curtis, 2 Bro. Rep. 620, where this point was very much considered.'

[4] Com. Dig. Chancery, 4 N. 3, Rent; Attorney-General *v.* Mayor of Coventry, 1 Vern. 713.

[5] Com. Dig. Chancery, 4 N. 3, Rent; Davy *v.* Davy, 1 Cas. Ch. 144, 147;

685. But in cases of rent where Courts of Equity do interfere, they do not grant a remedy beyond what, by analogy to the law, ought to be granted. As for instance if an annuity be granted out of a rectory and charged thereon, and the glebe be worth less per annum than the annuity, Courts of Equity will make the whole rectory, and not merely the glebe, liable for the annuity.[1] But they will not extend the remedy to the tithes, they not being by law liable to a distress.[2] So if a rent be charged on land only, the party who comes into possession of it will not be personally charged with the payment of it unless there be some fraud on his part to remove the stock, or he do some other thing to evade the right of distress.[3]

686. Before the statute of Anne (8 Anne, ch. 14) it was often necessary to go into a Court of Equity, in cases of a rent seck, for a suitable remedy.[4] But that statute and other subsequent statutes enable the party in all cases, whether the rent be a rent service or a rent seck or a rent charge, to distrain or bring his action of debt.[5] The remedy in equity is therefore in a practical sense narrowed, or rather it is less advisable than formerly. Still however (as Mr. Fonblanque has properly remarked) there are cases in which a resort to a Court of Equity may be salutary and perhaps indispensable ; as where the premises out of which the rent is payable are uncertain,[6] or where the time or amount of payment is uncertain, or where (as already hinted) the distress is obstructed or evaded by fraud,[7] or where the rent is issuing out of a thing of an incorporeal nature, as tithes, where no dis-

Champernoon v. Gubbs, 2 Vern. R. 382; Francis's Maxims, 6, § 3, p. 35 (edit. 1739), marginal note; 1 Fonbl. Eq. B. 1, ch. 3, § 3; Duke of Bolton v. Deane, Prec. Ch. 516.

[1] Thorndike v. Collington, 1 Cas. Ch. 79; Com. Digest, Chancery, 4 N. 2, Rent.

[2] Ibid.; Thorndike v. Collington, 1 Cas. Ch. 79 ; Francis's Maxims, 6, p. 25 (edit. 1739), in margin.

[3] Ibid.; Palmer v. Whettenhal, 1 Cas. Ch. 184; Com. Dig. Chancery, 4 N. 3, Rent; 1 Fonbl. Eq. B. 1, ch. 3, § 3, note (k) ; Davy v. Davy, 1 Cas. Ch. 144, 145; s. P. 3 Cas. Ch. 91.

[4] See 3 Reeves, Hist. of the Law, ch. 21, pp. 316 to 320; Litt. § 218.

[5] Stat. 4 Geo. II. ch. 28; 5 Geo. III. ch. 17; 3 Black. Comm. 6; Id. 230 to 233; Bac. Abridg. Rent, K. 6.

[6] Benson v. Baldwyn, 1 Atk. 598; ante, § 684; Com. Dig. Chancery, 4 N. 1, Rent.

[7] Champernoon v. Gubbs, 2 Vern. 382; s. c. Prec. Ch. 126; ante, §§ 684, 685.

tress can be made,[1] or where a discovery may be necessary, or where an apportionment may be required in order to attain complete justice.[2]

687. The beneficial effect of this jurisdiction in equity may be further illustrated by reference to the doctrine at law in cases of derivative titles under leases. It is well known that, although a derivative lessee or under-tenant is liable to be distrained for rent during his possession, yet he is not liable to be sued for rent on the covenants of the lease, there being no privity of contract between him and the lessor.[3] But suppose the case to be that the original lessee is insolvent and unable to pay the rent; the question would then arise whether the under-lessee should be permitted to enjoy the profits and possession of the estate without accounting for the rent to the original lessor. Undoubtedly there would be no remedy at law. But it is understood that in such a case Courts of Equity would relieve the lessor, and would direct a payment of the rent to the lessor upon a bill making the original lessee and the under-tenant parties. For if the original lessee were compelled to pay the rent, he would have a remedy over against the under-tenant. And besides in the eyes of a Court of Equity the rent seems properly to be a trust or charge upon the estate ; and the lessor is bound, at least in conscience, not to take the profits without a due discharge of the rent out of them.[4]

[1] 1 Fonbl. Eq. B. 1, ch. 3, § 3, note (*g*), and cases there cited.

[2] See North *v.* Earl of Strafford, 3 P. Will. 148, 151; Benson *v.* Baldwyn, 1 Atk. 598; Com. Dig. Chancery, 4 N. 3, Rent.

[3] Halford *v.* Hetch, 1 Doug. R. 183; 1 Fonbl. Eq. B. 1, ch. 3, note (*s*); Com. Dig. Chancery, 4 N. 5, Rent.

[4] See Goddard *v.* Keate, 1 Vern. 27; 1 Fonbl. Eq. B. 1, ch. 5, § 5, and note (*x*); ante, § 684; Com. Dig. Chancery, 4 N. 1, 4 N. 2, Rent.